TRAVEL CAREER DEVELOPMENT

Institute of Certified Travel Agents

Patricia J. Gagnon, CTC
and
Karen Silva, M.A.

Irwin
Mirror Press
Homewood, IL 60430
Boston, MA 02116

Fifth Edition

Library of Congress Cataloging-in-Publication Data

Gagnon, Patricia J., CTC
  Travel Career Development — 5th edition/Patricia J. Gagnon, CTC, Karen Silva, M.A.
  p. cm.
  Includes bibliographical references.
  ISBN 0-256-11977-5
  1. Travel agents — Vocational guidance. I. Silva, Karen.
  G154 G34 1993
  338.4'79102373 — dc20

                                                                    93-10507

Design: Julie A. Zimmer

Table of Contents

A Letter from ICTA's Chairman

Dear Travel Student:

Congratulations! By choosing a career in travel, you're saying "yes" to one of the country's most exciting and fastest growing industries. Travel and tourism account for close to seven percent of our total gross national product and by the year 2000, travel is expected to be the country's largest industry. Choosing a travel career now positions you in a field that will continue to offer exciting opportunities well into the next century.

Studying Travel Career Development, written by the travel and tourism education experts at the Institute of Certified Travel Agents (ICTA), is an excellent first step in establishing yourself as a travel professional. ICTA is the travel industry's leading educational organization, setting standards of excellence through our Certified Travel Counselor (CTC) Program, our Destination Specialist Program, and a host of other offerings and publications. Now in its fifth edition, Travel Career Development is the definitive introductory travel text. It gives you a thorough, up-to-date, and engaging overview of the travel and tourism industry.

Equally important is the fact that Travel Career Development is linked to ICTA's Travel Career Development Testing Program and — through that — to our prestigious CTC accreditation. By using Travel Career Development you become eligible to be tested for ICTA's Travel Career Development Certificate — your first professional travel credential.

I've been in the industry for more than 30 years, and I still find it full of exciting new challenges. I want to congratulate you once again on your decision and extend my best wishes for a successful and rewarding career.

Sincerely,

H. Wayne Berens, CTC,
Chairman,
Institute of Certified Travel Agents
Wellesley, MA
Vice-President, Industry Affairs
American Express TRS

Preface

This year, Americans will take over one billion trips. Whether we are traveling for business or for pleasure, alone or in groups, to get into the thick of things or to get away from it all, we are a nation on the move. And a dynamic, robust travel industry has grown up to help keep us moving.

The tremendous growth of the travel and tourism industry over the last quarter century has had at least two significant implications for travel professionals: Our business is more complex, and it's more competitive. Travel professionals must master an ever expanding body of knowledge and technical skills to attain proficiency in the field. Meanwhile, sophisticated travelers have become smart shoppers when choosing among travel products and services and the professionals who provide them.

In response to these developments, the Institute of Certified Travel Agents (ICTA) published the first edition of Travel Career Development in 1983. ICTA — the travel industry's only organization devoted exclusively to education — saw the need for an authoritative and comprehensive text to give future travel agents a systematic overview of the travel industry. The result was *Travel Career Development*, and its subsequent adoption by hundreds of colleges and schools attests to how well it has fulfilled its mission. Since its introduction, *Travel Career Development* has been widely used as a core text in introductory travel courses and as the centerpiece of a variety of programs on various aspects of travel and tourism.

Travel Career Development focuses on the pivotal role of the travel agent and the nature of the relationships between agents and supplier and between agents and their clients. It's the single-source text that gives students comprehensive and critical information on travel products and destinations, important business issues, and the technical and personal skills they need to begin a productive travel industry career.

The fifth edition carefully preserves the strengths of previous editions, while incorporating recommendations from travel instructors and travel industry professionals, and from ICTA's staff of professional educators. This edition boasts many learning aids and reflects the most important developments in the travel industry today including

- Cruise line consolidation
- Frequent guest awards
- Automation in the travel industry
- The handicapped traveler
- Customer service skills
- Airline fare structures

How This Book is Organized

To help students and instructors navigate the increasingly complex waters of the travel and tourism industry, *Travel Career Development* is divided into four parts that reflect key areas of concern for travel students: The Travel Product, Sales and Marketing, Agency Operations, and Travel Career Planning.

Part One — The Travel Product

This part presents the building blocks of travel,

from air travel and cruising to types of accommodation to passport and visa requirements. Students acquire the product knowledge that every travel professional needs. Part One also includes a primer on destination geography, with maps and geographic information on the world's most popular destinations.

Part Two — Sales and Marketing

Even the most knowledgeable travel agents can't be successful unless they market their services and close sales. Sales and Marketing covers key business and selling skills, including how to evaluate client needs, and what's involved in a successful sale. The section also addresses customized sales, marketing techniques, and sales follow-up.

Part Three — Agency Operations

A central skill required for success in the travel industry is communication. The key technology is automation. Part Three of *Travel Career Development* covers both. Agency Operations focuses on the importance of effective communication and writing skills. Students learn about automation technology, especially as it relates to reservations systems, and the section addresses the basic money management skills necessary for operating a travel agency.

Part Four — Travel Career Planning

Travel Career Planning helps students close the loop between theory and practice. It describes what they need to do to find travel industry jobs, and how they can turn those jobs into satisfying careers. Part Four presents examples of resumes and cover letters, and outlines successful strategies for interviewing. It also includes an appendix of travel and trade organizations — an invaluable resource for job seekers.

Learning Aids that Enhance the Book's Effectiveness

In addition to the core text, each chapter includes features that aid learning by putting key information at each student's fingertips.

Objectives and Vocabulary

A set of objectives and a vocabulary list begin each chapter. These inform readers of important industry terms and help ensure that students focus on the issues most important to a successful career in travel.

Career Information

While Part Four deals specifically with career planning and development, each chapter in Part One also includes career information related to the chapter topic. Chapter Three, "Air Travel," for example, includes information on being a flight attendant; "Tours," Chapter Eight, includes information on becoming a tour escort. These features help students identify career opportunities, as well as the requirements and growth potential associated with each job.

Historical Perspective

In such a fast growing field, the enriching knowledge of the past can easily be lost. Each chapter in Part One highlights a pertinent topic and sets it in historical context. In the discussion of "Cruising," for example, readers learn about the ships of a bygone era.

Sidebars, Chapter Summaries, and Chapter Wrap-ups

Whenever a particular subject warrants a closer look, boxed inserts are included which treat the information in greater depth. Information on communication skills and customer service — areas of great import in all travel professions — are just two of the many topics treated this way.

Each chapter ends with a summary of key points, followed by a wrap-up including review questions and discussion topics. These present thought-provoking scenarios that help students apply their travel knowledge to real-world situations.

Ticketing Appendix

In response to many requests, a Ticketing Appendix has been added to the fifth edition of *Travel Career Development*. This appendix provides detailed step-by-step instruction on manual ticketing procedures consistent with ARC guidelines. Exercises for student practice are also provided.

Rand McNally Quick Reference World Atlas

One of the most important additions to the fifth edition of *Travel Career Development* is the new *Rand McNally Quick Reference World Atlas* — a 64-page, full color atlas bound at the end of each book. This important reference will help students learn destination geography, and it's a tool they'll find useful for their entire travel careers.

The Student Workbook

The Student Workbook is an effective learning tool specifically designed for use with *Travel Career Development*. Its worksheets, objective tests, and practical exercises emphasize hands-on learning and cover such important topics as

- Reading train schedules
- Analyzing tour and cruise brochures
- Identifying airline and city codes
- Demonstrating geographical knowledge

The Instructor's Resource Manual

Travel instructors can use *Travel Career Development's* Instructor's Resource Manual to plan effective lessons and reinforce their teaching strategy. Among the tools included are

- Suggested lesson plans
- Testing materials
- Transparency masters
- Role-playing exercises
- Teaching tips
- Answers to Student Workbook exercises

The book also includes many articles that can form the basis for lectures, debates, or thought provoking classroom discussions.

ICTA's exclusive Travel Career Development Test

ICTA offers an optional testing service exclusively to students who complete a course of study using *Travel Career Development*. Students who pass the Travel Career Development Test — a 100-question multiple choice exam that is administered by instructors and scored by ICTA — receive ICTA's coveted Travel Career Development Test Certificate. The certificate is a recognized travel industry credential.

For more information about Travel Career Development Program testing, the Certified Travel Counselor Program, or any of the Institute's educational programs, contact

ICTA
148 Linden Street
P.O. Box 812059
Wellesley, MA 02181-0012
Phone   617 237-0280
FAX   617 237-3860

Acknowledgments

Many people have contributed to this project with valuable comments and suggestions drawing on their fields of expertise. Our special thanks to the following individuals whose assistance was particularly valuable: John Butters, CTC, Chris DeSessa, David Helmstadter, Gwenn Lavoie, Claudette Levesque, Arlene Lewis, Clare Lyne, Debra MacNeill, CTC, Marie Mooradian, and Michael Sabitoni.

We're grateful to Kevin Bast for preparing the Ticketing Appendix and to the following people who helped in the review process: Helen Pannes, Herkimer County Community College, Herkimer, NY; Fredericka Ferrell, CTC, Ambassador Institute of Travel, Madison, TN; Deborah Rietzen, Travel One Travel Academy, Cherry Hill, NJ; Janet Tooker, Massasoit Community College, Brockton, MA; and Sharon Lencki, Glendale, CA.

Introduction

The travel industry has an aura of glamour, excitement, and romance. Travel careers may involve exotic locations and can put you in touch with people all over the globe. But travel is also a multibillion dollar industry. With those kinds of stakes, it's imperative that travel professionals possess a range of skills and be responsive to the needs and demands of their clients.

Travel Career Development is your introduction to the information, strategies, and responsibilities that will help you succeed as a travel professional. Whether people travel for business or leisure, they expect their counselors to give them informed, objective advice on an enormous variety of products and services. The information contained in this book is your first important step to becoming the trusted professional travelers rely on.

What Does a Travel Professional Do?

By the year 2000, travel will be this country's largest industry. It's hard to generalize about an industry that employs so many in such a wide variety of jobs. For example, travel workers may earn the minimum wage or be among the nation's most generously compensated professionals. They may head airlines, or they may handle baggage. Travel professionals may be self-employed, or they may work for companies that employ thousands.

Travel Career Development introduces you to a range of jobs in the travel field, and while there is no universal job description or career path, all travel industry positions do share one trait: every

one is about providing service. Whatever role you choose for yourself in travel and tourism, remember that your primary responsibility is to offer service to your clients.

What Skills Does a Travel Professional Need?

The major goal of *Travel Career Development* is to give students a thorough and practical introduction to the travel industry. Many chapters discuss the skills required for a successful travel career, including those outlined below.

Interpersonal Skills

Almost all travel professions require an ability to work with clients. Counselors are salespeople. They must work well with others and retain a genuine enthusiasm and patience for the endless requests and questions that come their way.

Travel counselors must be empathetic. The ability to show concern for a client often marks the difference between an average counselor and a superb one. No client wants to be taken for granted, treated as a type, or ignored. *Travel Career Development* explains why every successful travel professional must be able to understand people, and to communicate that understanding effectively.

Technical Skills

Many travel jobs include routine but time-consuming responsibilities, such as constructing fares, generating tickets, and preparing invoices. With the right technical skills, travel professionals can streamline these functions, leaving more time for serving clients.

Travel Career Development outlines the technical skills travel professionals need in this increasingly automated industry. Designed to complement hands-on training, these technical lessons will prepare students for further learning.

Organizational Skills

At its core, a travel agency is an organized store of information. Information is essential for successful counseling and selling, and agents who lack the organizational skills to access information will not survive long.

Travel Career Development has culled organizational strategies from top industry professionals to help novice travel counselors maximize their effectiveness from the first day on the job.

General Business Skills

Most travel professionals are employed by companies. To perform successfully, these travel professionals must understand how their company works, what its goals are, and how they can contribute to these goals.

Travel Career Development explains both general, and specific business skills, including

- Writing effective business letters
- Handling money
- Filing records

The Role of a Travel Counselor

While there are many jobs available in the travel industry, *Travel Career Development* focuses on the pivotal role of the travel counselor. Counselors arrange travel for their clients, and doing that successfully means safeguarding two important relationships: between the travel agency and its clients, and between the travel agency and its suppliers.

Agents and Clients

Travel counselors have both ethical and legal obligations to their clients. Clients rely on travel counselors for their knowledge and count on them to be honest, informed, and able to secure the best rates and fares.

Travel counselors must stay abreast of the most accurate and current information available in the industry. In other words, a career as a travel counselor demands a lifelong commitment to continuing education. Agents must avoid exaggeration and deceptive practices, and they must never misrepresent facts or mislead clients in order to close a sale. Remember, counselors who behave unethically expose themselves and their agencies to legal liability.

Agents and Suppliers

Travel counselors represent different suppliers — airlines, hotels, car rental agencies, and so on — so that the counselor can promote and sell the suppliers' travel products. Travel agencies enter into contracts with suppliers — some written, others implied — in which counselors agree to represent suppliers fairly and objectively. These contracts set commission levels and specify under what conditions a counselor can sell the supplier's services.

Counselors are responsible for quoting accurate rates, schedules, and fares and for producing correct tickets.

A Commitment to Personal Service

This introduction outlines the nuts and bolts of what it takes to be a travel professional, but it barely alludes to what's at the heart of a successful career in travel. As you follow the lessons in *Travel Career Development*, even if you're absorbed in the details of customized selling strategies or agency automation, never lose sight of the fact that a career in travel requires more than a set of skills. It demands a commitment to personal service.

As a travel counselor, clients whom you barely know will entrust you to make expensive and complicated travel arrangements, and fulfilling their expectations may not always be easy. But if you are commited to providing responsible, intelligent, and professional service, all of the personal and professional rewards a travel career has to offer will be available to you.

The Travel Product

Part One

Past, Present, and Future
The Travel Industry
Chapter 1

CHAPTER OBJECTIVES

After completing this chapter, the reader should be able to
- Identify the contributions of three pioneers in the travel industry
- Describe Maslow's theory of human motivation
- Compare today's travel market with the past's
- Differentiate man-made attractions from natural ones
- Describe a typical familiarization trip
- List five sources of information for travel professionals
- Explain why destinations go in and out of fashion
- Discuss the features of a good travel video

VOCABULARY

After completing this chapter, the reader should be able to define
- Accessibility
- Fam trip
- Infrastructure
- Intangible need
- Man-made attraction
- Natural attraction
- NTO
- Personal bias

Introduction

Journeys have been important since the beginning of time. Religious and political migrations throughout the centuries have been recorded in secular and sacred literature. The French roots of the word travel (*travail*: work) suggest that there was little enjoyment in early journeys. Travel for pleasure is a more contemporary idea, resulting from the sweeping social and political changes and great technical advances in transportation that occurred during the early nineteenth century. The introduction of rail travel, the building of large steamships, the invention of the auto and then the motorcoach, and the development of air travel created the modern travel industry.

Origins of Travel

Our earliest ancestors depended on some degree of travel for food. This, of course, was not viewed as a leisure activity, but survival. The development of safe communities and settlements made travel less important. Dwellers were content to stay within their own environment. Hunters on foot were driven to search for prey only as a means of providing sustenance to their village.

Sledges were designed around 7000 B.C. to carry food along the tundra. Eventually, animals were used to drag these vehicles across the harsh terrain. However, it wasn't until the invention of the wheel, around 3000 B.C., that wagons and chariots were effectively used to transfer goods and passengers across the land.

Destination Careers

Cartographer
Tour Host
Tourist Board Representative
Travel Researcher
Travel Video Producer
Travel Writer

Travel Writer

Many people believe travel writing is the ideal way to combine their love of travel with their skill at writing or photography. This career conjures up images of relaxing, free trips to exotic lands. Unfortunately, this is usually not the case. Travel writers range from well-known professionals to people who write an occasional article. The professionals work long hours, catch countless flights, and must meet pressing last-minute deadlines.

The Society of American Travel Writers has a code of ethics to ensure that professional travel writers maintain their independence from all sectors of the industry so their judgments can be freely based on their own experiences. In other words, most writers must acknowledge reimbursement from outside sources. This helps ensure that their articles are free from bias.

Although travel writers provide valuable information about destinations, they also help the consumer understand the complex rules and regulations surrounding such matters as promotional fares, baggage, charters, and health requirements. Informational articles produce better-educated consumers who understand the travel product and work more effectively with their agents. Articles in travel magazines like *Travel & Leisure* or *Conde Nast* are consciously upbeat, romanticizing and glamorizing the destinations they describe. The magazines describe various destinations, concentrating heavily on advising readers where to stay, where to eat, and what to buy.

Travel writers may choose an area to specialize in, such as cruises or group tour packages, or a part of the world, like South America. Many concentrate on a specific medium — guidebooks or trade publications, for example. Novice writers should not overlook such modest beginnings as in-house brochures, itineraries, newsletters, or local newspapers to gain experience. Much can be learned by inspecting and analyzing the work of others. Additional course work in creative writing, editing, or journalism could prove helpful to the aspiring travel writer.

Water travel began around 4000 B.C. in ancient Egypt as civilization developed along the Nile and Tigris-Euphrates rivers. The Phoenicians built massive fleets to cross the Mediterranean for trade and commerce, and the Vikings, Celts, Greeks, and Romans used vessels to increase their military power. Using the stars as guides, Polynesians navigated the Pacific in canoes around 2000 B.C.

Beginning in 776 B.C., Greek citizens jour-neyed every four years to Olympia to worship the god Zeus. Thus began the first Olympics, com-plete with sports, lodging, food, and revelry.

Unlike other ancients, the Romans valued travel for its own sake. Favorable political, economic, and social conditions during the second century A.D., coupled with the Romans' willingness to learn, made travel attractive to the affluent. Pathfinders, precursors of modern tour guides, would recite legends and local history as tourists experienced first hand such cities as Naples, Athens, Delphi, Alexandria, and Troy.

After the fall of the Roman Empire and the resulting political instability, travel during the Middle Ages was limited and had a strong religious overtone. Pilgrimages to the Holy Land were taken by nobles, wealthy landowners, and prosperous merchants. Travel to Jerusalem, Bethlehem, and other Middle Eastern shrines later expanded to include the exotic bazaars and entertainment of the Moslem world.

In the 1200s Marco Polo traveled to such sites as Baghdad, the Gobi Desert, and the Forbidden City, where he encountered Kubla Khan. A fervent admirer of Polo, Christopher Columbus began the recorded history of transatlantic travel two hundred years later. Both were followed by explorers like Vespucci, Cabot, Drake, Magellan, and Cook.

On land, the Grand Tour became popular among the English aristocracy. The development of the stagecoach greatly increased land travel despite the poor condition of most roads. Following the Industrial Revolution, such technological achievements as the railroad further increased land travel.

Steamships and clipper ships began making regular transatlantic crossings in the early nineteenth century, and spas became popular during this time.

The Golden Age of hotels began in the 1900s with the dedication of properties like the Tremont House and the Waldorf-Astoria. Twenty years later, the Great Depression nearly destroyed the travel industry. However, the creation of Henry Ford's Model T during this same time period provided the impetus for future highway motels and family vacations. Orville and Wilbur Wright were experimenting with a winged bicycle that heralded the beginning of air travel in the early 1900s. Floating palaces, the backbone of transatlantic travel, were replaced when commercial air travel became a reality under Pan American Airlines. Tourism for the masses, rather than just the upper classes, was finally a reality.

Thomas Cook

Thomas Cook is frequently credited with being the father of the travel agency industry. Born in England in 1808, he grew up just as railroads came of age. He became involved in travel because he wanted to stamp out the evils of alcohol. On July 5, 1841, his first organized group tour took 570 teetotalers on a day's train excursion for a temperance meeting. As Cook recalled later in his biography, "What a glorious thing it would be if the newly developed powers of the railways could be made subservient to the cause of Temperance."

In the beginning Cook volunteered his services for the cause, but by 1845 he had opened a commercial excursion agency. He negotiated with the railroads to pay him a commission on each ticket. The railroads suggested that he surcharge his travelers, but Cook convinced them to pay him the commission by pointing out the volume of business that his sales methods produced. Thus he established the basic principle of commission that continues to this day.

Thomas Cook and Son dominated the early travel industry. The term "Cook's Tour" became part of our language. On the fiftieth anniversary of the founding of the firm, Cook was acclaimed by royalty for his contribution to English national life. The early escorted tours promoted by Cook opened up the world to the emerging British middle class. Protected by a Cook's Tour guide, unescorted women began to travel as well.

Other Pioneers

■ George Stephenson, considered the father of the rail system and steam locomotive, developed the *Locomotion* and the *Rocket* to handle passengers and cargo. In 1868, George Pullman refined this idea by developing a plush sleeping car complete with dining amenities.

■ American Express, a division of the Wells Fargo stagecoach line, already prominent for its domestic and international shipping, freight, and banking services, entered the travel market, initially as an agent for rail and steamship travel and later as a tour operator. It introduced the first traveler's cheques and expanded to provide travel bookings, credit cards, and other member-related services.

■ Conrad Hilton, one of the few hoteliers to remain solvent during the Depression, began his career renting out spare bedrooms in his father's house to traveling salesmen. His later purchases included the Plaza and the Waldorf-Astoria in New York. By 1950, Hilton corporation ranked as one of the three largest hotel chains in the United States.

■ Kemmons Wilson opened the first Holiday Inn in Tennessee after a disappointing family vacation. Today, the Holiday Inn chain is one of the largest in the United States.

■ Orville Wright made the first airplane flight at Kitty Hawk, North Carolina, on December 17, 1903. Although Americans were early air pioneers, England, France, and Germany took the lead in developing  commercial aviation. The shorter distances between cities and the availability of government subsidies gave European aviation advantages lacking in the United States.

■ Charles Lindbergh was the first to fly solo across the Atlantic. Soon after, the federal government began regulating commercial aviation. The Air Commerce Act laid down rules for the establishment of airports and the design and construction of aircraft. Each aircraft type had to be certified as fit to fly. Pilots had to pass tests and submit to regular re-examination. The act also standardized air routes and established methods of promoting air travel.

American Express introduced the first traveler's cheque in 1891.

The Hotel Porter

In the late 1920s, when the United States airlines began scheduled passenger service, the railroads were their prime competitors. Traveling salespeople used the railroads and stayed in hotels convenient to railroad stations. Travelers who wanted a train ticket often asked the hotel porter to go to the station to get it. The porter who did so received compensation from the railroad and a tip from the customer.

In big cities travel agencies were slowly appearing, selling steamship tickets and grand tours to the wealthy. Flying was still reserved for the mail and the adventurous few, until the development of planes like the DC-3 in the late 1930s permitted the airlines to offer safe and comfortable transportation. Service was limited at first, and it was only natural that the airlines turn to the existing distribution network of hotel porters and offer them 5 percent commissions to sell tickets. The porters did not need reference books or training. Airline tickets came with preprinted fares.

When travel agents started selling air tickets, the airlines responded by contending that agents were not creating new business, but merely servicing a demand that already existed. As air transportation rapidly grew more complicated, porters began to leave the industry or, sometimes, join it.

Two Boons to the Travel Industry — President Roosevelt's New Deal in the 1930s brought about shorter work weeks with increased leisure time, and the post– World War II unions began demanding mandatory vacation time for all employees.

The Travel Market Today

Today's traveler has different reasons for travel, and today's counselor must be responsive to those needs. Competition is keen. Veteran agents have witnessed both a social and a technological revolution: ocean liners have become cruise ships; the elegance of the Grand Tour has given way to

Historical Perspective

Great Dates in Travel History

The history of mankind is actually the history of travel. From earliest times driving factors such as hunger, curiosity, and need for shelter have caused mankind to spread across the earth. The Phoenicians, Greeks, and Romans built mighty warships to explore the Mediterranean. Aristocrats, scholars, and authors traveled miles to view the seven wonders of the ancient world. The fall of Rome may have briefly deterred travel, but the Crusades renewed pilgrimages to holy sites in Europe. History is replete with examples such as these.

Many events during the twentieth century have already had significant international impact.

1931	Formation of ASTA
1932	Depression forces travel agencies to introduce time-payment plans
1937	Crash of the *Hindenburg* ends dirigible travel
1939	World's Fair held in New York; first commercial flight crosses the Atlantic — Pan Am
1944	The *Queen Elizabeth* and the *Queen Mary* are used to ferry troops for the war effort
1950	Alaska Highway opens
1957	Beginning of Eurailpass
1958	American Express introduces its plastic charge cards
	First Holiday Inn opens in Memphis, Tennessee
1961	United States Travel Service is created to increase the number of foreign visitors
1964	ICTA is established
1970	Air-traffic controllers walk off their jobs
1971	Amtrak begins service; Walt Disney World opens in Orlando, Florida
1974	Oil embargo causes gas shortages and limits extensive travel plans
1976	First flight of the Concorde
1977	Last trip of the Orient Express
1978	Airline Deregulation Act becomes law
1980	United States boycotts Moscow Olympics
1981	Wedding of Prince Charles and Lady Di
	Birth of People's Express
1982	Recession in United States limits disposable income for travel
	EPCOT Center opens in Orlando, Florida
1984	Russia boycotts Los Angeles Olympics
1985	Hijacking of TWA flight 847
	Hijacking of the *Achille Lauro*
	Earthquake in Mexico City
1986	Statue of Liberty centennial celebration
	Chernobyl disaster
	United States attacks Libya
1987	Stock market crashes
1988	Russian policy of *glasnost* begins to open Eastern Europe
1989	Alaska oil spill
	Student massacre in China
1990	Removal of Berlin Wall
1991	Iraq invades Kuwait
1992	The breakup of the Soviet Union
	Euro Disney opens in France

discounted airfares; aircraft have evolved from small propeller-powered planes to jumbo jets.

Deregulation and automation have made it possible for airlines to change fares and routes abruptly. In this newly competitive atmosphere, airlines initiate radical new programs or rush to match those of their competitors. If the airlines have travel counselors confused from time to time, they often have consumers completely baffled. Passengers need somebody to explain it all and help them obtain value. The growing complexity of air travel has forced more clients to consult travel professionals for assistance and advice. Large companies view travel counselors as cost-effective because of their awareness of current airfares, bonus or incentive programs for frequent travelers, and other supplier discounts. Travel counselors are benefiting from the new competitiveness within the industry.

Counselors today also need to understand their clients' many different reasons to travel and match them to the variety of destinations. Understanding why people travel — in other words, their intangible needs — is the basis of all good counseling. It is key to providing such essential services as meeting planning, sophisticated destination information, or offering accessories like passport photographs or luggage.

Some clients will have very definite ideas of what they want in a vacation, and others will be distressingly vague. Clients may have very strong prejudices against certain places because of things they have heard or read. If a client is biased against a destination, it is usually futile to argue, even though the preconceptions are completely untrue. Clients who visit a place they expect to be unsanitary and full of rude people will be constantly looking for proof and very likely will find it. Such clients will be far happier visiting places about which they have no prejudices.

The noted sociologist Abraham Maslow developed a theory of human motivation based upon need satisfaction. He contended that human beings are motivated in their behavior and choices by their desire to satisfy a variety of needs. The needs are arranged in a hierarchy, or pyramid, ranging from the most basic to the most self-indulgent. Each successive level of the hierarchy does not come into play as a motivator until the levels preceding it have been largely satisfied.

Maslow's Hierarchy of Needs

"Hierarchy of Needs" from *Motivation and Personality* by Abraham H. Maslow. Copyright 1954, by Harper & Row, Publishers, Inc. Copyright ©1970 by Abraham H. Maslow. Reprinted by permission of HarperCollins Publishers.

Following Maslow, some agents would place the motivation for vacation and leisure travel fairly high on the hierarchy of needs. The desire to gain the respect or esteem of one's peers has a particular impact on destinations. Destinations remain fashionable as long as people can impress their friends by going there. Once a place becomes passé within a particular social group, it either begins to decline or adapts its appeal to a different group. In the 1950s, Jamaica was one of the most popular destinations in the Caribbean, and Montego Bay was a name that was every bit as magical and suggestive as Monte Carlo. But then the fashionable focus of the Caribbean shifted eastward to other islands, and Jamaica had to adapt to a new market composed, in part, of charter vacations and hedonistic beach clubs.

In a study about travel, Dr. Stanley C. Plog, president of the Behavior Science Corporation, suggests that all travelers can be placed somewhere on a spectrum of psychological types, ranging from those who prefer nearby destinations or familiar surroundings to those who seek new and exotic places to visit. The latter are always the first to discover new destinations that later become popularized by those who fall somewhere between the two extremes.

Plog suggests that some destinations may begin as exotic places for the few and become familiar to the many later. Bermuda shows this kind of development, especially for people living on the east coast of the United States. Once a very exclusive retreat, the island now offers hotels with recognizable American names, and its current advertising features people who return year after year.

Some destinations will never become extremely popular, either because of their distance from major populations or because of their specialized appeal. For Americans, the Seychelles and the Galapagos Islands are likely to remain remote. Conversely, the Catskills for New Yorkers and Hawaii for Californians are almost like home.

Developments in popular culture can affect the popularity of a destination. A television series, movie, or novel can pique interest in a particular country or city. Officials promoting tourism to Kenya reported that the movie *Out of Africa* increased inquiries about the country.

Since 1978, the number of travel agencies has increased from 6,700 to 33,000 in 1992.

Finally, as private industry and government investment developed such resort areas as Walt Disney World in Florida or Cancun in Mexico, other destinations lost popularity because of the competition. As more countries are enticed by the vision of tourism's economic benefits, the choice of destinations keeps growing. If the growth in tourism keeps pace, the total tourism market will always be distributed among countries in varying percentages. If not, the overdevelopment of destinations may lead to a worldwide surfeit.

Apart from developments that are reported by the news media and obviously influence the decisions of travelers, there are other factors that affect the popularity of a destination. There have been several attempts to explain these trends, and they focus as much on the characteristics of travelers as on the destinations themselves.

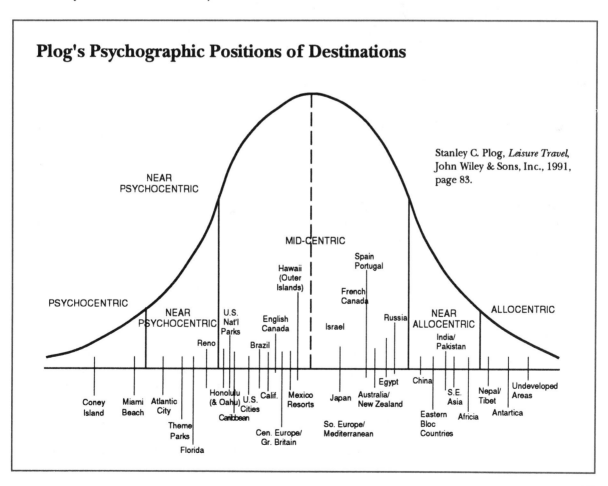

Plog's Psychographic Positions of Destinations

Stanley C. Plog, *Leisure Travel*, John Wiley & Sons, Inc., 1991, page 83.

Factors Important To a Vacationer's Destination Decision

According to a 1990 survey sponsored by *Travel Agent* magazine, vacationers base their destination decisions on the following variables:

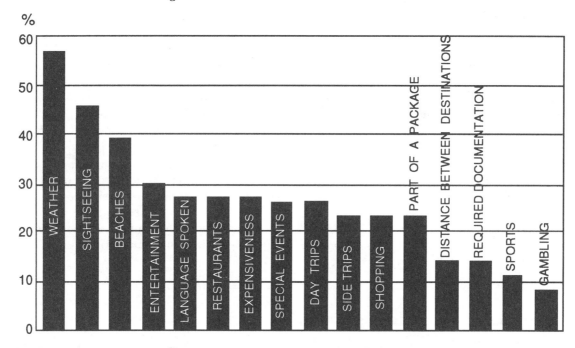

How Destinations Go In and Out of Fashion

For most people, distant destinations are the subject of fantasy escapes from daily routines. For those in the travel industry, however, such places are the focus of daily life. Travel professionals are expected to know about intriguing destinations and counsel clients wisely about their travel plans. Counselors use all of their skills to sell different products and present a clear picture of what clients will find at their destinations.

Destinations are like clothing. They go in and out of fashion. Periods of growth can be followed by periods of decline, which are sometimes never reversed. After a destination becomes fashionable, it then becomes popular. The adventurous early visitors are followed by the larger mass of tourists. Some destinations, like denim jeans, manage to retain their popularity. Others, like women's hemlines, rise and fall cyclically. Still others disappear seemingly forever, like starched collars.

The characteristic differences among destinations contribute to their popularity: ease of access, natural and man-made attractions, reasonable living costs, high health standards, a lively culture, an attractive climate, and a range of desirable accommodations and entertainment. Clearly, any marked deterioration in one of these elements will reduce tourism.

Attractions

Certain destinations boast attractions, either natural or man-made, that make them distinctive. Some have natural attractions so spectacular that they constitute the only reason for tourist activity. In the United States, the Grand Canyon draws millions of people to an area that otherwise would be virtually deserted. In Brazil, Iguassu Falls attracts tourists from all over the world even though one must fly two hours from Sao Paulo or go by train or riverboat for two days to view them. The Galapagos Islands are another natural wonder that attracts tourists despite the difficulty of getting there. These islands, mostly uninhabited, lie 650 miles off the coast of Ecuador and were the site of Charles Darwin's observations. They contain varieties of wild life not found anywhere else in the world.

The loss of or damage to natural attractions seriously affects a destination's popularity. According to experts, the national parks in the United States are threatened by pollution from nearby industries, from excessive camping that produces litter and the danger of fire, and from too many private cars. Development adjacent to the parks has also marred their attractiveness. The encroachment of private homes has spoiled the view. The National Park Service is concerned that the lands in its care may soon lose the qualities that caused them to be protected, victims to some extent of their own popularity.

Man-made attractions also draw visitors. The success of Disneyland in Anaheim, California, and Walt Disney World/EPCOT near Orlando, Florida, is well documented. Since they were first conceived and built, beginning with Disneyland in the 1950s, they have drawn millions of tourists each year. Other man-made attractions in various parts of the world are famous for their religious or

historical significance. The pyramids in Egypt and Mexico, Stonehenge in England, and the Taj Mahal in India attract tourists to locales that boast no other outstanding characteristics.

Cost and Standards of Living

Destinations vary widely in the cost of tourist goods and services. Although destinations like Bermuda are attractive because of their desirable climates and accessibility, rates for hotels and food are rather high. Bermuda must import nearly all the necessities and luxuries the tourist seeks.

Sometimes the availability or extremely high cost of certain items results from cultural differences between the local inhabitants and the tourists. In Saudi Arabia, where the population is Moslem and the style of dress tends toward the

flowing robe, the tourist will find alcoholic beverages forbidden by Moslem law and a man's shirt priced up to ten times what it might cost in the United States.

Some countries are too poor to afford luxuries either for tourists or their own citizens. Many Third World countries need to import basic foods and materials. Consequently, tourist items are rarely found and are very expensive.

The problem of meeting tourist wants and needs arises in varying degrees all around the world. The more exotic, remote, and undeveloped the destination, the more prepared the client must be to forgo some items that are commonplace at home or to pay an exorbitant price for them. Rates of currency exchange also affect the cost of living for tourists at any destination. The fluctuating relationships between currencies make it vital for travel agents to know when destinations are becoming more or less expensive for their clients.

Significant inflation in the local economy or unfavorable shifts in currency exchange rates may make destinations too expensive, and reports of health problems may deter many travelers. Philadelphia lost a number of individual, group, and convention visitors in the wake of an outbreak of Legionnaire's disease. Changes in political philosophy may adversely affect the level of investment in tourism facilities and may also affect the attitude of the inhabitants toward tourists.

A recent American Express survey predicted a growing interest in travel to Eastern Europe. However, Florida and England are still expected to be the top domestic and foreign destinations for U.S. travelers.

Accessibility

It may not be true for everybody that getting there is half the fun. Accessibility affects the traveler's vacation experience. Some people become very upset and confused if their trip begins with a series of flights, transfers, layovers, and changes in modes of transportation. For example, clients traveling from Dayton, Ohio, to spend a week at Club Med in Playa Blanca, Mexico, would drive very early in the morning to the airport; fly to Dallas; change planes for Puerto Vallarta; and then drive two and one-half hours to Playa Blanca. Some clients may like this kind of adventure; others may not. Clients who delight in finding their own way to remote corners of the world will obviously not be much concerned with how easy it is to get to a destination.

Many clients prefer an uncomplicated trip. A visit to Dallas, for instance, can be made on a direct flight from many cities in the United States. Despite the distance between the city and the airport, modern baggage- and people-moving systems and an efficient transportation network can deliver clients to their downtown hotels within an hour.

When terrorism, outbreaks of disease, or strikes occur in foreign countries, it is often difficult to obtain an accurate picture of the conditions for visitors. The agent needs to know exactly what the problems are. Clients may be completely unaware that air-traffic controllers are striking in a particular country and that flights are subject to diversion or delay. Here the counselor can assess the problems and prepare clients for them.

In most instances counselors should report to clients any questionable situation and allow them to decide whether they will postpone or alter their trip. An agent who feels that clients are overreacting to trivial incidents or misjudging the location of events would be very unwise to pressure them to travel against their will. On the other hand, the agent may feel impelled in a few instances to advise clients not to travel. Such drastic advice is usually necessary if other clients report an unpleasant situation on their return, or most particularly if the State Department issues an advisory warning U. S. citizens that travel to a particular country may be dangerous to their health, life, or liberty.

State Department advisories are sent to travel agencies when requested. Travel publications such as *ASTA Notes* also carry updates on these advisories. However, a travel agent's best policy is to read a daily newspaper and keep current on world events. If there is the slightest doubt about the situation in any destination, the agent should check with the nearest State Department office or with a carrier or tour operator offering flights and tours to the affected area.

Sources of Information

Continuing education and training represent opportunities for both personal enrichment and career development. *Travel Career Development* suggests ways to grow within the travel industry. Almost any form of education—formal or informal—will contribute to personal and professional growth.

A travel office is a microcosm of pooled knowledge surrounded by accessible resources. Interaction with experienced staff members and suppliers, within the office or at trade gatherings, is a stimulating educational experience. The successful travel professional builds a store of information and, more importantly, knows where to find more. In today's competitive environment, the ability to draw on knowledge and produce information speedily becomes increasingly important. This book is dedicated to that simple proposition.

Familiarization Trips

There is probably no substitute for a personal visit if an agent wishes to be truly well informed about the attractions, accommodations, and facilities at a particular destination. Carriers, tour operators, and governments operate familiarization (fam) trips to popular destinations so that counselors can inspect hotels and restaurants, sample the attractions, and experience the local culture. The agent's personal vacation trips can also supplement the knowledge gained.

Familiarization trips build the confidence and product knowledge so necessary for successful selling. Participants also meet other professionals, sometimes from different areas of the country, who provide interesting new viewpoints on the travel industry. No agent can personally visit each destination and hotel, so the sharing of updated, eyewitness accounts becomes very important. Certain counselors may become a source of information about a particular destination and will be consulted by colleagues when appropriate.

Suppliers routinely offer fam trips that enable counselors to visit destinations where they attend related workshops or seminars. Counselors may hear that fam trips are a vacation, a fringe benefit, or even a natural right, but these attitudes encourage irresponsible behavior that insults the hosts and defeats the trip's real purpose. Fam trips are enjoyable because they enable individuals to see exciting or new destinations firsthand, but they are primarily structured educational programs with a serious purpose extended as both a reward and an incentive.

It is clearly impossible for agents to visit every destination they sell. Destinations, accommodations, and facilities change over time, and to remain truly current, a visit at least every five years to each destination might be required. Travel counselors cannot refuse to sell a destination because they do not know it personally. They must rely on other sources of information, most printed, some automated, and others on video. A brief visit cannot provide a comprehensive and true picture of a destination's appeal and can never replace entirely the references that form the backbone of an agent's knowledge.

How to Get the Most Value Out of a Fam Trip

Certainly it is much more enjoyable to visit a destination than to merely read about it or listen to clients regale you with their exploits, but fam trips are also educational and cost-effective opportunities. Prior to the trip establish a clear objective — choose exactly what you want to do and what information you want to gain as a result of the experience. When packing, choose items appropriate for the climate and nature of the destination. (Hint: Be sure to pack a tape recorder or writing materials for notes). During the trip, be sure to introduce yourself to your fellow travelers. Ask appropriate questions — remember, your purpose is to learn. Evaluate your experiences at airports, transportation vendors, accommodations — how was the service? Gather important materials that will help you sell the destination when you return. If it's a long flight, transcribe your notes while the ideas are fresh in your mind. Upon your return, send thank-you notes — everyone likes to know that they've done a good job.

Associations and Tourist Offices

Closer to home, especially in large cities, suppliers, national tourist offices, trade associations, and other organizations schedule presentations, workshops, or seminars. Many companies designate one individual to attend and report back to the office at staff meetings. In addition, marketing representatives of suppliers may offer to brief a company's staff on new developments.

Many foreign governments maintain tourist offices that actively promote travel to their countries. Working closely with airlines and tour operators, the national tourist offices (NTOs) can provide sophisticated marketing assistance as well as a wealth of printed information. The staffs have an intimate knowledge of their countries and can assist anyone who would like to know more about how business is conducted in a country or how a school band can perform a series of concerts there, or answer more predictable questions about sun and sand.

Agents may see national tourist offices primarily as sources of brochures and informational pamphlets, but they are more than that. As agencies of their governments, NTOs develop, promote, and market tourism to bring the maximum economic benefit to their countries. Some divisions are responsible for keeping up-to-date destination information available in computer reservation systems.

Inside its own country, an NTO works to foster awareness of the benefits of in-bound tourism and to promote friendliness toward visitors. It formulates and implements official government policy. Working with carriers and tour operators, the NTO presents plans or recommendations for legislation to promote tourism. Thus, although NTOs can assist with individual bookings, they are especially helpful in developing groups because of the promotional aids, marketing expertise, and contacts they offer.

Addresses for national tourist offices are found in the OAG *Travel Planners* or in the *Travel Industry Personnel Directory*, published annually by *Travel Agent* magazine. As a rule, NTOs do not sell any travel arrangements except when a country's government is the tour operator. The primary responsibility of an NTO is to present its country in the best light. Most of them recognize, however, that the most valuable assistance they can provide is balanced advice and promotional support.

Written References

Travel agencies have many reference books, each addressing specific needs. Yet as travel counselors progress to more and more complex arrangements, their creativity and imagination in using these references are tested. A good atlas is a necessity and should be revisited frequently like an old friend. Reading the *National Geographic* helps in gaining a general knowledge of well-known and remote areas of the world. Other sources of more specific information about destinations exist within the office or at the end of the telephone.

All second-hand information, whether written or spoken, is subject to personal bias. Judgments, ratings, and even the selection of topics represent to some degree the values of the reporter. Travel professionals might be well advised to stick to facts about a destination were it not that destinations are very often distinguished by just those subtle nuances of culture and ambience that can be conveyed only through highly personal judgments. What agent would not like to have a thoroughly reliable guide to the Caribbean that recommended without any shadow of doubt the three best islands for scuba diving, for golf, for shopping, for tropical vegetation, for beaches? Such judgments inevitably express personal tastes and values.

Electronic Publishing

Within the next five to ten years, electronic publishing could eliminate the need for cumbersome printed materials. Does that mean that such tools as maps, OAGs, and travel guides will become extinct? Not yet, according to most experts. Computer directories like SABREvision provide ease of use for PC and modem owners who have made initial equipment and training investments. Such systems offer the benefits of immense quantities of data, color visuals, and audio at your fingertips. However, many travel vendors have yet to convert to this technology. Most agencies still favor standard print media for daily use. Most likely for the near future, publishers will change as they respond to competition.

Guidebooks

Almost all agencies carry copies of the best-known guidebooks, and travel agents should be  familiar with them if only to know where some clients are getting all their ideas. This is becoming increasingly difficult as more than 400 new titles come out yearly. To further complicate matters, guidebooks vary in quality by volume, edition, editor, and author.

Some general factors to consider when recommending guidebooks include ease of use, cost, photography and graphic design, and level of detail. Someone wishing to spend a summer in Europe may choose a very comprehensive book, while a weekend tripper to the Berkshires may want honesty and accuracy on a simpler scale. Clients appreciate recommendations, and matching the right book to the client can be invaluable PR.

One way to evaluate a guidebook is to read what it says about any attraction or hotel that you know very well and have recently visited. Compare the guidebook's description with your own experience. Look at factors such as prices and restaurant or hotel selections to check for accuracy.

Despite the fact that new editions of many guidebooks appear each year, much of the information remains the same. The cost of visiting every hotel or restaurant once a year would probably make the guides very expensive to produce. Nevertheless, it is sometimes disconcerting to realize the description of a highly recommended property may be several years old.

Most guidebooks are published for sale to the public, although some also enjoy a healthy distribution to travel agencies where they are used as invaluable research tools. Some authors specialize in niche marketing to budget-minded or adventure travelers. Others have chosen to focus on travel with children, the handicapped, shoppers, or allocentrics. Choosing the right guidebook (or video) for a client is often as important as recommending the right destination.

Trade Publications

Trade groups such as ASTA and PATA publish magazines or annual guides with up-to-date information about destinations. Similarly, trade news-

Leading Guidebook Series

Frommer Guides — Dollar-A-Day and City Guides both emphasize accommodations, restaurants, and sightseeing tips. Frommer's country and regional guides provide pricing information, walking maps, sightseeing information, as well as the author's personal insights and advice. Features in the newer editions include children's favorites, travel tips, suggested reading, cultural information, terminology, climate, currency, clothing sizes and metric conversions, and basic native phrases.

Baedeker Guides — Not to be confused with the original Baedekers that flourished in the late nineteenth and early twentieth centuries, this series concentrates on how to get there and what to see. These guides include color photographs; full-size, removable maps; and detailed touring and sightseeing attractions. Twenty-one country or regional listings for Europe, the Caribbean, Asia, and Africa are included.

Insight Guides — Designed for the armchair and the avid traveler. All contain color photography, essay-style cultural articles, maps, and planning orientations in short, encapsulated style. Currently, 129 destinations are covered.

Fodor Guides — A comprehensive series of guides to most destinations in the world. This series includes standard listings, affordable listings, bed and breakfast guides, and three-in-one travel kits. The three-in-one kits contain guidebooks, language cassettes, and phrasebook/dictionaries. Destinations are listed by city or country, depending on travelers' needs. Most include sightseeing, walking tours, attractions, hotel and restaurant reviews, nightlife, and shopping.

Michelin — Has been publishing guidebooks since 1900. Today it offers guidebooks, atlases, and maps to more than 200 cities, regions, and countries in the world. The *Red Series* lists hotels, restaurants, and garages (for tires) in the country or countries covered by the particular guide. The *Green Guides* provide detailed historical and sightseeing tourist information about destinations, as well as maps. *Green Guides* may deal with an entire country, a region of a country, or a single large city. Michelin concentrates on Western European destinations, although other areas, such as North America, are now appearing.

Birnbaum Travel Guides— The Birnbaum series concentrates on tourist services, sources of information, and brief descriptions of important sights. These works are contemporary and practical in nature, including details such as historical and cultural information, hotel and restaurant appraisals, shopping hints, day tours, and diversions.

The Best Places to Stay — This series discusses all types of hotel accommodations from budget B & Bs to romantic hideaways. Some lodging examples are cottages, farms, ski lodges, ranches, and island resorts. Included are local maps, cross references, recommended reading, and suggested itineraries.

papers like *Tour and Travel News, Travel Weekly, Travel Agent,* and *Travel Trade* contain destination articles and supplements in every issue. These are useful since they combine information about a destination with the names of suppliers who provide tours or special services. They also give information about new industry rules and regulations. Every other sector of the industry, be it hotels, restaurants, or recreation, has its own specific journals. A subscription to any of them would significantly supplement the contents of this book.

Brochures

Although brochures distributed by tour operators and suppliers are designed to present destinations in their best possible light, responsible tour operators, desiring to secure repeat business from satisfied clients, take care not to misrepresent the destinations they portray. In "General Information" sections, brochures often present information about local customs, health precautions, visa requirements, currency, and shopping. Cruise line brochures supply passengers with hints on what to wear.

Tour operators know the destinations they offer very well and can often provide advice over the telephone. They are not likely to volunteer information unless asked.

Every travel agency has its own filing system for tour brochures and informational literature. Most counselors keep a personal file with single copies of frequently used brochures. Some tour operators provide special agents' editions of their brochures, including specific booking instructions and facts about destinations and accommodations.

Travel Videos

Travel videos were primarily designed to sell travel to the consumer, but they have turned out to be a boon to the agent as well. The proliferation of home VCRs and the reduction in cassette prices allow the agent many creative uses.

More than 65 percent of all homes now have VCRs. A recent Roper poll indicated that travel tapes are the most popular video rental category after feature films.

Most videos are watched by upscale consumers who travel extensively. Originally developed for armchair travelers, today's productions contain practical information. These video guidebooks

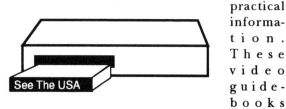

show clients where to stay, what attractions to see, and what souvenirs to buy. Often this type of tape is produced by single operators or commercial sponsors.

Other videos portray the flavor of the destination by creating certain moods. Rather than concentrating on specifics, they help travelers experience the atmosphere of the country. This type, often produced by tourist bureaus or independent production houses, is an excellent sales tool.

Travel agencies use tapes as resource libraries, loaning or renting them out to clients interested

in the destination. This service has an added advantage. Another sales opportunity arises when the client returns the video to the agency. In addition, the use of video signifies to the client that the agency is service-oriented and on the cutting edge of technology. Videos may help in upselling additional destinations or finalizing the sale of lesser-known destinations to clients who have only vague travel plans.

Ways to Use Videos Successfully

■ Training sessions for staff
■ Group presentations
■ In-house viewings
■ Gifts to clients
■ Revenue production through sales or rentals

How to Choose a Good Travel Video

Sometimes the wide choice of travel videos intimidates not only consumers but also agents when selecting exactly the right tape for their clients or staff. A good video should be professional in production, presentation, editing, and sound quality. For travel purposes, it should be relatively short in length and feature practical information such as maps. Music and narration should reflect the culture of the destination but should not obscure the message of the film. Images of people and places should sell the destination, not the sponsors' commercials. Finally, choose a video series that looks attractive on a shelf and will not be outdated quickly.

Travel videos often replace guidebooks for younger, more visually-literate clients. The old saying "a picture is worth a thousand words" certainly holds true for this new entry in travel promotion.

Other Sources

Novels, television, newspapers, and films help build an agent's knowledge of the world. To keep abreast of consumer needs, agents must be aware of the very latest trends and happenings, as well as the enduring and traditional images. Agents should never neglect their clients as sources of information about destinations. Those who have recently returned from a particular destination can provide up-to-date information and impressions. They are usually pleased to be asked for their opinion.

The Future of the Industry

Increasingly, governments around the world are becoming more interested in tourism as an industry capable of employing millions, of improving international relations, and of narrowing the gap between exports and imports. Visitors to a state or country spend money there. The prepayments they give to a travel agent back home eventually transfer to hotels and suppliers at the destination. These prepayments behave like exports, where payment made in another state or country goes to the place where the product was manufactured.

The travel industry relies on a network of supporting services and facilities called the infrastructure. Airports, harbors, roads, bridges, and water supplies must be capable of serving growing numbers of tourists.

Other factors will affect the travel industry in the near future. Some changes will be incremental, flowing naturally from events already known or set in motion. The availability and price of fuel will continue to concern all suppliers. The industry will counter by applying technology to mitigate the impact of shortages or rising prices on consumers. Cruise lines are building new ships designed to carry more people in greater comfort. The new generation of Boeing, McDonnell Douglas, and Airbus Industrie jets are up to 30 percent more fuel-efficient than the planes they are replacing. New ships and planes use recently developed metals that are stronger but lighter than steel.

The travel industry is inventive. More than most industries it can adapt to changing conditions. It has long been used to seasonality. Both agents and suppliers emphasize different destinations and services at different times of the year. Travel agents can be true entrepreneurs, sensing new needs and utilizing new markets as soon as they appear.

To retain the loyalty of their clients and to consolidate their importance within the industry, counselors need to look beyond today. It is crucial for them to do more than sell transportation and accommodations. They need to understand why their clients travel so they can provide a whole range of services.

Travel can create its own future. An area of undistinguished flatland near a sleepy little town in Florida became Walt Disney World, and Orlando emerged as one of the most futuristic areas in the world. The Mexican government selected a deserted stretch of shoreline on the Yucatan peninsula and created a new destination—Cancun. As long as the travel industry can discover or create reasons for travel and promote them successfully, the future remains bright.

Summary

Our earliest ancestors traveled primarily in search of food. As time progressed, other reasons for travel included trade, religious pilgrimages, and exploration. Early pioneers in the travel industry field included Thomas Cook, Conrad Hilton, and Charles Lindbergh.

The travel market today consists of travelers motivated by an endless variety of factors. According to a *Travel Agent* magazine survey, the top three reasons that vacationers gave for their destination decisions were weather, sightseeing, and beaches. Destinations may also rise or fall in popularity because of their reputations.

Travel agents must be equipped with as much education and as many resources as possible to address the needs of their clients. This can be achieved by going on familiarization trips, working with tourist offices, attending trade shows, and stocking the agency with appropriate guidebooks and brochures. Travel videos are one of the newest resources available to both agents and their clients.

The future will always offer the educated travel agent new challenges and opportunities.

Chapter Wrap-up

DISCUSSION TOPICS

Papua New Guinea

In Papua New Guinea life goes on much as it has for more than 8,000 years. The majority of the population of three million lives in clans or village communities. Some primitive tribes in remote regions have yet to be touched by modern society. Age-old mores are the norm rather than the exception. For example, drums have notches carved in them representing heads that have been hunted; the backs of young boys are scarred during initiations into manhood; and spirit houses open only to men remain the focus of village life. Naked children and half-naked adults live in villages where pigs wander loose, competing with strutting chickens and stray dogs for scraps of food. Modern electricity, plumbing, and other amenities usually associated with everyday living are not available. What type of client would enjoy such a destination? What effect would the discovery of oil off the coastline or in the interior have on such a destination?

Disasters

Many tourists are lured to destinations by an unusual local occurrence, a noteworthy event, or a natural disaster — the damage wrought by a hurricane in Hawaii, the site of former President Reagan's shooting in Washington, D.C., the oil spill off Alaska's coastline. Look through a local newspaper, examine the headlines, and consider areas of the world being affected by similar problems. Identify which disasters might actually increase tourism. How many others will cause irreparable damage to the tourism in the area?

Plog's Theory

Using Dr. Plog's chart as a guideline, choose two international destinations that would appeal to allocentric travelers; two destinations within the United States that would appeal to midcentric travelers; and two local destinations that would appeal to psychocentric travelers. Justify your answers.

Destination Geography

Chapter 2

CHAPTER OBJECTIVES

After completing this chapter, the reader should be able to

■ Discuss three types of geography
■ Identify map terminology
■ Relate the differences between weather and climate
■ Discuss some important regional sightseeing attractions in the United States
■ Identify popular worldwide tourist destinations

VOCABULARY

After completing this chapter, the reader should be able to define

■ Continent
■ Cultural geography
■ Gulf
■ Index
■ Island
■ Latitude
■ Legend
■ Locational geography
■ Longitude
■ Physical geography
■ Relief
■ Scale

Introduction

Travel counselors who lack basic geographic skills will not be able to give advice to their clients, plan trips, or construct itineraries. As doctors need to study medicine and lawyers need to study law, so do travel agents need to have a working knowledge of geography. Clients do not expect that agents know the whole world, but they do expect them to be acquainted with the popular tourist areas. In this chapter you will learn basic destination geography.

One chapter in a book cannot possibly provide a complete and detailed description of all the world's tourist destinations. After studying this chapter, however, you should become aware of the major tourism areas. Hopefully, this information will serve as a starting point as you continue to study and learn the destinations of the world.

Rand McNally Quick Reference World Atlas

Use the *Rand McNally Quick Reference World Atlas* in the back of the book to help you as you study this chapter.

Destination – Related Careers

Cartographer
Climatologist
Convention and Visitors
Bureau Representative

Tourist Bureau Representative
(local, regional, national)
Travel Photographer
Travel Writer

Convention and Vistors Bureau Representative

Convention and visitors bureau representatives are one of the most rapidly expanding segments in the field of travel. They come from all sectors of the service industry: hotel sales, tour guides, restaurant managers, meeting planners.

Bureau representatives perform a variety of duties. Membership managers are responsible for recruiting area businesses and sponsors in local promotional efforts. Sales and marketing managers coordinate all phases of meetings for associations and corporations from the initial sales proposal to servicing the actual function. Travel managers interact with local travel agencies and tourists to provide information about transportation, sightseeing attractions, hotels, and restaurants. Directors are responsible for the overall public-relations effort of the office as well as personnel and operational management. The daily duties of a representative may include telemarketing, conducting site inspections, organizing and participating in familiarization tours, dealing with the press, developing sales presentations, and performing clerical tasks.

Applicants should be organized and detail-oriented, with strong interpersonal and communication skills. Having computer expertise is also an advantage. One of the keys to this position is flexibility as functions are often held in the evening or on weekends. In addition to strong product knowledge, a good rapport with area vendors, local businesses and chambers of commerce is also important. Convention and visitors bureau representatives provide a vital sales and service link between travelers, delegates, and local businesses.

Types of Geography

Geography is a science with many branches. Travel counselors are primarily concerned with three of its aspects:

■ Locational

■ Physical

■ Cultural

Locational Geography

Locational geography seeks to answer two questions: "Where is it?" and "How do you get there?" The answers primarily lie in maps, atlases, and reference books. Counselors need to know where countries, regions, and cities are, as well as the location of the ports and airports that provide access to these areas.

For travel professionals, maps are invaluable sources of information about destinations. No map can show everything because it would be impossible to read, so every map is a simplified picture of what is really there.

Cartographers encounter major problems when they attempt to map a large area. A map is flat and two-dimensional; the earth is a sphere and three-dimensional. It is impossible to represent a spheri-

Map Terminology

■ **Title** — What the map is going to be about.

■ **Scale** — How much area and how much detail the map will cover. A large-scale map shows many details of a small area — for example, every road within a village. A small-scale map shows little detail — for example, states, countries, or continents.

■ **Relief** — The altitude of the area. Relief shows height and depth in relation to altitude above or below sea level.

■ **Legend** — An explanation of what symbols the map will use.

■ **Index** — A guide to where information can be located.

■ **Compass Points** — North, south, east, and west. Generally north is at the top of the map, but not always.

cal object on a flat surface without distortion. Cartographers have tried many methods to project the round earth onto flat paper, but none is completely successful. The only way to see the true relationship of both area and shape is on a globe.

Latitudes are parallel lines measuring distances north or south of the equator. Longitudes measure distances east and west of the prime meridian.

Physical Geography

Basic to physical geography is the study of climate and the description of terrain. Physical geography answers questions such as "What is the weather like?" "Is it worth driving through the countryside?" "When is the best time to go?"

The terms *weather* and *climate* are sometimes used interchangeably, but they refer to different things. Climate is the combination of temperature, precipitation, winds, and water currents that along with air pressure and elevation is studied over a long period of time. Weather is what is happening at a particular moment. A climatologist is engaged in the long-term study of the climate, but a meteorologist observes local conditions and gives information and predictions about what is going to occur for the short term.

Weather is probably the most consistent front-page news item in the daily newspaper. Such prominence shows the importance of weather in everyday life, especially to travelers.

Clients have different concerns about the weather depending on their reasons for travel. Off-season travel with its sharply reduced rates offers excellent bargains, but the counselor must be careful to investigate why off-season is off-season. Perhaps the weather make the destination unpleasant or unsuited for its principal attractions.

It is climate, however, that influences the larger patterns of mankind on the earth. A knowledge of the climate in various parts of the world helps the travel professional select a vacation spot for a client or advise the business or pleasure traveler. In some countries climate varies so greatly over short distances that knowing the patterns in the capital city may prove misleading for clients who wish to tour the country.

The annual revolution of the earth around the sun causes seasonal changes. Because of the way the earth tilts on its axis, the rays of the sun shine either more or less on specific portions of the earth at certain times of the year. The equator receives the most direct rays during the whole year and is the hottest part of the earth; the North and South Poles get the least amount of direct sun and are therefore the coldest.

Detailed city weather information is available through a variety of continuously updated weather hotlines. Many services are accessed through 900 telephone numbers. Some of the more detailed systems provide not only weather information, but also road conditions, tipping customs, foreign entry requirements, and financial data.

Cultural Geography

Cultural geography studies the division of the world into groups and contrasting societies. A knowledge of cultural geography permits the counselor to understand the distinctive political, historical, social, artistic, and religious characteristics of a country or region. Travel professionals use this knowledge to advise clients about what to do and see at the destination and to prepare them for any differences they will encounter.

Cultural characteristics — language, religion, politics, art, food — are the forces that have shaped the society and made it distinct from others. Culture is manifested in the variety of human behaviors and customs that tourists encounter every day. A society's culture profoundly affects the tourist's experience because it can encompass such things as attitude or which stores are open on Sundays.

Although many aspects of a society's culture are immune to change from contact with tourists, some are quickly altered. The arts, culinary traditions, or social customs and behavior may often be speedily and radically changed by tourism. For example, in some countries art that started as a pure expression of native traditions gradually has become commercialized to fit the desires of the tourist. On the positive side, however, tourism can also preserve native traditions that otherwise might decline from disuse.

Destinations

Every country in the world is a potential travel destination. Each area offers a combination of natural resources, man-made attractions, products, and services that render it unique. When discussing destination geography, it is important to match the unique features of a destination with the needs and wants of the individual traveler. The destination areas we will focus on are

- The United States
- Canada
- Mexico
- The Caribbean
- Central and South America
- Europe
- Asia and the Pacific
- Africa

Geographical Definitions

Land Masses

The earth is a sphere. If we divide the earth as geographers do, the sphere subdivides into hemispheres — northern and southern, eastern and western. Everything north of the equator is in the Northern Hemisphere, and everything south is in the Southern Hemisphere. Other definitions useful to the travel counselor are:

- **Continent** — A continent is one of the large land masses of the earth. The seven continents are Asia, Africa, North America, South America, Antarctica, Europe, and Australia. Within the continents, countries have established their own boundaries.

- **Island** — An island is a body of land completely surrounded by water. Islands are found in all shapes and sizes.

- **Mountains** — Mountains are composed of land that rises higher than the surrounding base land. Mountains were caused by the shifting of the earth's land mass.

Bodies of Water

Between most continents are bodies of salt water called oceans, seas, bays, or gulfs. A huge body of salt water covers nearly three-fourths of the surface of the globe. That great body has three major divisions — the Pacific, the Atlantic, and the Indian oceans.

- **Gulf** — A large body of salt water that is bordered by a curved shoreline.

- **River** — A moving body of fresh water that flows from a basin to its mouth, or termination point.

- **Sea** — Smaller than an ocean, a sea is a body of salt water surrounded by land mass.

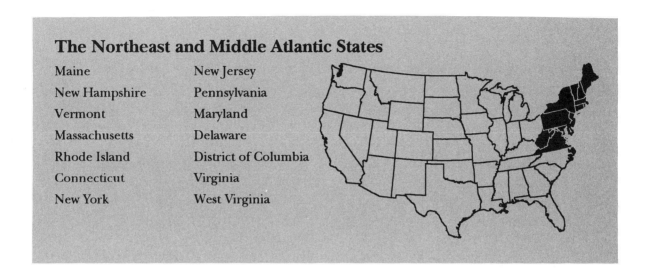

The Northeast and Middle Atlantic States

Maine	New Jersey
New Hampshire	Pennsylvania
Vermont	Maryland
Massachusetts	Delaware
Rhode Island	District of Columbia
Connecticut	Virginia
New York	West Virginia

The United States

It would be difficult to imagine a country with greater diversity in landscape and climate than the United States. The United States offers a blend of cultural traditions, many natural attractions, an advanced infrastructure, and a stable political climate. Sometimes referred to as a "melting pot," its appeal draws travelers from many countries.

The Northeast and Middle Atlantic States

Maine, New Hampshire, Vermont, Massachusetts, Rhode Island, and Connecticut make up the states of New England. Located in the northeastern corner of the country, much of New England maintains the charm and quaintness of its historic past. New England offers beautiful fall foliage, picturesque villages with quaint country inns, and skiing in mountain resorts. Other attractions include the rugged coastline of Maine, the historic sights in Boston, and the beautiful mansions in Newport, Rhode Island.

New York state has a wide selection of regions to visit, each offering unique sightseeing opportunities. The Finger Lakes region in central New York is an area of scenic vistas, gorges, and waterfalls, and the location of numerous wineries. Lake Champlain and Lake George are filled with resorts, and the Adirondack Mountains are popular for hiking, fishing, and camping.

New Jersey, although small in size, has hundreds of miles of beautiful beaches and natural parkland. Philadelphia is the historic heart of both Pennsylvania and the nation. It was in Independence Hall that the Declaration of Independence was signed and the Constitution drafted. Day trips from Philadelphia include Valley Forge State Park; Pennsylvania Dutch country, home to the Amish and the Mennonites; and the Poconos, a popular year-round resort area.

Maryland's tourist destinations range from the white beaches in Ocean City to the Inner Harbor in Baltimore. Delaware, the second smallest state in the nation, is mostly rural. Wilmington is the major city and is known as the capital of the chemical industry. Washington, D.C., is the center of a vast metropolitan area that also encompasses Maryland and Virginia.

Virginia's topography ranges from ocean beaches in the east to mountains in the west. Williamsburg is a restored, eighteenth-century town, home to crafts, and beautiful gardens. West Virginia is a beautiful mountain state that contains vast mineral resources, especially coal.

The Southeast

Kentucky is sometimes referred to as a border state — southern in history and make-up, but northern in economics. It's best known for horses, caves, and bluegrass. Lexington is a major horse-breeding center; Louisville is the proud host each year of the Kentucky Derby. Tennessee has plains on the west, a hilly center, and a mountainous east. Memphis is Elvis Presley's hometown and site of his Graceland Mansion. Nashville is considered the home of country music.

The Southeast

Kentucky	Florida
Tennessee	Alabama
North Carolina	Mississippi
South Carolina	Louisiana
Georgia	Arkansas

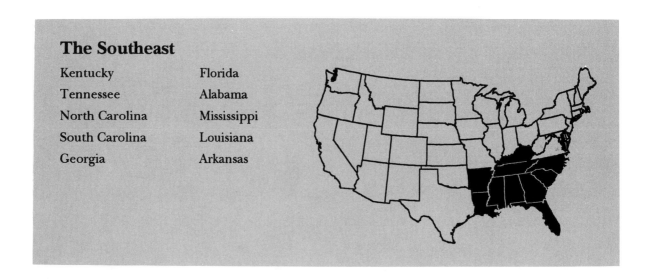

The coastal areas of North Carolina, South Carolina, and Georgia have miles of warm sandy beaches, championship golf courses, and charming cities such as Ocracoke, North Carolina; Charleston, South Carolina; and Savannah, Georgia. North Carolina is famous for the islands of the Outer Banks and the Cape Hatteras National Seashore. South Carolina features a rich history, beautiful plantations, and Civil War battlesites. Charleston, South Carolina, is an elegant and historic city. Atlanta, capital of Georgia, is a cosmopolitan city that is considered the cultural, financial, and entertainment hub of the South.

The main centers for tourism in Florida are the Gulf Coast, comprising the Tampa, St. Petersburg area; central Florida, most famous for the many man-made attractions in Orlando; the Gold Coast, home to Miami and West Palm Beach; and the Florida Keys, culminating in Key West, the southernmost city in the contiguous United States.

Alabama, Mississippi, and Louisiana are all located on the Gulf of Mexico. One of the largest space museums in the country, the Alabama Space and Rocket Center, is located in Huntsville, Alabama. Mississippi is noted for its pre-Civil War mansions, fine beaches, and scenery. Natchez has more than four hundred eighteenth- and nineteenth-century pre-Civil War mansions, many of which are open to the public. French traditions and language dominate much of southern Louisiana: the Creole culture is mainly experienced in New Orleans, and the Cajun culture is in the bayou country south of the city.

Mountains, valleys, and rivers make up the state of Arkansas. Hot Springs National Park is a resort and international spa.

The Midwest

The Midwest region is a mixture of agriculture and industry, often referred to as America's heartland. The largest cities are located along the shores of the Great Lakes. Boating, fishing, swimming, and all other types of summer water-related activities epitomize the lakes regions of Minnesota, Wisconsin, and Michigan. In winter, these states are blanketed by snow and offer a variety of winter-sports opportunities.

Ohio is largely an industrial state, home to nearly four-fifths of the nation's leading industries. Cleveland, one of Ohio's largest cities, is the headquarters of more than 30 major industrial corporations and numerous smaller companies. Michigan is divided into a Lower Peninsula, with its countless lakes and most of the state's population, and an Upper Peninsula, featuring a more rugged and hilly terrain. Detroit, Michigan's largest city, is the cultural and commercial center of the state and the center of automobile manufacturing in the United States.

Indiana, known as the "Crossroads of the Nation," is a typically American state. Every Memorial Day, the famous Indy 500 auto race takes place in the capital city, Indianapolis. Illinois, the "Land of Lincoln," features Chicago as the focal point of the state. Springfield, the state capital, was Lincoln's

The Midwest

Ohio	Wisconsin
Michigan	Minnesota
Indiana	Iowa
Illinois	Missouri

home for 25 years and there are several Lincoln attractions open to the public.

Wisconsin, a land of scenic beauty, is famous for dairying and paper-making. Milwaukee, Wisconsin's largest city, is the state's primary commercial and manufacturing center and is famous for its brewing industry. Minnesota is home to farmland, forests, and more than 11,000 lakes. The twin cities of Minneapolis and St. Paul share many cultural activities. St. Paul, the capital, is more historic; Minneapolis is more modern.

Iowa represents the epitome of farming in rural America — the heart of the cornbelt. Because of its location, Missouri is a melting pot blending the frontier West, the gracious South, the sophisticated East, and the industrial North. Branson, Missouri, in the heart of the Ozarks, is fast becom-ing the second country music capital in the United States.

Texas and the Plains

North Dakota, South Dakota, and Nebraska are rich in natural scenery, frontier history, and rural towns. North Dakota is the exact center of the North American Continent. The fabled Black Hills of South Dakota are where Mt. Rushmore pays tribute to four U.S. presidents, whose faces are carved in the mountain. Farm land and cattle ranges form the landscape of Nebraska.

Kansas is mostly agricultural, with vast fields of wheat. Kansas is the site of the terminus of the Old Chisholm Trail, where herds of cattle were taken during the frontier cowboy era.

Texas and the Plains

Texas	Nebraska
Oklahoma	South Dakota
Kansas	North Dakota

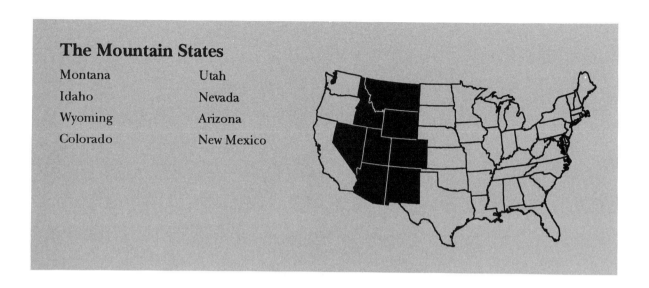

The Mountain States

Montana   Utah

Idaho   Nevada

Wyoming   Arizona

Colorado   New Mexico

Oklahoma and Texas benefit economically from oil reserves and natural gas deposits. The National Cowboy Hall of Fame and Western Heritage Center, located in Oklahoma City, features the art and history of the Old West. Big, bold, and colorful, Texas is second only to Alaska in size. Its three major cities are Houston, a modern city filled with high-rise buildings; Dallas, a commercial and cosmopolitan center; and San Antonio, a modern city retaining a flavor of its historic past.

The Mountain States

The Rocky Mountain range defines the topography of these states as it extends north from Mexico through Arizona, New Mexico, Colorado, Utah, Nevada, Wyoming, Idaho, and Montana and through Canada to the Arctic. This mountain range makes winters in the north cold and snowy and summers in the south dry and pleasant. The diversity in both climate and topography influences the economic and cultural activities available in each state, as well as the centers of population. Major cities are located at the confluences of rivers, areas of agreeable climate, and gateways to the far west.

Less than 50 miles wide in its panhandle and more than 300 miles wide in the south, Idaho is a state of contrasts. The Sawtooth Mountains and Craters of the Moon National Monument are names that convey its rugged beauty, contrasted with other parts of the state where you will find sagebrush and potato fields. Montana, known as "Big Sky Country," has relics of the past, like Custer Battlefield

National Monument — site of the Battle of Little Bighorn.

Known as the "Cowboy State," Wyoming's firsts exemplify the essence of the state: Yellowstone, the first National Park; Devil's Tower National Monument, the first area to be so designated; and the Shoshone National Forest, the first timberland to be reserved under the national forest system. The highest peaks of the Rocky Mountain range are found in Colorado, making the state one of the prime skiing areas in the country. Denver's state capitol building is a prime location to view the Rockies to the west, the Great Plains to the east, and the modern city sprawled below.

Utah is a state of great canyons and home to five national parks. Salt Lake City, the capital, is the international center for the Mormon Church and site of the famous Mormon Tabernacle. Nevada, except in the west, is a mostly unpopulated and arid state. The western part of the state is a glittering oasis featuring the entertainment and gambling centers of Las Vegas and Reno.

Arizona's dry climate and sunny weather make it a delight to visit. Phoenix is the cultural and commercial center of the state, and Tucson is a popular resort area, where one can visit nearby Saguaro National Monument, home of the giant Saguaro cacti. Pueblo Indian villages are located throughout areas of New Mexico and reflect its early history. Santa Fe, the country's oldest capital, has many art museums that chronicle the history of Indian arts and culture.

California and the Pacific Northwest

California   Alaska

Oregon   Hawaii

Washington

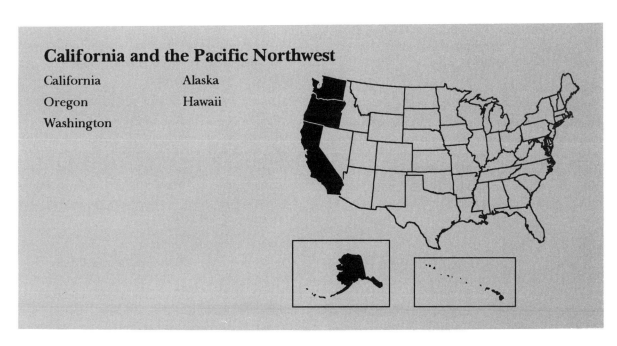

California and the Pacific Northwest

California, Oregon, and Washington are meccas for tourists because of their climate, location, and abundance of sightseeing opportunities. The Pacific coastline that they share provides spectacular scenery as well as beach and boating activities.

California has a diversity not found in any other state. In southern California travelers can experience San Diego, with its sunny climate and world-famous zoo, or Palm Springs, a chic desert resort. The coastal highway between Los Angeles and San Francisco affords breathtaking views high along the Pacific Ocean. Northern California sightseeing includes the grandeur of Yosemite National Park; the majestic redwood trees; and many delightful wineries.

Oregon and Washington occupy the northwestern section of the country. Few of Oregon's touring regions combine so much diversity into so small an area as the Portland - Mt. Hood - Columbia Gorge area located in the northwestern part of the state. They represent the state's largest city, its highest mountain, and one of its most magnificent riverways, all within seventy miles of one another. Coastal Washington exhibits shimmering bays on its Pacific coast and scenic trails and mountain climbing in the Cascade and Olympic mountains.

Hawaii and Alaska are in a class all their own. Hawaii, located 2,500 miles from the nearest continent, is a chain of more than 300 volcanic islands.

The eight major islands that constitute the state of Hawaii are noted for their lush vegetation, brightly-colored flowers, and beaches fringed with palm trees. However, each island has its own personality. Oahu is the chief island and contains Honolulu, Pearl Harbor, and the Polynesian Cultural Center. Alaska, located at the northwestern extremity of the North American continent is the largest of the fifty states. It is a land of rugged natural beauty, including glaciers, rivers, and mountains.

Spotlight on Cities in the United States

Boston, Massachusetts

Boston, known as the "Cradle of Liberty," is a combination of the old and the new. Almost all of Boston can be classified as historical. The most famous of its many sights have been marked for walking and bus tours along a route known as the Freedom Trail. Boston is also an educational and cultural hub. The Boston symphony is world-renowned, as are Boston's museums.

New York, New York

The nation's most popular city and the capital of business, communications, and theater. Nowhere are things done in such style and number as the "Big Apple," with museums, theaters, skyscrapers, and parks in abundance. Points of interest include the Statue of Liberty, United Nations Building, Empire State Building, Metropolitan Museum of Art, and Ellis Island.

Washington, D.C.

Our nation's capital was the first American city planned for a specific purpose. It has two major industries—government and tourism. Sightseeing possibilities include memorials to Jefferson, Lincoln, and Washington; federal buildings like the Mint, Supreme Court, Capitol building; and museums like the Smithsonian, the National Gallery of Art, and the National Air and Space Museum.

Orlando, Florida

Orlando lies in the heart of the citrus and lake country of central Florida. One of the best things about Orlando is its location; it's a short day's drive from many of Florida's attractions. Today, as host to Walt Disney World, it is also a growing metropolitan area offering more man-made attractions than perhaps any other area in the country.

New Orleans, Louisiana

Few cities compete with New Orleans' reputation for charm. Travelers come to dine in superb restaurants, listen to incomparable jazz, browse in Royal Street's fine antique shops, and dance in the streets during Mardi Gras. New Orleans has mastered the art of festivity.

Chicago, Illinois

Chicago, the nation's third largest city, is the financial, industrial, and cultural center of the Midwest region and a great mid-continental shipping point. Chicago is a port of entry; a major Great Lakes port; the busiest air center in the country; and an important rail and highway hub.

Los Angeles, California

Los Angeles is best known as the film-making capital of the world and a major tourist center. It's a sprawling city, comprised of canyons, foothills, mountains, and desert. It is beautifully situated — from the hills of Hollywood to the beaches in Malibu. Disneyland and Knotts Berry Farm are major tourist attractions.

San Francisco, California

San Francisco's setting is part of its allure — fog rolling in from the Pacific; cable cars clattering up and down hills; houses of infinite variety, perched on hills; the Golden Gate Bridge; and the broad sweep of the Pacific. The town's many cultures co-exist peacefully, yet each retains its identity and adds to the city's character.

Seattle, Washington

Seattle is among the youngest of the world's major cities. Nestled between Puget Sound and Lake Washington, its natural harbor welcomes commercial and passenger vessels. Seattle prospers from the products of its surrounding forest farms and waterways. It also serves as a provisioner to Alaska and the Orient.

Honolulu, Hawaii

Honolulu, the crossroads of the Pacific, is a melange of Polynesia, the Orient, and the contemporary mainland, and the country's most foreign metropolis. Famous for its beautiful setting and hospitable climate, it is the southernmost city in the United States. The beaches of Waikiki make Honolulu the ideal tourist destination.

Spotlight on U.S. National Parks

Each park in the United States national-parks system seeks to preserve the beauty and natural resources of the area. These retreats were established by the Congress of the United States for their unique historical, scenic, or geological features. The national parks offer popular family vacations and are best visited off-season to avoid bumper-to-bumper traffic that might otherwise detract from the experience.

Acadia National Park

New England's only national park, located in Maine, offers spectacular scenic drives that pass jagged cliffs and coves coupled with inland mountains and forests.

Great Smoky Mountains

Named for the haze that surrounds it during the early hours, this park on the Tennessee-North Carolina border is known for scenic parkways with beautiful rugged vistas.

Everglades National Park

A subtropical Florida wilderness, home to many rare and endangered species of birds, plants, reptiles, and mammals.

Glacier National Park

Adjoining Canada's Waterton National Park, this park in Montana covers over a million acres of territory. It is best known for its many glaciers, hiking trails, and grizzly bears.

Yellowstone National Park

The first and largest national park, shared by Wyoming and Montana, it is best known for the geyser "Old Faithful."

Mesa Verde National Park

Originally inhabited by Native Americans, this Colorado park is known for its original cliffside dwellings.

Grand Canyon National Park

Probably the world's most famous gorge, its primary Arizona feature is its vast scale and range of scenic sunrise and sunset views.

Carlsbad Caverns

In New Mexico, along the Texas border, this national park is famous for its limestone rock formations.

Yosemite National Park

Home to sequoias, wonderful waterfalls, and huge California monoliths. Made famous by mountain climbers is the monolith El Capitan.

Denali National Park

Mt. McKinley, North America's tallest mountain, towers over this Alaskan wilderness. The park is particularly known for its preservation of spectacular wildlife.

Spotlight on Attractions

Fall Foliage

Fall-foliage lovers eagerly await the natural wonder that annually transforms the northeastern and north-central regions of the United States into a rainbow of gold, red, orange, and brown colors. New England and the Great Lakes region begin their show in mid- to late September. The color continues south through the Blue Ridge mountains of Virginia and the Smoky mountains of Tennessee in October.

Gambling

Only a few states have legalized gambling. The most famous are New Jersey, with Atlantic City's casinos, and Nevada, with Las Vegas, Reno, and Laughlin. Illinois, Iowa, Mississippi, Louisiana, and Missouri have recently enacted legislation that will allow gambling on Mississippi river boats.

Skiing

The most popular ski areas in the eastern United States are in Maine, New Hampshire, Vermont, and New York. Cold temperatures, an excellent snow base, lighted ski areas, and close proximity to large population centers make low-altitude skiing popular in the Michigan and Wisconsin areas. The Rocky Mountain states of Colorado, Utah, Wyoming, New Mexico, and Idaho are considered by most to have the finest ski conditions and resorts in the United States. In addition, California's High Sierras offer excellent skiing opportunities.

Theme Parks

Man-made attractions enchant people of all ages. Most popular are the Disney properties in Orlando, Florida, and Anaheim, California. Six Flags has numerous locations throughout the United States, such as in Los Angeles, California; Atlanta, Georgia; and Chicago, Illinois. Busch Gardens — home of the famous Clydesdale horses — offers the Dark Continent in Tampa and a park with a European flavor in Williamsburg, Virginia. Sea World also offers a variety of aquatic life and activity. These attractions are located in San Diego, California; Cleveland, Ohio; San Antonio, Texas; and Orlando, Florida. Those who enjoy country music should visit Opryland in Nashville, Tennessee, or travel to Branson, Missouri.

Wine Country

The diverse climates of California and New York provide ideal conditions for wine production in the United States. The Napa and Sonoma valleys in California and the Finger Lakes region of New York offer many opportunities for touring, sampling, and purchasing. Washington state and Oregon are two other important areas in the production of wine.

Canada

Home of the Mounties and the maple leaf, our northern neighbor, Canada, is bordered by the Atlantic on the east and the Pacific on the west. Its

The East

Nova Scotia

New Brunswick

Newfoundland

Prince Edward Island

Quebec

Ontario

topography is similar to that of the United States, with rocky mountain ranges, lowlands, dense forests, glaciers, and mighty rivers. Since it is further north, winters are longer and more severe. Summer is the primary tourist season. Visitors concentrate their travel attentions on the cosmopolitan cities of Canada, its island hideaways, and natural attractions.

The maritime provinces—Newfoundland, Nova Scotia, Prince Edward Island, and New Brunswick — are known for fishing, picturesque overlooks, and miles of beaches. Nova Scotia's Cabot Trail offers spectacular coastal scenery. Other attractions in Nova Scotia include the French fortress of Louisburg, the artist colony at Peggy's Cove, and Evangeline country around Grand Pré. New Brunswick's Bay of Fundy has the highest tidal bore (record tides) in North America. Prince Edward Island provides the real-life setting of the novel *Anne of Green Gables*.

Quebec, Canada's French-speaking province, is one of the most densely populated regions of Canada. Cosmopolitan Montreal and historic Quebec City dominate the St. Lawrence River Valley.

Ottawa, the capital, located in the province of Ontario, has stately buildings, sparkling cleanliness, and much charm. Ontario is also the sight of Horseshoe Falls, located on the Canadian side of Niagara Falls. Toronto, Canada's largest city, is the financial and industrial heart of the nation.

Nearly all major Canadian cities, with the exception of Edmonton, are within a 250-mile radius of the U.S. border.

The prairie provinces of Saskatchewan and Manitoba are considered Canada's breadbasket. Canada's famous national parks — Banff, Lake Louise, and Jasper — are further west in Alberta. Edmonton and Calgary are the province's two most important cities. Mountainous British Columbia sweeps down to the Pacific Ocean. Off the coast is Vancouver Island, with the province's capital city, Victoria, one of the most English of the Canadian cities. On the mainland, the city of Vancouver is Canada's major Pacific port. Canada's northern territories, Northwest and Yukon, are sparsely populated and remain a pristine wilderness. Whitehorse, the capital of the Yukon, and

West

Manitoba

Saskatchewan

Alberta

British Columbia

Yukon Territory

Northwest Territories

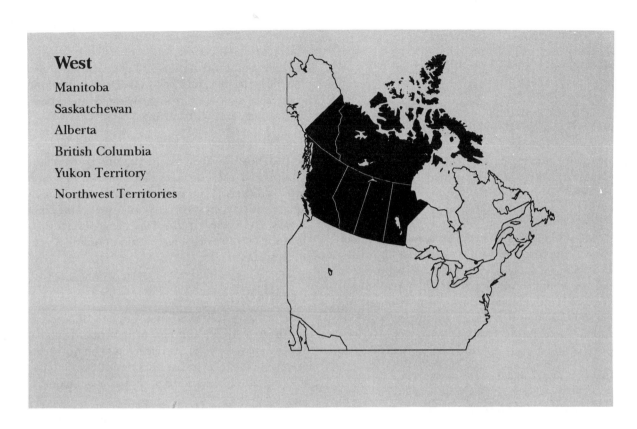

Dawson City became famous during the Klondike gold rush of 1898.

Spotlight on Canadian Cities

Victoria, British Columbia

Victoria is best known for its magnificent flower gardens, mild climate, turreted Parliament buildings, and ivy-covered Empress Hotel, and is home to the famous Butchart Gardens, fashioned from a limestone quarry.

Vancouver, British Columbia

Modern Vancouver is a cultural center containing the gorgeous Stanley Park. It is a gateway for Alaskan Inside Passage cruises and is Canada's doorway to the Orient. Grouse Mountain ski area is nearby.

Edmonton, Alberta

Edmonton is home to one of the world's largest malls and indoor amusement parks, the West Edmonton Mall. Edmonton is also known for its Space and Science Center and for being the site of Klondike Days carnival, held every July. It is also the gateway to the Northwest Territories. Edmonton is also Canada's oil capital.

Calgary, Alberta

The Calgary Stampede, a week-long western extravaganza, is held here annually during the month of July. It is also a major petroleum-producing area, was host of the 1988 Winter Olympics, and is an agricultural and ranching center.

Winnipeg, Manitoba

This city's diversity mirrors the many nationalities that have settled here. Winnipeg's folklorama, held every August, celebrates this diversity with food and festivities. This is Manitoba's capital city, complete with government buildings, the Royal Canadian Mint, and the Manitoba Museum of Man and Nature. It is also known as the "Gateway to Hudson Bay."

Toronto, Ontario

Toronto is home to the famous CN Tower, the world's tallest free-standing structure. Toronto also contains Ontario Place, a theme park on the edge of the city, and a lovely harborfront area. It is a popular family summer destination. Toronto is the banking and stock exchange center of the country and one of the fastest-growing cities of North America.

Ottawa, Ontario

Ottawa is a city dominated by gothic-style parliament buildings. The changing-of-the-guard ceremony performed on Parliament Hill is very impressive. Ottawa is also home to Rideau Canal, a family area with parks and open spaces, six national museums, and the National Arts Center.

Montreal, Quebec

Montreal offers a variety of historical and cultural attractions, as well as some of the finest shopping in Canada. It is essentially a European city, providing a traditional French experience. It contains Underground Montreal, a business, and residential complex. Also in Montreal is the famous Notre Dame Basilica, Place des arts — a performing arts center, and Man and His World.

Quebec City, Quebec

The only walled city in North American north of the Yucatan peninsula in Mexico. Quebec City provides some of the best examples of history and architecture in North America. The narrow cobblestone streets wind past such sites as the Citadel, Chateau Frontenac, and the Parliament buildings. It is the most vivid and tangible remnant of New France in America.

Halifax, Nova Scotia

Halifax is known for its coastal beauty and fishing. It is the commercial, administrative, and military center of Atlantic Canada. It is also the center of Canada's maritime industry. It is strongly English in culture and tradition.

Spotlight on Canadian Parks

Jasper National Park

Located in Jasper, Alberta, Jasper National Park boasts lofty peaks and alpine valleys, clear lakes and thundering falls that are a backpackers' paradise. All-weather parkways provide access to such scenic highlights as Mailgne Lake, Athabasca Falls, and the famous Columbia Ice Fields.

Banff National Park

This park, located in Banff, Alberta, contains Canada's most spectacular mountains, alpine meadows, glaciers, forested slopes, rivers, and lakes — including the incomparable Lake Louise. It also has hot sulphur springs, well-developed hiking trails, and canoeing, riding, skiing, fishing, boating, sailing, and scuba diving.

The Laurentians

Just northwest of Montreal, the Laurentians comprise a succession of ski communities, one after another. It is a region of charming French villages with lovely inns, pleasant resorts, and small hotels. The northern end of the string of ski resorts is Mont Tremblant — the premier Canadian winter resort.

Mexico

The topography of Mexico, our neighbor to the south, is a varied contrast of mountain ranges, valleys, coastal plains, and beaches. The northern section of the country has a dry desert-like climate, which gradually modifies to that of a wet tropical climate in the south.

Mexico offers countless resorts along its coastline. One can view ancient ruins hacked free from the clinging jungle, enjoy cities imprinted with a Spanish stamp, and follow the route of the country's struggle for independence. Shopping opportunities are varied: this is a land with an abundance of handicrafts.

From spectacular game fishing, skin diving and just plain resting in the sun to boating on high-plateau lakes to tackling the jungle on horseback — the range of activities is endless. In short treks from Mexico City, the country's metropolitan capital, visitors may see tranquil mountain spas, sparkling seacoast resorts, quaint and historically interesting towns, picturesque artist colonies, and awe-inspiring archaeological wonders.

Spotlight on Mexican Cities

Mexico City

Mexico City is the cosmopolitan capital of the country and the largest city in the hemisphere. Aztec, Spanish, and twentieth century architecture stand side-by-side in the city. Sightseeing attractions include the Zocalo, the metropolitan cathedral; the National Museum of Anthropology;

Chapultepec Castle; and the Shrine of Guadelupe.

Guadalajara

Guadalajara, Mexico's second-largest city, is an excellent base for exploring the country's colonial past. It is a unique blend of modern and traditional architecture, tree-shaded residential streets, temperate climate, and a cosmopolitan atmosphere. Mexico produces a tremendous amount of folk art — primarily handicrafts designed for household use. The region around Guadalajara is notably rich in these handicrafts, such as pottery, baskets, and sarapes.

Acapulco

Acapulco is the premier city of Pacific coastal resorts; it has the most visitors and the most hotels in Mexico. Winter is probably the best season to visit, but the resort is popular year-round. The weather never gets very cold, and the water temperature is always perfect. Vegetation is lush, fragrant, and tropical.

Oaxaca

Oaxaca is set in a broad valley and acts as the center for the surrounding Indian villages. It remains one of the most colonial of the Mexican cities. Its pace is low-key, and its small-town atmosphere is unspoiled. Oaxaca serves as a base for touring the pre-Columbian ruins of Monte Auban and the old Indian ceremonial center of Mitla.

Cancun

This is Mexico's premier luxury resort in the Caribbean. It contains crystal-clear seas, spectacular off-shore coral reefs, luxury hotels, golf courses, a marina, restaurants, and lots of shopping. The waters are ideal for skin diving, snorkeling, swimming, water-skiing, and windsurfing.

The Caribbean

Between the tip of Florida and the northern coast of South America lie the Caribbean islands. The islands are typically grouped into the Greater Antilles, located southwest of Florida in the northern part of the Caribbean Sea, and the Lesser Antilles, in the eastern part of the Caribbean Sea. Bermuda and the Bahamas are included here, although they are not geographically in the Caribbean.

The island-nations of the Caribbean provide travelers with an endless variety of cultures, languages, cuisines, and history. Although the sun, sand, and sea are the foremost attractions, the area is characterized not by sameness, but by incredible diversity. Various cultures and traditions are reflected in the French islands of Martinique, Guadeloupe, St. Martin, St. Barthelemy, and Haiti; the Dutch islands of Sint Maarten, Sint Eustatius, Saba, Aruba, Bonaire, and Curacao; the Spanish islands of the Dominican Republic, Puerto Rico, and Cuba; and the British-influenced islands of the Caymans, Jamaica, the British Virgin Islands, Antigua, St. Lucia, Barbados, and Grenada, to name a few.

Terrain may vary from deserts to lush green mountains traversed by sparkling streams. The ambience may range from the tranquility of a remote hideaway to the glitter of exclusive resorts, complete with casinos and nightclubs.

Spotlight on Caribbean Islands

Bermuda

Bermuda sits in the north Atlantic Ocean, 600 miles east of Cape Hatteras, North Carolina. British in style and customs, Bermuda's prime industry is tourism. Pretty as a postcard, Bermuda has pastel houses, turquoise seas, and pink sandy beaches.

The Bahamas

Starting with the island of Bimini, just 50 miles off the coast of Florida, the 700 Bahama islands spread in an arc for 700 miles to the southeast. The most popular tourist centers are Nassau and Freeport. Attractions include gambling, a glittering nightlife, and water sports of every variety.

Greater Antilles

Jamaica

The third-largest island in the Caribbean, Jamaica is mountainous and lush. The resort areas of Negril, Montego Bay, and Ocho Rios are located on the north shore of the island. Jamaica is known for its fine beaches, deluxe resorts, and reggae music.

Puerto Rico

Puerto Rico is a United States commonwealth, with a strong Spanish tradition. The island's interior is mountainous; the coastline is surrounded by wide beaches. San Juan, the capital, is the center for tourism, containing deluxe hotels and casinos as well as the historic Old San Juan section of town.

United States Virgin Islands

The United States Virgin Islands, formerly belonging to Denmark, consist of St. Thomas, St. Croix, and St. John. St. Thomas, the most commercially developed, is a major cruise port and shopping mecca. St. Croix, the largest, has many historical landmarks, and St. John, the smallest, is the least developed for tourism but home to the Virgin Islands National Park.

Lesser Antilles

St. Martin/Sint Maarten

St. Martin/Sint Maarten is the smallest island in the world to be shared by two nations — France and Holland. Each side of the island has its own personality. St. Martin is exemplified by French chic, complete with French restaurants, boutiques, and bistros. Sint Maarten is bustling, with glittering casinos. Each side has fine resorts and beaches.

Barbados

Although an independent island, Barbados retains British traditions from earlier rule. Often referred to as "England in the tropics," it contains neat gardens, parish churches, and narrow roads. The best hotels and beaches are on the calm west coast of the island.

The ABC Islands

Located between fifteen to fifty miles north of Venezuela, Aruba, Bonaire, and Curaçao are collectively referred to as the ABC islands. All reflect Dutch influence. Aruba is a well-developed island with casinos, white sandy beaches, and deluxe hotels. Bonaire is the least developed and primarily known as a scuba-diving destination. Curaçao, the largest of the three, most reflects the Dutch influence in its buildings and shops.

Central and South America

Central America is the narrow, southernmost portion of the North American continent, linked to South America by the Isthmus of Panama. It separates the Caribbean Sea from the Pacific Ocean.

Central America	South America
Guatemala	Columbia
Belize	Ecuador
Honduras	Peru
El Salvador	Bolivia
Nicaragua	Chile
Costa Rica	Argentina
Panama	Uruguay
	Brazil
	French Guiana
	Guyana
	Venezuela

The mountains of Central America have an active zone of volcanoes and earthquakes. Central America's climate varies with altitude from tropical to cool. The eastern side of the region receives heavy rainfall.

La Paz, Bolivia, at 12,001 feet, is the highest capital in the world.

South America is a continental land mass with a north-to-south extent of nearly 5,000 miles. The northern half bulges eastward then narrows to a cone shape in the south. Most of the continent lies east of the United States. One of the world's great mountain ranges, the Andes, runs parallel to the west coast of South America. East of the mountains, two large river systems and the plains they cross are dominant features. The equator passes through northern South America. Most of the major cities are located on high plateaus.

Spotlight on South American Cities

Bogota, Columbia

Bogota, the capital of Columbia, is located on a plateau in the Andes. It is a city of contrasts — old and new, wealth and poverty. Amid soaring skyscrapers visitors often see burro-driven carts right out of the colonial era. Art treasures from the past are housed in colonial churches and museums — buildings that stand alongside modern office buildings, posh nightclubs, and luxury hotels.

Quito, Ecuador

Quito, the capital of Ecuador, once the seat of government of the northern Inca empire, was destroyed and rebuilt by the Spanish. Now, many years later, the heart of colonial Quito is still largely untouched, with dignified colonial buildings, superb religious art, and beautiful Spanish architecture. It has been called the "Florence of the Americas." Its colonial treasures of art and architecture have earned Quito a place on the UNESCO list of world cultural heritage sights.

Lima, Peru

Government, finance, industry, and education are centralized in Lima, the capital of Peru. Lima's wealth of colonial buildings date to an earlier era, when the city served as the seat of government for New Spain. Today the city is a combination of old and new architecture, mountains in the distance, and a string of beautiful suburbs along the Pacific.

Santiago, Chile

Among Latin Americans, Chilean hospitality is legendary. Santiago is an architectural mixture of northern European elegance, North American suburbia, and South American culture. The city is surrounded by some of the most productive farmland in the nation and flanked on two sides by the towering Andes. Santiago is populated by a well-educated, cosmopolitan middle class.

Buenos Aires, Argentina

Acclaimed by both residents and travelers as the "Paris of South America," Buenos Aires, capital of Argentina, is one of the most attractive destinations on the continent. The city shares a number of architectural elements with its French counterpart: wide boulevards, flowers, large parks, and ornate buildings. The capital's lifestyle takes its rhythm from Paris, too. The Teatro Colon, one of the world's premier opera houses and concert halls, draws many international artists.

Rio de Janeiro, Brazil

Located on Brazil's Atlantic coast, Rio de Janeiro has golden beaches, along with graceful valleys and hillsides. Above the city, the world-famous sculpture of Christ the Redeemer spreads its arms to embrace city and sea. Rio's downtown area is bustling, hectic, and noisy, and though it has a number of hotels, restaurants, shops, and nightspots, the really chic establishments are concentrated in the fashionable beach communities of Copacabana and Ipanema. Rio's most important annual event is Carnival.

Sao Paolo, Brazil

The continent's largest city, Sao Paolo resembles a perpetual-motion machine. This city drives the economic locomotive that has pulled Brazil to its current place as the world's eighth-largest economy. In this state capital, the locals have joined agriculture with industry to create a thriving commercial center. Sao Paolo has one of South America's highest standards of living, some of the finest restaurants on the continent, and an active cultural and night life.

Spotlight on Attractions

The Galapagos

The Galapagos Islands, located 600 miles west of Ecuador and consisting of thirteen major islands and several small ones, may be the only remaining habitat of substantial size where huge quantities of wildlife have been preserved. Native species so unique that almost half of them cannot be found anywhere else on earth — and whose isolated development has provided the basis for our theory of evolution — reside here.

Iguassu Falls

Iguassu Falls, located on the Brazilian-Argentine border, is considered the widest waterfall in the world, extending well over four miles. The falls produce a roar that can be heard miles away and huge clouds of mist that rise over the jungle. A two-hour hike will take you past all of the falls visible on the Argentine side as well as through the tropical jungle.

Machu Picchu

Accessible by train from Cuzco, this incredible Inca complex of temples, houses, baths, hundreds of stairways, and a guard house rises 2,000 feet above the river valley. Discovered in 1911, it has more than a hundred acres of granite-block buildings, walls, and plazas.

The Amazon

The Amazon River, the second-longest river in the world, drains the heart of the South American continent. This region is one of nature's last preserves of wildlife, hosting 2,000 species of fish, 14,000 species of mammals, 15,000 species of insects, and 3,500 birds. The jungle's more-renowned inhabitants include the jaguar and the wild boar; exotic birds such as the macaw and parrot; reptiles, including the boa constrictor and alligator; and fish such as the piranha and the electric eel.

Europe

Europe has often been considered the birthplace of Western civilization. From the time of the ancient Greeks, European political ideas, scientific discoveries, religious beliefs, and cultural practices have spread to nearly every country. Today, Europe is a composite of countries and traditions that is rapidly becoming one nation under the European Economic Community (EEC). This step will eliminate passport controls and travel restrictions, and will standardize many items such as taxes and, perhaps eventually, currencies. A boon to its citizens because it will increase prosperity, a united Europe will also improve life for travelers.

The political situation in Europe is causing many changes in heretofore fixed borders.

British Isles

The British Isles is a geographical term referring to the group of approximately 920 islands that lie off the northwest coast of the European continent. Great manufacturing cities and thriving farms

British Isles

England

Scotland

Wales

Northern Ireland

Ireland

lie on the rolling plains of England. Deposits of coal and other minerals are mined in the hills and mountains of Wales. Scotland's famous Highlands are almost too rugged for anything except sheep and tourists; the Scottish Lowlands support large manufacturing and shipbuilding industries. The mild climate of Northern Ireland and the Republic of Ireland provide classic green beauty throughout the countryside.

England is one of the most popular international tourist destinations for Americans because of its similarity in culture and language. The regions of England offer sightseeing opportunities such as southern seaside resorts like Brighton; the rugged landscape of Devon and Cornwall in the southwest; the quaint villages of the Cotswolds; the romantic Lake District, home of many English poets and writers; the well-known university towns of Cambridge and Oxford; and the famous White Cliffs of Dover.

Scotland conjures images of bagpipes, kilts, and lochs, such as Loch Ness, home of the famous Loch Ness monster. Edinburgh is the capital and center for tourism, banking, and finance; Glasgow is the industrial center and is becoming a major cultural center. The Hebrides, the Shetlands, and the Orkneys are Scotland's most famous islands.

The principality of Wales is the smallest of the countries, with a distinctive language, customs, and scenery. The three principal areas are South Wales, including the capital, Cardiff; mid-Wales, with its coastal resorts and Cambrian Mountains; and North Wales, containing Snowdonia National Park and the island of Angelsey.

Northern Ireland, occupying approximately one-fifth of the entire land mass of Ireland, is primarily an agricultural country. North of Belfast lies the causeway coast, with its holiday resorts and the Giant's Causeway.

The Republic of Ireland is characterized by its varied terrain, with picturesque rolling pastures, peat bogs, and landscape in forty shades of green. Trinity College, Abbey Theatre, and Guinness Brewery are three of Dublin's major attractions. Waterford is famous for its crystal, and Blarney for its castle and famous kissing stone.

Scandinavia

Scandinavia is considered the land of the midnight sun because of its seemingly never-ending

Scandinavia

Iceland

Norway

Sweden

Finland

Denmark

days in summer. Geographically, it encompasses northern Europe and includes the countries of Denmark, Norway, Sweden, and Finland. Iceland is also considered to be in Scandinavia but is an island in the north Atlantic off the coast of Greenland.

Iceland features hundreds of volcanoes, many hot springs, glaciers, and geysers. Settled by Vikings, Iceland is also known for its sagas, wool outerwear, thermal power, and natural attractions.

Norway's most outstanding feature is its coastline, with deep fjords surrounded by high mountains. Bergen, on Norway's west coast, is gateway to the fjord country. Oslo, the capital, located on the Oslo fjord, is Norway's most important industrial, commercial, and shipping center.

Sweden, one of Europe's largest countries, is sparsely populated. Most people live in the south, amidst a landscape speckled with lakes and carpeted with meadows and forests. Lapland is found north of the Arctic Circle. Stockholm, its capital, built on a string of islands, is known as the "City Between the Bridges."

Finland, a country of lakes, streams, and forests, is often called the "Land of 100,000 Lakes." Finland is the home of the sauna. Helsinki, the capital, is the country's most densely populated region.

Denmark is the smallest and most densely populated of the Scandinavian countries. Except for the common land border with Germany, Denmark is surrounded by water. Hans Christian Andersen, the famous children's storyteller, was born in Odense.

Continental Europe

Europe amazes tourists with its diversity of cultures in such a small area. Although much of the diversity is a result of Europe's history, it also comes from its geography — the many peninsulas, islands, and mountain ranges that divide it.

Switzerland is the very heart of Europe. It is the meeting place for three great European cultures — Italian, German, and French. South of Switzerland and separated from the rest of Europe by the Alps is the Italian peninsula — site of Florence, the birthplace of the Renaissance; Venice, the city of canals; and Milan, a major banking center.

On Switzerland's north and east are the Germanic countries of Austria, Hungary, Czechoslovakia, Germany, and Poland. Every summer Salzburg, Austria, hosts its famous music festival; Hungary's Budapest is really two cities divided by the Danube River; Munich is the site of Germany's Octoberfest; Prague is often called the city of one hundred spires because of its many churches and castles; and Crakow, Poland, is a beautiful medieval town.

To the north and west of Switzerland are France and the Benelux countries. Nice, on the Mediterranean coast of France, is the heart of the French Riviera. Together Belgium, the Netherlands, and Luxembourg make up the Benelux. Brussels, the capital of Belgium, boasts magnificent Guild Square; Rotterdam, in the Netherlands, is Europe's largest port; and the Grand Duchy of Luxembourg is emerging as one of Europe's largest financial centers.

Other European areas are either peninsulas or

Continental Europe

Switzerland	Portugal
Italy	Albania
Germany	Yugoslavia
France	Romania
Austria	Bulgaria
Hungary	Greece
Czechoslovakia	Andorra
Poland	Monaco
Belgium	Vatican City
The Netherlands	San Marino
Luxembourg	Liechtenstein
Spain	

Historical Perspective

The Cote d'Azur

The mere mention of the French Riviera conjures up images of bikini-clad, oil-covered sun-worshippers adorning miles of sandy beaches and frequenting elite resorts such as Cannes, Nice, and Monte Carlo. Like other tourist areas, the Cote d'Azur evolved from an exclusive winter haven for the wealthy to a summer retreat for the masses.

Prior to 1914, the vacation trend along the French Riviera was toward prolonged winter stays, usually three to six months in duration, for therapeutic purposes. Similar to spa vacations, such trips were prescribed by the medical community for their wealthy patients. For reasons of health and propriety, seaside visitors remained clothed from head to foot. Social life revolved around hotel properties, where guests expected to be pampered. Soon, however, public gambling was introduced, and a new breed of pleasure-seeking tourist replaced the sedentary invalid.

The natives who had always depended on wine, fruit, olive oil, and fishing for their salvation began to realize that a profit could be made from these newly-arrived tourists. The subsequent rapid development of the area caused a decline in its natural beauty. Coupling this factor with the outbreak of the First World War and the subsequent shortages, inflation, and black market resulted in a risky seasonal economic base.

No sooner had the modern summer tourist begun to emerge during the 1920s than the Depression struck. The tourist business slumped immediately. Those who could afford to travel did so by auto rather than train and stayed at smaller private hotels or rooming houses. After the Depression, the French legislature introduced the paid vacation — two weeks' holiday with pay for all workers with at least one year's service. Soon working-class families flooded the Riviera, and package tours grew in popularity. In 1936 the franc was devalued, and the Paris Exposition opened. Conventions, business travelers, middle-class tourists, and foreign travelers all arrived at the French Riviera for the popular summer season. Vacations began to assume an important role in the French lifestyle.

Today the French Riviera's appeal amazingly remains intact — its Mediterranean coast inundated with tourists, its streets tied up with traffic jams, and its hotels filled to capacity. The annual mass migration continues to place incredible burdens on municipal services. The Riviera's dilemma now is how to maintain its international reputation and profitability yet balance it against the environmental hardships that result from such economic success.

offshore islands. For example, the Iberian peninsula is occupied by Spain and Portugal and extends west of France toward the Atlantic. Barcelona, Spain, is the country's second-largest city, its major commercial and industrial center, and one of the most important Mediterranean ports. Oporto, on Portugal's Costa Verde, is the center of the port wine industry.

Southeast of Switzerland is another peninsula — the Balkan. Albania, Yugoslavia, Romania, Bulgaria, and Greece make up this area. Albania, closed to the west since World War II, recently opened its borders. Yugoslavia is presently undergoing political turmoil as some seek to re-establish the independence of the former nations that comprise present-day Yugoslavia. The Transylvanian section of the Carpathian mountains in Romania evokes the memory of Count Dracula. Varna, Bulgaria, a quaint resort town on the Black Sea, has lovely beaches and good hotels. Olympia, the site of the first Olympic games, is an easy day excursion from Athens, Greece.

Andorra, Monaco, Vatican City, San Marino, and Liechtenstein, the continent's smallest countries, complete the European scene.

Spotlight on European Cities

London, England

London is rich in history, with a wealth of cultural and artistic attractions, sophisticated shopping areas, splendid parks and gardens, and varied architecture. Buckingham Palace, Parliament, Westminster Abbey, Piccadilly, the Thames, and the Tower of London are only a few of the sightseeing attractions available.

Copenhagen, Denmark

Copenhagen has many old buildings, fountains, statues, and squares, as well as two stellar attractions — the Little Mermaid statue in the harbor; and Tivoli, one of the world's liveliest amusement parks.

Paris, France

Paris, the capital of France, is often referred to as the "City of Light" because it is an international cultural center. The Eiffel Tower, the Louvre, the Champs Elysees, Notre Dame, and the Seine are only a few of this city's attractions. Expected to draw even more travelers to this area is Euro Disney, opened in 1992 and located twenty miles east of Paris. It is one-fifth the size of the city of Paris itself and is Europe's largest amusement complex.

Rome, Italy

Rome, "the Eternal City," is one of the world's richest cities in history and art and is a very important religious center. The Forum, Colosseum, and Pantheon all date back to the days of the Roman Empire. St. Peter's Basilica is the seat of the Roman Catholic Church.

Vienna, Austria

Located on the banks of the Danube River, Vienna's charm emanates from its parks, fine shops, hotels, and music. Schubert, Mozart, Strauss, Beethoven, and Haydn lived and composed here. The city thrives on concerts, operas, and theatrical performances. Two outstanding attractions are the Spanish Riding School, with its world-famous Lipizzaner White Stallions, and the Vienna Boys' Choir, who perform in the Hofburg Palace Chapel.

Berlin, Germany

Berlin, Germany's largest city, was united in November 1989 when the wall came down. Even though united, Berlin presents two faces — although the western sector is an intensely Americanized city, the eastern clings to the city's past.

Madrid, Spain

Madrid, the highest capital in Europe, is one of the newest of the great Spanish cities. Madrid is noted for the arts. The Prado Museum ranks as one of the outstanding art museums of the world. The Plaza de Toros presents bullfights every Sunday from March through October.

Lisbon, Portugal

Lisbon, Portugal's capital city, reaches out to the sea. The seven hills provide a varied setting, and charm is reflected everywhere in the city's tiled roofs, pastel-colored houses, inlaid-tile streets, and iron balconies accentuated with flowers. Portugal preserves its seafaring days in the magnificent Manueline Tower of Belem.

Athens, Greece

Cosmopolitan Athens is a museum of antiquity — a city of classical art and architecture. The

Acropolis, crowned by the Parthenon and the Eretheion, survives as a monument to Greece's Golden Age. The Benaki Museum houses art works from prehistoric to post-Byzantine periods.

Amsterdam, Holland

Water characterizes the cosmopolitan port of Amsterdam. Amsterdam's seventy islands are separated by canals and connected by 1,000 bridges. It is a modern city that has retained the traditions of its past. Because the Netherlands is a small country, the city is convenient to many major attractions, like the flower center of Aalsmeer, the cheese market at Alkmaar, and the picturesque fishing villages of Marken and Volendam.

Spotlight on Natural European Attractions and Sightseeing

Wine Country

France is the greatest wine-producing area in the world, both in quantity and quality, and has developed still wines and the finest sparkling wine — champagne. Bordeaux, Côte d'Or, the Loire and Rhone Valleys are the major wine-producing areas. The Champagne district is located in Epernay. Italy is the second-largest wine-producing country in the world. The best-known is Chianti, from the Tuscany region. Spain is the third-largest wine-producing country in the world and famous for sherry. Germany, particularly in the Rhine Valley, also produces fine wine. These wines are generally light, dry, and white, characterized by a fresh flowery bouquet. Portugal, best known for port and Madeira, produces excellent table wines.

The Alps

The Alps curve in a great arc from the Mediterranean coast of France through the South of France, Switzerland, southern Germany, Austria, and into present-day Yugoslavia. Mont Blanc is the highest peak. Switzerland's Matterhorn is also an Alpine peak. Tourism is based on the scenic attractions of the Alps, and the mountaineering and winter sports they provide is a major source of income. Among the more famous resorts are Chamonix (France); Zermatt and Davos (Switzerland); Innsbruck and Kitzbuhel (Austria); Berchtesgaden (Germany); Cortina d'Ampezzo and Bolzano (Italy).

The French Riviera

The Riviera, located on the Mediterranean, offers a perfect setting for the lifestyles of the rich and famous. It combines beaches, sensational weather, and superb dining. It is also a popular resort area for the French during their annual July and August holiday. St. Tropez and Cap d'Antibes are two of the smaller, more luxurious resorts. Cannes, famous for its international movie festival, has casinos and nightclubs. Nice, the largest city on the Riviera, is somewhat crowded but still charming. Nearby is Monaco, best-known for its Grand Casino and the Grand Prix auto race held each May.

The Rhine

The Rhine, one of Europe's principal rivers, rises in the Swiss Alps, flows north, and empties into the North Sea. The river carries more traffic than any other waterway in the world. South of Mainz, Germany, the Rhine flows through a steep gorge famous for its scenery, vineyards, and superb wines; castles surviving from times when tolls were levied on river traffic; and legendary landmarks such as the Lorelei and the Drachenfels. Various types and lengths of cruises are available.

Asia and the Pacific

Asia and the Pacific form a fascinating melting pot, a multi-racial and religious mix of Chinese, Japanese, Thais, Malays, Koreans, Indonesians, and Indians, and Buddhists, Hindi, Muslim, and Christians. And discriminating travelers flock to this area for one simple reason — there's nothing quite like it anywhere else in the world. A traveler can experience feudal Japan in Kyoto; the regal splendors of Siam in Bankgok; the beauty of Chinese arts in Taipei; the dignified remains of English colonialism in Hong Kong and Singapore; the imposing rituals of Islam in Malaysia and Java; the blending of manmade and natural beauty in Bali; the Maori way of life in New Zealand; and Australia's unique flora and fauna.

Australia

Australia is the world's largest island and smallest continent. Comparable in size to the United States (excluding Alaska), it is the only continent with just one nation on it, and geologically it is the oldest continent on earth. Seasons in Australia are the reverse of those in the Northern hemisphere. The topography ranges from rich-red plains to blue-green mountains, from deep-green pasturelands to turquoise-colored lagoons.

Spotlight on Australian Cities

Brisbane

Brisbane is the focal point for reaching Australia's seaside resort towns along the Gold and Sunshine Coasts. The city has a large number of parks, museums, government and civic buildings, and monuments.

Sydney

Sydney is the largest city in Australia and a bustling center for business, industry, and manufacturing, as well as a major world port. Sightseeing attractions include the controversial Sydney Opera House, the harbour bridge, and the Rocks — the original settlement in Australia that has been converted to shops and restaurants. Sydney's central location offers easy access to the Blue or Snowy Mountains, Hunter Valley wine region, Manly and Bondi beaches, and the Hawkesbury River.

Canberra

Canberra is the capital and the center of government for all of Australia. Parliament, Government House, the Royal Australian Mint, the National Library, and many embassies and legations are all found in Canberra.

Melbourne

Melbourne is a city of quiet dignity. There is a sense of culture, graciousness, beauty, and unhurried growth and prosperity. It is the financial hub of Australia, as well as a major fashion center. The Melbourne Cup, an internationally famous racing event, is held every November.

Spotlight on Attractions

Fauna

Animals are one of Australia's greatest attractions. The kangaroo family, including wallabies and quokkas, is unique to Australia. The duck-billed, webbed-footed platypus and the wombat, cousin to the cuddly koala, are also natives. Near

Melbourne, the Fairy Penguins of Phillip Island are another favorite.

Ayers Rock

Alice Springs, in the center of the outback, is the jumping-off point for Ayers Rock, the world's largest monolith. This rock — Uluru, as the Aborigines called it — was considered sacred. This was also the area where *Crocodile Dundee* was filmed. The best times to visit the rock are sunrise or sunset, when its colors are brightest. For the adventurous, it's possible to climb it.

The Great Barrier Reef

Australia's Great Barrier Reef, north of Brisbane, is 1,250 miles long and the world's largest living organism. It is inhabited by thousands of coral dwellers, sharks, and turtles. Daily flights, glass-bottom boat rides, and cruises provide tours of the reef, and those interested in snorkeling or diving can also enjoy its wonder.

New Zealand

Set in the vast southern seas, New Zealand is a land of awesome scenic beauty—it consists of a spectacular coastline, indented by tree-rimmed bays and inlets; magnificent glacial mountains, with fjords, lakes and streams; and volcanoes towering above an arid desert and subtropical forest. New Zealand consists of three islands — North, South, and Stewart. Both Auckland, its largest city and Wellington, its capital, are situated on the North Island. Important South Island cities are Christchurch and Queenstown.

Spotlight on New Zealand Cities

Auckland

Auckland is the commercial and industrial center of the country and the North Island's transportation hub. Mount Eden, Auckland's highest point, offers the finest view of the city and harbor.

Rotorua

Rotorua, on New Zealand's North Island, offers three exceptional attractions — an opportunity to learn about Maori culture, an intriguing variety of thermal activity (geysers, mudpots, and hot springs), and some of the country's best trout fishing.

Christchurch

Often called "New Zealand's most English city,"

Christchurch retains many features established by its Anglican settlers. Shaded by overhanging trees, the Avon River runs through the city, adding gracious old-world charm. Stately Gothic buildings constructed by early leaders house religious, educational, governmental, and cultural institutions. Christchurch Cathedral is located in the heart of the city.

Queenstown

Queenstown, South Island's principal resort, is the hub of the southern lakes district, a popular recreation area with lake and mountain scenery, exhilarating climate, and changing seasons.

Spotlight on a New Zealand Attraction

Fjords

Queenstown is the usual gateway to Fjordland National Park, which houses some of the most spectacular scenery in the South Pacific. Milford Sound is the best-known of New Zealand's fjords. The Milford Track from Lake Te Anau to Milford is described by some as the "finest walk in the world."

Pacific Island Groupings

Polynesia

Melanesia

Micronesia

Indonesia

Phillipines

The South Pacific evokes images of paradise with its isolated islands, complete with coconut palms and white sandy beaches. Hundreds of islands, from low coral atolls to high volcanic formations, dot the vast expanse of the Pacific.

Polynesia, covering an area of more than fifteen million square miles, is made up of French Polynesia, the Samoas, Tonga, and the Cook Islands. Hawaii and New Zealand are also part of Polynesia. This island group is popular with tourists because it offers a resort type of vacation with sun, sand, and surf.

Melanesia, often referred to as the "dark islands," extends from just north of Australia to the islands of Polynesia. The five main islands are Fiji, New Caledonia, Vanuatu, Solomon Islands, and Papua New Guinea. Since all of these island groups are located on or near the equator, the climate is hot and humid. Adventurous travelers enjoy exploring their remoteness.

Micronesia, a group of islands that includes the Carolines, the Marianas, the Marshalls, the Republic of Kiribati, and the Republic of Nauru, is located north of the equator and immediately east of the international dateline. All the islands share a tropical climate — hot and humid. The Marianas and Carolines played a strategic role in the naval and military operations of the United States during World War II. Remnants of war equipment remain both on land and at the bottom of the sea. Micronesia appeals to travelers seeking an out- of-the-way destination.

Indonesia consists of over 3,000 plush, tropical islands in a semi-circle straddling the equator — islands of unique sights, sounds, and tastes. Customs, dress, climate, ceremonies, arts, and handicrafts are almost as varied as the landscape that starts with Jakarta, the capital, and extends to the enchantment of Bali.

An archipelago of 7,000-plus islands, linked like a necklace along 1,150 miles, the Phillipines consist of three principal groups: Luzon, the site of Manila; Visagas, home of sugar cane plantations and fishing fleets; and the Muslim provinces of Mindanao.

When considering Russian geography in the 1990s, you need a scorecard and a map. The Commonwealth of Independent States (CIS) is the proposed name for the former USSR.

Asia can be divided into five regions, each possessing distinctive physical, cultural, and economic characteristics.

Southwest Asia (Iran and the nations of Asia Minor and the Arabian peninsula), long a strategic crossroads, is characterized by an arid climate, a rich agriculture, great petroleum reserves, and the predominance of Islam.

South Asia (Afghanistan and the nations of the

Continental Asia

CIS	Bangladesh	Singapore
Afghanistan	Myanmar	The People's Republic of China
Pakistan	Thailand	Taiwan (the Republic of China)
India	Laos	North and South Korea
Sri Lanka	Vietnam	Japan
Nepal	Cambodia	Mongolia
Bhutan	Malaysia	Hong Kong (BCC)
Iran	Iraq	Syria
Lebanon	Jordan	Israel
Saudi Arabia	Bahrain	The Republic of Yemen
Oman	Muscat	United Arab Emirates
Qatar	Dhahran	Kuwait

Indian sub-continent) is isolated from the rest of Asia by great mountain barriers and was once entirely under British rule.

Southeast Asia (the nations of the southeastern peninsula) is characterized by a monsoon climate, a maritime orientation, the fusion of Indian and Chinese cultures, and a great diversity of ethnic groups, languages, religions, and politics.

East Asia (the countries of China, Mongolia, Korea, and the islands of Taiwan and Japan) is located in the mid-latitudes of the Pacific Ocean, has strong indigenous cultures, and forms the most industrialized region of Asia.

Formerly-Soviet Asia (the central and northern third of the continent) accounts for about 75 percent of the area and is the largest section of Asia. With the recent break-up of the USSR, many of the former republics are clamoring for independence. This all-encompassing change will affect the political and economic climate of the region.

Spotlight on Cities

Tokyo, Japan

Sprawling along the shores of Tokyo Bay, the city is an intriguing composite of East and West. Tokyo is the head and the heart of Japan. It's a cosmopolitan city — the biggest, most chaotic, noisiest, and perhaps the most fascinating city.

Sightseeing attractions include the Ginza, the formal shopping district; Asakusa, a lively amusement center; the Imperial Palace; and Ueno Park.

Beijing, the People's Republic of China

Beijing, the capital, is the economic and political center of the country. Beijing's attractions include the Imperial Palace; the Forbidden City, a major architectural masterpiece; the Ming Tombs; the Summer Palace; the Beijing Zoo; and Tian An Men Square.

Bangkok, Thailand

Bangkok is the capital of Thailand and home to nearly 400 Buddhist temples. The most famous temples are those of the Emerald Buddha on the grounds of the Grand Palace; the Temple of the Reclining Buddha; and the Temple of the Golden Buddha. Wats (temples), klongs (canals), and palaces are three of the main reasons for visiting Bangkok.

Singapore, Singapore

Singapore, at the southern tip of the Malay Peninsula, is one of the world's great commercial centers and one of the world's busiest ports. Commerce has historically been the chief source of income. The city is prosperous, clean, and combines the modern with elegant colonial. Singapore boasts fine hotels, excellent dining, and shopping.

New Delhi, India

The city is a union of two cities — Delhi and New Delhi. Delhi was the capital of the ancient empire. New Delhi was planned and built by the British. New Delhi has massive government buildings, open green spaces, and urban plazas. Delhi forms a contrast with its serpentine streets and crowded bazaars.

Spotlight on Attractions

Taj Mahal

The Taj Mahal is considered one of the most beautiful buildings in the world and the finest example of the late style of Indian-Muslim architecture. It is in a walled garden adorned with fountains, marble pavement, and an oblong reflecting pool. This memorial honors love through its faultless structure and perfect proportions.

The Great Wall

The Great Wall, snaking across the southern edge of the Mongolian plain, was erected to protect China from northern nomads. It is a composite of many walls. Northwest of Beijing, the rebuilt wall is 30 feet high, 25 feet wide, with interspersed 40-feet-high guard towers; far in the distance, the ancient stones are crumbling and overgrown as the wall stretches away. It is one of the only man-made artifacts that can be distinguished from space.

Mt. Fuji, Japan

Mt. Fuji is an easily recognizable symbol of Japan. It is a sacred mountain and the traditional goal of pilgrimages. The beauty of the snow-capped symmetrical cone, ringed by lakes and virgin forests, has inspired Japanese poets and painters throughout the centuries.

Xian, the People's Republic of China

Xian, the capital of China during the course of eleven dynasties, profited from its location on the Silk Road and became one of the wealthiest and largest cities in the world. The discovery of Emperor Qin Shi Huangdi's burial site, with its army of life-size terra cotta figures, has made Xian an important tourist destination.

Africa

Known as the "Dark Continent," because of its late exploration, Africa still casts a spell of the mysterious and unknown over the worlds imagination. Images of Africa range from the barren dunes of the Sahara to the impenetrable jungles of the Congo, and from crowded, colorful bazaars surrounded by minarets and mosques to wide-open rolling grassland sprinkled with herds of zebra and giraffes. These contrasting images actually define the two separate worlds of Africa — Africa north of the Sahara and Africa south of the Sahara.

Spotlight on Attractions

Pyramids and the Sphinx

Located near Cairo, Egypt, the great pyramids of Giza and the Sphinx were considered one of the original seven wonders of the ancient world. There are three pyramids, the largest being over 450 feet high and containing some three million huge blocks of stone. One can explore deep inside the pyramids by means of tunnels and staircases. Light shows in the evening highlight their distinctive forms.

Nile Cruises

Week-long cruises on the Nile depart from Cairo, Egypt, bound for the city of Luxor, site of the awesome ruins of the Temples of Karnak and Luxor, as well as the Valley of the Kings and the Valley of the Queens. The valleys are the burial areas of ancient royalty. The termination of the cruise is Aswan, site of the famous Aswan Dam.

Victoria Falls

Victoria Falls is near the town of Livingston, on the border between Zambia and Zimbabwe. The falls are formed as the Zambezi River plummets into a narrow chasm, producing a loud roar and a mist perceptible from a distance of twenty five miles.

Game Parks

Kenya is the home of the world-famous parks Tsavo, Amboseli, Samburo, and Masai Mara, where visitors can see the entire range of big African game in their natural environments. Among the many lodges that serve visitors is the Treetops Hotel.

Summary

In today's ever-changing world, the need for complete and accurate geographic information has never been more important to travel professionals. The agent who can accurately match client needs to locational, physical, and cultural information is an invaluable resource. Locational geography answers the questions "Where is it?" and "How do you get there?" Those answers are usually available in maps and reference books. Physical geography answers questions such as "What is the weather like?" "When is the best time to go?" Cultural geography answers the questions "What is the food like?" "Does the country have a different language?"

This chapter serves to briefly summarize destinations of the world. The areas chosen are the United States, Canada, Mexico, the Caribbean, Central and South America, Europe, Asia and the Pacific, and Africa and the Middle East.

Chapter Wrap-up

DISCUSSION TOPICS

Climate

Most climatic conditions repeat themselves in different parts of the world. Mediterranean-type climates, for example, are found primarily on the southwest sides of continents between 30 and 40 degrees latitude. Using your atlas, locate four areas in the world found in this location. What characteristics do they share? Consider such elements as flora, fauna, mountain formations, rainfall, temperature, and wind patterns. How have these common characteristics impacted tourism to these areas?

Cultural Geography

National parks are one factor that might determine the popularity of a particular destination. Other cultural reasons might include sporting events, native cuisine, art, history, and so on. For example, New England is a popular destination for those who enjoy historical sights and natural beauty. Using the categories listed, choose domestic destinations that might fulfill each of the cultural reasons for travel.

The South Pacific

Clients have come into your office wanting to go to the South Pacific on their next vacation. How would you summarize to your clients the various groups of islands in the South Pacific? Which group offers sun, sand, and surf? Which islands attract adventurous travelers? Which islands are best for those seeking out-of-the-way destinations?

Itinerary

Prepare a two-week itinerary through Europe for each of the following groups:

■ A choral group
■ Art collectors
■ Skiiers
■ Hikers.

Air Travel

Chapter 3

CHAPTER OBJECTIVES

After completing this chapter, the reader should be able to

- Explain interline agreements and provide two examples of them
- Discuss the relationship between fares and classes of service
- Define promotional fares and relate three reasons for their use by an airline
- Describe the difference between a non-stop and direct/through flight
- Trace the history of the hub-and-spoke concept
- Explain the effect of deregulation on airline default

VOCABULARY

After completing this chapter, the reader should be able to define

- Bumping
- Circle trip
- Commuter airline
- Configuration
- Connection
- FAA
- Hub and spoke
- Open jaw
- Planned capacity
- Waitlist

Introduction

Man's desire to fly is recorded in the legends of the earliest known civilizations. In 1903 the American astronomer Simon Newcomb said, "Aerial flight is one of that class of problems with which man will never be able to cope." Before the year was out, however, Orville and Wilbur Wright coped with it over the windswept dunes of Kitty Hawk, North Carolina, in the first manned, powered flight. The air transportation industry has progressed tremendously since that day at Kitty Hawk and now represents the preeminent long-distance mover of people.

Regulation

From the start, the airlines in the United States were regulated as if they were public utilities. The government hoped to protect the fledgling transportation business. Government regulation aimed at two rather different goals: promotion and development of an integrated system and protection of the passenger's interests. To achieve these aims, an independent authority called the Civil Aeronautics Authority (CAA) was established in 1938. Two years later the authority was reorganized and renamed the Civil Aeronautics Board (CAB). The regulations introduced by the Civil Aeronautics Act of 1938 remained in effect until the 1970s.

Until 1938 there were few barriers to entering the airline business in the United States. But the only way to make any money was to obtain a contract to fly the United States mail. The postmaster general effectively controlled airline destina-

Airline Careers

Co-Pilot
Flight Attendant
Flight Engineer
Gate Agent
Ground Crew

Pilot
Reservations Agent
Sales Agent
Traffic Supervisor

Flight Attendant

Numerous employment opportunities exist in the airline industry. In addition to the pilot and the crew who fly the airplane, commercial airlines employ flight attendants who are trained to offer customer service and make sure safety regulations are observed. The number of attendants varies according to the number of passengers on board, the size of the plane, and the length of the flight. Bigger jets carry a dozen or more attendants. Domestic flights usually carry fewer attendants than international flights.

Flight attendants check in approximately one hour before departure. Their first on-board duty is to check the safety equipment: oxygen tanks, fire extinguishers, and first aid supplies. Their next step is to perform a galley (on-board kitchen) count. They count meals, note special diets, and prepare a liquor inventory. The meal count and liquor inventory must be verified, signed for, and returned to the gate agent. Each flight attendant has specific duties such as cabin supervision, safety announcements, liquor inventory, and forward and aft galley responsibilities.

The airline gate agent, not a flight attendant, has control over boarding procedures. These include the order of passenger boarding, seat assignments, initiation of boarding, and granting of standby and upgraded seats. Boarding usually begins fifteen to thirty minutes before departure. Normal boarding order (first to last) is usually: unaccompanied children, families with small children, people needing extra time, back rows of coach, and finally, front rows of coach. First-class passengers may board at any time.

After passengers are boarded, the gate agent closes the door and backs the jetway away from the aircraft. Inside the plane, a flight attendant engages the escape slide by dropping a bar into place at the bottom of the door. A red ribbon or similar signal is then snapped across the door window as a warning to the gate agent not to reopen the door. Should it be opened, the escape slide would rapidly inflate and could injure someone standing outside the plane.

One flight attendant begins the safety announcements while other members of the cabin crew perform the equipment demonstrations. On wide-body planes videos are frequently used for these safety demonstrations. Certain checks are required to ensure passenger safety. Seatbelts must be fastened, trays must be in an upright and locked position, and seats must be fully upright. Flight attendants make sure that hand luggage is stowed firmly beneath the seats or in overhead bins. Reminder: The amount of allowable carry-on luggage varies from carrier to carrier.

During the flight, the attendants serve beverages and meals, supply pillows and blankets, offer reading material, and help parents with small children. In case of in-flight emergencies such as sudden illness, they also provide assistance.

tions by awarding airmail contracts from the post office. In 1925 the Kelly Act permitted the airlines to compete openly for mail contracts.

From 1925 to 1938, through natural growth and mergers, American, Eastern, TWA, and United emerged as major airlines. Pan American World Airways dominated the international routes. Although no transatlantic service was available until 1938, Pan Am had already started service to Latin America and had begun experimental trans-Pacific flights.

ATC

In the mid-1940s the Air Traffic Conference (ATC) was established to lay the groundwork for an official relationship between airlines and travel agents. The ATC was a non-governmental body, a division of the Air Transport Association (ATA) and essentially a trade association of airlines. It appointed travel agents to sell air transportation and enforced a standard sales contract on behalf of all ATA members. It also developed agreements among airlines on such issues as interline travel and baggage, joint fares, and interline reservations. In most of its work, ATC enjoyed a special exemption from antitrust laws.

The great potential of air transportation created the modern travel agency. Before World War II any carrier could appoint an agent, and normally other carriers would follow suit, appointing the same agent or allowing the agent to deduct commissions from ticket sales. The system tended to limit the number of appointed agencies. Slowly the ATC established rules to formalize appointment procedures. After World War II, pleasure travel grew rapidly, and the airlines turned to travel agencies as their official sales outlets.

By the mid-1970s a regulatory structure was in place. The Civil Aeronautics Board decided whether an airline was fit to fly, which route it flew, how much airlines could charge, and what subsidies each should receive to encourage continued

service to the more remote areas. The CAB indirectly regulated travel agents because of its power to approve or reject agreements among the airlines. The Federal Aviation Administration (FAA) issued certificates of airworthiness to new aircraft, licensed pilots, and enforced reporting procedures designed to ensure passenger safety. The Airline Deregulation Act of 1978 changed this complicated structure.

The major regulatory acts affecting domestic airlines and consequently the travel industry were:

1938 Civil Aeronautics Act — Authorized a Civil Aeronautics Authority (CAA), an Air Safety Board, and an administrator to encourage and develop air transportation, to provide for safety and sound economic conditions, to promote a sound air transportation network, and to allow competition.

1940 Reorganization of the CAA to the CAB

1948 Reed-Bulwinkle Act — Established the Air Traffic Conference (ATC) to set airline rates, which were exempt from the antitrust laws. The airlines' cooperative relationships would have violated these laws were it not for the immunity granted to CAB-approved agreements.

1952 Act of July 14, 1952 — Brought all ticket distributors within the regulatory jurisdiction of the CAB for the purpose of preventing rebates, deceptive practices, and unfair methods of competition.

1958 Federal Aviation Act of 1958 — Recodified the general economic regulatory authority from 1938 and established the Federal Aviation Administration (FAA).

1967 The FAA moved to the Department of Transportation, and the National Transportation Safety Board was created to investigate accidents.

1970 Airport and Airway Development Act of 1970 — Provided for large-scale development and expansion of the nation's airport system.

1978 Airline Deregulation Act of 1978 — Removed government control and regulation from civil aviation in the United States.

1985 The Department of Transportation assumed the functions of the CAB, which was disbanded. The Airlines Reporting Corporation (ARC) assumed the responsibilities of the ATC travel agency program.

Deregulation

Airline deregulation became a popular political issue during the 1976 presidential campaign. Widely publicized hearings on airline deregulation were held by Senate subcommittees. Begun in 1976, the hearings continued for three years. President Carter saw how popular the issue had become and shortly after taking office in 1976 endorsed the Airline Deregulation Act.

The Deregulation Act did not specifically mention travel agents, but its effect on them was immediate. Uncertainty and confusion replaced security and stability as fare wars erupted, schedules changed frequently, and new airlines with similar names appeared. Inflation, escalating fuel costs, and the air-traffic controllers' strike of 1981 also contributed to the confusion.

In 1984 President Reagan signed legislation transferring CAB functions to the Department of Transportation (DOT). New laws preserved federal authority to protect airline passengers and to police unfair industry practices. The transfer included rules governing in-flight smoking, charters, denied-boarding compensation, baggage liability, handicapped travelers, and computer-reservations-systems bias. Travel agency programs previously controlled by ATC were placed under the jurisdiction of ARC (the Airlines Reporting Corporation), and new rules permitted individual airlines to appoint whomever they chose to sell their tickets.

In 1986, a shake-up — actually, a consolidation — of the airline industry began in earnest. Many carriers born through the assistance of deregulation died due to the pressures of trying to operate in a highly competitive, low-fare environment. Innovators such as People's Express and New York Air were absorbed by Texas Air Corporation. Western merged with Delta; Republic joined Northwest; and USAir absorbed Piedmont. The era of the mega-carrier arrived.

Mega-carriers operate from strategic hub cities and cover national and international routes. Smaller regional and commuter airlines increasingly aligned themselves with major carriers through marketing agreements that allowed the smaller airlines to act as feeders, bringing passengers from cities not served by the major carrier into the hub city. To gain a competitive advantage, the regionals and commuters take on an identity closely related to that of their major partner. This accounts for their adoption of such names as American Eagle, Delta Connection, United Express, Continental Express, or Trans World Express. The agreements have also led to the controversial practice of sharing airline codes between the major and regional carriers on connecting flights.

Airline Deregulation Act

The Airline Deregulation Act (1978) relieved airlines of the responsibility of publishing tariffs. Some people feared that each airline might revert to individual ticket stock as in the early days of the industry, thus making interlining difficult. In late 1982, recognizing the convenience of the standard ticket, the airlines adopted a procedure remarkably similar to what had previously existed. The standard ticket now refers to binding conditions of carriage even though the exact details of the complex contract are not on the ticket and may not be available at the place of purchase. Travel agencies do not need to keep copies of each airline contract. Agents should, however, be prepared to advise clients of the existence of such contracts.

Competition Through Service

Some airlines are designing programs to deal with customer service and satisfaction. Many offer employee training on such topics as attitude, appearance, and guest relations. Some are providing more amenities such as larger and fewer seats, more deluxe meal service, hot towels, free liquor and headsets, skyphones, and laptop computers. Some even include beauty therapists for first- and business-class passengers.

Proponents of deregulation claim that the skies are safer, more flights are offered, and bargain rates are still available. However, some members of the travel industry community blame deregulation for most of today's air service problems. They claim that many of the benefits of deregulation were short-term. Fare wars brought about sharp drops in prices. However, some feel that today's fare structure discriminates by charging higher fares to those travelers who have the least flexibility, the business travelers.

These same experts believe competition has actually declined since the enactment of deregulation. This is due, in part, to the wave of bankruptcies and mergers. Should monopolies control the industry, an increase in pricing and decrease in routing will be the results. The dominance of computer reservations systems by a few airlines has also contributed to this concern.

Types of Airlines

Until 1978, the Civil Aeronautics Board (CAB) regulated all airlines in the United States. The large airlines with long-distance routes were designated as trunk carriers. A second class of airline, called regional, served large areas within a certain part of the country. The third category, commuter airlines, operated short flights from small airfields, primarily to transport passengers to major airports for connections with the large carriers. Commuter airlines could be distinguished by the aircraft they flew. Unlike the trunks or regionals, which operated jets, the commuters usually used propeller aircraft because the CAB limited the number of seats the airlines could offer.

Since deregulation, the distinctions among the three types of carriers have become blurred. The large carriers still offer the same long-haul services but have elected to drop less profitable, often short-haul, routes. Regional airlines have expanded into areas where they were not permitted to fly before, often merging with other carriers to become major airlines. Commuter airlines have become recognized partners of major carriers and share designations and airport facilities. Domestic airlines are now divided for bureaucratic purposes into major airlines and large and small commuters, depending on annual revenue.

Hub-and-Spoke System

The growth of the hub-and-spoke concept and the trend toward mega-airlines with acknowledged partners have enabled trunk carriers to take on aspects of regional airlines. The hub-and-spoke system uses an airport as the center, or hub, at which as many flights as possible arrive from outlying cities at the same time. Passengers can make convenient connections and proceed to any one of many different destinations when the same planes depart about one hour later. Nearly two-thirds of all airline passengers pass through a hub to arrive at their destination.

Two major benefits result from the hub-and-spoke system. First, the airlines can provide convenient on-line service between a much greater number of cities and, by careful scheduling, ensure that they do not lose passengers connecting to other airlines. Second, they are able to maximize passenger loads from smaller cities and save fuel, since virtually all destinations can be served by a single departure to the hub city.

Large cities are natural hubs. Airlines establish administration centers and mechanical facilities in them. But the growth of air traffic has saturated many natural hubs. The busiest airports can handle no more slots (the time during which a plane lands, is at a gate, and then departs). Gate and runway holds are increasing everywhere. Airlines are buying and selling slots from each other. To

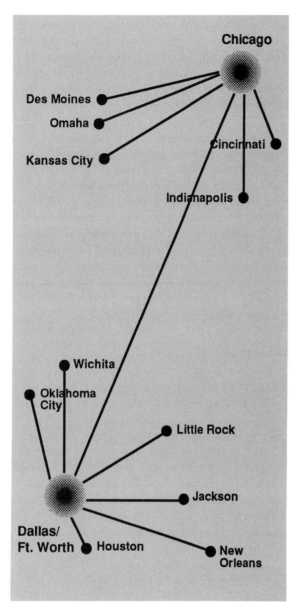

Charters

A charter flight operates under rules different from those governing scheduled air flights. Planes may be chartered from airlines that offer scheduled service or from a company that operates charters only. Airlines that lease a plane to an individual or a group impose a set of rules to protect both the airline and the passengers who book a seat on a charter. These rules vary from airline to airline.

The popularity of air charters has been dimmed considerably by deregulation, but there are still times when they can save clients money. Charters are not nearly as widespread as they were a few years ago. Deregulation of the airline industry has resulted in lower fares on scheduled carriers, attracting leisure travelers who once would have flown almost exclusively on charters.

When charters began in the early and mid-1960s, the airlines specializing in them were known as supplemental carriers because, as the term implies, they tended to go when or where scheduled service did not. During those early years charters were formed to supplement scheduled service to Europe during the peak summer travel months.

Soon after that initial surge in service to Europe, the supplemental lines began offering flights to the Caribbean and Mexico. Charter flights became so popular to those winter havens that resorts were built around the services. In the early days, connections to the Caribbean and Mexico were not what they are today. Charters were able to offer direct flights, which made them more attractive to travelers.

From the beginning of deregulation in 1978, new scheduled carriers that offered low fares, greater frequency, and better connections began to invade the market that was once almost exclusively charters. Since 1978 the charter business has been up and down, depending at least in part on the economy. For example, charters did very well to Europe during the summer months of 1984 and 1985. They were successful largely because the entire travel industry was doing well, particularly in travel to Europe. Then, with the sudden increase in terrorism, charters, along with travel to Europe in general, slumped. The future of air charters is tied to the future of the travel industry and closely dependent on the direction, up or down, that regular airfares take.

ease main-hub congestion, airlines are creating artificial hubs at smaller airports. People who live in hub cities benefit from the hub-and-spoke system. For example, in Raleigh/Durham in 1978, six airlines offered 61 daily flights to 23 destinations. In 1987, American designated Raleigh/Durham as a hub city, and as a result, in 1991 the airport accommodated 251 daily flights by five airlines to 67 destinations.

In a move to boost full-fare revenue and improve service, especially to the important business traveler, some airlines are shifting from hub-and-spoke routes back to non-stop or direct services.

Commuters

Commuter airlines serve the many smaller communities that large airlines cannot service economically, linking small airports with major hubs. Most fly smaller planes that typically seat from eight to forty passengers. Many commuter airlines operate through a formal feeder agreement with a major airline. However, the cost of being designated as an American Eagle, United Express, or Delta Connection can be high. Some agreements involve service contracts in which the major carrier charges the commuter airline for such items as reservations, advertising, and accounting.

Other agreements are based on a per-passenger payment to the major carrier. In addition to the fee, the commuter airline is often required to upgrade its equipment and operating standards. Demands might include repainting airplanes, retraining workers, or leasing or buying new aircraft.

In return, the major airline provides advertising, promotion, and accounting support; a sophisticated computer reservations system; and most important, it shares its name and image with the smaller commuter carrier.

Interline Agreements

The standard air ticket permits passengers to fly on many different airlines on one ticket rather than on a different ticket for each airline. This

Balloning

The first balloon was designed in France by Etienne and Joseph Montgolfier. Its first passengers were a duck, a rooster, and sheep. Upon learning of this success, the king of France chose a criminal to be the first man aloft. However, he was dissuaded from this, and on November 21, 1783, Pilatre de Rozier became the first balloonist. His 30-minute flight over Paris established balloons, or Montgolfiers as they were later called, in the history of aviation. Later, gas- and hydrogen-filled balloons complete with wicker baskets became popular for racing, experiments, and pleasure voyages throughout Europe. Today, the invention of liquid propane, coupled with the development of inexpensive and durable nylon, has made balloon trips increasingly popular among adventure travelers.

ARC

Since 1985, the Airlines Reporting Corporation (ARC) has managed the world's oldest centralized ticket processing and reporting system. ARC's goal is to help airlines and travel agents better serve their customers by providing a simple and unified system through which airlines can market their services. ARC provides three primary services to the travel industry:

- Travel agency accreditation.
- Printing and distribution of standardized ticket stock.
- Centralized reporting, processing, and settlement of tickets issued.

agreement is known as an interline agreement. Travel agencies report their sales of standard interline tickets to the Airlines Reporting Corporation (ARC), which arranges for each airline to receive correct payment. Airlines outside the ARC system provide their own individual ticket stock to agents.

The Airline Ticket

Purchase of an air ticket initiates a complex contract between the airline and the passenger. This contract is somewhat one-sided: the passenger does not negotiate directly with the airline. The airline states its terms or conditions for transporting passengers. Most passengers do not know that when they buy an airline ticket they are accepting these terms and conditions.

The Airline Ticket

Most travel agencies issue the automated ticket/boarding pass that combines an airline ticket and boarding pass. The following examples show an automated ticket and a hand written ticket for the itinerary-BOS/SFO/BOS.

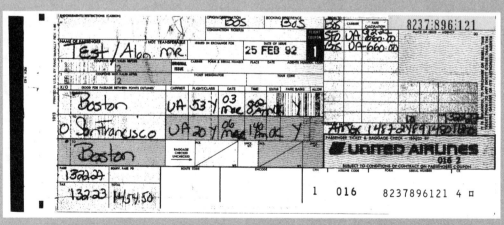

Airline Seating

All aircraft have different seating configurations. Note the differences between Delta Air Lines 757, serving short and medium domestic routes; and Delta Air Lines MD-11, used on long international routes.

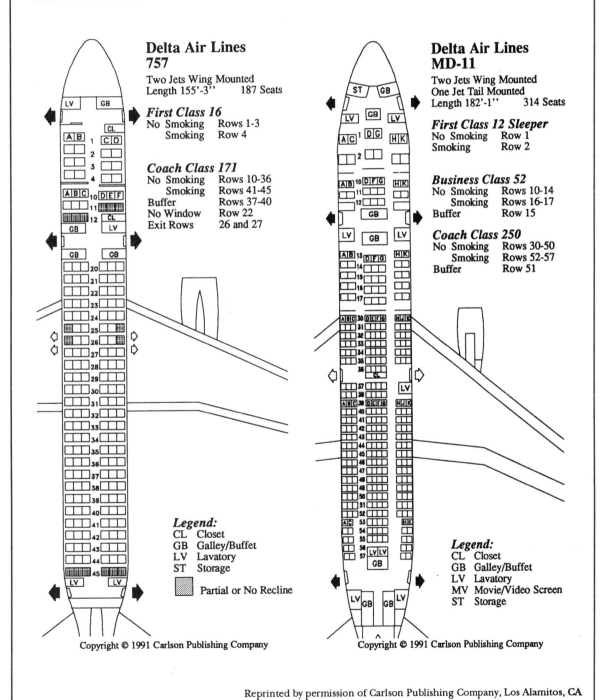

Delta Air Lines 757

Two Jets Wing Mounted
Length 155'-3"   187 Seats

First Class 16
No Smoking   Rows 1-3
    Smoking   Row 4

Coach Class 171
No Smoking   Rows 10-36
    Smoking   Rows 41-45
Buffer   Rows 37-40
No Window   Row 22
Exit Rows   26 and 27

Legend:
CL   Closet
GB   Galley/Buffet
LV   Lavatory
ST   Storage
▓   Partial or No Recline

Copyright © 1991 Carlson Publishing Company

Delta Air Lines MD-11

Two Jets Wing Mounted
One Jet Tail Mounted
Length 182'-1"   314 Seats

First Class 12 Sleeper
No Smoking   Row 1
Smoking   Row 2

Business Class 52
No Smoking   Rows 10-14
    Smoking   Rows 16-17
Buffer   Row 15

Coach Class 250
No Smoking   Rows 30-50
    Smoking   Rows 52-57
Buffer   Row 51

Legend:
CL   Closet
GB   Galley/Buffet
LV   Lavatory
MV   Movie/Video Screen
ST   Storage

Copyright © 1991 Carlson Publishing Company

Reprinted by permission of Carlson Publishing Company, Los Alamitos, CA

During an average daytime hour, between 95,000 and 100,000 people are airborne over the United States.

It would be impossible to state all the terms of these airline contracts on the ticket itself, particularly since no two airlines are exactly the same and a standard ticket must be valid for all passengers. Until recently, therefore, tickets summarized only the most important conditions, including liability in case of death, personal injury, or loss of baggage, and referred passengers to the published rules and tariffs that could be found in any travel agency or airline ticket office.

Today a standard ticket must identify the important areas covered in the contract: airline liability for personal injury and death; restrictions and procedures for filing claims; the right of carriers to change the terms of the contract without advance notice; the carrier's rights and liabilities for delays, schedule changes, reroutings, or failure to operate; the limitation of liability for lost or damaged baggage; and the availability of excess valuation insurance. Each airline's ticket office will make copies of its own contract available for inspection.

Baggage

In addition to the use of standard tickets, interline agreements also allow for the transfer of baggage from one airline to another. The free baggage allowance on domestic flights is based on the number of pieces of luggage and the size and weight of each piece. Domestic flights include those between and within the continental United States and parts of Canada, Puerto Rico, the Virgin Islands, Alaska, and Hawaii. Regulations vary somewhat from carrier to carrier, but in general, passengers are allowed to check two standard suitcases and one small one. Smaller commuter aircraft with limited baggage capacity may restrict passengers to only one bag. No piece of luggage may weigh more than 70 pounds, and the largest piece should not measure more than 62 to 80 inches in total dimensions. All checked baggage must include an identification tag on the outside bearing the owner's name and address. It is also advisable to put a tag inside luggage in case the outside one comes off.

If passengers will be carrying unusual baggage, the airline should be alerted beforehand. If a person has more baggage than permitted, an extra fee is charged. Charges vary from airline to airline. The amount of excess baggage an airline can accommodate is limited, but unless a passenger is carrying an extraordinary amount of luggage, the limit is unlikely to be reached. Most airlines will accept sporting equipment, including bicycles, surfboards, skis, and golf clubs. Charges for these items are the same as those for excess baggage.

Bags can sometimes be permanently lost or badly damaged. Popular soft-sided luggage is particularly susceptible to damage. On domestic flights, the liability of larger airlines is limited to $1,250 per fare-paying passenger. The airline may pay any amount up to that maximum, based on its assessment of the value of the loss or damage. When passengers check their baggage, they may declare a higher valuation and pay an additional charge. They may also purchase excess valuation insurance.

Suitcase dimensions —

To determine a case's total dimensions, add its length, height, and width. For example, a typical suitcase's longest side (length) might measure 28 inches, and it might be 20 inches high and 5 inches deep. The case's total dimensions would be 53 inches.

In 1970, H. Doyle Owens opened an unclaimed baggage center in Alabama. He began by purchasing lost and unclaimed luggage, along with the bags' contents, from passenger planes, reconditioning the merchandise, and selling it at discount prices. Today four such centers can be found in Alabama. Some of the most popular items are hairdryers, sunglasses, cameras, blue jeans, giftware, toys, toiletries, and jewelry.

The airlines will not assume any liability for damage to bags that the passenger carries on board. They will usually compensate for damage to checked luggage except when the passenger is responsible: for example, through overstuffing bags or packing fragile items improperly.

Bags that were placed on the wrong flight or that arrive on a later flight will be delivered to passengers at their home or destination as soon as possible. Most major airlines spend three to five days attempting to trace lost baggage. The passenger's claim is then forwarded to the carrier's central office, where it may be kept on file for up to three months. Most claims are settled before the expiration of the three-month period.

At the discretion of the airline's airport station manager, a small cash advance may be offered to passengers in transit who have lost baggage and need to purchase clothes or other necessary articles. Any such cash advance is deducted from the final liability settlement.

Pets

Airlines stress the necessity of making advance reservations for pets. Most airlines will transport animals either in the passenger cabin or as freight. Reservations are accepted for one small pet per passenger cabin on a first-come, first-served basis. The agent should request pet approval when making the reservation. If the pet is too large or if the cabin space has been promised to another person with a pet, the owner has the option of checking the animal as excess baggage in the cargo compartment or booking another flight with pet space.

If the routing requires connections to other carriers, pets are automatically transferred between flights. Passengers with pets should allow extra time at the airport for check-in. Animals are loaded last and unloaded first. At the destination, an airline employee will per-

sonally deliver the pet to the baggage claim area.

The charge for pets carried as cargo is based on excess baggage charges, and the cost of a pet accompanying a passenger is approximately $50. Seeing-eye and hearing-ear dogs are exempt from the rules forbidding larger pets from traveling in the passenger cabin. When accompanied by their owners and harnessed, these dogs are accepted on board without charge but may not occupy a seat or block aisles. Agents should request a bulkhead seat for passengers with such dogs so the animal has room to lie down.

Special Requests

If the airline through which a travel agent has made a booking has to contact another airline to secure a confirmed reservation, the necessary flight may be said to be on request. The request proceeds through the computer and is answered through the computer, taking from a few seconds to several hours or even days.

The primary airline may thus recontact the agent electronically after an original reservation is made to advise that a waitlist has cleared, a flight on request has been confirmed, or a schedule or flight number has been changed. If the agent has made the original reservation on the primary airline's own computer system, any changes in a passenger's status will automatically be sent to the originating agent.

Since one person's cancellation may be another's confirmation, travel agents should notify the airline immediately when a passenger cancels. Any changes that the client wishes to make in the itinerary should also be communicated as quickly as possible.

Planned Capacity

In the airline industry people who hold confirmed reservations and fail to check in or cancel the reservation are known as no-shows. Because of no-shows, people who are waitlisted for a flight or who are flying standby are often able to get on flights that had been listed as full. A serious impact of no-shows, however, is that flights apparently booked to capacity often depart with empty seats. These seats could have been occupied by passengers who were turned away because, according to the number of reservations, the flight was full.

Airlines try to compensate for no-shows by overbooking, taking reservations for more seats than are on the airplane. The airline term for this procedure is planned capacity. The airlines review each flight to see what its normal no-show factor has been. Some flights have high no-show rates, with up to as many as one out of three booked passengers not claiming their seats; others have as few as two passengers out of a hundred not arriving for the flight. The flights are also tracked for day of the week, time of day, and seasonal patterns, since all of these factors affect the no-show rate. Based on this information, an airline's inventory-management department statistically determines the probabilities of no-shows and cancellations on each flight and adjusts the seat inventory accordingly. In this way airlines lose as little money as possible because there are fewer empty seats.

Yield Management Strategy

Consumers typically call travel agents after seeing advertisements for low fares to desirable destinations. Seats at these low rates are usually limited, and percentages allotted to these fares vary daily. In theory, only seats that might otherwise remain unsold should be offered at these inexpensive fares. Therefore, when an agent checks with the airline reservationist, the agent may be told that the fare is already sold out. Customers frequently complain about this, yet by disclosing the limitation and restrictions, airlines have fulfilled their obligation. It is then up to the agent to explain this system of yield management to the client.

Denied-Boarding Compensation

In practice, planned capacity works well. As experienced travelers know, however, occasionally more confirmed passengers arrive at the departure gate than there are seats on the airplane. This situation is called being oversold. The common term for denied boarding is bumping, and it is strictly legal within the framework of airline contract rules.

HELP!!! — Passengers can contact the Consumer Affairs Office of the U.S. Department of Transportation for records of on-time performance and lost-baggage frequency. The Airline Passengers Association of North America gives members advice about compensation for delays, refunds, missing or damaged luggage, and cancellations. A booklet describing passengers' rights if a flight is cancelled, delayed, or overbooked is available from the Superintendent of Documents in Washington, D.C.

Bumped passengers are entitled to compensation only if they have a confirmed reservation and arrive at the departure gate at least ten minutes before the scheduled departure time for domestic flights. Longer and more variable check-in times are required for international flights. This compensation may be either in the form of a cash settlement or a voucher for future travel. Depending on airline and destination, bumped passengers may not be compensated in certain special instances. For example, the government may suddenly requisition seats in an emergency, or a smaller plane may have to be substituted for the scheduled carrier. Passengers who fail to reconfirm their reservations when required may also be bumped without compensation.

Passengers who have booked first class but cannot be accommodated are not entitled to denied-boarding compensation if they decline a seat in coach. They will, however, be given the appropriate monetary refund. Passengers who are accommodated on a flight that departs one hour or less after their scheduled departure time are also not eligible for denied-boarding compensation.

The most successful method of handling bumping is the volunteer program. Passengers who voluntarily relinquish their seats are compensated with a cash payment or a voucher for a future free trip, then are placed on the first available flight to their destination. If there are no volunteers, individuals who are bumped receive either alternative transportation and a free ticket or cash payment. As a general rule, early check-in is the best protection against being bumped.

If an airline delivers a bumped passenger to a

destination within an hour of the originally scheduled time, no compensation is required. But if arrival time is more than an hour later, but less than two hours (four hours on international flights originating in the United States), the passenger must be paid the face value of the ticket up to a maximum of $200. After more than two hours, the compensation doubles, to a maximum of $400.

Bumping

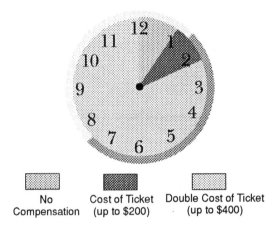

| No Compensation | Cost of Ticket (up to $200) | Double Cost of Ticket (up to $400) |

Regulations require that this payment be made by check or bank draft, delivered by hand or mailed within twenty-four hours of the occurrence. Passengers denied boarding may be provided with meals, hotels, and free phone calls at the discretion of the airline. Some airlines offer a voucher good for future free travel in place of cash; the vouchers usually have a higher value than the cash. They are normally good for one year from the date of issue, but only on the airline that issued them.

Cancellation of Flights

If a flight is cancelled because of weather conditions or some other situation over which the carrier has no control, the airline has no obligation to the passengers. However, some will offer free phone calls or lodging if necessary to stranded passengers. Airlines that cancel flights attempt to board passengers on the next flight to the destination, even if it happens to be on another carrier. This is another example of a helpful interline agreement. Frequently, if the airline must reroute the passenger in such a manner that the airfare is higher on the new itinerary, the passenger may not be charged any additional fare.

The airlines have no set rules for compensation when passengers are delayed. The airline responsible may, at its discretion, provide meals, drinks, and free telephone calls. A passenger delayed for more than four hours during the period between 10 p.m. and 6 a.m. is entitled to a free telephone call, a meal, and hotel accommodations.

Waitlisting

If a flight is full, the passenger can be put on a waitlist. As cancellations come in, waitlisted passengers are confirmed in the order in which their reservations were received. As insurance, waitlisted passengers should be confirmed on alternate flights.

Passengers can, theoretically, be waitlisted on up to three flights but must hold confirmed reservations on only one. People who hold duplicate confirmed reservations, sometimes made through different agencies and under different names, are the bane of the travel industry. This unethical practice should be discouraged.

Travel agencies that have good working relationships with particular carriers may occasionally request a priority waitlist for a certain client or in special situations. A passenger with a priority waitlist automatically jumps to the front of the line. For example, a client who has an itinerary composed of six or seven flights, all of which can be confirmed except one, might warrant a priority waitlist if the one waitlisted flight is vital to the rest of the itinerary. Long-standing and VIP clients may also warrant a request for priority. The decision to grant priority rests with the airline's reservations supervisor, and it is a privilege that agents should not abuse.

Children

The airline needs to know the ages of all children traveling. On domestic flights, children under 2 who do not occupy a separate seat fly free of charge and need no separate ticket. On international flights, infants must be ticketed and pay an over-the-water charge, even though they do not occupy a seat. Currently, the FAA is reviewing whether safety seats for babies and small children should be mandated on scheduled flights. This would require that children under the age of 2 be assigned their own ticket and seat.

Most airlines will refuse to accept children unaccompanied by an adult unless the child has reached a certain age; this differs from airline to airline but usually is in the 5- to 6-year bracket. Unaccompanied children who qualify for transportation must be escorted to the plane and met at their destination by an adult. Most children traveling alone are pre-boarded.

Once on board, trained flight attendants help the children to their seats, check on their well-being during the flight, and assist them in finding the adult who has arranged to meet them. The airline requires the names, addresses, and telephone numbers of the responsible adults at both origin and destination.

Handicapped Passengers

Since the passage of the 1990 Americans with Disabilities Act and the Air Carrier Access Act, air travel for the handicapped has become easier. These acts guarantee travelers with disabilities the same rights of service and access as those travelers who are not handicapped. Extensive training programs by the airlines have helped ensure compliance with these acts, and the Department of Transportation strictly enforces any violations or failure to meet these new standards.

Medical Problems

Airlines may deny transportation to some passengers. These ineligible passengers include women in the ninth month of pregnancy, people suffering from acute sinus conditions, and those whose health would be seriously threatened by the stress of normal air travel. Passengers with serious health problems should consult their doctors before flying.

Advance Seat Reservations

Most airlines allow passengers to choose a particular seat when making a reservation. If making the reservation directly with the airline or through an agency with access to the airline's computer system, the passenger may request the seat assignment several months in advance. Some airlines, however, limit the period of availability to no more than thirty days in advance of the flight date. Airlines also hold a certain percentage of seats for airport assignment, so passengers may not be able

to reserve a particular seat on a particular flight.

Fare Structures

The fare determines the class of service a passenger may travel in. Within a particular class of service, however, there may be many different fares. Passengers in the coach cabin on a domestic flight may be flying on fares ranging from full coach to free. Each passenger in a particular class receives the same service and amenities.

Not so long ago, air fares were set by carriers based on complicated formulas submitted to and approved by government organizations. The fares were disseminated to airline and travel agency rate desks in the form of books called tariffs. Airlines would generally match each other's air fares as soon as the fares were approved, and the counselor could confidently quote prices and tell clients that fares between city pairs were the same on major airlines. The client had a choice of fares: first-class, coach, or limited promotional fares introduced to encourage travel to vacation destinations. To compete, airlines used gimmicks such as on-board pianos, flight attendants wearing hot pants, and elaborate deli-buffets.

When deregulation took place, pricing competition heated up. The right to set fares reverted to each airline, and marketing departments seized on low fares as the way to promote sales. By 1986, the Air Transport Association reported that more than 90 percent of all passengers on major United States scheduled airlines flew on discounted fares. Only a computer could handle the volume and pace of the new fares. Paper tariffs gathered dust in corners as the need for access to fare information forced travel agencies to automate.

Promotional Fares

A promotional fare is intended to attract more passengers to a particular airline. Today's normal coach fare was the first promotional fare. It was  introduced in the 1950s as manufacturers developed bigger and better planes and airlines needed to fill more seats. As an alternative to first class, the coach fare was created to make air travel more affordable and was just as revolutionary and controversial then as many of its successors are today.

Promotional fares require more time to explain because of their restrictions. The reservations agent must be informed of all the rule changes. Airlines make quick decisions and implement them as speedily as possible. They use all available media to announce a new promotional fare, and sometimes agents discover that clients hear of a new fare before they do.

Promotional fares often bear strange ticketing codes and complicated issuing instructions. They may, in fact, seem needlessly complicated. Nevertheless, they represent the airlines' scientific marketing effort to increase their own revenues and also to produce more business for the travel industry. Promotional fares may fulfill a short-term goal, the production of instant cash for current commitments, or a long-term goal, the building of a new clientele who will be faithful repeat travelers.

Airlines Introduce New Fares for Three Main Reasons:

1. To stimulate bookings on a new route, particularly when an airline is competing with a long established carrier on that route. When promotional fares are restricted to certain routes, the relationship between fare and distance traveled can be destroyed. A special fare from St. Louis to Denver, for example, might be considerably less than the normal fare from St. Louis to Wichita, a much shorter distance.

2. To promote travel between particular destinations during the off-season: for example, between the Northeast and Florida during the summer.

3. To promote travel at certain times of the day or on certain days of the week when flights are not usually full. For example, the shuttle flights between New York and Boston cater primarily to business people and are very full Monday through Friday, early morning and late afternoon. Promotional fares for these flight are offered on weekends.

When an airline introduces a promotional fare, it is not always assured of increased profits. A discount fare represents a risk potential for either profits or large losses. So once introduced, the new fare must be promoted and all its features exploited to attract the largest number of bookings.

Many airlines do not willingly choose the discount fares they introduce; they often feel forced to match the innovation of a competitor. A so-called fare war develops. An airline analyzing the profitability of a new fare must consider that most competitors will probably match it to avoid losing their own passengers to the competition. A good promotional fare is thus designed to stimulate more travel and not simply to steal existing passengers from competitors. Moreover, it must be introduced quickly and without much warning so there is a lag before competition can react.

Discount fares stimulate air travel by making it more affordable or by making it a more attractive alternative to other forms of transportation. For example, intercity bus travel has diminished considerably since the introduction of low airline fares. Conversely, some travelers who might otherwise have paid full fare take advantage of the discount fare, and the airline loses money. The airline must thus feel confident that any new discount fare will stimulate enough additional revenue to compensate for any loss caused by the movement of full-fare passengers to the discount fare.

The first commercial flight to cross the Atlantic was between Port Washington, New York, and Lisbon, Portugal. Twenty-two passengers and a crew of twelve were aboard Pan American's Dixie Clipper for this historic event.

Discount Fare Restrictions

To ensure that only certain customers qualify for discount fares, the carriers impose restrictions on the purchase and use of discount tickets. Some restrictions exist simply to ensure that the discount-fare-buying passengers travel when the carriers have empty seats that need to be filled. Such restrictions as advance purchase, minimum stay, no interlining, no stopovers, cancellation penalties, non-refundable status, or a minimum group size discourage full-fare business travelers from switching to lower fares. These restrictions usually do not present problems for vacation travelers who plan ahead and visit only one destination.

Because airfares change so often, the lowest fare one day may not be the lowest fare the next day. No fare is confirmed until ticketing occurs. In addition, airlines no longer provide automatic refunds when fares are lowered.

By requiring payment in advance and imposing cancellation penalties, the airline is theoretically able to use the money for short-term investment or to meet current debts without borrowing. Without such restrictions, the airlines would not be able to direct the discount-fare-buying passengers to empty flights and would dilute the revenue from full-fare passengers.

Successful new discount fares rely heavily on the airlines' ability to predict which flights will have a large number of unsold seats. Any airline can adjust frequency of service and size of aircraft to compensate for broad seasonal fluctuations, but it is impossible to make these changes from day to day. Most airlines flying between the east and west coasts add service or change to larger aircraft during the summer months, but they cannot fly a large plane one day and a small one the next.

Some vacant seats are created by normal variation in demand and provide a safety margin to accommodate either last-minute passengers or an influx of unexpected passengers caused by a cancellation or the late arrival of a connecting flight. However, airlines dislike vacant seats because the opportunity to sell a seat on a particular flight occurs only once.

Once an airline has calculated normal demand, it must allow for holiday or vacation periods. Even normally uncrowded planes fill without promotional effort on certain days. Flights for the day before Thanksgiving, the busiest day of the year, are sold out months in advance. Discount fares will have blackout periods on such days.

Promotional airfares are symptomatic of a trend that tends to negate any relationship between distance and fare. Before deregulation, the further a passenger flew, the higher the fare. Now with airlines competing vigorously on popular routes, fares respond to free-market forces. As a result, it is not unusual to find normal fares lower between some cities than others the same distance apart.

Frequent-Flyer Programs

For years, airlines have devoted enormous effort to building and maintaining brand loyalty. One of their most effective techniques has been to entice frequent customers into bonus programs that reward consistent patronage. The prime target is the person who travels a great deal, usually on business. Although the names may vary, the programs are generally called frequent-flyer plans.

A Gallup poll revealed that frequent flyers account for 6 percent of all airline passengers and 38 percent of all trips. Average flyers take 3.4 trips per year; frequent flyers take more than 10 trips per year.

As passengers accumulate mileage on one airline, they can claim travel benefits ranging from a standby first class upgrade to a free international trip. Domestic airlines offer free or reduced-cost travel to other countries through reciprocal agreements with international carriers.

The frequent-flyer idea has also been widely adopted by hotel chains and national car rental companies. They now have agreements with one or more airlines whereby participants are credited with air mileage for using the hotel or car service.

All the plans work about the same way. First, the traveler has to sign up as a participant with the airline. Once enrolled, the flyer must make sure the mileage of each flight is recorded. The mechanics vary. With some plans, you put a sticker supplied by the participating airline on each flight coupon; with others you fill in a certificate and submit it at the gate with your ticket; and with others, you simply show a membership card or provide a number when you check in for a flight.

The airline records the total mileage and sends the participant periodic computer-generated summaries of accumulated credits. Most plans are keyed to annual mileage accumulations. Some, however, allow a passenger to carry over all or part

Planes Currently in Use in the United States

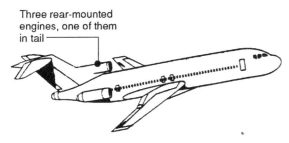

Three rear-mounted engines, one of them in tail

Boeing 727 (Narrowbody)

See it on: Short-to-Medium domestic routes, such as Dallas to Tampa.

Plane fact: New York's LaGuardia Airport dropped its ban on jet airplanes when the 727 began flying there in June, 1964.

Three flap track guides

Boeing 767 (Widebody)

See it on: Long domestic and some international routes, such as Washington to Paris.

Plane fact: The narrowest widebody jet in the air, the 767 is used on trans-Atlantic routes that lack enough passengers for a 747.

Engine housings extend in front of and behind wing

Boeing 737 (Narrowbody)

See it on: Short and medium domestic routes such as Houston to Dallas.

Plane fact: The 737 aircraft are the best-selling jetliner fleet in the world.

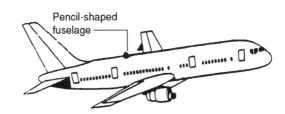

Pencil-shaped fuselage

Boeing 757 (Narrowbody)

See it on: Short and medium domestic routes such as San Francisco to Orlando.

Plane fact: The 757 is the Boeing's family late bloomer. The 757 is one of the quietest, most fuel efficient jetliners in the world.

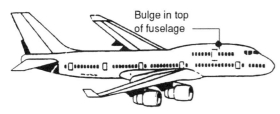

Bulge in top of fuselage

Boeing 747 (Widebody)

See it on: Long international routes, such as New York to London.

Plane fact: There are 15 different models of 747 jetliners. The 747-400 is the world's biggest jet.

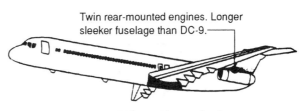

Twin rear-mounted engines. Longer sleeker fuselage than DC-9.

McDonnell Douglas MD-80 (Narrowbody)

See it on: Medium domestic routes such as Orlando to New Orleans.

Plane fact: There are five members in the MD-80 series.

Planes Currently in Use in the United States

Engine mounted at rear of each side of fuselage

A winglet on each wing tip

McDonnell Douglas DC9 (Narrowbody)

See it on: International domestic routes such as St. Louis to Des Moines.

Plane fact: An aging jetliner, the DC 9's numbers are steadily declining.

Airbus A320 (Narrowbody)

See it on: Medium to long domestic routes such as Los Angeles to Detroit.

Plane fact: The A320, the widest narrowbody jet flying, was the first commercial jet to replace the traditional cable controls with a fly-by-wire electronic system.

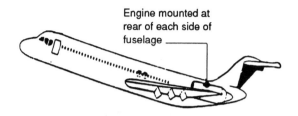

Winglets

Engine placement similar to DC10

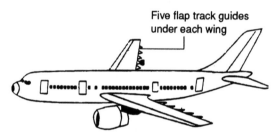

Five flap track guides under each wing

McDonnell Douglas MD-11 (Widebody)

See it on: Long international routes such as Seattle to Tokyo.

Plane fact: Successor to the DC10.

Airbus A300 (Widebody)

See it on: Long international routes such as New York to San Juan.

Plane fact: The A300 was the first twin-engine, wide body jet.

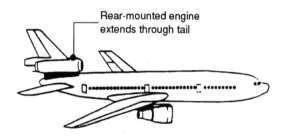

Rear-mounted engine extends through tail

Same features as A300 but body is 20 feet shorter, only four flap track guides

McDonnell Douglas DC910 (Widebody)

See it on: Long domestic and international routes such as Los Angeles to New York.

Plane fact: The DC10 is the most popular wide body jet flying in the USA, but it's close to retirement age.

Airbus A3010 (Widebody)

See it on: International routes such as Miami to Mexico City.

Plane fact: The A310 was the first jet to put a fuel tank in the horizontal tail, an innovation that increased fuel capacity and range.

of the unused mileage from one year to the next.

The most common frequent-flyer bonus is an upgrade from economy to first class. The maximum bonus is usually a pair of system-wide first-class tickets. Once frequent-flyer participants have received their first award, they are usually hooked. The public has become quite sophisticated about getting the most out of these programs. When a TWA plane was hijacked by terrorists a few years ago, a businessman was among those held hostage while the plane was flown four times between Lebanon and Algeria. His reaction on his release revealed him to be a true modern traveler. He demanded frequent-flyer mileage credits for the four unscheduled flights. TWA complied.

Although frequent-flyer programs are very popular, they are costly to operate at a time when most airlines can barely break even; the Internal Revenue Service may start taxing mileage awards; and the programs no longer give one airline a competitive edge over another.

In-flight Services

The interior of an aircraft is called the plane's cabin. Propeller planes do not fly very high, so air pressure inside their cabins does not differ noticeably from that on the ground. Because jets operate more efficiently at high altitudes, their cabin air pressure must be artificially increased to approximate the air pressure at ground level. Modern jets that fly at high altitudes have pressurized cabins.

The layout of the cabin has much to do with passenger comfort. Coach-class seating comfort has been decreasing steadily in recent years because the airlines have been under intense pressure to improve profitability. Two of the airlines' most common responses to financial pressure have had an adverse impact on comfort:

■ Crowding more and more coach seats into the cabin space.
■ Filling a higher percentage of the seats by offering attractive promotional fares to vacation travelers.

Probably the greatest determinant of comfort on any flight is how full the flight is. Even though passengers can sometimes select a flight the airline thinks will not be full, the luck of the draw in the seat-selection computer usually determines whether the adjoining seat is filled.

Seat space is determined by a combination of three factors: seat pitch, seat width, and configuration of the aircraft. Pitch is the airline term for the front-to-rear spacing of seat rows. Modern passenger planes are equipped with seat-mounting tracks in the floor, and the airline can adjust seat spacing. Seat pitch on planes on domestic routes averages between 31 and 33 inches; the typical pitch on transatlantic flights is 34 inches. The average pitch in first class is 40 inches, although in wide-body aircraft it may be as much as 57 to 60 inches.

Seat width, like seat pitch, is determined by airline policy. It is the total side-to-side space available at seat cushion or chest level and cannot be adjusted as easily as pitch. Cabin dimensions limit the number of seats an airplane can place across each row. The configuration of seats in each row also influences passenger comfort and the feeling of roominess. At any given width, seats installed in pairs provide the most comfortable arrangement. Every passenger has either an aisle or window on

Kinds of Journeys

One Way — A trip from an originating city to a destination city that can be made on one or more flights. The passenger may or may not have to change planes.

Example: Miami to Atlanta to New Orleans on Delta (DL).

Round Trip — A trip that begins and ends in the same city. In strict use, a round trip describes a trip from an originating city to a destination city and back via exactly the same routing and using the same carriers.

Example: Miami to Atlanta on DL; Atlanta to Miami on DL.

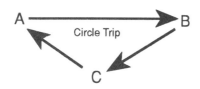

Circle Trip — Similar to a round trip except that the return trip may be via a different routing or on a different carrier.

Example: Outbound: Miami to Atlanta on DL; Atlanta to Minneapolis on DL.
Return: Minneapolis to JFK on NW; JFK to Miami on NW.

Knowing the difference between a circle trip and a round trip is important to the application of discount fares that may be applicable only on round trip and not on circle trip journeys.

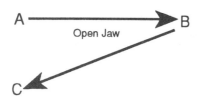

Open Jaw — Any trip essentially of a round-trip nature, but on which the passenger returns to a different city from the point of origin or departs for the return trip from a city other than the original destination.

Example: 1. Seattle to Boston to San Francisco.
2. Seattle to Boston via NW, Boston to New York by car, New York to Seattle via NW.

Kinds of Flights

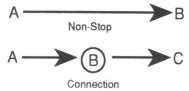

Non-Stop — A flight with no intermediate stops.

Connection — A flight from origin to destination with an intermediate stop. Passenger must change planes.

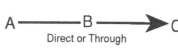

Direct or Through Flight — A flight from origin to destination with one or more intermediate stops. Passenger does not have to change planes.

Airline advertising of direct or through flights can cause passengers some confusion. When the airline advertises "Four direct flights from Seattle to New York each day," the client may think the airline means non-stop flights. Exceptions add to the confusion. Some direct or through flights require passengers to change planes at intermediate stops. Airlines will change equipment if one segment of a flight is more or less heavily traveled than another or if the flight changes from domestic to international.

Additional Charges

Add-on charges started years ago with an 8 percent federal ticket tax to be used for airport improvements. Then security surcharges were added and international departure taxes were imposed. In 1986, a $5.00 Immigration Service fee for all arriving international passengers was added. Other fees and taxes are continually proposed. The Customs and Immigration fees will be adjusted every two years to match costs. Ticketing agents must collect the fees and show the totals on the airline ticket. Fortunately, these add-on charges are automatically calculated by most computer reservation systems.

one side. Seats installed in groups of three or more have at least one middle seat in each row. In a full plane, a passenger in a middle seat is squeezed between two other passengers.

Selecting a seat may depend on the in-flight configuration of each class. The most common cabin configuration separates an aircraft into first, coach, and sometimes business-class sections. Passengers have their own ideas about which is the best seat. In first class, all seats should be equally comfortable. The first class section is located at the front of the plane or upstairs, if there are two levels of seating, and has from eight to twenty-four seats. Seats are wider than coach seats, usually more heavily padded, and are spaced to provide extra leg room. More flight attendants per passenger can provide a higher level of personalized service. Meals are more elaborate, have more choices, and are often served on china with cloth napkins, instead of the plastic and paper used in coach service. First class passengers receive free alcoholic

City and Airport Codes

Every city and airport served by an airline is given a three-letter code. If a city has one airport, the code will be the same for both the city and the airport — for example, BOS is the code for both the city of Boston and its airport. Cities served by more than one airport have one code for the city and others for the airports — for example, the city code for Washington, D.C., is WAS. The codes for the airports that serve Washington are IAD for Dulles International Airport and DCA for National Airport. Many times airport codes bear no resemblance to the city they are in but are derived from the name of the airport itself — for example, the three-letter code for McCoy airport in Orlando is MCO.

Examples of city and airport codes are

ATL	Atlanta, GA		LAX	Los Angeles, CA
BOS	Boston, MA		MIA	Miami, FL
DEN	Denver, CO		MSP	Minneapolis/St. Paul, MN
DFW	Dallas/Ft. Worth, TX		SFO	San Francisco, CA

Airline Codes

Every airline has a two-letter airline code. Some examples of these codes are

AA	American Airlines		NW	Northwest Airlines
AZ	Alitalia		SR	Swissair
BA	British Airways		UA	United Airlines
DL	Delta Air Lines		US	USAir

beverages and, on flights with movies, free headsets.

Business or executive class is halfway between first class and coach. In this class passengers receive many of the amenities of first class. Some airlines offer business class in addition to first class and coach; others substitute it for first class. Passengers flying on discount fares sit in the normal coach cabin.

In coach, some distinctions can be noted. Seats over the wings generally provide a smoother ride, but the view is obscured. Seats near emergency exits often have more leg room because the pitch must be adjusted to provide for access to the exit. For the same reason, seats in the row immediately in front of the emergency exits do not usually recline. Large jets have several compartments for coach seating.

Since most passengers travel coach, the airlines make every effort to make this section comfortable and enjoyable. Soft drinks and meals or snacks are served at no charge; coach passengers who desire alcoholic beverages usually must pay for them. Most carriers offer a choice of entree even in coach class. If movies are shown, coach passengers pay for the use of headsets.

On international flights, within each class of service most airplanes are divided into smoking and nonsmoking sections. The smoking section can be adjusted in size to reflect the preferences of the majority of passengers. Passengers are only allowed to smoke cigarettes; pipes and cigars are banned. United States and some international flights have a mandatory no-smoking rule.

In all cabins, movie viewing is best enjoyed from the middle rows. Aisle seats provide easy access to the bathrooms and a chance to stretch cramped legs. Although smoking sections are isolated in most aircraft, smoke drifts, and the nonsmoker may not be able to avoid contact with it, especially if seated directly in front of the smoking section.

Bulkheads are the partitions that separate the compartments of the plane. Bulkhead seats offer more leg room, but they have no space to stow carry-on luggage and offer no fold-down tables. Often, bulkhead seats are reserved for families with young children. A tired businessman sitting there might not appreciate the noise and confusion a 2-year-old can cause. Galleys and bathrooms are other sources of noise.

Airline Meals

Airline meals are designed with a wide range of passengers in mind. From a basic selection of diabetic, kosher, vegetarian, and low-sodium choices, they've expanded into Hindu, Moslem, fruit, child, infant, seafood, and other health, religious, and ethnic entrees. Northwest serves Makunouchi — a chilled Japanese meal, and Air Canada has considered the requirements of athletes and health-conscious passengers by offering special meals high in complex carbohydrates and low in fat. All the airlines ask for is advance notice that can range from four to twelve hours.

Passengers may also choose among aisle, center, or window seats. If passengers have not made an advance seat selection, they can make a choice at check-in at the airport. Sometimes passengers booked at low discount fares cannot make advance seat selections.

Oxygen masks have always been standard equipment aboard aircraft. Today, they are used only during emergencies. Prior to pressurization, however, it was necessary to wear the masks throughout the entire flight.

Airports

With carriers free to enter and exit destinations and to raise and lower fares at will, many airports, like the airlines, are caught in a financial struggle to survive. Airports are owned by local communities, and there are minimum costs involved in maintaining them. It costs the same amount to maintain a 7,000-foot runway whether planes use them thirty times a day or a hundred times a day.

Airlines rent space from the airport and pay fees for certain rights. Landing fees charged to an airline are affected by the number of landings it makes. The greater the number of landings, the lower the cost per landing, and thus the more attractive the airport.

The change to the hub-and-spoke pattern has

No Smoking

In February 1990, smoking was banned on all domestic flights lasting less than six hours. Yet, a study done by United Airlines in 1990 noted 159 incidents of illicit in-flight smoking. Apparently, rather than kicking the habit, smokers have been secretly disabling smoke detectors then lighting up in lavatories while in-flight. The FAA punishes such a violation by imposing a $1,000 fine and issuing warnings. Smoking in lavatories was banned in 1973 when a fire caused by a tossed cigarette broke out in a wastebin and 124 passengers were killed.

Internationally, associations such as the ATA, American Cancer, Heart, and Lung associations have been lobbying to eliminate smoking on all international flights by U.S. carriers. The International Civil Aviation Organization is considering a global solution to the problem.

been a boon to some airports and a disaster to others. It has forced passengers to spend time waiting for connections. Therefore, airports now emphasize ancillary services because of the revenues they bring and because the services please passengers. In addition to the traditional newsstands, banks, lounges, and gift shops, some airports now boast health clubs, business service centers, and mini-hotels in which passengers can rest or conduct meetings. Airports also provide meet-and-greet service and tour-group assembly areas.

Because passengers have become accustomed to making connections, they have also become more selective about the airports at which they choose to make these connections. Since much of airport revenue is generated by concessions (car-rental desks, stores, and restaurants in the terminals), airports have to attract many passengers to

make them profitable. American Airlines built an advertising campaign around the fact that its services connected through Raleigh, North Carolina, and stressed the convenience of that airport.

Many airports are located so close to others that there is intense competition for airlines and passengers. Orlando, Daytona, and Tampa airports, for example, all vie for the same traffic. Washington-Dulles, for a time, was considered a white elephant. It handled only 11 percent of the traffic into Washington because of other nearby airports. Then a task force was organized to inform airlines and travel agencies about the services and benefits of using the airport, notably its good roadway access and airport parking. The effort paid off as airport traffic has more than doubled.

International airports also battle for airlines and passengers as the market for overseas travel tightens. The competition is intense, especially in Europe where travel distances between hub destinations are short. International airport authorities — in most cases, extensions of government agencies — recognize the economic and political importance of modern airport facilities as a means of luring both vacation and business travelers.

The Physical Plant

Early air terminals were constructed with long, straight facades. The passengers drove up to the building, went in one side to go through the check-in process (which in the early days included weighing the passengers as well as their baggage), and exited the building on the other side to walk out to the plane parked on the tarmac. As traffic increased in the late 1940s, terminals were extended by the addition of piers, at first in a U shape and later becoming more complicated with increased growth.

Long piers meant walking long distances, so during the 1960s the satellite design evolved. Central buildings were attached to boarding areas by passages. The newest airports, like Orlando and Tampa, are connected by monorails. Some airports have moving sidewalks or electric carts to take passengers more comfortably the long distance from check-in counter to boarding area. Passengers can also walk conveniently from boarding areas directly onto aircraft through jetways that protect them from the elements.

Check-in Procedures

Whatever the specific layout, airports have airline check-in and ticketing desks located in the main departure area. Travel agents must be familiar with their local airports to direct their clients through the check-in procedure. The busier the airport, the more important this becomes.

Large metropolitan airports may have a terminal for each airline. Passengers should be directed to the departures area of their particular airline. This terminal will have gift and news shops and a variety of eating places and bars. International airports will also have duty-free shops and currency exchange centers. Some airports have as many shops as a good-sized shopping mall. Car-rental desks are usually found in the arrivals section near baggage pick-up carousels.

Check-in procedures differ for domestic and

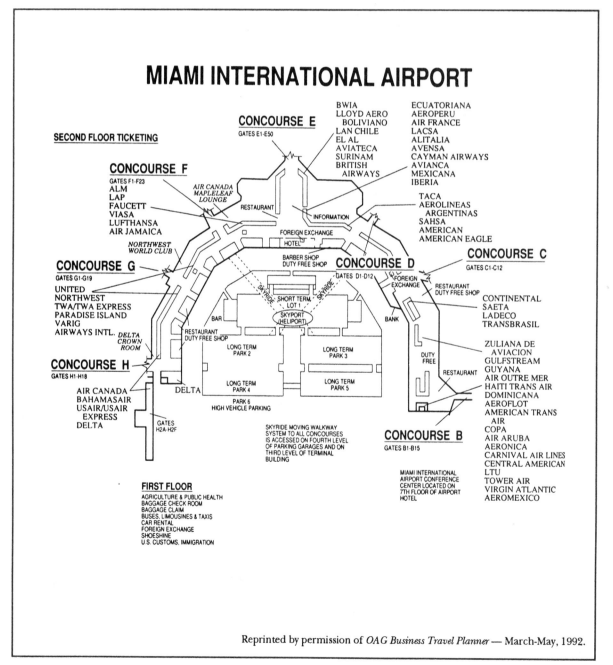

Reprinted by permission of *OAG Business Travel Planner* — March–May, 1992.

international flights. Ticketed passengers arriving at the airport for domestic flights can check their bags at curbside or at the check-in counter. Passengers for international flights must check their bags at the counter.

Checked luggage is tagged with the three-letter code of the destination airport and with any necessary connection information. Passenger tickets are checked, and pertinent flight coupons are removed. If the flight is an international one, the airline agent will check the passenger's passport and other necessary international documentation. International departure rituals differ from country to country. Passengers leaving a foreign country often must go through complicated passport control and security checkpoints.

Security

Since the late 1960s, when a wave of hijackings swept the air travel industry, all airports have been equipped with security guards and metal detectors. Passengers and guests must pass through them before going to the boarding area. Security is so tight at some airports that friends and relatives can no longer meet arriving passengers at their gates.

Passengers may not carry certain articles on board such as knife blades, scissors, cans of mace, and anything else that could be used as a weapon. There is an obvious ban on guns, bombs, and other such devices in carry-on luggage. Aerosol cans are also forbidden.

The X-ray devices used to screen carry-on baggage can cause streaks on undeveloped film and cause it to turn green or light-toned when developed. The X-ray dosage is cumulative and will become more damaging with each screening. Lead-lined bags protect films. Also, cameras can be handed to security people and thus avoid the X-rays. The same bag can be used for prescription drugs and recorded magnetic tape that can also be harmed. Wheelchairs and children's strollers must pass through the security check. Dogs are frequently used to sniff out drugs and other contraband in luggage areas, as well as to patrol with uniformed security personnel. In cases of tightened security, the numbers of both security and animal patrols are increased.

Minimum Check-in Times

Airlines request domestic passengers to check

Boarding Passes

The boarding pass permits the passenger to get on the plane. Some carriers issue boarding passes for all flights on a client's itinerary at check-in; others issue one pass at a time. Travel agencies can issue passes on all airlines. Pre-issued boarding passes are part of an airline's effort to smooth airport check-in procedures.

To board an airplane, the passenger must have
- A reservation for that particular flight.
- A ticket.
- A boarding pass.

Boarding passes can be obtained from
- Travel agencies and airline city ticket offices.
- Airline check-in counters.
- Airline club lounges.
- Airline departure gate agents..

in at least one hour before a flight so that baggage can be loaded onto the aircraft and boarding passes can be distributed. This may be modified at some airports. Lines at the check-in counters or at the boarding gates can be very long, especially at peak travel times at busy hub airports. Passengers who arrive at the airport an hour before departure sometimes find it will take that amount of time to reach the first check-in counter. The OAG *Travel Planner* and certain automation systems contain diagrams of the major airports with details of services found in each one. Having this information in advance can help speed up connections.

Foreign travel requires an airport check-in of at least two hours before a flight. Some, such as the Israeli airline El Al require an extended time period for their complicated security procedures.

Airline Club Lounges

The time spent in an airport is hardly the highlight of any trip. Finding a comfortable place to wait is not easy, and you are not likely to hear your

Security Precautions

During times of tightened security, such as the Iraqi war, U.S. airports react with heightened security measures.

- Parking within 100 feet of terminal buildings is prohibited.
- Vehicles left unattended near curbs are towed.
- Armed security guards, complete with helmets and flak jackets, patrol 24 hours daily.
- Unattended baggage left in airport terminals is removed, inspected, and may be confiscated.
- Individual body searches using metal detectors are standard procedure.
- Only ticketed passengers are allowed to enter secured areas.
- Carry-on luggage is opened and searched.

name being paged if someone needs to reach you.

There is an alternative to the airport crunch if the traveler is willing to pay. For about $100 to $150 a year, plus a one-time enrollment fee, the frequent traveler can join an airline-sponsored club that operates comfortable, convenient, members-only lounges at many large airports. Some airlines offer lifetime memberships as well as spouse memberships. Compared with the typical airline waiting-room and gate facilities, these clubs are quite comfortable. They provide a degree of personal service that has all but disappeared from mass travel.

The world's first scheduled supersonic passenger service began on May 24, 1976, when two Concorde jets from London and Paris landed within seven minutes of each other at Dulles Airport.

Personal Liability of Airlines

In the United States, the Federal Aviation Administration (FAA) is the government agency responsible for establishing rules and regulations designed to ensure the safety of the air transportation system. The FAA licenses all commercial pilots and oversees maintenance programs and procedures for all aircraft. In 1978, the FAA implemented major revisions to achieve equivalent levels of safety in small and large aircraft. Foreign governments have comparable agencies.

Outside the United States, the amount of compensation payable for aircraft accidents is limited by the Warsaw Convention (1929). Limits were established to prevent the airline industry from being destroyed and also because the lengthy process of establishing the cause of a crash penalized victims or relatives by making them wait for settlements. The Warsaw Convention struck a compromise whereby the airlines agreed to be liable for damages in all accidents; claimants did not have to prove negligence. In return, compensation was limited to an amount now corresponding to about $10,000 per passenger. Subsequent international agreements have raised that amount to $75,000.

Airline Clubs Offer

- An area with a quiet and relaxed atmosphere. Rooms are furnished with comfortable easy chairs and sofas.
- Copies of newspapers and magazines.
- A place to store coats and baggage while the passenger goes to eat or shop.
- Television, often in a separate viewing area.
- Bars. Soft drinks are available most of the time, and local liquor laws govern the serving of alcohol.
- Telephones and FAX machines.
- Check-in facilities, including seat assignments and boarding passes. Baggage must be checked at the curb or counter.
- Meeting rooms and check-cashing services.

Historical Perspective

Air Travel — In the Beginning

Human beings had always dreamed of creating wings and conquering the sky. By the beginning of the twentieth century, an entirely new form of transportation made this dream seem possible. Today, the airline industry carries millions of passengers annually and connects thousands of city pairs all over the world.

Since deregulation, however, many carriers have started and then terminated service. Mergers, buyouts, consolidations, and bankruptcies often seem the rule more than the exception. Yet was this always the case? For many years fledgling airlines began service with short local routes and expanded as funds and other routes became available. Closer examination reveals some startling similarities between the past and the present.

American — American Airways became American Airlines in 1930 when eighty-five airlines merged to form the new company. Charles Lindbergh had been a pilot for one of them.

Braniff — Braniff was started by two brothers from Oklahoma City, Tom and Paul Braniff, in 1927. Their company was soon absorbed by a larger corporation, but in 1930 the two brothers re-entered the industry and successfully began servicing an area from Texas to Illinois.

Delta — In 1925 Delta Air Service was a crop-dusting company. In 1929 it began carrying passengers, then returned to crop-dusting in 1930. In 1934 Delta acquired a mail contract that extended its airline operations. By 1961 the airline offered coast-to-coast passenger service throughout the south.

Eastern — In 1928 Eastern Airlines was an airmail carrier whose crew consisted of World War I flying veterans and barnstormers. Passenger service began in 1930 between New York and Virginia. The pride of the Eastern fleet, the Condor, had a top speed of 120 miles per hour.

Northwest — Northwest was founded by Charles Dickinson as an airmail service. A series of accidents convinced Dickinson to sell his airline. The buyer extended the service throughout the northwest.

Pan American — Pan Am began service between Florida and Cuba in 1927. They expanded their routes when Boeing's and Sikorsky's famous flying boats and Martin's clippers crossed the ocean. Scheduled air service from San Francisco to Manila then took only 60 hours.

Trans World Airlines — Thirty-four commercial airlines were already in service in the United States by 1930 when TWA was formed. It began with the merger of three other giants of the time, Transcontinental, Western Air, and Aviation Industries.

United — In 1926 a biplane began scheduled airmail service for Varney Airlines. Later Varney was absorbed along with three other carriers to become today's United Airlines.

Airline Default

Since deregulation, several airlines have filed for bankruptcy and ceased operations, leaving passengers with useless tickets. An industry-wide plan for assisting stranded passengers was implemented and almost immediately put to the test in 1982, when Braniff International filed for bankruptcy. The plan worked quite well on that occasion but subsequently fell apart when the participating airlines withdrew their support.

Travel agents who collect and forward client monies to a carrier that subsequently declares bankruptcy may find themselves in a difficult position. Their clients are technically creditors of the airline and may seek recompense in the bankruptcy courts. But confronted by angry and resentful clients, many agencies may decide to refund the money themselves, even though their own chance of recovering it from the airline is slim.

Insurance coverage will not protect clients against default. An alternative is to suggest credit card payments when purchasing tickets since many credit card companies will protect clients against default.

The major travel associations often install emergency hotlines to advise travel agents and passengers when an airline ceases operation. Before an airline bankruptcy occurs, telltale signs and rumors usually abound.

Summary

Deregulation has had a profound impact on the airline industry. The subsequent change to the hub-and-spoke system coupled with the increased use of computer reservation systems has changed the services provided to the traveling public.

Interline agreements, as listed on the airline ticket contract, cover such areas as baggage, pets, denied-boarding compensation, and medical problems. Other concerns include rules about waitlisting, cancellation of flights, and advance seat reservations. In-flight services generally differ based upon carrier and class of service.

Airlines have provided increasing benefits such as frequent-flyer options to compete in an increasingly difficult market. Airports, too, have been forced to deal with new security issues and better levels of service to grow during the 1990s.

Casualty List in the Airline Industry — *Airlines filing bankruptcy petitions*

1991	Braniff International
	America West Airlines
	Midway Airlines
	Pan Am Corporation
1990	Continental Airlines Holdings
	CCAir, Inc.
1989	Presidential Airways
	Braniff, Inc.
	Eastern Airlines, Inc.
1987	Royale Airlines, Inc.
1986	Frontier Airlines
1985	Provincetown/Boston Airline
1984	Capitol Air, Inc.
	Air One
	Air Florida Systems
1983	Continental Airlines
1982	Braniff International, Inc.
	Flight Transportation Co.
1981	Airlift International
	Frontier Airlines, Inc.

Source: Air Transport Association, January 1992

Chapter Wrap-up

REVIEW QUESTIONS

1. How has the hub-and-spoke system affected air travel in your area?
2. How much do you think people are influenced by the kind of plane they fly on? Why?
3. Which in-flight services might be most important to passengers?
4. Which current promotional fares advertised in the newspapers seem to achieve their aims best? Which do not? Why?
5. How important is it to be aware of the limits of airline liability?
6. What are the principal features of the nearest major airport? How would you advise people to get there?

DISCUSSION TOPICS

Lost Luggage

Sophie Snowbunny and Jack Rabbit of San Diego, CA, are just departing for a long ski weekend in the Rockies. Both are avid skiers who take their own equipment on these mini-vacations. On this trip they arrived in Salt Lake City (SLC), but their luggage and equipment went to Santiago, Chile (SCL). Needless to say, they are not pleased. The airline offered them a $300.00 clothing allowance and rental fees for the equipment. However, they feel that their inconvenience was not sufficiently compensated. What is the airline's responsibility? What is the agent's responsibility? Is the complaint justified? How can the situation be rectified?

Bankruptcy

The management of ABC Air has been negotiating with its largest union for weeks to avoid a possible strike or walkout by the employees. It has been unsuccessful, and today's news headlines have reported the airline's bankruptcy. Your agency has a group tour scheduled for departure tomorrow morning on ABC Air. How do you proceed? Consider the impact of cash versus credit card payment, trip cancellation insurance, and the land portion of the tour.

Bumping and Advanced Seating

Mr. and Mrs. Tom Collins requested advanced seating assignments in bulkhead seats. They received their boarding passes with these seat assignments confirmed from their travel agent. Therefore, rather than checking in, they went directly to the airport lounge to bolster their courage before the flight. Upon arrival at the gate five minutes before departure, they discover their seats have been reassigned and the flight is oversold. As the gate agent, what do you do?

Frequent Flyers

After their Thanksgiving wedding, Mr. and Mrs. Horatio Bliss plan to honeymoon in Hawaii. As frequent business travelers, they have accumulated sufficient mileage for upgrades to first class for the entire trip. They have been assured by the reservationist that this will not be a problem. However, upon check-in, every available seat in first class for the entire day is occupied. What can they do?

International Travel

Introduction

Domestic and international travel differ significantly. Internationally the traveler experiences exciting sights and sounds, exotic tastes and smells, and a myriad of rules and regulations. To help travelers with the practical aspects of these exciting changes, the counselor must be aware of the differences between domestic and international airfares and the government regulations that control travel between countries.

According to a survey of households with incomes of $100,000 or more conducted by Doyle, Graf, and Roper, the highest symbol of personal status is owning your own business: In second place is frequent travel abroad.

International Air

Internationally, the pricing of airline tickets is based on agreements among governments and incorporates set formulas for the computation of fares. International airfare pricing is not a result of competitive marketing decisions by carriers as in the United States. However, international deregulation has begun. In 1992 the European Economic Community expects to finish the process of dismantling the trade barriers established after World War II. This will create border-free skies, new airlines, lower fares, and more routes.

International Travel Careers

Air Courier
Attraction Employee
Foreign Service Officer
Film/Videomaker

Ground Operator
Interpreter
Tour Escort
Travel Writer

Foreign Service Officer

The Foreign Service is America's diplomatic, consular, cultural, and information service. Currently over 4,000 Foreign Service Officers (FSOs) serve as administrative, consular, economic, and political officers in United States embassies and consulates throughout the world. Administrative affairs involve the physical security of government areas, communications, and personnel. Consular employees work closely with the public. Among their duties are issuing passports, registering absentee voters, providing birth certificates to Americans abroad, and granting visas to foreigners. Economic officers deal in monetary trade, investment, and energy matters. Political representatives analyze and report on political matters that affect United States interests and maintain close contact with leaders of other nations.

Candidates for these positions require specific skills. Most importantly FSOs must have a strong command of the English language. Officers must also demonstrate proficiency in at least one foreign language. No specific degree is required, but a basic knowledge of history, politics, literature, culture, current events, and business is necessary. All prospective candidates must be at least 20 years of age, citizens of the United States, and must pass both written and oral examinations. Those who qualify must be available for immediate worldwide assignment.

Such an exciting career option has many benefits and some disadvantages. FSOs spend over 60 percent of their time abroad and move every two to four years. This can be rewarding and adventurous but difficult on family life. Sometimes remote locations have harsh climates and many health hazards. But the opportunity to represent the United States and enjoy enriching social, cultural, and travel experiences may far outweigh the drawbacks.

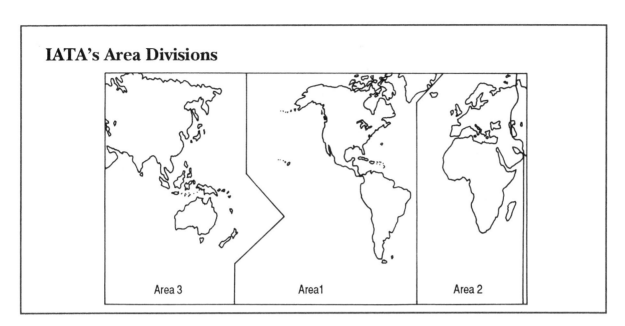

IATA's Area Divisions

Area 3   Area1   Area 2

International Air Transport Association (IATA)

The International Air Transport Association (IATA), first founded in 1919 and reorganized after World War II, is an association of international airlines whose aim is to create order and stability in the international aviation community. Between 1945 and 1985 IATA provided an agency program in the United States designed to ensure that travel agencies meet specific standards of integrity, competence, and financial stability. Member airlines required this before IATA would authorize an agency to do business on IATA's behalf.

IATA divides the world into three areas, or traffic conferences, and attempts to set rates and service levels within and between these areas.

- Area (Traffic Conference) 1: North and South America and the Pacific as far west as the international date line
- Area (Traffic Conference) 2: Europe, Africa, and the Middle East
- Area (Traffic Conference) 3: Asia, Australia, and the Pacific as far east as the international date line

Agreements among most IATA members are subject to approval by their governments. Because many foreign carriers are government-owned, their negotiating position represents government policy. They know in advance what fares or routings their governments will accept. The major United States international airlines, which are privately owned, are less certain that the Department of Justice, Department of State, Department of Transportation, and the White House (all of which can become involved in international air agreements) will approve the IATA agreements.

International Airlines Travel Agent Network (IATAN)

On December 31, 1984, legislation went into effect to bring about the general deregulation of the U.S. airline industry. The need for a service organization to promote integrity and professionalism in the travel community worldwide, however, was not in any way diminished by deregulation. On the contrary, the traveling public needed more than ever to know where they could obtain reliable, professional service.

In May 1985 the International Airlines Travel Agent Network (IATAN) replaced IATA as the organization that appoints United States travel agencies to sell tickets for international airlines serving the United States. IATAN is a private, not-for-profit, wholly-owned corporation, and operates as a financially self-sufficient sbsidiary of IATA. The primary difference between the former IATA program and the current IATAN is that the latter acts as a service organization.

Today IATAN forms the link between its international airline members and United States travel agencies. It acts on behalf of its subscriber airlines to appoint agents to deal in the airline product according to each airline's own standards. It also seeks to maintain professionalism among travel agents by endorsing them as official International Airlines Travel Agents.

Bilateral Pacts

The United States government has periodically challenged the authority of IATA to set airfare rates between the United States and other countries. The United States proposed that IATA agreements should exclude fare-setting and capacity control. Capacity agreements determine the number of airlines and the frequency of flights on particular routes. Finding opposition to its propos-

als, the United States government informed the United States flag carriers that it would make separate agreements with individual countries to supersede IATA's functions. These bilateral pacts (*bilateral* means involving two sides) permit fares to be set by the airlines in response to demand and other free-market forces. Capacity is unlimited although there are limits on the number of cities that can be used for international departures. As a result of bilateral pacts, airfares between the United States and other countries may vary.

The Six Freedoms of the Air

Air traffic between any two countries is negotiated as carefully as any trade pact. When the United States is discussing such an agreement with another country, the State Department, the Department of Justice, and the Department of Transportation are all involved. A framework for the negotiation is provided by the five freedoms outlined by the Chicago Convention (1944). One additional unofficial freedom governs the transportation of passengers between countries other than the airline's own.

■ **First Freedom:** The privilege of one country to fly through the air space of another country without landing

■ **Second Freedom:** The privilege of one country to land in another country to refuel, change crews, and so on, but not to do business

Publications

The *Official Airline Guide*, Worldwide Edition, sister publication of the *OAG*, North American Edition, contains schedules for flights between and within all countries in the world except the United States, Canada, Mexico, Bermuda, and the Caribbean. It also contains schedules between these countries and the United States, Canada, Mexico, Bermuda, and the Caribbean.

The Worldwide Edition contains information on credit card acceptance, baggage allowances, international time zones, airport duty-free shops, and exchange rates, in addition to features found in the North American Edition, such as minimum connecting times and flight itineraries.

The *OAG Travel Planner*, European and Pacific Area Editions, has a similar format. Information on how to reach many cities is combined with general facts about countries, hotel listings and locator maps, airport terminal diagrams, and details of reservations systems.

- **Third Freedom:** The privilege of one country to land in another country and discharge passengers, mail, and cargo taken on in its own country

- **Fourth Freedom:** The privilege of one country to take on passengers, mail, and cargo destined for its own country from the territory of another country

- **Fifth Freedom:** The privilege of one country to take on passengers, mail, and cargo in a second country destined for yet a third country and to discharge passengers, mail, and cargo from any such country

- **Sixth Freedom:** The privilege of one country to fly both from and to destinations other than the home country, passing through or stopping in the home country for brief periods of time

Agreements between countries usually specify the exact number of routes that will be permitted, the number of seats that can be offered, and the provisions for future expansion. Negotiation may include details such as which airport in a particular city may be used.

The free flow of citizens between countries possesses political and diplomatic significance. The flow reflects the relationship between two nations and is subject to foreign policy dictates. Each country must decide what documentation it requires of foreign nationals.

Many countries have one international airline. Many international airlines are referred to as their country's flag carrier, implying that they perform a significant political role simply by being seen around the world "showing the flag." Given the importance of the flag carrier and the substantial financial investment in it, many governments are eager to ensure that it is not put at a competitive disadvantage.

In the United States, the completion of negotiations is followed by a difficult decision. Which United States carriers will be designated to serve the new routes gained in the negotiations? After reviewing all applicants, the various government agencies make recommendations to the president, who makes the final decisions.

International Airfares

International airfares are considerably more complex than their domestic counterparts. Detailed construction principles govern the calculation of fares between countries. International fares and the rules governing them are found in computer reservations systems (CRSs).

The use of complex international airfare calculations by agents is limited, particularly in the highly automated airline and agency community in the United States. Most vacation trips are simple round trips from the home city to the vacation destination and back. They are made on non-stop flights or over the most direct routing possible, without stopovers. The agent uses the computer to find the best discount, promotional, or excursion fare. The air itineraries that require knowledge of fare calculation rules are principally those of business or vacation travelers who make a series of stops in different countries.

Most international air itineraries do not require

the travel agent to grapple with the complicated principles of airfare construction. Large agencies specializing in international travel have specific departments staffed with agents who receive special training in this area. Airline reservations systems have computer software that permits pricing of complex itineraries through the systems.

International airfares are set according to certain principles, outlined below:

■ **Mileage** — The cost of an international air ticket is typically related to the distance flown. This is in contrast to air travel within the United States, where the law of demand sets prices.

■ **Maximum Permitted Miles (MPM)** — IATA members establish maximum permitted mileage figures for every city pair in the world. Passengers who wish to travel additional miles by making more stops between the city pair are surcharged accordingly.

■ **Higher Intermediate Points (HIPs)** — This rule stipulates that if a fare between any two cities on an itinerary is higher than the fare between the origin and destination cities, passengers must pay the higher fare.

■ **Add-ons** — Add-on amounts are added to specific point-to-point fares to construct through fares.

■ **Neutral Units of Construction (NUCs)** — In 1989 IATA implemented a worldwide currency conversion system to establish an equitable method of calculating fares to account for currency fluctuations and to standardize fare construction. In tariff publications a unit value (NUC) is assigned to each fare and add-on.

Airline Rate Desks

The airline rate desk is a valuable resource for many agents faced with a complicated international itinerary. Airline rate agents will calculate the fare for any itinerary if the passenger is originating with their carrier or taking the first substantial international flight with it, provided the reservation has already been made. Carriers will not typically quote rates for unconfirmed itineraries, so if the client is requesting an approximate fare before committing to the trip, the travel agent must be able to supply a fairly accurate quotation. Airline rate agents are very busy and may take some time to come up with the information.

The airline rate desks should not become a crutch for travel agents who don't want to make simple calculations or consult the information available in the computer. Yet in an era when fares change rapidly, agents may often find it necessary to check a fare with a reservations agent of the originating international carrier or to refer a complicated itinerary to a rate desk. Rate agents perform a specialized function both for their own airline and for agents. Because their calculations involve interpretation of fare rules, they can indirectly instruct agents in the ways of international ticketing.

Each fare calculation provided by a rate agent bears an identifying number, which the agent should enter on the ticket. This number helps to guarantee the fare if it is ever challenged. For this reason, any complex fare calculated by an agent should be checked with the airline rate desk for verification, particularly if the calculated fare appears especially low for the complexity of the itinerary. Airport ticket counters have been known to require additional payments from passengers whose tickets are questioned for the lack of a rate number.

Regulation of International Travel

Whenever clients are planning to leave the United States and return, the travel counselor must make sure they will be permitted to enter the countries they wish to visit, that they will be allowed back into the United States, and that they do not unknowingly break any laws regarding the import or export of goods. In other words, clients may

Consolidators

For over twenty years, consolidators — or "bucket shops," as they're referred to in Great Britain, where they originated — have been offering deeply discounted airfares for international flights on a wide variety of airlines and to worldwide destinations. These fares are often seen as tiny ads in Sunday travel sections, typically showing a list of cities with prices next to it and no airline names. Consolidators provide substantial discounts on international routings by negotiating with major airlines to obtain discounted tickets and then selling these tickets to consumers, either directly or through travel agencies. Through consolidators, airlines sell seats that would otherwise have gone unoccupied.

Although this may sound like the answer to every international traveler's prayers, there are some drawbacks to these fares.

■ Severe penalties apply for any changes

■ No travel advice or counseling is available

■ Routings may be unusual and time-consuming, sometimes requiring several connections

■ Travelers may be required to use an airline with which they are not familiar

need to obtain passports, visas, tourist cards, or other documentation and be vaccinated against certain diseases. They will need to decide what to take with them, and they may want to make a shopping list of items to purchase abroad.

Most of the basic information about documentation for international travel can be found in airline reservations systems or publications such as the *OAG Travel Planner*. The international airline must ensure that each passenger has the appropriate documentation to enter the country of destination. If an airline transports a passenger who does not have proper documentation, it is subject to a fine and must provide return transportation to the passenger. Other sources of information about

changing requirements are visa services that specialize in obtaining the documents.

Passports

A passport is a formal document issued by a government to its citizens. It officially establishes an individual's identity and nationality and requests protection for the traveler while abroad. As its name suggests, a passport enables a traveler to pass through ports, or enter a country. Many countries require foreign visitors to have a valid passport, although less formal documentation is occasionally accepted. United States citizens, for example, may enter most Caribbean islands, Canada, certain United States territories in the South Pacific, and Mexico without a passport.

Applications for United States passports are available at most post offices and state and federal court buildings. They are also available from passport agencies in major cities where applications are processed. The following must accompany a passport application:

■ Proof of citizenship: a certificate of naturalization, a previous passport, or any official certificate on which the place of birth is stated, if a birth certificate is unavailable. A driver's license is not a proof of citizenship.

■ Two recent photographs (2" x 2").

■ Proof of identity: any of the same documents not being used as proof of citizenship. A driver's license that bears the applicant's signature and photograph or physical description will suffice as proof of identity.

■ Fee: currently $55 for applicants over 18 years of age and $30 for those under 18. First-time applicants pay an additional processing fee of $10.

The completed application form and accompanying documents are submitted to any designated post office, federal or state court building, or passport office. Passports are valid for ten years from the date of issuance except for holders under 18 years of age at the time of application. Their passports must be renewed after five years. Travelers should apply for a passport as far in advance as possible since processing time varies.

In an extreme emergency, a passport can be issued at short notice if the applicant has all the

The 24-Hour Clock

Although the travel industry uses the conventional a.m./p.m. system when dealing with the public, timetables for travel between or within foreign countries show times using the 24-hour clock. The counselor must understand this system and be able to explain it to the client. The 24-hour clock eliminates the a.m./p.m. distinction and provides a different figure for each hour of the day. Beginning with 0000 (midnight), the day progresses through each hour of the day from 0100 (1:00 a.m.) to 2300 (11:00 p.m.). Minutes are indicated in the conventional way so that 0645 is 6:45 a.m., 1845 is 6:45 p.m., and 2319 is 11:19 p.m.

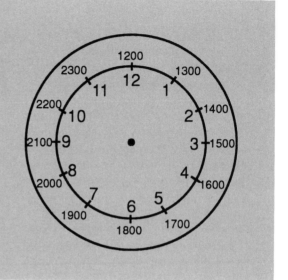

necessary documents and appears personally at a District Passport Office. These offices are currently located in Boston, Chicago, Honolulu, Houston, Los Angeles, Miami, New Orleans, New York, Philadelphia, San Francisco, Seattle, Stamford, and Washington, D.C.

A passport can be renewed by mail using a special pink form, provided that the previous passport is not more than eight years old. Agencies can obtain supplies of these pink forms from major post offices. If the passport is lost abroad, a temporary replacement is available from a United States embassy or consulate. Agents should advise clients to photostat pages three and four of their passports and to take these copies with them to facilitate reissues.

Visas

A visa is an endorsement or stamp placed in a passport by officials of a foreign government. It specifies the conditions under which the traveler may enter the country. Some countries require visas; others do not. A booklet from the Bureau of Consular Affairs in the State Department contains information on entry requirements of each country from passport and visa information to onward or return ticket and proof of sufficient funds.

Visas are issued for different purposes. Many countries do not require a visa for a stay of less than twenty-four hours or if the passenger is making a flight connection and does not leave the airport.

Some countries require all visitors, even those who are just passing through, to obtain a transit visa. If travelers are driving across a country, the transit visa permits enough time to make a direct journey without detours or unnecessary stopovers.

Before leaving the United States, tourists who plan to stay in another country should apply for a tourist or visitor visa. These visas are entered in the bearer's passport and may permit multiple entries to the foreign country. Visitor visas are usually valid for a specific period of time but can often be renewed without leaving the foreign country. Students who travel to study in a foreign country and stay for an academic year will normally require a student visa. Business people entering to conduct business may require a business visa. Once again, not all countries require all kinds of visas.

A visa service can obtain several visas in a relatively short time. Otherwise clients must submit their passports with each visa application and it might take months for an individual without the contacts enjoyed by visa services to obtain documents from several different embassies.

Visas may be obtained from the following sources:

- ■ The tour operator, if the client is traveling on a prearranged tour
- ■ A visa service in a major city
- ■ The consulate or embassy of the foreign country

Time Zones

The world is divided into twenty-four time zones with a one-hour time difference between each one. Time for each country is fixed by law and is based on the theoretical division of the world's surface into the zones, each occupying 15 degrees longitude (with some deviations due to frontiers or local option).

Each time zone is measured in relation to the prime meridian, a mythical line that passes from north to south through Greenwich, England. On the opposite side of the world in the Pacific Ocean is the international date line. The international date line separates one day from another. When it is noon in Greenwich on the prime meridian, it is midnight on the international date line. All time zones are expressed as plus or minus Greenwich Mean Time (GMT).

Within the continental United States there are four time zones: Eastern, Central, Mountain, and Pacific Standard Times. Alaska, the Aleutian Islands, and the Hawaiian Islands each have their own time zones.

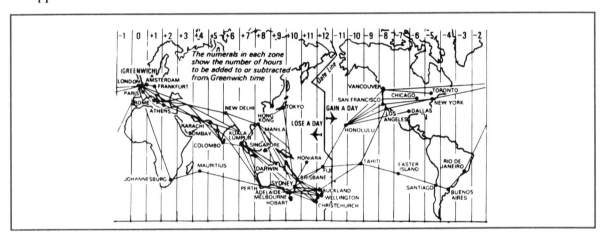

Time Differences

Using a Standard International Time Chart, find each destination's local time and its relationship (+ or -) to GMT.

1. If the local time at both points is on the same side of the international dateline, either ahead of GMT (GMT +) or behind GMT (GMT -), subtract the smaller from the larger figure.

Example:

| Bermuda | (GMT -4) |
| San Francisco | (GMT -8) |

Answer: 4-hour time difference

2. If the local time is ahead of GMT (GMT +) at one point and behind GMT (GMT -) at the other, add both figures together.

Example:

| Haiti | (GMT -5) |
| Rome | (GMT +1) |

Answer: 6-hour time difference

Elapsed Flying Time

Travelers always ask, "How long will the flight take to my destination?" Calculation of elapsed flying time is easy to do. Follow these simple steps:

1. Convert departure and arrival times to 24-hour clock time.

2. Subtract the departure time from the arrival time.

3. When traveling east, subtract one hour for every time zone crossed. When traveling west, add one hour for every time zone crossed. The resulting figure will be your elapsed flying time.

Example: Paris to Boston
Depart Paris at 12:15 PM (1215)
Arrive Boston at 1:25 PM (1325)

(plus)

1:10 represents a 1 hour and 10 minute difference
6:00 six time zones were crossed westbound

7:10 7 hours and 10 minutes is the flying time

Tourist Card

Some countries require a tourist card for entry instead of a visa or passport. For example, United States citizens need a tourist card to enter Mexico for stays of more than seventy-two hours. When applying for the card, the traveler must provide proof of citizenship. Both proof of citizenship and the tourist card must be presented upon arrival in Mexico. Cards are valid for six months and are provided free of charge at Mexican embassies and consulates, Mexican government tourist offices, travel agencies, airlines serving Mexico, and immigration offices at the border. Minors traveling alone or with only one parent must present a notarized letter of permission to enter the country signed by the parents or legal guardians.

Proof of Citizenship

Some countries accept proof of citizenship instead of a passport from American tourists who are staying less than a certain amount of time. A valid passport is always the best proof of citizenship, and clients who possess one should use it. Proof of citizenship requirements change, often without notice. Passengers should not leave the United States without first verifying that they are carrying the correct documentation.

Other acceptable proofs of citizenship include

■ An expired passport

■ A birth certificate with raised seal

■ A naturalization certificate

Travel professionals should not assume that all their clients are United States citizens. Many people reside permanently in this country without being citizens, and different requirements may apply to them.

Customs Regulations

Most people who leave the United States on a trip return with items they have purchased abroad. Each country is known for its specialities and bargains. But travelers must be aware that when they finally reach home, they may find there is a further price to pay. Every country in the world restricts the value and kinds of items that can be brought in and assesses a charge, called duty, on items whose value exceeds the permitted allowance. Travel agents should alert clients to the regulations published by the United States Customs Service. All returning residents of the United States, citizens or not, must observe these rules.

Duty-Free Exemptions

Each United States resident may bring back $400 worth of items purchased abroad duty-free. The duty-free limit is $600 for travelers returning from foreign countries in the Caribbean. If a client's itinerary includes the United States Virgin Islands, American Samoa, or Guam, the duty-free exemption is raised again to $1200.

The value of each item is based on its fair market value in the country where it was purchased, and receipts will be requested for substantial purchases. To qualify for this exemption, the items must have been bought for personal use and must accompany the client.

On the flight or cruise back to the United States, passengers complete a customs declaration that is examined by Customs on arrival. All items acquired abroad over the $400 limit must be itemized. Receipts for purchases should be kept with the declaration form. To qualify for the $400 exemption, clients must have been out of the United States for at least forty-eight hours. They qualify for the exemption once every thirty days. Liquor and tobacco products are not part of the exemption, but are treated separately.

A duty-free port is one located in a country or territory where goods may be less expensive because no duty or taxes are levied on them either entering or leaving the country. In St. Thomas in the United States Virgin Islands, for example, a Swiss watch is imported without any duty. It can then be sold to a visitor, who can take it out of St. Thomas without duty or tax. Duty-free ports can theoretically offer goods more reasonably than they are sold in countries where duty and taxes are levied. In reality this is not always true. The traveler contemplating a spending spree in foreign countries would be wise to comparison shop at home first.

It is important to remember that an item bought in a duty-free port or shop is only duty-free at the place of purchase. When brought back to the United States, the normal regulations apply. Just because an item is bought in a duty-free establishment, it is not necessarily duty-free entering the United States.

Liquor and Tobacco

In addition to the $400 duty-free exemption, passengers of any age may each bring in up to one hundred cigars and two hundred cigarettes duty-free. Passengers twenty-one years of age or older may also bring in up to one liter of alcohol. Some states have laws that prohibit the importation of alcohol or tobacco products regardless of federal regulations. State regulations and enforcement vary widely. A guide entitled "State Liquor Laws" is available from United States Customs. State government Alcoholic Beverage Control Commissions can provide further information.

Mailing Items Home

Clients may want to send gifts back home to friends or mail items to themselves, particularly when their bulging suitcases have reached their limits. Gifts purchased abroad and mailed back to the United States are not subject to duty if they do not exceed $50 in value. No household can receive more than $50 worth of items in any one delivery. Travelers cannot mail gifts back to themselves, but they can always mail home clothing or personal articles they do not need without paying duty. Items they buy and send back or have sent by the store cannot be counted as part of the $400 exemption and are subject to duty.

Forbidden and Restricted Items

Some items cannot be brought into the United States at all. These include narcotics and dangerous drugs, fireworks, switchblade knives, dangerous toys, and automobiles that do not conform to standards set by the Environmental Protection Agency. Clients may need to carry prescribed medicines that contain habit-forming drugs or narcotics. Cough medicines, diuretics, heart drugs, tranquilizers, sleeping pills, anti-depressants, and similar medicines should be clearly labeled and identified. Clients should carry only the amount they will need for the trip and also a copy of the prescription with a doctor's statement that the medicine is necessary for physical well-being. There are severe restrictions on other items, including firearms and ammunition; fruits, vegetables, and plants; meat, livestock, and poultry; money; and pets. More detailed information is available from the United States Department of Agriculture for those clients who wish to import some of these articles for personal or business purposes.

Special Warning

Anything the client takes from home can be brought back into the country duty-free. However, the client may have to prove to a customs officer that a foreign-made article was bought in the United States. For example, a Japanese camera, although bought in the United States, is liable for duty each time its owner returns to the country if proof of purchase cannot be provided. Owners of foreign-made articles should be encouraged to take the bill of sale with them or to register the item with a United States Customs office well before departure. Similarly, the client should take a bill of sale or appraisal for any items with a high value, such as furs or jewelry.

Travelers should be aware that the United States forbids the importation of any articles made from whale teeth, African ivory, tortoise shell, alligator skin, and furs, except for certain limited purposes with advance permission. Since such articles made from endangered species are regarded as contraband, they will be seized without reimbursement by U.S. Customs officers. Importation of these goods is a felony under U.S. law and may result in a heavy fine. Tourists must be wary of merchants falsely claiming that their merchandise is exempt from government prohibitions.

Value-Added Taxes (VATs)

Value-Added Taxes are basically surcharges or additional sales taxes placed over and above the cost of an item. Some countries in Western Europe encourage tourists to shop by offering a tax break in the form of a refund of VATs. The refund is on purchased goods, and most countries have complicated rules about collecting the refund. Each traveler must decide if the time and effort spent to obtain the refund is worth it. Some countries will allow refunds on the spot, others at the airport on departure; still others require an application to be sent back to the store where the purchase was

made. If the refund is to be applied for at the departure airport, extra time must be allowed.

Generalized System of Preferences (GSP)

The Generalized System of Preferences was devised to exempt from duty many goods bought in some developing countries, in an effort to help stimulate their economies. This system exempts items that would typically be subject to duty if the client exceeds the $400 limit. Some of the countries are the Bahamas, Dominican Republic, Barbados, and Peru. A pamphlet entitled "GSP and the Traveler" is available from the United States Customs Service.

Government Publications

Before traveling abroad, clients may want to contact U.S. Customs, P.O. Box 7407, Washington, D.C. 20044 or their local Customs office for free pamphlets that answer the most frequently asked questions pertaining to Customs regulations.

Government publications are also available from the Superintendent of Documents, U.S. Government Printing Office, Washington, D.C. 20402. These include booklets on such topics as how to protect against terrorism, advice for older Americans, and travel tips for specific countries.

Health Issues

A common-sense approach to health will permit the international traveler to minimize the dangers of serious illness or the discomfort of temporary disorders. The travel professional should not offer medical advice or attempt to substitute for a physician. However, the counselor should be able to give information on what is recommended. Even experienced travelers can become ill if they are careless. There is nothing like sickness to ruin a trip.

A relatively new specialty, travel medicine, has now emerged in response to the needs of the traveling public. Doctors in this field keep current with health conditions and patterns worldwide.

Technical medical questions related to travel should be addressed to these experts, who may be found in university medical centers or recommended by city, county, or state health departments. These professionals not only provide pre-departure counseling, inoculations, and preventive medications but also are well qualified to treat maladies that may result from international travel. Preparations for travel overseas should always include taking steps to prevent unnecessary illness.

Medical Assistance Abroad

Despite all precautions, sickness or accidents can still strike travelers abroad. In response to increased international travel, several health services have been developed within the United States to aid international travelers. These services vary in the benefits they offer and in the cost of membership.

One organization provides bracelets, necklaces, cards, tags, or other identification that explain the wearer's health problems and direct a hospital or doctor to the location of vital medical records.

Another program offers annual membership or insurance coverage to provide emergency medical assistance to travelers either in the United States or abroad. Services include emergency transportation and medical service.

A third group of organizations provides information about medical facilities in other countries and offers advice about what precautions to take before departure.

Health Precautions

Vaccinations against diseases are not typically required for direct travel from the United States to most countries, and the United States currently does not require any vaccinations for incoming or returning travelers. Most cities with major airports also have a division of the Federal Department of Health and Human Services that provides up-to-date information on vaccinations.

All vaccinations have an incubation period before they become effective. Some also require a series of shots, spaced several days apart. Many can cause mild fever and discomfort that may be aggravated by travel. For all these reasons, the traveler is advised to take any necessary or recommended shots well before departure.

Malaria is a serious and sometimes fatal disease that cannot be prevented by vaccination. Pills can prevent it, and drugs can treat any symptoms that travelers develop. Malaria is unpleasant and can linger in the bloodstream for many months following the traveler's return before it suddenly flares up. As with all recommended vaccinations or medicines, the traveler is urged to consult a physician or public health clinic.

Cholera and yellow fever are still present in some countries. However, travelers who follow well-planned itineraries and stay at tourist accommodations are virtually at no risk of infection.

The increasing awareness of the threat posed by the spread of Acquired Immune Deficiency Syndrome (AIDS) has led to an ongoing review of entry requirements by a number of countries. Some nations may require visitors to present documentation stating that they have been tested for and found free of this disease.

Common Problems

All travelers should carry a first-aid kit containing bandaids, aspirin, antiseptic, and any over-the-counter drugs they typically require. Prescription drugs should be carried in their original, clearly marked containers to avoid any suspicion that they might be illegal. People who wear eyeglasses or contact lens should carry an extra pair.

■ **Diarrhea:** This is usually caused by contaminated food or water. It is rarely serious or incapacitating, although severe cases may require medical attention. Canned fruit juices, especially clear juices, juice from fresh fruit prepared in sanitary conditions, hot tea, or carbonated drinks can be helpful to the sufferer. Over-the-counter drugs may treat some symptoms at the risk of aggravating others.

■ **Motion Sickness:** Travelers with a history of motion sickness can choose from a number of over-the-counter remedies or antihistamines that can be taken before departure. Most induce drowsiness and react with alcohol. A product called Transderm-V Scopolamine is available in the form of a small adhesive patch stuck onto the skin behind the ear. It requires a prescription in the United States. The patch releases medication slowly into the bloodstream for up to seventy-two hours. Sea-Bands are also

Historical Perspective

The Boeing Corporation

In 1903 Bill Boeing left Yale University and moved to Seattle, Washington, to enter the lumber business. Four years later, spurred on by an interest in aviation, he went to Los Angeles, California, to learn how to fly. Immediately after taking his first solo flight, he bought a plane and moved back to Seattle. Unhappy with the planes flying at the time, he hired engineers and designers in 1916 and set up an airplane factory whose first order of business was to build war planes. After the war Boeing designed and built a flying boat, the B-1, the first private commercial mail service in the United States. In 1927 Boeing was awarded a contract to operate an airline route for mail delivery from San Francisco to Chicago. Within five months, he had designed and built a fleet of twenty-five Boeing B-40s — bi-planes expressly designed for mail service.

From 1928 onward, Boeing's business developed and grew, building planes for both commercial and military use. Aircraft that were developed during this time included the big comfortable Stratocruiser in the 1940s and the Dash 80 in the 1950s. During World War II, most of the bombers that hit Germany and Japan were Boeings.

William Boeing died in 1956, but the Boeing Company today produces more commercial airplanes than all other aircraft companies combined. Among their aircraft are:

The Boeing 727 — The first trijet introduced into commercial service, the 727 was the best-selling airliner in the world during the first thirty-five years of jet transport service.

The Boeing 737 — Boeing's smallest jetliner, it is the best-selling jetliner fleet in the world. In twenty-four years of operation, the 737 fleet has flown the equivalent of ninety-four roundtrips between Earth and the sun.

The Boeing 747 — Six months after these superjets entered commercial service in 1970, a million passengers had been carried. There are fifteen models of the 747 in service.

The Boeing 757 — The first delivery of the 757 was in 1982. This aircraft is one of the quietest, most fuel-efficient jetliners in the world.

The Boeing 767 — Making its initial flight in 1981, it was the first Boeing airplane to replace 3,500 pounds of aluminum with 1,200 pounds of graphite.

The Boeing 777 — Slated to be ready to fly in 1995, the 777 will be the first jetliner to be 100 percent digitally designed and pre-assembled using advanced computer technology.

particularly effective in combatting motion sickness. These wristbands work painlessly and without drugs, exerting subtle pressure on a point inside the wrist, quelling the disconcerting sensation of motion sickness.

■ **Altitude Sickness**: All travelers should rest and take the first day easy when visiting high-altitude destinations. Many otherwise healthy persons become ill at altitudes over 10,000 feet. Individuals with heart and lung disorders should not contemplate such travel without first consulting their physicians. Doctors may prescribe drugs to overcome symptoms that include chest pain, shortness of breath, and severe fatigue.

■ **Food**: In areas of the world where hygiene and sanitation are poor, the traveler should avoid unpasteurized milk and milk products such as cheese. Cooked food is preferable to raw vegetables and fresh fruit, which should always be peeled. Salads, in particular, may look delicious but contain invisible contaminants.

■ **Water:** It is usually safe to drink water in major cities where it is treated with chlorine to protect against disease. In rural areas of less-developed countries or wherever chlorinated water is not available, the traveler should substitute carbonated drinks, bottled water, beer and wine, or beverages made with boiled water. If the water is questionable, ice should be avoided.

Jet Lag (Dysynchronosis)

Long international flights that cross several time zones lead to a disruption of normal sleeping and eating patterns and result in a phenomenon known as jet lag. The symptoms include irregular sleeping and waking, and mental and physical exhaustion. A person flying east to west finds a normal day extended, and the passenger flying in the opposite direction — west to east — loses hours of sleeping time in the middle of the night. Passengers can begin before departure to minimize the effects of jet lag by adjusting eating and sleeping schedules to the time zone of the country to be visited. If possible, arrivals should be scheduled close to the passengers' normal bedtime. Most importantly, passengers should not rush around on the day of departure and should arrive at the airport in plenty of time.

The actual experience of flying contributes to

Terrorism

In today's ever-changing and volatile world, we read and hear more and more about international terrorism. Terrorist attacks impact seriously on our industry; each in-flight bombing creates panic that results in a decline in bookings both for destinations and for the airlines flying to them.

Because airlines are viewed by terrorists as representatives of the governments of the nations for which they fly, they are frequently the targets of terrorist attacks. Therefore, airlines are shouldering much of the responsibility for thwarting these attacks. They are installing equipment and implementing procedures designed to prevent terrorists from planting bombs on aircraft.

In excess of one billion bags are checked onto flights each year, and inspecting each bag for explosives is a monumental task. Although the technology of detection equipment has become more sophisticated, the same can be said for the technology utilized by fanatical terrorist groups.

In response to the Aviation Security Improvement Act of 1990, the Federal Aviation Administration has placed federal security managers in major airports around the United States to oversee passenger protection procedures.

The travel counselor must inform and advise the client of the potential hazards of certain destinations, methods of travel, and activities. The best advice is to use common sense and, if possible, avoid areas and situations where there is the potential for political unrest.

fatigue. It may be difficult to understand why sitting for eight to ten hours should be so tiring, but the combination of high ozone content, low humidity, and constant pressurization in the cabin has a draining effect. Passengers will feel worse if they drink alcohol and overeat; they should drink plenty of non-alcoholic fluids, and if the flight occupies part of their normal night, they should try to sleep. If they do not sleep, they should try to exercise in their seats or walk around the plane. Sleeping pills, travel-sickness medicines, and other drugs aggravate jet lag.

The agent can assist the client in overcoming the effects of jet lag by ensuring that passengers who arrive short of sleep do not immediately rush into hectic schedules. Passengers may be too excited on arrival to go to sleep, but a short nap upon arrival may help diminish fatigue. The worst effects of jet lag are typically felt on the second and even third day of the trip. Typical recovery from jet lag is one day of recovery time for every one hour of time differential.

Four billion dollars was lost by the airline industry in 1990 due to the dramatic rise in fuel prices and to the threat of international terrorism, both directly related to the Persian Gulf War.

Foreign Currencies

Before clients leave the United States, they should become familiar with the currencies of countries they plan to visit and their value in United States dollars. In most foreign countries, only the local currency is acceptable, and the visitor must convert United States dollars to this currency.

Exchange Rates

Most currencies fluctuate daily in relationship to one another. In a country where inflation is high, the purchasing power of the currency is constantly declining, and its value on the world market decreases. These and many other social, economic, and political factors contribute to fluctuating currency rates.

Exchange rates typically do not change dramatically from day to day but could do so over a

Warnings Issued by the State Department

The U.S. State Department issues four different kinds of messages regarding foreign travel. Of the four, warnings and cautions are termed "advisories". During an extreme crisis, as when Americans were held hostage in Iran, all travel is banned.

■ A warning indicates that non-essential travel to a given country should not be undertaken.

■ A caution indicates that extra care should be taken when traveling in a certain country or area of the world.

■ A threat informs travelers about specific threats made by terrorists against an airline or location.

■ A notice on conditions warns of outbreaks of disease or other disasters in specific geographic locales.

Americans seeking information on travel advisories, passports, emergency services for citizens overseas, or health recommendations may call the Citizens Emergency Center at 202-647-5225.

lengthy trip or during the period between booking and departure. Exchange rates between the United States dollar and foreign currencies are quoted in such newspapers as the Wall Street Journal. Airline computers also display exchange rates and can perform exchange calculations.

When to Exchange Money

Clients who are traveling abroad can exchange their United States dollars into foreign money by

■ Obtaining the foreign banknotes they need before they leave

■ Buying travelers cheques in foreign currency before they go

■ Buying travelers cheques in United States dollars and exchanging them for cash as needed

■ Using a credit card for purchases and receiving bills later in United States dollars

Travelers should have enough foreign currency to cover expenses for the first day or so. Nobody wants to line up at the airport after a long flight and wait to get local money for a cab. Travelers arriving on weekends or after banks have closed will need to get extra.

Many countries limit the amount of their own currency that a visitor may bring in. Information about such regulations can be obtained from the national tourist office, consulate, or embassy of the country. The United States Customs Service requires that any United States citizen departing this country with more than $10,000 must report the fact on a Customs Form.

When foreign banknotes have to be exchanged for the currency of another country during a trip or when the client brings some home and wants United States dollars for them, loss occurs. Some countries forbid the export of their currency, and tourists must spend it all before leaving.

Only large banks in the United States or special banks located at gateway-city airports stock supplies of foreign currency. Ruesch International (1350 Eye St., NW, Washington, D.C. 20005) provides ten different services relating to international currencies and foreign-currency travelers' checks. The company also publishes a "Foreign Currency Guide" three times per year, which gives the value of twenty-four foreign currencies in relation to the U.S. dollar. It also publishes brochures of tips for travelers planning to go overseas.

Foreign–Currency Travelers Cheques

Many people feel that travelers cheques are safer than cash regardless of any other benefits. They can be replaced if stolen and require a duplicate signature to be cashed. Foreign-currency travelers cheques can be obtained from American Express, Thomas Cook, Visa, and foreign banks like Barclay and are subject to the same fluctuations as currency. In addition to paying a service charge or commission to the seller, travelers will also pay a charge each time they cash a check.

If foreign-currency travelers cheques are brought back to the United States, there will be some loss on the exchange to dollars. Foreign-currency travelers checks are, of course, exchanged at their full face value in their native country, less any service charges.

United States–Dollar Travelers Cheques

Clients who purchase United States–dollar travelers cheques pay a small service charge, although special offers sometimes waive this charge. Travelers cheques are exchanged for foreign banknotes abroad.

U.S.-dollar travelers cheques can be bought in denominations of $10, $20, $50, and $100. Although travelers do not want to be constantly signing cheques, they should not carry all large denominations. There is no point in having to cash a $100 cheque one day before departure when $20 is all that is needed.

Credit Cards

Major credit cards such as American Express, Diners Club, Visa, and MasterCard are widely accepted around the world in hotels, restaurants, and stores. Travelers still need some cash, but credit-card statements provide a useful record of all purchases. The traveler is eventually billed in United States dollars. Use of a credit card helps to spread payment for a vacation over time, because billing may not appear for several months after the purchase.

Before billing, the credit-card company translates the amount of the purchase into U. S. dollars on the posting date. Therefore, the rate used will almost certainly be different from the rate in effect on the day the purchase was made.

Where to Exchange

There are many places to exchange travelers cheques for cash in foreign countries. By and large, banks offer the best rates and the most reliable service. Banks, however, may have odd hours and be closed on local holidays. Stores, restaurants, and hotels usually accept travelers cheques as settlement of bills and give small amounts of change in local currency. Some hotels also cash travelers cheques as a service to guests but extract a service charge and use a conservative exchange rate. Exchange bureaus at airports often attract a captive and rather desperate clientele and do not offer very good rates.

Instant Cash

Travelers with large cash needs may choose to

establish credit at foreign banks or at American Express so they can obtain funds in the foreign country. They must make such arrangements before leaving home. In popular tourist areas, travelers can get cash from participating banks or American Express branches by using their credit cards. The client's account is billed the amount and a service fee.

The travel professional need not be a financial wizard to give some common-sense advice to travelers about the options for taking funds abroad. Clients who are planning to travel with large sums of money or who are taking foreign banknotes abroad should be aware of all governmental regulations. Ignorance of these rules might result in the airlines refusing to permit the clients to depart from the United States or in some foreign country's refusing to allow them to enter.

Summary

International travel is governed by many rules and regulations. Most of these policies are designed and coordinated by IATA or IATAN and involve such airline issues as mileage, add-ons, and units of construction. Airline rate desks employ specialists who compute intricate fares that conform to these rules.

One concern for international travelers is changing time zones. Therefore, a complete understanding of the 24-hour clock and elapsed flying time is essential for advising clients.

Clients also need valid documentation when traveling outside the United States. Some foreign countries require passports, visas, or proofs of citizenship from citizens.

Customs regulations relating to purchases outside the United States must also be adhered to.

Duty-free exemptions entitle travelers to purchase certain items, as well as liquor and tobacco, without paying additional taxes. On occasion, VATs are placed over and above the cost of items. Some gifts, however, are restricted or forbidden under any circumstances.

Travelers must also be concerned with inoculations and general health matters. Developing countries often have different standards concerning food and water. Jet lag, motion sickness, and altitude sickness are common occurrences and may require medical assistance abroad.

Often currency can be a concern. Travelers cheques and credit cards may be the best protection against fluctuating exchange rates. Banks and hotel lobbies provide the safest and best areas for exchange.

Chapter Wrap-up

REVIEW QUESTIONS

1. How has the United States government's international aviation policy affected service from your nearest international gateway?

2. Explain briefly what a duty-free port or a duty-free store is.

3. How can jet lag affect business travelers?

4. Are there any benefits to purchasing United States–dollar travelers cheques rather than foreign-currency travelers cheques?

5. How would fluctuations in currency rates affect supplier prices?

DISCUSSION TOPICS

Macchu Picchu

A new agent in your office has just returned from what she considered a disastrous fam trip to Macchu Picchu. It began with a one-hour delay before landing at Quito, Ecuador, due to fog; continued with altitude sickness in Cuzco; was followed by a labor strike of Inca drivers and hotel workers, and torrential rain at Macchu Pichu; and climaxed with a case of Montezuma's Revenge and a five-hour delay departing from Lima. As her manager, what advice might you give her about her experience before she begins working again? What can her clients learn from her experiences?

Visa Requirements

Mr. and Mrs. Sydney Koala from Boston, Massachusetts, are flying to Australia for their second honeymoon. They arrive at the gate in San Francisco and present their passports to board a Friday evening flight for Melbourne. The Qantas representative checks their documents and requests their Australian visas. The Koalas claim they were never informed of this requirement. Whom should the Koalas contact at this point? Why is timing such a key factor in this situation? Who should be responsible for the resulting unexpected expenses?

Proof of Citizenship

En route back from Montreal to New York, it is necessary for a tour group to clear customs in Vermont. Just prior to arrival at the border the tour guide routinely asks if there are any non-residents aboard or if anyone has purchased items while in Canada that exceed duty-free limits. Surprisingly two passengers indicate they have purchased items that fall into this category, have packed them in their luggage, and have not paid duty on them. Another couple remembers they have mistakenly left their documentation at the last coffee stop. What are the responsibilities of the tour guide under these circumstances? Consider passenger inconvenience, legality, return or connection times, and the reputation of the tour operator. What is the most appropriate course of action?

Missing Documents

Mr. and Mrs. Joe Triptick have begun a one-week package tour of Rio during Carnival. While they were swimming at the beach at Ipanama, their beach blanket and all of their personal belongings, including their hotel key, have disappeared. After walking back to their hotel, they discover their room has been ransacked. Their money, credit cards, travelers cheques, passports, visas, airline tickets, and gold jewelry are all missing. What is their course of action? Would there be a language problem? If this happened on Sunday what additional problems might arise?

Ground Transportation

Introduction

Ground transportation can provide a pleasant, relaxing, and often inexpensive alternative to air transportation. It can also be combined with air or water travel as part of a complete tour package. The variety of ground operators ranges from national train service to private automobile to chartered motorcoach. In this way the needs of all clients can be met.

Rail Transportation

Some people choose to travel by train rather than to fly or drive. A train trip gives passengers a  chance to sit back, enjoy the scenery, and move about the cabin. Train enthusiasts claim that getting there is as much a part of the travel experience as the destination itself. Train travel is also an alternative for the client who has a fear of flying.

The first steam locomotive made its appearance in America in 1830, and rail travel developed very rapidly during the remainder of the nineteenth century. The increase in automobile ownership during the period between the two world wars, however, had a tremendous impact on train travel. After World War II, fewer people depended on rail transportation to get them to their destinations; more and more people could afford automobiles. Air travel became more affordable and dependable for long trips once jet planes became widely used for commercial aviation.

Ground-Transportation Careers

Car-Rental Agent   Motorcoach Driver
Chauffeur   Reservationist
Dispatcher   Sales Representative
Lead Service Attendant   Ticket Agent

Lead Service Attendant (LSA)

Trains, like airplanes, have attendants, called lead service attendants, or LSAs, to serve the needs of their on-board clients. LSAs are responsible for all concession goods and services purchased from the commissary. They arrive one to two hours before departure to check stock, arrange merchandise, and set up their displays. Once passengers board, LSAs sell beer, soda, snacks, and other items, depending on the length of the trip. At the conclusion of the trip, the LSA recounts the stock, totals the daily sales, verifies all figures, and remits the necessary amount.

LSAs have one home base, such as Boston or Chicago, from which they begin their trips. Some trips are long and require stayovers before returning, so Amtrak covers the cost of lodging, food service, and transfer to the return train. On overnight train trips LSAs have private sleeping accommodations. Typical work schedules are two days on, then one or two days off, depending on the trips. A combination of trips guarantees the LSAs 180 hours of work per month.

Because Amtrak's on-board workers are unionized, seniority is extremely important. Beginning LSAs are on the "extra board," whereas senior attendants "own" their positions. This means senior attendants are given a first choice, or preference, of work assignments over new hires. Pay is also determined by seniority but, like the benefits package, is quite generous for an entry-level position. Tips and free rail travel in the United States are just a few of the incentives for this position.

The position of LSA is ideal for single individuals with a food- or transportation-service background. Applicants must pass a general math, English, and reading exam, have a high school diploma or G.E.D., have their own transportation to and from work, and be 21 years of age or older.

LSAs must be willing to work long hours and live out of a suitcase. Because this is a visible service position, a neat appearance and a pleasant attitude are important. A logical progression from this position is to on-board service chief, the supervisor of the train's on-board crews. After one year of service, LSAs can transfer to a different union within Amtrak if they want to progress in other parts of the company.

Amtrak

During 1970 most intercity rail systems in the United States joined to form the National Rail- road Passenger Corporation, known as Amtrak. Amtrak immediately began to improve track, train cars, and on-board amenities. Amtrak now carries twenty-two million passengers per year. The busi-

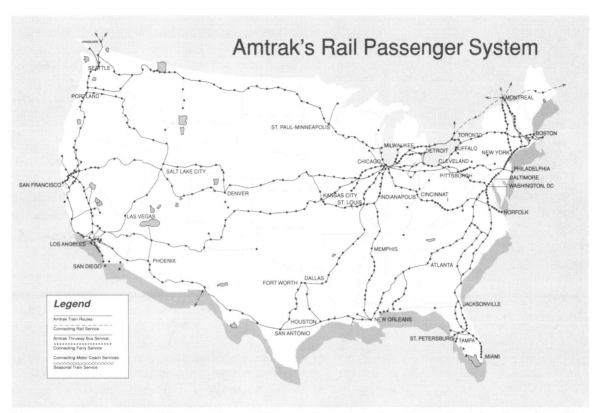

Amtrak's Rail Passenger System

Map provided courtesy of *Amtrak Express*, on-board publication of Amtrak trains, Pace Communication Inc., Greensboro, NC.

est routes include the Northeast corridor from Washington to Boston and the California coastal route from San Francisco to San Diego.

Although many train coach fares are lower than plane fares covering the same routes, sleeping accommodations require additional charges. So long train journeys should be considered land cruises rather than simply point-to-point transportation.

During the very early days of train travel, passengers in open carriages carried umbrellas to protect themselves from the rain of smoke, sparks, and cinders from the chimney stacks. Unfortunately, sometimes even the umbrellas disappeared in flames.

Although different kinds of trains appear in different parts of the country, Amtrak has completely modernized and standardized the equipment. The Metroliner offers high-speed service between New York and Boston; the bi-level

Superliner provides comfort and ideal visibility on long journeys in the West; and the Heritage Fleet features sleepers for overnight travel in the East. Standard coaches used for day travel are Amfleet or Horizon Fleet equipment.

Amtrak offers a variety of tour programs incorporating rail travel. The key to a good rail-tour program is to combine leisurely train travel with extensive stopover sightseeing and good living at fine hotels. A rail tour may combine various means of transportation: train and motorcoach, train and plane, or train and ferry. Amtrak's *Travel Planner* lists its rail tours.

National routes are principally for leisure travel, whereas corridor routes are commercially oriented. Superliners, used primarily in the West, offer lounges with large windows for panoramic views of the scenery. Eastern routes may have a variety of equipment.

The Official Railway Guide, available to travel offices by subscription only, gives detailed information about Amtrak's and VIA Rail Canada's timetables, fares, services, and the rules that govern them. In addition, schedules are included for

Types of Accommodations

■ Coach seats (also called Amcoach) are two reclining seats on each side of a center aisle. On many trains coach seats must be reserved in advance. Luggage racks are located above the seats.

■ All reserved first-class club service cars have wide, plush, reclining seats, two on one side of the aisle, one on the other, and provide luxurious seating and personal service at a surcharge.

■ Night coach seats have a leg rest that folds out from under the seat.

■ A slumbercoach is a sleeping room with toilet and washroom facilities, designed for day and night use It contains a single seat and a bed that folds down from the wall. A double slumbercoach has two berths, an upper and lower. The space for baggage is very limited.

■ A roomette is a slightly larger single room with toilet facilities. When the bed is folded down for the night, the facilities are covered.

■ A bedroom is designed for two adults and contains two berths, enclosed washroom facilities with toilet, luggage space for three average suitcases, and a small closet for hanging clothes.

■ Superliner, with its double-decked equipment, has deluxe bedrooms, special bedrooms for the disabled, family bedrooms, and connecting rooms that may be used as suites.

computer formats, with some modifications to accommodate the uniqueness of rail transportation, are also used to access Amtrak. Automated agencies are able to issue tickets on airline stock and report these sales just as though they were airline tickets. Although reservations are always necessary for persons desiring sleeping accommodations and special services, many trips on unreserved or conventional corridor trains need no reservations. It is always wise to check availability and restrictions prior to booking.

Amtrak offers a 50 percent discount on children's fares for youngsters up to age 15.

International Rail

When speaking of international rail travel, most people think of Europe. But trains operate all over the world, and the travel professional needs to know how to find specific information about any of them. The *Thomas Cook European Timetable* and the *Thomas Cook Overseas Timetable* are valuable resource books for finding the routes and times of trains all over the world. The *European Timetable* covers rail schedules for Europe and Britain, and the *Overseas Timetable* lists schedules for all the world except Europe and Britain. They each contain detailed instructions on how to read timetables, illustrate special features of each train, and include country maps with train routes marked. An assortment of other information is included: visa requirements, average temperatures, metric conversion, and time zones, as well as timetables and routes for ferries and steamers.

Rail Europe

In Europe, where large population centers existed long before the invention of the steam engine, the net-

work of rail systems grew rapidly to provide transportation for the dense population. The European economy, suffering from the effects of two wars, slowed the purchases of private automobiles while trains continued to improve and provide mass transportation. Today train travel is so popular in Europe that it can be an ideal way to meet people and enjoy the local countryside.

The cost of air travel for short flights within

the National Railways of Mexico and certain important international routes. The guide is issued eight times a year in a format resembling the *Official Airline Guide.*

Amtrak's Arrow reservation system is linked to four airline computer systems. In fact, nearly 75 percent of Amtrak agency reservations are made through computer reservation systems. In an automated agency Amtrak's fares and ticketing procedures are similar to airline procedures. The airline

Europe is much higher than in the United States, so European train service also provides transportation for the business traveler. Therefore, when traveling in Europe, especially between major cities, it is best to book reservations in advance. Many trains are crowded at peak travel times, and passengers without reservations can find themselves standing in the aisle.

Most trains in Europe offer compartment- (first-) and coach- (second-) class seating for day travel, as well as first- and second-class (couchettes) sleeping accommodations for the night. Seats in second class are perfectly comfortable, but first

class offers more space. Few night accommodations include private toilet facilities; bathrooms are located at the ends of each car. All sleeping accommodations require payment of a supplement in addition to the basic fare.

Because trains within one country rarely need to travel overnight, most sleeping accommodations tend to be on long-distance express trains. The cost of accommodations can be far less than a hotel. Sleeper charges vary depending on accommodations and distance, and the cost of a couchette is a flat fee. First-class sleepers accommodate one or two persons. Couchettes are composed of compartments with six bunk beds. These beds are assigned without regard to sex, and it is customary not to remove all of one's clothes. Some couchettes are limited to four berths, and triple couchettes containing three berths are reserved for families or members of the same sex. A recent innovation, hotel trains between Spain and Switzerland or Italy and Portugal, combine long-distance night travel with the privacy and comfort of a hotel room

It is a good idea to carry a bottle of drinking water; many European trains do not have potable water.

Many European trains have popular dining cars serving elegant and expensive meals. Some trains also have buffet and self-service cars with simpler, less expensive meals, and vendors who travel through the cars selling drinks and snacks. At many stations there are buffets where passengers can dine if they are changing trains. At stops along the way vendors sell food and beverages through the open windows of the train. Many Europeans pack a lunch at home before boarding.

Not only is it wise to verify the train station, since some cities have two or more, but travelers in Europe should also know that individual cars are often switched from train to train. A train from Paris to Rome may have only one or two cars going all the way between those two points. Other cars may be going only part of the way or may be switched to other trains en route. Once in the right place, passengers should not casually change seats. It is also wise to keep all tickets handy during the trip, because they are often inspected on the train and then collected at the outer gate. Passengers who misplace their tickets may be forced to purchase others.

Porters are not readily available in large cities and are nonexistent in small towns. Therefore, it is better to carry two small suitcases that can be easily handled, rather than one large, heavy case. Some trains have baggage cars where suitcases can be checked ahead, but there are often delays when numerous passengers disembark and wait for one or two porters to empty the baggage car.

Travelers should be warned that in some cities, particularly in London, they will be changing from one terminal to another. London has a number of mainline stations, all connected through the London Transport Underground system.

VIA Rail Canada

VIA Rail Canada Inc. is Canada's passenger-train network linking Canadian cities from the Atlantic coast to the Pacific coast.

VIA has three types of coaches: the LRCs (Light, Rapid, and Comfortable), VIA1s (First Class Affordable), and Transcontinentals. Sleeping accommodations vary from bedrooms with upper and lower berths and private facilities to roomettes, which are private one-person rooms, to semi-private coach-style seats.

VIA's western routes travel from Toronto, across the prairies, through the Rocky Mountains, to the Pacific Ocean. In this region the *Canadian* is a classic Transcontinental train that has been newly restored to its original 1950s style. It travels to Vancouver with stops in Sudbury, Winnipeg, Edmonton, and Jasper. Accommodations on this train include observation cars, smoking rooms, a dining car, a bar, and lounge. Sleeping cars on the *Canadian* may also contain drawing rooms. Hudson's Bay, the Arctic, and Vancouver Islands can also be reached through the western network.

Eastern routes link Montreal to the Atlantic coast and Maritime provinces. The *Atlantic* runs from Montreal through Maine to New Brunswick and Nova Scotia, and the *Chaleur* travels through the Gaspe Peninsula; the *Ocean* follows the St. Lawrence River.

Central Canada provides connections with other major regions, such as the Thousand Islands and Niagara Falls. Some of the principal cities serviced include Ottawa, Kingston, Windsor, and Quebec City.

VIA offers the Canrailpass, which provides unlimited coach train travel throughout Canada for thirty consecutive days. Sleeping accommodations can be purchased at an affordable extra cost. In addition, discount rates are available for car rentals at any Canadian location.

VIA rail-travel packages are offered by various tour operators since VIA does not maintain its own tour department. At present, VIA reservations must be booked manually, not through computerized reservation systems.

The Canadian Rockies offer some of the most spectacular scenery in the world.

Rail Passes

Rail passes can provide convenience and discounts to travelers throughout Europe. Each pass has its own particular advantages and restrictions. Some are available to anyone, some only to youths, some only to travelers older than 60 or 65. Some are valid only in one country, others in several. Some must be bought outside the country in which they are used; others are sold only within that country. Some must be paid for in American dollars, others only in local currency, still others in any money the traveler chooses.

Essentially there are two ways to get the best use of an unlimited mileage pass. One is to plot an itinerary following a continuous loop; the other is the hub-and-spoke approach. It means setting up several base cities, depending on the overall time allotted to travel, and fanning out from each city on a series of one-day trips. However, if the traveler plans only one major train trip, chances are a point-to-point ticket will be cheaper than buying an unlimited mileage pass.

Rail Europe, Inc., formerly FrenchRail, is one of the leaders in the distribution of European rail passes and rail-related products in North America.

They handle the French TGV network, Spanish AVE system, Austrian Rabbit Card, and a variety of specialized programs throughout Portugal, Greece, Germany, and Scandinavia.

In many countries, when dates are written the day precedes the month. For example, a rail ticket dated 12/5/92, which in the United States would be December 5, 1992, is May 12, 1992, in most other countries. To avoid any confusion, travel agents should always write dates out in full—December 5, 1992. Similarly, any incoming correspondence, confirmations, or documents that abbreviate the dates into numbers should be double-checked carefully.

Eurailpass

The Eurailpass is the granddaddy of passes, introduced in 1959 by a consortium of Western European railroads. For those who plan to take more than a few train trips during a specified time and for people who like to travel without a set itinerary, purchasing a Eurail Saverpass, Flexipass, or Youthpass can be an easy and economical way to travel. These passes provide unlimited train travel in the class indicated through seventeen participating countries: Austria, Belgium, Denmark, Finland, France, Germany, Greece, Holland, Hungary, Italy, Luxembourg, Norway, Portugal, Republic of Ireland, Spain, Sweden, and Switzerland.

A pass does not guarantee a seat unless a reservation has been secured in advance.

Eurailpasses must be purchased outside Europe. They are valid in five time denominations ranging from fifteen days up to three months. Eurail Youthpasses have the same restrictions, are available to anyone under 26 years of age, and are valid for one or two months. Saverpasses offer additional discounts to groups of two or more people traveling together on continuous days. The Eurailpass entitles the holder to first-class accommodations, and the Youthpass is good for second class. Both are nontransferable, and pas-

Booking Rail Tickets

United States travel agents do not issue tickets for any foreign trains except Canadian, but reservations can be made in a variety of ways. A guide to fares can be found in the *Eurail Tariff*. This reference book includes information about the travel time between European cities. Official fares are computed by the ticket-issuing office, but clients usually like to have estimates as soon as possible. Computer reservation systems are becoming increasingly more common for this type of booking and reservation information. For example, Rail Europe, Inc., provides toll-free computerized reservations for travel agents throughout the United States and Canada.

sengers must show their passports when presenting the pass.

The passes are also good for free or reduced-rate passage on many steamers (such as on the Rhine and Danube), ferries (between Ireland and France, Italy and Greece, or Finland and Sweden), and scenic bus trips throughout Europe. They do not include extra costs such as seat-reservation fees, charges for sleeping accommodations, meals, or port taxes. Passes are validated at the first station ticket office in Europe and stamped with the first and last valid date.

BritRail

Great Britain is excluded from Eurailpass, but British Rail offers its own versions. The BritRail Gold or Silver passes provide convenience, flexibility, and considerable savings over

point-to-point travel, and a Flexipass allows unlimited access to 15,000 daily departures in England, Scotland, and Wales for several (non-consecutive) days during a fixed time frame.

Both first- and standard-class coach service and sleeping accommodations are available via BritRail. First-class sleeping compartments accommodate one passenger, but standard-class cabins sleep two,

Historical Perspective

The Rail Way to See the World

It is hard to imagine that only 150 years ago no public railways existed in the United States. However, the environmental, economic, and social impact of trains has forever changed travel and transportation.

Paris - Istanbul — One of the most famous trains was the legendary *Orient Express* that traveled between Paris and Istanbul. The new *Venice-Simplon-Orient Express* is a specialty train that has become something of a destination in itself. Dressing for dinner in either black tie or period costume is considered standard procedure.

Scotland — The *Royal Scotsman* began service in 1985. It features restored vintage carriages, ornately decorated Pullman sleeping cars, and an observation car with an open veranda on which to sit and watch the Highlands pass by.

Australia — A sixty-five–hour journey aboard the *Indian-Pacific* has long been regarded as one of the world's great train trips. The train takes its name from the two oceans it bridges, the Indian Ocean, near Perth, and the Pacific Ocean, near Sydney.

Spain — Carriages for the *Andalusian Express* were gathered throughout Europe, then carefully refurbished. The bar car was built in France; the dining car once carried the British royal family; and one of the sleeping cars transported the Duke of Windsor on a regular basis.

Japan — The Japanese railway system is one of the fastest, safest, and most punctual in the world. The famous *Shinkansen bullet trains* and the Hikari super-expresses cross the country, sometimes reaching speeds of 171 mph. Not only are the trains high-tech, but they are extremely energy-efficient so that travel aboard these trains is nearly as exciting as the scenery.

France — The French *TGV* trains (Train a Grand Vitesse, or high-speed train) are models of comfort, able to cruise at over 186 mph and to reduce the travel time between Paris and Lyons (265 miles) from 4 hours to 2 hours, 40 minutes.

India — The *Palace on Wheels* travels for eight days past marble palaces, temples, and colorful markets that dot the countryside of India. Travelers enjoy Western or Indian cuisine, modern facilities, and luxurious service, just like the maharajahs of yesteryear.

Russia — The *Trans-Siberian Railroad* from Moscow to Nahodka is the longest overland train trip in the world. Russia's only private luxury train covers a distance of 9,438 kilometers (4,627 miles) and eleven time zones in nine days.

Mexico — The famous *Copper Canyon* travels from Chihuahua to Los Mochis, a twelve-and-one-half-hour trip through spectacular mountain scenery. The journey includes eighty-nine tunnels, thirty-seven bridges, and many hairpin turns.

South Africa — The *Blue Train* travels between Cape Town and Johannesburg, a distance of 1,600 kilometers in twenty-six hours.

using upper and lower berths. If you travel alone in standard class, you will be assigned a shared compartment.

Passes can be purchased for eight-, fifteen-, twenty-two-, or thirty-day periods. Rates for the passes vary, depending on number of days chosen, class of service, cities visited, age, and additional tours or sightseeing. BritRail specializes in suggested driving itineraries with discounted car rental.

Automation is making BritRail easier to reserve and process. Some passes require no reservations and may be issued on an American or United Airlines ticket via Apollo, Worldspan, PARS, SABRE, Datas II, Gemini, or System One.

The English Chunnel is scheduled to open in 1993, linking Folkestone, England, and Calais, France. It will be the first land connection between the two countries and will run beneath the English Channel. Travel will be via underground rail service.

Rental Cars

A rental car represents an alternative to local public ground transportation. Florida and California are destinations well  suited to car rentals because attractions are spread out and public transportation is scarce. On the other hand, recommending a car rental to the client staying at a hotel in the center of New York, London, Rome, or Cairo would demonstrate an ignorance of the cities' traffic congestion and public transportation systems.

Most car-rental firms make money in two ways: from the rental of the car and from its later sale. High maintenance and labor can significantly impact the cost of keeping unused cars. Recently, however, car manufacturers have offered favorable deals to rental agencies by reducing the sale price and guaranteeing a high resale return rate. In this way rental companies have increased their purchases and reduced their maintenance costs. Rental agencies now keep cars for periods of six months or less, or 10,000 to 25,000 miles. This has

been a bargain for the rental agencies but questionable for manufacturers who sell at deep discounts, then are forced to dispose of used cars at discount rates at auctions.

Car-rental firms have been increasing at a rate of nearly 10 percent yearly. Currently there are an estimated 5,000 in the United States, with Hertz, Avis, Budget, Dollar, and National holding the lion's share of accounts.

Renting an automobile is different from purchasing a plane or train seat or reserving a hotel room. The hotel room does not move away from its rental location, and the airplane and train have extremely well-qualified drivers. The car-rental firm loses control over the automobile the minute its unknown driver leaves the lot. Therefore it is only natural that the rental firm be interested in the car's welfare while it is on loan and in its safe return. These concerns are reflected in car-rental procedures.

Because car-rental clients are entrusted with a valuable vehicle, companies require renters to produce identification. To qualify, a client must

- Be of a certain age
- Have a valid driver's license
- Be credit-worthy
- Be personally responsible

Age

In the United States the client must usually be at least 25 years of age. A minor over 18 may qualify if he or she holds a charge card recognized by the car-rental company; if an acceptable purchase order or letter of authorization is received from the minor's business organization; or if a parent or legal guardian completes the form *Guarantee of Rental to a Minor* from the rental-car firm. Many companies insist on additional daily fees for renters below the age of 25.

Internationally, age requirements vary from country to country. Many countries have maximum age limits of 65.

Driver's License

Every renter must produce a valid driver's license. To be valid a license must be current, must not expire during the period of rental, and must

tion to a cash deposit, the car-rental company will need

■ Verification of the customer's address. The client must have a telephone number verifiable through directory information.

■ Verification of a customer's employment history

■ Verification of a savings account

■ References

Such stringent qualifiers often require between four to five business days. At the very least, clients are subject to inconvenience before they can get behind the wheel.

Nearly 20 to 25 percent of all rental reservations result in no-shows by the client, causing rental companies to lose business and travelers to be denied available autos.

have no erasures or alterations. The physical description or photograph on the license must match the appearance of the customer, and the signature must match the signatures on the rental agreement and credit identification. Car-rental companies in the United States will accept a license issued by a state or territory of the United States, foreign country, or an international driver's permit.

United States drivers who rent cars in certain foreign countries may need to obtain an international driver's permit. To do this, clients need to present a valid license, pay a fee, and submit two passport-sized photos. The American Automobile Association (AAA) issues these permits.

Credit Qualifications

Renters must produce a major credit card acceptable to the car-rental firm. If the client does not have an acceptable credit card, the travel agent may suggest the use of a prepaid voucher. A prepayment must include the total estimated rental charge, plus — usually — an additional 20 percent. Full payment of all rental charges is required when the car is returned.

Personal Responsibility

Renters who carry no acceptable credit identification and who are unable to use a prepaid voucher will have to be approved as cash clients at the rental site. This can be very difficult. In addi-

Automobile Partnerships

Car-rental companies often form relationships with hotels and airlines. This connection is especially beneficial to car companies as car rentals are almost always sold in conjunction with other travel segments. The major benefit of this partnership to the traveler is in the accumulation of frequent-flyer miles or other frequent-user benefits. Other special deals that are a result of these associations include discounts, upgrades, or special package rates.

The following is an illustration of a selection of these partnerships:

Car Company	Airline Partner	Hotel Partner
Avis	Air Canada; American; Delta; Midwest Express; Qantas	Best Western; Hilton; Hyatt; Sheraton; Stouffer
Budget	Air Canada; Alaska Airlines; America West; American	Hyatt
Dollar	TWA; United	Choice; Outrigger; Sheraton; Westin
Hertz	American; Northwest; United; USAir	Holiday Inn; Marriott
National	Alaska Airlines; Continental; Delta; Midwest Express; Northwest; United; USAir	Hilton; Radisson

Information reprinted with permission of Travel Agent magazine ® 1992.

Qualifying Clients

When qualifying a client, the travel counselor should consider the following key issues:

When and where will the client pick up the car?

Most car-rental companies provide cars at airports, in town, and at suburban locations. Sometimes rates depend on the pick-up point, and depending on the circumstances, a car is held for up to two hours. Although most airport car-pickup counters are located near the baggage-claim area, not all car-rental firms have in-airport counters. Some maintain off-airport facilities and usually provide some sort of courtesy transportation to their offices. Such arrangements often produce lower prices. If most business dealings are at a hotel property, car rental is usually unnecessary merely for transfers between airport and hotel because airport shuttles stop at major hotels. Some hotels offer their own limousine service, and taxis may be cheaper than rental cars.

When and where will the client drop off the car?

Rates vary widely among cities, and some companies charge extra if a car is taken out of state. Additional fees may be charged if a car is returned to a different city or location than its original pick-up point, a service called the Rent It Here/Leave It There (RIH/LIT) plan.

113

Choosing a Car-Rental Company

According to a survey commissioned by *Travel Agent* magazine, the following are the factors considered most important by vacationers in their choice of a car-rental company:

FACTOR	PERCENTAGE OF RESPONDENTS
Ease of getting car	65%
Return – location options	49%
Express return	47%
Airport location	47%
Directions to and from places	43%
Special discounts	43%
Mileage plan	42%
Reputation of company	39%
Additional charges	38%
Models offered	34%
Insurance	30%
Price of gas	29%
Part of package	28%
Frequent-flyer tie-ins	17%

Information reprinted with the permission of Travel Agent magazine ® 1992.

What kind of car does the client wish to rent?

The car-rental company will attempt to provide the make and model of car requested: subcompact, compact, economy, standard, deluxe. All classes of cars may not be available at all locations. If no particular make is specified, the car-rental firm will reserve a standard-sized car. As firms buy smaller cars with fewer options to reduce costs, it becomes difficult to know what type of car to request for a client. Car-rental firms try to help by providing charts showing models available within each class. The client who loves a big American gas-guzzler may not be happy in a small foreign im-

port, no matter how seductive the price. One way to match rental car and driver is to ask what type of car the client owns.

When and for how long will the client want to rent?

A rental charge applies whether the car is used or not. Clients should minimize the amount of time the rental car is sitting in a garage, parking lot, or driveway. Sometimes blackout dates are in effect during holidays so lower advertised rates will not apply. Regular rates generally include a charge for the day and a total mileage cap with an added amount for each mile driven over the cap. This rate includes oil, minor repairs, public liability insurance, and property damage insurance. Cars are rented on a twenty-four-hour basis. Rental charges are computed when the car is returned in order to give the client the least expensive rate. Many companies offer lower rates on weekends or a weekly rate versus a daily or hourly rate.

If the customer has a reservation and the confirmed car class is not available at the time of rental, the customer is usually given the next larger car class at the confirmed car class rate.

What additional charges might be added on?

Business clients may desire extras such as cellular phones or portable FAX machines, and families might want cribs or car seats. Leisure travelers might want extra room or equipment such as a bike or ski rack. Unlimited mileage could be important for clients choosing to drive longer distances. Fees for additional drivers and underage drivers can also add up. Special physical requirements or disabilities may increase costs or time of booking. Hidden gasoline charges, too, can prove costly. If the tank is returned empty, rental agencies may charge more than double the average rate per gallon. To avoid this fee, some car companies offer clients the option of purchasing a full tank in advance at cheaper prices. This may cut the cost per gallon in half.

Is the client eligible for discounts?

Car-rental firms offer a standard corporate discount to qualified companies based on rental volume. Also, frequent renters, like frequent flyers, are entitled to substantial discounts, privileges, and bonuses. Most plans are similar in nature and may be tied to frequent-flyer or frequent-stay plans. In 1972 Avis introduced its Wizard system, a computer-based on-line, real-time, global rental, reservation, and management information system. In 1988, Avis's Preferred Express program was introduced to provide a discounted rate tied to the computerized profile. National pioneered the field with the introduction of the Emerald Club, which also offers such perks as free travel and express rental. Hertz has the #1 Club Gold Service plan; Budget has Rapid Action; Thrifty has Fastrac; and

Car-Rental Practices

■ Credit-card holds or contingent charges may not be imposed without the client's consent.

■ Weekly rates must be available for the first week and for subsequent weeks of the same rental.

■ Daily rates must be available for a minimum of one day.

■ Unlimited mileage cannot be referred to as free mileage.

■ Mandatory surcharges such as cleaning must be included in the base price.

■ Car-rental firms must include all of the following in their print ads: airport access fees, mileage fees, geographical limits, blackout dates, and optional fees for additional drivers or early/late returns.

General offers the Executive Express Club.

Will the client need insurance?

Automobile liability coverage is included in the rental agreement at no extra charge. The rental agreement will state the specific initial amount the customer is responsible for if damage to the car occurs. To avoid such a charge a collision damage waiver (CDW) or a loss damage waiver (LDW) can be purchased. A CDW is the waiver of the rental company's right to charge the renter for damages if the rental car is involved in an accident. An LDW includes the waiver of responsibility for damages resulting from theft or vandalism as well as collision. Both waivers apply only to damages to the rental vehicle.

Because the amount of the renter's liability has been increasing, the daily fee for purchasing these options has been soaring, too. Car renters may now find themselves liable for the total value of the car unless they purchase a damage waiver. Many rental agencies require large cash deposits or a security amount charged against the client's credit card if the waiver is refused by the client.

The most important reason for purchasing a waiver is that it can buy peace of mind. If a car is

Club Membership

Club membership is intended to promote customer loyalty. Membership in the club costs nothing: no application fee, no annual fee, no renewal charge. When the client fills out a membership application, the car-rental firm has a permanent record of all the customer's credit and billing information as well as any special preferences. The client is assigned a number that can be quoted when making a reservation, enabling the car-rental company to complete the rental agreement before the client arrives to pick up the car. The customer merely signs and presents a driver's license and credit identification.

In an effort to speed the process even more, some car-rental companies offer an express service. Club members are assigned express numbers. By specifying at the time of reservation that they want express service and by quoting their number, they can, at certain airports in the United States, go straight from the baggage-claim area to the courtesy bus. Their car and rental agreement will be waiting for them.

totaled by a renter with protection, the onus is on the car-rental firm, not on the driver or the driver's personal insurance company. The car-rental firm is obligated to replace the car at its own expense. The damage-waiver client is protected in all cases except one: a violation of the car-rental contract. If the driver does something inexcusable — driving while intoxicated or allowing a minor to drive — the driver will still be charged.

Personal accident insurance provides coverage in the event of bodily injury to the renter. Like a collision damage waiver, PAI is optional; the premium is usually nominal. The amount of coverage is limited, and many people with life or health insurance are already covered. Some companies combine a collision damage waiver and personal accident insurance in a single package. In the event of an accident, the client should call the nearest rental office and ask for advice on what

procedures to follow. Parking and moving violations are the responsibility of the renting client.

International Car Rental

The motorist in a foreign country enjoys the freedom of venturing into many varied spots. Having a car allows the traveler to stay at small hotels off the beaten path and outside congested tourist centers. Most international car-rental requests are for Europe and Canada, although cars can be rented practically anywhere in the world. Reservations procedures are quite similar, but driving in certain countries is more foreign than in others, and some clients will need more preparation.

Tips for Car-Rental Insurance

Many individual collision policies will pay for damage to a rented vehicle, so drivers may already be insured against collision when they rent a car. However, some companies will not offer such coverage if the renter chooses a specialty car, such as a jeep.

Some credit-card companies provide free collision coverage to customers who pay for rental cars with their card. Although each company's policies vary, Master Card, Visa, ATC, and American Express cardholders should check with their particular banks to see if they are already covered.

It is important to determine if coverage is primary or secondary. Some credit plans provide secondary coverage only — that is, they will pick up what the driver's personal insurance policy does not. For example, if a driver has a collision policy valued at $10,000 and totals a rental car valued at $15,000, the secondary party will pay only what remains after the insurance company pays the original $10,000 and the driver pays his or her deductible.

Customers should check with their own protection plans to make the most informed decision possible.

Computerized Innovations

At some locations, automation is replacing human contact. National's Smart Key self-service, frequent-renter perk program enables customers to use a touch-screen computer to get their car. The newer version, Smart Key II, prints a receipt telling the customer where the car is parked in the lot. Avis is testing a program that provides renters with audiotapes prepared by the Financial News Network. Budget has introduced a computerized mapping direction system whereby customers can access a data base via a touch-screen terminal in any one of five languages. Automap is a similar software program that allows the user to map out a route between nearly any two cities in the United States.

Air conditioning is standard in the United States but usually not available, even by special request, in some other countries. Automatic transmission is standard in the United States, but it is a special request in foreign countries and costs more.

Driving outside major cities can be an adventure. Even the major centers may be a problem to the timid driver caught in rush-hour traffic. In Europe, for instance, traffic moves faster than in the United States. Cities observing the typical Mediterranean working and siesta schedule have four major rush hours. With these patterns, it is hard not to get caught in one rush hour or another.

Special points to remember:

■ Outside the United States the client will be renting a real foreign car. Rental fleets vary from country to country, but they generally feature cars that are popular locally. Orders are confirmed by car group only, and specific models cannot be guaranteed because rental fleets are continually being updated. The range is from small fuel-efficient economy models through minibuses and campers to top-of-the-

line luxury models.

Familiar cars may appear under strange names. To help the renter, firms specializing in European rentals publish pictures of their fleets in their brochures.

American drivers have become accustomed to smaller cars but still may find it necessary to restrict their luggage. Four adults and four suitcases in a standard-sized European car do not allow much room for impulsive purchases. If a roof rack is needed, it must be ordered in advance.

■ Automatic transmission is generally more expensive and must be specifically requested in advance.

■ Gasoline prices may be substantially higher than in the United States, and gas is often sold by the liter. One gallon is equal to 3.78 liters. Britain and places historically connected with British rule, such as Hong Kong, use the imperial gallon, 25 percent larger than the corresponding American unit. Gas stations in some countries may be few and far between, and their hours of operation depend on the customs of the country.

■ Distances are primarily expressed in kilometers. One kilometer is equal to 0.6 United States mile.

■ International currencies fluctuate. To simplify planning, the agent can reserve a car at a prepaid guaranteed United States dollar rate, sometimes called "common rates." The same rate is applied in all participating countries. Common rates are not discountable and are subject to frequent change.

■ Quoted rates may not include value-added taxes, which can range from 10 to 25 percent of the total rental charge.

■ Political situations affect car rentals. Cars rented in one country may not be allowed over a border to another. If the client is planning to cross borders, a special insurance document called the "green card" must be provided by the rental office.

■ Some countries require local driver's permits.

■ Only chauffeur-driven service is permitted in

some countries: Nepal and Pakistan, for example. Bermuda will not allow car rentals at all; vacationers can rent motorbikes, provided they wear helmets and remember to keep to the left.

- Clients who need a car for a month or more might consider leasing rather than renting. Leased cars come new from the factory and usually cost less over an extended period than rental cars. Furthermore, a leased car is not subject to the very high taxes levied on rentals in European countries.

International Car Purchase

International car purchase has certain advantages depending on the rate of currency exchange. In the past, savings from a European car purchase often paid for the trip. Buying a car at the beginning of a trip and driving it qualified the car as used when brought back to the United States. But fluctuating currency relationships, rising car costs, and changes in customs regulations have made the advantages less predictable, and any plans to buy abroad should be checked carefully. United States Customs now charges duty based on the actual purchase price. The car must be driven for six months or more to be considered used, and even then, the decision is up to the port-of-entry customs officer.

To make sure the client is receiving the most up-to-date information, it is wise to use an import-car dealer or a company that specializes in factory-delivered cars. These firms often offer a choice of purchase plans: factory-base plan that includes new car only; car-import package that includes new car plus all shipping costs and preparation; car-plus-air package that includes car purchase, shipping costs, and round-trip air tickets from United States gateway cities to Europe.

Summary

Ground transportation can provide an inexpensive and relaxing alternate way to see the country. Rail travel throughout North America includes the recently upgraded Amtrak and VIA rail systems. Reservations for both can be made through most computerized reservation systems. International rail in Europe is rapidly expanding, with new routings joining eastern and western capitals. Passes are available, offering many substantial discounts.

Rental cars appeal to those travelers seeking flexibility, freedom, and economy. Agency fleets are newer, and services more diverse. Rates vary by company, benefit package, and options. International services differ greatly from North American products. In short, ground transportation continues to remain popular in destinations throughout the world where accessibility is a key element.

118

Chapter Wrap-up

DISCUSSION TOPICS

Advertised Rates

The Entourage family of four, complete with their baggage and Great Dane, has just arrived at the airport location of Rent-a-Ride Autos in Orlando, Florida. They are requesting an advertised rate of $99 per week. They would like to return the car at the end of the week in Pensacola. The $99 rate is for a subcompact with no mileage included, obviously an inappropriate choice for such a group. What is the best course of action for the counter agent? What specific needs does this family have?

Train Travel

The Atrics family — Dr. Geri, his wife Psyche, and their son Pedi — traveled on Amtrak's Empire Builder in coach class from Minneapolis, MN, to meet their cousin Thea in Portland, OR. On the final leg of the trip they walked up to the observation car and fell asleep. Imagine their surprise when they awakened and discovered they were in the Seattle station. They have called their travel agent collect, long-distance to discover how they could have been booked on the wrong train. (Note — The Empire Builder is actually two trains: one destined for Portland, and one destined for Seattle, with Spokane as the division point.) What options do the Atrics have? What should the travel agent do? What responsibility does Amtrak have?

Transfers

Etta Lamb and Ida-May Fry waited for their included transfer at the Grand Hotel in Paris, which would take them to Charles De Gaulle Airport for their return to the States. They waited over an hour for their prepaid limousine service, which never arrived. Consequently they were forced to take a cab to the airport. Upon arrival at CDG they realized they had already exchanged all of their French francs. What should they do? Will they make their international flight? Whom should they contact regarding the trauma they have experienced and the reimbursement of funds?

Cruising
Chapter 6

Introduction

With the first non-stop transatlantic passenger flights from New York to Europe, the death knell sounded for the luxury ocean liner. The subsequent growth of jet travel forced famous shipping lines to retire the ships that had provided the only feasible continent-to-continent service for millions. Luxury ocean travel had to adapt to the new age, either by accepting that its market was permanently diminished, by concentrating on cargo rather than passengers, or by developing new markets. Unfortunately, many of the liners were not able to make graceful transitions, principally because they were uneconomical to operate. Others, by offering more space, more facilities, and a graciousness of bygone days, continue to attract faithful clientele.

The Cruise Market

In today's ever-expanding travel market the cruise industry has designed ships and itineraries to appeal to all ages and tastes. The fact that less than 5 percent of the North American population has ever taken a cruise has accounted for more creative destinations and shipboard amenities to attract the widest possible market. Carnival Cruise Line was the first to market cruising as a "vacation experience" rather than a mode of international transportation. The image of transcontinental luxury liners still raises some very persistent myths about people who choose to cruise. Some people maintain that cruising is only for the rich and famous or for the elderly who have unlimited time

Cruise Line Careers

Bridge Officer	Staff Captain	Entertainer
Captain	Cabin Steward	Host/Hostess
Chief Purser	Dining-Room Steward	Purser
Deck Officer	Engineer	Shore-Excursion Manager
Navigation Officer	Sailor	Casino Croupier
Radio Officer	Cruise Director	Photographer

Cruise Director

One of the most popular characters on the television show *The Love Boat* was Julie — the cruise director. From this series a glamorous picture of the cruise industry and the position of cruise director was drawn by millions of viewers. In reality, how accurate was this image?

Cruise directors are responsible for all social activities on board. Depending on the ship, their duties can range from calling bingo to setting up singles dances to actually performing in the evening show. Cruise directors may have assistants who help with these responsibilities, but all social-staff members must be willing to participate in activities. They are all responsible for ensuring that passengers have an enjoyable voyage.

This sounds like a tall order, and it is. In addition to the obvious people skills, cruise directors should have foreign-language experience, good time-management ability, and the stamina to withstand eighteen-hour work-days for weeks and months at a time. No specific degree program is required, although management, recreation, sales, and language courses are desirable and recommended.

Most cruise directors work their way up, beginning as hosts or hostesses and progressing to social coordinators, assistant cruise directors, and upward. Another common route of progression is through a land-based job requiring similar skills, such as a Club Med GO (Gentil Organisateur) or an activities coordinator at a major resort property. This sector of the industry is predominantly male with an average length of employment of two to eight years.

and money. In fact, there is a cruise for everyone.

There are many reasons why cruising is associated with the rich. The ships recall old luxury ocean liners with film stars and diplomats in full evening dress. Modern cruise lines exploit these associations, presenting cruising as an opportunity to experience unusual pampering and luxury. Finally, the price of a cruise, like the price of an escorted tour, appears high at first glance.

Few clients will feel out of their league on a one- or two-week cruise. Of course, the longer the cruise, the more expensive. The Cruise Lines In-

ternational Association (CLIA) has identified three types of potential clients: those with limited budgets and limited time; those with ample budgets but limited time; and those with ample budgets and ample time. There are cruises for each profile. In fact, the myth that cruises are only for the rich has helped to enhance the social status of many returning cruise passengers. Actually, 40 percent of today's cruise passengers earn less than $40,000 a year.

Some brochures discourage potential first-time clients because they show pictures of distinguished-looking gentlemen in tuxedos and elegant ladies in long evening gowns or trim members of both sexes relaxing on deck in bathing suits. Clients worry that they do not have either the wardrobe or the figure to go on a cruise. In fact, casual dress is normal during the day, and although some dinners are dressy, passengers dress as they would to dine in a good restaurant back home. Jacket and tie are perfectly acceptable for men at even the most formal of occasions on board; women will be comfortable in cocktail dresses. Most lines still have one or two formal nights when women may wear long dresses and gentlemen wear a tuxedo or dark suit. In general, resort chic is in vogue for the nineties. Because clients frequently ask for advice on what to wear in the evening and fashions do change, the agent should consult the individual line at the time of booking.

Older clients, so the argument goes, are more likely to be found on cruises because they have the time and money. Clearly, working people have less time than those who are retired. But the majority of cruises last from three to fourteen days, well within the normal vacation time allotted by most companies. CLIA's research indicates that the two- to five-day cruise itinerary is the fastest growth category in recent years. Generally speaking, the longer the cruise, the older the clients.

The range of activities on board indicates that the cruise lines are ready for younger clients, whether they are singles, couples, or families. Many provide babysitting service for a fee, special events, or even entire programs for children. Ships that cater to families offer children's fares.

Some cruise lines offer special singles get-togethers and take pains to find an appropriate roommate to reduce the single supplement fare. The policy of permitting crew members to mingle with passengers varies widely. On some ships, officers are encouraged to dance with passengers; on others they may not. A few cruise lines are experimenting with host programs that invite single male passengers to dance, play bridge, and host tables for unaccompanied female passengers in exchange for their fare. Policies for hosts are very strict.

Current statistics indicate that cruise passengers are getting younger. The most rapidly expanding group is between the ages of 25 and 39. Some cruise lines cater to young adults and stress a party-like atmosphere. By offering cabins with

CLIA

CLIA, the Cruise Lines International Association, consists of thirty-three member cruise lines and more than 20,000 travel agency affiliates. The stated function of CLIA is "to provide a forum where companies engaged in the marketing of the cruise and passenger liner industry in North America can meet and discuss matters of common interest and develop and agree on policies aimed at promoting the concept of shipboard holidays." In simpler terms, the function of CLIA is to promote the cruise product to both the selling agent and buying public through the broad activities of travel agent training, public relations, and advertising. CLIA's end objective is to raise awareness about the cruise experience.

double beds and Sunday departures, they also attract honeymooners.

What Is a Cruise Like?

Because cruise ships are direct descendants of

luxury ocean liners, they seek to preserve the traditions of elegance. Like an isolated resort, a cruise ship anticipates as many of the passengers' needs and desires as possible.

The ship functions as a complete resort hotel even while in port. Although all employees on board are collectively referred to as crew, the majority are, in fact, hotel staff. On most cruise lines it is the chief purser whose responsibility it is to ensure the smooth running of all services. The purser's office, like the front desk of a hotel, offers banking services, safety deposit boxes, postal communication, customs and immigration information, and is chiefly responsible for passenger accommodations.

Television programs, notably *The Love Boat*, led the public to expect spacious cabins. In reality, however, cabins are necessarily smaller than a comparable hotel room. Typical cabin configuration is two lower twin berths, but on newer and some refurbished ships, double, queen-, and even king-size beds are also available. Cabin size varies from ship to ship and significantly contributes to price. Larger cabins have both a sleeping area and a separate living space. Other accommodations offer beds that convert to sofas during the day or recess into the wall. In smaller cabins, suitable for single passengers or budget-minded couples, the second bed may be above the first one, providing an upper and lower berth arrangement and very limited floor space.

Cabins also contain a toilet, washbasin, and shower; passengers who prefer a tub usually have to choose a more expensive cabin. Luxury ships offer hair dryers, mini-bars, refrigerators, in-room safes, and terry bathrobes. All cabins have closets and a dresser with a mirror. Most outside cabins have portholes, but deluxe outsides and suites often have larger windows. All ships are climate-controlled; most offer radio or television entertainment in the cabins, and some even come equipped with VCRs. Older ships may not have appropriate plugs for small electrical appliances so adapters may be necessary.

Food Service

In the health-conscious nineties, cruise chefs are offering a passengers dining alternatives. Spa cuisine, lite fare, and heart-healthy choices endorsed by the American Heart Association are appearing on the menus of most cruise lines. Most diet restrictions (salt-free, fat-free, and so on) can be accommodated by the ship's galley if advance notice is given. Some cruise lines are experimenting with restaurant alternatives on board to provide passengers with as much choice as possible in dining. For a small surcharge passengers can dine in the intimacy of a small supper club or gourmet bistro when the mood strikes. Pizza parlors, outdoor barbeques, and make-your-own-sundae spots round out the selection of fare available.

Most cruise lines employ food and beverage

Time to Eat

Cruise ships are famous for the quantity and quality of their food. The reputation for cuisine varies from ship to ship, but all offer menus with lavish choices and an abundance of opportunities to eat. Anyone who is determined to indulge at every possible occasion could be faced with this arduous program.

6:30 a.m.
Coffee and pastries served on deck for early risers OR

7:00 a.m.–11:00 a.m.
Full breakfast or continental breakfast in bed OR

7:30–10:00 a.m.
Full breakfast served in the dining room OR

8:30 a.m.
Buffet breakfast served on deck.

12 noon–2:00 p.m.
Buffet lunch served on deck OR

12 noon–2:00 p.m.
Lunch in the dining room.

4:00 p.m.
Afternoon tea served on deck.

6:30–10:00 p.m.
Dinner served in the dining room.

11:45 p.m.
Midnight buffet served either on deck or in the dining room.

managers to arrange private parties, particularly popular on longer cruises. Continental breakfasts, sandwiches, cocktails, and mixers can be delivered to individual cabins by request on most ships around the clock.

Passengers should also indicate their preference for first or second sitting in the dining room. Early-to-bed and early-to-rise passengers will probably prefer first sitting; night owls, second sitting. Tables are assigned immediately after boarding. Some lines pre-assign tables, notifying passengers with a card left in the cabin. Dining rooms are arranged with a limited number of tables for two; tables for four, six, or eight are more typical. Any special request is more likely to be honored if the counselor follows up the telephone request by writing directly to the cruise line. ✦

Amenities

Although eating, sleeping, and relaxing may be the three most popular activities on a cruise ship, each vessel also features a full program of organized events from dawn to dusk and beyond. The cruise director and staff are responsible for arranging and supervising a non-stop flow of passenger activities. Evenings are busiest because ships generally sail between the hours of 6 p.m. and 6 a.m. Most ships have a large ballroom or lounge for dancing and the nightly show, featuring professional entertainers or fully-staged Las Vegas revues. Theme nights are a tradition on most ships: a Masquerade, a Passenger Talent Show, and so on. The Captain's Welcome-On-Board Cocktail Party and the Gala Farewell Dinner are the highlights and highest fashion nights of all evenings on board. When the ship is at sea, shops and casinos are open, as are smaller, more intimate bars and lounges featuring soft music; the library; and the card room. Most ships also have a cinema and discotheque.

A full program of daytime activities is scheduled if the ship is at sea for all or part of the day. Passengers are free to choose as many or as few as they please. They can jog around the deck, play ping-pong, try skeetshooting off the stern, or drive golf balls into the ocean, all under the watchful eye of an instructor. Other classes include dancing, flower arranging, tennis, and photography. For devotees, bridge, bingo, chess, scrabble, backgammon, and shuffleboard are available. Longer cruises or those that emphasize a certain theme or destination will often have special guest lecturers on board to present topics of particular interest on the days prior to port arrival. While the ship is in port, limited activities are featured for those who do not wish to go ashore.

Most cruise directors present a port talk each day to familiarize passengers with the attractions of the next destination. Topics include history, major sights, shopping hints, optional shore excursions, and local customs.

The Benefits of Cruising

Cruise ships are not merely a means of transpor-

tation to get people from point A to point B. To many experienced cruise passengers, specific ports are secondary considerations. The ship becomes their destination, and they go for the experience of cruising, the way of life on board. Some clients anxiously await inaugural cruises, so they can be among the first to sail on a new ship or a new itinerary. What appeals most to individuals varies, but a CLIA survey rated satisfaction with the cruise product at 85 percent, citing many of the following benefits.

Relaxation

The sea has a romantic allure. The combination of the constant, gentle movement of the ship, the brisk sea air, and the unhurried pace makes a cruise relaxing. Passengers are insulated from everything that reminds them of everyday responsibilities and pressures. Frequently they can be seen simply leaning over the rail watching the wake of the ship and the changing scenery. Everything is within easy walking distance, including good restaurants and evening entertainment, without the need for telephone calls, taxis, reservations, or additional expense; and as at a resort hotel, clients unpack and pack only once.

Those who enjoy being busy can participate in a variety of daytime activities and nightly entertainment. Others can be as lazy as they like without feeling they are missing the real experience of cruising. Couples or groups who cruise together often make their own entertainment, and clients who travel alone are never at a loss for opportunities to socialize.

Prepayment

Worry about money is largely removed. Virtually every charge is prepaid except for shore excursions, tips, drinks, and shopping. Clients can accurately predict the cost of their vacation and avoid carrying large sums of money.

Service

Although modern cruising does not quite compare with the luxury once enjoyed by the elite during the great age of ocean liners, cruise ships still pamper the passenger with personal service and gracious touches. A standard method of comparing service is to focus on the ratio of crew to passengers. Ships that are advertised as luxury cruises feature this ratio prominently, implying that the lower the ratio, the more specialized the attention. These ships may have a ratio as low as one crew member for every one and a half or two passengers.

At embarkation, passengers are advised to carry on board all hand luggage and fragile or valuable items. Suitcases are left on the dock, then transferred to the ship and delivered to the cabin.

The Ship Itself

Some experienced cruise passengers develop an affection for a particular ship or cruise line, returning year after year. Each ship has its own individual appeal and unique history. Whenever one is sold, its followers hold their breath hoping the new owner will not redecorate, rename, or otherwise modify it in such a way that it loses its personality.

The operation of a ship is always a source of fascination to passengers. Whenever one docks or leaves port, the decks are crowded with passengers watching each maneuver. Nothing can quite compare with the site of a huge ocean liner being tugged into position at a crowded dock or slipping gracefully away to sea.

Value

Like escorted tours, resort hotels, and any other vacation in which most features are prepaid, cruises look expensive at first glance. But their value compares favorably with other fully prepaid vacations and package tours.

Possible Disadvantages

As with any vacation, cruises are not for everyone. A typical cruise provides only fleeting impressions of the destinations visited. Passengers may have time to do little more than take a standard sightseeing tour, visit a beach, or check out local markets and stores. Some people are not interested in the local culture. All they want is sun, a beach, or a show designed especially for tourists. However, for passengers who want to experience

Seasickness Remedies

About with seasickness can ruin the best of cruise experiences. Even the heartiest of sailors can be affected by persistent rough weather. Passengers who experience motion sickness should try to stay as close to the center of the ship as possible, where the motion is minimal. Avoid liquids of any sort, especially alcohol, and take advantage of the crackers the crew will distribute throughout the ship during rough seas. Although ships come equipped with stabilizers to minimize the effect of the ship's movement, an ounce of prevention can equal a pound of cure. The following are commonly used seasickness remedies:

■ Dramamine, Marezine, and Bonine are over-the-counter drugs taken orally three to four hours before sailing as a preventive. Passengers complain most frequently of drowsiness with these drugs.

■ Scopolamine is available by prescription and comes as a small patch worn behind the passenger's ear for up to three days. Known more familiarly as "the patch," it is not recommended for the elderly, and its side effects are dry mouth and blurred vision.

■ The Sea-band is a band worn on the passenger's wrist that prevents motion sickness through acupressure. Sea-band is drug-free and is endorsed by CLIA. No side effects have been reported.

native culture in depth, a cruise with its brief exposure to each port is not recommended.

Some people are concerned that cruises are confining. Once on board ship at sea there is nowhere else to go. Those who tend to be claustrophobic about such limited space should be advised to avoid extended cruises.

The weather is also an important element. Although cruise ships provide entertainment and indoor facilities rain or shine, there is no doubt that prolonged rain or cloudiness can sharply reduce the passengers' pleasure. Rough weather can cause physical discomfort and make movement around the ship difficult. All cruise ships have stabilizers that are deployed to minimize the effect of the ship's normal roll. Whenever possible, the captain avoids storms and bad weather through the use of radar, but rough seas are always a possibility.

Tendering

Many small islands in the Caribbean and smaller ports all over the world do not have enough deep water or dock space to accommodate a large cruise ship. Ships anchor in the harbor, and passengers are transported to and from the shore in smaller boats called tenders. Disabled passengers may find tendering difficult because they have to negotiate steps or narrow gangways. Megaships have tenders that can carry upwards of 500 passengers.

What Most Ships Offer

Infirmary: The ship's doctor provides treatment for routine medical problems and is on call for emergencies. Hours and fees are posted in the daily news. Cabin calls are a costly extra. Anti-seasickness medication is generally available at the purser's office free of charge.

Duty-Free Shops: Open daily while at sea, selling gifts, clothing, souvenirs, tobacco, candy, and necessities. Comparison price shopping before arriving in port can result in considerable savings.

Beauty Salon and Barber Shop: Usually open both at sea and in port, these facilities are heavily booked, especially before a formal night such as the Captain's Cocktail Party. Facial and manicure services are usually available. Fee plus tip for most services.

Sauna: Some ships also have a masseuse on board. Hours and fees are posted in the daily news.

Gymnasium: Many ships offer a gymnasium with exercycles, nautilus, and other workout equip-

ment. There is usually no charge to use equipment or partake of aerobics classes. However, some spas at sea, such as Cunard's Golden Door or Norwegian Cruise Line's Roman Spa on the Norway, offer such extravagances as aromatherapy, hydrotherapy, and herbal wraps that are a definite extra. Special spa packages can be purchased in advance or once on board.

Laundry: Laundry and dry cleaning are offered for a fee. Items can be left with the cabin steward. This service normally takes two days. Some ships have free self-service laundries.

Religious Services: Some ships offer Jewish, Catholic, and interdenominational services. Others offer only interdenominational services conducted by a single chaplain. Service for particular religions or sects will be offered at special times like Christmas, Easter, or the High Holy Days. Special services are arranged for couples interested in renewing their marriage vows.

Communications: Each ship publishes a daily newspaper that summarizes news, sports, financial information, and shipboard activities. Telex and ship-to-shore telephone are available for a fee, as is the ship's radio while the ship is at sea. FAX capabilities are offered on some of the newer ships.

Library: Most ships offer a small library that may also include video rentals.

Television: Cable TV and VCRs are found in the cabins of some of the newer ships.

What Is Not Included

Some important individual costs are not included in the price of a cruise. For example, the cost of transportation between the passengers' homes and the port of embarkation will differ for everyone and is not necessarily included in the price of the cruise. Many cruise lines subsidize all or part of the cost of air transportation for those who fly to the port of embarkation.

Port Taxes: Lines that offer a variety of cruises calling at many different ports may find it impossible to state the port taxes for all sailings in the brochure. Therefore, port taxes for a particular cruise are quoted at the time of the booking. Fuel surcharges are sometimes tacked onto the price of the cruise as well.

Personal Expenditures: Personal expenditures in shops on board or on shore are not included.

Neither are certain medical expenses, casino gambling, use of some sports equipment or activities, or the enjoyment of special facilities like the beauty salon or sauna. These expenditures are clearly discretionary.

Liquor: Passengers pay for drinks and wine as ordered. Some cruise lines prefer passengers to charge drinks to their cabin and settle the bills at the end of the cruise. Drinks are often less expensive at sea than on shore.

All ships fly flags that indicate a variety of messages to those in the know. For instance, the blue-and-yellow vertically striped flag is a request for a pilot, and the half-red half-white flag means there is a pilot on board.

Tipping: Most cruise lines provide tipping guidelines in passenger documents or in each cabin. Tips to the dining-room steward, the busboy, and the cabin steward are normally given at the end of the cruise, either at the last dinner or the evening before leaving the cabin. The usual amount of these tips is from $3 to $5 a day per person. Some lines provide envelopes for the distribution of these tips. On long cruises, tips are given every week or every two weeks, not just at the end of the cruise. Bar personnel, wine stewards, and cocktail waiters are tipped the normal 15 percent whenever a tab is paid. Ship's officers are never tipped. Some cruise lines advertise a no-tipping policy. However, passengers may want to recognize outstanding service.

Shore Excursions: Unless specifically stated to the contrary, shore excursions are an additional option that passengers may purchase before or during their cruise. Selling shore excursions as part of the cruise package offers the travel counselor an opportunity to earn additional commission.

Shore excursions run the gamut from two-hour city tours to extravagant overnight land adventures exploring the depths of the Amazon or other exotic spots. They are conducted by local tour operators by arrangement with the cruise line.

On some cruises passengers may purchase all shore excursions as a package. This price is considerably less than the sum of the individual components purchased separately. Some excursions can be duplicated by individuals making their own arrangements. Clients should be warned, however, that when several cruise ships are in port at the same time, the services of taxis, limousines, and even rental cars may already be contracted to tour operators. Some shows and attractions become impossible to book for the same reason.

Cruising Areas

Several distinct cruising areas are available to clients. All are subject to some degree of seasonality, so cruise lines reposition ships frequently. Although life on board ship may vary little from area to area, the scenery, weather, customs, and pace of the cruise will vary.

Caribbean cruises leave primarily from East Coast or Gulf ports and are most popular among clients from the Northeast, Mid-Atlantic, and Midwestern states. Cruises to the Mexican Riviera, which leave from West Coast ports, are popular with clients from the West and Rocky Mountain states. Cruises in the South Pacific, because of the distance between ports, usually take at least two weeks and therefore appeal to those with ample time.

According to CLIA, the Caribbean is the number one destination for North American passengers, followed by western Mexico, Alaska, the Mediterranean, and trans-Panama Canal cruises.

The Caribbean

Readily accessible from Florida warm-weather ports, the Caribbean Islands are close enough to one another to permit a ship to visit one all day and sail on to another at night. Cruises to the Caribbean range from short two-, three-, and four-day voyages to the more popular one-week cruises. Longer cruises of the Caribbean may include the Yucatan Peninsula of Mexico, the coast of Venezuela, or a passage of the Panama Canal. These itineraries lie beyond the range of a one-week cruise.

A favorite one-week itinerary links San Juan, Puerto Rico, and St. Thomas, United States Virgin Islands, with either Nassau in the Bahamas, Puerto

Plata in the Dominican Republic, or ports in Haiti and Jamaica. San Juan and St. Thomas are popular with first-time passengers because they offer vestiges of home. San Juan provides Las Vegas–style entertainment, and St. Thomas has duty-free shopping and beautiful beaches. Both of these stops are so popular that many ships are usually anchored in the harbor at the same time.

Due to increased air service, San Juan is one of the principal ports of the Caribbean. By beginning a cruise itinerary here rather than in Miami or Port Everglades, the eastern islands of the Caribbean can be reached in one week; St. Maarten, Barbados, St. Lucia, Antigua, Guadeloupe, and Martinique, for example, fall within the one-week range. These islands represent a less crowded and unhurried atmosphere and provide opportunity for night life and shopping.

For many people one week simply is not enough time for a cruise. They no sooner start to relax than they are on their way home. Several cruise lines, therefore, offer itineraries lasting ten, eleven, or twelve days. Usually the extra days are used to push further eastward in the Caribbean, to travel further south to touch the coast of South America and return via the Netherlands Antilles, or to do a partial transit of the Panama Canal. Caribbean cruises rarely exceed two weeks, partly to accommodate the vacation schedules of North Americans, and partly because the area can be thoroughly explored within such a period. Most one- and two-week cruises leave and return on Saturday. Sunday departures accommodate honeymoon vacationers.

The reopening of Cuba to tourism in the 1990s may result in a demand for cruises as the preferred way to see the island. One cruise line is considering a Havana/Disney package from the west coast of Florida.

Peak season for Caribbean cruising runs from mid-December to mid-April, with many ships offering extended gala cruises during the Christmas and New Year period at slightly higher prices. Sometimes there is a lull in cruise bookings during January, particularly the first two weeks, and cruise lines may make promotional offers for this period. The official low season in the Caribbean is summer because of the greatly improved weather in the north. September and October are the traditional months for tropical storms, during which ships might be delayed or rerouted. Ships are frequently placed in dry- or wet-dock during these months for mechanical servicing and interior refurbishing.

Bermuda

Cruises to Bermuda typically last one week and provide four days in port and three days of cruising. The number of cruise lines serving Bermuda is strictly limited because of the time each ship spends in port and the size of the island and its harbors. Bermuda has three docking areas: the capital, Hamilton; St. Georges; and Dockyard. Most cruises to Bermuda leave from New York. The season begins in April and ends in October.

A cruise ship normally averages about 16 knots (18-1/2 mph) and has a maximum daily range of about 450–550 miles (approximately the distance from Boston to Washington, D.C., or from San Francisco to San Diego).

Mexico

Cruises sail for the Mexican Riviera from West Coast ports. Winter and spring are considered high season, and the principal ports of departure are Los Angeles and San Diego. Brief three- and four-day cruises embark from the West Coast to Ensenada.

On one-week cruises, ships may call at Mazatlan, Puerto Vallarta, Manzanillo, or Acapulco. Calls at Zihuatanejo and Cabo San Lucas are subject to tidal conditions. Ships must tender at both, even when the tides are right.

The Panama Canal

Some cruise lines have decided that if West Coast departures go as far as Acapulco, it makes sense to stretch the cruise to fourteen days or more and proceed through the Panama Canal. By the same token, ships cruising in the western Caribbean often extend itineraries to include a partial transit of the canal. In this way, clients experience two popular cruising areas and the unique passage between two oceans.

Transit through the canal takes a full day and is

usually done during daylight hours for maximum effect. Ships are boarded early in the morning by a pilot who navigates the intricate locks and a lecturer who enlivens the experience with a narration of the canal's history.

Hawaii/South Pacific/Orient

Regular one-week cruises of the Hawaiian islands are offered from Honolulu. Honolulu may also be a port of call on longer cruises originating in Los Angeles or San Francisco and proceeding to Tahiti or New Zealand and Australia, or even further to Singapore, Hong Kong, Japan, and China. Because of the length of these cruises, only occasional departures are offered.

Alaska

Over the last few years the popularity of cruises to Alaska has grown enormously, and the choice of accommodations has grown with it. Passengers can be pampered on the most deluxe of ships, or select a no-frills study tour that emphasizes learning about the people, history, and geography of the area. The season along the protected Inside Passage runs from mid-May to late September. The ship is never out of sight of snow-capped, mountainous land. Cruises feature the spectacular scenery of Glacier Bay; the once-rowdy frontier town of Skagway; the capital city, Juneau; Sitka, with its history of Russian domination; and the modern Canadian cities of Vancouver and Victoria.

Cruise lines reserve the right to change an itinerary if circumstances warrant. The changes are usually dictated by weather or political events. Adjustments are at the captain's discretion, and no refund is made to passengers

Canada/United States East Coast

Maritime Canada can be visited by cruise ships from East Coast ports. During regular summer sailings from New York, ships call at Nova Scotia, Prince Edward Island, Montreal, Quebec City, Bar Harbor, Boston, and Newport. In the autumn, several lines add special cruises for viewing foliage. On these cruises, passengers enjoy the smooth, protected waters of the St. Lawrence and Saguenay rivers. However, the crossing between New England and Nova Scotia can be rough.

Cruises to and from Canada call at ports on the New England coast. Smaller ships departing from these ports have added places like Gloucester, Nantucket, Martha's Vineyard, Portland, and New Bedford to the roster of cruise itineraries. Sensing a growing interest among Americans for the sights and history of their native land, other cruise lines have begun to operate further south, visiting such charming ports as Savannah, Charleston, Hilton Head, St. Augustine, and the small cities along the Chesapeake Bay.

South America

South America offers a variety of cruise experiences. A coastal trip along the eastern seaboard can combine calls on Forteleza, Recife, Salvador de Bahia, and stops at the notorious Devil's Island and Rio de Janeiro for Carnivale. A trip around the tip of South America that includes Tierra del Fuego, Beagle Channel, and Cape Horn is fast becoming the choice of naturalists and adventurers alike. Newest of the South American itineraries follows the west coast through the Chilean Fjords, calling on Guayaquil, and offers a day trip to Quito. An interior exploration of the Amazon as far as Manaus, Brazil, has been popular for several winter seasons.

Europe

Two major cruising areas are popular in Europe: the Mediterranean, including the Aegean Sea, and Scandinavia, including the Baltic Sea. Both areas are seasonal, with cruising lasting from April to October in the Mediterranean and from June to late August in Scandinavia. Europe is back as a popular destination, having recovered from the political unrest of the 1980s. The cultural diversity of the area combined with the changing political face of many European nations creates a wealth of opportunity for creative itineraries.

Mediterranean

Political events in the mid-1980s had a serious effect on the eastern Mediterranean cruise market. Fear of terrorist activity led major international cruise lines to eliminate this area from their itineraries. The market is strong, however, because this area offers some of the world's finest ports. As with any politically sensitive area, travel to this region should be evaluated on a continuing basis.

The eastern Mediterranean, particularly the Aegean Sea, offers regular departures from Piraeus, the port of Athens, and is more popular than the western Mediterranean. The lure of the Aegean is the abundance of small islands rich in history and myth that are within easy sailing distance of one another. The islands are the sites of legendary civilizations; they also provide beautiful beaches and a relaxed lifestyle.

In addition to the Greek islands, some cruises touch the coast of Turkey. Most cruise ships spend a complete day at Istanbul, but stops at other ports can be brief and are generally affected by tidal conditions. Other one-week cruises depart from Venice and call at Corfu in the Adriatic Sea, Palermo in Sicily, Valletta in Malta, Costa Smeralda in Sardinia, Portofino in Italy, and Nice, France.

Genoa is an ideal port of embarkation for a circle cruise including eastern as well as western Mediterranean ports. Other popular ports in the eastern Mediterranean include Cannes or Nice on the French Riviera, Barcelona, the islands of Malta and Sicily, and Naples and Livorno, close to Pisa. Regular cruises are also available during the summer from Southampton, England, into the Mediterranean or down the coast of Portugal to North Africa and the Canary Islands. These cruises range in length from one to three weeks.

Ships often communicate with one another by blasts of the ship's whistle. One blast means the ship is turning right. Two blasts mean a turn to the left. An oncoming ship acknowledges the signal by repeating it.

Scandinavia and Western Europe

As the market for cruises in the Mediterranean declined, a shift began to itineraries that included Britain, Portugal, the western coasts of France and Spain, Gibraltar, the Madeira Islands, and Scandinavia.

If the Aegean is Europe's Caribbean, the North Cape of Europe is the geographic and scenic equivalent of Alaska. From a port like Copenhagen or Hamburg, the cruise heads up the Norwegian coast as far as Tromso and Hammerfest in Lappland.

Here the midnight sun in late June and early July never dips below the horizon.

Other cruises head into the protected waters of the Baltic Sea, calling at major port cities like Leningrad, Helsinki, and Stockholm. Each Baltic stop offers a multitude of sightseeing and shopping possibilities, in contrast to the simple quiet of towns and settlements of the North Cape. North Cape and Baltic cruises generally last fourteen days.

Non-Traditional Cruises

There are a variety of popular cruising options that may be best defined as non-traditional. In some cases they provide creative options to the experienced cruiser and in others they are simply an alternative to other forms of transportation.

The Grand Tour

Political uncertainty has taken its toll on traditional around-the-world cruises. Where once several great liners would spend three or more months circling the globe, many now follow special itineraries that permit them to be based for short periods of time in such ports as Osaka, Hong Kong, Singapore, or Sydney. From these ports the ships make one- or two-week cruises to China or the South Pacific.

Longer cruises are making a comeback as clients express an interest in more exotic itineraries. The cruise industry has capitalized on this market segment. Some of the upscale ships with longer itineraries are moving toward a return to the golden era of the grand tour. Large luxury cruise ships are best suited to extended cruising because they provide spacious public rooms and a great variety of activities. Clients who cannot afford the time or money for a complete cruise can purchase shorter segments of an itinerary planned for 45, 90, or 120 days at sea.

Transatlantic Crossings

Some large liners still provide limited point-to-point service. The voyages are primarily designed to transport passengers from point A to point B with all the style and luxury of a cruise. The tradition of regular sea crossings between Europe and the United States is currently maintained only by

131

Historical Perspective

Great Ladies of the Sea — Where Are They Now?

Once considered "the only way to cross," most grande dames of the sea have been relegated to places in history and sent to the breakers, i.e., the scrapyard. But even today their names conjure up romantic images of a bygone age of elegance.

Many of these flagships served not only the idle rich but acted as passage for European emigrants seeking the promise of the American Dream. Others were painted battleship grey and transported United States troops during World War II. Afterward, some of them were refurbished to their former luxury and reconverted to passenger service. A few floating palaces, such as the *Queen Elizabeth 2*, remain, and new modern ships are on the horizon.

It is easy to understand the loyalty clients feel for specific ships and their nostalgia for this long-lost era. It is also interesting to research the fates of some of these great ladies of the sea.

- The *Normandie* — Once the pride of the French maritime, she burned and sank in 1942 while being converted to a troop ship.
- The *Andrea Doria* — This three-year-old Italian showcase sank off the coast of New England in 1956 after colliding with the *Stockholm*.
- The *Caronia* — The first post-war ship designed for cruising, she sank at sea during a storm.
- The *Queen Mary* — The last of the three-stackers, she is now a floating hotel in Long Beach, California. The ghosts of former passengers and crew are rumored to haunt her.
- The *Queen Elizabeth* — This ship was renamed the Seawise University in 1970 and destined for a new career as an ocean-going center of learning. Two years later she was sabotaged and sunk in Hong Kong harbor.
- The *Ile de France* — Sold to the Japanese in 1959 and damaged while being used as a floating prop for a film, she was finally sent to a scrapyard.

Cunard's *Queen Elizabeth 2*, which sails between Southampton, England, and New York. The cost is roughly equivalent to a first-class airfare.

Some passengers prefer a sea crossing; for others who typically would fly, transatlantic sailings provide practical benefits. For example, students or academics going to Europe for an extended course of study can take far more baggage by ship than by air. Passengers can take cars and household furniture for an additional charge. Furthermore, the sea voyage provides a gradual transition between cultures and no physical after effects from jet lag.

Royal Caribbean Cruise Line — m/s *Sun Viking*

The following illustrates deck plans from Royal Caribbean's m/s *Sun Viking*.

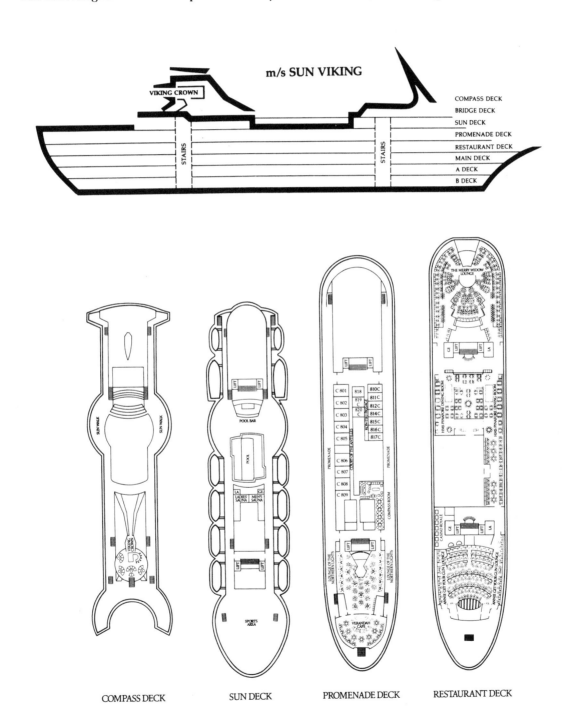

COMPASS DECK   SUN DECK   PROMENADE DECK   RESTAURANT DECK

1992 *CLIA Cruise Manual.*

Royal Caribbean Cruise Line — m/s *Sun Viking*

The following schedule demonstrates the full slate of activities available during one day aboard Royal Caribbean's *Sun Viking*.

Royal Caribbean Cruise Line	At Sea	Friday, March 20, 1992

8:00 a.m. — 9:00 a.m.	**NEWS BROADCAST** (In English, atmospheric conditions permitting) —Channel # 1 on your radio.	
9:00 a.m. — 8:00 p.m.	**SPORTS DECK OPEN FOR INFORMAL PLAY** — Sports Deck (6) Aft.	
9:00 a.m. — 4:00 p.m.	**TRIVIA** — Pick up your copy of today's Trivia in the Compass Card Room, Promenade Deck (5) Aft. complete it at your leisure, then check your answers at 4:00 p.m. In the Compass Card Room.	
9:00 a.m. — 2:00 a.m.	**SLOTS OPEN** — Restaurant Deck (4) Aft.	
9:15 a.m. — 9:45 a.m.	**WALK- A- THON** — $ Promenade Deck (5) Aft.	
9:45 a.m. — 10:00 a.m.	**MORNING STRETCH** — $ Sports Deck (5) Aft.	
10:00 a.m.	**SUN VIKING TRIATHALON $** — The most exciting sports event of the Cruise! Sports Deck (6) Aft.	

10:00 A.M. — 10:45 A.M. "Merry Widow" Lounge Restaurant Deck (4) Fwd.	***BINGORAMA # 8 *** The Snowball is about to be won!	10:00 A.M. — 10:45 A.M. "Merry Widow" Lounge Restaurant Deck (4) Fwd.

10:00 a.m.	**INFORMAL BRIDGE GET-TOGETHER** — Compass Card Room, Promenade Deck (5) Aft.
10:00 a.m.	**PASSENGERS TALENT SHOW REHEARSAL** — Please bring all music, tapes or props needed. "Annie Get Your Gun" Lounge, Restaurant Deck (4) Aft.
10:00 a.m.	**SKEET SHOOTING** — $ Restaurant Deck (4) Aft.

11:15 a.m "Merry Widow" Lounge Restaurant Deck (4) Fwd.	*** COOKING DEMONSTRATION*** Our Executive chef will bestow upon us some of his Culinary Expertise and perhaps a few secrets.	11:15 a.m. "Merry Widow" Lounge Restaurant Deck (4) Fwd.

11:30 a.m. — 12:30 p.m.	**MUSIC POOLSIDE** — Poolside, Sun Deck (6)
11:55 a.m.	**VOICE FROM THE BRIDGE** — The Captain reports our noon position weather forecast and points of interest for the afternoon

12:00 NOON SECOND SITTING "Merry Widow" Lounge Restaurant Deck (4) Fwd.	* SHORT TALK ON CUSTOMS AND LANDING PROCEDURES * with Robin your Cruise Director. Please don't miss this very important talk. At least one family member must attend In order to receive your Customs declaration card.	1:30 P.M. MAIN SITTING "Merry Widow" Lounge Restaurant Deck (4) Fwd.

1:00 p.m. — 6:00 p.m.	**CASINO ROYALE TABLES OPEN** — Open for your Gambling pleasure, Restaurant Deck (4) Aft.
2:30 p.m.	**SHIPSHAPE SPORTS AWARDS** — Medal Presentation for Tournaments, Poolside, Sun Deck (6) Aft.
2:45 p.m.	**CRAZY T-SHIRT CONTEST** — Wear your craziest T-Shirt for lots of fun and Prizes - Poolside, Sun Deck (6)
3:00 p.m. — 4:00 p.m.	**MUSIC POOLSIDE** — Poolside, Sun Deck (6), Aft.
3:30 p.m. — 4:00 p.m.	**LAST CHANCE TO REDEEM SHIPSHAPE DOLLARS FOR SHIPSHAPE T-SHIRTS** — Sports Deck (6) Aft.
3:30 p.m. — 5:00 p.m.	**FINAL BOOK RETURN** — at the Library, Promenade Deck (5) Aft.

3:45 p.m. — 5:00 p.m. "Merry Widow" Lounge Restaurant Deck (4) Fwd.	*** FINAL SNOWBALL BINGORAMA *** TODAY THE SNOWBALL JACKPOT MUST BE WON!!	3:45 p.m. — 5:00 p.m. "Merry Widow" Lounge Restaurant Deck (4) Fwd.

5:00 p.m. — 6:00 p.m.	**NEWS BROADCAST** (In English, atmospheric conditions permitting) — Channel # 1 on your radio.

5:15 P.M. BOTH SITTINGS "Merry Widow" Lounge Restaurant Deck (4) Fwd.	*** PASSENGER TALENT SHOW *** It's an All-Star Performance.	5:15 P.M. BOTH SITTINGS "Merry Widow" Lounge Restaurant Deck (4) Fwd.

8:00 p.m. — 8:45 p.m.	**DANCE DANCE DANCE** — With The Sun Viking Orchestra "Merry Widow" Lounge, Restaurant Deck (4) Fwd.

8:45 P.M. MAIN SITTING "Merry Widow" Lounge Restaurant Deck (4) Fwd.	*** THE SUN VIKING FAREWELL SHOW *** Featuring your Cruise Staff and our entire family of Entertainers for a farewell tribute for all of you, filled with Song, Music, Dance and Comedy. You'll never see another show like It!	10:45 P.M. SECOND SITTING "Merry Widow" Lounge Restaurant Deck (4) Fwd.

9:30 p.m. — 1:00 a.m.	**CASINO ROYALE TABLES OPEN** — Open for your Gambling pleasure, Restaurant Deck (4) Aft.
9:45 p.m. — 10:30 p.m.	**MUSIC FOR YOUR DANCING PLEASURE** - "Merry Widow" Lounge, Restaurant Deck (4) Fwd.

10:00 p.m. — 2:00 a.m. "Northern Lights" Lounge Promenade Deck (5) Aft.	*** DANCING TO THE TOP HITS *** Featuring: "Dawn & James"	10:00 p.m. — 2:00 a.m. "Northern Lights" Lounge Promenade Deck (5) Aft.

* TODAY'S MOVIES *
"ANNIE GET YOUR GUN" LOUNGE (Restaurant Deck (4) Aft.)

2:00 p.m.	**BEHIND THE SCENES** — A Royal Caribbean Cruise Line Documentary. Ends at 2:30 p.m.
2:30 p.m.	**SHATTERED** — Starring Tom Berenger and Bob Hoskins. Rated R. Ends at 4:08 p.m.
4:15 p.m.	**NECESSARY ROUGHNESS** — Starring Scott Bakula. Rated PG. Ends at 6:03 p.m.
7:30 p.m.	**LITTLE MAN TATE** — Starring Jodie Foster and Dianne Wiest. Rated PG. Ends at 9:09 p.m.
10:00 p.m.	**RAMBLING ROSE** — Starring Robert Duvall and Laura Dern. Rated R. Ends at 11:52 p.m.

ROYAL CARIBBEAN CRUISE LINE

MS SUN VIKING

BUILT: 1972
COUNTRY OF REGISTRY: Norway

SHIP SPECIFICATIONS

SPEED (in knots) 21
NORMAL CREW SIZE 320
NATIONALITY OF OFFICERS .... Norwegian
NATIONALITY OF CREW .... International
LANGUAGES SPOKEN BY CREW .... English
GROSS REGISTERED TONNAGE (cu. ft.) 18,556
LENGTH (in ft.) 563
BEAM (in ft.) 80
NUMBER OF PASSENGER DECKS 8
TOTAL CABINS 363
NUMBER OF ELEVATORS 4
TOTAL PASSENGER CAPACITY 846
REGULAR PASSENGER CAPACITY 726
SPACE RATIO PER PASSENGER (cu. ft.) 22
STABILIZED .... Yes

ACCOMMODATIONS

TYPE	INSIDE	OUTSIDE	SQ. FT.
Suites	—	9	163-425
Double/Queen Bed	—	—	—
With 2 Lowers	38	148	120-123
Convert to Doubles	12	34	—
Upper and Lower	68	54	—
Single Lower Only	—	—	—
Totals	118	245	—

FACILITIES FOR THE HANDICAPPED

In Public Areas: Ramps, handrails, wide doorways and elevators admitting wheelchairs

PUBLIC ROOM CAPACITIES

DINING ROOMS
HMS Pinafore 427
Verandah Cafe 125

Number of seatings for dinner: 2   Hours: 6:30 & 8:45
Formal Dress at dinner: Optional

BARS, LOUNGES, NIGHTCLUBS, THEATRE
Merry Widow Lounge 440
Annie Get Your Gun Lounge 384
Northern Lights Nightclub 239
Viking Crown Lounge 48
Casino Royale 25
Offering slots and blackjack

FACILITIES

Babysitting	Dry Cleaning	Meeting Room
Barber Shop	Duty-free Shops	Ping-pong
Beauty Salon	Exercise Classes	Pool
Bingo	Horserace on Deck	Putting Green
Boutique	Jogging Track	Sauna
Bridge	Laundry	Shuffleboard
Counselors	Library	Skeet Shooting
Dance Lessons	Liquor Store	Teen Activities
Driving Range	Masseuse	Tour Office
Drug Store	Medical Facilities	Valet Service

TIPPING GUIDELINES

Cabin Steward .... $3.00 per person per day
Waiter .... $3.00 per person per day
Busboy .... $1.50 per person per day

TYPES OF PAYMENT ACCEPTED ON-BOARD

American Express, MasterCard, VISA

TYPE OF CLIENTELE

Singles 50%
Couples to 35 .... 20%
Couples 35 - 55 .... 20%
Families 10%

SUN VIKING

DESCRIPTION: The Sun Viking is the smallest ship in the Royal Caribbean fleet but no less impressive than her larger sisters. In fact, her modest size and smaller passenger capacity are perfect for guests who seek the intimacy lost on larger cruise ships.

ACCOMMODATIONS: Cabins equipped with private bath, shower, convertible sofa, air conditioning, 3-channel radio, phone, wall-to-wall carpeting and 110AC power — Larger and deluxe staterooms equipped with sitting area and large wardrobe, some with refrigerator and tub — Many twin beds convert to doubles — 24-hour room service — Nightly turndown service.

DINING/ENTERTAINMENT: Cuisine and dining atmosphere change according to nightly themes such as Italian, French, Caribbean and American — Formal breakfast served in the dining room or casual breakfast buffet — Breads and pastries baked daily in the ships bakery — Midnight buffets culminating in the extravagant Gala Buffet — Las Vegas-style revues, live music and dancing in 4 lounges and bars — Stunning view from the window-lined Viking Crown Lounge, 9 stories above sea level — Plenty of hideaways for a quiet drink — Special evenings may include Passenger Talent Night, Ladies Night, Masquerade Party, Fifties & Sixties Night and Captain's Cocktail Party — First-run movies — Casino.

FACILITIES/SERVICES: ShipShape fitness program offers exercise classes and a variety of tournaments — Golf Ahoy! program arranges playing privileges at ports of call — Talks on topics of local interest given by Cruise Director — Conference facilities accommodating up to 427 people — Youth counselors organize special activities for teens and children — Medical Center.

Official Cruise Guide — publisher Christopher Schultz. Published by Reed Travel Group.

Repositioning Cruises

In addition to regular transatlantic crossings, some ships make repositioning cruises that cross oceans once or twice a year when the ships change location for the season. As the Caribbean season draws to a close, ships can be seen sailing northwest to Alaska or east to the Mediterranean. Later in the summer and early fall, when the weather turns cooler, these ships return to Caribbean ports. Rather than sail empty with a skeleton crew, cruise lines market these trips to special market segments that shun the ordinary. A repositioning cruise is also an ideal opportunity for veteran cruisers to try an unusual itinerary with their favorite ship. Repositioning cruises can offer substantial discounts for the educated traveler, especially on one of the super luxury ships.

Theme Cruises

Adding themes to attract passengers to repositioning cruises gave birth to the concept of theme cruises during slow periods for the cruise industry, traditionally late September through November, post-Christmas through January, and again in late April through early May. During these shoulder seasons cruise lines market their ships with themed events and special interest cruises. Among the offerings: pre-holiday shopping sprees, Theater at Sea with the New York Theater Guild, Improv at Sea Comedy, musical retrospectives, fall foliage tours, celebrity guest sailings, Murder Mystery at Sea, ethnic festivals, and beauty and fitness programs. Some passengers have become so enamored of these events that they return each year, making bookings difficult to get during these once slow seasons.

River Cruises

Many of the world's great rivers lend themselves to cruising. Passengers are in intimate contact with  the shore, and stops are frequent. The ships are smaller, often resembling large yachts. In the United States the *Delta Queen* and its sister, the *Mississippi Queen*, are the last overnight steamboats. They offer an opportu-

nity to experience some of the great rivers in the United States on three- to twelve-night cruises. The large paddle steamers call at antebellum plantations and large cities, all the way from New Orleans to Minneapolis and St. Paul. Special Expeditions' seventy-passenger *Sea Lion* sails the Sacramento and San Joaquin rivers and into San Francisco Bay, and allows passengers to visit some of Napa Valley's delightful wineries.

The Rhine is another favorite for cruising. The river is famous for the vineyards and castles that line its banks. Among the many other navigable rivers around the world are the Yangtze, the Danube, the Nile, and the Amazon. Other possibilities include sailing a cabin cruiser on the Thames in England or barging along the inland waterways of France.

Ecocruising

As the travel buzzword for the 1990s is *ecotourism,* for the cruise industry it is *ecocruising.* This philosophy urges travelers to "take only photographs, leave only footprints." In the wake of this new doctrine sails the latest in ecotechnology for cruise ships, the *Frontier Spirit.* The ship takes environmental-safety practices to new heights. All shipboard kitchen trash is separated, compacted, and refrigerated until proper disposal at port. Paper waste is incinerated; glass is ground and discharged into the sea. There is also an onboard sewage treatment plant. The captain of this vessel has the authority to deduct $50 from the paycheck of any crew member found throwing trash overboard. If all goes according to plan, this ship will also minimize the environmental impact of Antarctic exploration and set the pace for ecoships to follow.

Special Interest and Adventure Cruises

Each cruising area caters in some way to unique interests simply because of the lure of its civilization and culture. But many cruise lines go further in appealing to special interest groups by featuring activities or information that enhance the value of the vacation experience in some way for the traveler. These are often marketed as expeditions.

All are small vessels with luxurious amenities accommodating between 90 and 250 passengers. They resemble large luxury yachts except they are specifically designed to sail some of the most inaccessible waters in the world, such as the Arctic and Antarctic. These cruises feature expert lecturers in various fields. Expeditions of this sort appeal to passengers with the time and money for longer-than-average cruises and men and women of all ages with an insatiable curiosity about the obscure. An example of one such itinerary is an eighteen-day cruise departing from Auckland, New Zealand, tracing the voyage of the HMS *Bounty* through the South Sea Islands.

Yacht Charters

Yacht charters offer an alternative to large cruise ships. Of the 500 charter yachts in the world, 90 percent are found in the Caribbean, the Mediterranean, and off the coast of New England; the rest, around the Pacific and Scandinavia. Many of the larger yachts migrate seasonally from one place to another. The Caribbean season begins around Thanksgiving and runs through April, though peak time is Christmas week. The Mediterranean season begins in mid-May, peaks in July and August, and ends in October. New England charters are at their height in July and August, though the season runs from June through Labor Day.

In a typical yacht charter, groups of four to ten persons hire the boat for a certain number of days. They choose the itinerary, subject to the advice of the operator and the crew. A professional crew sails the boat and cooks the meals. The charterers often have the option of getting the boat fully provisioned with food; provisioned for breakfast and lunch (split-provisioned); or not provisioned at all, passengers bringing their own food or purchasing it from day to day.

Experienced sailors may charter yachts that they sail themselves. This is known as bareboat charter, meaning "without a professional crew." The boat operator will require evidence of sailing experience and expertise. Some administer a written exam or conduct a trial at sea. If the prospective skipper and crew pass all the tests, they receive their boat complete with charts, safety equipment, and everything necessary to sail the ship.

Windjammers

Windjammer cruises are not charters. Berths are sold to the public on a per-person basis. The itinerary is determined by the operator, who is also responsible for sailing the ship, serving meals, and providing the normal comforts of life. Passengers assist with deck tasks and often pick up a smattering of nautical knowledge. These usually appeal to the young at heart who have flexible schedules and free spirits.

Until recently, very few tall ships crossed the oceans of the world. But recently new ships and ship companies are entering the market each year. Cruising areas for these ships are exclusive to the coast of Maine, the Caribbean, and, to a lesser extent, the Mediterranean. Capacity on tall ships is limited.

Star Clipper's 196-passenger Star Flyer is the tallest sailing ship in the world. It features unique underwater lights mounted on the vessel's hull to allow passengers to view the fish and coral underwater.

A subset of the Windjammers are computerized sailing ships with both sails and motors. Windstar

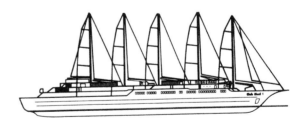

Sail Cruises has three vessels afloat, and Club Mediterranee, better known as Club Med, debuted *Club Med I* in 1989 and *Club Med II* in 1992. Classed officially as schooners, these ships take advantage of modern computer technology and sound motorized navigation without sacrificing the beautiful lines of a sailing vessel. Both companies advertise a relaxed ambience and sports-minded vacation experience in cozy and pampered surroundings.

Freighters

Many freighters sail regularly to carry goods, but typically they may also carry up to twelve passengers. They are best suited for those with time to spare, few fixed commitments, and the ability to stay friendly with eight to ten other people in fairly close quarters for three months. Ships that are licensed to carry more than twelve passengers are called cargoliners. Full information about freighter sailings worldwide is contained in *Ford's Freighter Travel Guide*, which is published semi-annually.

Most freighters are modern vessels with stabilizers, climate control, and some amenities. The cabins are comfortable, the food varied, but the on-board activity is limited. Table conversation may be entertaining, but passengers should take plenty of good books, plan their own shore excursions, and pack hand-washable clothing. Because freighters have few cabins, they are often booked months, even years, ahead.

Ferries

Regular ferry service offers an alternative to train or car transportation and in some instances air travel. Around the world ferries carry passengers, vehicles, livestock, and supplies on regular schedules. They can be as small as a rowboat or as large as some of the smaller cruise ships.

Ferries may be the only practical way to get to some destinations. Prince Edward Island, Nantucket, Catalina Island, the islands of the Philippines, and the Greek islands of the Aegean are almost all accessible only by ferry. Some of the most famous ferry trips in the world can be found in Hong Kong.

Ferries make a vital, if less glamorous, contribution to the global transportation network. Characteristically, such trips take less than a day, so sleeping accommodations are optional. It is tempting to say that where there is a body of water, somebody is sailing a ship across it.

The Price of a Cruise

In general, the price of a cruise is determined by four factors:

- The length
- The season
- The ship
- The cabin

Safety on Ships

All ships that serve United States and Canadian ports must meet government  safety requirements. Although many ships are registered in faraway places like Panama, Liberia, or the Netherland Antilles, the place of registration has no bearing on safety standards. All ships sailing from United States ports must meet the safety standards of the International Maritime Organization (IMO), an agency of the United Nations, as well as certification by the IMO Safety Of Life At Sea (SOLAS) Convention. Ships that operate exclusively from foreign ports may not be subject to such stringent standards. The agent's best guide in these situations is familiarity with the cruise line.

United States health inspectors regularly check the cleanliness of each ship sailing from a United States port. Inspections focus on standards of sanitation ranging from quality of water aboard to food preparation and general cleanliness.

The Length

The number of days devoted to any cruise itinerary will determine to some extent the price tag of the whole package. Cruise prices are often compared by the per diem (daily) cost per person. This formula helps put into perspective the all-inclusiveness of the cruise vacation. When the potential client considers that the total cruise fare includes transportation, accommodation, food, entertainment, and various other features and divides that cost by the number of days on the cruise, rates can be favorably compared with land-based resort vacations. The typical cruise price is in the range of $300–$400 per person per day, although luxury cruise ships with a full complement of shipboard amenities can be considerably higher.

The length of a cruise is also some indication of the shipboard ambience and passenger profile. Short cruises of three or four days tend to attract those looking for pure escape and exude an informal, often party-like atmosphere. Longer cruises place a greater emphasis on service, ports of call, and gourmet cuisine.

The Season

Cruise seasons used to be fairly easy to define. During the winter months the Caribbean was the hub of most activity, as North Americans sought to escape from the short, cold, gray days of December through March. In the spring most ships found their way to the Mediterranean for summer vacationers. However, as cruise lines compete for an expanding market share, seasons are now not always so clear-cut. New seasons emerge as cruise lines find opportunities to attract passengers in creative ways. New itineraries appear as the old stand-bys become saturated with new ships and passengers. Now we can add Alaska to the summer season and the Caribazon, a combination of the Caribbean and the Amazon, to the winter season. Short transitional periods or special celebrations also have become seasons, in a sense. Cruising has certainly become a year-round activity.

Fares are usually printed in cruise brochures for both the high and the off- and shoulder- seasons, also known as the value seasons. Value-season prices can represent a significant savings, as much as 20 percent less than regular prices.

The Ship

The price of a cruise is greatly affected by the history of the ship and the efficiency of its design. When Norwegian Caribbean Lines acquired the *France* and renamed it the *Norway*, several engines were removed to cut down fuel consumption. The ship is now assigned to a Caribbean itinerary where speed is not essential, and without these modifications, the ship would probably have proved to be uneconomical.

The newer ships, built specifically for short cruises, usually have many small cabins. They are more fuel-efficient and require fewer crew members. Older rebuilt ships have usually been modified either to become more fuel-efficient or to increase the density of passengers.

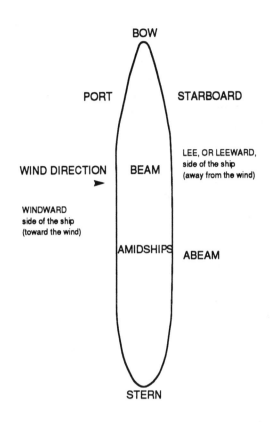

Other guides to the spaciousness and comfort of a ship are the gross tonnage (GRT) compared with the number of passengers and the ratio of crew to passengers. The GRT represents the amount of enclosed space on the ship and when compared with the passenger capacity gives some indication of size and spaciousness. By comparing the size of the crew with the number of passengers, some idea of the quality of service can be gained. A ship that offers more space and more crew members per passenger generally is more expensive simply because costs are higher.

The Cabin

The cost of a cruise also depends on the location of the cabin. Cabins, sometimes called "staterooms" or just "rooms," vary in location, size, design, and special features. To appreciate these differences, the counselor needs to study a deck plan of each ship.

Other considerations also affect the choice of a cabin. Proximity to elevators, stairs, and public areas can be helpful to clients with limited mobility. But such cabins may be noisier. On some ships with more than one dining room, the category or location of the cabin controls where the occupants dine.

■ **Decks.** Each deck is identified by a letter of the alphabet or a name. Usually the higher the deck is in the ship, the more expensive its cabins are and the closer they are to most public areas. Lower decks are closer to the engine room and consequently may be noisier.

■ **Forward or Aft.** The cost of a cabin is also dictated to some extent by its proximity to the bow (forward) or stern (aft) of the ship.

A center cabin is an ideal location for passengers prone to seasickness. Movement from side to side, called "roll," is the primary cause of seasickness and may be experienced least in the center of the ship. Movement up and down, called "pitch," may similarly be less apparent halfway between the bow and the stern. The efficiency of modern stabilizers is such that most passengers will be perfectly comfortable in cabins a fair distance each side of midship.

A ship's running lights are color-coded. The starboard light is green; the port light is red.

■ **Inside or Outside.** An outside cabin has a porthole, or window, that looks out over the ocean, whereas inside cabins have no access to natural light. Outside cabins are, therefore, always more expensive than inside cabins of comparable size and comfort. It is important to note, however, that portholes cannot be opened to allow fresh sea breezes into the cabin. In fact, on older ships caps are sometimes secured over the portholes on the lowest decks to make them safe for rough seas.

■ **Cabin Design.** Although all cabins are designed to accommodate two persons, some can accommodate more. Upper berths recessed into the walls above twin beds can be pulled out to provide sleeping accommodations for two additional persons. These cabins are popular with families and young people who wish to save money by traveling as a group.

Selling Cruises

Unlike other travel products that can be purchased by the public directly from the supplier,

such as airline tickets, cruises are sold almost exclusively through travel agents. For the travel counselor, one of the greatest benefits of booking a cruise is that it often requires just one phone call.

Selling a cruise requires special selling skills. Particularly when dealing with first-time cruisers, the counselor may have to overcome clients' misconceptions and misunderstanding of the cruise experience. Therefore, an agent may have to begin by separating fact from fiction. Additionally, the sheer number of cruise ships and itineraries can be overwhelming to clients and counselors alike. A successful travel counselor will need to match the right client with the right cruise.

A number of opportunities exist for travel counselors to get to know cruise products. Personal experience with every ship is ideal but impossible. Ship inspections, cruise nights hosted by sales representatives, travel trade shows, and cruise directories are but a few of the ways an agent can learn details about specific ships. Most travel counselors also keep a supply of brochures and videos to use as selling tools with their clients.

Cruise-Only Agencies

Today, more than 2,000 cruise-only agencies operate in the United States and many more full-service agencies are opening cruise-only departments. The National Association of Cruise-Only Agencies boasts a membership of at least 1,000. The success of these agencies lies in their ability to focus on a narrower product line and serve as experts to the clientele they serve.

Single Passengers

The number of single cruisers has grown consistently over the years, but the economic barrier to selling cruises to singles has changed little. Few cabins are designed for single occupancy. Therefore a single passenger usually pays between 50 and 100 percent more than the person in a double cabin of similar quality.

Some cruise lines offer to find a cabin mate for single passengers. They attempt to match compatible people but can guarantee only that occupants are of the same sex. Cabins may be changed once on board, but single passengers who are not tolerant and flexible should be discouraged from seeking an unknown companion.

Groups

On some cruise lines group bookings are becoming more frequent. The reservations are organized by a group desk eight to twenty months before the sailing date. Typically, a cruise line offers promotional assistance and discounts for groups booking ten to fifteen cabins. Other lines offer one free cabin for so many cabins booked.

Incentive groups are another growing market. Increasingly, smaller ships are entirely occupied by a single company for business seminars or as business perks. Or larger ships may be chosen for their prestige or private facilities, particularly function rooms.

Cruise Directories

It would be next to impossible to know every cruise ship afloat. The numbers of ships and shipping lines change constantly, along with their names, itineraries, sizes, schedules, and services. Instead, trust the growing number of reliable cruise directories to enhance and update personal knowledge. Guides can help travel counselors keep abreast of new developments in cruise products and serve as handy desk references that answer specific questions on departure dates, ports of call, and cruising areas. Some of the most dependable

Servicing the Cruise Client

Because cruising is associated with pampering and luxury, many travel counselors perform special services for cruise clients. Some agencies request that cruise lines place a bon voyage gift such as a bouquet, fruit basket, or bottle of champagne in their clients' cabins or have a waiter present a bottle of wine at dinner with the agency's compliments.

Travel agents should supply all of their cruise passengers with United States Customs and Immigration information before they depart. Although the cruise director typically explains this topic before the end of the cruise, clients should know what to buy and what receipts to keep. Similarly, the agent should ensure that clients have the necessary passports, proofs of citizenship, or visas required by each port and for re-entry into the United States.

of these are

- *CLIA Cruise Manual*
- *OAG Cruise and Shipline Guide*
- *Official Steamship Guide International*

Typically, cruise lines assign cabins within a particular category on a first-come, first-served basis, starting midship and working toward the bow and stern.

Paying On-Board Ship

All cruise ships accept travelers checks and cash as payment for bar bills, shore excursions, or any other kind of on-board service. But many will not accept credit cards or personal checks as payment for these services, nor will they offer cash advances

141

on credit cards. Major credit cards are, however, accepted in the shops on board. Payment policies are usually stated clearly in brochures. Several cruise lines establish a credit account for passengers as soon as they board the ship that allows them to sign for all services on board. These accounts are settled at the purser's office at the end of the cruise.

Fly/Cruise

The majority of cruise passengers fly to the port of embarkation. To diminish the cost of this additional transportation and to provide additional incentives for people to book cruises, cruise lines offer special fly/cruise arrangements. These come in three varieties:

■ **Transportation on scheduled airlines** — Cruise lines pay round-trip airfare on scheduled service from most major cities.

■ **Transportation on charter airlines** — Some cruise lines organize air charters from major cities to the port of embarkation and back. This option offers less flexibility.

■ **Air credit** — Using this alternative, the passenger is given an air credit. This provides the most flexibility: clients can choose their own air itinerary, class of service, and routing.

New Ships and Technology

More than thirty-five ships, new or refurbished, are planned for addition to the North American fleet by 1995. These ships will come in all sizes with a host of new and improved amenities available to lure passengers aboard. Advances in technology have improved navigation, safety, and cabin and public room design. Cruise lines vary in their perception of what passengers want, but the advantage for passengers, or would-be passengers, is that there is an ever-widening choice of ships to try and cruising areas that are broadening to accommodate them.

Mega-Ships

The "bigger is better" theory has taken its place in the cruise industry. Although small luxury ships have an established following, there is a segment that prefers the sheer magnitude of a mega-ship.

The *Radisson Diamond*

A company normally associated with land-based hotels has taken to the seas

with a radical new concept in both ship design and market segmentation. Radisson Hotel Corporation's brand-new *Radisson Diamond* enters the market by unleashing a ship-design concept that claims to all but eliminate shipboard rock and roll. The technology is called Semi-Submersible Craft (SSC), and the vessel looks almost like an oversized catamaran. The company will position its ship to capture the meeting and incentive market, a group that has been largely ignored by the cruise industry.

These vessels provide choice on a scale that a smaller ship cannot hope to offer. Entertainment rivals that found in some Las Vegas revues; spas are replete with the most exotic treatments and facilities; an entire deck may be devoted to the casino or shops; and there is often a wide choice of restaurants. Passengers can forget that they are actually on board a moving vessel; motion is reduced to a bare minimum.

However, there is another side to the size argument. Opportunity to get lost on board is increased, and opportunity to get to know many of the other passengers is greatly decreased. Ships of this size carry 2,000-plus passengers. Some examples of the new mega-ships are NCL's *Norway*, Carnival's *Fantasy* and *Ecstasy*, and RCCL's *Sovereign of the Seas* and *Monarch of the Seas*.

Cruise Line Consolidation

The cruise industry has grown by leaps and bounds in the past two decades. New ships were built, stretched, refurbished, or rebuilt. Cruise lines historically bought and sold, or leased, individual ships to one another, but in recent years as the industry became stronger, the cruise lines became bolder. Whole lines were sold intact to competing lines, who sometimes repainted the ships and positioned them in different markets. The ships of Home Lines now appear as a part of Premier's Disney fleet. Other companies diversified their markets by creating upscale divisions of the original cruise line and adding to its fleet by purchasing other lines that were struggling or tired of trying to keep up the pace. In addition to mergers, new ships arrive on the scene each year. Now Chandris Fantasy Cruises sports an upscale division known as Celebrity, and Commodore Cruise Line invented Crown Cruise Line by acquiring Bermuda Star Line. Dolphin Cruise Line followed suit with its Majesty Cruise Line. CLIA predicts a 45 percent increase in available berths by 1995. This represents thirty-five to forty new ships in the five-year period 1991–1995.

The top three lines — Kloster, Royal Caribbean, and Carnival — control approximately 50 percent of the industry. The remaining thirty-odd lines compete for a share of the remaining 50 percent. There will always be an opportunity for niche marketing in the cruise industry. Cruise lines will continue to diversify, seeking the ultimate product mix.

Summary

The cruise industry is enjoying a position of strength it has not previously known. New ships enter the market each year, with new passengers emerging to fill them. CLIA reports that the industry has tripled in size every decade since 1970, and predicts that by the year 2000, ten million passengers will cruise yearly. These predictions are based on careful market research that examines preferences in vacation products and trends in travel.

Selling cruises is a profitable business, as evidenced by the number of cruise-only agencies. Travel counselors can take advantage of the growing cruise market through creative marketing strategies and superior product knowledge. An abundance of sales tools are available to help travel counselors do just that. Cruise directories help navigate through the maze of products available, and advancing computer technology provides greater access to cruise lines for booking information and reservations. As new itineraries, new ship design, and more services are offered, the challenge for the travel counselor will be to find the right cruise for their clients.

Chapter Wrap-up

REVIEW QUESTIONS

1. Why might clients prefer one ship over another?
2. If you could take a cruise, where would you like to go, and why?
3. How does river or canal cruising differ from ocean cruising?
4. What makes cruises desirable?
5. Why might you purchase shore excursions in advance?
6. Which cruises attract older clients? Younger? Richer? Why?
7. For what reasons might clients prefer an inside cabin?

DISCUSSION TOPICS

Group Sales

As a sales representative for XYZ Travel, you have a potential group booking for forty senior citizens on the *QE2*. What are some important sales considerations with a group of this size and age group? What special arrangements should be made if any members are disabled? Why is the *QE2* a good choice for such a group?

Repeat Clients

Mr. and Mrs. Travelalot arrange all of their vacations with your retail agency. Therefore, you know they are extremely detail-conscious and like to confirm all arrangements as far in advance as possible. When you call the cruise line to request their reservations, the cruise agent informs you that he can guarantee you the category requested with the quoted rate but cannot give you the specific cabin number. You realize that Mr. and Mrs. Travelalot may be upgraded because of this, but you won't have any specifics about their cabin until about two weeks prior to sailing. How do you handle this situation?

Honeymoon Present

Your parents have given you a honeymoon cruise as a wedding present. You have always wanted to take a cruise, but your future husband is not so sure. His friends have convinced him that there is nothing to do on board and that it will still be an expensive honeymoon because the shore excursions, alcohol, tips, and, of course, souvenirs will not be included in the price. He would prefer to take the money and choose a different type of vacation. This would be totally unacceptable to your parents, so how can you allay his fears about cruising?

Bargain Rate

The Sunday newspaper contained a special section on cruising. On Monday morning your office was swamped with calls for the lowest-priced cruises featured in the advertisement. These minimum lead-in rates, however, are not available on the dates your clients want to travel. How do you keep these impulse buyers happy and make the sales?

Accommodations

Introduction

Studies show that clients ask their travel agents for advice on property selection more often than on any other aspect of their trips. A hotel must meet the requirements of its guests for shelter, security, food, and recreation. It must also meet a traveler's expectations for comfort and convenience.

Properties do differ. Even hotels built from the same plan, with identical furniture and features, will differ when located in other countries and cultures. Fundamentally, a good property is a combination of a well-kept building and a hard-working staff and management.

Hotels are not members of a conference system that formally appoints travel agencies. Antitrust regulations have inhibited sales agreements between hotel associations and the agency community. Thus, the agency-hotel connection is loosely knit and imposes no official controls or responsibilities on either side. The very diversity of the hotel industry makes procedural uniformity next to impossible.

Despite past impediments, the relationship between travel agents and hotels is getting better. Hotels are paying more attention to agents, and enlightened executives see the agency as an extension of a hotel's sales force. One reason is simple economics. There are more beds for rent than there were ten years ago. Hotels compete fiercely, especially for the corporate traveler who books through travel agencies offering hotel reservations as part of a total, automated travel service.

Hotel Careers

Accounting
Financial Management
Food and Beverage
Concierge
Front Office
Housekeeping

Meetings and Conventions
Reservations
Sales and Marketing
Human Resources
Security
Engineering and Facility Maintenance

Concierge

The term *concierge* comes from France where the position usually refers to a doorkeeper. Throughout most of Europe, however, the title refers to a multilingual hotel staff member who handles reservations, tours, luggage, mail, and any other guest service. The job is not so different in the United States, although some duties of this newly developing position may vary from hotel to hotel.

The role of the concierge is a demanding one requiring great resourcefulness, as well as public relations and managerial skills. Usually luxury hotels employ a concierge to provide extra services for their guests. This person must possess a wealth of knowledge and be able to satisfy a guest's every wish — from reservations, tickets, seasonal happenings, and gifts to information on an incredible variety of subjects. The concierge is also in charge of uniformed service personnel such as elevator operators, bell staff, and doorkeepers.

Some prerequisites for the career include in-depth knowledge of a particular city, usually through residency there, and understanding of the hotel industry, most often through a college degree in hospitality or a related field, or through extensive industry experience. In addition, proficiency in two or more languages is desired. After employment, specific in-house training for the position is conducted by hotel management. In addition to personal gratification from a job well done, rewards for this service may include tips, commission, or free tickets to local events, depending on the policy of the property.

Les Clefs d'Or is the professional society of concierges. To qualify for membership, individuals must have five years of industry experience, three years of which must be as a concierge. Currently, over twenty-four countries are represented internationally, including over 150 members from the United States.

Some properties have additional service positions, such as guest-service managers. These individuals take care of services within the hotel, rather than securing outside suppliers. The size of the property and its service-level standard will determine the need for such positions.

According to one survey, the top ten requests for concierge service are

- Confirmation of airline tickets
- Dinner reservations
- Limousine arrangements
- Car rentals
- Maps or directions

- FAX service
- Cellular phones
- Photocopies
- Portable computers
- Theater tickets

Dates in Hotel History

1829 In Boston, the Tremont Hotel allowed a guest to rent a single rather than a double room shared with strangers. (The Tremont was also the first hotel to have bathrooms.)

1881 The Prospect House in New York State was the first property to install electric lights.

1904 The St. Regis in New York City provided individual room settings for climate control.

1907 The Plaza Hotel in New York City installed telephones in each guestroom.

1908 The Gideons placed their first Bible in the Superior Hotel in Superior, Montana.

1927 Radio reception and broadcast programs were available to guests of the Boston Statler.

1955 Sheraton installed large-screen televisions in seven of their properties.

1981 500,000 guestrooms had in-room movies.

Agents are a relatively inexpensive distribution source. Hotels do not have to pay commissions (averaging 8 to 10 ___ agents until the guest a___ at the property.

A Brief Histo___ Accommoda___

The history of acc___ the many references to l___ aps the most famous be___ em. Later, travelers from a___ red to carry official docu___ at granted permission to travel and stay in private mansions. During the Middle Ages, *hostelry* was the term used to describe an inn where travelers could stop for the night and compare stories of their trips.

Transportation advances such as stagecoaches and railroads also had a great impact on the industry. Train tracks, in many instances, led to spas that were visited for their medicinal value. Resorts flourished during the 1900s, and legendary names such as Ritz, Statler, and Hilton soon became synonymous with the hotel industry.

The Depression of the 1930s nearly caused the demise of the industry. After World War II, however, the hotel/motel industry entered a major building phase. The railroads were deteriorating, air travel was expanding, and the city hotels were old and lacked sufficient parking facilities for increased automobile travel. The development of the interstate highway system began in 1956, and Americans who started taking to the roads, commercial travelers as well as vacationers, needed convenient hotels. Highway motel construction boomed. The small mom-and-pop cabins built in the 1920s could not compete with the new chains that offered amenities like swimming pools, TVs, and property-to-property reservations systems.

The rise in gasoline prices during the 1970s forced many travelers to switch to air travel. Urban renewal revitalized downtowns, and large hotels moved in. Today, chains, franchises, resorts, spas, and all-suite properties share the leisure and corporate markets.

The Organization of Accommodations

The legal structure of a hotel organization is complex. A hotel can be individually owned, a member of a chain, a franchise operation, a wholly owned subsidiary of a major corporation, or owned by one corporation and operated by another. Several large conglomerates have moved into the tourist business by purchasing existing hotels.

Although a hotel's corporate structure is important to its financial health, the travel agent must be more concerned with what a hotel can offer its guests. The choice of a hotel is a reflection of a client's self-image. All things being equal, a Hyatt customer is not interchangeable with a Days Inn customer, and hotel managers do not suppose that customers should be. Market segmentation in the hotel industry offers the client a wide choice and the travel agent a constant challenge.

Hotel Affiliations

A chain consists of a group of affiliated properties bearing the same name and following the same operating procedures, central reservations system, and standards. Among the largest hotel/motel chains are Holiday, Sheraton, Hilton, Marriott, Ramada, Days Inn of America, and Hyatt. Chains of luxury, medium-priced, and budget hotels and motels of every size and kind are available. To the travel agent these chains represent an easily accessible inventory of rooms with predictable standards. The chain property provides a sense of security; the agent knows what is being sold, and the client knows what is being bought. Reservations can be easily confirmed, and prices are competitive with other hotels of equal rating.

Best Western International Inc. is also among the largest hotel groups but is considered a membership organization rather than a chain because it consists of individually owned and operated hotels that have united to centralize reservations and to pool advertising costs. The individual properties in a membership organization differ widely.

A franchise hotel is permitted to use a well-known name in accordance with a legal agreement with the parent group. The franchisor provides many services, particularly at the beginning of the relationship. The franchisee actually owns the hotel but is expected to meet organizational standards. A fee is paid by the franchisee to the parent company for the shared benefits of a central reservations system, advertising, and use of the name.

The management-contract concept was developed in the 1950s by United States–based international chains wanting to expand overseas. Foreign hotel developers sought the management and marketing expertise of American companies. Their countries either prohibited investment by foreign owners or levied exorbitant taxes on them. Thus, major international hotel operators accepted contracts to manage hotels that often bore their names but were not actually owned by the parent corporation.

In the United States it was not until the 1970s that most major chains began using management contracts to supplement traditional ownership, joint-venture, and lease and franchise arrangements. The contract concept has three basic tenets: the operator has the right to manage the property without the owner's interference; the owner is responsible for all operating and financing costs; the operator is not liable for operating results except in the case of fraud or gross neglect.

Each country has its own name for an inn. In Japan an inn is called a "ryokan"; Spain has "paradores"; Portugal, "posadas"; England, "bed and breakfasts"; Germany, Austria, and Switzerland, the "gasthaus."

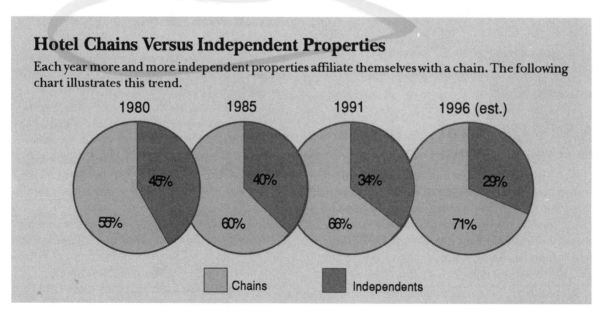

Hotel Chains Versus Independent Properties

Each year more and more independent properties affiliate themselves with a chain. The following chart illustrates this trend.

1980	1985	1991	1996 (est.)
45% / 55%	40% / 60%	34% / 66%	29% / 71%

☐ Chains   ■ Independents

Independent Properties

Individually owned properties continue to exist today, and many travelers seek them out at all price levels. Clients can stay in farmhouses, inns, castles, monasteries, rooming houses, and jungle camps. Some of the world's finest hotels operate independently. The high standards of these hotels make it a pleasure to recommend them to the client. Other individually owned properties may be less predictable, especially at the budget level. These unique properties vary from country to country and mirror the variety of the world.

Each hotel operates in ways indigenous to its nation and offers the client immersion in the local culture. Properties may be small in size but rich in history. The bathroom may be down the hall, but the possibilities for views, variety, and memories more than make up for any inconvenience. For business and reservation purposes many smaller properties belong to membership organizations. The grand-deluxe city hotel or the fashionable resort can be a unique property or a member of a prestigious chain.

The Lodging Industry

The lodging industry in the United States is a multi-billion-dollar industry; worldwide its impact is far greater. To see why, consider the following statistics:

■ The lodging industry employs more than 1.6 million people.

■ There are more than three million hotel rooms in the United States.

■ There are more than eleven million rooms worldwide.

■ Over the past ten years, industry employment has increased 43 percent.

■ The number of hotel rooms across the world increases at a rate of 3.4 percent annually.

■ About 76 percent of the world's hotel rooms are in Europe and North America.

■ Average occupancy in the United States is around 67 percent; internationally it is 69 percent.

Market Segmentation in the Hotel Industry

In recent years the hotel industry has responded to a saturated market by creating a wide variety of specialized types of accommodations. Some chains offer products at virtually every price level.

Types of segmentation include:

■ Motels
■ Budget properties
■ Economy properties
■ Full-service mid-priced properties
■ Full-service upscale properties
■ Luxury properties
■ Resort hotels
■ All-suites
■ Airport hotels
■ Commercial hotels
■ Spas

Motels

It was in 1926 that the word *motel* was invented by Arthur Heineman, who tagged his establishment on Route 101 in San Luis Obispo, California, the Mo-tel Inn. It was a mock Spanish mission with a bell tower and a sign that superimposed the M of Heineman's new linguistic coinage like a roof over the initial H of the word *hotel*. Heineman's word has come to mean not only the classic motel, with its rooms arranged under one long, low roof, but its predecessor, the motor court, and its successor, the motor inn.

The motel introduced Americans to all sorts of modern amenities. In the years before the reassuring familiarity of the chains, motel owners advertised reliable, nationally known products such as Congoleum floors and Simmons Beautyrest mattresses. The features promoted on hundreds of motel signs — steam heat, tile bathrooms, sliding glass doors, air conditioning, radio, and then television — were for many people their first experience with these niceties.

Motorists avoided hotels from the beginning of the auto age for several reasons. Hotels were expensive, and early motoring was seen as a modern form of camping. The first motorists felt dirty and dusty, and unfit to enter a fancy lobby. They were also reluctant to be separated from their vehicles, wanting them close by, preferably in sight. Hotels, for their part, disdained the motel business.

In the 1930s the Pure Oil Company developed a chain of motels. One of the operators of the chain was Colonel Harlan Sanders, who went on to start the Kentucky Fried Chicken operation. Another, and the most famous, of the early chains was Holiday Inn. It succeeded by combining a standardized unit, the room itself, with a fixed number of rooms, 120, and the franchising resources of one of the nation's leading home builders, Wallace Johnson.

The Typical Lodging Customer in 1991

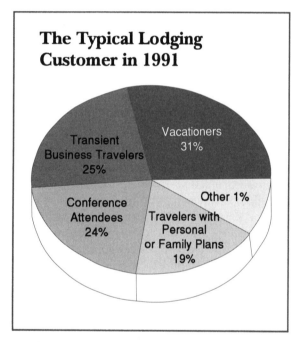

Budget Properties

The budget segment of the industry has experienced a rapid growth spurt, today representing 12 percent of the total number of hotel rooms in the United States. As the big chains have entered the market, this niche has become more competitive. Friendship Inns are in this category.

The benefit of the budget level is that these properties outpace their full-service rivals in profitability. Budget lodges do not have to provide restaurants, large lobbies, or meeting rooms. A budget property needs fewer workers, so it can break even by filling a lower percentage of its rooms.

Budget properties are very affordable, and clients receive a standard room, often with two double beds and a private bath.

Economy Properties

Economy properties offer more amenities, such as color televisions and ice machines. These properties cost a bit more than the budgets. The decor is expanded slightly to include armchairs and a table or desk. Bathroom facilities may provide such amenities as shampoos, lotions, and a shower cap. Econo Lodges and Sleep Inns are in this category.

Full-Service Mid-Priced Properties

As price increases, so does the number of amenities offered. Style becomes more detailed, and options such as a twenty-four-hour attendant, restaurants, lounges, room service, and bathroom amenities are all available. Often, mid-priced hotels are located near convention facilities to capitalize on the needs of corporate clients. Quality has many properties in this category.

Full-Service Upscale Properties

More luxurious surroundings account for the increase in price for this type of property. Amenities again increase to include twenty-four-hour room service, health clubs, swimming pools, perhaps even concierge service. High-quality restaurants are within the facility. Clarion Hotels and Quality Suites are in this category.

The Regent Beverly Wiltshire in Beverly Hills is rumored to have the most luxurious bathrooms in the world. They are made of marble from Greece, crystal from Italy and Hong Kong, and contain scales from Germany. The mirrors are framed in silver, and the dressing tables have silver candlesticks. Each bathroom cost approximately $35,000.

Luxury Properties

These properties boast lavish surroundings and impeccable service with lobbies of marble and brass. The facilities include health clubs, in-room mini-bars, haute cuisine restaurants, concierge, and many suites. Prices for such properties easily top $100 per night. Clarion Suites are considered part of this category.

150

Case Study — Market Segmentation

Choice Hotels International, formerly Quality International Inc, was formed in 1990 and is the world's largest franchise hotel company with more than 2,800 hotels, inns, resorts, and suites in twenty-eight countries. They have been very successful in segmenting their product, allowing them to market different kinds of hotel properties to different client types. There are seven brands under the Choice umbrella — Quality, Comfort, Clarion, Sleep, Rodeway, Econo Lodge, and Friendship. The following chart demonstrates their brand-positioning strategy.

Choice Hotels Brand-Positioning Strategy

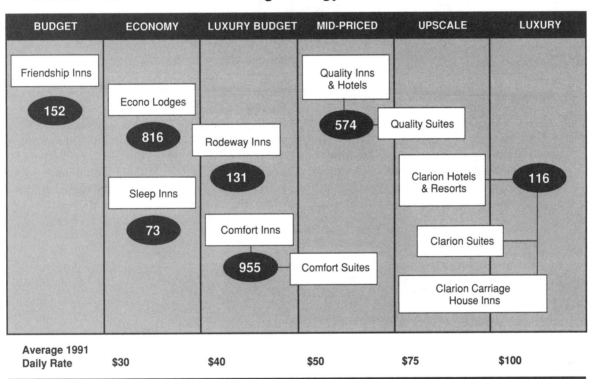

NOTE: Total properties: 2,817. Numbers reflect existing properties and those under development for each brand.

Resort Hotels

Resort hotels attract special market segments. In the 1950s resort hotels relied on families who stayed two or three months and came back year after year. Now, however, group and convention business is a staple for these traditional properties, and many new resorts are built with special meeting facilities. Elaborate facilities for golfers, scuba divers, and tennis players are staffed by big-name professionals. Beautiful natural surroundings, night life, and special attractions offer a wide variety of experiences.

The resort hotel wants to attract clients for a longer stay. Many resorts, especially in the Caribbean, will not accept guests for less than three nights. Properties like the vacation villages of Club Med may require a stay of one week and even specify that clients begin their vacation on a certain day of the week. Resort properties are one of the fastest-growing segments of the industry.

151

Club Med

Club Med is one of the largest resort hotel chains in the world. It started as a tent village on the Mediterranean island of Majorca and has grown into a family of international resorts. French management tries to make each resort as different as its location. The newer villages are designed to be self-contained vacation destinations. Meals and sports activities are included in the total price. Although it once targeted single "swingers," as the baby boom-population bulge moved through the century, Club Med kept up with demographic demand and now encourages all market segments.

All-Suites

Beginning in the early 1980s, the all-suite-hotel concept brought high expectations, high occupancies, and high consumer satisfaction. The all-suite concept has been outdistancing traditional hotel products in both occupancy rate and rate of growth. The typical all-suite-hotel unit in major cities incorporates a living room, sleeping area, and kitchenette. It is not unlike the popular rental condominium properties found in Hawaii, Florida, and other resort areas. On the Mediterranean coast, similar resort properties are described as self-catering apartments. The all-suites are ideal for the relocating executive, the employee on a long-term project, or the leisure traveler who wants cooking facilities and space separation.

Airport Hotels

The first airport hotel in the United States was built in 1929 at the Oakland Municipal Airport. Airport properties boast high occupancy rates even though they may be the largest hotels in town. Aggressive marketing has promoted their special features: amenities such as pools and recreational facilities; convenience for people with early morning flights; avoidance of downtown traffic; parking and meeting space for groups. Complimentary mini-bus service to and from the airport is usually provided. Special honeymoon packages are popular for couples departing early the next day. Business clients often hold meetings there. Most airport hotels are members of a major chain.

The Top Ten Corporate Hotel Chains in the World

RANK	ORGANIZATION	ROOMS	HOTELS
1.	Holiday Inn Worldwide	320,599	1,606
2.	Best Western International	268,140	3,348
3.	Choice Hotels International	201,048	2,102
4.	Accor	159,877	1,421
5.	Hospitality Franchise System	138,122	944
6.	Marriott Corporation	131,238	476
7.	ITT Sheraton Corporation	130,862	429
8.	Days Inn of America	129,907	1,112
9.	Hilton Hotels Corporation	94,232	263
10.	Hyatt Hotels	76,794	161

Rankings are based on total rooms open as of December 31, 1990.

to city and country to country. But wherever the hotel is, some constant factors affect the price of a room. The experienced agent evaluates these factors each time a hotel selection is made.

Factors That Affect the Price of a Room

- Yield management
- Property location
- Currency fluctuations
- Room location
- Room size and amenities
- Occupancy
- Length of stay and season
- Special rates
- Special features and marketing efforts

Commercial Hotels

The commercial hotel offers meeting space and support services for the business person. Many commercial properties have downtown locations so they are convenient to shopping, sightseeing, and local transportation. Large properties must pursue group and convention business to maintain high occupancy rates and profitability.

Spas

The word *spa* means a resort with mineral springs. Europe maintains its classic spas with their therapeutic orientation, many of which are on the sites of Roman ruins. Spas in the United States are generally different from their European counterparts. They are health resorts that specialize in diet and fitness regimens and even teach people how to manage stress. Dude ranches and ski resorts also fit into the health-resort category.

According to Hyatt Hotels, 78 percent of business executives believe that vacations are necessary to prevent burnout and view them as a psychological investment.

What Affects the Price of a Hotel Room?

One of the travel counselor's hardest tasks is to select the right hotel at the right price for each client. Hotels vary greatly in kind and cost from city

Yield Management

For a number of years airlines have used a pricing system called yield management. This practice of frequent price changes to keep airline seats filled, as determined by computer tracking of advance bookings, is now used by most hotels. This is based on the philosophy that a room night is a perishable commodity — if the room remains empty for that night, that revenue is lost forever.

The yield-management system relies on the sophistication of the supplier's computer reservations system to permit the adjusting of prices on a day-to-day, often moment-to-moment basis. As demand weakens, lower-price tiers, or discounts requiring advance bookings, come on the market. As demand builds, lower-price tiers are closed, and consumers are forced to pay more for the same product on the desired date.

Hotels measure how well they are doing by establishing average rates, then dividing this figure by daily rates and the number of rooms sold. The objective is to maximize rates and occupancy to come up with a higher daily average. In this way hotels get the maximum amount of revenue available on any given day.

Hotels list a variety of room rates based on such factors as season, day, location, and type of room. In addition, there are usually discounted rates depending on a guest's group affiliation, age, or business.

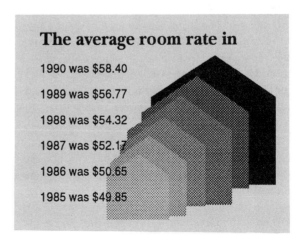

The average room rate in

1990 was $58.40

1989 was $56.77

1988 was $54.32

1987 was $52.17

1986 was $50.65

1985 was $49.85

Some properties have begun using another long-established airline practice — heavily discounted nonrefundable rates. Marriott, Forte International, and ITT Sheraton are just three of the industry leaders experimenting with this concept. The premise is that clients receive substantial discounts at participating properties, sometimes up to 60 percent off, by booking two to three weeks in advance. Substantial penalties are levied if clients need to cancel the reservations.

Property Location

The location of a property is the single most important factor influencing the cost of its rooms. Resort hotels located in a scenic area on a beautiful beach can command top prices. Similarly, commercial hotels located in the heart of a city close to convention facilities are the most expensive.

A hotel tends to be more expensive if there is no competition or if it is the only hotel in sight. An isolated hotel that is not ideally located, on the other hand, remains isolated and empty.

In many countries hotel development is stimulated and/or controlled by the government. A government can control the number and variety of hotels in a resort area to stimulate tourism or to ensure that overdevelopment does not result in low occupancy rates or damage to the environment.

A recent study indicated that shampoo is the most frequently used amenity, and suntan lotion is the least requested.

Currency Fluctuations

The price of a hotel room in a foreign country will vary with fluctuations in the currency exchange rate. If converted from local currency, dollar prices quoted in advance are not firm unless guaranteed. For clients who pay the bill in U.S. dollars or U.S. travelers cheques, the exchange rate will be the rate in effect that day, not the day of booking.

Currency fluctuations typically do not vary greatly from day to day or week to week but may change substantially over a longer period. If a foreign hotel shows a rate in U.S. dollars in a reference book or brochure, remember that this amount is only an approximation and reflects the rate on the

Female Travelers

In 1966 Hilton introduced the "Lady Hilton" program that included women-only floors. Many hotels have continued this tradition of catering to the needs of female travelers. This is not surprising, since studies indicate that women will account for half of all business travel by the year 2000. Today, female business travelers number over thirteen million and account for 39 percent of all business travel, or $23 billion. Currently, the average female business traveler is 43.5 years old, is in an executive or managerial position, and earns approximately $50,000 annually. Security is the primary concern of women choosing hotel properties. For this reason, rooms on upper floors and in-house restaurants or room service are important. Men have also benefited from many of the amenities that hotels have provided to attract female travelers, such as full-length mirrors, skin-care products, and sewing kits.

day the brochure or advertisement was printed. The agent should quote rates in local currencies if possible.

Room Location

Another factor affecting price is the location of a room within a hotel. Particularly in resort properties, the most expensive rooms are those with the best views. In some hotels the price of a room is affected by its proximity to sources of noise. Rooms on upper floors — far from public areas such as the lobby, the restaurants, or the pool — tend to be quieter. Rooms close to elevators are noisier, because of the opening and closing of doors and the sound of guests talking in the halls.

Room Size and Amenities

Most Americans take for granted that a hotel room will contain a comfortable bed, chairs, a dresser, desk, good lighting, a closet with hangers, a television set, telephone, a private bathroom with sink, toilet, bathtub with shower, and, of course, that the room will have heat and air conditioning. Throughout the world, however, standards differ, and the traveler needs counseling on what to expect from one country to another and from one hotel to another.

The size of the room and its amenities affect its cost. Newer hotels are planned so that almost all rooms are of equal size. The major factors affecting price in these hotels, therefore, are location and types of fixtures or decor provided. Older hotels have rooms of different sizes, and more luxurious hotels usually have suites or demi-suites that are more like small apartments. These suites can also be used for small meetings or receptions.

Hotel Services and Benefits

According to a recent survey by the American Hotel & Motel Association

- 82% of hotels have FAXing facilities
- 70% have cable television
- 7% have VCRs
- 86% cater to guests who need special diets
- 79% have non-smoking rooms

Occupancy

Most hotel rooms are designed for two people. A single person always pays far more than half the rate for two persons in the same room. When any room is rented as a single, a hotel loses revenue. A room with one double, queen-, or king-size bed or two twins usually has two rates: single (one person) and double (two persons). A room with two double, queen-, or king-size beds may have four rates: single, double, triple (three persons), or quad (four persons). Rates for more than four persons in a room are not offered, either by custom or because of local building laws.

Often friends or family members wish to stay in adjoining rooms. Adjoining rooms have separate entrances but no means of getting directly from

one room to the other. Connecting rooms, on the other hand, are linked by a common door inside the rooms. Most hotels can provide cribs or roll-away beds for small children sharing a room with their parents.

Length of Stay and Season

Other factors affecting the price of a hotel room are the length of stay, the season of the year, and the day of the week the guests stay. Some hotels, particularly in Europe, offer weekly rates at a savings to the client.

Rooms needed for a business meeting may be rented for a special day rate that permits guests to use a room during the day or to stay beyond normal check-out time. Other partial rates may be available. Day rates, sometimes called "use rates," are often half the regular rate.

In the United States many hotels that cater primarily to business travelers are busy on week-days but not on weekends. To smooth out their occupancy statistics, the hotels offer weekend prices that are simply discounts from the normal rate or are packages with some restrictions.

In resort areas subject to seasonal demand, hotel rates rise and fall with the seasons. These fluctuations are often a reliable indicator of the best time to visit a vacation area. High season for hotels often corresponds to peak season for airfares.

All destinations, even big cities, are affected to some extent by yearly cycles. Immediately after major holidays, especially Christmas, travel declines while most people worry about all the money they have just spent. Hotels offer special rates to attract guests during these slack periods. Like airlines, hotels have extremely expensive fixed overheads that must be met regardless of the number of guests. If occupancy rates begin to drop or tend to drop in a predictable way at certain times of the year, a hotel can act quickly to stimulate additional bookings by using a variety of attractive discounts.

Special Rates

Hotels frequently reduce the cost of rooms to their best clients. Typically, large companies are good clients of hotels, and their employees are given what is known as a corporate, or commercial, rate. A hotel that grants a corporate rate to the employees of a company hopes to become their automatic choice. Corporate rates represent a negotiable discount on the normal room rate and may not always be commissionable to travel agents.

If a company, organization, tour operator, or travel agency books a block of rooms for a group, the hotel usually offers a group rate for each room. Group rates represent a discount similar to the corporate rate.

An organization that arranges a convention or meeting in a hotel will expect the largest discount of all on the room rates. Conventions and meetings typically use so many other services of the hotel and give the hotel so many other opportunities to make money, particularly at the bar, that competition for them is keen.

Family plan originated in 1952 with the Westin Hotel organization, then called Western International. The plan permits children under certain ages to occupy their parents' room at no additional charge. A few hotels interpret family plan very liberally to include all children, regardless of age.

To maintain the baby-boomer market, hotels are beginning to target children. Properties such as Hyatt provide games, special menus, kids' passports, bonuses, and reduced rates. In addition, regional activities such as hayrides, swimming with dolphins, panning for gold, or trips to local sites are also planned.

Special Features

Hotels provide special features for guests, and these features affect room costs. Resort hotels compete to have the biggest pools, both indoor and outdoor, the most tennis courts lighted for night play, beach clubs, saunas, game rooms, and nightclubs. In many instances, use of these facilities is free, but it is not uncommon for hotels to charge to light the courts for tennis at night or require greens fees for the hotel-owned golf course.

Hotels also provide saunas, racquet clubs, scuba instruction, jogging tracks, and in-room movies. Special touches like round-the-clock room service or a small chocolate mint on the pillow add to the pleasure of a stay.

Hotel Perks

In a strategy similar to the airline industry's, some hotel chains offer frequent-stay incentives for guests who utilize their properties. Frequent-stay programs usually are packaged in one of four ways: awarding stays for accumulated stays (or points); awarding merchandise for accumulated stays (or points); the immediate reward of increased service during stays; or some combination of these. Benefits include additional amenities or upgrades in service. Business perks can include electronic mail messages, FAX service, morning newspapers, airline confirmations such as QuikTix, and video express checkout. Service upgrades could include corner or deluxe rooms, complimentary hors d'oeuvres, compact-disc players, or just fluffy feather pillows. Rewards are not always given on negotiated or discount room rates.

Finally, if a hotel has a particular history, some unusual architectural design, or subtle ambience, the rooms are likely to be more expensive than those in a hotel with less character. Guests should expect to pay more to sleep in a room that was once graced by George Washington or Henry VIII, to wander through a hotel that was a castle, or to eat in a revolving restaurant.

Typical published room rates are called "rack rates." A run-of-the-house rate (ROH) is a flat rate that a property agrees to offer a group for any of its available rooms at the time of arrival.

Government Grading Systems

Among countries where tourism regulation is a governmental function, some have established a system of monitoring and grading hotels. Yet no universal standards exist to permit direct comparison of hotels in different countries. Government grading systems reflect national standards and are

Meals

The room rate does not include meals unless specifically stated. Meal plans vary according to the customs of each country. In the United States meals are not normally included in the cost of the room. The room rate is said to be *EP,* which is an abbreviation for European Plan, meaning no meals. In other countries, particularly in resort areas, hotels offer a choice of meal plans.

EP:European Plan — No meals; typical in the United States and most big cities of the world.

CP: Continental Plan — Rate includes continental breakfast of rolls, jam, and coffee. This plan is affected by breakfast customs worldwide. Juice or fruit is not common with breakfast in many countries. Some hotels and tour operators make a special point of including juice as an attraction for the American tourist.

BP: Bermuda Plan — Similar to B and B (Bed and Breakfast). Rate includes full breakfast but no other meals.

MAP: Modified American Plan — Rate includes breakfast and one other meal, usually dinner. Popular in the resorts of the Bahamas, Bermuda, the Caribbean, and Mexico, where the breakfast provided tends to be American-style. In Europe this plan may be called "demi-pension," and breakfast is continental style.

AP: American Plan — Rate includes breakfast, lunch, and dinner. This plan is sometimes known as "full board" or "pension." Breakfast is either full or continental. Cruise ships and resorts such as Club Med offer American Plan.

Many hotels, even in exotic locations, have adopted an international menu that caters to the normal diet of the American traveler. Guests at a hotel in the Orient may be given a choice of Eastern or Western food. Certain local specialties remain. An Israeli breakfast often includes eggs and smoked fish. A Scandinavian breakfast includes fish and smoked meats.

Generally speaking, hotels that offer BP or MAP are in resort locations where guests are expected to stay a few days; hotels with EP have a high proportion of transients. Some hotels limit choice from the menu for MAP guests, and diners who want a specialty such as lobster pay a surcharge.

Because resort hotels in some areas offer guests a choice of EP, BP, or MAP, it is important to recognize the benefits of each. MAP is particularly beneficial if a hotel is isolated or if eating out is expensive. MAP guests save the cost and inconvenience of transportation and do not have to worry about making dinner reservations. Lunch at a hotel may be as simple as a sandwich. It is usually less expensive to eat dinner as an MAP guest than to pay a la carte. Furthermore, with MAP the total cost of the vacation can be predicted more accurately.

Dining in the same hotel restaurant can be dull even though menus are changed nightly. Some hotels provide a dine-around option that gives guests a credit toward dinner at another hotel or in some restaurants. EP and BP are designed to permit flexibility and freedom and are desirable whenever a variety of restaurants is nearby with competitive prices.

Historical Perspective

A Pioneer Hotel Guide to the Trade

In 1928 Elwood Ingledue created the Hotel Informant, a brochure rack with approximately seventy listings that appeared in member hotel lobbies. This system was limited to the size of the rack, so in 1939 Ingledue came up with an index to the Informant that evolved into today's *Hotel and Travel Index*.

In 1939, however, hotels were worlds away from what they are today. The first issue of the *Index*, consisting of sixty-four pages, noted that United Airlines had increased its fleet to sixty twin-engine airplanes. Another advertisement for the Hollywood Knickerbocker Hotel was endorsed by Kate Smith and listed the price of a double room at $6 per night. By the end of this first year, the *Index* claimed to have listings for all the reputable hotels in the eleven western states. By 1941 it had published a list of hotels in Hawaii and Mexico.

In 1946 the *Index* began listing its first European hotels and urged the creation of a "universal reservation form which can be used by all agents." Ingledue was the first to persuade hotels to pay agents commissions and to convince agents to consider hotels as important sources of income. In 1947 the *Index* began printing a symbol denoting the hotels that were paying commissions to agents. By 1950, it began listing its first hotels in the Orient, Asia, and the Pacific.

Ingledue remembers his first attempts at bridging the gap between hotels and travel agents. "The early days was an era when there were very few travel agents, and they sold only cruises." In 1986 Mr. Ingledue was elected to ASTA's Hall of Fame, a well-deserved honor for a pioneer of the travel industry.

Today, *Hotel and Travel Index*, published quarterly, is the world's largest and most widely used hotel directory.

---

affected by national pride. Many national tourist offices with branches in the United States can supply lists of hotels categorized by the government. The lists provide a useful starting point. Often the tourist offices can supply more detailed information about particular properties or direct agents to appropriate sources.

Making a Hotel Reservation

Nearly 80 percent of travel-agency hotel bookings are domestic United States reservations. Most travel-agency hotel bookings are made through toll-free 800- numbers and computerized reservations systems (CRSs). Hotel representatives, reservations services, and direct calls to hotels account for the remainder of the bookings. Travel agents use 800- numbers to book hotels for vacation travelers more than for any other type of client. They use hotel representatives or reservations services most often for international travelers, computerized reservations systems most often for business travelers. When time is short, the agent must choose the best method to check availability and price and to confirm the space quickly.

Guaranteed reservations will protect late arrivals but will also be automatically charged to a credit card if the customer does not show up.

Rep Firms

Rep firms, diverse organizations that represent and provide creative services for the world's hotels, are a steadily growing, integral component of the complex hotel industry. The firms' purpose is to accept reservations and provide marketing and sales help for the members of these groups of hotels. In this capacity they can be regarded as something of a huge sales force.

For a hotel they provide

- Reservations systems using 800- numbers
- A staff that works extended hours
- Tie-ins with airlines' CRSs
- Pooled marketing, including direct mail, sales calls to agents, advertising, and participation at trade shows
- The image enhancement of being represented by such firms as Leading Hotels of the World, Preferred Hotels, and so on

For travel agents they provide

- Ease of reservation
- Substantial discounts
- Speed of commission payments
- Liaison with independent properties

Hotels pay to belong to these organizations, typically with a one-time initiation fee and annual dues. In return they expect top-notch advertising and marketing support. Agencies that deal with hotels associated with these firms are reassured that they are selling quality properties, a real need if the area of a hotel is unknown. Commissions are paid promptly. Some firms even process agent commissions, relieving agencies of dealing with foreign-currency checks.

Because of centralized operations and inventory control, property managers are more willing to release rooms to the rep firm, improving agents' chances of getting last-room availability. In addi-

tion, toll-free numbers are a cost savings for agents and give them ready access to off-shore hotel availability. Confirmations can be immediate or, at most, available in twenty-four hours for remote properties.

The Sheraton Los Angeles Harbor Hotel in San Pedro, California, in June 1992 became the first United States hotel to let guests check in solely by inserting a credit card into a slot, with no human interaction at all. This practice is expected to become more common within the decade.

Common Agency Problems with Hotels

Not surprisingly, many agency problems relating to hotels concern commission. Listed below are a few common examples.

- A client with a guaranteed arrival who does not show up at the hotel is automatically charged for the room, but the agent who made the booking does not receive commission.
- Upon check-in the client receives a lower rate than originally quoted. The front desk creates a new booking at that rate, the agency booking becomes a no-show, and therefore no commission is received.
- The client directly contacts the hotel to change his arrival date. Again a new booking is created, and the original booking is deleted along with the commission.
- Often commission checks list only the parent holding-company name, so that the agent has no idea what client or hotel the money is for.
- The hotel books a number of rooms under one name, as one reservation. Commission is given only for one name rather than for numerous rooms.

Computer Reservations

A few years ago this was a familiar story: a travel agent trying to book a room at a chain hotel learns from the CRS that the property is sold out. Then the agent dials the toll-free number of the central reservations system of the hotel and is again informed that the hotel is full. Finally, the agent calls the hotel long-distance and easily manages to book the space.

Better computers are changing the story. Hotel managers, less fearful of overbooking their properties, are surrendering more rooms to airline systems and to hotel central reservations centers. This does not suggest that hotel managers do not always control the last rooms in a house. They do, and the agent who calls the right person at the right time can often break space for a client.

The large hotel chains, all of which have computerized central reservations systems, use one of two controls to keep track of space at their individual properties: status control or inventory control. Status control is the more primitive of the two methods. It gives a free sell right to the airline and central reservations computers until the hotel changes its status to sold out. Hotel managers tend to close out a property early to avoid the risk of overbooking, so the agent calling such a hotel directly stands a chance of finding space.

The Caribbean Hotel Association (CHA) has introduced its own computerized reservations system to service 200 hotels in the Caribbean. Called CHARMS, Caribbean Hotel Association Reservations and Management System, it provides travel agents with last-room availability and instant confirmation of rooms.

Inventory control, on the other hand, permits hotels to allocate a specific number of rooms to the computers, which automatically close out the properties once those rooms are sold. Hotel managers, knowing the maximum number of rooms the computers can sell, will surrender more rooms to a central reservations system than if they were operating under status control. Agents are less likely to find last-minute space by calling a hotel that practices inventory control than they would find at a property that relies on status control.

Why would any chain use status control if it is capable of keeping track of inventory? Because status control is easier for the individual properties. Under an inventory-control system, the hotel manager must constantly monitor the inventory given to the computers, adding to it or subtracting from it as the situation warrants.

Decisions to hold a room in reserve explain why an agent can sometimes find space through an 800-number, when the CRS screen shows that a hotel is sold out. Often, there is also a time lag between hotel and airline computers on booking and status messages, evoking the specter of overbooking. It is the policy of hotel chains to guarantee all bookings taken by an airline system even if a sold-out message is in the pipeline on the way back from the hotel to the agent's CRS.

Telephone or FAX

Surveys indicate that the more upscale the hotel, the greater the likelihood of travel agents using the telephone for bookings. This is primarily due to the fact that the complexity of the hotel booking increases for more upscale properties. Likewise, the majority of budget hotel bookings are made by telephone. This is due to the fact that many budget properties, especially the independents, are not in any CRS system.

Obtaining a telephone confirmation directly from the hotel can seem like a good idea, but the primary drawbacks are expense and time-zone differences. Controlling telephone expense is a major goal for most businesses. Individual office policies differ, but many travel agencies will not make long-distance hotel-request calls for clients until all other reservation channels have been tried. Agents who make such calls often ask permission to charge the cost to the client.

Large agencies or those that specialize in extensive foreign bookings have telex and FAX facilities. The use of a FAX machine to make a booking is increasing. Cost is about the same as a phone call, and the process avoids time-zone and language problems.

Sheraton introduced the first automatic electronic reservations system, Reservatron I, in 1958.

160

Hotel Reference Guides

Regardless of how hotel bookings are made, travel agents typically require additional hotel information other than that provided through the CRS or through the hotel representative.

Directories can present either objective or subjective information. Objective information consists of the facts and figures about a hotel, including the number and kinds of rooms and special features such as swimming pools, restaurants, and sports facilities. Subjective information consists of evaluations made about service and ambience.

The following is a brief description of the three most popular travel-industry references. See how each guide differs in the way they describe Marriott's Camelback Inn Resort in Scottsdale, Arizona.

Official Hotel Guide (OHG)

The *OHG* is published once a year in three volumes, each consisting of about 1,000 pages. In total, the books contain listings for about 30,000 hotels. The publication's features include a ten-category classification of properties, from moderate tourist class to superior deluxe, maps showing all the hotels for a particular area, and detailed reservation information.

● MARRIOTT'S CAMELBACK INN RESORT, GOLF CLUB & SPA

Superior Deluxe   Map Location **E-1/99**

ADDRESS 5402 E. Lincoln Dr. (85253)	PHONE (602)948-1700
AFFILIATIONS Marriott Hotels & Resorts	ROOMS 423	FAX (602)951-8469
CREDIT CARDS AE CB DC DIS JCB MC VISA	COMMISSION R-10	TELEX — — —

Description/Location: Secluded Desert Resort and Golf Club (1936) set on a 120-acre private estate, between the Mummy and Camelback Mountains — 3 miles from downtown Scottsdale; 12 from airport — Renovations 1990

Accommodations: Individual casitas with landscaped entrance, air conditioning, color TV, radio, phone, kitchenette and patio or balcony — Wheelchair accessibility

Facilities/Services: Restaurants include The Navajo Room for family dining, the gourmet, award-winning Chaparral Dining Room, the Oasis Lounge, and Sprouts Restaurant at the spa — 25 Meeting Rooms for up to 2200, theater-style and 1600, banquet-style — 36 holes of USGA Championship Golf — 25,000-square-foot European Health Spa — 10 Tennis Courts — 3 Swimming Pools

Awards & Distinctions: Mobil Five Stars 1968-1992 — AAA Five Diamonds 1976-1992

Rates: European Plan
Single/Double/Twin with Bath $95-130/175-275
Suite 155-395/260-835
Each Additional Person 10

Max rates Jan-Jun & Sep-Dec — Tax 9.05% — Trade Discount: 30%

RESERVATIONS:
Reps: UI MAR PSR₃ — Toll-Free: 1(800)24-CAMEL
CRS: Apollo, Datas II, Pars, Sabre & SystemOne

Reprinted by permission of
Official Hotel Guide, published by Reed travel Group.

Hotel and Travel Index

Published quarterly, the *Hotel and Travel Index* contains information about 45,000 hotels. It also provides details on hotel facilities, rates, commissions, and seasonal packages. The *Hotel and Travel Index* also contains destination maps that show regions, countries, and cities. It is also a great source for numerous hotel advertisements. The *Hotel and Travel Index* is a publication of the Reed Travel Group.

● **MARRIOTT'S CAMELBACK INN** 423 R SWB/DWB $225-275 (MAR)(UI)
5402 E Lincoln Dr, 85253, Tel: 602-948-1700, 800-228-9290, 800-831-1000 Ⓐ Ⓟ Ⓢ ♦
See Advertisement Page 53 and Map Page 46

Reprinted by permission of *Hotel and Travel Index.*

The Star Service

The Star Service is a subjective guide to more than 10,000 hotels and more than a hundred cruise ships throughout the world. They use paid travel writers and correspondents to update the reports on a regular basis. The reviews are very complete and can range from the size of a room's closets to the ambience of the lobby to decor of the rooms. Unlike the other guides, *The Star Service* accepts no advertising.

MARRIOTT'S CAMELBACK INN RESORT AND GOLF CLUB, 5402 E. Lincoln Dr., four miles from center, 11 miles northeast of Phoenix, near Red Lion's La Posada and Marriott's Mountain Shadows, is one of the Southwest's most admired deluxe convention resorts and able to please a wide range of clients, from groups, seminars, and conventions to discriminating individuals. Mountain views surround the complex of desert sandstone cottages in landscaped grounds. A large, inviting Western lobby with beehive fireplace breathes history, with paintings on adobe brick walls and stenciled beams on ceiling. One lounge features nightly entertainment and another overlooks a pool on several levels. One highly regarded restaurant offers Continental gourmet specialties and mountain views while another less formal room with a Southwest atmosphere serves all meals and features a buffet on the garden terrace at the north pool. Of the three pools, the large south pool has the most deck space and privacy. An elaborate spa center with a spectrum of treatments and services is the newest attraction here, complete with hot and cold plunge pools, Swiss saunas, and treadmills with built-in TVs. Two 18-hole golf courses are just five minutes away by car. Ten tennis courts (five lighted), lawn games, a playground, riding, cycling, game room, whirlpools, and shops complete the amenities. Golf cart service links low-rise accommodation buildings scattered on different levels. Accommodations, which have emerged recently from a thorough updating, are all privately owned and leased back to management for nightly rentals. Most casitas are large, flat-roofed stucco cottages of one or two stories with two double beds, refrigerators, wet bars, ranges, thermostats, and standard-size baths. Octagonal rooms with an Indian flavor have cathedral ceilings, muted earth tones, matching floral drapes and spreads, TVs, and solid Western wood furniture. Property exhibits more regional charm than its garden-club sibling, Marriott's Mountain Shadows, and leaves little to be desired overall. 423 units. $95-$290 single or double. Wynn Tyner, mgr. (C) Marriott. Phone (800) 242-2635, (602) 948-1700. Fax (602) 951-8469.

©1992 *Star Service.* Reprinted by permission of the publisher.

Marriott's Camelback Inn Resort, Golf Club, and Spa

**Marriott's Camelback Inn
Resort, Golf Club and Spa
5402 East Lincoln Drive
Scottsdale, Arizona 85253
(602) 948-1700
Fax: (602) 951-8469**

LOCATION	12 miles northeast of Phoenix Sky Harbor Airport in Paradise Valley. Minutes from downtown Scottsdale. Commercial shuttle service available to resort.
DIRECTIONS	Exit Hohokam Expressway, travel north to 44th St., turn left on Tatum Blvd. and right on Lincoln Dr.
423 GUEST ROOMS/ 50 SUITES	423 Pueblo styled casitas, including 50 sundecks and suites. Seven suites have private pools. Rooms have private patios, refrigerators, servi-bars, desks, sitting area, remote control TV, make-up mirrors, hair dryers, and in-room safes.
RESTAU-RANTS/ LOUNGES	The *Chaparral Dining Room,* one of the Southwest's finest continental restaurants. The *Navajo Room,* authentic Southwestern decor at breakfast, lunch and dinner. The *North Garden Buffet* specializes in exotic buffets. *Sprouts Health Eatery,* serves calorie controlled spa cuisine for breakfast and lunch. Spa cuisine served in all of our food and beverage facilities. *Dromedary's* and the *Oasis Lounge & Patio,* snacks and light fare. The *Chaparral Lounge,* dancing and entertainment nightly. The *Golf Club Restaurant* serves breakfast and lunch daily.
HEALTH SPA	25,000 square foot world class, European Health Spa. State of the art fitness and exercise facilities, beauty salon, indulgent body and beauty treatments, Wellness Center in association with Dr. Kenneth Cooper.
RECREA-TIONAL FACILITIES	Two 18-hole championship golf courses, clubhouse restaurant and pro shop, practice greens and driving range. Ten tennis courts, five illuminated for night play. Three outdoor swimming pools, jacuzzi's, children's playground, basketball, volleyball, table tennis, shuffleboard, 9 hole "pitch & putt" course, mountain hiking trail, bicycle rental.
SHOPS/ SERVICES	Gift shop, ladies boutique, mens shop, sport shop, swim shop, spa boutique. Beauty Salon, concierge staff, babysitting, children's programs, business services, Hertz desk, valet, washer/dryers, free parking.
PLACES TO SEE/THINGS TO DO	Shopping in old Scottsdale, Fifth Avenue shops, Scottsdale Fashion Square and the exclusive Borgata. Horseback riding, desert jeep tours, hot air ballooning. Heard Museum, Phoenix Zoo, Scottsdale Center for the Arts, Arizona State University, Phoenix Cardinals, Phoenix Suns, horseracing, greyhound racing, Grand Canyon and Sedona.

For details, rates, and reservations, call us direct at (602) 948-1700, your travel professional, or toll-free in the United States and Canada 800-228-9290.

Reprinted by permission of
Marriott's Camelback Inn Resort, Golf Club and Spa.

Group Hotel Reservations

Groups contribute greatly to the profit of an agency, and these bookings are eagerly pursued. Although the mechanics involved in making a group reservation are the same as for an individual, there are certain important differences. Hotel bookings for groups fall into several categories.

■ **A Request for Three to Ten Rooms.** With each hotel the minimum number of rooms that constitutes a group may differ. At a certain point the reservationist may transfer the travel agent to the group department. When a rate is quoted by a group department, the travel agent must inquire if the rate is net (non-commissionable) or gross (commission to agent included). If the rate is net, the agent adds the markup.

■ **Hotels as Part of a Tour.** The travel agency often puts together tour packages for small groups that involve one or more hotel bookings. Room reservations may be made directly with the individual properties or through a ground operator with experience in the area. Room rates are often quoted run-of-the-house (ROH) and will depend on the size of the group. ROH rates represent a discount from rack rates.

■ **Large Groups, Conventions, Meetings and Seminars.** Large groups that have many special needs are the province of the experienced meeting planner. Hotels are often booked years in advance. The meeting planner deals directly with the hotel, negotiating rates and making on-site inspections.

Even the largest group may be booked in one name although individual names (the rooming list) must be supplied to the hotel before arrival. The hotel will require a deposit and signed contracts.

A travel agent consistently involved with group hotel booking generally works for a larger agency, a tour operator, or an incentive house. Dealing with groups is a specialized field. The less-experienced agent should become thoroughly comfortable making individual hotel reservations before proceeding to groups.

American Hotel & Motel Association

The trade association that represents the lodging industry in the United States is the American Hotel & Motel Association (AHMA). It is the umbrella organization for local and state chapters, including the District of Columbia, Puerto Rico, and the U.S. Virgin Islands. It is located at 1201 New York Ave., NW, Washington, DC, 20005-3917.

Overbooking

To be assured of a full house each night, hotels overbook their rooms knowing that a certain number of guests with confirmed reservations will not show up. Although hotels carefully calculate how much to overbook according to the days of the week and time of the year, the practice still creates problems. Existing policies or legal remedies to prevent problems are inadequate. Hotels can alleviate the problem of no-shows by insisting on deposits or guarantees, but there are still people who are delayed or negligent about canceling their reservations.

Guests do not always check out when they are expected to and may stay additional nights that have been reserved for someone else. Most states consider that innkeepers have the right to request a guest's departure if the room is needed for an incoming reservation. In practice, hotels tend to evict only undesirable guests. As a result, hotels may be faced with more confirmed guests than available rooms.

In the event of overbooking, most hotels help clients secure alternative reservations. The policy varies from hotel to hotel, but typically when a hotel cannot accommodate a guest with confirmed reservations, it tries to substitute nearby accommodations of equal quality. This policy is called "walking the guest." The hotel also agrees to compensate for any difference in the room rates and to provide free transportation to the substitute hotel. As soon as space becomes available, guests may transfer to their original hotel.

These attempts do not always satisfy the disappointed guest. Unlike airlines, hotels are not required to reveal publicly that they occasionally overbook, so the shock to the client may be greater when it happens.

The biggest complaint about properties from business travelers is overbooking; pleasure travelers complain most about service.

The Future of Accommodations

By 2020, a partnership between the United States and Japan could create a new $28 billion space resort. The property, resembling a gyrosope, would contain sixty-four rooms. Guests would be carried back and forth from earth to the resort on a space plane. Once aboard, guests would be protected by artificial gravity. Tour options would include space walks, astronomical observation, space-experiment tours, space theater, and, later, moon excursions. As of today, no price tag has been developed for these packages.

Summary

A hotel is much more than just food and shelter. Some properties are members of chains, franchises, or management companies, and others are independent. Due to changing demographics, two of the fastest growing segments of the industry today are budget properties and all-suites.

Many factors affect the price of a room within a property. One of the most significant of these is yield management. Other variables include currency fluctuations, property location, room location, room size, amenities, length of stay, seasonality, and special rate structures. Meal plans may also be a consideration.

Hotel reservations can be made via a CRS, telephone, FAX, or rep firm. Guaranteed reservations help to eliminate overbooking on the part of the hotel property, ensuring client satisfaction.

Chapter Wrap-up

REVIEW QUESTIONS

1. Why is the choice of accommodations sometimes more complicated than the choice of transportation?
2. What hotel features would the following clients prefer?
   a. The business traveler
   b The vacationer interested in sports and relaxation
   c. The vacationer touring by car
3. Which factors most affect the cost of a hotel room?
4. Are there times of the year or days of the week when hotels in your area offer special rates?
5. At which destinations might MAP be a preferable option?

DISCUSSION TOPICS

Overbooking

Upon arrival at one of the casino resorts in Atlantic City, G. Whiz, the tour escort for a group of forty motorcoach passengers, has been informed that another group has extended its reservations for one additional night. Therefore, the property is overbooked and must accommodate the first group's extended stay and walk G. Whiz's group. G. Whiz has a copy of the original contract between his tour company and the hotel confirming a block of twenty-two rooms for a three-night stay. What options does G. Whiz have? Whom should he contact first? What can he tell the passengers who are waiting on the motorcoach? Could this have been avoided? If so, how?

World Travelers

Mr. and Mrs. Moneybags are seasoned world travelers. Their former travel agent has retired, and they are seeking a suitable replacement. They wish to take a three-month tour to see "the real United States" by train, plane, and rental car. What types of properties should a good counselor recommend? What amenities should such properties offer? Where should these properties be located? Where could the counselor search for additional information?

Neighbors

Every year Mr. Solitaire takes a summer vacation. This year his neighbors, the Joneses, have convinced him to try their favorite retreat, Camp Woodsy Resort. As a matter of fact, they already have reservations there for October so they know exactly what flights to take, what room to request, what meal plan to choose, and how much the trip will cost. To keep up with the Joneses, Mr. Solitaire called the resort and made his reservation. Upon arrival, he is amazed with what he has found and how much it will cost. What factors could have affected the price? Why is this property a good choice for the Joneses but not for Mr. Solitaire?

Lost Reservation

Mr. and Mrs. Dewey Dive and their two children arrived for their winter-escape vacation in Cozumel, Mexico. In addition to all of their scuba and snorkel equipment, luggage, and winter coats, they have remembered to bring their hotel confirmation supplied by their travel agent. As they check in, the front-desk clerk informs them in his halting English that he has no record of their reservation and the hotel is fully booked. How could this happen? Who is responsible for their inconvenience and possible incurred costs? What options might they have that they are unaware of?

Tours
Chapter 8

Introduction

At some point, many people purchase a stereo system composed of a receiver/amplifier, turntable, speakers, tape deck, and CD player. All of these different products may be purchased as separate components. Yet each component must be compatible with the others. Frequently they are bought as a single unit without substantial modification. In the same way, various travel components of transportation, accommodations, and sightseeing can be purchased from different suppliers through a single retailer, the travel agent.

Components of a Tour

The components of a tour are put together and packaged by a tour operator or tour wholesaler and offered for sale to the public through the travel agent. Some travel agencies also package tours that they sell exclusively. Although tours offer different features and options, all tour operators and wholesalers make money by selling the same tours to many different clients.

The major components of a tour are transportation (air, rail, motorcoach, ship), accommodations, meals, and other features such as transfers or sightseeing. Some of these features are difficult, even impossible, to reserve in advance. Some tours offer a minimum of features; others are all-inclusive. Yet all tours are alike in presenting a package of features for purchase as a single unit.

Most tours feature transportation as part of the package. For example, a fly/drive consists of air

Tour-Related Careers

Convention and Visitors Bureau
Representative
Host/Hostess
Marketing Representative
Operations Manager

Reservationist
Tour Guide
Tour Manager/Escort
Negotiator

Tour Escort

All escorted tours are accompanied by a tour escort, sometimes called a tour conductor, tour manager, tour director, or tour courier. Although many escorts know a great deal about the social, political, historical, and physical features of the places on the itinerary, their primary responsibility is to ensure the smooth operation of the tour. They act as the tour operator's representatives in the field and must be capable of making quick decisions, if necessary. The tour escort must be patient, adaptable, imaginative, good-humored, tolerant, and meticulous with details.

Any tour escort should know the contents of the brochure used to promote the tour — the precise itinerary, the features, the liability and responsibility clauses, and the refund and cancellation agreements. An escort needs to prepare even more carefully if the tour is not one of a regular series on the same itinerary using the same hotels, or if it is the first of a series of tours. Should any question arise once the tour is underway, the escort must be able to answer it accurately and must not erroneously admit error or liability on behalf of the operator.

The escort should have a list of all passengers, known as the "manifest," and a rooming list indicating singles, twins, and triples. Participants with disabilities or special dietary needs should be noted, and the escort should check that necessary arrangements have been made for these special needs with hotels and restaurants. Operators also provide the tour escort with a listing of vendor contacts and phone numbers in case of emergencies or changes.

Once en route the escort should know all the interesting sights between major destinations. A detailed road map, literature from state tourist boards, and the driver of the coach are especially useful sources of information. The driver may be able to supply specific information on road conditions, convenient rest stops, and the time it will take to get from point A to point B. It is important to establish a good relationship with the driver from the outset, in case of emergencies or special opportunities. Each itinerary includes allowances for meal and rest stops. As a rule of thumb, a motorcoach should not travel more than three hours without a stop. The escort must endeavor to show that all rules such as smoking and rotation policies are designed to benefit the participants and not the escort or driver.

Some companies require a daily report mailed by the escort while the tour is still in progress. At the conclusion of the tour, escorts can expect to be tipped for their services, but they should never indicate that tipping is required or expected. Some escorts may suggest to the group that a driver who has accompanied them throughout the tour would appreciate tips. As a guideline, many tour operators advise all passengers before departure that normal tips are a certain amount per day, per passenger, for both driver and escort.

transportation (airfares shown separately) and a car rental. An air/sea or fly/cruise combines air transportation (airfares shown separately) with a ship. A rail tour includes transportation by train. In fact, if sleepers are provided, trains, like ships, can be considered to offer both transportation and accommodations. Finally, a motorcoach tour uses buses to carry tour participants from destination to destination to visit major sightseeing attractions. Transfers are sometimes provided between airlines, cruiselines, or motorcoaches.

Clients may be interested in purchasing a tour to save money on an accompanying airfare, intending to use only some or, in some instances, none of the features. Features that clients deliberately don't use are known as "throw-aways."

Tours need hotel properties that are equipped to handle groups. If the tour visits a major city, the hotels tend to be large and well-known. They must be able to register groups efficiently and to serve group meals. Because all tour participants pay the same price, their rooms must be similar, and larger hotels are usually able to provide similar if not identical rooms. Other hotel considerations are proximity to sightseeing attractions, transfer services, parking for the motorcoach, and handicapped accessibility.

Some standard sightseeing attractions are usually included in a tour. In most cases these are recognizable tourist draws, such as Walt Disney World, Busch Gardens, and Cypress Gardens in Florida. Depending on the special interests of the group, other sightseeing can be added to the package. Most attractions are prepaid, and the tour escort will have tickets or vouchers for the passengers to enter the attractions. Sometimes these must be obtained at the attraction itself, in which case the tour escort precedes the group and pays the admission fee.

When meals are included in the package but not provided at the hotel, many are served at such well-known restaurants as Brennan's or Arnaud's in New Orleans. Often these establishments provide special tour menus or limit passenger choices to four or five entrees. More deluxe tours offer a la

IT Numbers

The International Air Transport Association (IATA) requires that tours outside the United States conform to certain regulations to qualify for special group airfares and IT numbers. IATA requires that the tour include

■ Air transportation on the flights of one or more IATA members.

■ Accommodations for the duration of the tour.

■ At least one other feature, such as transfers, a sightseeing tour, or a car rental. If tour participants leave from the United States, the cost of the tour must not be less than 20 percent of their airfare.

IATA must also approve the brochure that promotes the tour to the public. Once the tour is approved, it receives an identifying number that is either assigned by IATA or submitted by the tour operator. This number is published in the brochure and is known as the "IT number." In most cases IT numbers allow travel agents to receive a higher commission on the international air tickets issued in conjunction with the tour.

carte dining to clients. Meals may be prepaid, or the passengers may sign their tabs and the tour escort will pay the entire bill prior to departure.

Tour Operators

The components of a tour are packaged by a tour operator or tour wholesaler. The terms *operator* and *wholesaler* are often used interchangeably to refer to the company that contracts the suppliers of accommodations, transportation, and sightseeing, and packages the tour for sale through travel agencies. Tour operators may sell directly to the public and may, in some cases, own retail travel agencies, such as American Express. Typically, a tour wholesaler works exclusively with travel agents, acting solely as an intermediary and paying a commission or offering a net rate to the retailer.

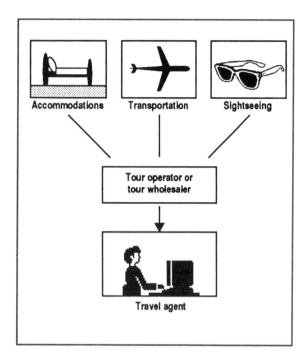

Accommodations   Transportation   Sightseeing

Tour operator or
tour wholesaler

Travel agent

Another distinction between operator and wholesaler is that the operator may actually operate aspects of the tour, own facilities or vehicles used on the tour, or employ personnel such as escorts and drivers. Wholesalers, on the other hand, leave operations to the individual suppliers or to a coordinating company at the destination, the ground operator. The tour operator/wholesaler produces a brochure describing the features of the tour and explaining cancellation penalties and the liability of all involved parties.

Suppliers can provide a shell to the tour operators or travel agencies who operate tours. A shell is an empty brochure that usually contains a photograph or two and some generic text with plenty of space for the operator to add the details of a particular trip. For example, an airline might supply a shell for a ski tour to the Rockies with photographs of snowy mountains and an aircraft. Tour operators insert the details of their tours and thus save time and expense.

The tour operator/wholesaler marks up the cost of the tour components before selling them to travel agents. Hotels and other suppliers typically reach an agreement with tour operators/wholesalers to reduce their prices when a predetermined volume of business has been generated. Since the selling price to the agent remains the same, the operator/wholesaler is rewarded for volume. But operators/wholesalers strive above all to earn a reputation for reliability, quality, and value in order to ensure repeat business.

Travel agencies also operate and sell their own tours, in effect blurring the distinctions between retailer and wholesaler. Some agency tours are uniquely designed for special groups and are offered annually or on a one-time basis. Others are intended for marketing to the general public and have a series of regular departures. All tours follow specific stages of development.

Stages of Tour Development

■ **Planning:** The idea for creating the tour can come from marketing inspiration, from an attractive offer by a supplier who would like group business, from a suggestion by a representative of an organization, or even from a repeat customer.

■ **Negotiation with Suppliers:** The services of suppliers must be secured. The agent negotiates prices and dates and an itinerary is created.

■ **Costing:** The tour must be broken down into its components and each cost factored. The selling price to the individual participant is based on a markup of the net cost, which should include all the costs of promotion and overhead.

■ **Promotion:** A brochure must be printed and the tour promoted through advertisements, direct mail, telemarketing, or group sales presentations.

■ **Documentation:** Incoming reservations must be processed, and tickets, vouchers, baggage tags, and so on must be sent to all confirmed participants.

■ **Operation:** The components of the tour must be coordinated by a tour manager, escort, host, or ground representative.

■ **Maintaining Good Relationships with Suppliers:** All suppliers must be given correct and final information, like rooming lists, names, and special needs of participants. Payment schedules must be established and followed.

Over fifty-six million travelers take tours or charters each year. Growth within this sector of the industry is expected to increase by 5 to 10 percent as the typical-group-traveler market continues to age.

Tour Costing

Negotiations require great skill. As tour operators develop good contacts with suppliers and their reputations grow, they are able to negotiate more favorable terms and include amenities that please clients.

Costing a tour is an art, relying on a realistic assessment of certain variables, most obviously the anticipated number of sales. In short, tour costing is based on that most dangerous of activities — assuming. Because certain costs are fixed, the risk of assuming can be minimized. This is especially true if the tour is broken down into its component parts so that an incorrect assumption in one relatively small area is not fatal to the entire tour.

Tour costing may proceed in a number of ways. Some tour operators establish the net cost to them for each individual participant. A markup sufficient to cover all promotional costs, staff salaries, overhead, and fair profit is then added to establish a selling price. The operator must still estimate the total number of tours to be sold before assigning these fixed costs fairly. The definition of fixed costs varies according to the kind of tour being operated. Motorcoaches, for example, cost a flat fee regardless of how many passengers are aboard.

Other operators, however, are able to negotiate agreements with suppliers whereby they only pay for what they use. A hotel room is a cost only if it is occupied. In industry jargon, some operators, therefore, are said to work from blocks of rooms, and others work with availabilities. The practice of blocking hotel rooms in advance means that sometimes hotels are available only through tour operators.

Staff salaries and brochure-production, marketing, and promotional costs are usually fixed costs and must be factored in before a single sale is made. Once reservations begin to come in, the costs become more variable and can be reduced or expanded as needed. If sales are high, more brochures are needed; if sales are low, more promotion may be needed.

Tour operators can economize in four main areas:
- Meal costs
- Hotel quality
- Length of stay in principal cities
- Sightseeing

The cost of meals is a significant item in any tour. By omitting meals and requiring tour participants to pay for their own, a tour operator can substantially reduce the cost of a tour. The kind of meals offered can also be adjusted. A tour operator who includes five dinners and five lunches is offering more than an operator who includes ten breakfasts. A tour operator who permits unlimited choice from the menu (a la carte) is offering more than an operator who arranges a set menu or limited choice. Escorted tours typically start after breakfast on the first day and conclude before dinner on the last. By using this rule of thumb, it is possible to calculate how many meals have been left out by the operator and what their total cost might be.

The quality of hotels is a second significant factor affecting the price of a tour. A deluxe tour will use better, more centrally located hotels with a wider range of services and facilities. Thrifty tours will use less expensive hotels and favor nights in smaller cities.

The hallmark of a good tour is a relaxed pace. On a deluxe tour participants remain longer at principal destinations. As a rule, tour operators try to avoid more than ten hours of travel or 350 miles in any one day. The quality of the roads and the terrain can significantly affect the distances that can be covered comfortably. Within the United States, ICC regulations limit drivers of motorcoaches to ten hours of driving per day.

Finally, the tour operator will look at the sightseeing to be included. Reductions in included sightseeing can significantly lower the cost of a tour. An indication of this reduction may be phrases in the itinerary such as "Balance of the day at leisure" or "Today you are free to explore. . . ."

Travel agents should identify those tour operators who include the entrance fees to sightseeing attractions and who transport their clients to them. Paid entrances can add up to a considerable sum of money, and major benefits of escorted travel are lost if the group does not arrive together at a museum or other sightseeing attraction.

Costing tours is a detailed process based on educated assumptions. It is only one step but perhaps is the most vital in the production of a tour. Travel agents who want to operate their own tours should study costing closely before committing to the effort.

Kinds of Tours

A distinction should be made between prearranged, or package, tours and custom-made tours. The rise of the tour operator who arranges package tours can be traced to several causes: the tremendous growth in the number of people at lower income levels who became interested in traveling; the economies that could be passed on to the consumer when tour operators could guarantee a certain volume of business to travel suppliers; and the recent inflation of prices that has made independent travel so expensive. Until the mid-1960s almost all vacation travelers had their arrangements custom-made by travel agents. The vast majority now purchase some kind of prearranged tour. The art of designing these custom-made tours involving many separate interlocking arrangements is now practiced by a relatively few skilled travel counselors.

Package Tours

Three major kinds of prearranged package tours are

- Independent tour
- Hosted tour
- Escorted tour

The Independent Tour

The independent tour is prepackaged but characterized by a minimum of structure and scheduled activities. Participants may not even realize they are on a tour because they do not travel with a group. They may depart and return any day; and the length of the tour can be adjusted to suit individual requirements. The purpose of the independent tour is to enable clients to obtain all the benefits of volume discounts and of prearranged, guaranteed rates without sacrificing independence and flexibility. Independent tours typically offer the minimum number of features required to qualify the arrangements as a tour.

In some independent programs participants can choose accommodations at different hotels listed in the brochure at different prices and can arrive any day of the year, although there are surcharges during especially popular periods. The tour can be extended indefinitely by adding a fixed extra-night rate for each additional night beyond the number specified in the tour.

According to the Environmental Protection Agency (EPA), a motorcoach vacation is an example of environmentally responsible travel. For example, if forty people travel together on one motorcoach, the trip is less harmful to the environment than if the same forty people took twenty individual automobiles.

Car rental permits flexibility; therefore such tours clearly cater to travelers who like to set their own pace, make their own way, and arrange each day to suit themselves. They are not committed to anything in terms of sightseeing or other prearranged features. The car provided is usually standard or economy size but can be upgraded to a larger model for an additional cost. The benefits to this type of independent tour are that participants select in advance a hotel to suit their budget, arrive independently on the day they choose, and travel each day in their own rental car.

Another kind of independent tour, the fly/drive, permits tour participants to stay at a number of different hotels rather than be based in a single one. This kind of tour is designed for those who wish to tour a particular region, stopping at a different place every one or two nights. Often the tour operator makes an agreement with a hotel chain so that participants can stay at any of its properties. Even as part of a tour, arriving unannounced is not recommended, particularly during high season.

The fly/drive is not the only kind of independent tour, although it is, perhaps, the most flexible and provides participants with the most freedom. There are many tours that simply provide participants with transportation to a destination, round-

170

Guides and Hosts

The term *guide* is often used to distinguish specialists in dispensing in-depth knowledge about a particular region, city, or building. On many escorted tours, a guide, sometimes called a "step-on guide," may join the tour for a day or half-day to conduct sightseeing of a particular city. These guides are highly trained, competent in several languages, and usually qualified by a difficult test as an official guide.

Instead of escorting tours that travel by motorcoach, train, or plane from destination to destination, travel agents may be asked to escort a group to a single destination. Once there, the agent becomes the equivalent of a host and dispenses information about optional sightseeing tours and local sights, and deals with any problems or emergencies that arise. The preparation for this kind of tour differs only slightly in that the escort/host must be more fully informed about a single destination.

trip transfers from the airport to their hotel, and accommodations for the number of nights they choose at a single hotel. Typically, these kinds of independent tours are popular in big cities where public transportation and sightseeing tours are plentiful or in resort areas where vacationers want only to relax.

The Hosted Tour

A hosted tour varies slightly from an independent tour. A host is available at each major tour destination to assist participants in planning their activities and to arrange excursions or sightseeing for them. Typically the hosts, who are representatives of the tour or ground operator, can be found at desks in the lobbies of all hotels featured on the tour.

On a hosted tour, participants can often arrive on the day of their choice and choose from a range of hotels. The length of stay may be adjusted. In contrast to the fly/drive programs, hosted tours typically offer sightseeing or entertainment features as part of the tour. The hosts will also offer many optional tour arrangements for purchase so that each day can be filled with organized events.

Such programs are similar to fly/drives, but without a rental car tour participants rely on the services and offerings of the host to enhance their vacation. The host does not typically accompany participants on any sightseeing tours and may only be personally available for an hour or so each day. When the host is not at the hotel, tour members can receive assistance and advice by calling the tour operator's local representative.

Hosted tours may visit more than one destination. In each city, participants normally receive round-trip transfers from airport to hotel, one sightseeing tour for general orientation, and the services of a host to help organize two or three days of free time. Major sights are briefly visited or noted, and travelers get a sense of where everything is and what they might want to revisit.

The Escorted Tour

Participants in an escorted tour enjoy a structured program of sightseeing, meals, transportation, and accommodations. As members of a group, they must schedule their arrival at the destination city to coincide with the tour departure. From that moment on, they travel together, usually by motorcoach, and are accompanied at all times by a professional escort.

The escort's responsibility is to ensure that the program operates properly. Specialized sightseeing tours of cities, museums, or art galleries can be given by local guides. Many cities require that all sightseeing tours be led by locally licensed guides. This is not to say that tour escorts lack knowledge. On the contrary, they are usually a gold mine of information on a wide variety of topics.

Unlike many independent or hosted tours during which participants spend several nights in the same city and hotel, escorted tours are characterized by movement. They may stop in a different city each night.

On independent and hosted tours, clients can

171

New England

9 Days - Escorted Tour NE from $1099

Plymouth • Newport • Mystic • White Mountains • Kennebunkport

15 Meals: 7 Breakfasts, 1 Lunch, 7 Dinners

Itinerary

Day 1: Arrive Boston
Welcome as you join Collette for a great vacation featuring all six of the scenic New England states, from the mansions of Newport to the rugged coastline of Maine. Today you arrive in BOSTON to start the tour.

Day 2: Plymouth - Newport
This morning you motor to PLYMOUTH, MASSACHUSETTS, where you will visit PLYMOUTH ROCK, the site of the Pilgrims landing in 1620. You will also tour a replica of the ship THE MAYFLOWER and then enjoy an interesting visit to PLIMOTH PLANTATION. Here you will see how the Pilgrims lived many years ago. Late this afternoon you will arrive in the seaside city of NEWPORT, RHODE ISLAND, where you will visit THE BREAKERS, one of Newport's fabled mansions and the home of Cornelius Vanderbilt. You will also travel along the rugged coastline of OCEAN DRIVE featuring fantastic views of coastal scenery. Your hotel is located in the very heart of Newport. Meals included **B, D**.

Day 3: Mystic Seaport Village - Vermont
Today you will travel into the Nutmeg State of CONNECTICUT. Your first stop will be MYSTIC SEAPORT VILLAGE. Here you are transported back to the days of whaling when many New Englanders were seafaring. This afternoon you motor through Connecticut, Massachusetts and into the Green Mountain state of VERMONT. Meals included **B, D**.

Day 4: Bennington - Newfane
Your sightseeing this morning includes a visit to BENNINGTON, where you will see the gravesite of ROBERT FROST and the

BENNINGTON BATTLE MONUMENT before driving over the world famous MOLLY STARK TRAIL. After lunch you will visit the quaint village of NEWFANE, considered by many to be the most beautiful of all New England villages. Meals included **B, D**.

Day 5: Vermont - New Hampshire
Today you will leave the Green Mountains of Vermont and travel into the WHITE MOUNTAINS of NEW HAMPSHIRE. You will pass traditional white steeple churches, quaint villages and tree covered mountainsides. This afternoon you will travel to FRANCONIA NOTCH and view THE OLD MAN OF THE MOUNTAIN. Meals included **B, D**.

Day 6: North Conway - Boothbay Harbor
This morning a short stop will be made in NORTH CONWAY. This bustling town features many factory outlet stores. Then you travel into the great state of MAINE to one of the state's prettiest coastal towns, BOOTHBAY HARBOR. Meals included **B, D**.

Day 7: Boothbay Harbor
Your day begins as you motor out to OCEAN POINT. Here the open ocean crashes over huge rocks which are so typical of the rockbound coastline of Maine. Then you depart on a two-hour narrated cruise of Boothbay Harbor. This afternoon you will enjoy a real DOWNEAST MAINE CLAMBAKE, featuring 2 lobsters, clams, corn and all the fixin's (steak and chicken substitutes are available). Tonight dinner and a broadway show are included at the CAROUSEL THEATRE. Meals included **B, L, D**.

Day 8: Boothbay Harbor - Boston
This morning you will travel to Freeport and visit the L.L. BEAN STORE. Time will also be available to browse this town which has many other factory outlet stores. Next you will travel

to the village of KENNEBUNKPORT for lunch and shopping, before journeying back to MASSACHUSETTS and the picturesque fishing village of ROCKPORT. Next you will view the FISHERMEN'S MEMORIAL in GLOUCESTER. Meals included **B, D**.

Day 9: Depart from Boston
Today you are homeward bound with many pleasant memories of your New England vacation.

Due to tour scheduling, flights home should not be booked prior to 12 noon.

YOUR HOTELS	
Day 1	Boston Park Plaza, Boston
Day 2	Viking Hotel, Newport
Day 3, 4	Stratton Mountain Inn, Stratton
Day 5	Town & Country Hotel, Gorham
Day 6,7	The Tug Boat Inn or the Ocean Gate Hotel, Boothbay Harbor
Day 8	Colonial Hilton or Vista International

*On some dates, alternate hotels may be used.

Land Rates Per Person*

	Twin	Single	Triple	Child
Sept 1-15	$1099	$1599	$1069	$599
Sept 26-Oct 12	$1199	$1699	$1169	$699
Oct 17-30	$1099	$1599	$1069	$599
Rest of Year	$1159	$1659	$1129	$659

*These prices are land only. See inside back cover for low air fares available with this tour.

Departs — August to October

THIS TOUR AVAILABLE AS A PRE-PLANNED FLY/ DRIVE VACATION. SEE INSERT FOR DETAILS.

control costs by selecting from a generous list of hotels ranging from inexpensive to deluxe. However, it is clearly impractical for a motorcoach on an escorted tour to drop off participants each night at different hotels and pick them up again in the morning. The time available for traveling and sightseeing would be sharply reduced. Clients, therefore, choose a grade of escorted tour that offers a certain level of accommodations throughout. Tours may be classified as Budget/Thrifty/Top Value/Economy at one end of the spectrum and Classic/Grand/Deluxe at the other. To reduce the selling price of a tour, the operator may eliminate certain meals or other features.

It may be difficult on an escorted tour to respect the religious commitments of all passengers. In many instances the escort can make arrangements for individuals to attend services. Sometimes, however, this may result in an unacceptable delay of the tour

Profile of an Escorted Tour Passenger

Typical escorted tour passengers

■ Come from households with annual incomes of more than $20,000.

■ Are 55 years of age or older.

■ Spend more time, more money, and travel further than independent travelers.

■ List their five top vacation choices as

Natural wonders/National parks

Historical sites

Warm weather/Beaches

Fall foliage sightseeing

Special events/Festivals

Special Benefits of Escorted Tours

Escorted tours offer some unique benefits.

■ **Relaxation:** Although popular myth suggests that escorted motorcoach tours are exhausting, they are, for many people, the most relaxing form of transportation. When the motorcoach starts in the morning, the sightseeing begins, and when it stops, it is magically in the right place for a visit, a meal, or an overnight stay. Border crossings, airport arrivals and departures, hotel check-ins, and baggage are all handled by someone else. Comfortable, modern, air-conditioned motorcoaches have large tinted windows, reclining seats, and lavatories. Some have domes in the roof to provide more spectacular views. Seating is rotated on most tours to ensure that everybody gets a chance to sit up front.

■ **Efficiency:** Escorted tours are carefully planned by tour operators who know the areas intimately. Besides providing their clients the benefit of volume purchasing, tours can maximize the use of time. Escorted tour participants are off to their first destination of the day while other travelers are still lingering over a cup of coffee trying to decide where to go. Each day's itinerary has been tested many times to ensure that the required mileage can be comfortably covered.

Special Prearranged Tours

Some special kinds of prearranged tours are worth mentioning. These are usually independent packages arranged to suit the needs of a particular group. Most of these programs focus on air arrangements, ground transportation, and a minimum of sightseeing.

Incentive Tours

An incentive tour is one offered as a prize or reward to employees of a company, usually for productivity or sales performance. Companies that offer incentive travel can set targets for their employees that will virtually ensure that the costs of the trip are covered by the increased sales or productivity.

The success of an incentive tour depends on the allure of travel as a motivating agent. Usually resorts, spas, or cruises are possible first choices for incentive destinations. Programs are developed through close cooperation between the travel agent, tour operator, and sponsoring company. Incentive tours represent a marketing area of great potential. When the group travels together, company spirit and loyalty are built. The company is prominently displayed as the host of every facet of the tour.

Spa vacations, one of today's more popular travel trends, are really nothing new. Stressed-out travelers have been journeying to such areas as Saratoga Springs since the late 1800s.

Convention Tours

Convention tours are designed for members of associations or corporations attending a convention, trade show, fair, exhibition, conference, or similar gathering. Like incentive tours, they are not typically advertised to the public but only to a special group. The travel counselor works very closely with a representative of the club, organization, or corporation and travel suppliers. Meeting planners are frequently asked to negotiate convention contracts.

Special Interest Tours

All over the world, people join together in

173

Survey on Escorted Tours

The bus had a flat tire, the food was unpalatable, the hotels were adequate at best, but everyone had a good time. Sound impossible? According to the National Escorted Tour Survey, this analysis is not only possible, but probable. The survey was designed to see why people choose escorted tours, what their expectations are, and, upon completion of the tour, how satisfactory the overall experience was. The survey revealed that in most cases, expectations are based on the destination itself and the reputation of the tour operator; satisfaction level is determined by the community relationship established en route.

Similarly, the National Tour Association (NTA) funded a survey in which people were asked their opinion of escorted tours.

■ 98 percent said that value is important when traveling.

■ 96 percent said it was important to feel safe in an unfamiliar place.

■ 93 percent said the opportunity to learn was an important reason for traveling.

■ 92 percent said the opportunity to share the travel experience was an important aspect of the trip.

clubs, societies, teams, or informal groups to pursue and discuss a particular interest or hobby. Many of these interests virtually demand travel. Photographers and painters, skiers and scuba divers, people learning a language or writing a book all find travel a natural part of their activities. Other special interest groups find reasons to travel. Bridge players attend tournaments; fans of *Star Trek* attend Trekkie conventions; devotees of Elvis Presley make pilgrimages to Graceland in Memphis.

Special interest group travel is a diverse but specialized field. It requires keen attention to detail, and many tour operators feel only those who share the interest can really design a successful tour. Some operators, however, choose to concentrate on special interest tours of all kinds.

Weekend Tours

Three-day, two-night motorcoach tours to nearby vacation resorts, usually scheduled over a weekend, are growing in popularity. For example, a tour operator located in Providence, Rhode Island, might offer regular weekend tours to Montreal, a resort in the Catskills, New York City, or an Atlantic City hotel. The motorcoach reaches these destinations as quickly and as inexpensively as the clients could drive to them. Although these tours have been traditionally and somewhat unfairly associated with older clients, weekend tours also attract younger people and are introducing a new generation to the advantages of this form of recreation.

Custom-Made Tours

Although tours permit great flexibility and choice of options, some clients still request arrangements custom-made to their individual requirements. A custom-made tour is known usually as an FIT. These initials originally stood for Foreign Independent Tour; today, however, the term is used to represent both foreign and domestic independent tours. The travel agent must either be an FIT specialist, work through an FIT department within the travel agency, or contact a tour wholesaler specializing in FIT arrangements. Individual agents who take on the task act as the personal wholesaler for these special clients.

Some agencies are equipped to do FITs, and some are not. Typically an agency that handles group tours of some kind and is used to acting as a tour operator can also handle FITs. Without the contacts and experience gained from group travel, the construction of an FIT is not cost-effective. The average retail agent who takes on an FIT will find the time spent and detail work far outweigh the financial return.

The FIT is almost exclusively pleasure travel. Because individual travelers do not benefit from the group savings a tour operator gets through volume, the FIT is more expensive than any packaged equivalent. The client pays for the expert

Historical Perspective

The Grand Tour

As the Renaissance took hold in the fifteenth and sixteenth centuries, tourism became a more secular activity. The Grand Tour, first popularized by the Elizabethan English, exemplified this change. Lasting between one to five years, the tour was a complete educational and cultural immersion for the sons of the well-to-do. The circuit generally began in the Low Countries, followed the Rhine into Switzerland, and involved a tedious crossing of the Alps en route to an intensive tour of central and southern Italy. The tour concluded after visits to southern France and Paris.

The young aristocrat toured with an entourage that included several servants and an enormous amount of paraphernalia. The party was led by a male tutor who was the forebear of today's tour guide. His knowledge and experience were crucial to the success and safety of the trip. Problems such as obtaining passports, exchanging money, handling reservations at inns and coffee houses, obtaining necessities, and repulsing would-be thieves were all part of the travel experience.

By the eighteenth century those participating in the Grand Tour benefited from an infrastructure developed to meet the needs of the European traveler. Regular horse-drawn coaches were available in parts of France and Italy, and an extensive network of scheduled passenger boats was offered to travelers on the Rhine, Loire, and other prominent rivers and canals. Travelers making brief stops en route were no longer limited to the primitive inns and hostels that were the legacies of medieval times. A number of quality hotels had sprung up along prominent tourist routes and in major cities. Even the age-old problems associated with currency exchange and credit arrangements were improved as local banks saw the advantages of providing such services. Thomas Nugent published the first guidebook for these travelers, entitled appropriately *The Grand Tour*.

At the height of its popularity, approximately forty thousand Englishmen made the Grand Tour. Then during the late eighteenth and early nineteenth centuries the Grand Tour went into decline. The Seven Years' War, the French Revolution, and the Napoleonic Wars all contributed to its demise. Tourist routes were ravaged by battling forces, and travel became difficult and hazardous.

When discretionary travel again became popular in the mid-1800s, a streamlined and very different Grand Tour was one of many travel options. Family travel replaced the traditionally male Grand Tour, and mass tourism replaced its elite exclusivity. Entertainment rather than education became the focus of such a tour to the Continent. Today, the extensiveness of the Grand Tour has been severely limited due to time and money constraints. Its remnants are package circle tours, the flavor of which is reminiscent of the cultural extravaganza of yesteryear.

New York City

3 Days - Escorted Tour NY from $379

Radio City Music Hall or Broadway Show • Statue of Liberty • Ellis Island • Chinatown • South Street Seaport

4 Meals: 2 Breakfasts, 2 Dinners

Day 1: Arrive New York City
Today you will travel to America's largest and most exciting metropolis, NEW YORK CITY. Upon arrival in New York, you will be free to shop. Then you will check into your hotel which is located in Manhattan. After dinner you will enjoy a performance at RADIO CITY MUSIC HALL featuring the Rockettes*. When Radio City is closed, a top BROADWAY SHOW is substituted. Meals included **D**.

Day 2: Statue of Liberty - Ellis Island
After breakfast, you will travel to Battery Park for a short ferry ride to LIBERTY ISLAND. Time will be allowed to visit the STATUE OF LIBERTY. Next you will travel via ferry from Liberty Island to ELLIS ISLAND. After a six-year, multi-million dollar restoration, Ellis Island is now a monument to the millions of immigrants who passed through its doors upon arrival to America. You will view the GREAT HALL as it looked in 1918. The remainder of the day is at leisure to explore the city at your own pace. Tonight dinner is included at a favorite New York restaurant. Meals included **B,D**.

Day 3: Sightseeing - Depart for Home
You begin the day with an outstanding, included breakfast at either the TAVERN ON THE GREEN RESTAURANT or WINDOWS ON THE WORLD. This is sure to be a highlight of your tour. After breakfast, a local tour guide will take you, via motorcoach, on an interesting sightseeing tour of Manhattan. You will pass through such areas as GREENWICH VILLAGE, THE WALL STREET DISTRICT, LITTLE ITALY, and CHINATOWN. You will also view the UNITED NATIONS, THE WORLD TRADE CENTER, THE EMPIRE STATE BUILDING, and THE CHRYSLER BUILDING, as well as countless other famous New York landmarks. Following your tour, you will travel to SOUTH STREET SEAPORT in the FULTON MARKETPLACE. Here you are free to explore the many unique shops and restaurants in this newly restored area reminiscent of Boston's Quincy Marketplace. You may catch up on some last minute shopping before departing for home. Meals included **B**.

Radio City Music Hall:
Easter Show—March
Christmas Pageant—Nov-Dec

Broadway Shows:
Top shows included such as
Will Roger's Follies
Phantom of the Opera
Miss Saigon

Reprinted by permission of Collette Tours.

---

services of the tour operator's staff.

FIT wholesalers/operators work with retail travel agents on the basis of a minimum number of arrangements. As a general rule, an FIT must consist of at least three destinations and a total of at least six nights' accommodations, in addition to transfers and sightseeing at each destination.

The FIT wholesaler/operator typically requires a nonrefundable deposit before beginning work. The FIT specialist then sends a suggested itinerary and a cost quotation to the agent. This quotation is based on local prices converted into dollars and may contain other contingent charges. At this stage FIT operators guard against the possibility of adverse currency fluctuations by adding in a small amount. Finally, they include their own markup. Once the client accepts the itinerary and the price quotation, the FIT operator secures confirmations of all arrangements.

Postcards have been popular mementos for more than a century. "Wish you were here... having a wonderful time."

Benefits of a Tour

Tours often have negative connotations for clients, the phrase "package tour" even more so. They seem to evoke nightmares of ruthless early-morning awakenings, regimented sightseeing conducted by tireless guides, and unceasing hustle and bustle. To clients who think of themselves as individuals or who resent being told they fit a mold, this misconception means that the travel counselor may do well to avoid the term "tour." Many tours permit so much flexibility and freedom that clients may never realize they are on one. Unfortunately, some agents also share this misconception. They ignore the obvious advantages each different kind of tour can offer both to clients and to themselves.

Benefits to the Client

■ **Prepayment:** Because tours are prepaid, remaining travel costs can be accurately calculated in advance. Clients will need to carry less money to purchase accommodations, sightseeing, meals, or other included features. They are protected against unfavorable currency fluctuations and will not find their funds running short because they have miscalculated the cost of necessary items.

■ **Peace of Mind:** Clients do not have to worry about getting from airport to attractions or waste time each day finding hotels. Because the cost of many tours includes tips, clients are spared the problems of local tipping procedures.

■ **Volume Discounts:** Although clients on an independent tour and, to some extent, on a hosted tour may not feel part of a group, they are. Their group is composed not just of others traveling with them at the same time, but of all the individuals who purchase similar tour arrangements throughout the year from the same operator. The operator's ability to produce volume business for each supplier permits negotiated discounts. These discounts are passed on to clients who benefit from being part of a group they may never see.

■ **Assured Entrances:** Tour operators make block purchases of tickets to attractions and events to ensure that their clients will have them. Individual travelers may find it impossible to obtain tickets that are available to tour participants. For very special events like the Oberammergau Passion Play, the Olympic Games, or La Scala, tour operators represent the best avenue of entrance for most would-be travelers. Tour participants also avoid lines. In popular tourist areas where accommodations are in short supply, tour operators may have essentially cornered the market.

■ **Reliable Sightseeing/Features:** Tour operators, through long experience, design tours to provide tried-and-true sightseeing attractions and other activities. In this way clients can be certain they visit the right places. Tour operators also schedule visits when attractions are open or at their best. Clients on a tour are assured that the operator knows where to take them and that local advice and assistance are also available for special tastes. On escorted tours, the escort or tour director often points out customs, traditions, and unusual phenomena that independent travelers miss.

Benefits to the Travel Agent

Many of the benefits to the agent follow naturally from the benefits to the client. All counselors appreciate the opportunity to provide clients with arrangements that have been tested over time and enable them to take advantage of volume discounts. Some other real benefits to agents are:

■ **Speed:** The features of a tour can be purchased from a single source—the tour operator. If arranged separately, booking the components would require numerous telephone and written communications, disbursement of separate payments, and complicated documentation. Dealing with a tour operator, however, usually involves one telephone call, one written communication, and one payment. Documentation is prepared by the operator.

■ **Maximum Earnings:** Tours permit agents to book and prepay features that are included in the cost of the tour, such as meals, special events, tips, and taxes that clients would otherwise pay for directly at the destinations. The tour operator then pays a commission to the agent based on total cost. Agencies that develop an ongoing relationship with a reliable tour operator are rewarded with commission overrides based on the volume of bookings made.

■ **Objective Advice:** Operators specialize in particular destinations, and they know their territory. They can develop close working relationships with productive agents by providing them with advice, not only about accommodations and sightseeing, but also about climate, culture, and current trends.

How to Choose a Tour

The process of matching clients with the right tour is not easy. The agent normally contacts the tour operator directly for a brochure and further details of an unusual tour. But for many destinations, reference books show a profusion of tours differing in inclusive features, cost, and length of stay. The travel agent's task is to choose among tours and tour operators to satisfy most closely the client's needs.

Experience and Reputation of Tour Operators

The travel professional must trust the tour operator to provide all arrangements as advertised and, if unforeseen circumstances arise, to intervene and provide substitute arrangements of the highest possible quality. A travel agent will usually look for an operator who is experienced in operating tours to the client's destination, enjoys a good reputation with other agents in the office, or is known to be bonded and financially stable. An ideal tour operator fulfills all three criteria.

Gradually, agents develop working relationships with particular tour operators who are especially responsive to their needs. Clients benefit from these close relationships in the form of better accommodations, superior service, and acceptance of last-minute changes or payments. The agent can maximize earnings for the agency by concentrating bookings with proven tour operators. It would be unsound business practice to use the services of a tour operator who is inexperienced, undercapitalized, and unreliable, regardless of the earnings potential.

If possible, travel agents should try to determine whether an escorted tour operator has a history of cancelling scheduled departures. Clients who are faced with last-minute cancellations and changes are justifiably upset. Agents should also be wary of operators who raise their prices between the date of reservation and departure, forcing the agent to ask the client for more money. Experienced and properly capitalized tour opera-

tors who plan correctly can absorb temporary currency fluctuations or adjust expenses to avoid passing on last-minute price increases. But some unforeseen rises in cost may force a tour operator to announce broad-scale price increases with fair warning.

It is also possible to identify tour operators who specialize in particular markets. These operators tend to know their product in depth. Some experienced escorted motorcoach tour operators have never offered any other kind of tour. These and many more are specialists either in a kind of tour or a particular destination.

In the travel business, longevity can be a meaningful measure of a company's quality. The older tour operators have, during their years in business, established relationships with their suppliers, and clients traveling on their tours receive preferential treatment. Certain tour operators, because of their contacts, their experience, and the repeat business they provide, are able to insist on special arrangements and considerations for their clients.

There are some objective standards by which travel agents may judge tour operators. Agents should be familiar with the following organizations:

The United States Tour Operators Association (USTOA)

The United States Tour Operators Association (USTOA) is a professional association for the tour operator industry whose members conduct business in the United States. It serves as a voice for the industry, particularly when communicating with governmental agencies. The organization's goals relate to consumer protection, education, and industry communication. Before applying for membership, companies must have been successfully operated by the same ownership or management for at least three years, must handle a certain volume of bookings, must post an indemnity bond of $250,000, and must participate in USTOA's $5 million consumer protection plan. The purpose of the plan is to reimburse consumers for any tour payments or deposits lost as a result of a member's bankruptcy or insolvency.

Applicants for USTOA membership must present references from within the travel industry and from a financial institution to attest to their professional reputation and financial stability. USTOA publishes a consumer protection booklet describing the duties and responsibilities of tour operators. It also offers guidelines on how to select a package tour and a listing of members' programs, services, and destinations.

The National Tour Association (NTA)

The National Tour Association (NTA) includes primarily those tour operators who offer escorted tours within North America. Members must post a $1 million professional liability insurance policy and comply with the NTA Code of Ethics as requirements of membership. Clients are thus protected from fraudulent claims or mistakes in brochures, statements, or other promotional information from tour operators. Clients are protected up to the amount of $100,000 should an NTA operator file bankruptcy. NTA represents 575 tour company members, 2,100 supplier members, and 750 destination marketing organization members.

American Society of Travel Agents (ASTA)

Membership in the American Society of Travel Agents (ASTA) is another important indicator of the stability and reliability of a tour operator. ASTA has instituted a voluntary Tour Protection Plan (TPP). Tour operators who participate post a $250,000 bond, which is held in trust. These funds are used to reimburse travelers booked by ASTA agents with ASTA operators in case the operator files bankruptcy before prepaid services are provided. ASTA has established an independent Litigation Center to assist members in disputes with service providers. ASTA also works in close cooperation with other member associations such as AHMA and CLIA to improve industry relations.

How to Read a Brochure

Tour operators design their brochures to appeal to the consumer and to act as valuable sales tools for the travel agent. In theory, the counselor should know the details of every tour in every brochure in the office and be able to lead the client deftly through the features of each. In practice, because of the sheer volume of brochures, travel counselors must limit their detailed knowledge to the offerings of the tour operators whose products

Terms and Conditions

In the back of the brochure, operators must disclose to the client the provisions of the contract. The details of this contract are extremely important, and although clients should be encouraged to read each part of the brochure carefully, the travel agent cannot assume that this has been done. The agent should take the initiative in summarizing and explaining these provisions and make sure the client understands them. Five important areas are:

■ A general statement of what each tour does and does not include

■ The deposit and payment schedule for all tours

■ The cancellation and refund policy

■ The limitation of the tour operator's responsibility and liability

■ The status of fares and rates published in the brochure

they sell frequently. Travel professionals must develop a technique for quickly reviewing both familiar and unfamiliar brochures.

To be effective, a brochure should enable the agent to answer or anticipate the client's questions about the tours it promotes. In response to consumer and agent suggestions, many tour operators have improved their presentation of important information by explaining unfamiliar terminology, more clearly stating included features, and displaying disclaimers and liability more prominently.

A well-designed, clearly written brochure is another indication of a reliable tour operator. The front portion of a typical brochure might contain a section in which the operator displays credentials and experience, emphasizes the general features that characterize the tours, and explains some of the terminology used throughout the brochure: transfers, continental breakfast, luxury motorcoach. Some operators even explain how to compare their tours with those of their competitors.

In the main section of the brochure, various

tours are listed. The operator normally provides a table of contents with page numbers. Tours may be arranged in the brochure according to kind of tour (independent, hosted, or escorted); grade of tour (deluxe, first-class, thrifty, or similar categories); length of stay; destinations visited; and special interest (tennis, honeymoon, and so on).

What Is Not Included

When reading a brochure, a client must assume that a feature is not included unless it is clearly stated to be. Many tour operators state explicitly what is not included. Many meals provided on escorted tours offer a menu with limited choice. Although these items seem minor, they can be sources of aggravation and embarrassment if the tour participant is unaware of them. By reading the tour operator's statement of what is and what is not included, the travel agent can gain new knowledge, appear well-informed to the client, and avoid complaints over small matters.

Deposit and Payment Schedule

All tour operators require a deposit. On independent and hosted tours, space at particular hotels may be limited; on escorted tours the capacity of the motorcoach determines the number of participants. To prevent cancellation, the deposit must be received by the tour operator within seven to fifteen days following the date of the reservation. The balance, or final payment, is due no later than thirty to forty-five days before departure, or as specified in the brochure. Once the deadline for final payment has passed, reservations can continue to be made for most tours.

Cancellation and Refund Policy

Tour operators reserve the right to cancel a tour before departure. Occasionally political events, social conditions, or weather make a trip inadvisable or impossible. Escorted tour operators also cancel tours when there are insufficient participants for a particular date. Their cost for hotel accommodations, sightseeing, and the motorcoach is based on a minimum number traveling together.

If clients cancel before departure, they are usually liable for a cancellation penalty, particularly if the cancellation is made close to departure. Unavoidable cancellations on the part of the client present good opportunities for agents to suggest trip cancellation or interruption insurance.

If the tour operator or a carrier, hotel, or agent contracted to supply services decides to cancel part of the tour, clients are typically entitled to receive a refund for the value of the portion missed. Most tour operators reserve the right to substitute features on the tour with or without notice. If the substitution involves accepting a lower grade of accommodations or other tour elements of lesser quality, the client will receive a refund, either on the spot or after returning home.

Most escorted tour operators reserve the right to expel tour participants for due cause once the tour is under way without compensation.

The Limitations of the Tour Operator's Responsibility and Liability

Tour operators are always careful to point out that they are not airlines, hotels, bus companies, or any kind of supplier and that they cannot be held responsible for the actions of these companies and their employees. The companies whose services the tour operator uses are all independent contractors. Tour operators disclaim responsibility or liability for the acts of their suppliers. They also disclaim responsibility for any loss, damage, or delay occasioned by events outside their control or by acts or omissions by passengers.

The Status of Fares and Rates Published in the Brochure

Most tour operators set their rates for one entire year. Land rates apply for the effective dates covered by the brochure and do not typically change if the tours are within the United States and are quoted in dollars. The land rates for tours outside the United States are also usually quoted in dollars, even though all costs to the tour operator are in local currencies. Most tour operators, for their own protection, reserve the right to adjust the prices of their tours if currency fluctuation affects them. Some tour operators guarantee their land rates, and most do not impose any surcharge once final payment has been received.

Summary

Tours combine the components of transportation, accommodations, and sightseeing to provide the best package to suit clients' needs. In this way, customers receive the benefits of volume discounts, prepayment, and assured entrances. Travel agents benefit by receiving speed, maximum earnings, and objective advice.

Tours can vary from independent packages to hosted programs to escorted trips. Some customers are interested in specialty tours such as convention packages, incentive tours, or weekend specials. Choosing the right level of services is key in meeting the needs of clients.

Regardless of its type, any tour requires planning, negotiating, and promotion. One of the most crucial areas in this process is costing.

Choosing the correct wholesaler or operator is important in assuring the success of the tour. Members of USTOA, NTA, and ASTA are recognized as respected leaders in the industry. The money sent to such representatives is guaranteed by the parent organization.

Chapter Wrap-up

DISCUSSION TOPICS

Closed Attractions

A recent twelve-day motorcoach tour through the deep South encountered a tropical storm that devastated one of the scheduled attractions. The gardens, which were one of the highlights of the tour, were closed due to gale-force winds. The group leader, Mrs. Dogood, scheduled alternate arrangements for the forty-four passengers. However, most of the group is still upset about missing this "once in a lifetime" opportunity. What is the responsibility of the operations manager of the tour operator? What options might be presented to appease the group members? Can you equate customer satisfaction with profit?

Brochure Advertisement

Mr. and Mrs. I. Rate have just returned from a cherry blossom tour to Washington, D.C. They have walked into the travel agency with itineraries and sales brochures firmly in hand. They claim the brochures and itineraries were misleading because they indicated the traveler would "see such historical monuments as the Washington, Lincoln, and Jefferson Memorials, as well as the Library of Congress, the Supreme Court, and the Archives." The word "see" indicated "visit" to them, and although they did ride by the buildings, they were never allowed off the tour bus to actually "see" them. Consequently, they are demanding a refund for this portion of the tour. What is the travel agent's course of action? (Please note, none of these attractions have entrance fees.) Is the brochure accurate?

Seat Rotation

Two groups, Swinging Seniors and Stuffy Yuppies, have purchased space on a fourteen-day National Parks tour. Each group has requested to remain on its own side of the bus. Tour policy, which is stated clearly in the tour contract, states that all passengers must rotate seats at the discretion of the tour guide. A couple from the Yuppies group have just mentioned that they have motion sickness and must have the front seat. The group leader of the Seniors has already informed her group that she automatically gets the front seat because she organized everyone, so she will not rotate. What are the responsibilities of the tour guide? What recourse does the guide have? What are the possible repercussions of the guide's actions?

Sales and Marketing

Part Two

Sales Techniques

Chapter 9

Introduction

Good salespersons are made, not born. Successful selling comes from extensive product knowledge and such skills as asking the right questions, controlling the conversation, listening effectively, countering objections, stressing benefits, and closing the sale. Salespersons need to structure their approach for each client; a set pattern or single style will not serve for all. Some clients like to make quick decisions and concentrate only on broad concepts. Others like to move more slowly, clarifying every detail and making sure they have anticipated all eventualities and considered every option. The agent depends on certain techniques, perhaps even certain phrases, but not on a pre-packaged presentation.

The Sales Personality

Counselors can develop behavioral characteristics that complement acquired selling skills and help produce an attractive sales personality. Agents impress clients when they first establish rapport by listening, making recommendations, solving problems, and selling customers what they want to buy. Experts stress the importance of winning the client's trust as an integral part of making sales and keeping customers. Service before, during, and after the sale is vital to continued success.

When counselors radiate self-confidence, they instill trust in their clients. Confidence derives from being up-to-date and knowing the answers — or where to find them. Travel professionals are alert to developments within the industry and its political, economic, and social environment. When change becomes a challenge, it can be mastered and even enjoyed.

Counselors must be aware of where they can get help and be willing to seek it. Seeking help from colleagues does not compromise or belittle a competent agent. The most experienced professionals regularly consult each other; doctors suggest second opinions. Consultation with colleagues is vital to an agent's professional growth.

Clients, too, can provide assistance and information. Selling is a cooperative venture between counselor and client. Counselors should not be afraid to ask well-traveled clients their opinions about destinations, hotels, or suppliers, even their recommendations for future clients.

Airlines and travel agencies set guidelines for dress and general appearance. Some provide uniform clothing. Combined with the decor, noise level, and pace of work in the office, the attitude

Interpersonal communication skills and customer service

Customer service representatives used to be individuals who dealt with services or products that customers found unsatisfactory. More companies today, however, are increasing their sales volume by anticipating clients' needs rather than dealing with problems later. This approach suggests that sales and service are really one entity. In other words, if customers perceive that counselors are offering value and quality service, the sale will be a natural follow-through.

The following list provides some helpful common-sense hints:

■ Greet customers when they enter the office. Use eye contact and a friendly smile to show that you are genuinely pleased to see them. If you remember someone's name, use it frequently. If not, be sure to ask and then use it during the course of your conversation. Stand to introduce yourself and extend your hand to welcome your clients, perhaps directing them to a seat. Remember, the first 30 seconds can make or break a sale!

■ If you can't greet clients immediately because you're on the phone or talking with another customer, acknowledge their presence and let them know you'll be with them soon. Provide reading materials such as brochures, photograph albums, or scrapbooks while they are waiting. No one likes to feel ignored.

■ Look at your office and workplace from the customer's viewpoint. Is the area messy?

noisy? cluttered? dirty? If so, what kind of service will customers feel they're getting?

■ Look at your own appearance. Is it professional? Does it reflect the attitudes of your clientele?

■ To begin the sale, try to establish a comfortable rapport with the clients. Ask about previous travel experiences, what areas they are most interested in, what they most enjoy — anything that makes them feel you care about their feelings and ideas.

■ Use a moderate tone of voice. Adjust it to the speed of your customers.

■ Provide alternatives if problems arise. Suggest options that indicate product knowledge and client concern. If a client is over budget, say so. Conversely, if a customer will be dissatisfied with less expensive surroundings, make positive suggestions and explain your course of action.

■ Don't waste time. If you don't know an answer, find someone who can help. Keep frequently used resources close by.

■ Don't bring out brochures that are inappropriate or unfamiliar. Don't read an entire brochure to a customer. Brochures are just sales tools that visually demonstrate the vacation you are suggesting.

■ End your sale on a positive note. Thank the clients for their time, assure them that the purchase (if made) is a good one, shake hands, use their names, and be prepared to follow up with a phone call, note, or mailer if needed.

and appearance of the staff create the all-important image of the workplace that clients see.

Most companies like a counselor to greet a client with an offer of assistance and to begin and end each conversation with a smile. In any successful sales presentation, agents need to know what to say, when to say it, and how to say it. They should try to phrase questions to elicit a positive answer. When recapping, the agent should concentrate on what clients have indicated they want to do.

Agents should not apologize for circumstances beyond their control. It is not their fault that an airline restricts travel on an excursion fare. Although the agent may sense the client's disappointment, constant apologizing creates the same effect as a negative attitude, and also implies that the agent is to some degree responsible.

Counselors should refrain from criticizing other agencies, even if the client voices complaints about them. It is not good policy to recommend one supplier at the expense of another or to contrast suppliers in ways that belittle them.

Customers must also be advised of their own responsibilities. Before traveling they must find out if visas or shots are required and be aware of restrictions on airfares that might affect their freedom of movement. The agent should always identify who stipulates these requirements (a government, an airline) and tell clients how they can easily comply. Clients may become apprehensive or resentful when ordered to do things, or worried if they think their trip presents difficulties or problems. Diplomacy is essential.

Clients should know how much a successful trip depends on the agent's knowledge and hard work. Yet the agent should avoid giving the impression that the trip is extraordinarily difficult or likely to be mishandled. Stressing what can be done and tactfully solving problems together constitute the elements of positive behavior.

The Importance of Travel

Travel is a vital part of many people's lives. Although it is often referred to as discretionary, this term is misleading. A dramatic reduction in

Why People Travel

For many inexperienced travel counselors, the spirit may be willing, but the flesh is weak. They would like to sell, but they find it difficult. Often the difficulties spring from fear. Some shrink from asking clients to spend so much money. After all, isn't travel really rather frivolous compared with the necessities of life? Some lack confidence in themselves and fear exposure. They are sure nobody would buy from them. Still others see selling as a rather disreputable activity. Don't travel agents have to be manipulative, fast-talking, and deceitful to be successful?

To counter these feelings, here are two important principles to remember:

1. Travel is important.
2. Clients want to travel.

prices or the appearance of an obviously good value stimulates travel that would not otherwise take place. The ability to travel is simply suppressed during periods when people cannot afford it.

Travel is discretionary in the sense that the demand is elastic and price-sensitive; it will increase during periods of prosperity and decrease during inflationary times. Business travel, however, is usually necessary and therefore inelastic.

As the airlines know, many people must travel. Most business travel is obligatory. With the advent of sophisticated teleconferencing and telecommunications systems, companies scrutinize all executive travel so that only the absolutely essential is arranged. The agent should view this market with appropriate seriousness.

Family travel constitutes another large segment of the market. It is no coincidence that on holidays airports are crowded, and train stations, bus depots, hotels, and cruise ships are full. Those who claim that this travel is discretionary have never

185

experienced the obligations that family members feel to attend such gatherings. Grandchildren have done more for the travel industry than the Wright brothers.

Leisure or vacation travelers make up a third important segment. Countless surveys and much computer time have been devoted to the question of why people go on vacations. Beyond the obvious reasons are more profound needs — some psychological, some emotional, some intellectual — that explain the importance individuals place on their annual vacation. Sophisticated and successful advertising taps these needs.

Many other people travel for serious and important reasons. They may be seeking specific knowledge by attending courses or joining a tour led by an expert lecturer. They may be convalescing from illness or seeking a cure. They may be making a pilgrimage or performing some other act of religious affirmation. Beyond these specific kinds of trips, any travel is widely seen as broadening an individual's understanding of self and the world. Many clients believe that travel can significantly enrich their lives. Their vacation also serves as a respite from routine, a chance to restore drained energy and enthusiasm. Travel can promote intellectual growth, emotional satisfaction, and psychological balance.

The Value of Travel

People budget for travel. The travel counselor should not feel  guilty about asking people to spend money. A vacation that costs $2,000 and fulfills all the client's expectations represents an investment. A vacation that costs $1,000 but fails to deliver is a total waste and may cause lingering feelings of loss and hostility. Remember that a travel experience lasts much longer than the duration of the actual trip. Memories, both good and bad, are lasting impressions.

Desire to Travel

Successful selling implies a partnership between client and counselor. The client wants to travel. The counselor wants to sell a trip and satisfy the customer. The variety and flexibility of the travel product relieve the agent, to a great extent, of the need to pressure clients to buy a particular trip. Constrained only by the limits of creativity and knowledge and by the need to use time efficiently and profitably, the agent can select products appropriate to the client's needs.

Clients seek a price that represents a good value. Value should not be confused with price. Low-cost arrangements that do not meet a client's needs do not represent good value. Sometimes clients may be willing to compromise or eliminate choices for reasons of price, but they must understand that they are sacrificing something. Value is a highly personal concept. To the couple who wish to celebrate their twenty-fifth wedding anniversary by returning to their honeymoon hotel in Hawaii, for example, the price to be paid is simply a necessity to duplicate the experience.

Clients who comparison shop are really searching for a travel counselor who will make arrangements that best suit their needs. Not even the rich want to be overcharged. When counseling, travel agents must be on guard against imposing their own values on the client. Often agents sell arrangements they can not afford themselves, but if the trip represents value to the clients, the partnership has worked.

Elements of a Successful Sale

■ **Introduction**
    Qualifying the client
    Listening Effectively
■ **Presenting features and benefits**
■ **Closing the sale**
    Making recommendations
    Recapping
    Overcoming objections
    Offering to book

Steps of a Sale

Many veteran travel counselors who are successful salespersons say that they learned to sell through experience and that they now instinctively know how to handle clients. To the uninitiated, selling appears to be a mystic art. Yet all good salespersons follow a structure, flexible enough to respond to individual situations but designed to encourage progress toward a sale. These elements of a successful sales presentation can be analyzed and discussed.

Qualifying the Client

Most conversations between agent and client start as a request for information. Travel professionals dispense information all day long, but they must be extremely careful not to think of that as an end in itself. The travel agent must view questions as evidence of a client's positive interest in taking a trip.

 Agents who simply answer questions and do not initiate their own presentation are doomed to frustrating, busy days with few sales. It is vital to understand that a request for information indicates a desire to travel.

To consult with a client and sell the right trip, counselors must qualify the client by asking a series of questions to determine the person's wants and needs. These questions are very simple.

1. When are you going?
2. Where (exactly) are you going?
3. Who/How many are going?
4. How long are you staying?
5. What kind/class of service or arrangements do you require?

Sometimes clients reveal the answer to one or more of these questions in their opening statements. Some answers need to be pursued further. Right from the start of the conversation with any vacation clients, agents must begin to build excitement. They must express enthusiasm, establish credibility, and convey empathy before proceeding to what should be a rewarding and interesting booking. If an agent cannot be genuinely enthusiastic about the trip, the client will remain apathetic about the arrangements offered.

Benefits of Qualifying

Assistance — The more information the client provides, the easier it is to find answers from reference materials, colleagues, or supplier representatives. Careful questioning will elicit this information.

Logic — Agents can become involved in long, inconclusive discussions about arrangements without ever establishing how and when the client will get to the destination. In any complicated booking, a good rule is to do first the things that are simple and that precede other arrangements.

Control — Controlling a conversation is not the same as dominating it. In fact, the agent controls a conversation best by asking questions and letting the client do the talking. Controlling the conversation means leading it toward the desired end.

Commitment — Not everybody who walks into an agency will purchase travel arrangements before leaving. Some may simply be shopping. By asking the five questions, the agent is able to ascertain the client's degree of commitment.

Counselors can frame questions to direct the conversation. An open-ended question enables the agent to discover more about a person's general tastes and needs. Occasionally a client may respond to an open-ended question with a precise answer, but usually a good question simply encourages clients to open up. Some typical open-ended questions are:

- What do you have in mind?
- What kind of vacations have you enjoyed before?
- What do you like to do?
- What particularly attracted you to the idea of a cruise?

Close-ended questions, on the other hand, are designed to narrow down possibilities. They elicit precise answers like "Yes" or "No." In this way the agent prompts the client to supply precise information. The five questions "When?" "Where?" "Who or how many?" "How long" "What kind or class?" are examples of close-ended questions.

Finally, the agent uses feedback questions to confirm details that have emerged in the conversation. The client can simply respond, "Yes," offer some minor corrections, or object in a way that reveals that the agent has misunderstood. These feedback questions are particularly useful when the open-ended and close-ended questions have been asked.

Before asking any question the agent must be sure of the kind of answer it will provoke. Questioning will not hypnotize clients into buying something they do not want. But it will provoke a thoughtful consideration of desirable alternatives and help them to focus. For the agent a question imparts a structure to the sales situation. Questioning should never sound like cross-examination, and the agent must always remain courteous and helpful.

Often clients' answers to the five important questions are vague and require follow-up to focus more clearly on their precise needs. Occasionally the agent will meet clients who know everything. They immediately announce in precise detail what they want. In some instances this extraordinary knowledge results from shopping at other agencies. Bearing in mind that the clients may be shopping again, the agent should, nevertheless,

- Confirm that the clients' information is correct.
- Be certain that the arrangements meet their needs.
- If they are making a mistake, present alternative recommendations.

Listening Effectively

Successful selling depends on asking questions, but simply asking is not enough. Counselors must learn to listen. The purpose of asking questions is to understand the client's needs and to empathize with them. Agents may not share these needs, values, tastes, or income, but their job is to understand, not change, them.

Clients must be allowed to talk freely, even as the agent controls the conversation and guides it into relevant areas. In this way the agent focuses on the client and avoids making recommendations or suggestions until the complete picture emerges.

Budgets

Some agents like to add "How much do

you want to spend?" or "Do you have a total budget in mind for this trip?" to the five essential questions. They maintain that the answer enables them to focus more quickly on the kind of arrangements or destinations to offer. They also point out that they might embarrass or alienate clients by suggesting arrangements that cost far more, or far less, than they intend to spend.

However, there are an equal number of good reasons for not asking about a budget or, at the very least, postponing it until the end of the conversation. The question assumes that clients have a clear idea of the cost of travel in general or, more precisely, the cost of what they want to do. Studies have shown that many people wildly overestimate the cost of travel—notice the oohs and aahs uttered by television game show audiences when a travel prize is given away. On the other hand, determined bargain hunters may deliberately understate how much they are willing to spend in an attempt to get the best deal. In short, the client's off-the-cuff response to this question may be totally misleading. Furthermore, if price is divorced from benefits, it tends to be meaningless.

All clients want to spend as little as possible to get exactly what they want. In fact, if an agent concludes a conversation by offering clients exactly what they want and they still seem unwilling to commit, it's almost certain that the principal objection is price. Then the agent may suggest ways in which the cost could be reduced without sacrificing too many benefits.

While listening, agents should give visual and verbal clues to reassure clients that they understand. Nodding, eye contact, phrases like "I see," all indicate that the agent is listening. Sometimes agents reinforce decisions clients have essentially already made. Agents who feel that clients have selected the wrong destination may attempt to alter their ideas. The clients may accept an agent's suggestion because it is based on an understanding of their needs. In fact, effective listening may result in the agent eliciting a decision or a commitment from clients. Yet the result seems to be a shared decision arising directly from the client's own statements.

Effective listening sounds easy. After all, people do it instinctively. But tests have shown that the average listener really hears only about 25 percent

For the sake of convenience, travel agents often distinguish the products and services of the different suppliers according to the features they offer and, not surprisingly, tend to sell travel arrangements by pointing to these features. Clients may be impressed by features, but they will not be motivated to purchase them unless the benefits are clear. A feature is an inherent characteristic, but a benefit indicates what the features mean to clients. Clients rarely upgrade arrangements or purchase optional features unless the benefits are clear.

Although the travel agent may know that a certain feature is highly desirable, the client may not. The agent must translate features into benefits so the client understands how the feature will directly affect the enjoyment of the trip.

Tips for Effective Listening

1. Limit your own talking. Ask questions and listen to the answers.
2. Listen for ideas.
3. Shut out distractions. Focus on what the client says.
4. Don't interrupt even if the client pauses for a long breath.
5. Take notes.
6. Reflect the client's own language in your comments and questions.
7. Don't let what clients say or how they say it irritate you.
8. Don't jump to conclusions.
9. Use verbal and nonverbal signals (body language) to indicate you understand and are paying attention to what the client says.
10. Watch the client's body language.
11. Listen and look for subtle inflections and overtones that imply attitudes or biases.

of what is said. That is, the listener hears but does not understand the significance of what is being said. Effective listening requires a concentrated effort. It is as much a vital part of selling as the essential questions are. They complement each other.

Presenting Features and Benefits

Travel suppliers compete with each other, offering features to induce travelers to choose their services. A feature is a product or service offered or any fact about that product or service that is always true. Tour operators commonly list the features of each tour in their brochures.

First, the agent must convert all travel jargon into everyday language. Do clients really know what round-trip transfers are? They will surely understand and begin to see the benefits if the agent says, "You will be taken from the airport directly to your hotel and back again at the end of your stay in time for your flight."

The description of the feature explains its use and the advantage of purchasing it and once the advantage appears, the benefits emerge. The agent's challenge is to make clients see the benefit of every feature before it is used.

One feature can have several benefits. Different people may purchase the same arrangements for

187

different reasons. Some may choose a particular cruise because they wish to relax, others because it offers nonstop entertainment. The agent emphasizes the features and benefits most appropriate to the individuals. A half-day sightseeing tour of Hong Kong enables some clients to see places they would not know how to find on their own. For others it serves as an orientation tour preliminary to their own sightseeing plans. Knowing which benefits to suggest to each client comes from careful qualifying and listening.

Closing the Sale

There are techniques, procedures, even specific phrases that can be used to close a sale effectively. By offering to book, the counselor is allowing clients to do what they want to do. Many salespersons worry about appearing pushy and aggressive. Yet not offering to book is potentially more dangerous. Every successful sale, in a travel agency or anywhere else, benefits both seller and buyer. Any missed sale benefits neither. If the five essential questions are answered, the agent can begin to close the sale.

Tips for Closing the Sale

■ When you feel the client seems ready to book, start to write a sample itinerary. Assume that the sale is imminent if no questions are asked and the client seems comfortable with the arrangements.

■ Ask the client about preferred method of payment. This may be an opportunity to suggest alternate payment methods.

■ Check availability of the travel arrangements. This creates pressure to decide.

■ Be positive. Reassure the client that the selection made is a good one.

The closing includes three distinct steps:
■ Presenting recommendations and setting priorities
■ Recapping
■ Overcoming resistance or objections

Features/Benefits of a Travel Agency's Services

Feature: Reservations and ticketing for all airlines.

Benefit: *Unnecessary to call several airlines to find one that serves your destination. One call to the agency for any destination. More convenient, saves time.*

Feature: Escorted tours are prepaid in full.

Benefit: *Clients can calculate more exactly the cost of their vacation, need to carry less money with them, and worry less about loss or theft. They have fewer reasons to change money and will not be left with too much foreign money at the end of the tour.*

Feature: Ticket delivery service.

Benefit: *Saves time, energy, and money.*

Feature: Trained fare experts.

Benefit: *Agency personnel knowledgeable in all fares — can keep travel arrangements within company or personal budgets.*

Feature: Car and hotel reservations.

Benefit: *Saves time and costly phone calls.*

Recommendations

Presenting information differs from presenting recommendations. Agents begin presenting information early in the conversation once they know the answers to some of the five essential questions. In presenting information the agent relies on facts and uses sales aids present in the office, particularly brochures, maps, reference books, and general information pamphlets.

The agent should never assume that clients know the attractions of destinations. As clients react to information, the agent gains valuable clues to their motives for traveling. The ability to present recommendations lies at the very heart of selling. Agents who are confident that they know what the client wants, that the arrangements to be recommended are of the very highest quality, and that they meet the client's desires can proceed confidently and enthusiastically to making a recommendation.

Ideally the agent has built enthusiasm, and the choice has become evident. But whenever the client is undecided or seems to be making a wrong choice, the agent may have to present recommendations. The client may request a recommendation directly ("Which of these two should I take?") -or may insist on arrangements that the agent feels are inappropriate. When presenting recommendations in either of these situations, the agent should

- Emphasize the benefits the client seeks and link the recommendation directly to them.

- Incorporate the client's own statements or refer to them when presenting recommendations.

- Refer directly to brochures, itineraries, or maps when presenting the recommendations so the client can see the points the agent is making.

When presenting recommendations, agents must seek to establish priorities. By giving each possibility its due, the agent can recommend what is best for a client without eliminating all the others. The agent must temper the ideal with the possible. The real world of full flights, full hotels, full tours, and full cruises intrudes. No recommendation should be so confined and so exclusive that the client will cancel the trip if one element cannot be booked.

Dangers to Avoid

Some dangers counselors should avoid when presenting recommendations are

- Exaggerating or lying. "It's the greatest value in New Orleans."

- Guaranteeing enjoyment by referring to some other client, named or unnamed, who enjoyed what the agent is recommending: "I know you will enjoy this trip because Mr. and Mrs. Jones did." Even when many clients have enjoyed particular arrangements, they may have done so for reasons totally different from the current client's expectations.

- Guaranteeing anything beyond control: the weather, the service, or the availability of attractive, unattached members of the opposite sex. "You'll love it" could be the most dangerous expression an agent can use. The clients may not.

Personal Recommendations

Once the client has reserved and paid, the agent can safely offer personal recommendations if they seem appropriate. Now is the time to mention the little restaurant, an unusual museum, a spectacular view, some local native handicraft. Now is also the time to recount personal experiences and personal likes. Such recommendations, made after the sale, do not impose the agent's personal taste on the client's choice of a trip. Like the recommendations in a guidebook, they can be accepted or rejected.

These recommendations contribute to the client's enjoyment and increase respect for the agent's expertise. They may help redeem a trip that goes wrong for some reason. Honest recommendations can derive from a number of different sources: colleagues in the agency, information from seminars or trade presentations, advice from previous clients. The agent should simply state the source of the recommendation.

Recapping

Recapping is an essential part of effective listening. The recap enables the agent to pull together details from the conversation and provides the client an opportunity to comment on, upgrade, or add to the arrangements. If the client agrees with the recap, the agent may proceed immediately to offer to book. The recap may uncover some disagreements or objections. Sensing that the moment for a decision is coming closer, the client may hedge on previously firm commitments. These disagreements or objections need resolution before the agent can offer to book.

It is dangerous to confuse the client with too many possibilities. A good way to avoid such confusion is to delay discussing any options until after the five questions have been asked. The recap should resolve any confusion over options still lingering in the client's mind.

Recapping has two other benefits for the agent. It reduces the possibility that a disappointed client may later accuse the agent of not having explained things clearly. An accurate recap also starts the client saying "yes" and can lead easily into the agent's offer to book.

Objections and Resistance

Not every client who enters an agency and talks to a travel professional makes a reservation. Some present objections or put up resistance that the agent is unable to counter. Frequently, agents mistake the real nature of these objections and do not counter them effectively or, admitting the reality of the objection, fail to act positively in any of the ways still available to them.

Some clients answer all five essential questions specifically and yet still raise objections when the agent offers to book. Several kinds of possible objections or resistance need to be recognized and countered.

An obvious resistance to booking would arise if the client were unable to answer, even after careful questions and recommendations from the agent, any of the five essential questions. In such instances the agent may offer a tentative or conditional reservation that protects the client against disappointment. It also saves the agent the bother of scrambling to get space at the last moment when the client finally decides. However, certain promo-

tional fares with their immediate payment demands and stringent cancellation penalties prohibit the use of any type of conditional reservation. Offering a conditional reservation can never be a substitute for careful qualification of a client. The agent must always try to get a firm decision.

The agent should set a date by which the client must confirm the conditional arrangements and offer to contact the client on that date. It is unfair to suppliers not to cancel reservations as soon as possible if the client decides not to travel.

Clients may resist the agent's offer to book because they feel pressured. This is a form of psychological resistance. Perhaps the agent has moved too quickly. Most people prefer to delay decisions, especially those that cost money. As the moment of decision draws nearer, they may forget all the benefits of purchasing or the extent to which they need something.

If the agent encounters unexpected resistance to the offer to book that seems to spring directly from the client's desire to postpone a decision, the agent should

- Stress that the decision has been reached by mutual agreement of agent and client.
- Point out how the arrangements meet the client's needs.
- Explain that a decision now can avoid disappointment later.

This momentary drawing back at the moment of decision is characteristic of many people. Some agents think they are doing their clients a favor by advising them to go home and think it over. Given such advice, most leave. But making a decision is usually followed by a great sense of relief and expectation. Travel agents help their clients overcome that last psychological barrier.

Frequently, clients feel they must consult a spouse or traveling companion before committing to final arrangements. This is a perfectly natural form of social resistance. The agent should fully describe the arrangements and their benefits so the client can explain the trip positively at home, then set a date to call back and check that they are definitely traveling. If everything has been explained clearly, further changes or consultation should not be necessary.

Sometimes agents encounter objections that arise from the client's ignorance or prejudice.

If the client does not know...	The agent can...
Where	Review needs with the client. Provide more information. Make suggestions. Make an appointment for the future.
When	Make transportation reservations (air, cruise, and so on) on the most likely dates, provided there is no cancellation penalty.
How long	Make definite reservations for outbound transportation and reserve on the most likely return date, or leave the return temporarily open.
Who/How many	Make reservations for the greatest number likely to travel. It is always easier to cancel one person from a party than to get a duplicate booking for another traveler later on.
What kind/class	Ask more questions. Provide more information.

Often these objections are amusing or understandable; sometimes they are unpleasant. Just as clients may have wrong ideas that lead to requesting inappropriate arrangements, so they may have wrong ideas that prevent them from wanting something that would actually suit them. Information, tactfully introduced, can help change a client's perception.

Yet when ignorance is firmly rooted, it resists reason. However strongly the agent may disagree privately, any attempt to correct the client will guarantee the loss of the booking. Agents can choose between making the point and losing the client.

Sometimes clients resist the offer to book because they do not fully understand what the agent is recommending. They need more information, or they need information repeated. The agent must supply additional information.

Another last-minute objection arises when clients suddenly feel guilty about taking the trip. When the moment comes to commit funds, a little voice asks whether they should be spending money on themselves. By reviewing how the suggested arrangements meet the client's expressed needs, the agent can help overcome feelings of guilt.

When benefits are stressed, the focus is on value, the antidote to price shock.

Some clients are quite willing to book, but they want just one last concession from the agent. Viewing the conversation as a kind of negotiation, these clients need to feel that they had the last word and struck the best possible deal. Sometimes this objection appears as a request for an impossible guarantee or an additional service not usually provided. These objections are not really serious, and the agent who hears one should consider it a signal to move forward confidently and offer to book.

Rather than use the word cancel, *suggest that clients can always* change *reservations should the need arise.*

Offering to Book

Offering to book is composed of two separate decisions: when to offer and how to offer. Ideally, the right moment occurs when the client agrees with the recap, agrees with the recommendations, and agrees with the agent's answers to any objections. Unfortunately, these moments are often not as clear-cut in real life as they appear on a diagram. The agent may make several offers to book at different times, discovering from each attempt to what point things have progressed.

Clients are often ready to commit before agents offer to book. Many more sales are lost by delaying than by offering too soon. If the agent's offer is rejected, the client may be indicating an objection that can be uncovered and countered. The first offer to book often takes place after the recap. The agent is testing the waters at this point and should be prepared for objections or resistance. Indeed, agents may uncover objections or a request for recommendations only when they offer to book.

Unfortunately, closing a sale is a concept often ignored by many agencies. In up to 90 percent of all sales situations, surveys indicate, salespeople fail to ask for the business. Keep in mind that travel agencies are not charitable institutions; they are not information booths; they are not merely counseling services. Travel agencies sell travel. They inform, counsel, and advise within the context of selling travel. A sale is not made until the client has paid or signed on the dotted line.

Selling Up

The scope of the original sale can be increased with a little effort. Usually this type of suggestive selling is done as the sale is being completed. The client is in a buying frame of mind and may readily make another purchase if it is presented as a time-saver or a good value. Up-sell the travel product by suggesting

- A stopover en route to the destination.
- An upgraded hotel room.
- A city tour or excursion.
- A car rental.
- Insurance.
- Transfer service from the airport.
- Theater tickets.

Gestures	Buying Signals	Non-buying Signals
Physical actions	Touching a brochure.	Refusing to touch brochure or even look at it; reading brochure very closely, indicating need for more information.
	Relaxed posture; open hand.	Leaning forward; legs crossed. Arms folded; hands clenched.
Facial expressions	Smiling/Sparkling eye. Stroking chin with hand.	Frowning/Wandering eye. Covering mouth with hand.
Verbal expressions	"It sounds great." Any specific inquiry about price or included features; e.g., "Did you say tips were included?" Any question or statement indicating the trip is mentally sold; e.g., "Will we need a passport?" or "How can I pay for this?"	Silence. An objection to price or features.

Summary

In the travel industry sales techniques need to be developed and practiced daily. No one is born with a sales personality that enables them to sell useless items to customers unready or unwilling to buy. Rather, sales techniques are learned and, when coupled with product knowledge and interpersonal communication skills, can be powerful tools to increase revenues.

Every sale has certain specific elements that contribute to its success. These include qualifying the customer through effective listening, presenting features and benefits, making recommendations, recapping, overcoming objections, offering to book, and closing the sale. To become effective, travel counselors must practice each of these steps until they become natural in style and conversational in tone.

By providing optimum service, counselors can successfully and confidently match clients with appropriate destinations. In this way, both customer and counselor will be satisfied.

REVIEW QUESTIONS

1. Why is it advisable to postpone presenting recommendations until you are ready to close the sale?

2. How should agents present recommendations to clients? What should they avoid?

3. What are the major benefits of recapping?

4. What are the advantages and disadvantages of offering conditional reservations?

5. There are many reasons why clients resist or object to the agent's offer to book. Which do you think are the most common: psychological resistance, social objections, prejudiced objections, informational resistance, guilty objections, guarantee objections?

6. How could you find out how much clients want to spend on a particular trip?

7. The travel agent typically performs a number of services for clients. How would you rate the following services in order of importance: informing, recommending, persuading, convincing?

DISCUSSION TOPICS

Qualifying

What type of questions has the counselor asked in the following discussion? Which of these answers need to be pursued further? Is this approach effective?

Client — How much is the fare to Denver?

Counselor — When would you like to go?

Client — The first week in April.

Counselor — Are you traveling alone?

Client — No, my wife and daughter will be with me.

Counselor — How old is your daughter?

Client— Ten.

Counselor — How long will you be staying?

Client— About two weeks. We are visiting my wife's family.

Budgeting

Suppose an agent asked clients who wanted to go to Canada how much they wanted to spend. They say, "About $1,000." What does this really mean? $1,000 per person? for everything? for transportation and accommodations only? Only by discussing the trip can the agent illuminate all the clients' needs and present a meaningful price and benefits package. For example, which of these two advertisements is more meaningful? More important, which is the better value? Why?

HAWAII
$599
And Up

HAWAII
- Round-trip jet
- Seven nights hotel
- Transfers
- Sightseeing
- Taxes, Tips

$699

Customized Sales

Chapter 10

CHAPTER OBJECTIVES

After completing this chapter, the reader should be able to

- ■ Describe the differences between inside and outside sales
- ■ Describe two types of groups
- ■ Define incentive travel
- ■ Identify four local business clients
- ■ Note the special needs of handicapped travelers

VOCABULARY

After completing this chapter, the reader should be able to define

- ■ Affinity group
- ■ Blocked space
- ■ Charters
- ■ Group profile
- ■ Incentive trip
- ■ Inquiry
- ■ Inside sales
- ■ Outside sales
- ■ Pied piper
- ■ Specialization

Introduction

The steps involved in selling are universal, regardless of product or market. However, certain types of selling require additional skills. Continued practice of these skills assures successful selling. Some individuals become more proficient in only one type of sales, and others enjoy a variety of situations. Most sales can be divided into two basic categories: inside or outside.

Inside Sales

Inside sales are comprised of selling to a customer either in the office or on the telephone.

Face-to-face encounters with potential clients are sometimes easier for agents to handle, because the opportunity to use such visuals as brochures, pamphlets, and maps may greatly enhance the sales presentation and inspire an immediate, positive response from the client.

However, today's busy consumer will often choose to use the telephone rather than drive to a travel agency. Because of the money agencies spend advertising their telephone numbers in newspapers, in the Yellow Pages, and on business cards, they would be alarmed if their phones did not ring. Some companies select a location designed to encourage more calls than walk-in clients. They find that selling on the telephone is as effective and efficient as selling in person.

Shopper and Buyers

Clients may decide to telephone rather than make arrangements in person if they fall into one of these two categories:

■ **Shoppers** — They are unprepared to discuss their plans in detail and merely want information. They may simply be checking prices or shopping for service; or

■ **Buyers** — They may be absolutely definite about what they want and are prepared to book.

Typical phone shoppers respond to an advertisement and request a brochure or further information. These shoppers often call on impulse. Agents should speak to them exactly as if they had come into the agency and should assume that they wish to travel. Some travel agents regard shoppers as a nuisance. They argue that a serious client would visit the agency personally. They do not recognize that many people go through several stages in planning any project, particularly one that involves unusual expense. Information gathering is a perfectly rational first step. For agents who treat a request for information purely as a request for information, these callers will indeed be an annoying and time-consuming interruption. Those agents who see a request for information as an indication of a desire to travel view the telephone inquiry as an opportunity to sell. Shoppers are potential buyers.

Using a phone conversation to ask questions, the agent can select a few relevant brochures to mail. The agent should include a cover letter explaining briefly how to read the brochures and stressing the benefits of recommended programs. If the cover letter is effective and the brochures carefully selected, the client may call again to book, thus becoming a buyer. After offering to mail material, the agent should invite the client to make an appointment to discuss the trip further. If the invitation is accepted, the appointment can then be confirmed in the cover letter accompanying the brochures. Alternatively, the agent might offer to call the client back at some later date to

review the material, answer questions, and make more definite plans.

Buyers tell the agent what to do. Typically, this caller is either an experienced traveler or one who has discussed the trip previously and wants to book or change some already existing arrangements. When taking a reservation over the telephone, agents must make sure they get all the facts they need during the first call.

Agencies that handle a large number of commercial accounts usually receive calls from buyers who know when, where, and how they want to go. Because most commercial agencies deliver tickets, their clients may never visit the agency or meet the individual who handles their arrangements.

Most agents work with the computer or complete a reservation card as the caller speaks. Those working directly with a CRT can enter the information, check availabilities, and confirm arrangements on the spot for most air itineraries and several other kinds of arrangements without needing to call back later with confirmations. Agents without a CRT should check the accuracy of the client's information quickly. Even if the trip is fairly straightforward, the agent should call back to confirm the arrangements.

More complicated plans require call-backs. Agents should always remember to discuss alternative arrangements for the client's second choice when appropriate. Knowing this in advance can save a considerable number of frustrating calls to both clients and suppliers.

More Questions to Ask

To the five familiar questions should be added

■ What is your business/home telephone number?

■ What is your address?

■ How will you be paying for this trip?

■ When will you be picking up your tickets/documents?

■ Do you have any special requests?

Outside Sales

Many outside sales opportunities begin within the office environment, frequently through telephone contact. This is particularly true of group sales. Travel agents sell to groups who have very different reasons to travel. Affinity groups, those not formed for the purpose of taking a single trip and including social, fraternal, religious, or educational organizations, often travel for specific reasons, like attending conventions or meetings. Destinations and travel dates for these groups are often predetermined. However, for these and other types of groups, an agent can offer to put together a total vacation package to be sold exclusively to the membership.

Agents should also take advantage of opportunities to sell group travel to their commercial clients. Many companies send their employees to sales meetings, conventions, and conferences. The agent can also design a trip to be used as an incentive for a company's employees, as a reward for the achievement of specified levels of sales or furthering other company goals.

Selling to Groups

Soliciting travel business from organizations requires careful consideration of the group's  makeup. To start, construct a profile of the average member in terms of age, economic status, background, social and cultural interests, and whatever other factors may have led the person to join the group. Then target the presentation to the average member. The profile can help the seller determine what approach to take, what choices to offer for destinations, and what specials needs of the members to consider.

When dealing with any group, it is important to establish a working relationship with the key decision maker who will act as group contact. This decision maker may well be what tour operators term a "pied piper," someone whom others will follow, whose opinions others will respect. These individuals are effective recruiters and, if satisfied, will travel frequently with an ever-growing number of followers. VIP treatment must be extended to this person who may be single-handedly filling the seats or cabins that the agent has blocked. This individual will communicate the desires of the group to the agent and relay information from the agent to the group's members. This one-to-one approach lessens the chance of confusion and misunderstanding in the planning stages of a trip.

It is virtually impossible for an agent to go before a group with a random selection of trips and expect agreement in an open meeting. A more effective approach is for the agent, after discussion with organizers of the group, to use a target profile and prepare a single trip package. The preliminary work of establishing destination, dates of travel, and price must have been completed prior to the presentation. Then the agent can guarantee that travel and accommodations are available. Otherwise, there is the risk of not being able to deliver what is promised, losing the sale, and also forfeiting the chance of any future business.

Group travel operations present interesting perspectives on the agent-supplier relationship. Although in theory it seems as easy to book a reservation for forty people as it is for one, in practice the administration of a group reservation is not quite so simple. Most suppliers (airlines, cruise lines, hotels) have departments that specialize in handling group business. It is through these group desks, rather than through the regular reservation channels, that agents must work. Group bookings have special payment procedures, cancellation penalties, negotiated pricing, and require multiple travel arrangements if the members of the group originate in more than one city.

Group sales require the blocking of space to accommodate all participants. Assuring the availability of arrangements and accommodations may take a year's lead time. Schedules must be drawn specifying due dates for reservations, deposits, final payments from participants, payments to suppliers, mailings of rooming lists to hotels, and issuance of tickets and deposits. Generally, all arrangements for group travel must be completed within thirty days of the departure date.

Pricing of group travel also differs from that of individual travel. Airlines either establish special group rates or offer discounts off normal fares. In some situations, a carrier might offer a free seat for each specified number of paying passengers, up to an agreed maximum. The agency can earn an override commission on the group's tickets.

Similarly, hotels may negotiate incentives to attract group business, especially during periods when occupancy may be low. Incentives can include free accommodations, the number depending on the total number of rooms occupied. One of the rooms may be upgraded to a suite at no additional charge. The hotel might also offer amenities like wine or fruit in each room or provide a cocktail party for the group at no charge. The agent negotiates with suppliers for such incentives.

Incentive Groups

Companies use travel to reward employees who have contributed to successful marketing efforts or dealers and distributors who have achieved a certain level of sales. When an agent designs a trip for an incentive group, the mechanics of transportation and accommodation planning are much the same as for any other group. However, making arrangements for the activities of the group at the destination requires creativity. Theme dinners, cocktail parties, special sporting events such as golf or tennis tournaments, or tours of locations that have some connection to the host company's activities are features that can be included in an incentive trip.

This type of planning requires working closely with the destination's tour operators and hotels. In some cases, prepackaged tours or regularly scheduled events are available. In other cases, the agent and supplier must design features that are unique.

Meeting Planning

Corporate meeting planners and travel counselors arrange meetings and conventions for various groups and companies. Depending on the size and duration of the meeting, the planner may be involved in transportation and accommodations for participants, preparation of the meeting space, planning of meals and functions, sightseeing, and often, pre- or post-meeting tours.

Participants may come to the meeting from a number of cities. The planner must coordinate reservations and ticketing so that documents can be mailed out on time. Airport transfers and hotel check-ins must mesh with the various schedules.

Organizers work with the group sales departments of hotels to coordinate a meeting. The head of the department is usually the convention sales/services manager. At some properties it is necessary to deal with several departments, such as sales for planning and pricing, catering for meals and functions, and reservations for accommodations. The planner acts as the intermediary conveying the wishes and requirements of the group to the supplier and assuring the group that the requirements are met.

Special Services

Many clients have special needs. Frequent business travelers, for example, usually need special treatment from counselors and suppliers, as do handicapped travelers, families with children, senior citizens, members of certain religious groups, and honeymooners.

Business Travelers

Although businesspeople are among the most experienced travelers, they can often be the most demanding and intolerant of delays or problems. They frequently know exactly what they want, yet  simultaneously demand care and attention. Contrary to popular opinion, business travelers usually travel because they must. Some may enjoy the experience, especially initially; others may view travel as an unpleasant, tiresome chore. Because travel represents a means to an end, business travelers need an agent who is quick, accurate, and efficient.

Although business travel is commonplace, it still denotes prestige and status within an organization. Business travelers often make reservations, changes, or cancellations close to departure or en route, so agencies that specialize in this kind of travel have developed services to accommodate them. Agencies may deliver tickets to an office or to a special box at the airport. Most business travelers use corporate credit cards. The agency may present recommendations designed to get a company better value for its money. Finally, agencies may install a WATS line available only to business travelers who may wish to change arrangements while they are traveling. The agency may join a consortium that offers a worldwide network of service available twenty-four hours a day. If there is sufficient volume to justify it, the agency may even agree to establish a branch office within the company.

Agencies that court business travelers point to several distinct benefits. Business travel takes place year-round, free from the seasonality that affects vacation travel. It can provide a steady source of income and help eliminate potentially damaging peaks and valleys in the agency's annual business. Furthermore, some agencies claim that business travelers request relatively straightforward arrangements that do not require much research, rarely need a selling presentation, and tend to repeat familiar itineraries.

Business travel can create additional revenue. Business travelers frequently use the same agency for their vacations. As a result of handling normal business travel, an agency may extend its services to the lucrative field of arranging meetings and conventions. Finally, an agency may develop incentive travel programs for its clients' employees.

Of business travelers, 13 million (39 percent) are women; 20 million (61 percent) are men. On an average, the corporate traveler takes 16 business trips annually and incorporates some vacation time into 23 percent of those trips.

Since corporate accounts are such desirable ones, the competition among agencies to secure them is fierce. Maintaining these accounts, therefore, is essential and can only be achieved through attentive, conscientious customer service, the primary factor that keeps clients returning to the same agency. At the first sign of apathy or disinterest, business travelers will take their accounts elsewhere, in search of more personal service.

As with any group, business travelers present agencies with special challenges. Any agency intending to service them needs completely computerized reservation, accounting, and bookkeeping systems. The agency must monitor accounts receivable carefully and avoid sudden cash shortages. Finally, each agency must study the cost of providing services such as ticket delivery to determine whether they are profitable.

Handicapped Travelers

Today, the likelihood of an agent needing to secure travel services for handicapped clients is great. Currently, there are nearly forty-three million handicapped persons in this country, and the number is expected to increase.

 On January 26, 1992, the public accommodations section of the 1990 Americans with Disabilities Act took effect, an act that guarantees the handicapped access to the same services enjoyed by those without disabilities. The provisions of this act will make travel far less problematic for those persons with physical limitations.

Travelers with disabilities represent an enormous, virtually untapped market, and the agents and suppliers who understand their special requirements and can respond to these needs with appropriate services will find a lucrative market and great personal satisfaction. By the broadest definition, handicapped travelers have impaired mobility and require special arrangements. For the travel industry such a definition may include people in wheelchairs, the visually or hearing impaired, the very elderly, or those who require oxygen or a respirator.

Although airline procedures regarding handicapped travelers have been regulated by the Air Carrier Access Act of 1990, and hotels and restaurants are required to adhere to standards set down in the 1992 additions to the Americans with Disabilities Act, travel counselors would be well advised to check with each supplier as the need arises and as far ahead as possible. Provided there is sufficient advance notice, the itinerary is carefully chosen, and suppliers are fully aware of the client's condition, handicapped travelers may go almost anywhere and see almost anything.

Great strides have been made, particularly in the United States, to accommodate handicapped travelers. The general norms that apply to wheelchair travelers and to deaf, or blind travelers, can be briefly summarized.

Air Travel: Airlines require advance notice, normally a minimum of forty-eight hours, to accommodate handicapped passengers. Many special services are available, some provided automatically by the airline, others requiring initiative on the part of the agent. Several computer codes are used to alert the airline to the client's special requirements and are entered in the PNR. These special services may include advance boarding, wheelchair availability, storage of canes and crutches, "meet and assist" escort service, dietetic meals, fully reclining seats, and accommodation for seeing-eye dogs. Airlines permit a seeing-eye dog to travel in the passenger cabin free of charge. The agent must check international flights carefully, however, because some foreign countries quarantine all arriving animals.

Many people treat people with disabilities either by being overly solicitous or distant and rude. The best rule to follow is to treat every client with dignity and assume that every client, regardless of disability, can competently convey his or her travel likes, dislikes, and requirements.

First-class seats are ideal, but if this is not an option, agents should consider booking aisle seats in coach, which may provide more leg room. Airlines usually try to leave the middle seat in a row of three empty if a client is occupying one of the others. By law, carriers may not exclude any qualified handicapped person from any seat in an exit row or any other location, except to comply with FAA safety regulations that govern the procedure for the emergency evacuation of the aircraft.

Rail Travel: Turboliners and Amfleet equipment marked with a stylized wheelchair provide one seat per car specially designed for handicapped passengers and have a storage space for wheelchairs nearby. There are also special bathrooms in these cars. Certain sleeping accommodations on Superliners are adapted for the handi-

capped. On all other Amtrak rolling stock, seats are usually wide enough and accessible, with ample aisle space to negotiate a wheelchair 26 inches wide. On many Amtrak trains, passengers may order food and drinks at their seats. Bathrooms on these trains are not suitable.

Once again the agent should relay reservations and special requests for handicapped passengers as early as possible. Amtrak supplies a Special Services Request Form on which the agent and client provide pertinent details of the special accommodations and services being requested.  Amtrak will carry seeing-eye dogs at no charge and, except on Metroliners, offers a discount to handicapped passengers. For further details on Amtrak's services and procedures for handicapped travelers, travel agents should consult the *Amtrak Sales Guide.* For foreign railroads the travel agent should consult the relevant office in the United States.

Car Rentals: Some major car-rental companies can, with about forty-eight hours' advance notice, provide cars with hand controls for handicapped drivers. If transfer from the terminal to the car is difficult, the car can be waiting outside the baggage claim area if airport regulations permit. Some smaller cars, particularly in Europe, may not have room for a wheelchair in the trunk. Other transportation companies now specialize in renting vans with power lifts, raised roofs, and sophisticated tie-down systems designed to carry one or two wheelchair-bound travelers and up to five other passengers.

Motorcoach Tours: Some tour operators specialize in tours for the handicapped and use motorcoaches with hydraulic lifts and enlarged baggage compartments. Most other tour operators will not accept handicapped passengers without a companion and a full written statement of the degree and nature of the disability. On escorted tours, so many different hotels, restaurants, rest stops, and sightseeing excursions are included that many tour operators feel only specialists should handle handicapped travelers. Such specialists are increasing in number, and tour packages of all kinds, ranging from trips to Disney World to African safaris and around-the-world air tours, are now available from many American tour operators who have expertise in providing travel for the handicapped. Gone are the days when travel was an option only for the fully mobile and able-bodied.

Hotels: Hotels can pose a number of problems for wheelchair clients. The entrance should be level or provided with a ramp. If no rooms are available on the ground floor, there must be elevators big enough to accommodate a wheelchair.

Some smaller European hotels have only very small elevators with narrow entrances. Carpets impede a wheelchair's progress, and door sills are difficult to negotiate.

Within the room, light switches, thermostats, air-conditioning controls, and locks must be low enough to be reached from a sitting position. The bathroom must have a tub with safety bars. There should be enough room in the bathroom to accommodate the wheelchair with the door either open or closed. The bed should be the same height as the wheelchair to permit easy transfers. In case of emergency a bedside telephone is vital.

In response to the 1992 addendum to the Americans with Disabilities Act, hotels will be required to provide accessibility to all public areas of the hotel, including front desks low enough to be comfortably reached from a wheelchair, and will need to modify existing guest rooms to better meet the needs of handicapped guests. Failure to do so will result in stiff fines.

Cruises: Cruises may pose the biggest barriers to travelers with disabilities. Many cruise lines refuse to accept the very elderly or passengers with a history of illness without a doctor's certificate. In the event of sudden and serious deterioration in their condition, it might take longer than usual to reach a hospital. Most ships will not carry animals of any kind, including seeing-eye dogs, and quarantine regulations apply at foreign ports.

On older cruise ships, cabin doors are often quite narrow and are sometimes entered at an angle from narrow passageways. Space inside the normal cabin does not permit easy maneuvering of wheelchairs. It is only with the latest generation of ships that consideration of the needs of the wheel-chair-bound passenger has been addressed by providing some cabins designed to accommodate a handicapped person. Even on these newer ships tendering is next to impossible for wheelchair passengers.

Nevertheless, if these difficulties can be reduced or eliminated, cruising offers an excellent vacation for the handicapped. The proximity of restaurants, entertainment, planned activities, and open deck space enables the handicapped passenger to be virtually independent.

Further Reference

The Society for the Advancement of Travel for the Handicapped (SATH) is an organization of travel agents and suppliers devoted to encouraging the development of special tours and facilities. The society publishes a number of informative brochures and pamphlets, available from SATH, 347 Fifth Ave., Suite 610, New York, NY 10016.

Travel for the Disabled, a valuable collection of lists of resources for the disabled, may assist agents and the travelers themselves in making suitable travel arrangements. It is available through Twin Peaks Press, Vancouver, WA 98666.

The *International Directory of Access Guides* provides listings and descriptions of publications that contain information about facilities around the world for handicapped and elderly travelers. It is available from Rehabilitation International USA in New York City.

The *OAG Travel Planner* contains information about suppliers and facilities that provide specifically for handicapped passengers. It also contains a list of publications describing facilities for the handicapped in different countries.

Families with Children

Children are welcome on all modes of transportation and in most hotels. Many suppliers provide special rates for children accompanying their parents. Cruise lines frequently accept the third and fourth occupants of a cabin at considerably reduced rates, or even for free. Some hotel chains allow children under 18 to share a room with their parents at no charge.

Airlines frequently offer discounted fares to children flying with a parent. Airlines normally preboard families with young children and can serve children's meals if they are requested in advance. Baby strollers will fit through the aisles in the cabin and are stowed in the overhead bins, beneath the seat, or in a baggage compartment. Although flight attendants can heat milk for babies, it is unfair to expect them to look after or feed a child. Children on planes are their parents' responsibility.

Some cruise lines offer special programs of activities for children. The parents are then free to leave them for almost the entire day, if they desire. Most cruise lines offer babysitting services subject to the availability of crew members.

Senior Citizens

Senior citizen travel is an area of specialization for many tour operators and travel agents. Once again, provided there is sufficient advance planning and written notice to the operator, senior citizens can travel with great freedom. In general, people tend to underestimate the stamina and interests of senior citizens.

Senior citizens represent a growing and important market for travel suppliers. Possessing leisure time and disposable income, America's older citizens travel in great numbers and are a significant source of repeat business for the suppliers of travel services who succeed in meeting their unique travel requirements.

Religious Groups

Members of some religious groups may require special attention. They need to attend services on a particular day or at a particular time each day. They may have restricted diets. In some instances they are not able to travel on certain holy days. Since religious beliefs are intensely personal, agents

may expect that clients will volunteer this kind of information. Usually they do. Yet it does no harm, if the agent senses that a client is interested in any of these topics, to ask if there are any other special observances. Clients who request particular foods may be indicating other needs that they do not think of expressing.

Honeymooners

Even in difficult economic times, honeymoon travel remains relatively stable. Perhaps it's the idea that the wedding trip is a "once in a lifetime" proposition or because a getaway is greatly needed after the stressful wedding preparation period, but newlyweds are rarely willing to forego a honeymoon of some sort. Naturally their requirements will vary depending on budgetary considerations and the age and interests of the couple, but conscientious agents can succeed in making arrangements for a perfect honeymoon trip if they know the right questions to ask and take the time to research appropriate options. Working on honeymoons is often very time-consuming, but couples who have had memorable wedding trips are excellent sources of repeat business and will speak glowingly of their agency to family and friends, all of whom are potential clients.

Statistics furnished by bridal magazines indicate that honeymooners today spend more on their trips than they once did, because many are marrying later and therefore tend to be more financially stable.

Charters

Most people think of airlines, railroads, cruise lines, and motorcoach operators as companies that offer only regularly scheduled departures to the public. But suppliers also offer trains, airplanes, ships, and buses for charter, and some companies charter exclusively.

Occasionally travel agencies, particularly those that specialize in groups, find it necessary or profitable to charter equipment rather than book a block of seats on scheduled service. A charter differs from scheduled transportation in that the agency purchases the complete use of the equipment at a net price. The price depends on when

Chartering a Cruise Ship

Suppose a travel agency charters a cruise ship for seven days to sail from Los Angeles to Puerto Vallarta and back, calling at two other ports. The cruise line quotes a net rate of $350,000.

The ship has 350 cabins with a maximum capacity of 600 passengers. The net rate includes all costs except port charges, tips, shore excursions, and personal items. The charterer must project the costs of publicity and promotion, including the production and distribution of brochures, the preparation and placement of media advertising, and the staff time needed to process bookings. The charterer must also decide whether to pay commissions to other agents who might want to sell cabins. These additional costs might total $100,000.

In establishing the selling price of this charter to individuals, the travel agent will be influenced by several factors: the price of similar cruises; the price of alternative kinds of vacations; a sense of what the market will bear. The main concern will be to get a substantial return on the $450,000 investment. Divide this investment by 600 passengers and the per person cost is $750. But suppose not all the cabins can be sold? If only 450 tickets are sold, the per person cost then becomes $1,000. The agent could now say that every booking in excess of 450 represents pure profit; or the price could be increased to, say, $1,099 per person, thus ensuring a lower break-even point of just over 400 bookings.

This example would be complicated by many other variables. For example, it is important to calculate the percentage of more expensive to less expensive cabins in establishing selling prices and the break-even point. But, basically, that is how charters work. Risks, rewards, and losses are all potentially greater than if scheduled service is used.

and where the charterer wants to go. Often the agency charters on behalf of a group or organization and adds other arrangements to form a complete tour. Chartering is more risky than scheduled service, and the chances for greater profits or losses are correspondingly higher.

Travel professionals can become involved with charters in one of two ways: the agency charters equipment directly from a supplier, or agents sell individual seats on a train, ship, plane, or bus chartered by another agency or tour operator.

Charter Motorcoaches

Increasingly, agencies are discovering that motorcoach charters represent a low-risk opportunity with the chance of a respectable return. Chartering a motorcoach never requires the large sums of money necessary for cruise ships or airplanes. Moreover, motorcoach operators usually have far more equipment available for charter. Cruise ships and airplanes are heavily committed to scheduled service. Stringent government regulations once severely restricted the marketing of motorcoach charters, but with recent relaxation in the licensing laws, the practice has grown rapidly.

Summary

Most sales situations can be divided into two categories: inside or outside. Inside sales consist of an agent selling to a customer face-to-face or on the telephone. However, not every telephone call results in a sale — many calls are from "shoppers." Using proper telephone skills, many times shoppers can be converted into buyers.

Opportunities for sales exist outside the office as well. Selling to groups is a very profitable business. Different types of groups include incentive, conventions, or affinity. Identifying the correct decision maker in a group and presenting a trip that is tailored to its specific needs will lead to success.

Travel agents who understand the special requirements of handicapped travelers and respond to those needs with appropriate plans are tapping a lucrative market. The 1990 Americans with Disabilities Act has guaranteed travelers with disabilities access to the same facilities and services as those with no disability.

Chapter Wrap-up

DISCUSSION TOPICS

Telephone Sales

Searching for information by telephone, if handled incorrectly, can be extremely annoying to both the client and the counselor. In each of the following scenarios, something is definitely lacking on the part of the counselor. Review each situation and suggest a better counselor response; continue the role play to the point of sale.

Client — How much is the fare to Denver?

Counselor — $69 is the cheapest fare.

Client — I have a group of forty senior citizens who want to go to Mexico. What packages do you have?

Counselor — Hold on and I'll go and look for a brochure.

Recommendations

It is a counselor's job to help clients select programs suitable for their needs. Suppose a repeat business client has asked for help in choosing a hotel property.

Agent — Oh, Mr. White, I'd really recommend the Belvedere rather than the Hartford. It is much more centrally located. The rooms are bigger, and the airport limousine stops right at the door. The Hartford overlooks a smelly paint factory and really doesn't look very nice in this brochure. I don't think you would want to stay there.

What would happen if the Hartford turned out to be the only downtown hotel available when Mr. White wants to stay? How could the agent possibly handle that situation after her original conversation? How could this have been avoided?

Special Client Needs

Compose a list of hotel services needed for the following groups or individuals:

- Forty senior citizens on a deluxe air package tour
- Three busloads of junior high school students on an overnight field trip
- A family reunion of fifty relatives ranging in age from 3 to 87
- Three handicapped couples traveling together

As an agent, would you sell all of these groups the same property at the same time if space was available? Why or why not? What other special considerations would be needed to successfully sell transportation to any of these groups?

Follow-Up
Chapter 11

CHAPTER OBJECTIVES

After completing this chapter, the reader should be able to

- Explain three ways clients change plans
- Describe four emergency situations
- Discuss four types of specialized travel insurance
- Determine how much insurance to sell to a customer
- List the steps involved in a reissue
- Relate the importance of a client profile
- Compare the differences between a written and an oral contract

VOCABULARY

After completing this chapter, the reader should be able to define

- Contract
- Coverage
- Double indemnity
- Errors and omissions
- Itinerary
- Liability
- Policy
- Premium

Introduction

A sale is not complete until the clients depart on their trip with all payments made and documents received. A sale may last several weeks or even several months. For example:

April
Clients discuss trip.
Clients return later to book.
Agent makes reservations.
Clients make deposit.

May
Clients make final payment.
Agent receives documents from supplier.
Agent generates tickets.

June
Clients depart.

Changes after the Sale

A travel agent, by offering to book a trip, promises to deliver the arrangements that the client has requested. The offer implies that the travel agent will make correct reservations, issue the necessary documents, look after the client's interests, and inform the client of payment deadlines. Failure to follow through, whether through negligence or incompetence, breaches this implied contract.

Additional services such as the reissue of documents may also be necessary when clients wish to change or cancel features of their original booking. Changes are part of every agent's daily responsibilities. The ability to make changes quickly and efficiently is one of the basic reasons why consumers — in particular, business travelers — use agents.

Before altering arrangements, agents should make sure that the changes are in the client's best interests. The agent should ask the reasons for the changes, restate the benefits of the original choice, quote rates for the new choice, and inform the client that the new choice may not be available. When changing arrangements, an agent should never cancel any reservation until the alternative has been confirmed.

Clients May Change Arrangements in Three Ways:

1. Add to them.
2. Exchange one arrangement for an identical or different one.
3. Cancel without rebooking.

Common Reasons for Changes in Plans

From the time a trip is booked up until departure, emergencies may force a client to cancel or change plans. Strikes, bankruptcies, political upheavals, earthquakes, and other natural disasters are all reasons for alteration or cancellation of arrangements. Many agencies have emergency policies and procedures in place to help agents decide when and how to make necessary changes.

Airline reservation systems can help in emergency situations by quickly identifying clients who may be affected. Through the agency's terminals, an agent can request identification of the PNRs by agent, airline, flight number, travel date, departure, or arrival city. These PNRs are then sent electronically to a specified queue number for review. This process is known as a queue sort.

Strikes

Strikes are among the most common disruptions to a client's trip. Since an airline strike affects a number of clients, speed is vital to secure alternative arrangements. The last-minute scramble to re-book can wreak havoc by tying up phones and computers. During most strikes, alternatives are usually available, providing the same, or virtually the same, arrangements. Strikes hit hardest whenever they make it necessary for a trip to be cancelled. A strike by air-traffic controllers or dock workers is crippling. Although some strikes can be anticipated, many get little advance publicity and are difficult to predict.

Bankruptcies

Although airline bankruptcies have been in the spotlight in the 1990s, tour operators, cruise lines, hotels, and other suppliers also slip into Chapter 11 (bankruptcy/reorganization) and possibly into Chapter 7 (liquidation). Agents have the responsibility to choose suppliers carefully in an effort to protect their client's interests, as well as their own. It is always prudent to inform the client of the Chapter 11 status of a supplier.

To guarantee that there will be no loss of monies, clients should always use a credit card to pay for travel. This will protect customers under the Fair Credit Billing Act, so that they do not have to pay for a service they have not received.

Other Emergencies

No less disastrous to a client's plans are coups, civil wars, political violence, epidemics, and natural catastrophes like earthquakes and hurricanes. No supplier can take responsibility for acts of God. On the other hand, no responsible supplier or agent would purposely expose a passenger to dangers of this kind. Agents should keep up-to-date on threatening weather forecasts and political upheavals. The State Department in Washington, D.C., issues regular travelers' advisories for countries that are in political upheaval or where conditions may be dangerous to American citizens.

Occasionally, an emergency develops after clients have left on their trips. In most instances, tour operators, airlines, and even United States foreign-service officers take the lead in assisting affected passengers. United States embassies and consulates are charged with the responsibility, within reason, of assisting citizens who get into trouble while traveling abroad. Government offi-

---

United States embassy or consulate employees could be of some assistance in these situations.

1. A Denver businessman has his passport, money, and credit cards stolen.

Most United States embassies can issue temporary emergency passports and arrange for funds to be transmitted quickly from the United States. Through the Citizen's Emergency Center in Washington, D.C., the embassy or consulate can provide small government loans to assist travelers until private funds arrive.

2. A Houston couple touring by car leaves no itinerary at home and cannot be located when there is a sudden family emergency.

The Citizen's Emergency Center can relay a request for assistance to the nearest consular official who will attempt to trace the travelers. Frequently, disasters such as earthquakes, floods, or crashes prompt numerous inquiries to the center about Americans believed to be living or traveling in the affected area.

3. A college student from Missouri is arrested for possession of narcotics.

Depending on the local situation, consular officials may visit the student arrested by a foreign government and advise him of his legal rights. The officials can arrange legal counsel and contact the prisoner's family. Beyond that, they must respect the legal system of the host country.

4. An elderly tourist from New Jersey falls seriously ill.

The Citizen's Emergency Center can transmit details of the patient's medical history and transfer funds to pay for medical care.

---

cials must respect the laws of the host country, even if the laws are fundamentally different from the American system. Embassies cannot intervene in private legal disputes or provide tourist services such as hotel or transportation reservations, check cashing, or sightseeing information.

Death

If a client dies while aboard a ship or aircraft or while traveling in a foreign country, the travel agent may be called on to assist the family in returning the body to the United States. If a client dies on board a ship, the ship's doctor can arrange to fly the body home from the next port. Burials at sea are not common. If the client were traveling alone, the cruise line would inform the agent of the death because the line would probably have no other reliable contact. The agent could then be responsible for checking all arrangements and costs and informing relatives.

If a client dies on a plane, the airline arranges for transportation of the body. The pilot radios the news of the passenger's death to the proper ground authorities, and they contact the next of kin or the travel agent and make necessary arrangements for the shipment of the body according to the wishes of the family.

The death of clients in a foreign country can involve the agent directly. Arrangements for transporting the body back to the United States for burial involve a lot of bureaucratic complications and customs problems. The agent should direct the family to contact the nearest American embassy or consulate, which will send an official to mediate with the host government, either for local burial, if desired, or transport of the body. The embassy or consular office will also know local requirements and costs for such arrangements. The Citizen's Emergency Center in Washington, D.C., can assist in contacting United States officials abroad.

Client Protection Against Changes

Travel counselors may act as agents for various insurance companies and offer travel insurance as a service to clients. The commission received from the sale of insurance can also be a significant source of revenue for agencies. The four basic types of insurance can be purchased separately, in combination, or as a part of a complete package.

Types of Travel Insurance
- Flight
- Travel Accident/Health
- Baggage and Personal Possession
- Trip Cancellation or Interruption

Flight Insurance

Flight insurance is a form of accident insurance. It is sold by travel agencies and tour operators; insurance companies sell it from booths and machines at airports; and it is also automatically provided as a benefit when tickets are charged on some credit cards. Flight insurance provides short-term coverage for accidents that occur during travel. Premiums are very low and reflect the safety record of the airlines.

The coverage applies to flights on both scheduled and chartered carriers. Flight insurance offers benefits up to $1,000,000 for accidental loss of life, limb, or sight occurring while the insured is riding as a passenger on a flight or while on airport premises or on other forms of transportation used by an airline to transport passengers, such as mo-

bile lounges or transfer buses. The client chooses the time limits of the insurance when purchasing the policy. Coverage begins when the client leaves home and includes the ride to the airport. Coverage ends when flights are completed or after 180 days, whichever comes first. Coverage is extended if any delays that are beyond the client's control occur because of scheduling changes by the carrier. Flight insurance is similar to life insurance. In the case of death, benefits are paid to a beneficiary chosen by the insured.

Travel Accident/Health Insurance

Some insurance companies combine flight and health and accident insurance, although the two should be separated. Flight insurance is bought frequently but collected on rarely; health and accident insurance is often needed. In the United States health insurance up to age 65 is privately purchased, either individually or through company-sponsored health plans. Each plan has different rules about policy-holder treatment away from home. Most people do not know what would happen to them if they became suddenly ill or had an accident while outside of the United States.

As a general rule, the larger and more modern the foreign city, the better the health care. Conversely, the more remote the area, the worse the medical resources. Public hospitals in countries with socialized medicine will not turn away a traveler in need, but neither will the treatment be free, with few exceptions.

Most foreign hospitals will not honor American health insurance plans. The client should not count on paying the bill with a credit card. Payment must be made on the spot with cash or travelers cheques. The patient should keep complete and accurate records in case a home health plan will reimburse.

Finding an English-speaking doctor is not always easy either, though the hotel staff and United States embassy or consulate can be of help. A person who is ill may choose to go home by emergency evacuation instead of being hospitalized in

Travel Insurance

Here is an example of travel insurance plans offered by the Edmund A. Cocco Agency.

GlobalCare Everywhere℠*

A. ✈ Trip Cancellation/Interruption Protection

- **Trip Cancellation/Interruption Insurance** — Covers non-refundable payments for hotels, side tours, airfare, cruiselines, trains or buses up to the level of coverage selected, if your trip is cancelled or interrupted due to illness, injury or death of you, a traveling companion or family member; bankruptcy or default of a tour operator, airline or cruise line; or terrorist incident.
- **Travel Delay Insurance** — Covers additional travel expenses and accommodations due to delay of 12 or more hours ($100 a day for a maximum of 5 days).
- **Accidental Death Insurance** — Provides 24-hour protection for loss of life during your trip (up to $10,000).
- **24-Hour Emergency Message Center****

B. Medical Protection

- **Emergency Medical Expense Coverage** — Covers medical costs due to accidental injury and/or illness with no deductible.
- **Accidental Death Insurance**
- **Medical Transportation** — Arranges and pays for transportation to a more appropriate facility or back home, if medically necessary.
- **24-Hour Hotline** for medical referrals and on-the-spot hospital payments.
- **Collision/Loss Damage Insurance**** (optional with medical protection only)— Provides up to $25,000 coverage for collision/loss damage to a rental car ($5.00 for each day the car is rented).

C. Baggage Protection

- **Baggage Insurance** — Covers lost, stolen or damaged baggage up to the level of coverage selected, during your entire trip, not just on a common carrier.
- **Baggage Delay Insurance** — Covers emergency purchases if baggage is delayed 24 or more hours (up to $100).
- **24-Hour Travel Hotline** for emergency cash and lost document assistance.

*This is a partial description of benefits. See the back cover for a more detailed explanation of GlobalCare insurance benefits, including some restrictions and limitations.

**The Emergency Message Center and Collision/Loss Damage Insurance are for travel in the U.S., Canada, the Caribean and Mexico only.

Call **1-800-821-2488** for more information on GlobalCare Travel Insurance.

GlobalCare Everywhere℠

For emergency use only
Services provided by Access America, Inc.

To get HELP when you travel, call:
1-800-654-1908
(in the U.S., Canada, Puerto Rico
and the Virgin Islands)
or
(202) 822-3948-collect
(from Alaska, Washington, D.C.,
and all other locations)
Telex Number: 706305 ACCESS WSH
(in Washington, D.C.)

Insurance benefits underwritten by BCS Insurance Company
(in the state of TX dba Medical Indemnity of America, Inc.)

Please Cut Out and Keep in Your Wallet

Travel Protection Programs

The three GlobalCare programs can be purchased separately or in any combination.

A. Trip Cancellation/Interruption Protection

The Trip Cancellation/Interruption Program can be purchased at **$5.50 for each $100** of coverage. **A $300 minimum purchase per individual or family is required.**

Coverage can be **purchased in $100 increments** up to a maximum of $10,000. Some pricing examples appear below:

Amount of Coverage	Price
$ 300 (minimum)	$ 16.50
$ 400	$ 22.00
$ 1,000	$ 55.00
$ 3,000	$165.00
$10,000 (maximum)	$550.00

B. Emergency Medical Protection

The Medical Program can be purchased separately by **each** traveling individual.

	Plan I	Plan II	Plan III
Medical Coverage	$ 2,500	$ 5,000	$ 10,000
Accidental Death	$25,000	$75,000	$150,000
Medical Transportation	$10,000	$25,000	$ 50,000
Prices (Per Individual):			
Travel Days	**Plan I**	**Plan II**	**Plan III**
1-5	$15	$19	$ 26
6-10	$25	$32	$ 42
11-18	$37	$48	$ 63
19-24	$50	$65	$ 86
25-30	$62	$80	$103
Daily Rate for trips over 30 days	$ 2	$ 3	$ 4

C. Baggage Protection

The Baggage Program can be purchased at **$5.00 for each $100** of coverage. **A $300 minimum purchase per individual or family is required.**

Coverage can be purchased in $100 increments up to a maximum of $3,000. Some pricing examples appear below:

Amount of Coverage	Price
$ 300 (minimum)	$ 15.00
$ 400	$ 20.00
$1,000	$ 50.00
$3,000 (maximum)	$150.00

Reprinted by permission of Edmund A. Cocco Agency

a foreign country. Unless the person has insurance for such a service, the cost is likely to be prohibitive. Most airlines have rules about transporting people who are ill, and these rules are fairly strict.

Many insurance packages offer emergency medical assistance. By calling one number, the client can get all the help needed — a doctor, hospitalization, and emergency evacuation. These plans also provide payment to the doctor or hospital and save the patient the burden of finding extra cash.

Health and accident insurance protects the client from travel- and non-travel-related accidents and sickness at all times while away from home. For accidents, the amount the client or beneficiary receives depends on how the loss occurs. The terms *principal sum* and *double indemnity* on accident premium charts refer to the benefits payable. *Double indemnity* means that the insurance company will pay twice the principal sum if an accident is completely beyond the individual's ability to avoid.

Most policies exclude coverage for death or illness caused by acts of war or other dangerous activities. Individuals who participate in "dangerous activities" such as mountain climbing, skiing, or hang gliding may wish to purchase additional special-coverage insurance.

Baggage and Personal Possession Insurance

This coverage protects clients against loss or damage to baggage and personal possessions while traveling and picks up where the responsibility of  a carrier ends. Many travel insurance policies cover only losses in excess of the airline's responsibility.

Normally, only items owned by clients and taken for personal use are covered. Some policies cover items borrowed from other people just for the trip. Benefits are payable at actual cash value, up to specified limits, if baggage or personal possessions should be lost, stolen, or damaged. One premium covers all family members. There are very specific exceptions and limitations to baggage coverage,

and clients should read these carefully. Most companies limit the amount they will pay for loss of jewelry, furs, or cameras. Additionally, clients should be made aware of the reporting procedures necessary at the time of loss to ensure payment of their claims. These are detailed in the brochure and the policy.

Many homeowner insurance policies cover loss or damage of personal possessions even away from the home. Clients with such insurance may not be interested in additional baggage insurance. It should be noted that in contrast to most homeowner policies, baggage insurance rarely has a deductible and often covers mysterious disappearances that homeowner policies generally do not.

Trip Cancellation or Interruption Insurance

The fourth and perhaps most important coverage is trip cancellation or interruption protection. Many clients already have some form of health, accident, and personal possession coverage, but travel agencies are among the few sources from which to obtain trip cancellation insurance. Trip cancellation or interruption protection should be offered to all clients.

Trip cancellation or interruption insurance will reimburse clients for nonrefundable prepayments if they must cancel for a covered reason. It will likewise cover clients for any nonrefundable portion of their trip and the cost of their transportation home should they have to discontinue their trip once underway. It will also pay for transportation back to a group if clients remain behind temporarily because of a covered accident or illness.

Most policies reimburse clients or their beneficiaries for cancellation penalties or additional costs if they fall ill, suffer an accident, or die. Some policies also cover cancellation if clients are summoned for jury duty, served with a subpoena, or forced to vacate their home for some reason.

Some policies provide for upgrading before departure. Suppose that two clients are taking a cruise and they have both purchased trip cancellation insurance. If one cancels for a covered reason but the other decides to go on the cruise, the insurance would defray the cost of any single supplement.

Recent Innovations

In response to the changing travel industry, some insurance companies have introduced new coverages. These include

■ Coverage against being stranded or losing a prepayment if a supplier defaults

■ Coverage for extra expenses incurred as a result of a plane hijacking, unexpected airline strike, or cruise line bankruptcy

■ Reimbursement for emergency purchases if baggage is lost or delayed

These can be combined with the traditional coverages — health and accident, baggage, trip cancellation or interruption — in a single package.

Selling Travel Insurance

Many agents feel uncomfortable selling travel insurance because it tends to emphasize all the things that might go wrong on a trip. Conversely, travel insurance is a positive product for clients because it can protect their investment in a vacation. Travel representatives are concerned with customer service and want to make sure all aspects of a client's travel experience run smoothly. Insurance can offer that protection.

In many instances, travel insurance, particularly trip cancellation insurance, offers a client low-cost protection and an agent relief from liability. In the increasingly competitive environment of travel, supplemental products such as insurance can help determine an agency's profitability.

Whenever insurance seems advisable, clients should check their existing health and homeowners' policies to see what coverages they already have. They may want to insure their baggage only for the amount of the deductible on their homeowners' policy. If clients have no policy protecting them outside the United States, they may require more coverage.

Medicare insurance does not cover senior citizens outside the United States.

In addition to protecting the client's interests, the offering of travel insurance protects the travel agent. Clients have a right to know that protection is available and may hold an agent liable for losses that are incurred if the offer is not made. Including a brochure describing kinds of travel insurance with tickets or documentation mailed to the client may constitute an offer. The inclusion of a reference or recommendation in the selling presentation is more effective and more clearly an offer in a legal sense. If insurance is offered and refused, the fact should be noted in the client's file, and the client should be asked to initial a spot on the final invoice indicating that an offer has been refused.

Although it is dangerous to generalize, there are some occasions when travel insurance would appear highly desirable:

■ Any tour, cruise, airfare, and so on, with high cancellation penalties

■ All charter arrangements

■ All escorted tours where baggage may be left out overnight for early-morning pickup

■ Touring by car

Travel insurance is primarily sold through airline automated reservations systems. The agent keys insurance-coverage information into the client's PNR, accepts the client's premium, and gives the client a memorandum of coverage (insurance policy) provided by the insurance firm. The sale is transmitted to the insurance company, and confirmation of the sale is queued back to the agency. At the end of the month the agency receives a computer printout and billing statement listing all sales for the month, commissions earned by the agency, and a bill for the net premium due to the insurance firm. A selling agent's sine, or initials, appears on the computer printout, enabling the agency to track agent productivity.

Record Keeping

Automated agencies consider the PNR (Passenger Name Record) the basic client file, but complicated itineraries continue to require a physical receptacle for special correspondence and for the safekeeping of documents received on the client's behalf. Automation plays an important role in the elimination of excess paper. The queue system has replaced reminder calendars for ticketing dates, and the development of automated client profiles has eliminated index cards.

Once the trip is over, a file becomes the reference if a refund is necessary because of any discrepancy between what was promised and paid for and what was provided. The agent can make a hard copy of the information stored in the computer before the record is automatically erased. For a fee, carrier systems provide a microfiche record of an agency's reservations and eliminate the need to keep hard copies. In an emergency any agency can obtain a copy of the itinerary as originally confirmed by the airline.

The records of previous trips constitute the most basic data for the agency's marketing research. By reviewing these files, agencies can identify frequent travelers and their tastes; develop mailing lists of clients with special interests; and determine exactly where an agency's clientele live, who they are, and where they go. Hotels have for many years used registration forms for similar purposes. Automated back-office systems and personal computers permit the convenient storage of a large amount of information on either disk or tape. An agency can rapidly compile data lists on many subjects.

Under no circumstance may agents reissue tickets without receiving the originals back from the clients.

How Much Insurance to Sell

The amount of trip cancellation or interruption insurance that clients should purchase depends on the greatest possible loss that can be anticipated. It is relatively easy to calculate the total of all nonrefundable portions of prepaid arrangements. These cancellation penalties are clearly stated in the rules of airline fares or in brochures. For example, a client booking a two-week escorted tour involving full land prepayment of $1000 may be liable for a 20 percent penalty if cancellation occurs within twenty-one days of departure. The client may also have a $500 airfare with a 10 percent penalty if cancellation occurs within twenty-one days of departure. The maximum cost of cancellation here is $250 ($200 + $50).

If the client is forced to leave the tour once it has begun, the following costs might also arise:

■ The cost of returning to the United States at full fare from the most distant point on the itinerary

■ The cost of any unused, nonrefundable tour arrangements that have been prepaid

Some clients purchase insurance after considering what is probable rather than theoretically possible. When speaking with clients the counselor should also check the tour operator's brochure for refund policies. Should the tour operator, for example, refund 50 percent of unused land arrangements, the client would need to purchase less insurance. There are many variables to consider. The agent should present all the options in a clear way and allow the clients to determine what is best for them.

The Profile System

Through the use of computer profiles and other permanent records, agencies maintain information about the tastes and demands of frequent travelers. By consulting the ever-growing profile, an agent is able to anticipate preferences. Clients become dependent on the agent or the agency for seeing to it that their needs are met without their having to enumerate them for each reservation. By properly using client profiles, the travel agent has changed from an order-taker to a professional organizer who provides a real and recognized service.

Types of information besides name, address, and phone numbers that can be kept in a client's file could include

- Seating preference
- Frequent-flyer membership information
- Billing preferences
- Favored hotel chains or car-rental companies
- Special airline meal requests

Reissues

ARC and IATA ticketing manuals specify the procedures for reissuing tickets. When the supplier provides tickets or documents, the originals must be returned before new ones are issued. Depending on the change clients make, the agent may

- Reissue and collect additional funds
- Reissue at the same price (even exchange)
- Reissue and refund

Agents must be particularly careful if the reissue calls for a refund. On ARC ticket reports agents receive an immediate credit for airline refunds, but other suppliers can take some time to send a check. Normally agencies do not reimburse clients until the supplier sends a refund.

ARC rules currently prohibit reissuance of air tickets originally issued at another agency or by an airline, unless the airline involved specifically

agrees. Reissues that involve refunds are never approved in such circumstances.

Reissues constitute one of the biggest sources of fraud in the travel industry. Thieves who steal tickets frequently try to exchange them, and tickets can be altered by revalidation stickers to indicate a higher fare. Besides deliberate frauds, some refund calculations are so complicated that agents make honest mistakes. For these and many other reasons, agencies will not normally reissue a document unless they issued the original.

Itineraries

Whether a trip is simple or complicated, every client needs an itinerary. Airline tickets contain abbreviations that are confusing to the average traveler. Agency computer systems generate itineraries that clarify travel jargon.

Tour operators provide travel agents with detailed itineraries for the land portion of their clients' trips. FIT wholesalers also provide full itineraries. In addition to the information about transportation, accommodations, and sightseeing, the agent may want to add to or adapt these by including such things as average temperature, clothing suggestions, and shopping tips. A good itinerary builds anticipation for the trip, and this anticipation is one of the great delights of travel, almost equaling the experience of travel itself.

Contracts

Written contracts exist in the travel industry, but implied contracts are more common, especially between agent and client or supplier and client. Most charter operators require that all clients sign the charter agreement, which the travel agent must explain. Tour operators state in their brochures the conditions under which they will accept reservations. A client booking a tour can see these terms and agree to the contract. Because the client does not formally acknowledge the contract in writing, it is considered an implied contract. Airlines state the conditions of their contracts with passengers on the front and back covers of the ticket. Purchase of a ticket implies assent to the contract. Cruise lines operate much the same way. Car-rental companies always present a contract for signature.

Unless stated in writing on the invoice, ticket

jacket, agency documents, or displayed prominently somewhere in the office, the contract between agent and client is also considered to be implied. Basically, the client expects the agent to confirm reservations, send deposits, check timings, issue correct documents, and so on. Failure to execute any of these required steps is a breach of the implied contract. Clients expect the agent to protect their interests by negotiating on their behalf with suppliers for the best possible arrangements at the best possible price.

Because an implied contract is more open to misinterpretation or misunderstanding than a written contract, the agent must make sure that the client understands the nature of their relationship. Although some courts have taken the view that clients ought to know certain things, agents would be wise not to assume anything. By disclosing the agency-supplier relationship, the agent may limit potential liability. Agents can protect themselves from potential litigation problems by retaining a Consumer Disclosure Notice.

A written or oral disclaimer of responsibility for the actions of suppliers does not release the agent from the responsibility of checking all suppliers and arrangements carefully. Nothing protects an agent from negligence.

Handling Complaints

Because agents sell the products of various suppliers, their control over the elements of a trip is minimal or nonexistent once the client departs. How the suppliers perform will affect future relationships. Clients complain whenever they find discrepancies between what they thought they had bought and what is actually provided. The higher the expectations, the greater the frustration and disappointment. The agent, like the airline flight attendant or customer-service representative, the hotel desk clerk, or the cruise director's staff, is part of the front-line that receives the full force of these feelings regardless of where the problems originate.

Courtesy itself is a form of self-insurance. People who are helpful and courteous, even in the most trying circumstances, can frequently defuse a complaint. Discourtesy, on the other hand, often provokes complaints in circumstances that are far less serious.

Disclaimer Statements

Many travel agents include a consumer disclaimer notice on their invoices, ticket  jackets, or itineraries. By doing this, they have protection from clients who may have otherwise sued for misrepresentation. The following is an example of this kind of disclaimer:

[NAME OF TRAVEL AGENCY] is acting only in the capacity of an agent for the various suppliers of travel services listed on your travel documents and itinerary. This agency is not liable for any personal injury, property damage, or other loss, accident, delay, or inconvenience caused by any supplier or any party not under its control. Your acceptance of travel documents indicates your understanding and agreement to this.

For clients who refuse to take advice from their travel agent, the following is a disclaimer of liability that many travel agents have their clients sign and date. This can avert a lawsuit as well.

I have personally selected the travel suppliers (airlines, tour operators, hotels, car-rental companies, etc.) for the travel arrangements that I purchased from [NAME OF TRAVEL AGENCY]. I have been advised of the possible difficulties and am also aware that [NAME OF TRAVEL AGENCY] cannot be held responsible for any losses or inconveniences that I might encounter as a result of my purchase of travel arrangements from these suppliers. I agree that any claims that I might have regarding these services shall be made only to the travel service suppliers and not to [NAME OF TRAVEL AGENCY].

Although clients who travel may be unaware of the distinction or even unwilling to make such a distinction, there are two kinds of complaints. Some arise from errors of omission or commission by travel agents. Others result from dissatisfaction with suppliers. The agent should listen carefully to the client's full explanation of what occurred. Before assigning blame, hazarding guesses, or apologizing, the agent must obtain all the facts and must clarify any uncertainties by asking questions. Agents should never admit liability or responsibility for whatever went wrong without discussing the client's complaint with the agency manager. Offering a client a small sum of money to compensate for hurt feelings or missed features could be interpreted as an admission of responsibility.

The agent should take notes and make the client feel that the complaint is being taken seriously, even if it appears to be relatively minor. Often the agent must delve beyond the client's immediate emotions to the actual source of the problem. The agent should accurately restate the complaint to prove it has been understood.

Besides listening, the agent should try to empathize with the client's own feelings of disappointment. Even if the complaint appears unjustified, the client can still be upset. Clients who honestly report problems are valuable sources of information about suppliers and destinations. The agent should explain what action can be taken and should follow through. Even if the client is temporarily satisfied with the agent's explanation, any complaint must be referred through appropriate channels. All agencies lose clients from time to time. But clients who feel that an agency has not even gone to bat for them can spread their dissatisfaction among acquaintances.

If possible, steps should be taken to see that the problem does not recur. At the very least, the agent should stress that the source of the complaint is under study. The client should be informed of the ultimate resolution of the problem.

Misrepresentation

Although most agents do not knowingly misrepresent hotels, destinations, or other travel services, they may thoughtlessly provide blanket assurances to clients. Misrepresentation can take different forms and have different levels of seriousness. It can range from white lies ("it's always lovely at this time of year") to more profound mistruths ("yes, the hotel is right on the beach") to reckless generalizations ("you don't have to worry about malaria; you'll never catch it in a week").

Brochures paint a rosy picture of destinations or hotels. The camera can lie. An agent who spots these inaccuracies should draw the client's attention to them. By offering the brochure to the client, the agent is taking responsibility for the truthfulness of its contents. By misrepresenting the supplier's product, or by being a party to the supplier's misrepresentation of a product, the agent can become legally liable for any problems that the client encounters.

Errors and Omissions

Even the most conscientious agent will occasionally make a mistake. Swift and decisive action may be necessary to correct the mistake or to limit its impact. Ideally, a mistake is corrected before the trip begins and preferably before the client is aware of it. Mistakes on documents, itineraries, or instructions commonly fall into this category. It is most important to check everything twice, particularly documents arriving from suppliers. Mistakes that the client sees, even if they can be easily corrected, can cause the agent embarrassment. Such a mistake might include misspelling a client's name on a voucher or ticket or neglecting to provide proper identifying baggage tags. Travel agents can also substantially reduce their risks by keeping as informed as possible about world and industry events.

More serious mistakes result in discomfort, worry, or anger. Some common mistakes include

■ Routing clients into one airport in a particular city and out of another without realizing it. Clients may arrive at Orly Airport in Paris with a connection departing from Charles de Gaulle Airport on the other side of the city.

■ Making a car or hotel reservation for the wrong day. Clients who depart New York on the evening of November 1 will require a car-rental or hotel reservation in London on November 2, the day the flight arrives.

■ Assuming that clients know that passports are required for overseas travel.

■ Failing to mention the need for proof of citizenship or visa for travel to certain countries.

217

Errors and Omission Insurance

Most travel agencies also protect themselves by obtaining errors and omissions insurance. It protects the agency by covering claims for damages suffered by the client for financial loss, inconvenience, embarrasment, or other injuries because of an error or omission on the part of the travel counselor. Even simple mistakes could trigger a lawsuit. Considering the high cost of travel, a client's expectation is likely to be equally high, so the risk of dissatisfaction is also present. Errors and omission insurance covers not only actual and possible compensatory damages awarded by the courts, but also the cost incurred in defense of the travel agency.

Summary

No sale is complete until clients have successfully departed on their trip. Until that time, many things can happen that may change their plans. Bankruptcies, strikes, death, illness, and many other emergencies can affect a sale.

To protect against some of these emergencies, a good travel agent should suggest the purchase of waivers and insurance. Some types of insurance include accident or health, flight, baggage, and trip cancellation or interruption insurance. Contracts also help protect both the agent and client.

Should any unforeseen problems occur during the trip, an agent must handle the resulting complaint in a professional and courteous manner. In this way, customers become repeat customers.

Chapter Wrap-up

REVIEW QUESTIONS

1. What items might be kept in a client file for a couple taking an escorted rail vacation in California?

2. Do complaints have any positive features? What can we learn from them?

3. Should agents consider travel insurance primarily as a source of income, a protection for clients, or a way to protect themselves from liability if clients are assessed cancellation penalties, lose baggage, or suffer some other loss that insurance would have covered?

4. What steps can agents take to reduce the risk of being sued by clients?

DISCUSSION TOPICS

Insurance

Lucky Break was the tour guide on an eight-day California circle tour via motorcoach. On day four the tour was traveling along the Los Angeles freeway when a heavy object was dropped from an overpass, shattering the front window of the motorcoach. The vacuum created by the smashed window caused a strong wind that shattered the back window also. Fortunately, the driver was able to maintain control and pull into the breakdown lane without further mishap. However, the flying glass cut a number of passengers sitting in both the front and rear of the coach. Who is responsible for this incident? the motorcoach operator? driver? tour operator? tour guide? travel agent? What type of insurance would cover such an accident? What if passengers have no insurance? What effect will this incident have on the remainder of the tour?

Client Profile

Choose someone you know well and create a client profile for him or her that could be entered into a permanent computer record. Consider such factors as favorite types of destinations (climate, activities, previous vacation spots), preferred accommodations, forms of transportation and seating preferences, special needs, and budget. What other factors should be considered to complete the profile? Suggest a new vacation destination for this client, and provide reasons for your recommendation based on the profile you have created.

Complaints

Irma Grump is a perpetual complainer. She takes at least six extended trips a year and grumbles about every one of them. However, she continues to travel and continues to book her tours with Such a Deal Travel Agency. On a busy Monday morning she has just entered the office, which is full of clients and short-staffed due to vacation schedules, and demanded to see the manager immediately. She is already muttering to other clients about her terrible trip. How should she be handled? Who should deal with her? with the phones? with the other clients? Could her visit have been avoided?

Marketing

Chapter 12

Introduction

Before discussing what marketing means to travel agencies, it is vital to understand the role of the agency in the travel distribution system and the relationships between agencies and suppliers. An agent acts on behalf of suppliers, usually with the power to commit them to agreements with clients. Agents agree to sell related products for particular vendors in a certain area. The agency promotes the products but also benefits from the advertising and promotional support of the airline, cruise line, hotel, and so on.

Marketing and Selling

Travel agencies are businesses. This may seem to be an obvious statement, but for years there was a perception by many, both inside and outside the industry, that all a travel agent had to do was plan trips, issue tickets, receive commissions, and take advantage of the many travel benefits. Deregulation shattered that illusion with a deafening crash. In today's environment of low airfares, increased competition for the traveler's dollar, rising costs, and reduced benefits, the only way any travel agency can survive is to operate on a sound business basis, exploring every opportunity to increase revenues and reduce costs.

Determining what product to sell—how, where, when, and to whom — is the function of marketing, and convincing a client to buy is the function of selling. Developing a marketing plan is critical to the success of any business. Successful marketing strikes a subtle balance between the needs of clients and the needs of the agency. At one extreme, agents cannot sell at a loss to satisfy client needs; at the other, agencies cannot concentrate on high-profit items if clients are not interested in buying them. An agency needs to match what it wants to sell with what clients want to buy.

Inventory

Most retail stores purchase inventory at net cost to sell at a profit. Travel agencies normally maintain no inventory unless the agency prepurchases blocks of airline seats, cabins, hotel rooms, and so on, for resale. They place an order on a client's behalf only when the client definitely decides to buy. Thanks to computers, the sale can be confirmed immediately. The product is delivered on the day of travel. The lack of inventory has advantages and disadvantages. On one hand, the travel agency does not risk money acquiring products it may be unable to sell. On the other hand, the agency must usually check with a supplier before selling anything. The agency does not control its inventory; its suppliers do.

Representing Suppliers

Suppliers in any industry prefer an agent dedicated only to their particular interests and welfare, rather than one who splits time and energy among other similar suppliers. However, most travel agencies represent all suppliers. Through what is known as the conference system, groups of suppliers appoint an agent to sell their products and use a

single standard contract. For example, a travel agency appointed by the International Airlines Travel Agent Network (IATAN) is authorized to sell transportation on, and receive commission from, any one of the network's members. As yet no agency enjoys the exclusive right to represent any one IATAN member in a particular area.

Exclusivity has a special significance for travel agents. Only those appointed travel agencies that continue to meet conference standards may sell the products of conference members and receive a commission. Leading conferences that appoint travel agents are IATAN, ARC (Airlines Reporting Corporation), Amtrak, and CLIA (Cruise Lines International Association). For further details on the standards and procedures for appointment, agents must contact the conferences directly.

Flexible Pricing

Travel agencies compete with one another for clients. But historically, agreements between travel agents and suppliers have forbidden agencies from competing by rebating, discounting, or in any way deviating from published rates. Since the Airline Deregulation Act (1978), flexible pricing through the use of net fares, discounts, rebates to clients, and similar concepts has become more acceptable.

Dual Distribution

Travel agencies frequently face direct competition from the suppliers that appointed them. Passengers may reserve and pay for air or rail transportation, hotel accommodations, tours, and car rentals by contacting the supplier directly, although nearly all individual companies advise consumers, "See your travel agent." At present, identical arrangements cost consumers the same whether purchased from an agent or directly from a supplier.

The reason for this dual distribution of travel products is that the travel agent does not purchase inventory. Therefore the supplier must retain some method of selling whatever agents do not sell. Moreover, the supplier's inventory is highly perishable; today's airline seat or hotel room cannot be sold tomorrow. The supplier must make the product as available as possible.

Suppliers might also be tempted to sell directly if it would reduce their selling costs. Studies seem to indicate that most suppliers prefer to pay commissions to travel agents rather than employ large sales and reservations staffs of their own. Although figures vary from airline to airline, statistics indicate that travel agents sell nearly 75 percent of all domestic air and up to 90 percent of international air booked in the United States. Advances in automation may change suppliers' patterns in the future. Even now, ticket machines and satellite printers allow suppliers to deliver products directly. The service role of the agent takes on new importance as people compete with machines for sales.

What image does this business card convey?

Image

Although developing an image is very complex, the word may be simply defined. A company's image is the impression it makes and the associations its name evokes in the mind of the individual consumer.

Travel agencies create an image in many ways. Are telephones answered promptly and courteously? What impression does a caller receive? What associations and impressions does the agency's name evoke? How is the agency decorated and furnished? Most of all, what impression does the staff communicate? Are they interested, alert, knowledgeable, well-groomed? What image do the business cards suggest?

Clients form an opinion of an agency the moment they walk through the door or make a telephone call. If the appearance of the office is frantic, messy, or disorganized, then they will assume that is the type of service they will receive. However, if the decor is pleasing, with orderly brochures, neat desks, and an overall professional appearance, their first impression will be positive.

Successful agencies go a step beyond what is necessary by providing information, brochures, and additional services to their clients. They know their target market and cater to it exclusively. The keys to a successful image are understanding your company's goals and marketing niche, providing good employee guidelines, then communicating policies and procedures clearly. This will ensure projecting a positive image to employees and customers alike.

Travel as a Sales Product

A travel agency can be defined as a retail business selling travel arrangements and products. For most agencies sales mean transportation — air, rail, car, ship, limousine, motorcoach — supplemented by accommodations. Some agencies also sell travel insurance, luggage, passport photographs, and other products that accompany the sale of transportation and accommodations.

Many people dispute such a simple description of a travel agency. They claim that an agency does not sell travel at all. They also quarrel with the word *product* because an agency does not sell a tangible product as do hardware stores, dress shops, or most other retailers. Although agencies talk of selling airline seats or selling cruise cabins, they really assist clients in leasing them temporarily. Thus, the definition raises two important questions: what is it that travel agencies sell and what kind of industry is travel?

Intangibles

If agencies do not sell travel, what do they sell? Some travel agents reject the notion that all they sell is transportation and accommodations. They claim that most travelers actually purchase intangible and private benefits; travel agents who specialize in leisure travel often say they sell dreams. Unlike the products bought in many retail stores, travel arrangements cannot be felt, tasted, or tried before buying. Advertising plays a big part in explaining the benefits of travel. The credibility and trustworthiness of the travel agent are also of great importance. In few other businesses do clients pay for something before they have seen or tried it, without any guarantee of their money back if not satisfied.

Nor do consumers interact quite so personally with most of their purchases. A dress that looked wonderful in the store may, under different lights, be disappointing, but a refrigerator usually works as promised. In travel, as with other purchases, the expectations and daily moods of the travelers are crucial to their satisfaction with the product. It falls to the travel professional to explain the intangibles, to make them clearly understood and alive for the client.

Service

Some travel agents offer another view of what they sell. They believe travel professionals do not sell transportation and accommodations or dreams and intangible benefits; they sell themselves. The travel agent is a source of counsel, information, and service that enables clients to purchase arrangements to meet their needs. In short, the agent sells a counseling service.

Clients come to travel agents with their needs and dreams partly formed, but not necessarily easy to explain. The agency has the information, knowledge, contacts, and expertise to translate these needs and dreams into travel arrangements. Without the agent, travelers would be committed to endless letter writing and telephone calls, with no assurance that they are on the right track or beginning to exhaust the possibilities.

The level of service and the kind of service provided differ from client to client because some clients know what they need or want and others do not. The agency's overall reputation and success depend on creating a consistent level of service, and agencies tend to compete with each other by offering more, better, or distinctive services. A successful service company must fill needs better than a competitor. Training and quality control are therefore vital in travel agencies.

The Process of Marketing

Marketing is a series of decisions and actions

that a seller implements to shift consumer preference to a particular product or service. Each step contributes in a unique way to the total marketing effort.

External Factors That Can Affect Market Research

When analyzing data, managers should look for trends or changes in society that will affect their marketing plans. The agency does not control or plan any of these influences but must be ready to react to them with an effective marketing strategy. Predicting general shifts and trends is important to the continued success of any agency.

■ **Social Change** — Social trends such as the declining birth rate, the dramatic change in the family unit, the high divorce rate, and the graying of the population greatly affect marketing plans.

■ **Legal Change** — Marketing is also affected by state and federal statutes. Specific laws dictate how services and products can be advertised, how contests must be structured, and who can and cannot gamble.

■ **Political Change** — Unrest in a foreign country will affect both business investments and travel.

■ **Economic Change** — Marketers should be aware of these four main trends: slowdown in real income growth, continued inflationary pressure, low savings and high debt, and changing consumer expenditure patterns.

■ **Technological Change** — Advancements such as more efficient transportation, video imaging, and the proliferation of computers all affect what and how clients buy.

Market Research

Travel industry marketing managers need up-to-date research information to help plan successful marketing strategies. Market research is the systematic design, collection, analysis, and reporting of data relevant to a specific marketing situation facing a company. Specifically, it involves surveying and questioning clients, reviewing past bookings, and considering social and economic trends in an attempt to predict what clients will buy. Market research tries to view travel through the eyes of the consumer and takes into account the volatile environment outside the travel agency.

Market research is vital because this information helps travel managers make decisions. Managers can plan, operate, and control more efficiently when they have pertinent facts. Research also helps to pinpoint significant problems and isolate areas that need improvement. In this way research keeps a company in touch with its markets. It identifies trends and changes so that policies can be based on facts, not hunches or intuition. Often, these trends result in new product offerings and new sources of profit.

Research also reduces waste. For instance, the energy crisis led to research that provided dramatic savings in aircraft fuel requirements. Perhaps the biggest benefit is that research creates goodwill. Consumers react favorably to it because they feel that a company really cares about trying to create a product or service that will meet their needs.

An agency can determine the composition and preferences of its clientele by collecting and studying primary and secondary data. Primary data consists of information originally collected for the specific purpose at hand. Sending a questionnaire to discover your client base and most popular products or services would be an example of collecting primary data. Secondary data consists of information that already exists somewhere, already having been collected for some other purpose. Consulting a standard reference work will provide accurate secondary data about income levels, social and ethnic affiliations, and purchasing power of specific zip code areas.

Once data is collected it must be coded, tabulated, and analyzed. This must be done with great care for there is a distinct possibility of error if these phases of research are not done properly.

Usually computer printouts containing statistical conclusions are used for analysis. Next, interpretation involves developing the data into action plans and recommendations. Finally, the data is used to determine which market segments are best served by the particular agency.

Database management software can offer agencies a competitive edge by rapidly converting research data. It is especially helpful in creating customer profiles and providing agents easy access to stored information. When choosing a system, managers should consider factors such as economy, ease of operation, the ability to import and export data to and from programs, sorting and searching abilities, business capacity, and labeling capability.

Market Segmentation

Some agencies try to serve the needs of the greatest possible number of clients. Others have a specialty of some kind, either because it suits the talents of the staff or interests of the owner/manager or because of the composition of the local population. Few agencies actually turn business away, but most do specialize to some extent. Consciously or unconsciously, agencies hire staff, develop selling styles, create advertising, and emphasize products to appeal to particular segments of the total population.

Market segmentation concentrates on identifying, separating, and clustering individuals with similar travel needs into groups or target markets. Where many agencies are close to and competing with each other, there is a greater tendency for each to select certain market segments for particular attention.

There are many ways to segment the total market: by age group, sex, ethnic origin, marital status, religious belief, and so on. For example, married couples whose children have grown up and left home are often called *empty-nesters*. Tour operators can select travel arrangements or emphasize certain benefits to suit the needs of this group.

Many tour operators appreciate the potential of senior citizens and offer motorcoach tours targeted at this segment. The product-oriented

Niche Marketing

Would you go to a Mercedes car dealership if you were in the market for a used Ford wagon? Of course not. Today, much like car dealerships, many travel agencies have decided to specialize in certain types of travel. Frequently you will see cruise-only agencies or those dealing with up-scale travel, budget travel, or any other of a myriad of specific travel products only. Finding a niche in today's competitive atmosphere has caused most smaller agencies to take a closer look at their marketing strategies. Being all things to all people is becoming increasingly difficult. Larger agencies tend to create special departments within the office and have certain agents deal with specific types of travel.

Many cruise-only agencies decorate in a nautical theme — from deck chairs to a ship's wheel — to create the right selling atmosphere. Niche marketing not only makes it easier for the agent to sell to a particular group, but it becomes easier for the traveler to choose an agent and a product.

marketing strategy senses the profitability of motorcoach tours and then searches for people to fill them. The market-oriented strategy defines needs within the target segment — senior citizens, for example — and then designs tours to meet these needs. Often the two approaches produce the same result, but the market-oriented company

enjoys the advantage of knowing that the chosen product will sell.

However carefully a company conducts market research, the success of a new venture or strategy is never absolutely guaranteed. Test marketing permits limited experimentation with an idea. An agent might approach a senior citizen group and offer to arrange a tour. The experience gained enables the agent to improve or abandon the marketing concept of senior travel to a particular destination.

Types of Segmentation

Knowing your customers and understanding what motivates them are the keys to successful competition. Many companies design statistical profiles of their clients to better handle their specific needs. Segmental analysis determines whether resources are being allocated efficiently and allows management to determine how changing the market mix can affect each segment. Some ways of researching and segmenting the market include:

■ **Demographic Segmentation** — Characteristics such as age and income (senior citizens, carriage trade)

■ **Psychographic Segmentation** — Segmenting groups by their attitudes, interests, and beliefs (allocentrics, psychocentrics)

■ **Benefit Segmentation** — Considers the needs of travelers (business travelers seek speed, efficiency, and personal service)

■ **Geographic Segmentation** — Determines how far clients are willing to travel to come to your business (mileage radius of telephone and walk-in business)

■ **Usage Segmentation** — Why customers use your company (purpose, frequency)

■ **Price Segmentation** — How value-conscious your customers may be (ability to pay)

Case Study – Club Med

Established in Europe shortly after World War II, Club Mediterranee introduced vacations featuring fun, sun, and joie de vivre. Today, with 110 properties in thirty-three countries, Club Med's spirit remains the same, but the product has evolved to reflect contemporary demographic changes.

Originally, Club Med catered to young, unmarried, economy-minded tourists. The company's promotional activities emphasized a "swinging singles" ambiance. Now Club Med's customer profile is only 50 percent single and is more sophisticated than in past years. Baby Clubs (for infants) and Mini Clubs (for children up to age 11) are available in several family villages.

In another innovative move Club Med continues to pursue the upscale segment of the cruise market by promoting Club Med I, the world's largest sailing vessel. The 610-foot ship is designed to keep the youth-oriented image, attracting the affluent with a median age in the 30s.

Marketing Strategy and Marketing Plan

Through constant contact with clients, the individual agent is able to gather vital information about tastes, trends, and attitudes that affects the development of the agency's marketing strategy. Both agents and management know what sells, but the front-line agent is able to detect subtle shifts in why it sells and who is buying it. The agent may detect a developing interest in a destination among an age group not normally interested in the area. The agent on the scene sees why a client is interested in this destination. A new market for the destination may be growing, implying a totally new promotional approach. The individual agent conducts informal market research every time a client answers a question.

At the other end of the marketing process, the agent ensures the final success of the strategy by performing the personal selling. Selling activities make the agency's marketing plan work. The marketing plan gives direction and logic to daily decisions about what products to sell and how to sell them. For many suppliers, the travel agent, as the focal point of their distribution system, is often responsible for the success or failure of their sophisticated and expensive marketing strategies. The individual agent who understands marketing concepts and knows the marketing plan will know that he or she is not acting in a void without guidance or objectives.

Segmental Analysis

Segmental analysis is the process of systematically studying divisions of the agency's business to determine which ones are the most profitable. To a salesperson, the volume of sales is all-important: the more the better. To a marketing person, the profitability of sales is all-important. Decisions about place, price, product, and promotion depend on segmental analysis. No agency wants to sell unprofitable items. If the agency plans to grow, it must emphasize growth in profitable areas.

The segmentation of an agency's product often resembles the divisions by supplier — domestic air, international travel, ships/cruises, rail, car rentals, charters, hotels, and tours. Most agencies also count a miscellaneous segment that includes insurance, guidebooks, luggage, passport photographs, and similar items. A good accounting system can furnish information about the gross volume and commission income derived from each of these sources. It is difficult, however, to allocate costs precisely to each source.

A more accurate method of analyzing costs would focus on the percentage of total staff time necessary to generate the sales in each segment. If agents spend 13 percent of their time selling cruises, then 13 percent of all costs would be attached to cruise sales, even if they accounted for only 10 percent of total sales volume.

The same segment may not be as profitable for one agency as it is for another. An agency that is highly automated can handle a much greater volume of domestic air, hotel, and car rental reservations than an agency relying on the telephone to call suppliers. The former agency might find domestic air profitable; the latter might find it marginal. Segmental analysis tells an agency its sources of current income and suggests segments that

Components of the Travel Marketing Mix — The Four Ps

In deciding what products to emphasize, most agencies ask a series of questions relating to the four Ps of classic marketing. Each of these four areas may receive different degrees of attention. Because the areas interact, an answer to one question influences the response to another. An agency that specializes in selling to groups may not need to pursue the same number of promotional avenues as an agency that sells only to individual clients.

PRODUCT

Do we sell all travel products or do we specialize?

What services or products apart from travel arrangements do we offer?

With which suppliers do we openly identify?

Do we offer our own tours, group programs, incentive programs?

Do we sell intangibles? Dreams?

PRICE

What price range of travel do we want to sell?

Do we want to sell high-priced travel?

Do we want to sell economy travel?

On what terms do we extend credit?

Do we apply service charges?

Are we associated with expensive or budget arrangements?

PROMOTION

How and where do we advertise?

What special promotions and sales efforts do we employ?

What public relations activities do we undertake?

What image are we creating?

How do we make people aware of us?

PLACE

Where do we want to sell travel?
In the office?
In front of groups?
In our clients' offices?
In private homes?
Over the telephone?
On television?

PRODUCT

Quality

Features

Packaging

Service

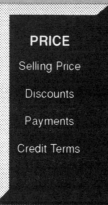

PRICE

Selling Price

Discounts

Payments

Credit Terms

PROMOTION

Advertising

Sales

Publicity

Image

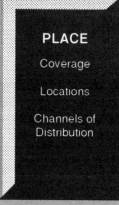

PLACE

Coverage

Locations

Channels of Distribution

TARGET MARKET

might be ripe for growth.

Segmental analysis contributes to marketing strategy from a financial point of view. It suggests where an agency could most profitably focus its marketing efforts. Concentration of sales enables retailers to obtain higher commissions and more clout with suppliers. Service levels are higher because product knowlege is better and time is available to provide special attention to customers. The key is to select high quality products consistent with the agency's image and appropriate to its clientele.

A Case Study in Market Development for Standard Travel

Standard Travel has never offered incentive travel programs to its current corporate clients or to companies not using Standard's services. Segmental analysis leads the agency to believe that these programs could prove profitable, considerably increasing revenues while requiring minor increases in costs. How might Standard Travel proceed?

STEP 1

Market Research. Standard might begin by finding which industries most frequently use travel as an incentive. Usually industries that sell or manufacture something are apt to offer incentives to encourage employees to achieve sales or production goals. Companies that sell insurance, automobiles and accessories, office equipment, computers, or farm equipment offer incentives to their employees. Manufacturing companies offer incentives to the dealers who distribute their products.

Standard Travel identifies the local companies that fit this profile. It gathers information on them from a variety of sources: the local newspaper, stock exchange reports, the Chamber of Commerce, local business people, friends, employees, and neighbors.

STEP 2

Benefit Segmentation. Incentive travel programs benefit companies in different ways. They increase sales, accelerate sales of a new product, help sell slow-moving items, reward productivity, reduce absenteeism, increase safety standards, and promote company loyalty. Standard Travel must know which benefits would appeal to a particular company.

The results of doing a survey can either deter or encourage Standard Travel. Standard may discover that companies are eager to offer incentive travel and cannot understand why no agency has approached them. On the other hand, Standard may find general ignorance, even apathy, about incentive travel programs. As a local travel agency, Standard might encounter resistance from companies that think big incentive programs need specialized incentive firms.

STEP 3

Promotional Decisions. Assuming that Standard still views incentive travel as a profitable and positive new direction to take, the agency must now decide how to promote it. Will a representative call on each company to present proposals? What materials will the representative need? Will a brochure by mail and a follow-up telephone call be better? How does Standard propose to promote its program to the employees and maintain their interest?

STEP 4

Test Marketing. Standard must also decide whether to test market its new product with a single company or to contract with as many companies as possible. Clearly, Standard must weigh the costs of adding or training staff; acquiring such fixed assets as computer terminals, telephones, or extra space; and of producing promotional material. Finally, Standard must develop a reliable method to measure the success of its new venture.

Promotion

Although marketing as a total strategy is, for some travel agents, a new concept, almost all have used elements of marketing for some time. Promotion and public relations consistently receive the most attention. Ideally, the choice of promotional techniques and the design of promotional aids depend on the agency's overall marketing strategy. Agencies can choose from many media to reach prospective clients, each of which has benefits and disadvantages.

Direct Mail

Many agencies use some form of direct mail and consider it most effective. Agencies send letters, postcards, flyers, brochures, questionnaires, and newsletters to past and potential clients. They use mailing lists compiled from their own records, from local directories, or from mailing list companies. Direct mail tends to use the agency's own talents, resources, and records more than any other kind of advertising.

Direct mail offers distinct advantages. It reaches identifiable segments of the total market. An agency could send a special announcement to all clients who have taken a cruise, to all persons living in a certain part of town, or to all clients who have not taken a trip in the past year. The advertisement can be tailored to the audience and identify individual needs.

Direct mail permits an agency to advertise when it needs to advertise. The agency does not have to sign a contract committing to a series of insertions or airings of its message. Furthermore, by inserting a response card or return reply envelope, the agency can measure the effectiveness of the promotion. A direct mail piece stands alone, unlike the newspaper advertisement that competes with other ads for the consumer's attention. A mailing piece can contain far more information than any other kind of advertisement; it may remain accessible for several days before being discarded; and it may be passed on to others not included in the original mailing.

Needless to say, direct mail is not entirely free of disadvantages. It requires time, effort, and expense. More staff time is required to prepare the message, organize the mailing lists, address labels, and stuff envelopes. The mailing list must be accurate and, more important, targeted correctly. Nevertheless, if done well, direct mail usually produces a greater response than any other form of advertising, even though the initial costs can seem expensive.

In addition to letters, brochures, flyers, or questionnaires, agency newsletters are popular. Although time-consuming to produce, a newsletter mailed to clients accomplishes a number of purposes. The agency can describe and promote travel arrangements. Staff members can contribute reports on destinations they recently visited. Clients are encouraged to contact a staff member who has specialized knowledge, recent travel experience, or a liking for certain kinds of travel.

A newsletter contains news, too. The agency may have acquired a new computer system with resulting benefits for clients. Staff members may have completed special training courses. The agency can present updates on conditions in troubled areas of the world. By featuring a client who has recently returned from an interesting trip, the agency is assured that a single newsletter copy will find its way into many hands. To be most effective, a newsletter should appear on a regular basis.

The best time to promote via direct mail is during an agency's slow period. Consider the lead time necessary, then establish a time frame for response. Consumers usually respond to first class mail in between nine to eleven days. First-time mailings to repeat customers should be sent four to six times a year, and general response mailings should be sent twice a year. Letters that arrive midweek have a higher chance of response. Most customers look at the top and bottom of a letter for seven seconds or less to determine if they will bother reading it at all.

Print Advertising

A travel agency's approach to print advertising often depends on the length of time the publication will last. Newspaper readers normally discard a paper immediately after reading it. Newspaper advertising tends to deliver a specific message of short-term validity to advertise a specific tour, airfare, or destination and tends to motivate readers to call or come into the agency immediately. Because deadlines are relatively close to publication date, the agency can change its message frequently while retaining a format or advertising design that, through repetition, makes the agency itself memorable. Newspaper advertisements commonly contain prices that may be valid for a brief period only.

Yellow Pages advertisements are more conventional and their messages must be valid for a year. The agency makes general statements about service, experience, and expertise. *Yellow Pages* advertising reaches a more specific segment than newspapers. Only people desiring travel arrangements turn to the pages where the advertisements appear.

Magazines tend to attract readers from specific market segments. Apart from the large news magazines like *Time* and *Newsweek*, many are devoted to special segments of the population: *Sports Illus-*

trated, Family Circle, Seventeen, Working Woman, Hot Rod Monthly. Each magazine, for its own purposes as well as for its advertisers, conducts extensive demographic research to determine the tastes and lifestyles of its readership. Agencies may know with some certainty which market segments are likely to read magazine advertisements. National magazines may not be suitable for an agency that expects to draw clients from its local area.

An agent should know what products the agency is advertising. Many agencies advertise in the Sunday papers, and agents can reduce Monday morning stress by advance research of the products being offered. Agents who see their agency's advertisements in advance will feel more confident dealing with clients who respond to them. Occasionally typographical errors creep into print advertisements, and it is vital to correct them.

Some clients reveal almost at once that they are responding to an advertisement. In other instances the agent may only suspect that the client has seen a particular advertisement. The agent may need to ask, "Did you see our advertisement for this destination in last Sunday's *Advertiser*?" By logging the number of responses and the number of bookings, an agency is able to measure the effectiveness of print advertising.

Travel suppliers, particularly cruise lines and tour operators, will share the cost of print advertising with the travel agency if the agency is promoting one of their products. For a portion of the total cost, agencies can associate themselves with a supplier's products by placing their names and addresses inside the advertisement as a contact for reservations. This arrangement is known as cooperative advertising.

Radio and Television

Fewer agencies use radio as an advertising medium than use direct mail or print. Fewer still use television. A radio or television advertisement is short-lived, lasting 30 to 60 seconds. It cannot be clipped, saved, or found again. Although a single effective newspaper advertisement can produce a significant response, experts agree that only repetition ensures the success of a radio or television advertisement. These advertisements require several airings to register on the consumer's consciousness. In smaller towns, radio may be the prime medium and may be no more expensive than other forms of advertising despite the need for repetition. In large metropolitan areas, the cost of repeated radio advertising exceeds the average travel agency's budget.

Consumers will not buy or keep buying a product that does not meet their needs no matter how creative the advertising.

Advertising rates and production costs are high for television. Agents who feel comfortable designing newspaper advertisements or writing radio copy will not be permitted to write, direct, and edit for film or videotape. Consultants, production assistants, and studio rentals inevitably add to the costs. Viewers measure television advertisements by the standards of professional advertising agencies handling multimillion-dollar accounts. Amateur television advertisement seldom measures up.

Although the same production costs apply, advertisements on cable television can be directed at particular segments of the market. Some cable television channels devote all their programming to one subject — sports, for example, or news.

Many cable companies offer assistance in the preparation of commercials that reach only local community subscribers. Cable TV offers opportunities to promote travel destinations and firms that feature the area. Several programs feature travel and give suppliers opportunities to advertise their specific products.

VCRs have become integral parts of home entertainment systems. Specialized companies produce destination videos for the active or armchair traveler. For a relatively low price, people can buy or rent a 60-minute video to preview their next vacation.

Special Promotions

Agencies can also stage special events. The agency can either be the primary sponsor or simply a participant in an event sponsored by someone else. Some agencies hold regular travel nights at which they show films, present interesting speakers, and promote corresponding travel arrangements. They might combine a film about Morocco with a selection of tours. These travel nights become a way of identifying market segments interested in a particular kind of travel.

Suppliers often cooperate with agencies to produce shows for the public. Cruise lines, for example, might participate with an agency for a cruise night. Each participant sets up a booth and shares the costs of the evening. Besides material about specific cruise arrangements, general information about life on board and cruising areas is offered. These shows are popular with the public, particularly if prizes are awarded.

Other shows can embrace more than travel. Bridal shows are designed for engaged couples and feature presentations by clothing stores, realtors, jewelers, houseware retailers, as well as travel agents offering honeymoons. On such occasions the agency often secures exclusive rights to present travel arrangements.

Promotions may be linked to some unique event such as the opening of a new branch office or a holiday. It is possible to arrange with certain suppliers for selected prizes to attract the public. Special promotions present the opportunity for personal selling.

Although promotions are expected to increase sales, they also serve simply to inform and entertain the public. They are often inappropriate occasions to counsel clients and accept payments, but they help establish an agency's image.

How does an agency create the one-of-a-kind name that becomes an instantly recognizable household word? The name must promote the products or services of the company, protect against copycat imitations, and generate profit. It must be distinctive and appealing to be easily remembered and to earn a valuable reputation.

Public Relations

Public relations is any activity that an agency conducts to establish recognition and respect within the local community. The major costs are staff time, creative talent, and organizational effort. Public relations efforts are only effective if they receive publicity. Perhaps a local newspaper will report the cruise night. A travel agency may regularly submit press releases to the newspaper describing interesting trips taken by local residents.

Other releases may explain recent developments in the government's regulation of the industry or announce the acquisition of new computer equipment. This kind of publicity can be viewed as free advertising. Obtaining publicity requires skill, practice, and contacts. Many agencies feel that publicity and public relations are the equal of any advertising at a far lower cost.

Summary

The travel industry relies on successfully marketing and selling not only products but also intangible services and dreams. Unlike other industries, it stocks perishable commodities such as airline seats and hotel rooms. The revenue from these items can never be recouped if they are not marketed properly.

To accomplish this a series of steps must be followed, including research, segmentation, strategy, and analysis. This allows for better planning, execution, and monitoring of results.

The industry attempts to get its message across through a variety of media. Promotions like discounts and coupons are popular methods. Radio, television, and print also reach specific target markets. Many agencies, however, rely on good public relations and word-of-mouth advertising to most effectively reach and keep their customers.

Chapter Wrap-up

REVIEW QUESTIONS

1. What is the relationship between an agent and a supplier?
2. What distribution channels might exist for airline tickets besides travel agencies and the airlines themselves? What possible benefits can travel agencies offer the consumer that other distribution channels cannot?
3. What do you think a travel agency sells?
4. What are the main differences between selling a tangible product and an intangible one?
5. What is the difference between marketing and selling?
6. Can you give an example of social change that is affecting travel right now? Legal or political change? Economic change? Technological change?
7. What is the major purpose of segmental analysis?
8. According to some opinions, direct mail is best for reaching former clients, and other forms of promotion are more likely to attract new clients. Do you agree?
9. What, in your opinion, constitutes an effective direct mailing?
10. Publicity is really free advertising. How could a travel company get publicity?

DISCUSSION TOPICS

Niche Marketing

For years the Generic Family Travel Service has been offering all types of programs to its clientele. Two mega-agencies have relocated within close proximity, and the owners of the GFTS are worried about maintaining business, so they have decided to specialize. Using your own community as the location for GFTS, choose an appropriate niche for the agency based on area demographics.

Design

■ The appropriate interior of the office to correspond to this market segment

■ An appropriate direct mail promotional piece

Image

An agency's image is the outward, most obvious manifestation of its marketing strategy. Business cards are a simple part of that marketing strategy. Design a business card for your agency. Consider such elements as design, shape, name, lettering, size, and logo.

Promotions

Agencies use various advertising promotions to attract their clientele. Choose one example of print advertising from a newspaper, one from the *Yellow Pages*, and one from a magazine. Examine each sample and consider its graphics, photos, headline, placement on the page, and use of color. How effective is the overall presentation? What could be done to improve it?

Marketing Research

Social, political, economic, and technological changes affect consumer buying patterns. Using the Sunday edition of your local newspaper, select two stories relating to each of these categories and discuss how these issues could influence travel marketing. How must the industry react in terms of an effective marketing strategy?

234

Agency Operations

Part Three

Automation

Chapter 13

CHAPTER OBJECTIVES

After completing this chapter, the reader should be able to

- Explain the various components of a computer
- Describe why computers are important in the travel industry
- Relate the history of automation in travel
- List three widely used computer reservations systems
- Define bias and how it can affect airline bookings

VOCABULARY

After completing this chapter, the reader should be able to define

- Access
- ARINC
- CPU
- CRS
- Hardware
- Input
- Keyboard
- Memory
- Modem
- PNR
- Program
- Software

Introduction

One of the most important changes in the travel industry has been the impact of the computer. Automation arrived on the travel scene in the 1970s. Today 95 percent of all United States travel agencies use computers to book airline reservations, hotels, cars, and other suppliers. When an agency is automated, tasks are completed more efficiently and accurately, resulting in better service for clients. In fact many clients today assume and expect their travel agent to produce computerized tickets, itineraries, and invoices.

Components of a Computer System

Computer systems are composed of two parts: hardware and software. Computer hardware includes the physical components that can be touched, seen, and heard. Software is the program or instruction that tells the computer what to do with the information it has.

Hardware

The central processing unit (CPU) is the operations center of the computer. It performs all tasks by taking information that it receives, treating it according to programmed instructions, and returning an answer to the sender. Memory is a kind of holding area where all the information and instructions about what to do with the information are assembled before entering the CPU.

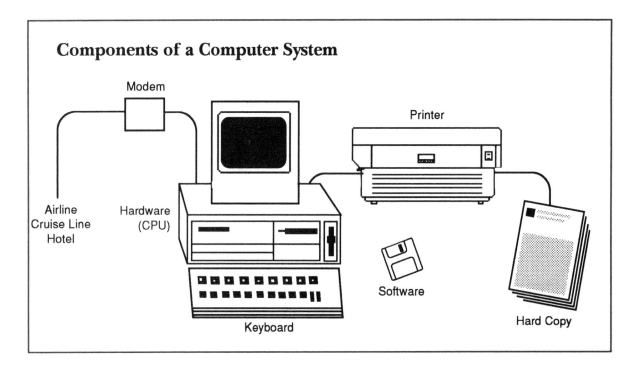

Components of a Computer System

Modem

Printer

Airline
Cruise Line
Hotel

Hardware
(CPU)

Software

Keyboard

Hard Copy

Peripherals are the devices connected to a computer to provide communication or auxiliary functions. The keyboard looks like a typewriter and is the operator's way of communicating with the computer system. Through the keyboard the operator generates input. Other methods of input can be voice-activation, a mouse, or joysticks. When the computer answers, it employs other peripherals, usually a printer or a video display. It can use both simultaneously when the operator requests a print or a hard copy of what appears on the screen. The CPU communicates with remote input and output devices by using a modem, a type of transformer that permits signals to travel over normal telephone lines. In this way a transmitter in New York can interface with a receiver in Paris.

Software

Software refers to the instructions or programs that tell a computer what to do. Computers can do nothing with the data entered unless they are given precise instructions. To do this the operator must activate a program. For example, a stereo system would be useless unless there is an album, C.D., or tape to play on it. The album is, in this example, the software, a program written to make the computer work. Software is stored on tapes or disks.

User friendly *is a term used to describe software that can be used even by a novice with little difficulty.*

History of Automation

In the beginning, each airline set up a central control system showing all their flights in separate books or on large boards. When another airline requested a seat, a counter indicated whether or not it had been sold. When this manual system became too cumbersome, the airlines evolved the system called "free sale." Other airlines were allotted a certain number of seats on each flight that they could sell without consulting central control.

The advantages of applying computer technology to produce an automated reservations system first became apparent in the 1950s. A few airlines had begun to use computers to keep track of the number of seats available on some of their busy flights. The travel agencies who called these carriers found they were able to confirm their clients' reservations promptly. At first, the computers simply kept track of the number of seats sold on flights.

An important breakthrough in automated airline reservations came with the ability to match a seat sold with a passenger's name and thus to

236

create a complete record. But because of the differences among the systems, when one carrier needed to make a reservation on another, the request for space could not be granted immediately. A teletyped message had to be sent to the carrier.

Each airline chose a different automated system, making coordination of the entire reservations network extremely difficult. A few major carriers entered individually into agreements with separate vendors of computer equipment and software. Then they proceeded to develop their own automated systems, which they eventually marketed to other segments of the travel industry. Still, the airlines needed to find a way to let their computers talk directly to each other.

ARINC

Even before the advent of automation, the airlines used a communication switching system called Aeronautical Radio Incorporated (ARINC) to make reservations and to handle other operating matters by teletype. The ARINC system became the vehicle for automated communication and is used today to store flight availability, provide interline confirmations, change and cancel reservations, and perform many other functions. ARINC is a corporation owned jointly by the airlines.

As the airline industry continued its rapid growth in the 1960s and 1970s, it became increasingly apparent that both carriers and travel agencies would benefit if agents were able to communicate directly with the airline computer rather than with a reservation agent. Calling in reservations, cancellations, and changes was time-consuming and costly for agent and airline alike. But most travel agents needed to contact all airlines and obviously could not afford, and did not have the room, to store a computer terminal for each one.

Efforts to develop a common reservations system available to travel agencies, incorporating all major airlines, ran into difficulties. Despite much research and considerable financial investment by the American Society of Travel Agents (ASTA) and

some airlines, agreement on a common industry-wide system finally collapsed in 1976. Shortly afterwards United, followed by American and TWA, began to install their own competing systems in travel agencies.

At this time, some agencies had teleticketing machines, printers connected via telephone lines to an airline computer system. A travel agent made an airline reservation by asking for the ticketing information to be relayed directly to the teleticketing printer in the travel agency. Special ticket stock was fed into the printers and the information was captured in the correct format.

Agencies have now discarded the teleticketing machine in favor of airline systems that permit acquisition of more hardware and two-way automated communication. As a result, agents now spend less time calling airlines and waiting on hold, and much less time typing or writing. They put information directly into the system using their keyboards and entering special formats. The airlines can communicate with individual agencies or agents by using a queue format.

Reservations systems have printers that produce tickets, invoices, and itineraries. The printers differ from the teleticketing machine in that the agent, not the airline, sends the instructions to print the ticket.

The majority of travel agencies now purchase or lease hardware from one, or occasionally two carriers. All have become vastly more sophisticated and now provide instant communications between a variety of airlines, hotels, car rental companies, and other suppliers.

Hosts, Co-Hosts, and Multi-Hosts

The airline that markets its own computerized reservations system, the host system to agents, offers other carriers the opportunity to participate in its system in a number of ways. A co-host carrier signs agreements to participate with the host to market and install the host's system in areas that may lie outside the airline's normal markets. In return, the host gives preferential treatment to the co-host's flight listings and other pertinent data. The two lines often take steps to increase data flow with direct access to each other's data base.

Multi-host partners have access to the host system but cannot themselves be directly accessed by another subscriber. Unlike the co-host carriers, which maintain their own automation systems, multi-host carriers have access to the same data base as the host system but limit information about their own flights to themselves.

Finally, there are pseudo-hosts, including hotels, car rental firms, and cruise lines. For pseudo-hosts, the host system handles every aspect of a reservation, including answering telephone calls. Pseudo-hosts can be accessed directly.

Through these host arrangements, airlines have established direct communication links that bypass ARINC's message-switching systems, thereby increasing speed and accuracy. Some direct communication links provide the desired last-seat availability on segments of flights.

Bias

Airlines derive revenue from leasing their systems. Consequently, they compete fiercely to install their systems in as many agencies as possible, encouraging them to sign up or switch from a competitive system. Each airline expects to secure more bookings from an agency using its system, because it can deliberately program characteristics to influence the user's choice. The easiest way to influence a booking is to control the display of available flights on the screen. An agent may feel more secure making a reservation on the host carrier knowing that the information has been programmed directly.

Most travel agents begin a transaction by asking the computer to indicate flight availability between two cities on a specific day at a specific time. The screen normally displays a maximum of six to eight flights. Although it is possible to request additional availability and see more flights, studies indicate that over 75 percent of all bookings are made from the first display. Unless a client requests a specific carrier or routing, the agent really has no reason to go beyond the first display unless all flights shown are full. Airlines that program computerized reservations systems could influence agents by positioning their own service prominently on the first display. This preferential positioning of flights is known as bias.

Some systems claim to be unbiased. Others admit bias in their favor but claim a computerized reservations system is simply another marketing tool, and bias is justified to help recoup the expense of developing the system. Furthermore, any system that is too biased would be useless to travel agents who need to serve their clients properly. Any airline that goes too far would make its system unattractive to agents.

The bias saga is not over yet. The government may still decide that no airline should own a controlling interest in a reservations system designed for travel agents. Forcing airlines to divest their systems might bring back the concept of a single industry system owned by a neutral outsider.

Access

Bias is only one side of the story. Access is also important. An unbiased system may have limited access to the computers of other airline systems. Therefore the agent would not be able to sell the last few seats on all flights shown on the screen. Ideally, travel agents would like the same freedom to reserve seats on any flight as the sponsoring airline's reservations agents.

Any airline can elect to participate in a reservations system in one of four different ways. The choice may depend on the sophistication of their in-house computer system.

■ The least expensive level of participation permits a display of schedules but not of availability. The travel agent looks at the CRT to select a flight but must confirm the reservation by telephone or some other method and enter the information manually into the PNR.

■ A second level of participation permits a carrier to display schedules and availabilities, but reservation requests must be transmitted via ARINC. The agent must wait for a return message from the airline confirming the reservation.

■ A third level enables travel agents to confirm reservations instantly.

■ At the fourth and most sophisticated level, an airline becomes a Designated Direct Access, Direct Link, or Total Access carrier. These names indicate that the travel agent can directly access a carrier's database and obtain last-seat availability and boarding passes.

Last-Seat Availability

Each airline maintains last-seat availability on its own flights in its own reservations system. Agencies use the systems of more than one airline to have last-seat availability for more than one airline.

Because airlines permit flights to be sold in segments, they must have a way to keep these segments from being oversold. They thus establish levels at which a flight is closed for interline sales. When only six seats remain on a segment of Airline A's flight, their computer might send out a closed message to all its interline partners. Without this caution, two travel agencies might request those seats at the same time through different airline computer systems and each receive confirmation. With control of last-seat availability at a certain point reverting to the host airline, only agencies with Airline A's computer in their offices can obtain those final seats. Agencies without Airline A's computer would have to call the airline directly to obtain any last-minute seats.

From 1991 CRS estimates: Travel agents made approximately 42% of their air bookings through SABRE, 28% through Apollo, 18% through Worldspan, and 12% through System One.

Computer Reservations Systems (CRSs)

Because most travel agencies have computer reservations systems (CRSs), manual reservation procedures are not often used. The computer is now an integral part of the reservations process. Scheduled airlines in the United States have adopted a standard format for making reservations. This format, explained in detail in the ARC *Industry Agents' Handbook*, follows the order in which information must be entered in an airline reservations computer. To reduce the chances for misunderstanding, the computer format must also be used when calling an airline. Airline computers will not accept a reservation that is entered incorrectly.

With a computer, an airline reservation can be made in either of two ways:

■ By requesting an availability display and choosing flights from the display.

■ By requesting space directly with already-known flight numbers.

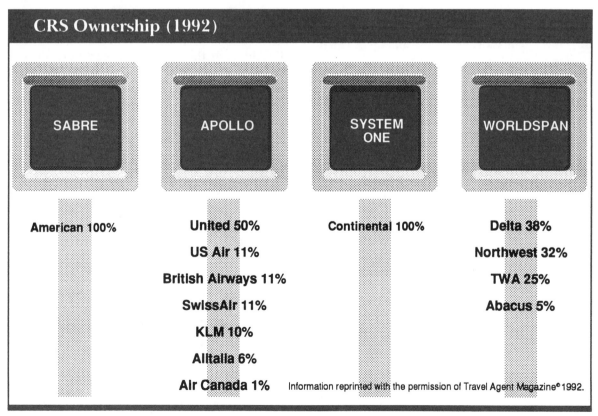

CRS Ownership (1992)

SABRE	APOLLO	SYSTEM ONE	WORLDSPAN
American 100%	United 50%	Continental 100%	Delta 38%
	US Air 11%		Northwest 32%
	British Airways 11%		TWA 25%
	SwissAir 11%		Abacus 5%
	KLM 10%		
	Alitalia 6%		
	Air Canada 1%		

Information reprinted with the permission of Travel Agent Magazine® 1992.

The PNR

The Passenger Name Record (PNR) is the complete record of a reservation displayed on the computer screen. It contains flight information, passengers' names, telephone numbers, ticketing and invoice information, and eventually the applicable fare. In computer jargon, these bits of information are called the mandatory fields of a PNR. Additional fields (hotel, car, cruise, and so forth) may eventually become part of the passenger's record, but they are not mandatory. A typical PNR may have a record of changes (a history).

Components of a PNR

- Airline name
- Flight number
- Class of service
- Date of departure
- Departure city
- Destination city
- Desired number of seats

When the itinerary segments are confirmed, the following information is added:

- Passengers' family names, initials, and titles
- Passengers' home and/or business telephone numbers
- Travel agency's name, phone, and agent's identification code (sine)
- Ticketing information, the date by which the passenger must pay for and pick up the ticket or lose the reservation (option date), and the form of payment
- Received field (person who phoned in the reservation)

The key components of a PNR can be represented by the word "PRINT":

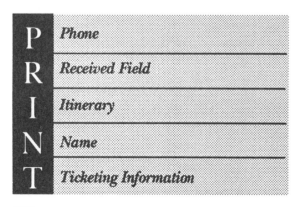

P	*Phone*
R	*Received Field*
I	*Itinerary*
N	*Name*
T	*Ticketing Information*

No-Recs and Unable to Sell

The volume of messages sent between airlines and the heightened expectations of agencies for system perfection have highlighted two recurring problems. Reservations, changes, and messages can occasionally be lost or delayed between airlines. These failures lead either to a no-rec or an unable to sell. Travel agents may receive these responses either on their own CRTs or when they contact an airline by telephone.

To complete a PNR or any change in a PNR, the user must press a key on the CRT to end the transaction. This key indicates that the transaction is complete and that messages should now be sent to all involved suppliers. If the booking agent does not officially end the record, the entire PNR will disappear, resulting in a no-rec.

Assuming that the agent ends the PNR correctly, there are four reasons for no-recs or unable to sell:

Reasons for no-recs:

- Malfunction of the system that results in garbled messages.
- A traffic jam on ARINC.

Reasons for unables to sell:

- Although the message is sent correctly and received promptly, an airline computer rejects it because of some internal controls.
- Schedule changes appear in one computer before another.

When a message is rejected, it is stored in a file of other rejects. Airline experts study each message in turn to see why their computer rejected them. Depending on the volume of rejects, a message may wait several days. In rare instances, it may not be seen until after the flight in question has departed.

Computers rarely lose messages, although they may delay them. It may not help a frustrated agent much to know this, but no-recs are most likely simply to be slow-recs waiting their turn, along with the unable to sell, either in an airline's reject file or in the ARINC system. Reservation requests and other communications sent to co-hosts of systems that proceed directly and bypass ARINC may be less subject to delay.

Computers are not perfect nor were they meant to replace the human element. Travel agents need to display common sense when using them and know when it is appropriate to question information.

Other Participants in CRS

Communication between travel agents and their non-air suppliers has also been affected by automation. The 800- number is gradually being replaced by direct computer linkups between agents and vendors and by vendor offerings in the airline-owned CRS. Airlines have given impetus to this trend, incorporating more services into their systems to make them more attractive to travel agents. Many hotel chains and car rental firms report that more than half their trade bookings are now coming over CRSs. Cruise lines, railroads, and tour operators have followed this trend.

Cars: Many car rental companies report that more than half of their bookings are received through a CRS. However, some programming restrictions affect the information that agents receive. For example, not all of the numerous car rental rates can be displayed in a CRS. A given CRS may display only one fare per car type when several rates may be available under certain conditions.

Hotels: Hotels have used automation for their bookings for many years. Holiday Inn was a pioneer in the field, introducing its Holidex system in 1965. Today, travel agents make hotel reservations through their computers as a matter of course. Some hotel computers can communicate directly with CRTs, and others communicate directly with the airline CRS.

Cruise: Increased automation has made the cruise industry more accessible to travel agents. In 1989 Royal Caribbean Cruises introduced CruiseMatch 2000, a direct-access computerized reservations system for cruise bookings. Travel agents who use CruiseMatch can check availability, make reservations, and directly select the cabin they want to book. A PC-based version of CruiseMatch with color graphics is being tested.

Rail: Amtrak has direct access in the airline computer systems. In fact, about 75 percent of agents who book Amtrak use a CRS to do so. Their participation in agency automation has had a ma-

jor impact on their sales. Amtrak is essentially booked in the same way as airlines since they use ARC ticket stock. Eurail Passes and BritRail passes can also be booked through an agent's CRS.

Back-Room Systems

Back-room systems are computerized accounting systems that perform back-up tasks and are often physically found in the back room. These systems are available from vendors of reservations systems or related companies who lease accounting systems that interface directly with other systems. The back-room system can automatically print an invoice and itinerary, drawing on the information in the PNR. It performs all the tasks of a bookkeeper and prepares management reports. The following is a list of just some of the features of a good back-office system:

- Prints invoices
- Records client payments
- Keeps track of accounts receivable
- Tracks supplier commissions and traces overrides
- Maintains agency payroll
- Stores and prints client mailing lists
- Prepares management reports for corporate accounts

The Paperless Agency

Some people mistakenly believe that a fully automated agency is a paperless agency. The term is used, however, to refer to the reduction of unnecessary paper formerly used to keep handwritten information and notes that due to automation can be stored in a CRS. Total elimination of paper can never be achieved as agents must keep items such as tickets, coupons, invoices, and brochures, but paper use can be substantially reduced. This can only be achieved when agents trust their computers enough to store information in them and have confidence that the necessary information will be available when needed.

According to an ASTA survey, in 1985 25 percent of travel agencies had back-office automated accounting systems. That figure grew to 52 percent in 1991.

Computers and the Future

Computers represent the most efficient way of communicating information about new fares, new programs, sudden emergencies, or any of the daily changes that occur in the travel industry. Agents can either review the latest events on the screen or receive a hard copy of all new information that has been entered into the computer in the preceding 24 hours. Different branches of the same agency can now communicate with each other through the computer, rather than tie up telephone lines designed for incoming calls.

Cruise lines, hotels, and car companies are all looking for ways to increase their accessibility to agents through automation. New PC enhancements allow agents to show four-color photographs of hotel lobbies, rooms, and meeting facilities. Agents are now also beginning to access color maps, charts, and diagrams that can be printed and included in clients' documents.

Pressure from travel agents and their clients' needs will dictate even more automation in the future. Automation will allow agents to do things that we can't even imagine at this point. The technology is there, and the demands of the industry will drive new developments.

Automation's Capabilities

Automation allows the agent to

■ Check flight availability on any of the world's major carriers nearly a year in advance.

■ Display schedules and connecting service between city pairs.

■ Display the schedules of hundreds of airlines.

■ Quote domestic fares, extensive international fares, and many special constructed fares.

■ Book the reservation and automatically price most itineraries.

■ Assign reservations to queue for ticketing on the appropriate date

■ Print the ticket, provide an invoice, and prepare the passenger's itinerary

Automation systems also can

■ Check the availability and confirm reservations for hotels.

■ Confirm car rental reservations.

■ Reserve and ticket Amtrak.

■ Provide international rail information.

■ Access cruise information.

■ Provide such information as weather conditions, theater offerings, ski conditions, and availability of convention facilities.

■ Keep files on frequent travelers and their preferences.

An improvement to an existing computer reservations system is called an enhancement.

Staff Training

Managers can install the most sophisticated computer system, but unless the agents know how to utilize the system to its full capacity, it is a waste of money. To get the most out of any computer system, the agents must be given as much training as possible to ensure that the system is used to its full capabilities.

Agents should take advantage of the classes offered by the host airline for computer training. They should attend as many sessions as they can. Since it is not always possible to have staff members out of the office, agents should also take advantage of in-house training offered by the reservation systems.

In addition, each airline system has its own form of computer-based instruction. These are prepared lessons which can independently lead an employee through the various programs/enhancements. The lessons can be quite useful, especially for a new employee.

As helpful as formal instruction is, each agency should designate one staff member to be an auto-

Computerized Itinerary/Invoice

Here is an example of a typical computerized itinerary and invoice issued to a client by a travel agency. All details of the client's trip are clearly itemized.

QD 2CYZA1F  229 BERKELEY STREET
BOSTON, MA 02116
(617) 247-0088
FAX (617) 247-4145

```
                                        ITINERARY INVOICE
                                        PAGE NO.  1

                                             TICKET JACKET
```

```
    MR. ALAN TEST
    100 MAIN STREET
    EVERYWHERE MA 02186
```

```
    TEST/ALAN.MR.
```

AGENT	CONTACT	CUSTOMER NO.	ACCOUNT NO.	DATE
ARLENE			C3/3	25FEB92

DAY	DATE	CITY - AIRPORT	TIME	CARRIER	FLIGHT-CLASS STATUS	SERVICE-AMOUNT
A TU	03MAR	LV BOSTON	802A	UNITED	53Y OK	BREAKFAST
		AR SAN FRANCISCO	1129A			OSTOP D10
		SEAT		32-G **BOARDING PASS ISSUED**		
				TEST/ALAN.MR.		
C TU	03MAR	SAN FRANCISCO CALIFORNIA		HERTZ TERMINAL		
DROP	06MAR		415-877-1600	SAN FRANCISCO INTL AP		
		VEHICLE TYPE		COMPACT CAR		
		RESERVED FOR		TEST ALANMR		
		DROP TIME		1300		
		GUARANTEED		DAILY .00MI		USD 35.99
		CONFIRMATION		80910380509		
H TU	03MAR	SAN FRANCISCO CALIFORNIA		SHERATON		
	06MAR			WHARF		
				2500 MASON ST		
				SAN FRANCISCO CA 94133		
				415 362 5500		
				NBR ROOMS 1*KING BEDDED		
				RATE PER DAY 185.00		
			CONFO-C425040038			
A FR	06MAR	LV SAN FRANCISCO	140P	UNITED	20Y OK	LUNCH
		AR BOSTON	1000P			OSTOP D10
		SEAT		32-J **BOARDING PASS ISSUED**		
				TEST/ALAN.MR.		

```
                    TICKET NUMBER(S):   0161523770193

                                AIR FARE               1322.27
                                TAX                     132.23
                                TOTAL AIR FARE         1454.50
                                AMOUNT                 1454.50

THIS AMOUNT WILL BE CHARGED TO CREDIT CARD: AX3782 1234 561 007
```

CODE: A-Air H-Hotel T-Tour C-Car	CLASS: F; P-First C-J-Business Class	STATUS: OK-Confirmed RQ-Request
S-Surface V-Other Travel Service	Y, B,H,M,Q,K,S,V,L-Coach/Economy	WL-Wait List

DMS 00176 02/251829

RECONFIRM RETURNING AND CONTINUING RESERVATIONS 72 HOURS IN ADVANCE FOR INTERNATIONAL FLIGHTS AND SUGGEST 48 HOURS IN ADVANCE FOR DOMESTIC FLIGHTS. CAUTION: TICKETS HAVE VALUE IF UNUSED, PLEASE RETURN FOR CREDIT OR REFUND.

mation specialist. This should be someone who is comfortable with and interested in the latest enhancements and is willing to share this information with others in the office. Once selected, this agent should be responsible for keeping abreast of changes or enhancements offered by the CRS.

After evaluating this information, he or she should condense and summarize it in order to relay it to the appropriate staff members. Programs such as American Airlines' "Train the Trainer Program" offer classroom instruction on practical methods of teaching others to use the computer.

Summary

Nothing has changed the travel industry as dramatically as computers and automation. Ninety-five percent of all United States travel agencies use computers for their bookings. The PNR is the complete record of a reservation displayed on the computer screen. The typical components of a PNR include the airline name and flight number, class of service, departure date, departure and destination city, and desired number of seats.

Agents use their CRS to book cars, cruises, hotels, and train travel, as well as airline seats. Because a computer is as good as the information that is entered in it, managers should ensure that their staff have proper training and trust in the system.

Automation has come a long way since the mid-1970s. Future advancements in automation are limitless.

Chapter Wrap-up

DISCUSSION TOPICS

Unable to Sell

Airline A announces on April 30 schedule changes due to go into effect May 25. It programs the new schedules into its computer. Airline B, however, does not program these changes until May 15 when it receives the tapes. During the intervening period what happens to messages sent by B's computer requesting flights on A's old schedule? How can this be avoided?

PNR

Mrs. Haltwhistle and Miss Nunsuch of your hometown are planning a trip to Kearney, Nebraska. They wish to leave on the Tuesday before Thanksgiving and return on the following Sunday. They prefer morning flights, first class service, and window seats. Both work for the largest bank in your hometown. As an agent for Try Us First Travel, use an OAG or an airline simulated reservations system to design their PNRs. What additional information must be supplied?

Record of Changes

Jane Nomind has just received her tickets from your agency for her next trip. As usual, she is unable to translate the documents. What can you tell her about her reservation?

AA 615Y 07 JUN BOSBDA 950A 1249P

AA 632Y 14 JUN BDABOS 445P 532P

If the AA 615 changed to arrive at 12:51 p.m., the 632 changed to arrive at 5:47, then the 632 was withdrawn completely and passengers were rebooked on flight 63, how would the history look?

Automation

Your boss, Mr. Fussbudget, has consistently rejected any attempts by staff to automate his agency. A new automated travel office is opening (in six months) across the street and you are concerned that many of your clients will be swayed by the new agency's capabilities. You want to convince your boss that now is the time to automate, before the new office opens. How can you persuade him that automation will help his business?

Industry Communications

Chapter 14

CHAPTER OBJECTIVES

After completing this chapter, the reader should be able to

■ List five instances when a travel counselor should use a letter

■ Recall the most crucial step in letter writing

■ Review five guidelines to letter writing

■ Explain when to use overnight mail

■ Summarize the ways fax machines are used in travel agencies

■ Demonstrate proper telephone etiquette

■ Explain the purpose of a policy and procedure manual

VOCABULARY

After completing this chapter, the reader should be able to define

■ Deadline

■ Fax

■ Jargon

■ Prepayment

■ Refund

■ Telegram

■ Telex

■ Voucher

Introduction

Travel industry arrangements depend on effective communications. Clients communicate their needs to travel counselors who, in turn, describe arrangements that meet these needs. Then, in making reservations for the client, counselors communicate with suppliers, usually by computer or telephone. To confirm arrangements the travel professional may communicate orally or in writing several more times with vendors and clients. Clearly, good communications skills are essential for success in the travel industry.

Oral Communications

Despite the efficiency and popularity of computers, there are times when agents must still use the telephone to call suppliers. Not only do they call suppliers for information, but many feel more comfortable making a reservation over the phone than via the computer.

One key to successful telephone reservations is having all of the necessary information at hand before calling the supplier. This saves time for everyone concerned — the client, the supplier, and the agent. Most often, suppliers request information from agents in the order that best suits their automated system. Often, when agents are put on hold, suppliers have a recorded message that prepares them for the information that will be required. Many times, a supplier will begin by asking agents their ARC number that automatically triggers basic agency information.

Client Information

In most reservation situations, the following information is needed by the agent from the client:

- Name(s), complete with appropriate title(s)
- Home and/or business address and telephone number(s)
- Number of people traveling
- Ages of clients (if applicable)
- Dates and times of reservation (if applicable)
- Specific reservation information such as tour information, flight numbers, and so on.
- Method of payment
- Special requests or restrictions
- Special discounts

Some additional client information is necessary, depending on the travel product:

Cruises

- Category, deck, or cabin number preference
- Early or late seating
- Special meal restrictions (if necessary)
- Optional tours or extended stay information

Accommodations

- Type of room
- Location of room
- Check-in and check-out times
- Frequent-stay information

Airlines

- Seat request
- Passenger age (if applicable)
- Frequent-flyer information
- Special meal requests

Car Rentals

- Pick-up and drop-off times
- Age of renter (if applicable)
- Club membership information
- Additional driver information

Successful agencies will keep much of this information updated in their CRSs in the form of client profiles. This can save time and effort when making reservations for repeat clients.

Agent Information

In most reservation situations, the following information is needed by the agent from the supplier:

- Reservation or confirmation number
- Name of reservationist and date
- Price quote
- Hidden extras (tax, service charges)
- Cancellation policy
- Deposit and final payment dates
- Commission amount

Preferred Suppliers

Vital to the reservation process is the choice of the correct supplier to suit the needs of each individual customer. The choice is made easier if clients come to the agency after having gone through the selection process. If the clients show no definite preferences, however, agents book them with their own preferred suppliers. Using a preferred supplier system benefits both the agency and the client.

Using preferred suppliers permits agents to know a few select products very well and eliminates the problem of having just a vague familiarity with a vast number of products. As agents become more knowledgeable, they also become more secure in their selling techniques. Preferred suppliers provide financial incentives to agents in the form of higher commissions. As agents make more reservations, they develop a closer relationship so they feel comfortable addressing special customer needs and requests. In short, preferred suppliers enable agents to provide better service to their clients.

Consortiums

An agency unable to negotiate a direct preferred supplier override arrangement often will join a consortium, an organization formed to provide collective buying power and increased remuneration to its members. Through the consortiums' ability to negotiate on behalf of their membership, a small-volume agency can enjoy the same override commissions as a larger one. Typically, agents pay a one-time charge to belong or an annual fee that can range from $200 to $500. Today, nearly 50 percent of all United States agencies are members of consortiums.

Written Communications

Many travel services must be prepaid and confirmed in writing. The travel agent needs a written record of the client's payment, as well as a method of transmitting payment to the supplier. The client also needs a written record of payment to present to the supplier in exchange for prepaid services. All of these receipts are necessary to ensure accurate verification and proper service.

Vouchers

In 1874, when Thomas Cook first devised his unique system for introducing clients to distant suppliers, a voucher was the logical, expedient step in his organization of worldwide travel arrangements. Cook visited suppliers personally and arranged to have his clients' prepaid forms recognized as payment. He devised the first prepaid voucher to enable customers to leave for foreign destinations with the assurance that their reservations would be honored.

Today, for prepaid arrangements other than air transportation, cruises, or rail travel (where suppliers provide or issue tickets), many travel counselors use a voucher. Vouchers can be written by hand, typewritten, or generated by the computer directly from the client's record.

Letters

Vouchers contain specific information about deposits, full prepayments, and confirmed arrangements. The travel agent must also communicate with suppliers on matters that go beyond the scope of a voucher.

Many offices use three-part message/reply forms, especially for shorter communications. Anything typed or written on the top copy of the form automatically appears on the two beneath. The agent uses one-half of the page to send a message, leaving space for a reply on the other half.

A letter is most important whenever changes or additions to standard arrangements are being confirmed, such as clients requesting king-size beds, meeting a tour on the second day, or requiring adjoining rooms. The agent may also want to confirm complicated arrangements in writing and advise clients of other important information including deadlines for future payments, visa requirements, shots, and so on.

If clients cancel certain travel arrangements and a refund is in order, the agent may have to write and enclose any negotiable documents the client received. If clients return from a trip with unused prepaid vouchers, these too must be submitted with a written request for refund. Travel agents are responsible for assisting clients to obtain refunds.

Clearly, travel professionals compose letters for various purposes. They need form letters that cover the more common occurrences and can be modified for individual needs. Form letters can be stored in computers to be used repeatedly. These letters should observe the fundamental principles of business correspondence by communicating information as briefly and clearly as possible. Appearance and content are equally important.

A business letter should gain the reader's attention and convey a message that elicits a response. A good letter helps convey that the agency is professional. Attention to spelling, grammar, and neatness enhances that image and makes the agency's statements more credible. The most crucial step in writing a letter is organization.

A Letter Is the Best Way to

■ Request special services in connection with a reservation.

■ Explain the details of the payment schedule.

■ Seek refunds on behalf of a client.

■ Put agreements or understandings in writing as protection against future liability.

■ Thank the client for a reservation.

■ Promote sales.

■ Welcome clients home from a trip.

The following examples illustrate types of letters.

Letter to a Client Confirming Arrangements

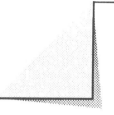

November 7, 1992

Mr. John Anderson
Post Office Box 189
San Diego, California 92399

Dear Mr. Anderson:

We are pleased to confirm reservations for you and your wife at the Camino Real Hotel in Cancun at a daily rate of $176, arriving Saturday, February 7, and departing Saturday, February 14.

The enclosed voucher confirms your reservation and should be presented at the hotel. This rate does not include meals, but several popular restaurants are close by. The hotel imposes a penalty of 50 percent of your total payment if you cancel within seven days of your scheduled arrival. We will be happy to discuss trip cancellation insurance with you.

We have also confirmed flights, as you requested. We strongly recommend that you reconfirm flight times directly with the airline on the day before your flight. The enclosed flight schedule contains full details. Please call our office before January 20 to let us know if you will be paying by cash, personal check, or major credit card. We will then issue your tickets.

You will need proof of citizenship and a tourist card to enter Mexico. Please complete the enclosed application form and return it to us. As soon as we receive it, we will issue the tourist cards to you.

Thank you for using the Travel Center for your travel arrangements. If you have any further questions, contact me or, in my absence, any of our travel consultants. We look forward to serving you again in the future.

Yours truly,

Ann Moore, CTC
Enclosures

Letter to a Client Enclosing Brochures

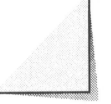

June 12, 1992

Mary French
20 Lakeside Drive
Wellesley, Massachusetts 02181

Dear Ms. French:

Thank you for your letter requesting information on a Caribbean cruise next November. We are pleased to enclose brochures for cruises that seem best suited to your needs.

You can select from a number of attractive ships with one-week itineraries. Cruise rates depend on the type of cabin selected and the luxury of a particular ship.

We are also enclosing a brochure with general information about cruising. It includes some fascinating details on the delights of a cruise vacation, as well as practical information about what to wear.

All of us at the Travel Center have sailed on cruise ships and will be happy to help you choose the one that will be best for you. Please call to make an appointment to discuss your trip. We recommend that cruise arrangements be made at least six months in advance to ensure the best choice of cabin.

Thank you again for your inquiry. We look forward to being of service to you.

Yours sincerely,

Betty Smith, CTC
Enclosures

Mail Services

Increasingly, electronic mail is replacing regular postal service when speed is a priority. Cost may also be a deciding factor. Like regular letters, electronic mail provides hard copy confirmations of communication for the agent, client, and supplier.

Telegrams

Telegrams have a minimum charge for up to 15 words. Beyond that the cost increases per word. Consequently, telegrams place a premium on succinct expression. Prepositions, conjunctions, and articles are frequently omitted. Strange compound nouns are invented to express several ideas. For example, "Mr. and Mrs. Jones have been delayed and will now arrive on Monday, February 22" becomes "JONES TWOPARTY NOW ARRIVING FEBRUARY 22. RESERVATIONS GUARANTEED." Symbols or abbreviations count as one word, so they are also omitted. Telegrams are transmitted instantly, and agents can request a hard-copy confirmation. An overnight telegram is less expensive per word than a regular telegram.

Telex

If both parties subscribe to a teleprinter or teletype service, the message can be typed, transmitted, and received in the same instant. The most widely used teleprinter service in the United States is Western Union's telex. Using a teletype machine, each subscriber can dial the number of another subscriber and transmit a message on a typewriter keyboard. The receiving machine automatically turns on to record the message and prints it on a continuous paper feed. Telex messages are also transmitted through airline computer systems. The message is typed on the agent's CRT and then queued to a central point where the message is relayed to the addressee. Replies are similarly processed and queued back to the agency from the relay point. Each subscriber has a unique number so there is no confusion in communications. Telex numbers can be found in reference books like the *OHG* or *Hotel and Travel Index*.

Overnight Mail

Overnight mail services, such as Federal Express or the post office's Overnight Mail service, continue to be a popular choice for rapid delivery. These offer the convenience of guaranteed, timely pickup and delivery of items of nearly any size. In addition, such couriers provide tracking of your parcel and notification of delivery. These services are especially useful for larger delivery packets containing group tickets, clients' bon voyage or honeymoon gifts, and corporate mailings.

Fax

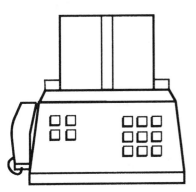

Fax, short for *facsimile*, machines are the newest form of electronic mail. From an obscure technology a few years ago, the fax machine has in many cases replaced the use of telegrams, telexes, and overnight mail. "Just fax it" or "What is your fax number?" have become as routine a request as "Drop me a letter" once was. Fax machines are part telephone, part copier, and part computer. They scan, digitize, and transmit images over phone lines and reprint a hard copy of the transmission at another fax station within minutes. Some can be directly attached to personal computers or voice-activated telephones. Most have memory features to keep track of transmissions. In the majority of cases, however, fax machines are used to transmit handwritten, typed, or printed data; photos; or illustrations across town or across the world. Fax numbers are commonly found on stationery, invoices, tour documents, and agency reference books.

Today, fax machines are nearly as prevalent as computers. From an agent's perspective using a fax has distinct advantages. It offers savings in time and money, simplicity, convenience, and accuracy over traditional mail services. It saves time because rates can be confirmed immediately on paper, urgent complaints are responded to more quickly, and clients and suppliers aren't put on hold. In addition, it is less expensive than most other traditional mail services.

Many cruise lines and tour operators immediately fax to travel agencies a copy of confirmations made on the telephone. Airlines send messages of new fares and routes via fax as well as invitations for fam trips.

Security concerns have thus far kept tickets and other accountable documents from being distributed via fax, but that may eventually change. Airport lounges, car rental offices, and most hotels have fax machines, some even in guest room areas. New fax networks are being established, where customers can use a separate fax booth or public terminal to send their message. These are as easy to use as telephones and can be credit-card activated.

Fax machines can run from $200 to $2,000. Some things to consider, besides price, when choosing a fax include speed, the amount of training and service provided by the vendor, types of paper used, timers, and volume capability.

Fax Facts — Ways fax machines are used in travel agencies

■ Making reservations with foreign vendors

■ Sending rooming lists or other last-minute information

■ Preparing itinerary proposals for corporate clients

■ Following up on proposals or commission requests

■ Ordering ticket stock

■ Booking cruises

■ Banking and invoicing

Just as junk mail can be a time-waster, so can junk fax. However, legislation has been passed in some states and is pending in others to regulate this nuisance. Some manufacturers have even developed blocking options on their machines to limit acceptance of unauthorized items.

Interoffice Communications

Travel agencies are information centers. Information comes in from suppliers in a variety of forms: reference books, brochures, computer queues, trade publications, and so on. This information must be speedily relayed to an office staff.

Although no office wants to drown in a sea of paper, written or typed memos are often the best way of imparting new information. The alternative is usually word of mouth, which is subject to distortion. Letters or electronic mail of interest to all can be circulated with a sign-off sheet. Information that is needed immediately cannot wait for a formal staff meeting. New fares, changes in a political situation, and messages for colleagues who are away from their desks or out of the office require written memos.

Each major airline computer system permits users to place messages, reminders, or instructions on queue for themselves or others. Electronic messages can be sent back and forth. Agents "work their queues" periodically to retrieve notes they left for themselves or messages from suppliers and co-workers. Daily briefings programmed by the office automation supervisor and the travel suppliers include updated industry information.

Telephone Techniques

Nothing more vividly reflects the atmosphere and personality of an agency than the telephone. A phone conversation is often the first contact clients have with the agent; it may create a lasting impression. To ensure that this impression is positive, managers should acquaint their staff with basic telephone techniques.

Phones need to be answered promptly, usually by the third ring. This alleviates office noise and tension, eliminates distractions to walk-in customers, and gratifies the caller. Since most agencies are busy, a proper balance needs to be reached between walk-in business and telephone callers.

When answering the phone, you need to identify the agency, yourself, and the caller. Be sure to pronounce names correctly and get the proper spelling. Professionalism is the key to proper telephone etiquette.

Frequently agents take telephone messages for co-workers. Most agencies supply specially printed forms for recording these messages that identify callers, their numbers, and brief relevant information.

Some important general guidelines should be remembered when taking messages. Perhaps the caller does not really need the person requested. By asking, "May I help you?" the agent answering may be able to take appropriate action without the need for a callback.

The answering agent should also make some attempt to find out briefly why the client is calling. A message indicating simply that somebody called does not allow an agent to call back fully prepared with the information the caller needs. The message should clearly state the caller's name (spelled correctly), telephone number, day and time the call was received, and time zone of the caller.

Although most people are used to being put on hold, they do not enjoy it. In fact, studies have shown that the average person grows impatient after less than 30 seconds. He or she may either hang up or, more likely, be less enthusiastic, less cooperative, more aggressive, or more angry when finally connected. In a busy office it is easy to condemn callers to everlasting hold and simply wait until the blinking light goes out. But the courtesy with which callers are put on hold helps build the agency's professional image and creates goodwill. Some procedures help to alleviate the irritation of being put on hold.

■ The receptionist should ask callers if they wish to hold and should wait for a reply. Sometimes callers are abruptly told to hold. Sometimes they are asked but put on hold before they can answer.

■ The person should explain why they are putting the caller on hold. "Could you please hold for a moment? I will check to see if she is available."

■ Agents should estimate how long the caller will have to wait. "She should be with you soon. Do you wish to hold?" Or, "She will be a few minutes. Do you wish to hold?"

■ Finally, if possible, the agent should check with callers who are holding, to reassure them they have not been forgotten, to see if they wish to continue holding, or to offer to take a message.

Telephone Tag

A recent study noted that the average career business person spends nearly two years of his life involved in the no-win game of telephone tag. Some ways to stop wasting this valuable time are:

■ Call busy people early in the morning, mid-week, and mid-month. These are the best times to reach most individuals.

■ Develop secondary contacts who can help you if the person you're trying to reach is unavailable.

■ Ask when the best time would be to return the call, use that information, and record it for future usage.

■ Leave detailed messages so others can help relay your information.

■ Be available when you tell others you will be. Nothing is more frustrating than waiting to return a call then finding no one there to take it.

Once the domain of mega-agencies, 800-numbers are becoming increasingly popular with smaller companies. These numbers are especially helpful for getting and keeping corporate and convention business clientele. Even leisure clients enjoy the convenience and savings offered by 800-lines.

Staff Meetings

Most agencies schedule regular staff meetings. These meetings enable counselors to discuss office procedures and propose changes. Agents who have recently returned from trips can brief their col-

leagues on hotels, sightseeing, and destinations. Upcoming promotions and recent advertisements can be discussed. The manager may wish to examine certain proposals and solicit staff input. A particular crisis may necessitate group action with the agency staff working as a team. Staff meetings can become merely opportunities for complaints or can, ideally, contribute positively to the agency's operations.

Policies and Procedures Manual

It is important for a manager to know that all employees are following the same basic procedures. Many times such information is relayed in meetings, but every business should also have routine policies in written form so that employees can easily access the information. Such a handbook could include issues like vacation leave, salary reviews, bonus and commission policies, fam trip information, acceptance of checks, and other reference material.

More elaborate information, often given during an employee's orientation, should include the history of the company, its philosophy or mission, and its objectives. An organization chart could also be included to familiarize new employees with management. Personnel policies should be listed to indicate fair and equitable treatment for all employees in areas such as dismissal, smoking policies, performance appraisals, liability, and outside employment.

Benefits to address might include

■ *Pay issues*—Bonuses, holidays, lunch and break times, overtime and comp pay

■ *Travel benefits*—Fam tours, contests and incentive travel, vacation time

■ *Health care*—Insurance, pension plans, dental and eye care, sick days

Such a manual can save time and money, particularly during initial orientation and training. In addition it provides legal advantages by proving that certain policies are part of standard operating procedures. If the information is stored in the computer, revisions are easy, and the handbook can remain current. However, the best handbooks are useless if employees do not have the time or lack the motivation to read them.

Summary

Effective communication between industry suppliers, agents, and clients is vital to the success of the travel industry. Written communication commonly appears in the form of vouchers and letters. These methods are used when written records are necessary in exchange for services. Certain guidelines should be followed to ensure that written correspondence is as productive as possible.

Many methods of mail service are used to convey this written communication. Reliance upon regular mail, telegrams, cables, and telex has been lessened by the success of fax and overnight mail services.

Oral communication, whether by telephone or in person, is equally important to travel counselors. Telephone skills are vital in maintaining good industry, peer, and client relations. Staff meetings are one method of relaying timely information to large groups of employees. When routine information needs to be consistently handled, policies should be recorded in a handbook readily available to all workers.

Chapter Wrap-up

1. The text suggests seven situations in which you might write a letter. Can you suggest any others?
2. When do you think three-part messages/reply forms would be inappropriate?
3. What major features would you want in a telephone system?
4. Putting callers on hold courteously is a key part of telephone etiquette. Can you summarize the major procedures without referring back to the text?

DISCUSSION TOPICS

Letter Writing

Mr. and Mrs. Noshow have canceled their one-week trip with No Frills Cruise Lines. They had been scheduled to leave on February 12 and return on February 20 via Seat of Your Pants Airways. The night of the 19th would have been spent at Harry's Hideaway Hotel. All suppliers had received $100 deposits from your travel agency. Do you have enough information to write letters of cancellation to the vendors? If not, supply the missing information and create sample letters of cancellation for the Noshows' trip.

Telephone Messages

Your office has just hired a new switchboard operator who is having problems adjusting to your telephone system. Consequently everyone has been receiving incomplete messages that require return calls. Most messages include only phone numbers, some incorrect, some incomplete, or a first or last name, and no messages. How can you begin researching these mystery callers? How can you impress on your new employee the importance of accurate telephone messages?

Staff Meeting

As the office manager of a busy travel agency, it is your responsibility to organize the weekly departmental meetings, the monthly business meetings, and the annual staff meetings. The office consists of accounting, computer, retail, group sales, operations, transportation, personnel, and tour guide departments. Consider topics each division might have for these three meetings. What additional information should be considered weekly, monthly, and annually?

Money Management

Chapter 15

CHAPTER OBJECTIVES

After completing this chapter, the reader should be able to

- List five sources of agency commissions
- Explain three types of expenses
- Understand the influence of time on money
- Analyze credit-card and check payments
- Compare financial statements
- Review a balance sheet

VOCABULARY

After completing this chapter, the reader should be able to define

- Asset
- Balance sheet
- Cash flow
- Commission
- Debit memo
- Equity
- Invoice
- Liquidity
- Profitability
- Receipt

Introduction

Owners and managers need financial information to help plan and control the activities of their businesses. A company must keep track of its finances by recording, classifying, and summarizing financial activities in a useful manner.

Bookkeeping and Accounting

The actual recording of daily transactions in a travel agency is performed by a bookkeeper. This person keeps a record of checks issued, deposits and transfers made, automatic cash withdrawals, and interest payments, usually using a system designed by the bank and incorporated in the checkbook register. A travel agency uses a more sophisticated system because it needs to identify precisely the sources of income and to relate its invoices to receipts. Once the actual recordings of daily transactions are made, an analysis of these transactions is necessary.

Accounting is the analysis of the everyday bookkeeping transactions. Accounting, the "language of business," is used to describe economic activity. This study of business transactions may be done manually or, more often, on a computerized accounting system.

Basic Financial Statements

Financial statements are the main source of financial information about a business. They are used by management as well as by investors, customers, employees, and government regulatory agencies to evaluate the financial strength and future of a business. The two most widely-used financial statements are the income statement and the balance sheet.

The Income Statement

The income statement is a report generated to evaluate the performance of a business by matching its revenue (or income) and related expenses for a particular accounting period. It is used to judge how well a company is doing by showing the net income or net loss. The income statement is used to prepare the balance sheet.

	INCOME (Revenue): the inflow of cash and receivables
Minus	EXPENSES: the cost of the goods and services used to earn revenue
	NET INCOME

Travel agency income is derived from a number of sources, but principally from commissions. Commissions do not represent earned income until the client has traveled, since arrangements can be cancelled or changed before departure or even while traveling. Clients returning from a trip may also submit documents for refund.

A special form known as a debit memo is used by airline suppliers to recall commissions that were incorrectly taken.

Expenses

Expenses are the cost of goods and services used up in the process of earning revenue. Travel agency expenses fall into three categories: fixed, variable, and semi-variable.

Fixed expenses remain unchanged despite changes in volume. They are predictable and can be controlled to some degree.

Some examples of fixed costs are

- Telephone
- Utilities
- Rent
- Insurance premiums

Sources of Agency Income

- Commission on sales of air transportation
- Commission on sales of cruises
- Commission on sales of tours
- Commission on sales of accommodations
- Commission on sales of travel insurance
- Miscellaneous income from cancellation penalties, service charges, passport photographs, travel guides, luggage, and accessories
- Override or bonus payments from suppliers for achieving a certain level of sales
- Income from custom-planned programs (FIT)

- Subscriptions to reference books
- Computer equipment lease(s)
- Trade association, cooperative, franchise, consortium membership fees
- Furniture and equipment
- Depreciation (the declining value of owned assets, such as typewriters)
- Accounting fees

Travel has been ranked as one of the top five expenses in 33 percent of Fortune 500 companies. Many companies now place travel costs right behind payroll and data processing expenses. Therefore, the need to control travel costs has become a top priority of such companies.

Variable expenses are costs that increase and decrease directly and proportionally with changes in volume. They are difficult to predict, but easy to control. Variable expenses should increase when business is good and decline when business is bad.

Variable expenses include

- Familiarization trips
- Corporate dividends
- Part-time salaries
- Commissions of outside salespersons

Semi-variable, or mixed, expenses change in response to a change in volume, but they change by less than a proportional amount. To the extent that they are unavoidable, they are fixed. To the extent that they vary with sales volume and can be quickly terminated, they are variable.

Semi-variable expenses include

- Office supplies
- Cost of advertising
- Postage
- Professional fees

Here is an example of a simple income statement. The source for the statement's figures is the financial data accumulated by the accounting system.

Carefree Travel, Inc.

Income Statement For Period October 1 – December 31

Commission Income:

Domestic Air	$40,162
International Air	17,531
Tours	8,025
Cruises	11,100
Hotels	2,813
Rental Cars	3,656
Miscellaneous	412
TOTAL	$83,699

Expenses:

Rent	$16,200
Telephone	1,800
Utilities	925
Computer	3,750
Furniture/Equipment	180
Salaries	39,250
Fees	400
Depreciation	1,500
Subscriptions	250
Insurance Premiums	790
Office Supplies	1,423
Advertising	3,600
Postage	950
Miscellaneous	525
TOTAL	$71,543

Excess of Income over Expenses:

	$83,699
Minus	$71,543
	$12,156

The Balance Sheet
(or, Statement of Financial Condition)

The balance sheet is a statement used to show the financial position of a business at a particular point in time. A balance sheet has two sides. One side lists assets, which are usable resources that the agency owns. The other side lists liabilities, which are claims that other companies or individuals have against the agency, and equity, which is the excess of assets over liabilities. The simple rule is that a change in the amount of assets on one side of the balance sheet necessitates an equal change in the amount of liabilities and equities on the other side. Through this method of double entry for each business transaction, the sum of all assets remains constantly equal to the sum of all liabilities and equities.

ASSETS: the economic resources owned by a business

Minus   LIABILITIES (Obligations)

OWNER EQUITY: the resources invested by the owner

Every agency has different kinds of assets and different kinds of liabilities and equities. At any given time, most agencies have some cash in a checking account and some short-term investments in certificates of deposit or treasury bills that can be turned back into cash in the near future. In addition, clients owe agencies money. These are clearly assets.

An agency may pay salaries every two weeks in advance. If the moment in time chosen for the balance sheet is the day after payday, each employee would owe the agency a certain number of work days. These days become assets of the agency. The agency owns furniture, office supplies, perhaps a car for ticket deliveries, maybe even the building it occupies. All these are assets of one kind or another.

At the same time, agencies may owe money to a bank or to some suppliers of furniture or equipment. They probably owe money to industry suppliers, particularly if an air sales report is nearly due. Agencies may owe salaries for days that employees have already worked, and they may owe

payroll taxes to the government. These are all liabilities.

The agency owner put some capital into the agency to get it started and may have injected more money periodically. Any excess of assets over liabilities represents the owner's equity. If liabilities exceed assets, the owner will have to inject more capital soon.

An agency formed as a corporation raises capital by selling shares in the company to investors. Owner equity then becomes known as stockholder or shareholder equity. Stockholder equity is always shown as the total value of all the stock at the time it was purchased. If the agency does well, total assets exceed liabilities and stockholder equity combined. This difference is then called retained earnings and represents the amount of cumulative increase in stockholder equity. If the agency does poorly, total assets may amount to less than liabilities plus stockholder equity. Stockholders in these circumstances contemplate a deficit in their equity that shows how much their investment has declined in value.

Both assets and liabilities are listed in the order they are expected to be used or fall due. Current assets are either cash or assets that can be converted into cash soon, usually within a year. A fixed asset, like a copying machine, is unlikely to be turned into cash in the near future unless the agency decides to replace it or goes out of business. All financial statements are prepared on the assumption that the agency will stay in business and is a going concern. Otherwise, all assets would be current.

Intangible assets, like goodwill, can never be turned into cash unless the agency is sold, because they tend to represent the difference between the agency's assets and the amount the owner paid to purchase the agency or the difference between total assets and what the owner thinks the agency is worth. If the agency has never changed hands, goodwill represents the owner's subjective judgment.

Assets are arranged on a balance sheet in order of declining liquidity. Liquid assets, those immediately available to meet current liabilities, are listed first. Liabilities are listed on the same principle. Debts the agency must pay soon, normally within a year, are listed first. Long-term debts follow. An owner will not realize equity until the agency is sold

Grace Travel Balance Sheet

Note — A balance sheet is usually prepared internally for the information of management and ownership. A statement prepared by an outside auditor and required for calculating taxes may differ in several respects from the statement shown.

Grace Travel
Balance Sheet
June 30, 1992

ASSETS			LIABILITIES AND EQUITIES		
Current Assets			*Current Liabilities*		
Cash	$59,000		Accounts Payable	$61,000	
Marketable Securities	15,000		Accrued Salary Payable	6,000	
Accounts Receivable	18,000		Accrued Taxes Payable	2,000	
Inventory	3,500		Deposits from Clients	4,500	
Prepaid Expenses and			Total Current Liabilities		$73,500
Deposits	10,000				
Total Current Assets		$105,500	*Long-Term Liabilities*		
			Notes Payable	25,000	
Fixed Assets			Total Long-Term Liabilities		25,000
Automobile	6,500				
Furniture and Equipment	10,000		*Owner's Equity*		
Less Accumulated			Invested Capital	25,000	
Depreciation	(3,000)		Retained Earnings	3,500	
Total Fixed Assets		13,500	Total Owner's Equity		28,500
Intangible Assets					
Goodwill	8,000				
Total Intangible Assets		8,000			
TOTAL ASSETS		$127,000	TOTAL LIABILITIES & OWNER'S EQUITY		$127,000

and he or she is the last person to have a claim against the agency's assets.

All financial statements are open to interpretation. One travel agency's balance sheet can be fairly compared only to those of other very similar travel agencies.

A favorite method of analyzing balance sheets involves the use of ratios: the comparison of certain items directly with others. The importance attached to ratios varies according to the information sought. When interpreting the balance sheet, four important questions should be asked.

Liquidity   Can the agency meet short-term liability from current assets?

Efficiency   Is the agency using its assets efficiently?

Solvency   Is the agency generating enough cash to meet long-term liabilities? Will it be able to stay in business for the foreseeable future?

Profitability   How profitable is this agency?

Time Value of Money

In an ideal world, income would always precede the expenses associated with it. The benefit of receiving income immediately is enormous. Every agency wants to accelerate cash inflow and delay

263

cash outflow as much as possible. Money received immediately is worth more than the same amount promised for some date in the future, simply because money can be invested in any number of ways to produce income.

Some businesses surcharge accounts receivable by a certain percentage if they remain unpaid beyond a given period. Other businesses may discount the amount due if payment is received immediately. These inducements to pay early are not widely found in the travel industry because they may violate current agreements between agents and suppliers.

The cost of extending credit may also include second invoices, past-due notices, and eventually bad debts. Some agencies encourage clients who wish to postpone payment to use a credit card. Using a credit card, individuals and companies usually obtain up to thirty days' credit automatically. They may also stretch payments with installments. The travel agency receives immediate income for the sale when a credit card is used.

Because agencies pay the airlines for all tickets issued during the preceding week, they do not want their agents preparing tickets for clients who do not come in to pay for them. Although a client's tickets should always be ready, agents should not issue them unless they are certain that they will be paid for before the air report is due. Agencies void unpaid tickets to avoid reporting them as sales unless these tickets are nonrefundable. Such fares must be reserved, ticketed, and paid for within a twenty-four-hour period.

Cash Flow

Air transportation and cruises enable agents to receive income at the point of sale. In the case of

car rentals or hotels, the agency receives commission income only after the client has used the service, unless it is part of full prepaid arrangements. Commission should never be deducted from deposits. Car-rental companies tend to remit consolidated commissions with a monthly check. Hotels usually send a check for individual clients shortly after checkout. These practices cause agency income to lag.

Any agency that specializes in groups or charters must anticipate considerable expense before realizing any income. Group tours must be promoted, and suppliers need deposits to secure accommodations and other arrangements. Charter contracts usually specify payments at certain intervals, regardless of whether revenue has yet reached the agency. Agencies offering group tours or charter programs require greater capitalization to meet expenses incurred in anticipation of revenues. Credit-card sales also affect a travel agency's daily cash flow.

Why Agencies Need Cash

An agency needs cash for several reasons. It needs to be able to meet short-term cash expenses, particularly salaries. Liquidity is so important that accountants generally produce a financial statement to measure it. The statement, called statement of changes in financial condition, shows how cash was earned, how it was spent, and the amount of cash on hand to meet expenses. Given the current high cost of borrowing money, liquidity is vital to travel agencies. Most agencies have both liquid assets (cash) and fixed assets (furniture, computer). Technically, an agency could raise cash by selling fixed assets, but not without harming its ability to stay in business.

Cash is necessary to invest in future business. New programs and growth have to be financed internally with the agency's surplus cash or the agency must seek a loan. If the agency secures a loan, it then needs to generate cash to repay it. Cash can also be used for short-term investments to generate additional income. Agencies are finding ways to earn interest on extremely short-term deposits. The further ahead of departure a deposit or full payment comes in, the larger the cash float that a travel agency, tour operator, cruise line, or other supplier can invest.

Cash flow is vital to an agency, and each individual agent can affect it. By requesting early deposits and payments from clients, by ticketing at the right time, by encouraging cash or check payments, the agent can help preserve liquidity. Many companies have been forced into bankruptcy, not because they were not doing well or because they did not have a bright future, but simply because they had no cash to meet current expenses.

Handling Money

Agents handle large sums of money. As conduits between clients and suppliers, they assume the role of trustees while funds are in their possession. They must keep accurate and complete records of money received and disbursed and must take every precaution to protect the financial interests of their clients and suppliers.

Invoices, Receipts, and Extended Billing

At one time travel agencies and airlines were not permitted to compete on the basis of price. Instead, travel agencies used to offer generous delayed payment options by carrying accounts for periods of thirty to sixty days. This practice was risky and tied up substantial amounts of money that might be used for other purposes. In agencies that continue to follow this procedure, the counselor must perform a substantial amount of record-keeping, filing, correspondence, and invoicing. The invoice is an important part of the process. To treat it casually is to invite serious and costly errors. An invoice constitutes an implied contract between the agency and the client for services rendered in exchange for payment.

An invoice indicates the amount due. Usually the agency does not release any tickets or other documents until they have been paid, unless the account is one to which credit is extended. A receipt is an invoice with a different purpose. All receipts indicate the amount paid. Many clients pay for tickets or documents when they pick them up at the agency. They do not need an invoice in advance. They need a receipt indicating the amount paid and the method of payment.

When clients who receive an invoice pay the amount due, they receive a receipt. If they pay only part of an invoice, the amount received and the amount due need to be shown, and a combination invoice/receipt issued. Agency computer systems can produce either invoices or receipts.

A standard invoice may carry notices and advice to the client that limit the agency's liability, remind the client about reconfirming international flights, and suggest the purchase of insurance. The remainder of the information on an invoice depends on the agency's standard practice. It is normal to include the serial numbers of tickets and vouchers, as well as some indication of the itinerary. Computers produce a combined invoice/itinerary containing more complete information. An invoice must be clear, concise, easy to read, and free from abbreviations that may mean nothing to clients.

Payment Options

Most agencies offer clients a number of payment options depending to some extent on the suppliers' policies. Cash is always acceptable. As a precaution, it must be counted, recounted, and receipted in the client's presence. Personal checks, company checks, travelers cheques, and credit cards require even more care. Because checks and credit cards are commonplace, it is easy to forget that they can be forged, stolen, or invalid for other reasons.

Many major companies learn from sad and costly experience not to make assumptions about a client's honesty and integrity. Travel agencies are in the same predicament. It may be a natural inclination, but not good business judgment, to trust every client who walks in the door.

Credit Cards

Agency policy on the acceptance of credit cards is largely dictated by the policies of suppliers. Some airlines do not accept certain credit cards, or they accept them only with certain provisos. A guide to airline acceptance of credit cards is found in ARC's *Industry Agents' Handbook* or in the computer. Some cruise lines accept most major credit cards as forms of payment whereas others accept none at all.

Because of this lack of unanimity, some agents become credit-card merchants themselves, even though it means paying a percentage of each sale to the issuing credit-card company. They may then accept credit cards from clients for any purchase regardless of supplier policy. The decision to become a credit-card merchant must balance the benefit of generating additional business against an additional cost of doing business.

ATC

The Air Travel Card (ATC), the world's first charge card, was developed by the airline industry in 1936. It is currently issued by over 30 airlines and is accepted by more than 200 airlines worldwide. Unlike other major charge cards, the ATC is limited to charges for air and rail travel only. The ATC red card is limited to travel in North America, and the green card can be used for domestic and international travel. Those cards marked with a P can be used only by the person to whom the card is issued, and those marked with a Q can be used for travel by any employee, associate, or client in the same company.

Agents who accept a credit card on behalf of a supplier may be liable for any problems the supplier encounters in collecting payments unless important steps have been followed.

- The agent must ask the credit-card holder to establish proof of identification (a picture I.D. that also lists a current home address).
- The agent must check the charge card's expiration date.
- The card holder must sign the charge form in the agent's presence.
- The agent then compares this signature to the signature on the credit card.
- The agent now validates the charge (on the actual date).
- The agent obtains authorization and shows an authorization code on the charge form.

Travel agents must be on the lookout for credit-card fraud. Occasionally thieves try to charge tickets to a stolen credit card and later resell them. Suppliers and travel agencies are reluctant to reveal much about these problems for fear of giving ideas to potential thieves. As it is, the methods of credit-card and airline-ticket robbers reveal a thorough knowledge of agency procedures.

Through computer information, such as multiple bookings made the same day by the same person using the same credit card, suppliers can detect possible fraud. Seasoned criminals concentrate on ordinary travel arrangements, but amateurs tend to try first-class travel or prepaid tickets (PTAs) destined to be picked up by partners in different cities. Take care not to give cash refunds for tickets originally charged to a credit card.

Many agents believe that credit-card holders can authorize a spouse or child to use their cards. In fact, this is not possible. Only the card holder may sign a charge form, using the authorized signature that appears on the back of the card.

Checks

Personal checks must be handled carefully. Proper identification is essential, and the client should sign the check in the agent's presence. Most agencies do not accept checks that are larger than the amount of the sale or checks from out of state.

Agents should be wary of second-party checks, personal checks that do not bear the printed name and address of the signer, and checks with low serial numbers. Agents should also be suspicious and alert if clients wish to pay by check for last-minute, rushed arrangements. Quite a few agents discover the hard way that the check accepted from a stranger late on Friday afternoon has been written on a nonexistent bank. Criminals often show up when their potential victim is preoccupied and distracted.

Without exception, agents should never accept pre-signed travelers cheques. Clients must sign travelers cheques in the agent's presence. Because these cheques are easily negotiated, the signatures on them should be carefully inspected to make sure that they match those on the proof of identity. Agents should accept only cheques from a reputable, recognized company. If there is any doubt or if the cheques are in such large denominations that they far exceed the amount of the actual sale, the agent should advise the client to cash them at the nearest bank.

The agent should write the client's address and telephone number on the back of the personal check or travelers cheque, as well as details of the driver's license or other proof of identity produced. This information provides one more record of the client in the event a problem develops.

To preserve goodwill between agent and client, verification of identity should be accomplished as a matter-of-fact, normal procedure. The careful balance of caution and discretion will keep the client from taking offense. If properly handled, such actions are accepted by most people as a natural business practice.

Sending Payment to Suppliers

Most suppliers accept payment for individual reservations by agency check. The airlines, however, have established a special remitting system for travel agents.

The Area-Bank Settlement Plan

Every week each agency must report its sales of airline tickets and other accountable documents and must pay the airline the gross amount less commission. Each sales report contains adjust-

ments, either in the agency's favor (for refunds made to clients or for commissions on credit-card sales) or in the airline's favor (commission recalls on refunded tickets or debit memos for overcharges). Each agent should know something about the air report since it controls to some extent the rhythm of work in an office, the policies and procedures followed, and the order of tasks performed. The air report is usually prepared by the agency's bookkeeping staff or by a designated employee under management supervision.

Whether the clients come in to pay or not, the agency has to pay the airline for the tickets within a week of making a reservation. No agency can last very long if it is always paying out money before any comes in.

Agencies report all sales to a central-processing bank in their area, and the bank disburses money to the appropriate carriers. The remittance time for the sales report is changing as ARC is allowing new arrangements that permit agencies to negotiate for a longer time between reporting periods.

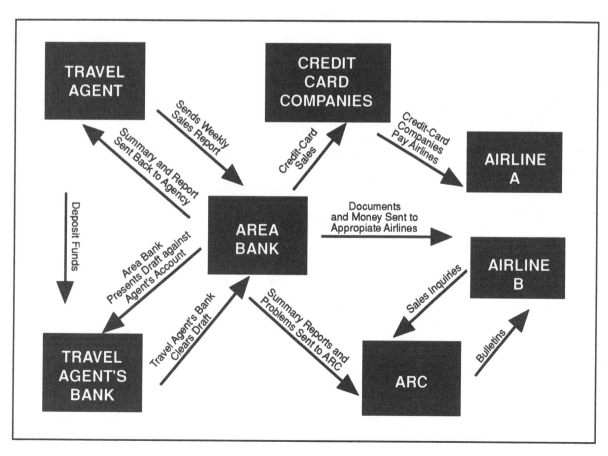

The diagram shows the agent mailing the sales report to the area bank within two days after the end of the business week. Currently, Sunday is the last day of the business week. The agency reports all cash, check, and credit-card sales of airline documents. Since credit-card sales involve no cash collection, the commission on them is deducted from the cash amount that the agency owes the airlines. The area bank will make similar adjustments for refunds, credit memos, and debit memos submitted by the agency.

The area bank receives the agent's report, calculates the total amount due the airlines, and presents a demand for that money (called a draft) directly to the agent's bank. To protect against miscalculations by the area bank, the agency notifies its bank each week of the maximum amount that can be withdrawn from its account. The area bank also forwards all credit-card billings to the credit-card company and reimburses the airlines directly.

ARC reports that among the most common errors on agency sales reports are

- Incorrect or illegible commission-code entries on tickets
- Tickets not reported
- Agent's coupons submitted instead of or with auditor's coupons
- Illegible credit-card transmittal forms
- Credit-card refunds submitted as cash refunds
- Credit-card numbers on the transmittal form that are not the same as the credit-card numbers indicated on the ticket

Mistakes like these can result in a delay in the agency's receiving proper credit. ARC regularly publishes a Travel Agent Bulletin designed to alert agencies to changes or common problems in the reporting system.

Either manually or through an automated system, the travel agent delivers the auditor's and agent's coupons for each document to the individual in the office who prepares the report. The coupons should legibly reflect the fare, commission percentage, and tax rate, unless this information is the bookkeeper's responsibility. Ensuring that no tickets are written prematurely, that commissions are correct, and that fares are accurate are vital tasks of the travel agent. A full description of the reporting procedure and the area bank

settlement plan is contained in ARC's *Industry Agents' Handbook*.

Through the area-bank system, an agency pays for all air transportation weekly. To pay suppliers not on the ARC system, agencies issue checks.

Agency Checks

Before issuing or authorizing a check, the agent should be satisfied that the client has paid in full and that the form of payment is valid. Rarely will agencies send checks to suppliers on the strength of a client's promise to pay. The agent remits the deposit in full to the tour operator and at a later date, submits a check to the tour operator for the balance, less commission. A record of monies received and disbursed on behalf of a client should be part of the client's file.

Authorized signatures of checks should be limited to one or two individuals. In most agencies, the owner or manager signs all checks. Agents often submit check requests to a single source, usually a full-time bookkeeper. In other offices the agent may fill out the check completely except for the signature and submit it to the authorized person for signing.

A cover letter or voucher clearly describes what the check is for and how the amount has been calculated if the agency is remitting net. This information should also be on a check request if the bookkeeper issues the check.

When making overseas prepayments, many agencies send a regular check on their United States bank account for what they calculate to be the dollar equivalent of the foreign amount owed. This practice can lead to problems. The solution to these problems may be to send a check in local currency. Some international-currency specialists write drafts in local currency drawn on foreign banks. Local banks also provide this service but at a higher charge than the foreign-currency specialist.

Service and Cancellation Charges

Suppliers reimburse agents for their services by paying them a commission. Most suppliers specifically forbid travel agents to charge clients more than the published rates. Nevertheless, agencies can impose their own charges for services to clients for which they receive no commission from a supplier. Service charges might be imposed for the preparation of a lengthy and involved foreign independent tour (FIT), a noncommissionable hotel reservation, visa-handling fees, the sending of a FAX, or long-distance telephone calls.

In the deregulated environment of the airline industry, travel agencies must deal with extremely low air fares. The commission an agency receives often does not cover the cost of writing the ticket. In some instances, agencies are charging a fee for writing these very low-revenue-producing tickets. The imposition of this type of fee on the sales of airline tickets is controversial and dependent on the competitive market in which an agency is located.

Service charges lie within the discretion of the agency owner or manager, but if they are adopted, the schedule of such fees must be prominently displayed in the agency. Once an agency begins to charge service fees, it must be careful to guarantee that the charges are equitably and consistently applied to all clients.

Security

Tickets and vouchers are essentially blank checks. In the wrong hands they constitute a dangerous source of fraud. So important is the security

of negotiable, accountable documents such as ticket stock that agencies often require agents to sign for airline tickets before issuing them to clients. Agencies take security seriously, and at the end of their business day they usually follow very exact procedures for securing ticket stock, tickets issued and awaiting pickup, undeposited checks and cash, and all other items of value. A fireproof safe, as described in the *Industry Agents' Handbook*, holds all the agency's valuables, and a specified individual is responsible for locking the office.

Security specialists recommend that nothing of any value be left in the open, especially if a window provides an easy view inside the agency. They further urge that routine procedures be varied to

The ARC *Industry Agents' Handbook*

The ARC *Industry Agents' Handbook* is an important reference source. Agents refer to it to check procedures and regulations governing the sale of air transportation. The *Handbook* was developed and is periodically revised by ARC's Agency Administration Department. It contains the ARC Passenger Sales Agency Agreement and specifies the exact business relationship between the airlines and their appointed agents. Since the regulations and procedures flow from the agreement, the *Handbook* affects the daily operation of every agency.

The *Handbook* has a list of telephone numbers for emergencies or complex problems. Any agency requiring immediate answers to questions involving application for ARC approval, bank account changes, changes of name or location, change of ownership, defaults, reduced rate transportation, and a number of other subjects will find telephone numbers for the appropriate personnel at ARC headquarters in Washington.

Various sections of the *Handbook* explain the procedure for writing a standard airline ticket and the format for making reservations and reporting air sales using the Area-Bank Settlement Plan. Other sections deal with the acceptance of credit cards, refunding, the use of documents like tour orders and MCOs, reduced rate transportation for agents, and bonding requirements. The information includes the most basic facts on ticketing and reporting as well as explanations of complex and unusual topics.

confuse potential thieves; the agency should not have the same individual depositing cash every night, at the same time, at the same bank. A light left on in the agency can prevent a thief from roaming without fear of detection. All locks should be checked. The main entrance should have an especially secure lock. Although these precautions may thwart the amateur thief, there may be no certain way to defeat the determined professional.

Agents can be held liable for lost or stolen tickets unless theft by persons other than the agency owner or employees is proved. ARC officials must determine that the agent "exercised reasonable care," including compliance with ticket-security rules. Airline-ticket stock is highly marketable. Often, a burglar loots an agency and sells the tickets to criminal groups specializing in the resale of stolen documents. Agents must control the number of tickets left unattended in the office and should never reveal to clients the amount of business they do in a day.

Burglaries often occur on weekends. If one occurs, the staff should react calmly, make certain that nothing is moved or touched, and alert the owner, manager, and police immediately.

The police will request descriptions of any curious strangers who have been in the agency asking questions prior to the burglary. They will also need a list of all stolen property, including the serial numbers of tickets and other accountable forms. The police can list the stolen ticket numbers with the National Crime Information Center in Washington, D.C. The Airlines Reporting Corporation must be notified immediately, and the agency must complete the burglary-report form found in the *Handbook*.

Negotiable Documents

Besides airline tickets, travel agents must also report Miscellaneous Charges Orders (MCOs), Prepaid Ticket Advices (PTAs, or prepaids), and Tour Orders. These are all negotiable and accountable documents.

Miscellaneous Charges Order (MCO)

An MCO is issued when standard ticket stock cannot be used. It is most often used to record deposits and full prepayments for air transportation, surface transportation, tour packages, supplemental charges, car rentals, hotel accommodations, or additional collections. A clear description must be indicated on the MCO for the type of service for which the MCO was issued.

In this example, Mr. Test paid his travel agent for Delta Senior Coupons. He will present this MCO (valued at $516), issued by his travel agent to Delta Airlines, in exchange for the discounted Delta tickets that this promotion allows.

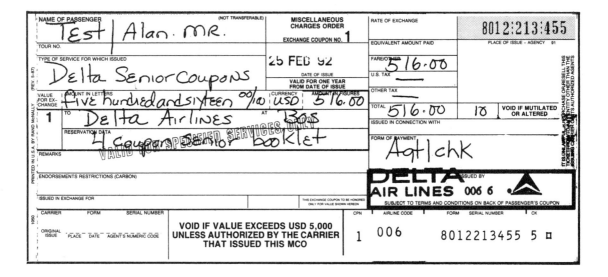

Tour Order

A Tour Order records payments for advertised air tours. In most cases, it serves as the actual tour document that the clients hand-carry to their destination and exchange for services. As each flight coupon on an airline ticket shows specific flight segments, each line on a tour order is used for specific services.

In this example, Mr. Test paid his travel agent $950 for the Maui Magic Tour in Hawaii, provided by American Airlines Flyaway Vacations. When he arrives at the airport in Maui, he will present coupon #1 to Orchid Tours in exchange for a transfer to his hotel. He will also receive a return-transfer voucher from Orchid Tours for his return to the airport at the end of his trip. He will present coupon #2 to the Hyatt Regency Hotel in exchange for his hotel accommodations.

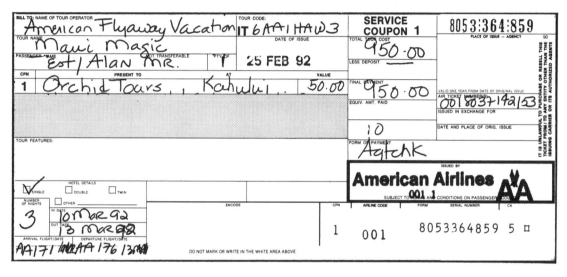

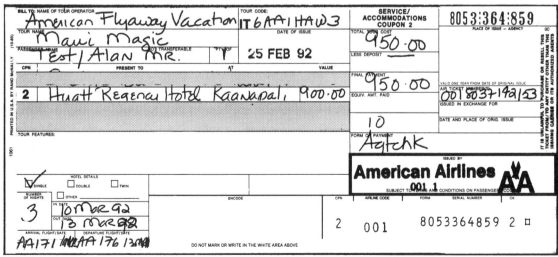

Prepaid Ticket Advice (PTA)

A PTA is an authorization that allows the issuance of an airline ticket at a point other than the point of payment. It is most often used when someone in one city wants to pay for the airline ticket of someone in another city and there is no time for the travel agent to issue and send the actual ticket.

In this example, The Big Corporation in New York called the travel agent on February 25 to book Mr. Test on a flight departing from Boston on February 26. After the agent made the booking and issued the PTA, she transmitted the booking details, including the PTA number, to the airline. The airline was then able to issue the actual airline ticket to Mr. Test at the airport.

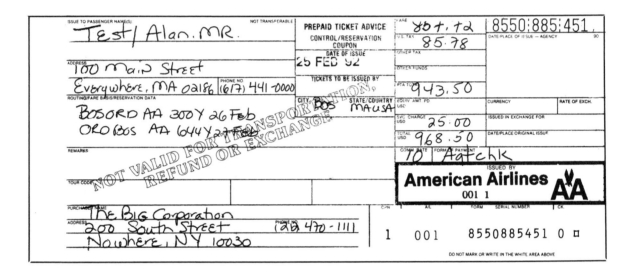

Summary

Financial management is important to the long-term stability of a company. Two basic financial statements — the balance sheet and the income statement — can be used to interpret the financial position of an agency at a given point in time. The income statement deals with fixed, variable, and semi-variable expenses. The balance sheet considers assets, liabilities, and equity.

Agencies need cash to continue to be successful. Sources of agency income usually include commission, service charges, overrides, and bonuses. Such payment options as customer credit cards and personal checks ensure timely client payments.

Once payment has been secured, agencies submit reports to area banks using agency checks. At this point, security issues concerning negotiable documents are extremely important.

Chapter Wrap-up

DISCUSSION TOPICS

Credit Cards

M.C. Visa, one of your VIP commercial clients, has arrived at your travel agency to pick up the tickets for his upcoming trip to Italy. He has decided to charge the balance of the ticket on his personal Diners Club Card. When you phone to get a routine authorization for the payment, the Diners Club representative tells you to seize and destroy his charge card. What do you do? How will any action that you take affect your relationship with your commercial account, as well as with the preferred client?

Negotiable Documents

One afternoon during lunch time, Mr. and Mrs. Lightfingers arrive at your agency needing information about flights to Las Vegas. During the sale, Mrs. L. becomes ill and asks to use the rest room. Since you are alone in the office you point her in the direction of the facility and continue to make recommendations to Mr. L. about the trip. A few moments later, Mrs. L. returns and informs you that she feels so indisposed that they must leave immediately. Mr. L. assures you that he will return to complete the reservation later. At closing, when the manager tabulates the ticket stock used for the day, she notices that ten tickets are missing. You have been asked if you remember any unusual clients or circumstances. What should you do? How do you try to recover this loss? Who is responsible for the stolen items?

Cash Flow

As the manager of a small, busy agency, you discover that money is sometimes missing from petty cash; first in small amounts, then in larger amounts. Since each of the five agents is responsible for collecting deposits and final payments for their own clients, each has access to the cash box. Consequently, all are under suspicion. The culprit is finally caught when it is discovered that several deposits were never sent to tour operators and no copies of receipts were recorded. The accused agent claims that he will sue for slander because nothing can be proven. What is your course of action? Can you recover the money? How will you change your office procedures to avoid this type of situation in the future?

Travel Industry Careers

Part Four

Career Development

Chapter 16

CHAPTER OBJECTIVES

After completing this chapter, the reader should be able to

- Identify types of resumes
- List four main parts of any resume
- Create a useful cover letter
- Explain the importance of follow-up
- Discuss three prospective job search sources
- Choose three personal and two business references
- Develop five questions to ask during an interview

VOCABULARY

After completing this chapter, the reader should be able to define

- Application form
- Benefits
- Career path
- Follow-up
- Information interview
- Interview
- Leads
- References
- Resume
- Screening
- Support services
- Training

Introduction

Ask most prospective employees why they want to enter the travel industry and they will answer that they enjoy working with people and want to travel. Although both of these involve necessary skills, many other abilities are more important to the individual who wants to secure and maintain a successful career in travel.

Career Planning

Success and career happiness depend upon careful planning and conscious development as you acquire new skills through training and experience. Invariably it is necessary to master basic entry-level skills before moving on to more advanced positions. One of the attractions of a career in travel is that it gives you the opportunity not merely to study but to grow by experiencing and sampling an incredible array of cultures, foods, crafts, and products as you travel around the world.

The travel industry is one of the largest employers worldwide. It includes food service, lodging, transportation, support services, as well as tour operators and travel agencies. In such a diverse market it should be relatively easy for anyone to find a job, but this is not always so. Anyone who has ever tried to secure a position in this expanding industry will verify that it is not simple, particularly for someone without experience. This does not mean that jobs are non-existent or unattainable, but simply that the industry is becoming more sophisticated and selective in choosing its representatives.

Components of the Job Search

Successful applicants need not only a combination of knowledge, experience, eagerness, and tenacity, but also a well-designed strategy for attaining their goals. Some components of this strategy include oral and written communication skills plus intangibles such as networking expertise, the ability to track down leads, and knowing how to dress for success.

Time is an important consideration when beginning the job search. Experts recommend that you begin your search three to six months in advance. Nine months to a year is an appropriate time interval for graduating seniors. During this time you can develop a plan of action. Select your strategy based upon personal style, opportunities available, and the amount of time you are willing to invest.

Where to Find a Job
- Employment agencies
- Newspaper ads and trade publications
- Friends in the industry — network
- Industry representatives
- Travel-industry trade shows
- College placement services
- Telemarketing
- Temporary part-time positions
- Direct mailings
- Cold calls

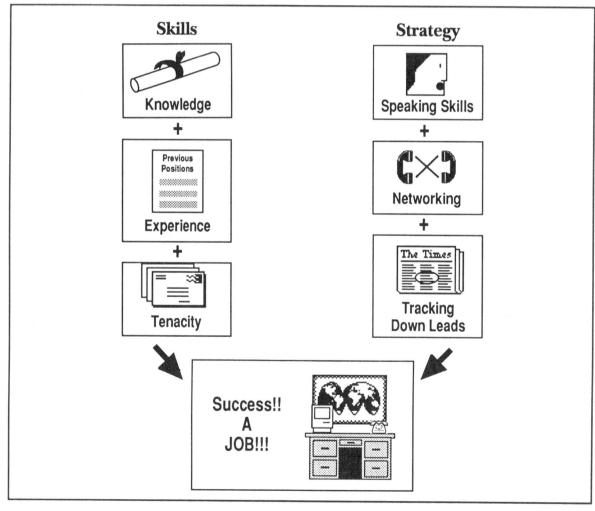

Effective writing is easy for some individuals and difficult for others. Practice helps. By following some simple rules, nearly anyone can successfully use writing to attain desired positions. Key to any written communication are consistency, conciseness, and clarity.

Intangible Skills

Getting a job requires much more than speaking and writing skills. It cannot be assured by obtaining a degree. It depends on many additional intangible elements such as networking, self-analysis, and perseverance.

Before beginning a job search, set individual goals based on careful self-evaluation. Analyze the skills that are necessary for a job in the area of travel and tourism. Also consider what important skills you may be lacking. This will help establish priorities and focus on the right career path.

Next, analyze what areas of growth exist in the job market. Consult trade journals, local experts, personnel agencies, school counselors, and other sources that help in evaluating the present position and future advancement of the industry.

Network with friends and relatives who are in travel or who know someone in the industry. Talk to various travel representatives and enlist their aid in finding out about jobs that may not be advertised. Knowing someone on the inside can help a great deal in obtaining your first position.

Don't be discouraged if it takes longer than expected to receive an offer. Finding a job in any industry is difficult and requires time and patience. It is better to wait for something interesting than settle for a totally unsuitable position. Perseverance and preparation can go a long way in uncovering opportunities that others might miss.

The Resume

An important written tool is the resume. If written correctly, this personal data sheet can open many doors. Its purpose is to introduce applicants to prospective employers through a summary of experience and qualifications. A resume should create an accurate and comprehensive impression of an individual's skills and background at a glance.

Travel careers are professional business posi-

tions. They demand resumes that are professional in both tone and layout. They should be grammatically correct, have no typing or spelling errors, and should be typed on heavy white or light-colored bond paper and sent in a matching envelope.

Although there are many styles of resumes, most contain the same basic information:

- A heading
- An objective
- An education summary
- Work experience
- Other relevant information
- References

The heading normally includes an applicant's name (in capital letters), address, and telephone number. It is always placed at the top of the paper and may be centered or placed to the far left or far right. A resume makes a statement about the individual sending it, so it must be easy to read and attractive to the eye.

A career objective should be clear-cut. An employer should not have to guess what position the applicant is seeking. The objective should not be so narrow that it will exclude future advancement, or so generic that an employer will offer anything. With word processing, a resume can include an objective tailored to any position.

The education section can either appear at the beginning or end of a resume depending upon its focus and should include all degrees beginning with the most recent. Each institution and its address should be included along with any major study concentrations and the degree earned. If the grade point average is high, it should also be included. List all course work in progress as well as field studies and internships.

Two common formats for the work experience section are the chronological format and the functional format. The chronological format lists each position held, the employer's name and address, major responsibilities, and the accomplishments of each job with the most recent position first. A functional format is usually written by people with a long work history of similar job experiences, many short-term jobs, or with periods of unemployment. It lists work by skills rather than by company although it still contains the same information. In either case, this section of the resume can become very lengthy. The entire resume should not exceed one page. Two are acceptable if the experience and education are relevant.

Other relevant information can include any honors or awards received, any professional associations, community involvement or volunteer experience, or any special skills that relate to the field. Employers look for well-balanced employees who demonstrate attractive qualities through personal activities and interests. It is not necessary to include personal information such as date of birth, marital status, political party, religion, or race. However, if this information might help prospects for a particular position, it should be included.

Usually a simple line stating that references are available is sufficient to end the resume. It is not essential to list them by name. Rather, it is more acceptable to forward a list of references, their addresses, and telephone numbers when requested. It is important that the individuals chosen as references can accurately assess skills and abilities. Employers, teachers, other travel personnel, and personal references make excellent choices. Caution — references should affirm their willingness in advance to speak on the applicant's behalf.

The Cover Letter

The cover letter is a letter of introduction that accompanies a resume and is designed to obtain an interview or an application form. It should be typed on paper that matches the resume and the envelope. Because this letter usually gives the first impression to a prospective employer, it should be businesslike and professional.

Most cover letters are included in responses to blind ads such as those in newspapers or trade journals or if the desired position is in another area of the state or country. Any cover letter should indicate that a resume is enclosed and note the specific job being sought, the skills the applicant has that meet the needs of this position, and a request for a personal interview, phone conversation, or application form.

It is preferable to address the letter to a specific individual using a correct title. It is vitally important to use correct spelling, punctuation, grammar, and sentence structure. The letter should be arranged in logical order and include a heading and introductory address, a salutation, the body of the letter, a closing, and signature. The letter design should be inviting and easy to read.

General Guidelines for Resumes

■ Stress accomplishments and results — illustrate goal orientation.

■ Use short paragraphs and phrases with widely spaced margins.

■ Have other people proofread the final copy.

■ Avoid gimmicks such as unusually colored paper, fancy lettering, and so on.

■ Avoid making exaggerated claims — let accomplishments speak for themselves.

■ Avoid jargon and slang.

■ Avoid unnecessary information.

■ Organize and highlight information — don't make the employer dig for facts.

■ If there is a change of address, be sure to send a forwarding address or update.

■ Don't use abbreviations.

■ Don't be repetitious with details.

■ Design the resume for easy scanning by using underlines, capitals, bold print, or bullets.

■ Center and balance the resume using plenty of white space.

Jane Doe

100 Main Street
Anywhere, MA 12345
617 555-3486

Objective:

To obtain a sales position with a supplier to the retail travel industry

Experience Summary:

- Extensive experience in the retail travel industry
- Experience selling leisure, corporate, affinity, and group travel
- Consistent record of top sales performance

Relative Experience:

4/85 to Present   ABC Travel, Maintown, MA

Cruise Department Manager

10/87 to Present
- Responsible for managing sales, marketing, and training operations for the Cruise Department
- Established the department and supervised the growth of ABC Travel's largest profit producer
- Negotiated with preferred suppliers for overrides to ensure profitability
- Established training seminars and incentive programs for the department sales staff
- Developed and executed aggressive marketing seminars, mailings, and advertising strategies

Director, Group and Incentive Travel

6/87 to 10/87
- Responsible for identifying and closing the sales of group travel
- Built marketing programs to attract groups
- Developed unique group travel events for ABC Travel's current and future customers
- Organized incentive programs for corporate accounts

Assistant Manager

5/86 to 6/87   Responsible for daily operations, including sales and personnel management

Travel Consultant

4/85 to 5/86   Responsible for selling corporate and leisure travel

***XYZ Tours*, Pawtucket, RI**

2/84 to 3/85   Travel Consultant Trainee — Responsible for sales of leisure travel

Education:

Travel Education Center
Boston, MA — 1986

Boston College
Boston, MA
B.A., French and Economics — 1984

References:

Available on request

John Smith

5 Elm Street
Anywhere, MA 06789
(617) 555-2425

Education

Providence College, Providence, RI
B.S. Business Administration, May 1986
Major: Business Management

Travel Industry Experience

1/88 to present   DEF International, Boston, MA
Client Services Representative

Primary Responsibility
- Provide assistance to a client base of approximately 1,000 travel agencies utilizing DEF International products and services, and act as their key contact.

Other Responsibilities
- Manage the operational administration of programs from point of application through enrollment to delivery.
- Act as liaison providing client information to all operational departments, and process client requests, changes, inquiries, and cancellations.
- Maintain current files on each client. Responsible for account status.
- Actively represent company at trade shows, generating sales leads and client contact.
- Represent company at all service training seminars, and conduct tours of operational facilities.

Administrative Assistant, Marketing
6/86 to 1/88
- Organized and managed service training seminars, coordinated client hotel reservations, organized seminar materials, attended seminars.
- Supervised part-time assistant.
- Managed mailings for all departments.
- Managed distribution of marketing materials.
- Organized in-house news source.
- Contributed articles to company newsletter.
- Employee Activity Planning Board Representative.

Other Experience

Kenneth Associates, Inc., Hartford, CT
Administrative Assistant, Summer 1985

References

Furnished upon request.

General Guidelines for Cover Letters

- Limit cover letters to less than one page in length.
- Be specific — list the exact position being sought.
- Sell yourself — illustrate how specific skills and experience meet the demands of the position.
- Be aggressive but polite — request a personal meeting or follow-up call for an appointment.
- Be creative and professional.
- Note the date available to begin work and a willingness to relocate if this is a job requirement.
- Use the active — not passive — voice.

Most employees are chosen based on the initial impression they create first with their written correspondence and then with their oral presentation during an interview. Therefore, preparation for face-to-face meetings is especially vital during a job search.

Other Written Documents

Prospective applicants often want information about specific companies or positions, but not an actual employment interview. An information request letter is similar to a cover letter in that it is addressed to a specific individual and contains facts about the applicant's skills and experience. It may be used to obtain written data about the company or to obtain an information interview. It should follow the suggested guidelines for cover letters.

Wings Travel

Name

Address

City   State

Phone

Current Position

Title

Many companies require applicants to complete an application form prior to employment. These forms usually request the same type of information provided by a resume, except in more detail. For example, on a resume the line "References Furnished on Request" is quite acceptable, whereas an application form will require the names, addresses, and telephone numbers of specific references.

Application forms provide other information. They illustrate neatness, thoroughness, the ability to follow directions, and knowledge of the law. Application forms may request more personal information than would be provided on a resume. Some questions, however, may be discriminatory.

What employers look for on an application or resume

- Gaps in employment
- Salary consistency
- Number of jobs and length of stay
- Questions that are left blank
- Incorrect spelling
- Reasons for leaving a job

Illegal pre-employment questions

(This information is not required unless the employer can demonstrate that the data is necessary for business.)

- Sex
- Age
- Race
- Religion
- Marital status
- Criminal record
- Number of children
- Height/weight
- Military service
- Friends or relatives in the company
- Citizenship
- English language skill
- Current economic status

Interviews

For most positions, a series of interviews is necessary before a decision is made. The preliminary interview is usually a screening device to eliminate applicants who are obviously unsuited for the position. Subsequent interviews obtain a deeper understanding of the applicant and fit to the job. In each situation applicants have approximately twenty to thirty minutes to convince the interviewer that they should be hired.

No matter what position the interview is for, certain preparations are expected. No employer wants to wait for an applicant, so it is important to arrive early, even if it means a wait. If unsure of directions, candidates should try a test run before the interview to acquaint themselves with the area and to time the ride. If the appointment requires flying or long-distance travel, arrangements should be made in advance, allowing ample transfer time to the interview site. If the long-distance interview is scheduled during a holiday period or during a time of unpredictable weather, it is wise to arrive a day early.

It is also important to research the company and interviewer, if possible, before the interview. This can be accomplished by studying trade journals, brochures, or stock and annual reports that are available to the general public. These publications provide background information on the philosophy of the company, its officers, its products, and its place in the market. Conducting such research shows an eagerness to learn more about the potential employer and inspires confidence during the interview.

Appearance is also important, particularly because many travel positions require personal contact. Clothing should be neat, clean, professional, and appropriate to the weather. Shoes should be polished, hair should be neat, and nails should be clean. Try to project a conservative but stylish image. Interviewers are trained to look for small inconsistencies that might affect their hiring choice.

At the interview site be courteous and polite to any staff members. Often a secretary or receptionist will be asked about candidates' actions in an outer office prior to the interview — were they visibly nervous? rude? impatient? Always strive to project self-confidence and assurance. On leaving the interview be equally friendly and polite.

The actual interview usually has three parts — introduction, questioning, and conclusion. During the first stage the interviewer will break the ice and provide basic information about the company and the specific position. It is important to listen during this period to be able to ask intelligent questions during stage two. In the questioning stage, the interviewer will try to obtain more information about the candidate's background, qualifications, and personality. At the end of this stage the applicant will be expected to ask intelligent questions about the company and the position. Finally, when both parties have finished their questions, the interviewer will indicate that the interview is over by making a closing statement.

The interviewer is concerned with what the candidate has to offer the company. The single biggest mistake made by job candidates is underestimating the competition. The more effective the applicant's communication skills are, the better prepared he or she will appear. Each interview can be a rewarding rather than an intimidating experience.

General Guidelines for Interviews

■ Relax but remain alert and interested — read a magazine or book while waiting, but don't bring company with you.

■ Be confident — offer a firm handshake, maintain eye contact, use a clear steady voice, don't slouch or fidget.

■ Listen carefully and ask appropriate questions.

■ Do not smoke or chew gum or candy.

■ Do not criticize former employers.

■ Respond with more than a yes or no answer.

■ Be sincere.

■ Use the interviewer's name during the interview.

■ Ask when the position will be filled.

■ Don't ask questions only about benefits.

■ Speak correctly — don't use slang or inappropriate expressions.

Questions candidates might ask in an interview — *if not already discussed*

- What are the daily responsibilities of the job?
- What is the most important responsibility? What is the least?
- Is training provided?
- To whom would I be reporting?
- Who are the other people I would be working with?
- Are there advancement opportunities?
- What other skills are required?
- Where do you see the company five years from now?
- When can I expect to hear from you regarding the position?
- Why have you gone outside the company to fill this position?

Any questions regarding salary, benefits, and so on, should wait until the second interview or at the time of the job offer.

Thank-You Notes

It is common courtesy after an interview to follow up by sending a thank-you note to each interviewer. This reminds interviewers of continued interest and brings the applicant's name back to their attention. Depending on the organization, the notes may be either formal — typed on a word processor and signed — or informal — handwritten on appropriate stationery. These brief notes should thank the individuals for their time and information and stress either the applicant's continued interest or lack of interest in the position. In either case, thank-you notes should be mailed no later than one week after the original interview. If multiple interviews are necessary, thank-you notes should be written after each one. Even if no offer is made, thank-you notes should still be written in case the job opens up later or another opening becomes available.

General Guidelines for Thank-You Notes

- Keep them short and personal — refer to a specific incident during the interview.
- Address them correctly to each interviewer.
- Make sure they are timely — don't wait two or three months to mail them even if there is no interest in the position.

Nine to Five

Long-term career success depends upon how well you do in the real world once you have landed a position. Many people find good jobs and begin work with high expectations, energy, and enthusiasm, only to be disappointed with the end results. New hires often prepare zealously for interviews but don't understand what it takes to successfully enter a new organization and stay there.

The first year of employment is critical to a career. It is a transition stage between student status and professionalism. The key to its success is having appropriate expectations and attitudes so you can learn how to establish yourself and earn credibility and respect.

No one enjoys the uncomfortable feeling of being new. However, the more you know about this role, the easier the adjustment will be. Recognize how much you don't know. Managers realize that schools and colleges only provide you with part of what you need to be successful. To make intelligent suggestions you must understand the nuances of the corporation.

Every company has its own unique culture and personality. Many of its rules and norms concerning behavior are unspoken and informal. Organizations expect successful employees to accept and emulate these behaviors.

Making a good impression is important as you begin to progress through your career. You can establish a proven track record by building good relationships with colleagues, exercising sound judgment, demonstrating respect for experience, keeping a positive mental attitude, and being realistic about your role and contributions.

It is your responsibility to make this transition a success. Once you accept the uniqueness of this period, you're on your way to a successful and rewarding career.

Tips for Securing and Beginning New Jobs

■ Look for a role model or mentor, someone who can give you advice and help you adapt.

■ Don't pretend to know something when you don't. Know what you don't know, then learn it.

■ Admit mistakes. Make the right ones — not those that come from immaturity or impatience.

■ Demonstrate initiative. Go the extra mile, no matter how trivial it may seem.

■ Be a team player.

■ Don't try to change things overnight. Avoid making a big splash before understanding the corporate culture.

■ Invest in your own career. Build a track record by finding opportunities to excel.

Building a Career

Many sectors of the travel industry face slow growth. Yet the Bureau of Labor Statistics projects a 46 percent increase in travel agency positions by the year 2000. In order to remain competitive, management will need to develop more fully service quality and the continued efficiency of automation. Agents will need to work harder to maintain profits. It will also become increasingly important to attract, select, and retain valued employees.

Job security and paychecks no longer guarantee peak performance. Incentives help motivate employees to perform better and thus increase profits. When properly structured, incentives can com-

municate management philosophy and convert fixed operating costs to variable costs. Common incentives in the travel industry include fam trips, cash bonuses, free or reduced-fare travel, health and life insurance.

Many agents love their jobs, are content with their pay, but are concerned about their overall career path. Lateral changes can often provide new experiences and challenges. One way to change direction laterally is to specialize. Choosing an existing niche, such as cruises or upscale clients, can offer an expansion of career options. Another way is to shift to nontraditional compensation, such as commission only or incentive pay. Developing a special skill — for example, computer expertise or meeting planning — can also provide a change of pace.

A final way to expand your horizons is by continually polishing your professionalism and expertise. Education doesn't end once you obtain a job in the travel and tourism field. Industry professionals recognize the need to update and refine skills. Currently, more than 1,100 schools in the United States offer degree programs in travel and tourism. Several hundred are proprietary schools, but many junior colleges and universities offer comprehensive curricula for majors in tourism.

Experiential learning through work-education programs provides new opportunities during undergraduate education. Some programs include work-study, internships, externships, cooperative education, or volunteerism. All of these build in real-world work experience in an area of career interest.

After completing undergraduate work, some individuals consider graduate school as an option. The most common advanced degree in the travel industry is an M.B.A. Such a degree can give a person the tools that will lead to effective management. It will also give broad exposure to business and its job functions, problem solving, and administration fundamentals.

Many professional organizations offer training sessions for industry representatives. For more than twenty-five years, the national nonprofit Institute of Certified Travel Agents (ICTA) has been recognized as the educational resource for travel industry members at all career stages. The Institute strives to offer education that suppliers and agents can continually apply to work situations.

ICTA is constantly developing new programs to help its members perform effectively during this time of vast technological changes and increasing consumer demands.

The CTC Travel Management Program

This program offers two tracks of study — sales skills and management skills — both of which lead to the prestigious Certified Travel Counselor (CTC) designation. The CTC designation has become the hallmark of the true travel professional, respected by travel executives and clients alike. The program helps front-line salespeople counsel clients more effectively and managers lead their companies more profitably. Both tracks provide agents with the necessary tools to cope with constant industry change, serve customers well, and turn new travel trends into opportunities to redirect or expand their businesses.

The Destination Specialist Program

The Destination Specialist program is designed to equip front-line salespeople with in-depth destination knowledge so they can counsel travelers expertly and professionally. The program is divided into courses focusing on different areas of the world: the South Pacific, the Caribbean, Western Europe, and the United States and Canada.

Summary

A career in travel offers many exciting employment opportunities. However, landing that first job requires a well-designed strategy that includes knowing where to track down leads, using effective writing and speaking skills, and persevering.

The most important written tool is the resume. It introduces applicants to prospective employers and should create a good impression of an individual's skills at a glance. An accompanying cover letter should also be businesslike and professional.

Because most employees are selected during the interview process, preparation is vital. Qualities that should be displayed during the interview include confidence and intelligent questioning. You need to convince the interviewer that you are the best person to fill the position.

After you are hired it is important to have a good work ethic and try to find opportunities to excel and advance. Many opportunities for continuing education are provided by the Institute of Certified Travel Agents.

Chapter Wrap-up

REVIEW QUESTIONS

1. Why are good writing and speaking skills so important in the job search?

2. How does information on a resume differ from that on an application form?

3. Under what circumstances would you feel comfortable using a formal thank-you note? An informal note?

4. Whom would you choose as personal references? Professional references? Would they differ depending on the job being sought? Why or why not?

5. Where might you consider going for an information interview? What criteria did you use for choosing this company?

DISCUSSION TOPICS

Scene #1 — *A travel agency*

Characters:

The agency manager and a potential employee.

Subject:

Job interview.

Question:

Why do you want to become a travel agent?

Answer:

I like helping people.

Question:

Do you have any experience?

Answer:

No, but I have traveled a lot.

Scene #2 — *A party*

Characters:

A travel agent and a restaurant owner.

Subject:

A typical conversation.

Restaurant owner:

Oh, let's talk about your job. It must be great to do all that traveling.

Travel agent:

How about your job? It must be great to do all that eating!

Discuss the implications of these two scenes. Do you think they dramatize myth or reality? How would you better answer the question from the potential employer in scene #1? Do you think scene #2 represents the view most people have of the travel industry?

Interview

You have a preliminary interview scheduled with ABC Travel for a week from Monday. Compile a list of tasks relating to this interview that you must complete before next Monday.

Self-Appraisal

One of the most important aspects of a job search is an honest self-appraisal. First, compose a list of relevant skills for the travel industry. Then, with the help of a colleague, prepare a list of your own skills and accomplishments. How closely do they match? What particular area of the industry are you most suited for? Least?

Ticketing Appendix

Introduction

Computer reservations systems (CRS) are used by a majority of travel agencies in the United States today. Current systems are so reliable that a system user can depend on the computer's functioning practically 24 hours a day, 365 days a year. However, systems sometimes malfunction, and CRS users must plan for certain "down-time" to load new fares and to update functions. In addition, telecommunications can occasionally cease in the middle of a transaction. Computers and machines (especially printers) have a tendency to break down at the worst possible moment. It is at these times that the manual ticket becomes essential to a travel professional.

Manual ticketing allows the agent the flexibility of immediately accommodating the client or passenger without depending solely on automation. In a worst-case scenario, customers could still obtain their ticket from an office or ticket counter even if there was an electrical blackout. At other times, agents may not be able to produce a computerized ticket due to system limitations or their own lack of understanding of a particular format. Finally, by understanding the components of the manual ticket, an agent will better understand the areas of information included in the automated version.

Manual and Automated Ticket Stock

The differences between automated and manual ticket stock are striking. Most easily identifiable is the difference in the packaging of the tickets. Automated stock arrives in larger quantities due to the way the forms are printed. A typical box of automated ticket stock contains 1,000 tickets. Each ticket is attached to the others, separated only by perforations in the paper. Manual ticket stock normally arrives in smaller amounts, with tickets being composed of independent booklets of coupons for customer use. The manual ticket has ticket numbers issued for each ticket, with the ticket number printed on each coupon. An automated ticket has a stock control number that is entered into the computer prior to the loading of the ticket stock. When the ticket is issued, the computer prints the ticket number on each of the coupons.

Tickets are generally divided into three types: Automated Ticket/Boarding Pass (ATB), Transi-

tional Automated, and manual tickets. Each ticket, whether manual or automated, may look different but contains the same information. The ticket must include the passenger's name and other passenger data, date of issuance, payment information, itinerary information, and a calculation area used to show the cost of each segment and surcharge.

Automated Ticket/Boarding Pass

The Automated Ticket/Boarding Pass ticket (Figure 1) is simply that - a ticket and a boarding pass all in one. This form is easily distinguished not only because of the boarding pass printed on the ticket itself, but also because of the type of paper it is printed on. The paper is a very stiff, almost cardboard type of stock. This form is useful because it allows passengers to have their entire itinerary ticketed and the boarding pass issued on one document.

Four Flight Transitional Automated Ticket

The Four Flight Transitional Automated ticket (Figure 2) is more colorful than the ATB stock. Traditional ticket paper is used for printing, making this type of ticket easy to distinguish from the ATB. Also, the Four Flight Transitional Automated ticket does not print a boarding pass with the

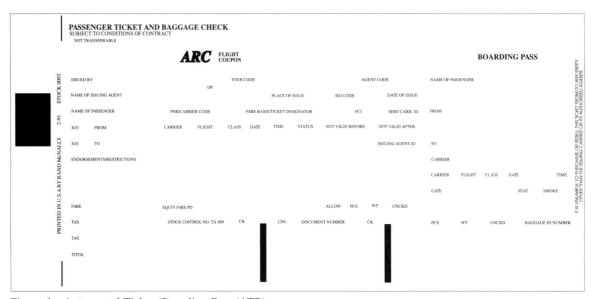

Figure 1 – Automated Ticket/Boarding Pass (ATB)

ticket, so the airline or agency must staple the boarding pass form to the ticket itself.

Manual Ticket

The rest of this section is devoted to manual ticketing. Each part of the ticket (Figure 3) will be described in detail.

Parts of a Manual Ticket

An airline ticket is a booklet that contains pages

caled coupons. Each coupon serves a purpose and is carbonized so that the information held on the front coupon is copied to subsequent coupons.

The Ticket Cover

The cover of the ticket booklet (Figure 4) identifies the type of ticket and serves as the "conditions of contract" between the airline and the passenger. In previous chapters you read briefly about the

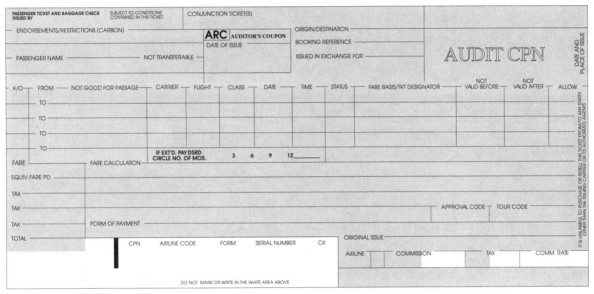

Figure 2 – Four Flight Transitional Automated Ticket

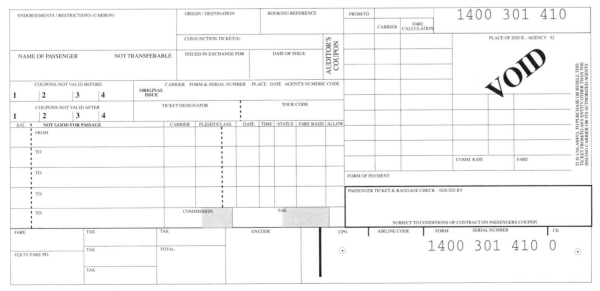

Figure 3 – Manual ticket

contract agreed upon between the airline and the passenger. By purchasing the ticket, in essence, the passenger has agreed to the conditions of carriage posted on the first two pages of the ticket. The front cover must be attached to the ticket to allow the passenger to travel.

The Auditor's Coupon and the Agent's Coupon

The Auditor's Coupon (Figure 5) is a green-colored coupon and is the first coupon in the booklet. The agent will write on this coupon. It is essential to press firmly when completing the ticket

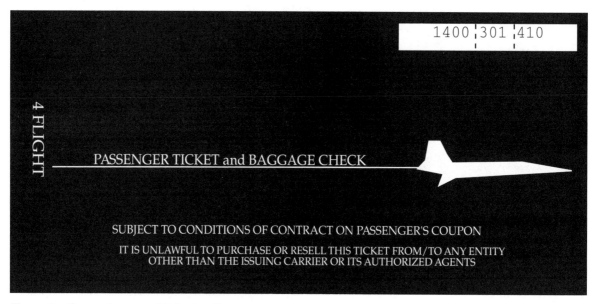

Figure 4 – Cover of a manual ticket booklet

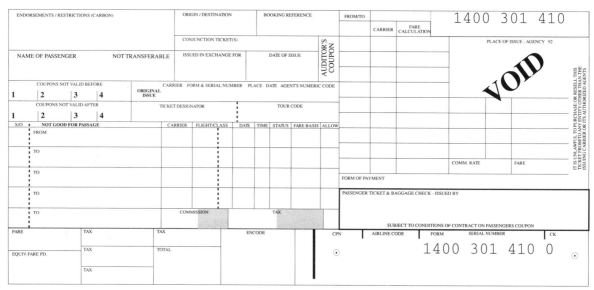

Figure 5 – The Auditor's Coupon

since there are six coupons behind the Auditor's Coupon. The Auditor's Coupon will be included in the weekly sales reported to the ARC, so it is also important to print very legibly.

The second coupon of the ticket booklet is the pink-colored Agent's Coupon. It is identical to the Auditor's Coupon except for the color and the words "Agent's Coupon." It is kept by the agency for record keeping.

The Flight Coupons

The Flight Coupons are the multicolored coupons used by the passenger for boarding authority. Without these coupons, the passenger cannot get on a flight. Each coupon is shaded to indicate which portion of the ticket is being used.

The first coupon (Figure 6) is shaded to show that the first segment of the itinerary is being flown.

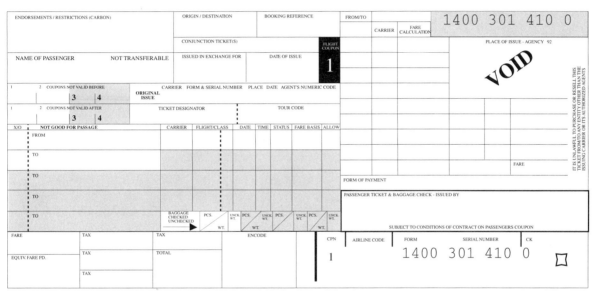

Figure 6 – A Flight Coupon for the first segment of an itinerary

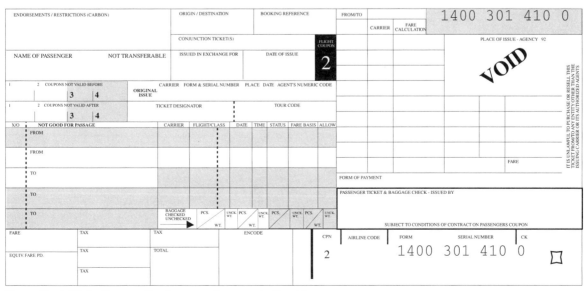

Figure 7 – A Flight Coupon for the second segment of an itinerary

When the ticket is filled out, the first flight will be the only section left unshaded. The shading shows the reader that the remainder of the ticket is not to be used at that time.

Compare the first coupon (Figure 6) with the second coupon (Figure 7) and notice the difference in shading. The second coupon has shading in all but the second and third lines of the flight information. If the passenger was using this ticket to fly from Milwaukee to Chicago to Miami, the second coupon would provide the information from Chicago to Miami. The remaining coupons continue in the same pattern of shading until the final coupon.

The Passenger's Coupon

The Passenger's Coupon (Figure 8) is a white coupon located in the back of the ticket booklet. This is the receipt that passengers may use for their own purposes. It is also required to be attached to the ticket booklet during travel.

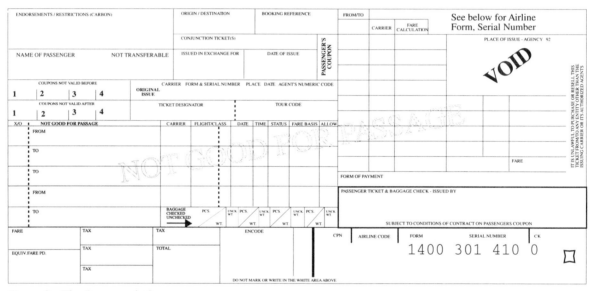

Figure 8 – The Passenger's Coupon

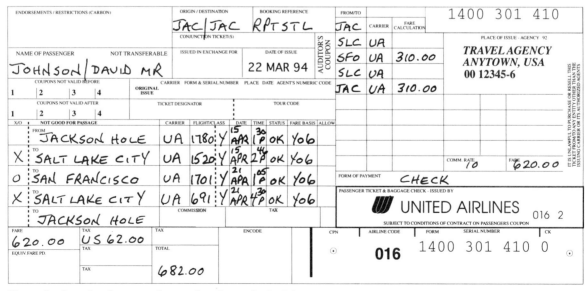

Figure 9 – Sample of a properly completed round-trip ticket

A Completed Round-Trip Ticket

Each area of the ticket should be filled out in a specific way (Figure 9). If an error is made on the ticket, it could prevent the passenger from completing the journey or could result in a debit memo for your office. If you make a mistake while filling out the ticket, void the entire ticket and start again. Complete each area of the ticket with uppercase (capital) letters. You must use a ballpoint pen with blue or black ink. One other important note to remember is that tickets must be used in numerical order. If the ticket stock is out of sequence, you invalidate the ticket by writing the word VOID across the first coupon (Auditor's Coupon) of the ticket. The agency should then file the Agent's Coupon in storage and destroy or store the remaining coupons, depending on the agency's policy. You may find it helpful to keep a personal record of the voided ticket numbers in case you need to reference the information in the future.

Sections of the Ticket

We will now describe the sections of the ticket (Figure 10) and how they should be filled out properly.

Name of Passenger ①

Write the passenger's last name first followed by a slash, first name (or initials), and appropriate title

(MR; MRS; MS; MISS; MSTR; PFC; COL; and so on). Our passenger's name is Mr. Fran Carlson, as shown in (Figure 11).

ENDORSEMENTS / RESTRICTIONS (CARBON)		ORIGIN / DESTINATION
		CONJUNCTION TICKET(S)
NAME OF PASSENGER NOT TRANSFERABLE		ISSUED IN EXCHANGE FOR
CARLSON/FRAN MR		

Figure 11 – Sample of a properly filled-in *Name of Passenger* Box

If an unaccompanied child is traveling, enter the letters UM and the child's age in brackets following the name. For example: JACKSON/STEVE MSTR (UM09).

If an infant travels for free without a seat assignment, the FAA requires that a record be kept of their travel. Mark the words PLUS INFANT or an abbreviation on the ticket of the accompanying adult. For example: LARSON/LINDA MRS PLUS INF.

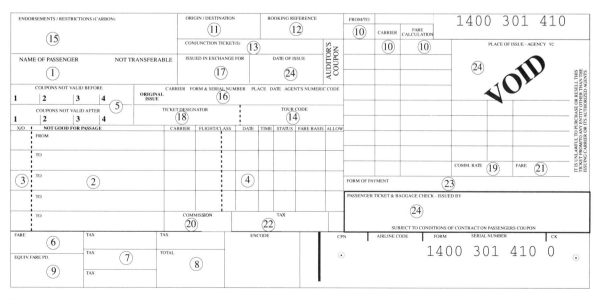

Figure 10 – Sections of the ticket that must be filled out by the agent

Before continuing, ensure that the passenger's name is correctly spelled and the appropriate title is used. After entering the passenger's name in the appropriate box, the next logical step is to complete the passenger's itinerary and flight information.

From and To ②

The *From and To* portion of the ticket indicates where the passenger is departing from and where they are going to. Enter the full name of the passenger's origin city in the *From* box. Print each stopover/connection or destination city in the boxes below the origin city box. Do not use city codes. In the event that the origin city has multiple airports (for example, Houston), you must indicate the airport name (Figure 12).

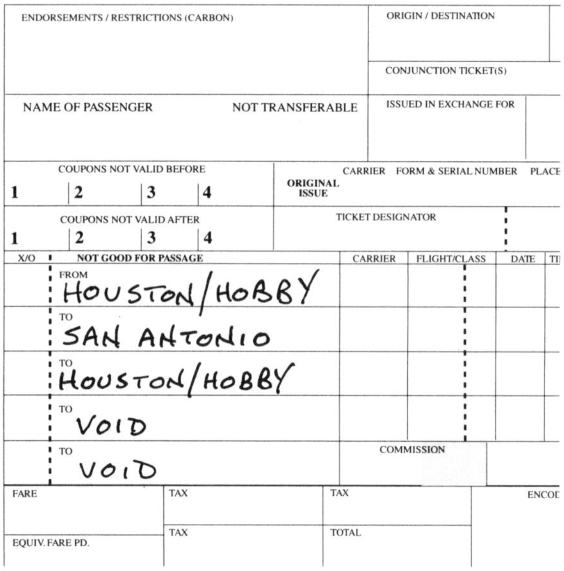

word VOID in any blank boxes and removing the coupons from the booklet. This makes the ticket easier to read and prevents any fraudulent use of blank coupons.

In the example (Figure 14) the passenger is only flying from San Jose, California, to Salt Lake City, Utah. The remaining *To and From* boxes are voided to prevent the use of blank coupons.

Stopover Indicator Box ③

If the fare that the passenger is using allows a stopover in an intermediate city (between the origin and ultimate destination), you print the letter O in the small column labeled X/O to the left of the stopover city. If the fare only allows a connection, you place the letter X in the indicated box.

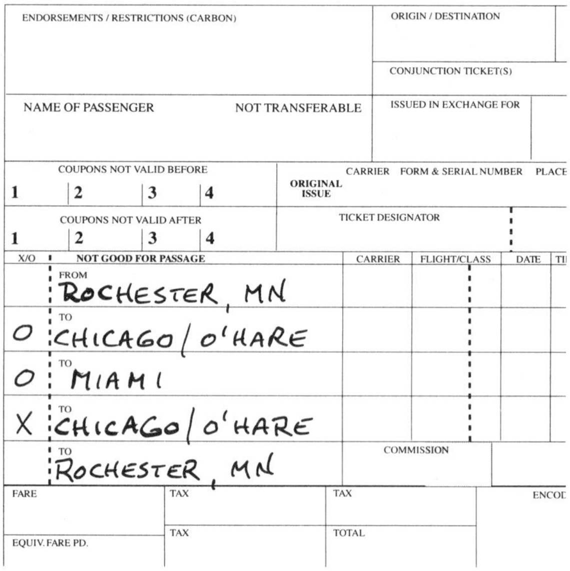

Figure 12 – Sample of properly filled-in *From and To* boxes

Figure 13 – Sample of a two-letter state code used to clarify a city's location

If one of the cities in the itinerary has an identical name to another city in a different state or country, you should enter the two-letter state code to clarify the selection. In the example (Figure 13), the two-letter code for Minnesota is used to differentiate Rochester, Minnesota, from Rochester, New York.

If the itinerary does not fill the boxes supplied after entering all the cities for the itinerary, you indicate the end of the itinerary by marking the

Example: Seattle - Dallas/Fort Worth (no stopover) - San Antonio - Dallas/Fort Worth (no stopover) - Seattle (Figure 15).

Example: Chicago O'Hare - Denver (connection) - Gunnison (destination) - Denver (stopover) - Chicago O'Hare (Figure 16).

Reservation Data ④

After entering the passenger information and listing an itinerary, the next step is to fill in complete

ENDORSEMENTS / RESTRICTIONS (CARBON) | ORIGIN / DESTINATION | CONJUNCTION TICKET(S)
NAME OF PASSENGER | NOT TRANSFERABLE | ISSUED IN EXCHANGE FOR
COUPONS NOT VALID BEFORE 1 2 3 4 | ORIGINAL ISSUE | CARRIER FORM & SERIAL NUMBER PLACE
COUPONS NOT VALID AFTER 1 2 3 4 | TICKET DESIGNATOR
X/O | NOT GOOD FOR PASSAGE | CARRIER | FLIGHT/CLASS | DATE | TI
FROM SAN JOSE, CA
TO SALT LAKE CITY
TO VOID
TO VOID
TO VOID | COMMISSION
FARE | TAX | TAX | ENCOD
EQUIV. FARE PD. | TAX | TOTAL

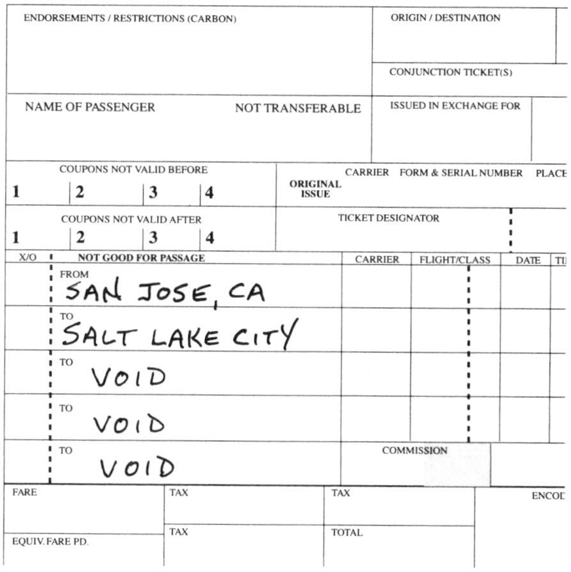

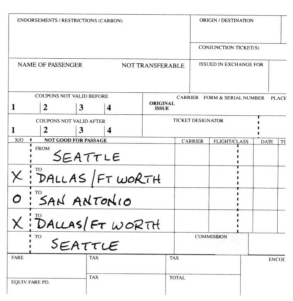

Figure 14 – Sample of voided *From and To* boxes

ENDORSEMENTS / RESTRICTIONS (CARBON) | ORIGIN / DESTINATION | CONJUNCTION TICKET(S)
NAME OF PASSENGER | NOT TRANSFERABLE | ISSUED IN EXCHANGE FOR
COUPONS NOT VALID BEFORE 1 2 3 4 | ORIGINAL ISSUE | CARRIER FORM & SERIAL NUMBER PLACE
COUPONS NOT VALID AFTER 1 2 3 4 | TICKET DESIGNATOR
X/O | NOT GOOD FOR PASSAGE | CARRIER | FLIGHT/CLASS | DATE | TI
FROM SEATTLE
X TO DALLAS/FT WORTH
O TO SAN ANTONIO
X TO DALLAS/FT WORTH
TO SEATTLE | COMMISSION
FARE | TAX | TAX | ENCOD
EQUIV. FARE PD. | TAX | TOTAL

Figure 15 – Sample of stopover indicators

information about the flights (Figure 17).

Carrier: Print the official two-letter code of the applicable carrier for the segment.

Flight/Class: Enter the flight number and the appropriate reservation booking code for the segment.

Date: Enter the two-digit number indicating the boarding date above the standard three- letter abbreviation for the month (JAN, FEB, MAR, APR, MAY, JUN, JUL, AUG, SEP, OCT, NOV, DEC).

Time: The scheduled departure time needs to be entered using standard clock hours. Use A for a.m., P for p.m., N for noon, and M for midnight. A 24-hour clock format can be used (for example, 1300 for 1:00 p.m.).

Status: The status of the reservation indicates whether the client is confirmed or waitlisted for a particular flight. You will normally use only two codes:

OK indicates that the passenger holds confirmed space.

RQ indicates that the reservation is requested, or waitlisted.

ENDORSEMENTS / RESTRICTIONS (CARBON) | ORIGIN / DESTINATION | CONJUNCTION TICKET(S)
NAME OF PASSENGER | NOT TRANSFERABLE | ISSUED IN EXCHANGE FOR
COUPONS NOT VALID BEFORE 1 2 3 4 | ORIGINAL ISSUE | CARRIER FORM & SERIAL NUMBER PLACE
COUPONS NOT VALID AFTER 1 2 3 4 | TICKET DESIGNATOR
X/O | NOT GOOD FOR PASSAGE | CARRIER | FLIGHT/CLASS | DATE | TI
FROM CHICAGO/O'HARE
X TO DENVER
O TO GUNNISON
O TO DENVER
TO SEATTLE | COMMISSION
FARE | TAX | TAX | ENCOD
EQUIV. FARE PD. | TAX | TOTAL

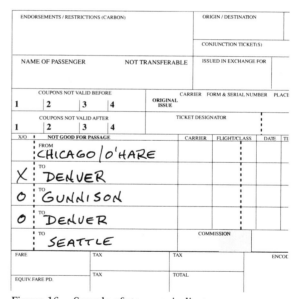

Figure 16 – Sample of stopover indicators

Fare Basis: The fare basis code is a combination of letters and numbers indicating the type of fare used. The fare basis code is obtained from the CRS in use, the appropriate tariff book, or directly from the airline.

Allow: When the free baggage allowance for the flight is anything other than a per piece allowance, you enter the appropriate allowance in the *Allow*

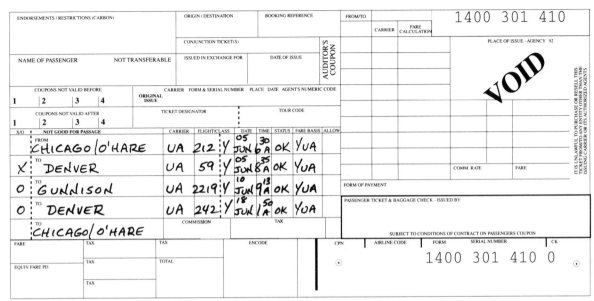

Figure 17 – Sample of properly filled-in flight reservation information

box. Generally, anything other than a per piece allowance is registered by weight. Indicate that in the box by using KG or K for kilograms or L or LB for pounds. If the fare used does not allow any baggage, enter NIL, NO, or XX. The *Allow* box is left blank on domestic U.S. tickets.

Not Valid Before/Not Valid After ⑤

Tariff rules may restrict the dates allowable for travel on some special fares. The *Not Valid Before* and *Not Valid After* boxes are used to indicate any special date restrictions applied to a special fare (Figure 18). You will note that each section has four blanks, one blank for each coupon. Date restrictions applied to the first coupon are entered in the space numbered 1, date restrictions applied to the second coupon are entered in blank 2, and so on.

Not Valid Before Boxes:

Tariff rules for a special fare may not permit return travel to begin before a particular date. If the passenger is traveling on a special fare that restricts return travel, you must fill out the *Not Valid Before* box of the ticket. You should enter the earliest return date using the same method used in entering the date in the itinerary portion of the ticket. When the tariff governing a fare does not

restrict travel, no entry is required.

Not Valid After Boxes:

If the tariff applied to a passenger's itinerary requires that a portion of travel involving a special fare or an expiring fare must be completed at a certain time, or within a certain number of days, you must enter the date by which travel must be completed across all of the applicable boxes. You

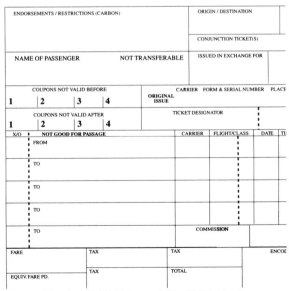

Figure 18 – *Not Valid Before* and *Not Valid After* boxes

296

enter the date in the same fashion that you do for the *Not Valid Before* boxes.

Fare ⑥

The *Fare* box is used to enter the applicable fare for the complete itinerary in the currency of the country of origin, excluding tax. If travel is outside the United States, the appropriate currency code (for example, FRF for the French Franc) should be entered within the box directly to the right or above the fare you printed.

Tax ⑦

The *Tax* box is used to enter the amount of taxes, fees, and charges, if any. If the tax, fee, or charge is for a country other than the one in which the ticket is issued, include the International Standards Organization (ISO) two-letter country code. Taxes for a single country can be combined into one amount.

Note: The following taxes and fees must be identified separately on a ticket:

CA	Canadian Tax
MX	Mexican Domestic Transportation Tax
US	U.S. 10% Domestic or $6.00 International Departure Tax
XA	Animal Plant Health Inspection Service Tax (APHIS) (U.S. charge)
XD	Mexican International Airport Departure Tax (Mexican charge)
XF	Passenger Facility Charges (PFC) (U.S. charge)
XG	Goods and Services Tax (Canadian)
XI	Insurance Surcharge (international)
XN	VAT Tax (Norwegian)
XO	Mexican International Transportation Tax
XS	VAT Tax (Swedish)
XT	Combined Taxes
XV	Mexican Domestic Airport Departure Tax
XY	Inspection Fee (U.S. fee)
YC	Customs Fee (U.S. fee)

If more than one tax, fee, or charge applies, show each amount in a separate tax box. For example, consider the Passenger Facility Charge (PFC). A PFC is a tax charged by the U.S. government to help offset the cost of airport maintenance and upkeep. The government allows an airport to charge a one, two, or three dollar fee to any passenger departing from the authorized airport. This charge is added to the ticket. When a PFC is collected, the airport code of the collecting airport and the dollar amount collected (enter 1 for USD 1.00, 2 for USD 2.00, or 3 for USD 3.00) are shown at the end of the *Fare Calculation* area to help distinguish what charges are being applied. No more than two PFCs are permitted on a one-way ticket, and no more than four on a round-trip ticket. An example of a PFC in the *Fare Calculation* area will be shown later in this section.

Total ⑧

The *Total* box contains the complete amount of payment required for the ticket. In this box you enter the sum of the fare and taxes, fees, and charges applicable to the entire itinerary. Below is an example of a simple domestic ticket with the *Fare, Tax,* and *Total* boxes filled in (Figure 19).

Figure 19 – Sample of properly filled-in *Fare, Tax,* and *Total* boxes

If an international ticket is issued in the United States and at least two types of taxes or fees are being collected for the same country, you combine them as a single amount. Be sure to use the appropriate ISO country code.

Below is an example of a multiple *Tax* column (Figure 20).

Figure 20 – Sample of a multiple *Tax* column

Equivalent Fare Paid (9)

The *Equivalent Fare Paid* box is used when payment for the ticket is made in a currency other than the one shown in the *Fare* box, or when payment is made in a currency other than the currency of the country of payment.

If the situation requires it and you need to complete this box, convert the fare value into the currency of payment. After it is converted, enter the amount, making sure that the appropriate currency code is entered (USD for U.S. Dollar, CAD for Canadian Dollar, etc.).

The Fare Calculation Ladder (10)

After completing the itinerary, flight information, and fare and tax portions of the ticket, you may need to complete the *Fare Calculation* area. This area is quite often referred to as the *Fare Calculation* ladder. It illustrates the methods used to calculate the fare of the ticket.

Calculating the Fare: Special Conditions

The *Fare Calculation* area of the ticket must be completed when any of the following special conditions occur:

- If tickets are issued in conjunction (two or more ticket booklets used because more than four flight coupons are needed for the itinerary)
- If a ticket is reissued in exchange for another ticket (reissue)
- If a surcharge, differential, or stopover charge is applicable
- If the fare is calculated by using mileage principles (international tickets)

If none of the conditions exist, you are not required to complete the *Fare Calculation* ladder of the ticket. When it is required, you must complete the three columns, making sure that you print three-letter city codes in sequence, beginning with the origin city and ending with the final destination city. You place the official two-letter carrier code opposite the segment to which it applies. In the last column, you enter the applicable fare information next to the segment to which it applies.

It is important to remember that the fare amounts shown in the *Fare Calculation* area are calculated without tax. The tax is added as a final result. In the example below (Figure 21) we are required to show the *Fare Calculation* area of the ticket because the itinerary requires two tickets to be issued in conjunction since six segments (six flight coupons) are required.

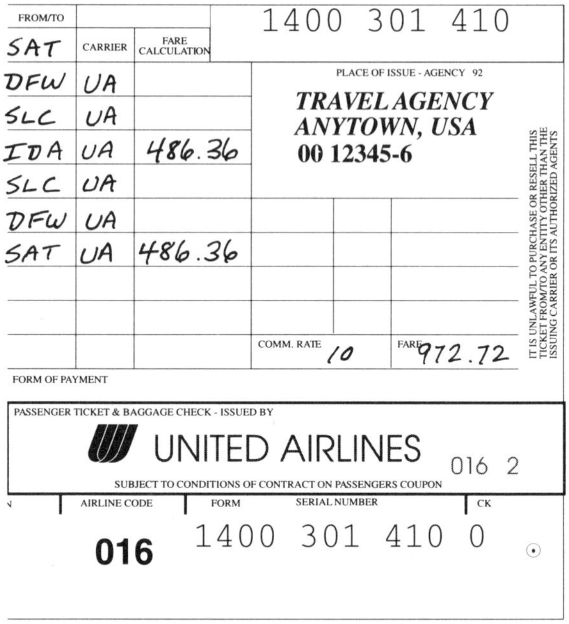

FROM/TO	CARRIER	FARE CALCULATION
SAT		
DFW	UA	
SLC	UA	
IDA	UA	486.36
SLC	UA	
DFW	UA	
SAT	UA	486.36

1400 301 410

PLACE OF ISSUE - AGENCY 92

TRAVEL AGENCY
ANYTOWN, USA
00 12345-6

COMM. RATE 10 FARE 972.72

FORM OF PAYMENT

IT IS UNLAWFUL TO PURCHASE OR RESELL THIS TICKET FROM/TO ANY ENTITY OTHER THAN THE ISSUING CARRIER OR ITS AUTHORIZED AGENTS

PASSENGER TICKET & BAGGAGE CHECK - ISSUED BY

UNITED AIRLINES 016 2

SUBJECT TO CONDITIONS OF CONTRACT ON PASSENGERS COUPON

AIRLINE CODE | FORM | SERIAL NUMBER | CK

016 1400 301 410 0

Figure 21 – Sample of a properly filled-in *Fare Calculation* ladder

When filling out the *Fare Calculation* ladder, you will be using many of the same principles that you used when completing the itinerary/reservation portion of the ticket. To signify a connection, instead of placing an X in the box, you leave the fare amount box blank. For instance, if a passenger is flying the following itinerary, the *Fare Calculation* ladder would like like that in (Figure 22).

MKE CHI RDU MYR
452.33 (AA local base fare)

MYR ATL
119.22 (DL local base fare)

ATL CHI MKE
392.22 (UA local base fare)

Other Forms of Transportation

When a passenger travels from one destination to another using various modes of transportation,

Figure 22 – Sample of a properly filled-in *Fare Calculation* ladder when there are connecting flights

Figure 23 – Sample of a ground segment indicated in the *Fare Calculation* ladder

you need to illustrate the entire journey on the ticket. For example, if a passenger flew from Miami to Orlando, then caught the Amtrak train to Washington, D.C., stayed in Washington, D.C. for a week, and flew back to Miami with a stop in Atlanta, Georgia, all of these segments must be indicated on the ticket. To illustrate a ground segment (also known as a surface segment or ARUNK segment, meaning ARrival UNKnown), you simply enter an X in the *From/To* column to indicate the transport from the city above to the city on the line below.

The following *Fare Calculation* ladder illustrates this idea (Figure 23):

Passenger Facility Charge

It was mentioned earlier that PFCs are shown in the *Fare Calculation* area of the ticket. When a Passenger Facility Charge is collected, the airport that is charging the PFC, and the amount charged, must be indicated at the end of the *Fare Calculation* area on the ticket. A heavy line is first drawn to separate the two areas. Write the XF in the *From/To* box. Place the amount charged for the Passenger Facility Charge in the *Fare Calculation* area (see Figure 23).

There is no need to include the carrier identification in the PFC indicator since the airport is surcharging the fee, not the airline. In some cir-

cumstances, a city will charge a surcharge other than a PFC (such as a fuel surcharge).

In the event that a passenger's itinerary travels through a city charging a fuel surcharge, the letter Q is placed in the *Fare Calculation* ladder following the last city of the surcharged sector, as shown below (Figure 24).

Figure 24 – Sample of a fuel surcharge

TICKETING EXERCISE

Exercise 1 – Completing a *Fare Calculation* Ladder

Let's test your knowledge of what we've learned so far. Using the itinerary and other information below, fill in the blanks of the *Fare Calculation* ladder.

COS - PHX	Y	DL	222.53
PHX - LAX	Y	HP	302.49
LAX - SAN	Y	AS	98.87
SAN - PHX	Y	HP	313.42
PHX - COS	Y	UA	249.32
	TOTAL		1186.63

Origin/Destination (11)

After completing the *Fare Calculation* area, complete the *Origin/Destination* box of the ticket. It is mandatory that this box be completed when the itinerary requires that two or more tickets be written in conjunction.

Origin = City where transportation begins

Destination = City where transportation ends

Booking Reference (12)

The box to the right of the *Origin/Destination* box contains the Passenger Name Record (PNR) record locator. The record locator is the file number issued by the airline's reservation system to allow easy access to the passenger's flight information. The *Booking Reference* box contains these letters and/or numbers.

Conjunction Ticket(s) (13)

The box labeled *Conjunction Ticket(s)* allows the agent issuing the ticket to include the ticket number of the next booklet to indicate that they are to be used in conjunction with one another. This is used in the event that the booklets are separated for some reason. This area is only to be filled out when more than one ticket booklet is used to complete one itinerary.

Tour Code (14)

The *Tour Code* box is used when the passenger is using this ticket as part of a tour package. This box contains the necessary information for the Airlines Reporting Corporation to credit the appropriate companies involved in the tour.

Endorsements/Restrictions (15)

The *Endorsements/Restrictions* box allows the ticket issuer to enter the restrictions regarding the fare onto the ticket. During ticket rewrite, the *Endorsements* box is specifically used. During some exchanges the airline may require information to be entered into the *Endorsements* box. Generally this is limited to airport personnel entering the agent's identification number and the message required to transfer authority from one carrier to another.

At other times fare restrictions are entered into the box. For example, *For Use On United Airlines Only* may be entered to limit the use of the ticket. The entry can be modified to meet the specific situation.

Original Issue (16)

When exchanging a ticket, the information from the ticket being used for exchange is placed in the *Original Issue* box. The information from the original ticket includes the two-letter carrier code, the form and serial number of the ticket, the place the ticket was issued, the original date the ticket was written, and the numeric code for the agent who issued the first ticket.

Issued In Exchange For (17)

The *Issued In Exchange For* box indicates specific information when exchanging tickets. The most important information includes the date of issue of the original ticket and remaining information.

Ticket Designator (18)

The *Ticket Designator* box is used in conjunction with the additional ticket information when using one ticket in exchange for another. If the fare used for the ticket is a percentage of a full published fare, the alpha code for the discounted fare is entered here (for example, senior citizen).

Comm. Rate (19), Commission (20), Fare (21), and Tax (22)

Enter the commission, base fare, and tax information into the appropriate boxes. Remember that the ARC depends on the agent to enter this information accurately. Commission rates depend on variable factors and are always subject to change and fluctuation. Throughout this appendix we have used a 10 percent commission rate.

The remaining tax information is crucial during auditing and particularly during ticket reissue. Incorrect information in any box could complicate the procedure in the event the passenger wishes to modify the itinerary and ticket.

Form Of Payment (23)

The *Form Of Payment* box indicates the method of payment (cash, credit card, check) used for the ticket. If a reissue is being written, the original form of payment is entered in the new ticket's box.

Validating Plate Information (24)

The process of validating the ticket completes the remainder of the ticket. Placing the agency and airline identification plates in the validating machine and processing the ticket fills in the *Issued By* (airline information), *Place Of Issue* (agency information), and *Date Of Issue* boxes.

Filling out a Ticket: An Actual Example

To view the complete process, examine the passenger information listed below and note the completed tickets shown in Figure 25.1 and Figure 25.2.

Passenger Name	Mr. Chris Miller
Itinerary	BWI (Baltimore/Washington International) on AA 420
	IAH (Houston Intercontinental) on Continental 1190
	DFW (Dallas/Ft. Worth International) on AA 429
	ORD (Chicago O'Hare) on TWA 313
	STL (St. Louis) on TWA 501
	ORD (Chicago O'Hare) on United 222
	LAX (Los Angeles) on United 101
	IAD (Washington Dulles Airport)
Times	Leave BWI at 4:45 p.m. on May 5
	Depart IAH at 8:10 a.m. on May 8
	Leave DFW at 2:12 p.m. on May 12
	Leave ORD at 9:10 p.m. on May 15
	Depart STL at 1:15 p.m. on May 19

301

	Depart ORD at 4:10 p.m. on May 22
	Leave LAX at 8:00 a.m. on May 25
Record Locator	RPPOST
Form of Payment	Check
Fare Basis	Y26 on all American Airlines flights YPNUT on Continental Airlines Y25 on all Trans World Airlines flights YUA on all UA flights
Fare	The base fare from: BWI to IAH is $448.18 IAH to DFW is $71.82 DFW to ORD is $396.36 ORD to STL is $252.73 STL to ORD is $252.73 ORD to LAX is $691.82 LAX to WAS is $725.45
Tax and Surcharges	The tax charged on this itinerary is $284.81 There are 4 PFCs - one each at BWI, DFW, ORD, and LAX - for a total of $12.00. There is a fuel surcharge in Chicago of $4.55
Total Tax and Surcharge	The total tax and surcharge amount is $296.81
Total Fare	The total fare is $2,848.19
Commission	10 percent (10%)
Conjunction Tickets	Ticket numbers end in 410 and 411

Read the conjunction tickets(Figure 25.1 and Figure 25.2) and note the placement of all the information.

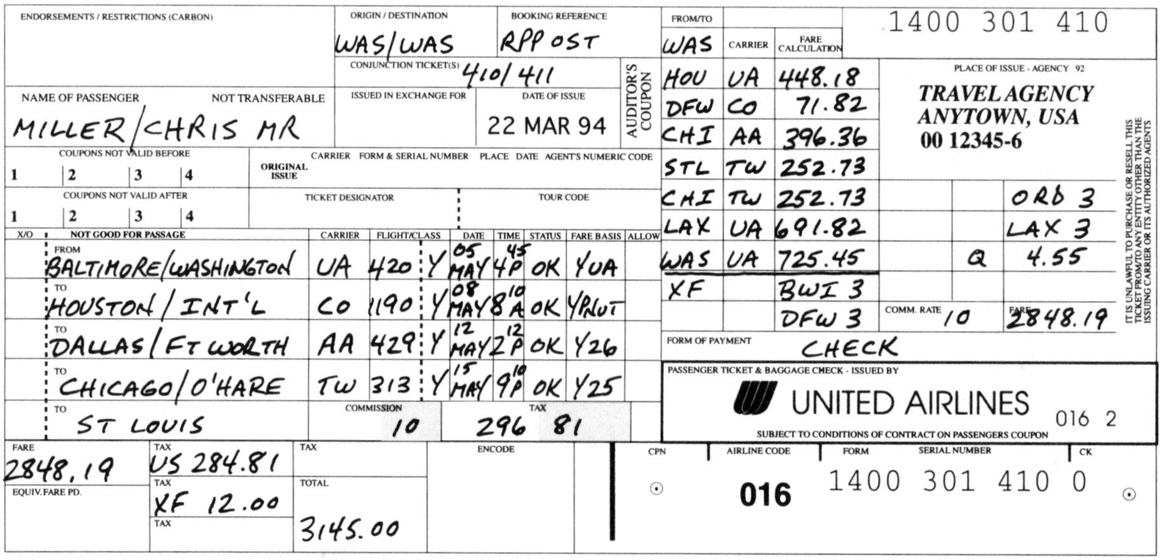
ENDORSEMENTS / RESTRICTIONS (CARBON)
ORIGIN / DESTINATION WAS/WAS
BOOKING REFERENCE RPPOST
CONJUNCTION TICKET(S) 410/411
NAME OF PASSENGER NOT TRANSFERABLE MILLER/CHRIS MR
ISSUED IN EXCHANGE FOR
DATE OF ISSUE 22 MAR 94
AUDITOR'S COUPON
COUPONS NOT VALID BEFORE 1 2 3 4
ORIGINAL ISSUE CARRIER FORM & SERIAL NUMBER PLACE DATE AGENT'S NUMERIC CODE
COUPONS NOT VALID AFTER 1 2 3 4
TICKET DESIGNATOR
TOUR CODE

X/O	NOT GOOD FOR PASSAGE	CARRIER	FLIGHT/CLASS	DATE	TIME	STATUS	FARE BASIS	ALLOW
	FROM BALTIMORE/WASHINGTON	UA	420 Y	05 MAY	445P	OK	YUA	
	TO HOUSTON/INT'L	CO	1190 Y	08 MAY	810A	OK	YPNUT	
	TO DALLAS/FT WORTH	AA	429 Y	12 MAY	122P	OK	Y26	
	TO CHICAGO/O'HARE	TW	313 Y	15 MAY	910P	OK	Y25	
	TO ST LOUIS							

COMMISSION 10 TAX 296 81

FARE 2848.19
TAX US 284.81
TAX XF 12.00
TAX
EQUIV. FARE PD.
TOTAL 3145.00
ENCODE

FROM/TO	CARRIER	FARE CALCULATION
WAS		
HOU	UA	448.18
DFW	CO	71.82
CHI	AA	396.36
STL	TW	252.73
CHI	TW	252.73
LAX	UA	691.82
WAS	UA	725.45
XF		BWI 3
		DFW 3

ORD 3
LAX 3
Q 4.55
COMM. RATE 10
FARE 2848.19
FORM OF PAYMENT CHECK

1400 301 410
PLACE OF ISSUE - AGENCY 92
TRAVEL AGENCY
ANYTOWN, USA
00 12345-6

IT IS UNLAWFUL TO PURCHASE OR RESELL THIS TICKET FROM/TO ANY ENTITY OTHER THAN THE ISSUING CARRIER OR ITS AUTHORIZED AGENTS

PASSENGER TICKET & BAGGAGE CHECK - ISSUED BY
UNITED AIRLINES 016 2
SUBJECT TO CONDITIONS OF CONTRACT ON PASSENGERS COUPON

CPN	AIRLINE CODE	FORM	SERIAL NUMBER	CK
	016	1400	301 410	0

Figure 25.1 – Sample of properly filled-in conjunction ticket

ENDORSEMENTS / RESTRICTIONS (CARBON)		ORIGIN / DESTINATION	BOOKING REFERENCE	FROM/TO			1400 301 411

Figure 25.2 – Sample of properly filled-in conjunction ticket

TICKETING EXERCISE

Exercise 2 – Completing a Manual Ticket

Now that you have seen each part of the ticket, complete the manual ticket above using the following passenger itinerary and information:

Passenger Name   Donald Smith

Itinerary   DCA (Washington National Airport) on United Airlines -111

ORD (Chicago O'Hare Air-

303

	port) on United Airlines 259		The passenger is flying coach on all segments
	COS (Colorado Springs Municipal Airport) on United 849		There are no date restrictions
	ORD (Chicago O'Hare Airport) on United 24	**Fare**	The base fare from WAS to COS is $607.27
	DCA (Washington National Airport) on United		The base fare from COS to WAS is $607.27
Times	Leave DCA at 9:08 a.m. on April 25		The total base fare is $1,214.54
	Connect in ORD departing at 11:05 a.m.	**Tax and Surcharges**	The tax charged on this itinerary is $121.46
	Leave COS on April 29 at 12:30 p.m.		There are PFCs of $3.00 charged in WAS, CHI (twice), and COS (total PFCs of $12.00)
	Connect in ORD departing at 4:50 p.m.		The total tax and surcharge amount is $133.46
Record Locator	The record locator for the reservation is R6J239		There is no fuel surcharge in ORD since it is a connection
Form of Payment	Check	**Total Fare**	The total fare is $1,348.00
Fare Basis	YUA		

Other Manual Forms

There are a number of ARC documents besides the ticketing form that need to be completed by hand for passengers. Each ARC document has detailed information on how to complete the form. It is essential to follow the guidelines printed for the document and complete the forms as required. All ARC documents are listed, explained, and documented in the ARC Industry Agent's Handbook. Contact the ARC for details on purchasing the support manual and materials. Let's take a detailed look at four particular forms:

Miscellaneous Charges Order (MCO)
Prepaid Ticketing Advice (PTA)
Tour Order
Refund Exchange Notice (REN)

Miscellaneous Charges Order

A Miscellaneous Charges Order , or MCO (Figure 26), comes in a booklet similar to a ticket booklet. The MCO can act either as a ticket or as a form of payment for items involved in the passenger's travels.

The MCO is generally used in two circumstances:

1. If the agency runs out of ticket stock, the MCO can be used as a form of payment that may be issued in exchange for a ticket at a later date. The use of the MCO as payment for a ticket is not customary.

2. The MCO is more commonly used as a deposit tool (for tours, etc.), a form of payment for additional collection, or as a receipt of payment for excess baggage.

Examine the parts of the MCO on the example coupon (Figure 26):

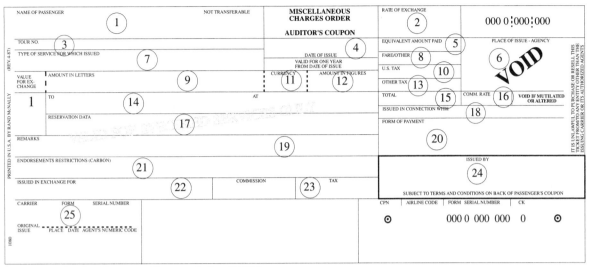

Figure 26 – A Miscellaneous Charges Order (MCO)

Each box of the MCO is filled out by following the steps below.

Name of Passenger (1)

The name of the passenger is placed in this box in the same manner as the manual ticket: last name, mandatory slash, initials or first name, and title of the passenger.

Rate of Exchange (2)

If the MCO is written in currency amounts other than U.S. Dollars, enter the currency code and rate of exchange for the currency used.

Tour No. (3)

If the MCO is written for a tour, place the tour IT number in this box.

Date of Issue (4)

This box is completed when you place the proper airline plate and agency identification plate in the ticket imprinter and validate. The date that appears in this box is the date of issue.

Equivalent Amount (5)

If the MCO is written in foreign currency, place the equivalent amount in U.S. Dollars in this box.

Place of Issue (6)

This box is also completed when you validate the MCO.

Type of Service (7)

This box contains a clear description of the type of service or purposes for which the MCO is being issued.

Fare/Other (8)

This box contains the base fare written with numbers.

Amount in Letters (9)

This box shows the total value of the MCO with any applicable tax, written in words.

U.S. Tax (10)

This box shows any taxes applicable for the United States.

Currency (11)

The type of currency used to issue the MCO is shown here. The three-letter ISO code is used (for example, USD).

305

Amount in Figures (12)

The total value of the MCO is shown in numerical figures in this box.

Other Tax (13)

Any foreign city or country taxes are included in this box.

To/At (14)

The name of the carrier or vendor involved in the MCO and their location requested to honor the exchange coupon are entered in this box.

Total (15)

The value, all taxes, and any fees are added together and placed in this box.

Commission (16)

The commission rate or code is included here.

Reservation Data (17)

The flight, class of service, date, three-letter city codes of the itinerary, and the status of the reservation are placed in this box.

Issued in Connection With (18)

Another ARC accountable document may be issued in conjunction with the MCO. If a conjunction document is issued, enter the document number in this box.

Remarks (19)

This box is used when additional descriptions are needed to explain or qualify the use of the MCO.

Form of Payment (20)

This box indicates the method of payment.

Endorsements/Restrictions (21)

The item or service being purchased by the MCO may require some type of restriction. This box is used to explain the restriction.

Issued in Exchange For (22)

If the MCO is issued in exchange for another document, enter the form and serial number of the original document.

Commission/Tax (23)

The commission and tax information is included in these boxes.

Issued By (24)

The airline plate will be carbon copied into this box automatically when you validate the MCO on the office ticket imprinter.

Original Issue (25)

If the MCO is issued in exchange for another document, enter the date and three-letter city code of the place of issue and the original ticket number in this box.

Prepaid Ticket Advice

A Prepaid Ticket Advice, or PTA (Figure 27), is an authorization that permits the ticket to be issued at a point other than the point of payment. For example, a PTA allows an individual in Orlando to purchase a ticket for a person in San Francisco without having to be physically present in San Francisco. Generally, the passenger and the purchaser are two different people. There is a nonrefundable service charge for PTAs.

TICKETING EXERCISE

Exercise 3 — Completing the MCO Form

Use the following information to complete the MCO form:

Your client, Ms. Deborah Lucas, will be renting a luxury car in San Francisco, CA (SFO) from Alamo Rental Car. She will pick up the car on June 2 and will drop it off four days later on June 5. The daily rate is $84.00 with unlimited mileage. She will pay for the rental with a check.

Arrange for Ms. Lucas to surrender the MCO to Alamo at the service counter in SFO when she picks up the car.

She will be flying into SFO on United Airlines (validate the MCO with UA). Alamo awards a 10% commission. There is a 10% sales tax (prepaid).

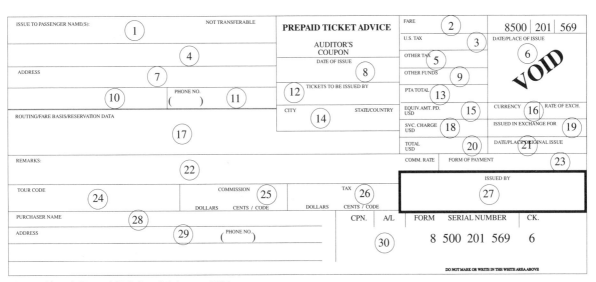

Figure 27 – A Prepaid Ticket Advice, or PTA

Each box of the PTA is filled out by following the steps below.

Passenger Name(s) 1

The name of the passenger is entered in the standard format: last name, mandatory slash, initials or first name, and title of the passenger.

Fare 2

The base fare of the prepaid ticket is entered in this box.

U.S. Tax 3

U.S. applicable taxes that fall under U.S. tax codes are entered here.

Extra Line 4

The extra line allows for additional passenger names to be included on the PTA.

Other Tax 5

Insert any tax collected on behalf of a foreign country or PFC charges from applicable airports.

307

Date/Place of Issue (6)

The agency validation plate automatically complete this box when the PTA is validated.

Address (7)

Enter the passenger's address in this box.

Date of Issue (8)

This box will be completed when the PTA is imprinted on the office ticket validator.

Other Funds (9)

This box is used to indicate additional amounts that are being prepaid for the passenger.

Extra Line (10)

This area allows completion of the passenger's address.

Phone No. (11)

Insert the passenger's phone number here.

Tickets To Be Issued By (12)

Complete the name of the carrier and the location where the PTA is to be honored.

PTA Total (13)

The total amount including taxes is placed in this box. It is important to remember, however, that the service charge amount is not to be included in this box.

City/State/Country (14)

Complete the city and country location where the PTA is to be honored.

Equiv. Amt. Pd. (15)

If the PTA is issued in another currency, enter the equivalent amount paid in U.S. Dollars in this box.

Currency (16)

Indicate the type of currency used (using the three-letter ISO code) and the current rate of exchange if the currency used is other than the U.S. Dollar.

Routing/Fare Basis/Reservation Data (17)

Enter the full itinerary and status of the reservation.

Svc. Charge (18)

Enter the amount of the service charge for the PTA.

Issued In Exchange For (19)

This box is used in the event that the PTA is issued in exchange for any other ARC accountable ticket.

Total (20)

Enter the total amount of the PTA in U.S. Dollars.

Date/Place Original Issue (21)

If the PTA is being paid for by another document, the date and place of original issue is included in this box.

Remarks (22)

This box usually contains the remark *Refundable To Purchaser Only*.

Form of Payment (23)

Enter the method of payment.

Tour Code (24)

Enter the tour designation IT followed by the tour number code if required by the carrier detailed in the PTA.

Commission (25)

If using a commission code (percentage), place it in the highlighted area. If no code applies, enter the commission amount after removing the Agent's and Auditor's coupons.

Tax (26)

If indicating a tax code or a percentage of 0 or 10, place it in the highlighted area; otherwise, the dollar amount will be placed in the TAX box.

Issued By (27)

The carrier plate for validation will be carbon copied onto the PTA when the ticket is run through the ticket imprinter.

Purchaser Name (28)

The purchaser's name is entered here.

Address/Phone Number (29)

Enter the purchaser's address and telephone number.

Airline Code (30)

The airline code will be carbon copied during imprinting.

TICKETING EXERCISE

Exercise 4 — Completing the PTA Form

Use the following information to complete the PTA form:

Your client, Ms. Melinda Sweetwater, would like to purchase a PTA for her friend, Dawn Heffer.

The carrier for the flight will be United Airlines (validate the PTA with UA). United Airlines charges a $30.00 service charge for a PTA. The date of the PTA issue is October 20, 1995. Ms. Sweetwater lives at 1520 Liberty Drive, Revere, MA; her telephone number is (617) 555-1329. She will be paying for the document with an American Express credit card (AX) number 372 3942 59112. The credit card is valid through October 1996. Ms. Sweetwater is the cardholder. The approval code for the transaction is V222.

Ms. Heffer lives at 1322 Mockingbird Lane, Denver, CO. Her phone number is (303) 555-1520. She will be flying UA round trip from Denver to Boston, MA. She will depart on July 20 at 10:35 a.m. on UA 352 in coach. She will return on July 26 at 11:15 a.m. on UA flight 569 in coach class.

The base fare of the ticket from Denver to Boston is $715.45. There is a $1.82 fuel surcharge from Denver. The base fare from Boston to Denver is $715.45. There is a $2.27 fuel surcharge from Boston. The fare basis code for both flights is YUA. Passenger Facility Charges of $3.00 are charged in Denver and Boston. The total base fare of her ticket is $1,434.99. The standard 10% tax applies.

ISSUE TO PASSENGER NAME(S):	NOT TRANSFERABLE	**PREPAID TICKET ADVICE**	FARE
		AUDITOR'S COUPON	8500 | 201 | 569

(PTA form — VOID)

ISSUE TO PASSENGER NAME(S): — NOT TRANSFERABLE

ADDRESS

PHONE NO. ( )

ROUTING/FARE BASIS/RESERVATION DATA

PREPAID TICKET ADVICE
AUDITOR'S COUPON
DATE OF ISSUE
TICKETS TO BE ISSUED BY
CITY — STATE/COUNTRY

FARE
U.S. TAX
OTHER TAX
OTHER FUNDS
PTA TOTAL
EQUIV. AMT. PD. USD
SVC. CHARGE USD
TOTAL USD

8500 | 201 | 569
DATE/PLACE OF ISSUE
VOID
CURRENCY — RATE OF EXCH.
ISSUED IN EXCHANGE FOR
DATE/PLACE ORIGINAL ISSUE

REMARKS:

TOUR CODE | COMMISSION — DOLLARS — CENTS / CODE | TAX — DOLLARS — CENTS / CODE

COMM. RATE | FORM OF PAYMENT
ISSUED BY

PURCHASER NAME

ADDRESS — PHONE NO. ( )

CPN. | A/L | FORM — SERIAL NUMBER | CK.
8 500 201 569 — 6

DO NOT MARK OR WRITE IN THE WHITE AREA ABOVE

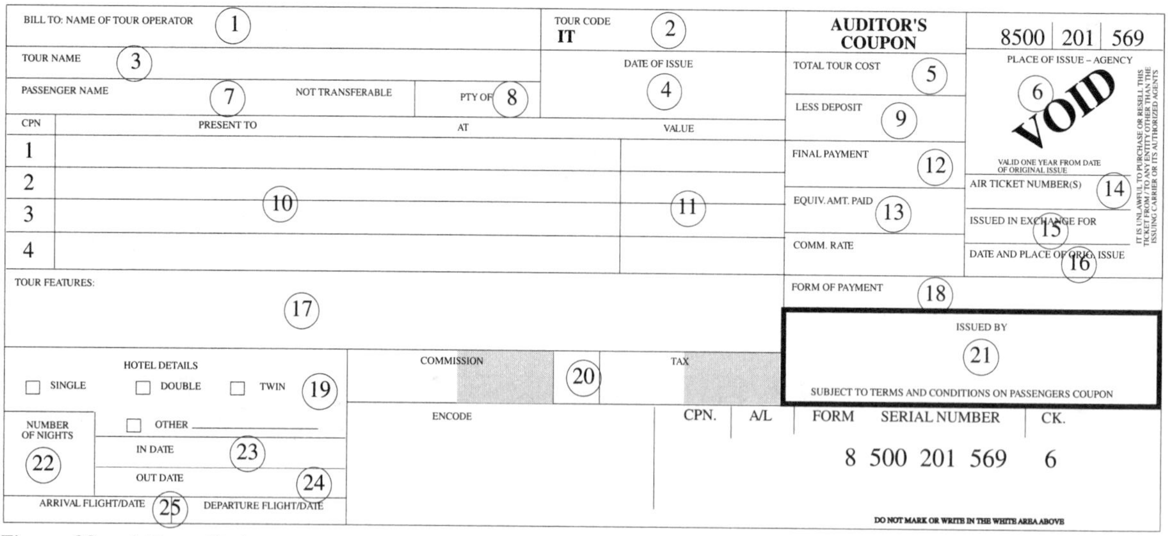

Figure 28 – A Tour Order

Tour Order

The Tour Order is used to cover payments on advertised tour packages, usually both air and land. A Tour Order is shown above (Figure 28).

To complete this form, each box must be completed by following these steps.

Name Of Tour Operator (1)

Enter the name of the tour operator.

Tour Code (2)

The approved tour code is placed in this box.

Tour Name (3)

Tour operators name the various tours they offer. The name of the tour reserved for the passenger is placed in this box.

Date Of Issue (4)

The date of issue is automatically entered when the tour order is validated in the ticket imprinter.

Total Tour Cost (5)

The total value of the tour, including tax, is included in this box.

Place Of Issue (6)

This box is automatically completed when the ticket is validated.

Passenger Name (7)

Enter the passenger's name in the standard format.

Pty Of (8)

The total number of passengers completing the tour is placed here.

Less Deposit (9)

When a prior deposit has been made on the tour, enter the amount deposited in this box.

Present To (10)

Information regarding the tour itinerary is included in these four boxes. The first box contains the name of the airport transfer company or rental car company and the name of the city where service will commence.

Box number 2 contains the name of the tour operator or hotel as specified in ticketing instructions, as well as the name of the city where the tour ends.

The boxes labeled 3 and 4 allow you to enter the name and location of additional services provided on the tour.

Value (11)

The value of the service rendered is entered in this column, as it applies to the vendor supplying the service.

Final Payment (12)

The total value of the tour is entered here. The deposit amount is subtracted if a deposit was made.

Equiv. Amt. (13)

If payment is made with a currency other than U.S. Dollars, complete this portion. The percentage of commission is included in the box below.

Air Ticket Number(s) (14)

If air tickets are written in conjunction with the tour order, include the number in this box.

Issued In Exchange For (15)

This box contains the appropriate number of the document used in exchange.

Date And Place Of Original Issue (16)

If a document is used in exchange for payment for the tour order, the original issue information must be included in this box.

Tour Features (17)

This box allows you to enter the services included in the package as specified by the tour operator.

Form Of Payment (18)

Enter the method of payment in this box.

Hotel Details (19)

Check the type of hotel occupancy purchased.

Commission/Tax (20)

Commission and tax information is placed here.

Issued By (21)

This area will be completed during the validation process.

Number Of Nights (22)

The number of nights purchased at the hotel are included in this box.

In Date (23)

Enter the check in/arrival date at the hotel.

Out Date (24)

Indicate the check-out/departure date at the hotel.

Arrival/Departure (25)

The flight information for arrival and departure is included for reference.

TICKETING EXERCISE

Exercise 5 — Completing the Tour Order Form

Use the following information to complete the Tour Order form:

The client, Mr. Jim Alex, is purchasing a Las Vegas tour package called "The Vegas Weekend Escape." He will be arriving in Las Vegas on September 13 and departing September 16. He will be staying a total of three nights at the Excalibur Hotel. Since he is the only one in the party, he would like a single room. The tour operator is Excalibur Hotel & Casino. The tour code is NV-PESDS.

Mr. Alex will be arriving on American Airlines light 213 on the 13th. He will take American Airlines flight 542 on the 16th for his return trip.

The tour includes the following deluxe accommodations, admissions, $300 in gaming chips, gratuities, and taxes.

The total cost of the tour is $492.00. Mr. Alex will pay by check. You will receive a 10% commission from Excalibur.

Mr. Alex's ticket was purchased one week ago, and the ticket number is 0015297227598.

BILL TO: NAME OF TOUR OPERATOR			TOUR CODE **IT**		AUDITOR'S COUPON	8500 | 201 | 569

TOUR NAME

DATE OF ISSUE · TOTAL TOUR COST · PLACE OF ISSUE – AGENCY

PASSENGER NAME · NOT TRANSFERABLE · PTY OF · LESS DEPOSIT

CPN	PRESENT TO	AT	VALUE
1			
2			
3			
4			

FINAL PAYMENT

EQUIV. AMT. PAID

COMM. RATE

VOID

VALID ONE YEAR FROM DATE OF ORIGINAL ISSUE

AIR TICKET NUMBER(S)

ISSUED IN EXCHANGE FOR

DATE AND PLACE OF ORIG. ISSUE

TOUR FEATURES:

FORM OF PAYMENT

ISSUED BY

SUBJECT TO TERMS AND CONDITIONS ON PASSENGERS COUPON

HOTEL DETAILS
☐ SINGLE ☐ DOUBLE ☐ TWIN

COMMISSION · TAX

NUMBER OF NIGHTS · ☐ OTHER _____ · IN DATE · OUT DATE

ENCODE

CPN.	A/L	FORM	SERIAL NUMBER	CK.
		8	500 201 569	6

ARRIVAL FLIGHT/DATE · DEPARTURE FLIGHT/DATE

DO NOT MARK OR WRITE IN THE WHITE AREA ABOVE

Refund Exchange Notice

The Refund Exchange Notice, or REN (Figure 29), is used in the event that a ticket is being exchanged or refunded. Let's examine a sample REN form.

To fill in this form, follow these steps.

Total Cost Of New Ticket(s) (1)

In this box, include the PFCs, base fare, and all taxes from the new ticket.

Base Fare Of Old/Refunded Tickets (2)

Enter the base fare of the old ticket or, on a partial refund, the base value of the unused portion of the old ticket.

Individual Taxes (3)

The taxes from the old ticket are entered in the boxes labeled C, D, and E. On a partial refund, the amount entered would be the unused tax amounts.

Same as above (4)

Same as above (5)

Total Cost Of Old Ticket(s) (6)

Copy this figure from the original ticket.

Line G (7)

In the shaded box you must circle the correct

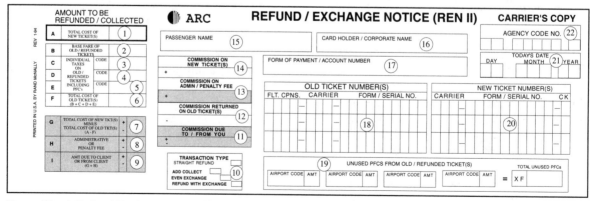

Figure 29 – A Refund Exchange Notice, or REN

sign. A plus sign (+) indicates that an additional collection is occurring. A minus sign (-) indicates that a refund is due. Calculations are required for this portion of the REN. Note that this box requires that you take the total cost of the new ticket(s) (line A) and subtract the total cost of the old ticket(s) (line F).

Administrative Or Penalty Fee (8)

Enter the administrative or penalty fee on this line. A penalty fee is an amount charged by an airline during the ticket exchange process. Some airlines will not provide a refund for the difference between a more expensive ticket and a new ticket. When this occurs, the difference between the new ticket and the old ticket is entered on line H and is considered a penalty fee.

Amt Due To Client Or From Client (9)

Line I will contain either a refund amount or an additional collection amount depending on the results of your calculation. If the final number is a positive number (+), an additional collection is required. If the final result is negative (-), the amount is refunded. If the end result is a zero (0), the process is considered an even exchange.

Transaction Type (10)

Notice there are four transaction types to choose from. You must select one of the transactions: Straight Refund, Add Collect, Even Exchange, or Refund with Exchange.

Commission Due To/From You (11)

This box shows the final result of calculations made from the tickets. To calculate this number add the commission on the new ticket, plus the commission on any penalty or administrative fee, and subtract the returned commission on the old ticket. As in previous calculations, if the number is positive, the commission is due to you. If it is a negative number, the commission is due from you.

The remaining areas of the REN II concern the various commission amounts.

Commission Returned On Old Ticket(s)

Enter the dollar amount of the commission from the old ticket.

Commission On Admin/Penalty Fee (13)

Indicate the dollar amount of the commission charged on the administrative or penalty fee.

Commission On New Ticket(s) (14)

Enter the dollar amount of all the commission from the new ticket.

Passenger Name (15)

The passenger's name is placed here.

Card Holder/Corporate Name (16)

If the ticket is being paid with cash, this box may be left blank. When the passenger's name is different from the individual's name on the credit card, this box should be completed. In some cases, a corporation may purchase a ticket. In that event, place the corporation's name in the box.

Form Of Payment/Account Number

This box is used to describe the form of payment used (cash, check, or credit card) If a credit card is used, enter the account number.

Old Ticket Number(s) (18)

This area is used to note the ticket numbers used as exchanges. Notice that you may enter up to four flight coupons per line. Transcribe the numbers from the old tickets to the appropriate boxes to indicate the coupon number, the carrier code, and the form and serial number of the tickets to be exchanged.

Unused PfCs From Old/Refunded Ticket(s) (19)

Write the appropriate airport code on the left-hand side with the dollar amount shown on the right. Remember that PFCs can be in amounts of $1.00, $2.00, or $3.00.

New Ticket Number(s) (20)

Enter the new ticket numbers from the tickets you have written. They are entered in the same format as the Old Ticket Number(s).

Today's Date (21)

The date is important to the ARC. This date is the actual date that you fill out the Refund Exchange Notice.

Agency Code No. (22)

The Agency Code Number or ARC number is entered here.

The REN is a relatively simple form to fill out if the directions are followed accurately.

TICKETING EXERCISE

Exercise 6 — Completing the REN document

Use the following information to complete a REN document.

Ms. Renée Schmidt has a round-trip, nonre-stricted ticket from Denver, Colorado, to Boston, Massachusetts. She can no longer complete her journey and would like a refund. Return the applicable commission to the carrier. Complete the REN II form by using the information on the facsimile of her ticket.

ANSWERS TO TICKETING EXERCISES

Exercise 1 — Completing a *Fare Calculation Ladder*

Your Fare Calculation should look like this:

FROM/TO	CARRIER	FARE CALCULATION	1400 301 410
COS			
PHX	DL	222.53	PLACE OF ISSUE - AGENCY 92
LAX	HP	302.49	*TRAVEL AGENCY*
SAN	AS	98.87	*ANYTOWN, USA*
PHX	HP	313.42	**00 12345-6**
COS	UA	249.32	

IT IS UNLAWFUL TO PURCHASE OR RESELL THIS TICKET FROM/TO ANY ENTITY OTHER THAN THE ISSUING CARRIER OR ITS AUTHORIZED AGENTS

COMM. RATE **10**   FARE **1186.63**

FORM OF PAYMENT

PASSENGER TICKET & BAGGAGE CHECK - ISSUED BY

UNITED AIRLINES 016 2

SUBJECT TO CONDITIONS OF CONTRACT ON PASSENGERS COUPON

	AIRLINE CODE	FORM	SERIAL NUMBER	CK
	016	1400 301 410		0

Exercise 2 — Completing a Manual Ticket

ENDORSEMENTS / RESTRICTIONS (CARBON)	ORIGIN / DESTINATION	BOOKING REFERENCE	FROM/TO	CARRIER	FARE CALCULATION	1400 301 410
	WAS/WAS	R6J239	WAS			
	CONJUNCTION TICKET(S)		CHI	UA		PLACE OF ISSUE - AGENCY 92
NAME OF PASSENGER NOT TRANSFERABLE	ISSUED IN EXCHANGE FOR	DATE OF ISSUE	COS	UA	607.27	*TRAVEL AGENCY*
SMITH/DONALD MR		22 MAR 94	CHI	UA		*ANYTOWN, USA* **00 12345-6**
			WAS	UA	607.27	
COUPONS NOT VALID BEFORE	ORIGINAL ISSUE	CARRIER FORM & SERIAL NUMBER PLACE DATE AGENT'S NUMERIC CODE	XF		DCA 3	
1 2 3 4					ORD 3	
COUPONS NOT VALID AFTER	TICKET DESIGNATOR	TOUR CODE			COS 3	
1 2 3 4					ORD 3	

X/O	NOT GOOD FOR PASSAGE	CARRIER	FLIGHT/CLASS	DATE	TIME	STATUS	FARE BASIS	ALLOW
	FROM WASHINGTON/NAT'L	UA	111 Y	25 APR	9 03A	OK	Y26	
X	TO CHICAGO/O'HARE	UA	259 Y	25 APR	11 05A	OK	YUA	
O	TO COLORADO SPRINGS	UA	849 Y	29 APR	12 30P	OK	Y26	
X	TO CHICAGO/O'HARE	UA	24 Y	29 APR	4 30P	OK	YUA	
	TO WASHINGTON/NAT'L							

COMMISSION **10**   TAX **133 46**

FORM OF PAYMENT CHECK

COMM. RATE **10**   FARE **1214.54**

FARE 1214.54	TAX US 121.46	TAX	ENCODE
EQUIV. FARE PD.	TAX XF 12.00	TOTAL 1348.00	

PASSENGER TICKET & BAGGAGE CHECK - ISSUED BY

UNITED AIRLINES 016 2

SUBJECT TO CONDITIONS OF CONTRACT ON PASSENGERS COUPON

CPN	AIRLINE CODE	FORM	SERIAL NUMBER	CK
	016	1400 301 410		0

IT IS UNLAWFUL TO PURCHASE OR RESELL THIS TICKET FROM/TO ANY ENTITY OTHER THAN THE ISSUING CARRIER OR ITS AUTHORIZED AGENTS

Exercise 3 — Completing the MCO Form

Your MCO should look like this:

NAME OF PASSENGER	NOT TRANSFERABLE	MISCELLANEOUS CHARGES ORDER AUDITOR'S COUPON	RATE OF EXCHANGE		000 0 000 000

LUCAS / DEBORAH MS

TOUR NO.

TYPE OF SERVICE FOR WHICH ISSUED
PAYMENT FOR ALAMO RENTAL CAR

DATE OF ISSUE
VALID FOR ONE YEAR FROM DATE OF ISSUE

AMOUNT IN LETTERS
THREE HUNDRED SIXTY NINE DOLLARS 60/100

CURRENCY   AMOUNT IN FIGURES 369.60

EQUIVALENT AMOUNT PAID
FARE/OTHER 369.60
U.S. TAX
OTHER TAX
TOTAL 369.60   COMM. RATE 10

PLACE OF ISSUE - AGENCY   VOID

VOID IF MUTILATED OR ALTERED

VALUE FOR EXCHANGE 1

TO   ALAMO   SAN FRANCISCO, CA   AT

ISSUED IN CONNECTION WITH

RESERVATION DATA
PICK UP JUNE 2 - DROP OFF JUNE 5 / LUXURY

FORM OF PAYMENT

REMARKS
UNLIMITED MILEAGE

ENDORSEMENTS RESTRICTIONS (CARBON)   ISSUED BY

ISSUED IN EXCHANGE FOR   COMMISSION 10   TAX

SUBJECT TO TERMS AND CONDITIONS ON BACK OF PASSENGER'S COUPON

CARRIER   FORM   SERIAL NUMBER   CPN AIRLINE CODE FORM SERIAL NUMBER CK

ORIGINAL ISSUE PLACE DATE AGENT'S NUMERIC CODE   000 0 000 000 0

Exercise 4 — Completing the PTA Form

Your PTA should look like this:

ISSUE TO PASSENGER NAME(S):   NOT TRANSFERABLE
DAWN HEFFER
1322 MOCKINGBIRD LANE
ADDRESS
DENVER, CO
PHONE NO. (303) 555-1520

PREPAID TICKET ADVICE
AUDITOR'S COUPON
DATE OF ISSUE   20 OCT 96
TICKETS TO BE ISSUED BY   UA

FARE 1434.99   8500 201 569
U.S. TAX 143.51   DATE/PLACE OF ISSUE
OTHER TAX XF 6.00   VOID
OTHER FUNDS
PTA TOTAL 1584.50

ROUTING/FARE BASIS/RESERVATION DATA
UA 352 Y 20 JUL DEN BOS OK
UA 569 Y 26 JUL BOS DEN OK

CITY   STATE/COUNTRY
DENVER   CO
XF DEN3 BOS3
Q - BOS - 2.27

EQUIV. AMT. PD. USD
SVC. CHARGE USD 30.00
TOTAL USD 1614.50

CURRENCY   RATE OF EXCH.
ISSUED IN EXCHANGE FOR
DATE/PLACE ORIGINAL ISSUE

REMARKS:
REFUND TO MELINDA SWEETWATER ONLY

COMM. RATE FORM OF PAYMENT AX 372 3942 59112
ISSUED BY

TOUR CODE   COMMISSION 161 45 DOLLARS CENTS/CODE   TAX 149 51 DOLLARS CENTS/CODE

CPN. A/L FORM SERIAL NUMBER CK.

PURCHASER NAME MS MELINDA SWEETWATER
ADDRESS 1520 LIBERTY DRIVE PHONE NO. (617) 555-1329
REVERE, MA

8 500 201 569 6

DO NOT MARK OR WRITE IN THE WHITE AREA ABOVE

316

Exercise 5 — Completing the Tour Order Form

Your Tour Order should look like this:

BILL TO: NAME OF TOUR OPERATOR *EXCALIBUR HOTEL + CASINO*	TOUR CODE IT *NV-PESDS*	AUDITOR'S COUPON	8500	201	569

TOUR NAME *VEGAS WEEKEND ESCAPE*
DATE OF ISSUE
PLACE OF ISSUE – AGENCY
TOTAL TOUR COST *492.00*
VOID

PASSENGER NAME *ALEX/JIM MR* NOT TRANSFERABLE   PTY OF
LESS DEPOSIT
VALID ONE YEAR FROM DATE OF ORIGINAL ISSUE
AIR TICKET NUMBER(S) *001 529 7227 598*

CPN	PRESENT TO	AT	VALUE
1	*VOID*		
2	*EXCALIBUR HOTEL*	*LAS VEGAS*	
3	*VOID*		
4	*VOID*		

FINAL PAYMENT *492.00*
EQUIV. AMT. PAID
ISSUED IN EXCHANGE FOR
COMM. RATE *10*
DATE AND PLACE OF ORIG. ISSUE

TOUR FEATURES: *DELUXE ACCOMMODATIONS ADMISSIONS, $300 GAMING CHIPS GRATUITIES, TAXES*

FORM OF PAYMENT *CHECK*
ISSUED BY
SUBJECT TO TERMS AND CONDITIONS ON PASSENGERS COUPON

HOTEL DETAILS: ☑ SINGLE ☐ DOUBLE ☐ TWIN ☐ OTHER
COMMISSION   TAX
ENCODE

CPN.	A/L	FORM	SERIAL NUMBER	CK.
		8 500	201 569	6

NUMBER OF NIGHTS *3*
IN DATE *13 SEP 95*
OUT DATE *16 SEP 95*
ARRIVAL FLIGHT/DATE *AA 213 13 SEP*   DEPARTURE FLIGHT/DATE *AA 542 16 SEP*

DO NOT MARK OR WRITE IN THE WHITE AREA ABOVE

Exercise 6 — Completing the REN document

Your REN document should look like this:

REFUND / EXCHANGE NOTICE (REN II)   CARRIER'S COPY
ARC

	AMOUNT TO BE REFUNDED / COLLECTED	
A	TOTAL COST OF NEW TICKET(S)	*0*
B	BASE FARE OF OLD / REFUNDED TICKETS	*1434.99*
C	INDIVIDUAL TAXES ON OLD / REFUNDED TICKETS INCLUDING PFC's CODE *US*	*143.51*
D	CODE *XF*	*6.00*
E	CODE	
F	TOTAL COST OF OLD TICKET(S) (B + C + D + E)	*1584.50*
G	TOTAL COST OF NEW TKT(S) MINUS TOTAL COST OF OLD TKT(S) (A – F)	- *1584.50*
H	ADMINISTRATIVE OR PENALTY FEE	+ -
I	AMT DUE TO CLIENT OR FROM CLIENT (G + H)	+ - *1584.50*

PASSENGER NAME *SCHMIDT / RENÉE MS*
CARD HOLDER / CORPORATE NAME

COMMISSION ON NEW TICKET(S) +
FORM OF PAYMENT / ACCOUNT NUMBER *CHECK*

COMMISSION ON ADMIN / PENALTY FEE +

COMMISSION RETURNED ON OLD TICKET(S) - *143.51*

COMMISSION DUE TO / FROM YOU ⊙ *143.51*

AGENCY CODE NO. *0 0 1 2 3 4 5 6*

TODAYS DATE
DAY	MONTH	YEAR
24	*APR*	*95*

OLD TICKET NUMBER(S)			
FLT. CPNS.	CARRIER	FORM / SERIAL NO.	
12	*016*	*1400301410*	

NEW TICKET NUMBER(S)		
CARRIER	FORM / SERIAL NO.	CK

TRANSACTION TYPE
STRAIGHT REFUND ☑
ADD COLLECT ☐
EVEN EXCHANGE ☐
REFUND WITH EXCHANGE ☐

UNUSED PFCS FROM OLD / REFUNDED TICKET(S)				TOTAL UNUSED PFCs
AIRPORT CODE *DEN* AMT *3*	AIRPORT CODE *BOS* AMT *3*	AIRPORT CODE AMT	AIRPORT CODE AMT	= X F *6.00*

REV 1-84
PRINTED IN U.S.A. BY RAND McNALLY

Resource Appendix

Travel Industry Organizations and Associations

Resources for Further Information

Airlines Reporting Corporation (ARC)
1709 New York Avenue, NW
Washington, DC 20006-5288
Telephone 202 626-8000
Fax 202 626-8029

Air Transport Association (ATA)
1709 New York Avenue, NW
Washington, DC 20006
Telephone 202 626-4000
Fax 202 626-4181

American Automobile Association (AAA)
1000 AAA Drive
Heathrow, FL 32746-5063
Telephone 407 444-7000
Fax 407 444-7380

American Bus Association (ABA)
1015 15th Street, NW #250
Washington, DC 20005
Telephone 202 842-1645
Fax 202 842-0850

American Car Rental Association (ACRA)
2011 Eye Street, NW, 5th Floor
Washington, DC 20006
Telephone 202 789-2240
Fax 202 371-1467

American Hotel and Motel Association (AHMA)
1201 New York Avenue NW, 6th Floor
Washington, DC 20005-3917
Telephone 202 289-3100
Fax 202 289-3199

American Society of Travel Agents (ASTA)
1101 King Streeet
Alexandria, VA 22314
Telephone 703 739-2782
Fax 703 684-8319

AMTRAK
60 Massachusetts Avenue, NE
Washington, DC 20002
Telephone 202 906-3000
Fax 202 906-2493

Association of Retail Travel Agents (ARTA)
1745 Jefferson Davis Highway, Suite 300
Arlington, VA 22202-3402
Telephone 703 553-7777
Fax 703 486-0228

BritRail Travel International
1500 Broadway - 10th Floor
New York, NY 10036
Telephone 212 382-3737
Fax 212 575-2542

Canadian Institutes Of Travel Counsellors
(CITC)
Shipp Center, Suite 2880
3300 Bloor Street W.
Etobicoke, ON M8X 2X3
Telephone 416 239-4891
Fax 416 233-7064

Caribbean Tourism Organization (CTO)
20 East 46th Street
New York, NY 10017
Telephone 212 682-0435
Fax 212 697-4258

Cruise Lines International Association (CLIA)
500 Fifth Avenue, Suite 1407
New York, NY 10110
Telephone 212 921-0066
Fax 212 921-0549

Institute of Certified Travel Agents (ICTA)
P.O. Box 812059
148 Linden Street
Wellesley, MA 02181- 0012
Telephone 617 237-0280
Fax 617 237-3860

International Airlines Travel Agent Network
(IATAN)
300 Garden City Plaza
Garden City, NY 11530
Telephone 516 747-4716
Fax 516 747-4462

International Air Transport Association (IATA)
2000 Peel Street
Montreal, PQ H3A 2R4 CAN
Telephone 514 844-6311
Fax 514 844-5286

National Tour Association (NTA)
546 East Main Street
P.O. Box 3071
Lexington, KY 40596
Telephone 606 253-1036
Fax 606 231-9837

Pacific Asia Travel Association (PATA)
1 Montgomery Street, Suite 1750
San Francisco, CA 94104
Telephone 415 986-4646
Fax 415 986-3458

Rail Europe
230 Westchester Ave.
White Plains, NY 10604
Telephone 914 682-2999
Fax 914 682-2821

Society for the Advancement of Travel
for the Handicapped (SATH)
347 Fifth Avenue, Suite 610
New York, NY 10016
Telephone 212 447-7284
Fax 212 725-8253

Society of American Travel Writers (SATW)
1155 Connecticut Avenue, Suite 500
Washington, DC 20036
Telephone 202 429-6639
Fax 202 452-8654

Society of Incentive Travel Executives (SITE)
21 West 38th Street, 10th Floor
New York, NY 10018
Telephone 212 575-0910
Fax 212-575-1838

Society of Travel Agents in Government (STAG)
6935 Wisconsin Avenue, NW #200
Washington, DC 20815
Telephone 301 654-8595
Fax 301 654-6663

Travel and Tourism Research Association
(TTRA)
P.O. Box 58066
Salt Lake City, UT 84158-0066
Telephone 801 581-3351
Fax 801 581-3354

United States Department of Transportation
(DOT)
400 Seventh Street, SW
Washington, DC 20590
Telephone 202 366-2435
Fax 202 366-3694

United States Tour Operators Association
(USTOA)
211 East 51st Street, Suite 12-B
New York, NY 10022
Telephone 212 944-5727
Fax 212 421-1285

United States Travel Data Center
Two Lafayette Center
1133 21st Street, NW
Washington, DC 20036
Telephone 202 293-1040
Fax 202 293-3155

United States Travel and Tourism Administration
(USTTA)
14th and Constitution Avenue, NW
Washington, DC 20230
Telephone 202 377-0136
Fax 202 377-4279

VIA Rail Canada
2, Place Ville-Marie, Suite 4000
Montreal, PQ H3B 2C9 CAN
Telephone 514 871-6349
Fax 514 871-6657

World Association of Travel Agencies
(WATA)
37 Quai Wilsons
Geneve, Switzerland 1201
Telephone 022 731 47 60
Fax 022 732 81 61

World Tourism Organization (WTO)
Captain Haya, 42
Madrid, Spain 28020
Telephone 5710628
Fax 571 37 33

Glossary

AAA American Automobile Association. An organization offering a variety of travel and motoring services. AAA is composed of regional clubs that own and operate travel agencies.

ABA American Bus Association. A trade association for motorcoach owners and operators. The association issues certificates of approval to companies that carry adequate insurance and post a performance bond.

Access Time A computer term that refers to the time between the instant the operator sends an instruction to the computer and the instant the information returns.

A La Carte Free choice in a restaurant among all the items on the menu.

Add-On A fare component that is added to a specified fare to construct a through fare.

Adjoining Rooms or cabins sharing a common wall but not necessarily connected by a common door.

Affinity An organization formed by people with common interests.

Aft Near, toward, or at the rear of a ship or the tail of an aircraft.

Agent Identification Plate A small metal plate provided by ARC to each approved travel agency. It is used to validate manually written tickets and other ARC documents.

AH&MA American Hotel and Motel Association. This organization represents trade associations in the lodging industry in the United States, Canada, Mexico, Central America, and South America.

Air Report An accounting of a travel agency's weekly sales of airline tickets.

Air/Sea Arrangements that combine air transportation to and from a port of embarkation with the cruise itself; sometimes called *fly/cruise.*

All-Inclusive Package A vacation package in which the traveler pays one price that covers all of the trip expenses.

Allocentric Personality The type of personality that seeks adventure, variety, and excitement.

All-Suite A type of hotel that offers units that include a living room, kitchen, and bedroom.

Amenity Something conducive to comfort or convenience, for example, special soaps or shampoos in a hotel room.

Amtrak The National Railroad Passenger Corporation, a government-subsidized corporation that operates almost all passenger train service in the United States.

AP American Plan. Referring to a hotel rate that includes three meals a day — usually breakfast, lunch, and dinner. Cruises and resorts such as Club Med offer American Plan.

APEX Advance Purchase Excursion fare. A fare or price quoted that requires advance purchase.

ARC Airlines Reporting Corporation. An independent corporation jointly owned by most of the major United States airlines. ARC collects payments for tickets sold by travel agents and distributes the monies to the airlines. ARC also supervises rules governing the appointment of travel agents to sell domestic air transportation.

ARINC Aeronautical Radio Incorporated. The communication network owned by major airlines that links different airline computer systems with each other.

ARTA Association of Retail Travel Agents. A trade association open only to retail travel agents.

ASI American Sightseeing International. The business name of the American Sightseeing Association. The association is composed of local tour operators offering sightseeing tours, transfers, and charter transportation.

ASTA American Society of Travel Agents. A major travel trade association. Its principal membership is composed of United States travel agents, but the organization also includes allied members drawn from all categories of travel suppliers.

ATA Air Transport Association.

ATB Automated Ticket/Boarding pass.

Attraction Natural and man-made features that attract tourists to a destination.

Availability The state of being obtainable, ready for immediate purchase. A CRT shows the availability of a supplier's product.

Back-Office system A computer system used for behind-the-scenes business operations.

Back-to-Back A series of tours or flights on which one group leaves as another group arrives, perhaps using the same aircraft.

Bareboat Charter The chartering of a boat without a crew or provisions.

Batch Mode A way of processing information whereby certain repetitive functions are performed in groups or batches.

B and B Bed and Breakfast. A room rate, in a guest house or private home, that includes sleeping accommodations and a full breakfast.

Berth A bed on a ship, train, or plane. Also, a place for a ship to dock.

Bias The deliberate programming of displays in a computer to favor one airline's service over another's.

Blocked Space Group space reserved on aircraft, cruise ships, in hotels, and so on, by retail agencies, wholesalers, or tour operators, which they hope to resell.

Boarding Pass A permit for the traveler to board or enter a ship, plane, train, or other form of transportation.

Bond Insurance or guarantee that protects a third party. For example, ARC requires each travel agency to purchase a bond to protect the airline in case the agency defaults on payment for tickets issued.

Bow The front or forward portion of a ship.

BP Bermuda plan. A hotel meal plan that includes a full American breakfast but no other meals.

Bridge The navigational and command control center of the ship.

BritRail Pass A pass used for train travel in Great Britain.

Brochure A printed folder that describes a hotel, tour, or package and gives details of the offering.

Buffer Zone A fare-construction term referring to the areas of Canada and Mexico within 225 miles of the continental United States.

Bulk Fare A net-fare contract for a certain number of seats.

Bulkhead A partition on an airplane or ship separating compartments.

Bullet Trains High-speed Japanese trains.

Cabana A small room near the beach or pool, usually separated from the hotel's main building.

Cabin A room on a ship, also called a *stateroom*.

Capacity-Controlled A fare available for only a certain percentage of seats on a flight.

Carrier A company that transports passengers or freight on air, sea, or land.

Central Processing Unit (CPU) That part of the computer in which the work actually takes place; technically, it alone is the computer.

Charter A plane, ship, bus, or other form of transportation used for nonscheduled operations. The verb *to charter* means to obtain the use of such transportation.

Check-In The point at which clients must present tickets, vouchers, and so on, at a hotel, airport, cruise terminal, or tour operator's facility.

Check-Out Formalities, usually including payment, associated with leaving a hotel, motel, resort, and so on.

Checked Baggage Baggage carried in the cargo compartment of an airplane and not accessible to a passenger during the flight. The passenger receives a receipt when the baggage is checked in.

Circle Trip A round-trip journey in which the outbound routing, class of service, and/or airline are not the same as on the return routing, service, and/or airline.

Class of Service The interior of an aircraft is divided into sections, each with a different level of service and amenities. Common classes of service are first, business, and coach.

CLIA Cruise Lines International Association. An organization offering promotional materials, training guides, reference books, and seminars on behalf of cruise lines. CLIA appoints travel agencies to sell cruises and receive commissions on behalf of the steamship companies that are members of the association.

Co-Host An airline that purchases the right to preferential display in another carrier's automated reservations system.

Commission The amount that a travel agent receives from a supplier for selling transportation, accommodations, or other services.

Common-Rated A fare-construction term referring to destinations having the same fare.

Concierge The hotel employee who attends to guests' needs for special information, theater and restaurant reservations, or any other requests.

Conditional Stopover A stopover restricted in some way, either by government or airline fare agreements.

Condominium An apartment, villa, townhouse, or hotel space rented from a company acting on behalf of the owner. Rental includes access to all the amenities of the development.

Conference An association of suppliers formed to establish rules and procedures to facilitate dealing with each other and their agents. Also, a meeting usually established to deal with a problem.

Configuration The arrangement of seats, bathrooms, galleys, and other areas inside a plane or motorcoach.

Confirmation Verification of a confirmed reservation either orally or in writing. Most confirmations are subject to certain conditions.

Congress An international gathering.

Connecting Any two things that are directly linked to each other. Connecting flights enable a client to change planes to complete a journey. Connecting rooms or cabins allow guests to move from one to another without going out in the hall.

Consortium A group of independent companies that join together to gain greater profits.

Consulate A branch office of an embassy that is located in a major city other than the capital.

Continental Breakfast A light breakfast of coffee, rolls, butter and jam, and sometimes juice.

Control Tower The area from which air-traffic controllers direct planes in the air and on the ground.

Convention A meeting involving a general group session usually followed by committee meetings in breakout sessions.

Convention and Visitors Bureau An organization that promotes travel to the city it represents and assists in servicing conventions and trade shows held in the city.

Co-op Advertising Advertising that promotes and is sponsored by two or more companies.

Corporate Rate A special rate negotiated between a supplier and employees of large companies.

Couchette A sleeping berth in a publicly shared compartment on an international train. Typically, a compartment has four first-class or six second-class couchettes.

Courier A term used in Europe as a synonym for *tour escort.*

CP Continental Plan. A hotel rate that includes continental breakfast.

CRS Computer Reservations System. A computer system that provides information about schedules, seat availability, and fares, and permits travel agents to make reservations and print itineraries and tickets.

CRT Cathode Ray Tube. The computer screen that displays information and permits communication with the central computer's data base.

CTO Caribbean Travel Organization. An organization supported by various Caribbean governments to promote tourism to the region.

CTC Certified Travel Counselor. A designation awarded by the Institute of Certified Travel Agents to travel professionals with five years or more industry experience who have completed a two-year, graduate-level travel management program.

Currency Code A three-letter code for the monetary unit of a country.

Cursor A symbol on the CRT screen that indicates the next position in which the computer will display something.

Customs The government agency, domestic or foreign, charged with collecting duty (taxes) on specific imported items and restricting the entry of forbidden items.

Day-Rate A special rate for use of a hotel room by day only.

DBA Doing Business As. Used when the corporate name is different from the business name.

Deadheading Operating any vehicle, plane, or ship empty to reposition it.

Debarkation Getting off a ship, plane, train, and so on.

Dedicated Line A communications line. For example, a telephone line devoted to one use, linking something such as a travel agency's CRT to an airline's central computer.

Demographics Statistics and facts, such as age, sex, marital status, occupation, and income, that describes a human population.

Denied Boarding The practice of refusing to accept confirmed passengers, usually because space is filled by the time they arrive at the check-in point. These passengers may or may not be eligible for compensation, depending on the circumstances.

Departure Tax A tax that visitors to a country must pay when they leave the country.

Deposit The partial payment required to confirm a reservation.

Deregulation Removal of government control over the operation of an industry.

Dine-Around Plan A meal plan that allows guests to dine at a variety of restaurants using vouchers.

Direct Flight A flight from origin to destination that makes one or more intermediate stops. Passengers do not have to change planes. (Also called a *through flight.*)

Discretionary Travel Travel undertaken voluntarily.

Documentation Papers used to identify travelers.

DOT Department of Transportation. The federal agency of the United States that regulates domestic transportation.

Double A hotel room with one double bed. Sometimes used to mean a room designed to accommodate two people.

Double Booking The practice of making reservations for two or more identical sets of arrangements as a type of insurance. Considered unethical by travel agents and carriers.

Double/Double Hotel room with two double beds.

Double Occupancy Hotel accommodations for two people sharing a room.

Downgrade To move a passenger to a lower class of service or accommodations.

Downtime Period when a computer is not operating.

Drop-Off Charge A fee charged for dropping a rental car at a different location from where it was picked up.

Duty-Free Shop An airport store in which departing international passengers may purchase items free of import duty (tax).

Efficiency A hotel or motel room with housekeeping facilities, usually including a stove, refrigerator, and sink.

Embarkation The process of boarding a ship, plane, train, and so on.

Embassy The official residence of an ambassador in a foreign capital.

Emigration The process of leaving one country to settle in another.

English Breakfast A full breakfast that could include fruit or juice, cereal, bacon, eggs, sausage, toast, butter, marmalade, and tea or coffee.

Enhancement An improvement to an existing computer reservations system.

EP European Plan. A hotel rate that excludes meals.

Escrow Account An account supervised by a bank or a financial institution. Funds paid into the account are frozen for safekeeping until the service has been provided.

ETA Estimated Time of Arrival.

ETD Estimated Time of Departure.

Excess Baggage Baggage in excess of specified size or weight of a particular carrier.

Excursion A journey where the traveler returns to the original point of departure.

Extension An optional addition to specified arrangements.

FAA Federal Aviation Administration. The agency of the United States Department of Transportation responsible for civil aviation. The FAA concentrates on passenger safety, aircraft certification, pilot licensing, and air-traffic control.

Familiarization Trip (Fam Trip) Trips designed for travel agents to acquaint them with a destination and its facilities or with a particular travel product.

Family Plan A hotel rate that allows children to stay in a room with their parents at no additional charge.

Fare Construction The process of computing airfares.

FAX A machine that allows the transmittal of facsimiles of documents from one location to another.

FIT Foreign Independent Tour. A custom-designed, prepaid tour with many individual components.

Flag Carrier Any carrier designated by a country to serve its international routes. Most countries have only one official flag carrier. The United States has many.

Flight Coupon A section of the airline ticket. The passenger must have one coupon to present to the airline gate agent for each flight involving a separate aircraft.

Fly/Drive A package that includes air transportation and use of a rental car.

Forward At or near the front part, as of a ship.

Free Sale The ability to confirm a reservation without consulting the supplier. Free-sale reservations will be honored provided the supplier is notified within a specified time.

Frequent-Flyer Program An airline program that allows travelers discounts, upgrades, or free tickets for traveling a number of miles on an airline.

Frequent-Stay Program A program that awards discounts or upgrades to travelers who use a particular hotel chain frequently.

Galley A kitchen on a ship or plane.

Gateway The city, airport, or area from which a flight or tour departs.

GIT Group Inclusive Tour. An airfare available to individual clients who purchase a tour package and its included features.

GMT Greenwich Mean Time. The reference point for the world's time zones as measured from Greenwich, England.

Gratuity A tip. Optional payment for services, as to a waiter or chambermaid.

Ground Time The time spent on the ground waiting for connecting flights.

GRT Gross Registered Tonnage. A measurement of a ship's enclosed space.

Guaranteed Air Fare A fare, guaranteed not to increase, charged for tickets purchased in advance. A cancellation or change may involve a financial penalty.

Guaranteed Departure A statement by a tour operator that a tour will depart no matter what.

Gulf A large body of salt water that is bordered by a curved shoreline.

Hardware The name for pieces of physical equipment used in the automation process. A CRT is considered hardware, for example.

Head Tax A fee some countries charge each arriving or departing passenger.

History Computer jargon signifying the record of reservation changes.

Hospitality Suite A room, or suite, in a hotel used for entertaining during meetings or conventions.

Host System An airline's computer reservations system (CRS) that is marketed to agencies.

Hotel Representative A person or company that represents a hotel, accepting group and single reservations, distributing literature, and assisting in the hotel's promotion to the public.

Hotel Staff That part of a hotel's or cruise ship's staff concerned with serving clients/passengers directly.

Hovercraft A high-speed boat that rides on a cushion of air over the waves.

Hub-and-Spoke The airline practice of using certain cities as connecting centers for feeder flights.

Hydrofoil A high-speed boat whose entire hull is raised clear of the water when moving and is supported by fins or foils.

IATA International Air Transport Association. An association of international airlines whose aim is to create order and stability in the international aviation community. Headquarters are in Geneva.

IATAN International Airlines Travel Agent Network. The organization that appoints United States travel agencies to sell tickets for international airlines serving the United States. IATAN is a private, not-for-profit, wholly-owned corporation, operating as a financially self-sufficient subsidiary of IATA.

ICTA Institute of Certified Travel Agents. Located in Wellesley, Massachusetts, ICTA is a nonprofit organization providing educational resources for the travel industry. ICTA administers the CTC and the Destination Specialist programs.

Immigration The formalities associated with entering a country.

Inaugural The first service over a new route or with new equipment.

Inbound Travel Return travel from the destination back to the original point of departure. Also refers to foreign travelers visiting the United States.

Incentive Trip A trip offered as a prize or bonus for superior performance. Certain travel companies specialize in incentive trips, setting up contests to promote sales so that superior performers may win incentive trips.

Incidentals Personal items such as dry cleaning, telephone calls, and bar bills that are usually excluded from the price of a tour, hotel room, or cruise.

Infrastructure The network of highways, utilities, airports, entertainment, stores, and so on, that makes tourism possible.

In-Plant A branch of a travel firm located on the premises of another company, servicing the travel needs of that company only.

Inside Sales Sales efforts inside the travel agency.

Interface Links between different computer systems that allow the systems to communicate with each other.

Interline Agreements Agreements between two or more airlines covering the transportation of passengers and the transportation and transfer of baggage. Interline agreements allow a passenger flying on two different airlines to use just one ticket.

Island A body of land completely surrounded by water.

IT Number Inclusive Tour Number. The code used to identify a tour that conforms to IATA regulations.

Itinerary A planned route for a trip.

Joint Fare A special through fare that permits travel on two or more different airlines.

Junior Suite A large hotel room usually with a partition separating the bedroom from the sitting area.

Kilometer A measure equal to 3,280 feet, or 5/8 of a mile.

Knot A measurement of speed at sea: 20 knots=23 miles per hour.

Lanai A room with a balcony or patio that is close to or overlooks water or a garden. The term originated in Hawaii, originally referring to a porch furnished as a living room.

Latitude Parallel lines measuring distances north or south of the equator.

Leeward The direction away from the wind. The leeward side of an island is the less windy side. The Leeward Islands are a group in the Caribbean.

Leg The portion of a journey between two scheduled stops.

Lido A term used internationally for a fashionable beach resort.

Load Factor The ratio, expressed as a percentage, of carrier capacity sold to total capacity offered for sale.

Local Currency The currency designated as legal tender within a country.

Longitude Parallel lines that measure distances east and west of the prime meridian.

Lower A berth on a ship or train that is underneath another berth.

Manifest A passenger list.

MAP Modified American Plan. A hotel rate that includes two meals, usually breakfast and dinner.

Marketing Determining what product to sell how, where, and to whom.

Market Research The gathering and analyzing of information.

Maximum Permitted Mileage (MPM) The maximum amount of air miles allowed between two cities. Established by working committees of IATA.

MCO Miscellaneous Charges Order. An accountable document issued by a travel agent or an airline as proof of payment for specific surface transportation, land arrangements for inclusive tours, car rental, hotels, and deposits.

Meeting Assistance The services of a local representative to help travelers on arrival at an airport, train station, and so on.

Mid-Centric Personality A type of personality who enjoys traveling to familiar destinations.

Midships (Amidships) The center of a ship from front to back. Generally used in reference to the middle of a ship.

Mileage The cost of an international air ticket is typically related to the distance flown. Mileage is the term used to express distance.

MPI Meeting Planners International. A professional educational association for corporate and association meeting planners.

Multi-Access A computerized reservations system that permits the user direct access to the data base of more than one carrier.

Murphy Bed A bed that folds into the wall when not in use.

Net Rate A rate given by a wholesaler to a retailer to which the retailer adds a markup before selling the product to a customer.

Non-stop A flight from origin city to destination city with no intermediate stops.

No-Rec No Record. When a supplier can find no record of a reservation for a client who holds tickets that indicates all is in order, this situation is called a no-rec.

No-Show An airline passenger or hotel guest who fails to use or to cancel a reservation.

NTA National Tour Association. A trade association of United States tour operators and wholesalers. Members operate within the United States and Canada.

NTO National Tourist Office. An agency sponsored by the government of its country, dedicated to promoting tourism and shaping tourism policy.

NTSB National Transportation Safety Board. An autonomous government agency that develops safety standards for all public transportation and investigates accidents.

Observation Car A railroad car specially designed for sightseeing.

Occupancy Rate The percentage of the total number of available beds or rooms actually occupied.

Off-Line Referring to a destination that a carrier does not serve.

One Way A trip from origin to destination with no return to origin city. A one-way trip can be made on one or more flights.

On-Line Referring to a destination that a carrier serves.

Open Jaw A trip essentially of a round-trip nature but different because the trip includes a surface segment.

Open Ticket A ticket that is valid for transportation between certain points but has no specific flight reservation.

Option A tour activity offered at extra cost.

Option Date The date by which a person must make a financial commitment to an airline, cruise line, or tour operator or lose the space.

Outbound Travel from the point of departure to the farthest destination.

Outside Salesperson A travel industry salesperson who works outside the office to generate group or individual business.

Overbooking The practice of accepting more reservations than there are airline seats or hotel rooms available to ensure against no-shows. Hotels that are overbooked usually try to find alternative but equal accommodations for a client.

Override Additional commission paid to agents as a bonus for productivity and/or volume or as an incentive to book particular arrangements.

Package A number of arrangements put together and sold at a single, all-inclusive price.

Parlor Car A railroad car, and sometimes a motorcoach, with individual swivel seats and food and bar service.

Passport The basic official document issued by a person's own country, necessary for travel to most foreign countries.

PATA Pacific Area Travel Association. Organization of government and business representatives that promotes travel to the Pacific area.

Per Diem Per Day. A daily charge, or the cost of the whole divided by the number of days to obtain an average daily cost.

Pitch The distance between rows of seats on an aircraft. Also, the rise and fall of a ship at sea.

PNR Passenger Name Record. The computer term for the automated client file.

POE Port of Embarkation.

Point to Point Refers to the fare-construction principle of charging from one stopover point to another.

Port The left side of a ship when you are facing the bow. Also, the place in which ships dock.

Port Charges Charges levied by a port on each arriving or departing passenger. Port charges are not typically included in the cruise price.

Porterage The handling of baggage at airports and in hotels. Usually included in the cost of a tour for a specified number of bags only.

Positioning Moving an aircraft, ship, bus, or other transport vehicle to another location.

Pre-Registration The completion of the registration paperwork process before a guest's arrival. This service is useful for handling tours and meeting groups.

Principal The owner of a travel business: airline, hotel, cruise line, travel agency, and so on.

Printer The piece of computer hardware that prints the information stored in the computer onto the ticket, invoice, or voucher.

Promotional Fare A fare designed to attract passengers who would not otherwise travel.

Proof of Citizenship A document that establishes nationality to the satisfaction of a foreign government. Such a document is necessary for obtaining a passport.

Pseudo-PNR A phrase used to describe information stored in an airline computer using a PNR format. It does not include an air reservation but deals with cars, hotels, tours, cruises, insurance, and so on.

PTA Prepaid Ticket Advice. A form used when an individual in one city wishes to pay for an air ticket to be picked up by an individual in another city.

Psychocentric Personality A type of personality who does not travel far from home.

Pullman A sleeping car on a train.

Qualifier The person in each travel agency who qualifies the office to open and stay open for business by meeting ARC's requirements for demonstrated knowledge and experience.

Queue A computer's electronic tickler file.

Rack Rate The official posted rate for each hotel room.

Rate Desk The department of an airline in which complex airfares are computed.

Reception Agent A tour operator or travel agency that specializes in providing services to incoming passengers. Also known as the *ground operator*.

Reconfirmation Particularly on international air itineraries, passengers are required to indicate their intention of using the next leg of their itinerary by contacting the appropriate carrier before departure.

Registry The country under whose laws a ship and its owners are obliged to comply.

Repositioning Cruise A cruise that transfers a ship from one cruising area to another between seasons.

Responsibility Clause The section of a brochure that details the conditions under which the brochure's arrangements are offered for sale.

Return In Europe, a round trip.

Revalidation The authorized alteration of a ticket or other document.

Revalidation Sticker A sticker placed on a ticket to indicate an authorized change.

ROE Rate of Exchange.

Roll The sway of a ship from side to side.

Round Trip A trip that begins and ends in the same city. In strictest terms, a round trip describes a trip from an originating city to a destination city and back via exactly the same routing and using the same carrier.

Routings Airline road maps. A list of the intermediate points between origin and destination cities in geographical sequence.

Run-of-the-House (ROH) A flat rate for which a hotel offers any of its available rooms to a group.

Satellite Ticket Printer A machine that allows travel agents to send tickets electronically to a client.

SATH Society for Advancement of Travel for the Handicapped. An organization that provides information and advice to people organizing tours for travelers with disabilities.

Scheduled Transportation Service operated in accordance with a published timetable.

Seasonal Rates A pricing structure that allows prices to vary depending on the time of year or consumer demand.

Seat Rotation A system used on motorcoach tours to ensure that passengers have an equal opportunity to sit up front. Passengers change seats frequently according to a pre-announced pattern.

Sector The portion of travel between two fare-break points. Sectors are made up of one or more segments, or legs.

Segment A leg, or group of legs, of essentially continuous travel.

Service Charge A fee added to a bill, usually in a hotel or restaurant, to cover the cost of certain services as a substitute for tipping. Also, an advertised fee that agencies may elect to charge clients for services.

Shell A brochure provided by a supplier, complete with artwork and graphics, but with space for a travel agency or tour operator to imprint an itinerary, price, and booking information.

Shore Excursions Land tours of ports of call sold by cruise lines or tour operators to cruise passengers.

Shuttle Continuous bus transportation between airport terminals or a no-reservation, guaranteed air service on heavily traveled routes.

Sine A set of initials or numbers that constitutes a reservation agent's identification symbol.

Single Accommodations designed for one person, or in Europe, a one-way journey or ticket.

Single Supplement The additional amount charged the single traveler for a private hotel room or cruise cabin.

SITE Society of Incentive Travel Executives.

Slot The time a plane lands, is at a gate, and then departs.

Software Computer programs that tell the machines how to manage data.

Space Availability of seats or accommodations.

Space Available Confirmation of a reservation, subject to availability at the last moment.

Split Charter A charter shared by several groups.

SS Steamship. This abbreviation precedes a ship's name.

Stabilizer A device on a ship that is used to reduce and eliminate roll (side-to-side movement).

Standard Ticket An air ticket issued by travel agents that is valid for travel on any ARC member airline and on other designated carriers.

Standby A passenger on a waitlist, or one prepared to travel if space becomes available at the last moment.

Starboard The right side of a ship when you are facing the bow.

Stateroom A cabin on a ship.

Step-on-Guide The guide who steps on a motorcoach at a destination to give the local sightseeing tour. Also called a *local guide*.

Stern The very rear of the ship.

Stopover An international interruption of a journey. In the United States, a stopover occurs when a passenger arrives at a transfer point and fails to depart within four hours.

Studio A hotel room with couches that convert into beds.

Supplement An additional charge for special needs. The price of most tours is based on double occupancy, and single passengers pay a supplement.

Supplemental Carrier An airline that offers charter service only.

Supplier The source of travel arrangements: an airline, hotel, cruise line, car-rental firm, tour operator, and so on.

Surcharge An additional payment imposed by a supplier, either at certain times of the year, or to meet exceptional circumstances (rising fuel prices), or to provide special arrangements for a client.

Surface Segment Referring to a section of trip itinerary traveled on land in combination with airline flights.

Table D'Hote A complete meal of several courses offered at a fixed price. Sometimes called *prix fixe*.

Tariff A published fare or rate. Tariff is also used to describe the supplier's official publication containing fares, rates, and the rules that govern their applicability.

Teleticketing The issuing of airline tickets by a machine connected to an airline reservations system.

Tender A boat used when docking is not possible to transport passengers from ship to shore and back.

TBA To Be Assigned, or Advised. When specific arrangements are pending confirmation or cannot be confirmed in advance.

TGV Tres Grande Vitesse: high-speed French trains.

Terminal Another word for a desk-top computer.

Theme Park Man-made tourist attractions, such as Disneyland, Disney World, Knott's Berry Farm.

Through Fare A fare between two cities that is constructed over intermediate connecting and/or stop-over cities.

Throwaway An item in a tour or land package that the passenger pays for but does not intend to use. Usually included to qualify the passenger for a lower airfare.

Ticket When completed and validated correctly, the ticket is the contract of carriage between a carrier and the customer.

Ticketing Deadline The date by which a person must pay for a ticket or lose the reservation.

Ticket Imprinter A device that validates a manually written ticket with the date of issue, the identification of the issuing agent, and the name of the carrier for which the ticket is issued.

Ticket Stock Blank airline tickets used by airlines and travel agencies that become contracts of carriage upon proper completion.

Time Sharing A condominium concept whereby clients purchase the use of accommodations for a certain period each year. Other people own the space during the rest of the year.

Tour-Basing Fare An airfare available to passengers who purchase tours.

Tour Escort The individual who accompanies a tour throughout and is responsible for its smooth operation. Also called *tour manager,* or *courier.*

Tour Guide The individual with a special knowledge of a destination who joins the tour only while it visits that one area. Also called a *local,* or *step-on, guide.*

Tourist Card A kind of visa issued to travelers before they enter certain countries. This card may or may not be required in addition to a passport or other proof of citizenship.

Tour Leader Strictly speaking, an expert lecturer or specialist whose reputation attracts tour participants. Loosely used as an equivalent of a tour escort.

Tour Operator The company that organizes the travel components into prepackaged, inclusive arrangements and then sells these tours through travel agencies. Often used interchangeably with *tour wholesaler.*

Tour Organizer An individual who organizes a group tour. The organizer can be a professional travel agent or outside salesperson, or an officer or member of a group who has no professional ties to the travel industry.

Tour Wholesaler A company that packages tour components for later sale through retail outlets. Often used interchangeably with *tour operator.*

Transfer Transportation between airports, docks, railroad stations, and hotels.

Travel Agent An individual working in the travel industry, serving as a counselor to the traveling public and as a salesperson of the travel product for industry suppliers.

Twin A hotel room with two beds, designed for two persons.

UATP Universal Air Travel Plan. An airline-sponsored credit-card system.

Upgrade To move to a better class of airline service, cruise cabin, or hotel room.

Upper A berth on a ship or train above another berth.

USTOA United States Tour Operators Association. A trade association of tour operators who are based in the United States, offer tours all over the world, and work mainly through retail travel agents.

Validate To imprint an airline document with the identifying mark of an airline or agency. This procedure is necessary to make a ticket a legal document.

VAT Value-Added Tax. Government-imposed tax.

Visa A permit to enter a foreign country, issued by the government of that country. Recorded in a person's passport.

Voucher Documents issued to confirm arrangements. Vouchers may be used to introduce clients, confirm a deposit, or indicate full prepayment.

Waitlist A list of people seeking a travel service that is sold out. As other clients cancel, waitlisted clients are confirmed in the order in which their reservations were received.

WHO World Health Organization. An agency of the United Nations that reports on communicable diseases and health conditions around the world and advises governments on vaccination requirements.

Windjammer A sailboat with multiple sails.

Windward Toward the wind, to the direction from which the wind blows.

WTO World Tourism Organization. With headquarters in Madrid, Spain, the WTO is a member organization of national tourism organizations.

Yacht A boat specifically used for private pleasure excursions.

Yield Average amount of revenue earned per passenger mile; computed by dividing total passenger revenue by the total number of passenger miles flown.

Index

An Exclusive Career Opportunity

The Travel Career Development Test Certificate

Students who complete a course of study using *Travel Career Development* have a unique opportunity for career advancement. It's the Travel Career Development Test Certificate.

When students pass the Travel Career Development Test, they receive ICTA's Travel Career Development Test Certificate — a nationally recognized travel industry credential. ICTA circulates the names of certificate recipients among travel professionals nationwide. Here's how the process works:

Step One

Students complete a course that is based chiefly on *Travel Career Development*.

Step Two

Students who want to participate in the testing program fill out an Application for Testing (see next page) and pay a $25 administrative fee. The instructor then submits the applications along with a Test Request Form to ICTA's headquarters located at 148 Linden Street, PO Box 812059, Wellesley, MA 02181-0012.

Step Three

Instructors receive and administer copies of the Travel Career Development Test. The test consists of 100 multiple-choice questions, and students have up to two hours to complete it.

Instructors return completed tests to ICTA for scoring. ICTA awards a passing grade to students who earn a score of 70 percent or better.

Step Four

Students who earn a passing grade receive the Travel Career Development Test Certificate from their instructor. The certificate is recognized by travel industry employers nationwide. ICTA also publicizes the names of certificate recipients among industry professionals. The certificate gives beginning travel professionals a competitive edge in the marketplace.

Application For Testing

I understand that:

1. I must submit $25 to my instructor to be eligible to take the Travel Career Development Test.

2. I will be allowed up to two (2) hours to complete the exam that consists of 100 multiple-choice questions.

3. To earn a passing grade I must score 70 percent or better.

4. I will receive the Travel Career Development Test Certificate when I earn a passing grade.

5. If I miss my assigned test date for any reason, I will be charged $25 to reschedule. If I fail the test, I may retest for $15. All application fees are nonrefundable.

When I earn a passing grade, my score will be mailed to my instructor along with the Travel Career Development Test Completion Certificate.

_____

Signature   Date

_____

Name   (Please print your name as you want it on your certificate.)

_____

Address

_____

City   State   Zip

_____

School

_____

City   State

 Institute of Certified Travel Agents
148 Linden Street, P. O. Box 812059, Wellesley, MA 02181-0012

RAND McNALLY

QUICK
REFERENCE

WORLD
ATLAS

Contents

Quick Reference World Atlas
Copyright © 1995 by Rand McNally & Company.

Printed in the United States of America

Library of Congress Catalog Number: 95-067031

World Political Information Table

This table gives the area, population, population density, political status, capital, and predominant languages for every country in the world. The political units listed are categorized by political status in the form of government column of the table, as follows: A—independent countries; B—internally independent political entities which are under the protection of another country in matters of defense and foreign affairs; C—colonies and other dependent political units; and D—the major administrative subdivisions of Australia, Canada, China, the United Kingdom, and the United States. For comparison, the table also includes the continents and the world. All footnotes appear at the end of the table.

The populations are estimates for January 1, 1994, made by Rand McNally on the basis of official data, United Nations estimates, and other available information. Area figures include inland water.

Region or Political Division	Area Sq. Mi.	Est. Pop. 1/1/94	Pop. Per. Sq. Mi.	Form of Government and Ruling Power	Capital	Predominant Languages
Afars and Issas see Djibouti						
† Afghanistan	251,826	16,595,000	66	Islamic republic................................A	Kābul	Dari, Pashto, Uzbek, Turkmen
Africa	11,700,000	683,700,000	58			
Alabama	52,423	4,202,000	80	State (U.S.)	Montgomery	English
Alaska	656,424	597,000	0.9	State (U.S.)	Juneau	English, indigenous
† Albania	11,100	3,424,000	308	Republic................................A	Tiranë	Albanian, Greek
Alberta	255,287	2,599,000	10	Province (Canada)................................D	Edmonton	English
† Algeria	919,595	26,780,000	29	Provisional military government..........A	Algiers (El Djazaïr)	Arabic, Berber dialects, French
American Samoa	77	53,000	688	Unincorporated territory (U.S.)..........C	Pago Pago	Samoan, English
† Andorra	175	58,000	331	Parliamentary co-principality (Spanish and French)................................B	Andorra	Catalan, Spanish (Castilian), French
† Angola	481,354	11,040,000	23	Republic................................A	Luanda	Portuguese, indigenous
Anguilla	35	7,000	200	Dependent territory (U.K. protection)......B	The Valley	English
Anhui	53,668	58,850,000	1,097	Province (China)................................D	Hefei	Chinese (Mandarin)
Antarctica	5,400,000	(1)				
† Antigua and Barbuda	171	64,000	374	Parliamentary state................................A	St. John's	English, local dialects
† Argentina	1,073,519	33,635,000	31	Republic................................A	Buenos Aires and Viedma (4)	Spanish, English, Italian, German, French
Arizona	114,006	3,943,000	35	State (U.S.)	Phoenix	English
Arkansas	53,182	2,438,000	46	State (U.S.)	Little Rock	English
† Armenia	11,506	3,743,000	325	Republic................................A	Yerevan	Armenian, Russian
Aruba	75	68,000	907	Self-governing territory (Netherlands protection)................................B	Oranjestad	Dutch, Papiamento, English, Spanish
Ascension	34	1,000	29	Dependency (St. Helena)................................C	Georgetown	English
Asia	17,300,000	3,385,900,000	196			
† Australia	2,966,155	17,950,000	6.1	Federal parliamentary state..............A	Canberra	English, indigenous
Australian Capital Territory	927	303,000	327	Territory (Australia)................................D	Canberra	English
† Austria	32,377	7,913,000	244	Federal republic................................A	Vienna (Wien)	German
† Azerbaijan	33,436	7,481,000	224	Republic................................A	Baku (Bakı)	Azeri, Russian, Armenian
† Bahamas	5,382	270,000	50	Parliamentary state................................A	Nassau	English, Creole
† Bahrain	267	572,000	2,142	Monarchy................................A	Al Manāmah	Arabic, English, Farsi, Urdu
† Bangladesh	55,598	115,240,000	2,073	Republic................................A	Dhaka	Bangla, English
† Barbados	166	260,000	1,566	Parliamentary state................................A	Bridgetown	English
Beijing (Peking)	6,487	11,365,000	1,752	Autonomous city (China)..............D	Beijing (Peking)	Chinese (Mandarin)
† Belarus	80,155	10,380,000	129	Republic................................A	Minsk	Belarussian, Russian
Belau see Palau						
† Belgium	11,783	10,050,000	853	Constitutional monarchy................................A	Brussels (Bruxelles)	Dutch (Flemish), French, German
† Belize	8,866	205,000	23	Parliamentary state................................A	Belmopan	English, Spanish, Mayan, Garifuna
† Benin	43,475	5,292,000	122	Republic................................A	Porto-Novo and Cotonou	French, Fon, Yoruba, indigenous
Bermuda	21	76,000	3,619	Dependent territory (U.K.)................................C	Hamilton	English
† Bhutan	17,954	1,707,000	95	Monarchy (Indian protection)..........B	Thimphu	Dzongkha, Tibetan and Nepalese dialects
† Bolivia	424,165	7,582,000	18	Republic................................A	La Paz and Sucre	Aymara, Quechua, Spanish
† Bosnia and Herzegovina	19,741	4,442,000	225	Republic................................A	Sarajevo	Serbo-Croatian
† Botswana	224,711	1,424,000	6.3	Republic................................A	Gaborone	English, Tswana
† Brazil	3,286,500	151,310,000	46	Federal republic................................A	Brasília	Portuguese, Spanish, English, French
British Columbia	365,948	3,354,000	9.2	Province (Canada)................................D	Victoria	English
British Indian Ocean Territory	23	(1)		Dependent territory (U.K.)................................C		English
British Virgin Islands	59	13,000	220	Dependent territory (U.K.)................................C	Road Town	English
† Brunei	2,226	279,000	125	Monarchy................................A	Bandar Seri Begawan	Malay, English, Chinese
† Bulgaria	42,855	8,813,000	206	Republic................................A	Sofia (Sofiya)	Bulgarian, Turkish
† Burkina Faso	105,869	9,922,000	94	Republic................................A	Ouagadougou	French, indigenous
Burma see Myanmar						
† Burundi	10,745	6,015,000	560	Republic................................A	Bujumbura	French, Kirundi, Swahili
California	163,707	31,905,000	195	State (U.S.)	Sacramento	English
† Cambodia	69,898	10,010,000	143	Transitional government................................A	Phnum Pénh (Phnom Penh)	Khmer, French
† Cameroon	183,568	12,845,000	70	Republic................................A	Yaoundé	English, French, indigenous
† Canada	3,849,674	27,950,000	7.3	Federal parliamentary state..............A	Ottawa	English, French
† Cape Verde	1,557	414,000	266	Republic................................A	Praia	Portuguese, Crioulo
Cayman Islands	100	32,000	320	Dependent territory (U.K.)................................C	George Town	English
† Central African Republic	240,535	3,089,000	13	Republic................................A	Bangui	French, Sango, Arabic, indigenous
Ceylon see Sri Lanka						
† Chad	495,755	6,149,000	12	Republic................................A	N'Djamena	Arabic, French, indigenous
Channel Islands	75	149,000	1,987	Dependent territory (U.K.)................................B		English, French
† Chile	292,135	13,795,000	47	Republic................................A	Santiago	Spanish
† China (excl. Taiwan)	3,689,631	1,184,060,000	321	Socialist republic................................A	Beijing (Peking)	Chinese dialects

Region or Political Division	Area Sq. Mi.	Est. Pop. 1/1/94	Pop. Per. Sq. Mi.	Form of Government and Ruling Power		Capital	Predominant Languages
Christmas Island	52	1,300	25	External territory (Australia)	C	The Settlement	English, Chinese, Malay
Cocos (Keeling) Islands	5.4	600	111	Territory (Australia)	C	West Island	English, Cocos-Malay, Malay
† Colombia	440,831	35,085,000	80	Republic	A	Bogotá	Spanish
Colorado	104,100	3,528,000	34	State (U.S.)	D	Denver	English
† Comoros (excl. Mayotte)	863	508,000	589	Federal Islamic republic	A	Moroni	Arabic, French, Comoran
† Congo	132,047	2,403,000	18	Republic	A	Brazzaville	French, Lingala, Kikongo, indigenous
Connecticut	5,544	3,272,000	590	State (U.S.)	D	Hartford	English
Cook Islands	91	19,000	209	Self-governing territory (New Zealand protection)	B	Avarua	English, Maori
† Costa Rica	19,730	3,285,000	166	Republic	A	San José	Spanish
† Cote d'Ivoire	124,518	13,930,000	112	Republic	A	Abidjan and Yamoussoukro (4)	French, Dioula and other indigenous
† Croatia	21,829	4,796,000	220	Republic	A	Zagreb	Sebo-Croatian
† Cuba	42,804	11,015,000	257	Socialist republic	A	Havana (La Habana)	Spanish
† Cyprus	2,276	574,000	252	Republic	A	Nicosia (Levkosía)	Greek, English
Cyprus, North (2)	1,295	193,000	149	Republic	A	Nicosia (Lefkoşa)	Turkish
† Czech Republic	30,450	10,400,000	342	Republic	A	Prague (Praha)	Czech, Slovak
Delaware	2,489	700,000	281	State (U.S.)	D	Dover	English
† Denmark	16,639	5,181,000	311	Constitutional monarchy	A	Copenhagen (København)	Danish
District of Columbia	68	576,000	8,471	Federal district (U.S.)	D	Washington	English
† Djibouti	8,958	579,000	65	Republic	A	Djibouti	French, Arabic, Somali, Afar
† Dominica	305	87,000	285	Republic	A	Roseau	English, French
† Dominican Republic	18,704	7,715,000	412	Republic	A	Santo Domingo	Spanish
† Ecuador	105,037	10,515,000	100	Republic	A	Quito	Spanish, Quechua, indigenous
† Egypt	386,662	56,820,000	147	Socialist republic	A	Cairo (Al Qāhirah)	Arabic
Ellice Islands see Tuvalu							
† El Salvador	8,124	5,179,000	637	Republic	A	San Salvador	Spanish, Nahua
England	50,352	48,320,000	960	Administrative division (U.K.)	D	London	English
† Equatorial Guinea	10,831	379,000	35	Republic	A	Malabo	Spanish, indigenous, English
† Eritrea	36,170	3,540,000	98	Republic	A	Asmera	Tigre, Kunama, Cushitic dialects, Nora Bana, Arabic
† Estonia	17,413	1,608,000	92	Republic	A	Tallinn	Estonian, Latvian, Lithuanian, Russian
† Ethiopia	446,953	54,170,000	121	Provisional military government	A	Addis Ababa	Amharic, Tigrinya, Orominga, Guaraginga, Somali, Arabic
Europe	3,800,000	709,300,000	187				
Faeroe Islands	540	48,000	89	Self-governing territory (Danish protection)	B	Tórshavn	Danish, Faroese
Falkland Islands (3)	4,700	2,200	0.5	Dependent territory (U.K.)	C	Stanley	English
† Fiji	7,056	759,000	108	Republic	A	Suva	English, Fijian, Hindustani
† Finland	130,559	5,056,000	39	Republic	A	Helsinki (Helsingfors)	Finnish, Swedish, Lapp, Russian
Florida	65,758	13,855,000	211	State (U.S.)	D	Tallahassee	English
† France (excl. Overseas Departments)	211,208	57,680,000	273	Republic	A	Paris	French
French Guiana	35,135	134,000	3.8	Overseas department (France)	C	Cayenne	French
French Polynesia	1,359	211,000	155	Overseas territory (France)	C	Papeete	French, Tahitian
Fujian	46,332	31,375,000	677	Province (China)	D	Fuzhou	Chinese dialects
† Gabon	103,347	1,127,000	11	Republic	A	Libreville	French, Fang, indigenous
† Gambia	4,127	919,000	223	Republic	A	Banjul	English, Malinke, Wolof, Fula, indigenous
Gansu	173,746	23,445,000	135	Province (China)	D	Lanzhou	Chinese (Mandarin), Mongolian, Tibetan dialects
Gaza Strip	146	745,000	5,103	Israeli territory with limited self-government			Arabic
Georgia	59,441	6,875,000	116	State (U.S.)	D	Atlanta	English
† Georgia	26,911	5,646,000	210	Republic	A	Tbilisi	Georgian, Russian, Armenian, Azeri
† Germany	137,822	80,930,000	587	Federal republic	A	Berlin and Bonn	German
† Ghana	92,098	16,595,000	180	Republic	A	Accra	English, Akan and other indigenous
Gibraltar	2.3	32,000	13,913	Dependent territory (U.K.)	C	Gibraltar	English, Spanish, Italian, Portuguese, Russian
Gilbert Islands see Kiribati							
Golan Heights	454	29,000	64	Occupied by Israel			Arabic, Hebrew
Great Britain see United Kingdom							
† Greece	50,949	10,500,000	206	Republic	A	Athens (Athínai)	Greek, English, French
Greenland	840,004	57,000	0.1	Self-governing territory (Danish protection)	B	Godthåb	Danish, Greenlandic, Inuit dialects
† Grenada	133	91,000	684	Parliamentary state	A	St. George's	English, French
Guadeloupe (incl. Dependencies)	687	424,000	617	Overseas department (France)	C	Basse-Terre	French, Creole
Guam	209	147,000	703	Unincorporated territory (U.S.)	C	Agana	English, Chamorro, Japanese
Guangdong	68,726	65,830,000	958	Province (China)	D	Guangzhou (Canton)	Chinese dialects, Miao-Yao
Guangxi Zhuangzu	91,236	44,285,000	485	Autonomous region (China)	D	Nanning	Chinese dialects, Thai, Miao-Yao
† Guatemala	42,042	10,510,000	250	Republic	A	Guatemala	Spanish, Amerindian
Guernsey (incl. Dependencies)	30	63,000	2,100	Crown dependency (U.K. protection)	B	St. Peter Port	English, French
† Guinea	94,926	6,274,000	66	Provisional military government	A	Conakry	French, indigenous
† Guinea-Bissau	13,948	1,078,000	77	Republic	A	Bissau	Portuguese, Crioulo, indigenous
Guizhou	65,637	33,985,000	518	Province (China)	D	Guiyang	Chinese (Mandarin), Thai, Miao-Yao
† Guyana	83,000	732,000	8.8	Republic	A	Georgetown	English, indigenous
Hainan	13,127	6,867,000	523	Province (China)	D	Haikou	Chinese, Min, Tai
† Haiti	10,714	6,411,000	598	Provisional military government	A	Port-au-Prince	Creole, French
Hawaii	10,932	1,167,000	107	State (U.S.)	D	Honolulu	English, Hawaiian, Japanese
Hebei	73,359	63,940,000	872	Province (China)	D	Shijiazhuang	Chinese (Mandarin)
Heilongjiang	181,082	36,945,000	204	Province (China)	D	Harbin	Chinese dialects, Mongolian, Tungus
Henan	64,479	89,520,000	1,388	Province (China)	D	Zhengzhou	Chinese (Mandarin)
Holland see Netherlands							
† Honduras	43,277	5,206,000	120	Republic	A	Tegucigalpa	Spanish, indigenous
Hong Kong	414	5,890,000	14,227	Chinese territory under British administration	C	Victoria (Hong Kong)	Chinese (Cantonese), English, Putonghua
Hubei	72,356	56,480,000	781	Province (China)	D	Wuhan	Chinese dialects
Hunan	81,081	63,580,000	784	Province (China)	D	Changsha	Chinese dialects, Miao-Yao
† Hungary	35,919	10,295,000	287	Republic	A	Budapest	Hungarian
† Iceland	39,769	262,000	6.6	Republic	A	Reykjavík	Icelandic
Idaho	83,574	1,089,000	13	State (U.S.)	D	Boise	English
Illinois	57,918	11,750,000	203	State (U.S.)	D	Springfield	English
† India (incl. part of Jammu and Kashmir)	1,237,062	906,770,000	733	Federal republic	A	New Delhi	English, Hindi, Telugu, Bengali, indigenous
Indiana	36,420	5,733,000	157	State (U.S.)	D	Indianapolis	English
† Indonesia	752,410	198,810,000	264	Republic	A	Jakarta	Bahasa Indonesia (Malay), English, Dutch, indigenous

Region or Political Division	Area Sq. Mi.	Est. Pop. 1/1/94	Pop. Per. Sq. Mi.	Form of Government and Ruling Power	Capital	Predominant Languages
Iowa	56,276	2,827,000	50	State (U.S.) ... D	Des Moines	English
† Iran	632,457	63,940,000	101	Islamic republic ... A	Tehrān	Farsi, Turkish dialects, Kurdish
† Iraq	169,235	19,335,000	114	Republic ... A	Baghdād	Arabic, Kurdish, Assyrian, Armenian
† Ireland	27,137	3,563,000	131	Republic ... A	Dublin (Baile Átha Cliath)	English, Irish Gaelic
Isle of Man	221	72,000	326	Crown dependency (U.K. protection) ... B	Douglas	English, Manx Gaelic
† Israel (excl. Occupied Areas)	8,019	4,950,000	617	Republic ... A	Jerusalem (Yerushalayim)	Hebrew, Arabic
† Italy	116,324	56,670,000	487	Republic ... A	Rome (Roma)	Italian, German, French, Slovene
Ivory Coast see Cote d'Ivoire	...	...	...	...	...	...
† Jamaica	4,244	2,538,000	598	Parliamentary state ... A	Kingston	English, Creole
† Japan	145,870	124,840,000	856	Constitutional monarchy ... A	Tōkyō	Japanese
Jersey	45	86,000	1,911	Crown dependency (U.K. protection) ... B	St. Helier	English, French
Jiangsu	39,614	70,210,000	1,772	Province (China) ... D	Nanjing (Nanking)	Chinese dialects
Jiangxi	64,325	39,550,000	615	Province (China) ... D	Nanchang	Chinese dialects
Jilin	72,201	25,815,000	358	Province (China) ... D	Changchun	Chinese (Mandarin), Mongolian, Korean
† Jordan	35,135	3,858,000	110	Constitutional monarchy ... A	'Ammān	Arabic
Kansas	82,282	2,568,000	31	State (U.S.) ... D	Topeka	English
† Kazakhstan	1,049,156	17,190,000	16	Republic ... A	Alma-Ata (Almaty) and Akmola [4]	Kazakh, Russian
Kentucky	40,411	3,813,000	94	State (U.S.) ... D	Frankfort	English
† Kenya	224,961	28,280,000	126	Republic ... A	Nairobi	English, Swahili, indigenous
Kiribati	313	77,000	246	Republic ... A	Bairiki	English, Gilbertese
† Korea, North	46,540	22,735,000	489	Socialist republic ... A	Pyŏngyang	Korean
† Korea, South	38,230	44,250,000	1,157	Republic ... A	Seoul (Sŏul)	Korean
† Kuwait	6,880	1,734,000	252	Constitutional monarchy ... A	Kuwait	Arabic, English
† Kyrgyzstan	76,641	4,645,000	61	Republic ... A	Bishkek	Kirghiz, Russian
† Laos	91,429	4,601,000	50	Socialist republic ... A	Viangchan (Vientiane)	Lao, French, English
† Latvia	24,595	2,556,000	104	Republic ... A	Rīga	Latvian, Russian, Lithuanian
† Lebanon	4,015	3,566,000	888	Republic ... A	Beirut (Bayrūt)	Arabic, French, Armenian, English
† Lesotho	11,720	1,907,000	163	Constitutional monarchy under military rule ... A	Maseru	English, Sesotho, Zulu, Xhosa
Liaoning	56,255	41,325,000	735	Province (China) ... D	Shenyang	Chinese (Mandarin), Mongolian
† Liberia	38,250	2,901,000	76	Republic ... A	Monrovia	English, indigenous
† Libya	679,362	4,917,000	7.2	Socialist republic ... A	Tripoli (Ṭarābulus)	Arabic
† Liechtenstein	62	30,000	484	Constitutional monarchy ... A	Vaduz	German
† Lithuania	25,212	3,777,000	150	Republic ... A	Vilnius	Lithuanian, Polish, Russian
Louisiana	51,843	4,332,000	84	State (U.S.) ... D	Baton Rouge	English
† Luxembourg	998	401,000	402	Constitutional monarchy ... A	Luxembourg	French, Luxembourgish, German
Macao	6.6	380,000	57,576	Chinese territory under Portuguese administration ... C	Macao	Portuguese, Chinese (Cantonese)
† Macedonia	9,928	2,198,000	221	Republic ... A	Skopje	Macedonian, Albanian
† Madagascar	226,658	13,110,000	58	Republic ... A	Antananarivo	Malagasy, French
Maine	35,387	1,245,000	35	State (U.S.) ... D	Augusta	English
† Malawi	45,747	8,942,000	195	Republic ... A	Lilongwe	Chichewa, English
† Malaysia	127,320	19,060,000	150	Federal constitutional monarchy ... A	Kuala Lumpur	Malay, Chinese dialects, English, Tamil
† Maldives	115	246,000	2,139	Republic ... A	Male	Divehi
† Mali	482,077	8,922,000	19	Republic ... A	Bamako	French, Bambara, indigenous
† Malta	122	365,000	2,992	Republic ... A	Valletta	English, Maltese
Manitoba	250,947	1,118,000	4.5	Province (Canada) ... D	Winnipeg	English
† Marshall Islands	70	52,000	743	Republic (U.S. protection) ... A	Majuro (island)	English, indigenous, Japanese
Martinique	425	377,000	887	Overseas department (France) ... C	Fort-de-France	French, Creole
Maryland	12,407	5,006,000	403	State (U.S.) ... D	Annapolis	English
Massachusetts	10,555	6,106,000	578	State (U.S.) ... D	Boston	English
† Mauritania	395,956	2,142,000	5.4	Republic ... A	Nouakchott	Arabic, Pular, Soninke, Wolof
† Mauritius (incl. Dependencies)	788	1,110,000	1,409	Republic ... A	Port Louis	English, Creole, Bhojpuri, French, Hindi, Tamil, others
Mayotte [5]	144	91,000	632	Territorial collectivity (France) ... C	Dzaoudzi and Mamoudzou [4]	French, Swahili (Mahorian)
† Mexico	759,534	90,870,000	120	Federal republic ... A	Mexico City (Ciudad de México)	Spanish, indigenous
Michigan	96,810	9,550,000	99	State (U.S.) ... D	Lansing	English
† Micronesia, Federated States of	271	119,000	439	Republic (U.S. protection) ... A	Kolonia and Paliker [4]	English, indigenous
Midway Islands	2.0	500	250	Unincorporated territory (U.S.) ... C		English
Minnesota	86,943	4,539,000	52	State (U.S.) ... D	St. Paul	English
Mississippi	48,434	2,646,000	55	State (U.S.) ... D	Jackson	English
Missouri	69,709	5,266,000	76	State (U.S.) ... D	Jefferson City	English
† Moldova	13,012	4,425,000	340	Republic ... A	Chişinău (Kishinev)	Romanian (Moldovan), Russian
† Monaco	0.7	31,000	44,286	Constitutional monarchy ... A	Monaco	French, English, Italian, Monegasque
† Mongolia	604,829	2,314,000	3.8	Republic ... A	Ulan Bator (Ulaanbaatar)	Khalkha Mongol, Turkish dialects, Russian, Chinese
Montana	147,046	830,000	5.6	State (U.S.) ... D	Helena	English
Montserrat	39	13,000	333	Dependent territory (U.K.) ... C	Plymouth	English
† Morocco (excl. Western Sahara)	172,414	28,095,000	163	Constitutional monarchy ... A	Rabat	Arabic, Berber dialects, French
† Mozambique	308,642	16,585,000	54	Republic ... A	Maputo	Portuguese, indigenous
† Myanmar (Burma)	261,228	43,630,000	167	Provisional military government ... A	Yangon (Rangoon)	Burmese, indigenous
† Namibia	318,253	1,555,000	4.9	Republic ... A	Windhoek	English, Afrikaans, German, indigenous
Nauru	8.1	10,000	1,235	Republic ... A	Yaren District	Nauruan, English
Nebraska	77,358	1,635,000	21	State (U.S.) ... D	Lincoln	English
Nei Monggol (Inner Mongolia)	456,759	22,495,000	49	Autonomous region (China) ... D	Hohhot	Mongolian
† Nepal	56,827	20,660,000	364	Constitutional monarchy ... A	Kathmandu	Nepali, Maithali, Bhojpuri, other indigenous
† Netherlands	16,164	15,320,000	948	Constitutional monarchy ... A	Amsterdam and The Hague ('s-Gravenhage)	Dutch
Netherlands Antilles	309	192,000	621	Self-governing territory (Netherlands protection) ... B	Willemstad	Dutch, Papiamento, English
Nevada	110,567	1,375,000	12	State (U.S.) ... D	Carson City	English
New Brunswick	28,355	755,000	27	Province (Canada) ... D	Fredericton	English, French
New Caledonia	7,358	179,000	24	Overseas territory (France) ... C	Nouméa	French, indigenous
Newfoundland	156,649	587,000	3.7	Province (Canada) ... D	St. John's	English
New Hampshire	9,351	1,167,000	125	State (U.S.) ... D	Concord	English
New Hebrides see Vanuatu	...	...	...	...	...	...
New Jersey	8,722	7,915,000	907	State (U.S.) ... D	Trenton	English
New Mexico	121,598	1,608,000	13	State (U.S.) ... D	Santa Fe	English, Spanish
New South Wales	309,500	6,117,000	20	State (Australia) ... D	Sydney	English
New York	54,475	18,375,000	337	State (U.S.) ... D	Albany	English
† New Zealand	104,454	3,486,000	33	Parliamentary state ... A	Wellington	English, Maori

Region or Political Division	Area Sq. Mi.	Est. Pop. 1/1/94	Pop. Per. Sq. Mi.	Form of Government and Ruling Power	Capital	Predominant Languages
† Nicaragua	50,054	4,267,000	85	Republic .... A	Managua	Spanish, English, indigenous
† Niger	489,191	8,754,000	18	Provisional military government .... A	Niamey	French, Hausa, Djerma, indigenous
† Nigeria	356,669	94,550,000	265	Provisional military government .... A	Lagos and Abuja	English, Hausa, Fulani, Yorbua, Ibo, indigenous
Ningxia Huizu	25,637	4,855,000	189	Autonomous region (China) .... D	Yinchuan	Chinese (Mandarin)
Niue	100	1,900	19	Self-governing territory (New Zealand protection) .... B	Alofi	English, indigenous
Norfolk Island	14	2,700	193	External territory (Australia) C	Kingston	English, Norfolk
North America	9,500,000	444,600,000	47			
North Carolina	53,821	6,955,000	129	State (U.S.) .... D	Raleigh	English
North Dakota	70,704	632,000	8.9	State (U.S.) .... D	Bismarck	English
Northern Ireland	5,461	1,605,000	294	Administrative division (U.K.) .... D	Belfast	English
Northern Mariana Islands	184	49,000	266	Commonwealth (U.S. protection) .... B	Saipan (island)	English, Chamorro, Carolinian
Northern Territory	519,771	172,000	0.3	Territory (Australia) .... D	Darwin	English, indigenous
Northwest Territories	1,322,910	56,000	0.1	Territory (Canada) .... D	Yellowknife	English, indigenous
† Norway (incl. Svalbard and Jan Mayen)..	149,412	4,301,000	29	Constitutional monarchy .... A	Oslo	Norwegian, Lapp, Finnish
Nova Scotia	21,425	922,000	43	Province (Canada) .... D	Halifax	English
Oceania (incl. Australia)	3,300,000	28,000,000	8.5			
Ohio	44,828	11,155,000	249	State (U.S.) .... D	Columbus	English
Oklahoma	69,903	3,242,000	46	State (U.S.) .... D	Oklahoma City	English
† Oman	82,030	1,659,000	20	Monarchy .... A	Muscat	Arabic, English, Baluchi, Urdu, Indian dialects
Ontario	412,581	10,315,000	25	Province (Canada) .... D	Toronto	English
Oregon	98,386	3,009,000	31	State (U.S.) .... D	Salem	English
† Pakistan (incl. part of Jammu and Kashmir)	339,732	126,090,000	371	Federal Islamic republic .... A	Islāmābād	English, Urdu, Punjabi, Sindhi, Pashto
Palau (Belau)	196	16,000	82	Republic .... A	Koror and Melekeok [4]	Angaur, English, Japanese, Palauan, Sonsorolese, Tobi
† Panama	29,157	2,592,000	89	Republic .... A	Panamá	Spanish, English
† Papua New Guinea	178,704	3,989,000	22	Parliamentary state .... A	Port Moresby	English, Motu, Pidgin, indigenous
† Paraguay	157,048	4,297,000	27	Republic .... A	Asunción	Spanish, Guarani
Pennsylvania	46,058	12,145,000	264	State (U.S.) .... D	Harrisburg	English
† Peru	496,225	23,305,000	47	Republic .... A	Lima	Quechua, Spanish, Aymara
† Philippines	115,831	66,190,000	571	Republic .... A	Manila	English, Pilipino, Tagalog
Pitcairn (incl. Dependencies)	19	100	5.3	Dependent territory (U.K.) C	Adamstown	English, Tahitian
† Poland	121,196	38,540,000	318	Republic .... A	Warsaw (Warszawa)	Polish
† Portugal	35,516	9,961,000	280	Republic .... A	Lisbon (Lisboa)	Portuguese
Prince Edward Island	2,185	140,000	64	Province (Canada) .... D	Charlottetown	English
Puerto Rico	3,515	3,801,000	1,081	Commonwealth (U.S. protection)........ B	San Juan	Spanish, English
† Qatar	4,412	502,000	114	Monarchy .... A	Doha	Arabic, English
Qinghai	277,994	4,618,000	17	Province (China) .... D	Xining	Tibetan dialects, Mongolian, Turkish dialects, Chinese (Mandarin)
Quebec	594,860	7,070,000	12	Province (Canada) .... D	Québec	French, English
Queensland	666,876	3,111,000	4.7	State (Australia) .... D	Brisbane	English
Reunion	969	643,000	664	Overseas department (France) C	Saint-Denis	French, Creole
Rhode Island	1,545	1,012,000	655	State (U.S.) .... D	Providence	English
Rhodesia see Zimbabwe						
† Romania	91,699	22,770,000	248	Republic .... A	Bucharest (Bucureşti)	Romanian, Hungarian, German
† Russia	6,592,849	150,500,000	23	Federal republic .... A	Moscow (Moskva)	Russian, Tatar, Ukrainian
† Rwanda	10,169	8,196,000	806	Republic .... A	Kigali	French, Kinyarwanda, Kiswahili
St. Helena (incl. Dependencies)	121	7,000	58	Dependent territory (U.K.) C	Jamestown	English
† St. Kitts and Nevis	104	45,000	433	Parliamentary state .... A	Basseterre	English
† St. Lucia	238	151,000	634	Parliamentary state .... A	Castries	English, French
St. Pierre and Miquelon	93	7,000	75	Territorial collectivity (France) C	Saint-Pierre	French
† St. Vincent and the Grenadines	150	115,000	767	Parliamentary state .... A	Kingstown	English, French
† San Marino	24	24,000	1,000	Republic .... A	San Marino	Italian
† Sao Tome and Principe	372	125,000	336	Republic .... A	São Tomé	Portuguese, Fang
Saskatchewan	251,866	1,006,000	4.0	Province (Canada) .... D	Regina	English
† Saudi Arabia	830,000	16,585,000	20	Monarchy .... A	Riyadh (Ar Riyāḍ)	Arabic
Scotland	30,421	5,130,000	169	Administrative division (U.K.) .... D	Edinburgh	English, Scots Gaelic
† Senegal	75,951	8,522,000	112	Republic .... A	Dakar	French, Wolof, Fulani, Serer, indigenous
† Seychelles	175	72,000	411	Republic .... A	Victoria	English, French, Creole
Shaanxi	79,151	34,455,000	435	Province (China) .... D	Xi'an (Sian)	Chinese (Mandarin)
Shandong	59,074	88,450,000	1,497	Province (China) .... D	Jinan	Chinese (Mandarin)
Shanghai	2,394	13,970,000	5,835	Autonomous city (China) .... D	Shanghai	Chinese (Wu)
Shanxi	60,232	30,075,000	499	Province (China) .... D	Taiyuan	Chinese (Mandarin)
Sichuan	220,078	112,250,000	510	Province (China) .... D	Chengdu	Chinese (Mandarin), Tibetan dialects, Miao-Yao
† Sierra Leone	27,925	4,538,000	163	Transitional military government .... A	Freetown	English, Krio, Mende, Temne, indigenous
† Singapore	246	2,834,000	11,520	Republic .... A	Singapore	Chinese (Mandarin), English, Malay, Tamil
† Slovakia	18,933	5,342,000	282	Republic .... A	Bratislava	Slovak, Hungarian
† Slovenia	7,820	1,986,000	254	Republic .... A	Ljubljana	Slovenian, Serbo-Croatian
† Solomon Islands	10,954	376,000	34	Parliamentary state .... A	Honiara	English, indigenous
† Somalia	246,201	6,541,000	27	None............................... A	Mogadishu (Muqdisho)	Arabic, Somali, English, Italian
† South Africa	471,010	42,320,000	90	Republic .... A	Pretoria, Cape Town, and Bloemfontein	Afrikaans, English, Xhosa, Zulu, other indigenous
South America	6,900,000	304,500,000	44			
South Australia	379,925	1,495,000	3.9	State (Australia) .... D	Adelaide	English
South Carolina	32,007	3,657,000	114	State (U.S.) .... D	Columbia	English
South Dakota	77,121	726,000	9.4	State (U.S.) .... D	Pierre	English
South Georgia (incl. Dependencies)	1,450	(1)		Dependent territory (U.K.) C	Grytviken Harbour	English
South West Africa see Namibia						
† Spain	194,885	38,640,000	198	Constitutional monarchy .... A	Madrid	Spanish (Castilian), Catalan, Galician, Basque
Spanish North Africa [6]	12	142,000	11,833	Five possessions (Spain) C		Spanish, Arabic, Berber dialects
Spanish Sahara see Western Sahara						
† Sri Lanka	24,962	17,970,000	720	Socialist republic .... A	Colombo and Sri Jayawardenapura	English, Sinhala, Tamil
† Sudan	967,500	28,900,000	30	Provisional military government .... A	Khartoum (Al Kharţūm)	Arabic, Nubian and other indigenous, English
† Suriname	63,251	418,000	6.6	Republic .... A	Paramaribo	Dutch, Sranan Tongo, English, Hindustani, Javanese
† Swaziland	6,704	854,000	127	Monarchy .... A	Mbabane and Lobamba	English, siSwati
† Sweden	173,732	8,747,000	50	Constitutional monarchy .... A	Stockholm	Swedish, Lapp, Finnish

Region or Political Division	Area Sq. Mi.	Est. Pop. 1/1/94	Pop. Per. Sq. Mi.	Form of Government and Ruling Power	Capital	Predominant Languages
Switzerland	15,943	7,001,000	439	Federal republic . . . . A	Bern (Berne)	German, French, Italian, Romansch
† Syria	71,498	13,695,000	192	Socialist republic . . . . A	Damascus (Dimashq)	Arabic, Kurdish, Armenian, Aramaic, Circassian
Taiwan	13,900	20,945,000	1,507	Republic . . . . A	T'aipei	Chinese (Mandarin), Taiwanese (Min), Hakka
† Tajikistan	55,251	5,720,000	104	Republic . . . . A	Dushanbe	Tajik, Uzbek, Russian
† Tanzania	364,900	27,450,000	75	Republic . . . . A	Dar es Salaam and Dodoma	English, Swahili, indigenous
Tasmania	26,178	483,000	18	State (Australia) . . . . D	Hobart	English
Tennessee	42,146	5,058,000	120	State (U.S.) . . . . D	Nashville	English
Texas	268,601	17,925,000	67	State (U.S.) . . . . D	Austin	English, Spanish
† Thailand	198,115	58,960,000	298	Constitutional monarchy . . . . A	Bangkok (Krung Thep)	Thai, indigenous
Tianjin (Tientsin)	4,363	9,235,000	2,117	Autonomous city (China) . . . . D	Tianjin (Tientsin)	Chinese (Mandarin)
† Togo	21,925	4,142,000	189	Provisional military government . . . . A	Lomé	French, Ewe, Mina, Kabye, Dagomba
Tokelau	4.6	1,500	326	Island territory (New Zealand) C		English, Tokelauan
Tonga	288	104,000	361	Constitutional monarchy . . . . A	Nuku'alofa	Tongan, English
† Trinidad and Tobago	1,980	1,288,000	651	Republic . . . . A	Port of Spain	English, Hindi, French, Spanish
Tristan da Cunha	40	300	7.5	Dependency (St. Helena) C	Edinburgh	English
† Tunisia	63,170	8,605,000	136	Republic . . . . A	Tunis	Arabic, French
† Turkey	300,948	61,540,000	204	Republic . . . . A	Ankara	Turkish, Kurdish, Arabic
† Turkmenistan	188,456	3,935,000	21	Republic . . . . A	Ashkhabad	Turkmen, Russian, Uzbek
Turks and Caicos Islands	193	13,000	67	Dependent territory (U.K.) C	Grand Turk	English
Tuvalu	10	10,000	1,000	Parliamentary state . . . . A	Funafuti	Tuvaluan, English
† Uganda	93,104	18,425,000	198	Republic . . . . A	Kampala	English, Luganda, Swahili, indigenous
† Ukraine	233,090	52,240,000	224	Republic . . . . A	Kiev (Kyyiv)	Ukrainian, Russian, Romanian, Polish
† United Arab Emirates	32,278	2,692,000	83	Federation of monarchs . . . . A	Abū Ẓaby (Abu Dhabi)	Arabic, Farsi, English, Hindi, Urdu
† United Kingdom	94,249	57,960,000	615	Parliamentary monarchy . . . . A	London	English, Welsh, Scots Gaelic
† United States	3,787,425	259,390,000	68	Federal republic . . . . A	Washington	English, Spanish
Upper Volta see Burkina Faso						
† Uruguay	68,500	3,181,000	46	Republic . . . . A	Montevideo	Spanish
Utah	84,904	1,842,000	22	State (U.S.) . . . . D	Salt Lake City	English
† Uzbekistan	172,742	22,240,000	129	Republic . . . . A	Tashkent	Uzbek, Russian
† Vanuatu	4,707	160,000	34	Republic . . . . A	Port-Vila	Bislama, English, French
Vatican City	0.2	900	4,500	Monarchical-sacerdotal state . . . . A	Vatican City	Italian, Latin, other
† Venezuela	352,145	20,460,000	58	Federal republic . . . . A	Caracas	Spanish, Amerindian
Vermont	9,615	585,000	61	State (U.S.) . . . . D	Montpelier	English
Victoria	87,877	4,566,000	52	State (Australia) . . . . D	Melbourne	English
† Vietnam	127,428	72,080,000	566	Socialist republic . . . . A	Hanoi	Vietnamese, French, Chinese, English, Khmer, indigenous
Virginia	42,769	6,485,000	152	State (U.S.) . . . . D	Richmond	English
Virgin Islands (U.S.)	133	97,000	729	Unincorporated territory (U.S.) C	Charlotte Amalie	English, Spanish, Creole
Wake Island	3.0	300	100	Unincorporated territory (U.S.) C		English
Wales	8,015	2,905,000	362	Administrative division (U.K.) . . . . D	Cardiff	English, Welsh Gaelic
Wallis and Futuna	98	14,000	143	Overseas territory (France) C	Mata-Utu	French, Wallisian
Washington	71,303	5,188,000	73	State (U.S.) . . . . D	Olympia	English
West Bank (incl. Jericho and East Jerusalem)	2,347	1,460,000	622	Israeli territory with limited self-government		Arabic, Hebrew
Western Australia	975,101	1,703,000	1.7	State (Australia) . . . . D	Perth	English
Western Sahara	102,703	208,000	2.0	Occupied by Morocco C		Arabic
† Western Samoa	1,093	168,000	154	Constitutional monarchy . . . . A	Apia	English, Samoan
West Virginia	24,231	1,816,000	75	State (U.S.) . . . . D	Charleston	English
Wisconsin	65,503	5,058,000	77	State (U.S.) . . . . D	Madison	English
Wyoming	97,818	467,000	4.8	State (U.S.) . . . . D	Cheyenne	English
Xinjiang Uygur (Sinkiang)	617,764	15,865,000	26	Autonomous region (China) . . . . D	Ürümqi	Turkish dialects, Mongolian, Tungus, English
Xizang (Tibet)	471,045	2,250,000	4.8	Autonomous region (China) . . . . D	Lhasa	Tibetan dialects
† Yemen	203,850	10,840,000	53	Republic . . . . A	Şan'ā'	Arabic
Yugoslavia	39,449	10,730,000	272	Republic . . . . A	Belgrade (Beograd)	Serbo-Croatian 95%, Albanian 5%
Yukon Territory	186,661	28,000	0.2	Territory (Canada) . . . . D	Whitehorse	English, Inuktitut, indigenous
Yunnan	152,124	38,720,000	255	Province (China) . . . . D	Kunming	Chinese (Mandarin), Tibetan dialects, Khmer, Miao-Yao
† Zaire	905,446	41,675,000	46	Republic . . . . A	Kinshasa	French, Kikongo, Lingala, Swahili, Tshiluba, Kingwana
† Zambia	290,586	8,625,000	30	Republic . . . . A	Lusaka	English, Tonga, Lozi, other indigenous
Zhejiang	39,305	43,455,000	1,106	Province (China) . . . . D	Hangzhou	Chinese dialects
† Zimbabwe	150,873	10,605,000	70	Republic . . . . A	Harare (Salisbury)	English, Shona, Sindebele
WORLD	57,900,000	5,556,000,000	96	. . . .		

† *Member of the United Nations*
. . . *None, or not applicable.*
(1) No permanent population.
(2) North Cyprus unilaterally declared its independence from Cyprus in 1983.
(3) Claimed by Argentina.
(4) Future capital.
(5) Claimed by Comoros.
(6) Comprises Ceuta, Melilla, and several small islands.

Map Symbols

In a very real sense, the whole map is a symbol, representing the world or a part of it. It is a reduced representation of the earth; each of the world's features–cities rivers, etc.–is represented on the map by a symbol. Map symbols may take the form of points, such as dots or squares (often used for cities, capital cities, or points of interest), or lines (roads, railroads, rivers). Symbols may also occupy an area, showing extent of coverage (terrain, forests, deserts). They seldom look like the feature they represent and therefore must be identified and interpreted. For instance, the maps in this atlas define political units by colored tints. Neither the colors nor the boundary lines are actually found on the surface of the earth, but because countries and states are such important political components of the world, strong symbols are used to represent them. On the maps in this atlas the surface configuration of the earth is represented by hill-shading, which gives the three-dimensional impression of landforms. This terrain representation conveys a realistic and readily visualized impression of the surface. A complete legend to the right provides a key to the other symbols on the maps in this atlas.

In this atlas a "local-name" policy generally was used for naming cities and towns and all local topographic and water features. However, for a few major cities the Anglicized name was preferred and the local name given in parentheses, for instance, Moscow (Moskva), Vienna (Wien), Prague (Praha). In countries where more than one official language is used, a name is in the dominant local language. The generic parts of local names for topographic and water features are self-explanatory in many cases because of the associated map symbols or type styles.

Cultural Features

Political Boundaries

International

Secondary: State, Provincial, etc. (Second order political unit)

Disputed de jure

Cities, Towns and Villages
(Note: On maps at 1:45,000,000 and smaller the town symbols do not follow the specific population classification shown below.)

PARIS — 1,000,000 and over

Milwaukee — 250,000 to 1,000,000

Huntsville — 100,000 to 250,000

Bloomington — 25,000 to 100,000

New Meadows — 0 to 25,000

BUDAPEST — National Capitals

Springfield — Secondary Capitals

Other Cultural Features

Research Stations

Ruins

Transportation

Primary Roads

Secondary Roads

Railroads

Topographic Features

Nev. Sajama 21,463 — Peaks
Elevations are given in feet

Water Features

Lakes and Reservoirs

Fresh Water

Fresh Water: Intermittent

Salt Water

Other Water Features

Rivers

Rivers: Intermittent

Reefs

Ice Shelf

ARCTIC OCEAN

GREENLAND
(Den.)

Baffin
Bay

ICELAND

ALASKA
(U.S.)

Dawson

Anchorage

Reykjavik

NORTH

Hudson
Bay

IRELA

Juneau

CANADA

Edmonton

ALEUTIAN IS.

Winnipeg

NEWFOUNDLAND

Vancouver

Montréal

St. John's

Seattle

Ottawa

AMERICA

Detroit

AZORES
(Port.)

PORTUG

UNITED STATES

Chicago

New York

San Francisco

Washington

GIBF

Los Angeles

Atlanta

CANARY ISLANDS
(Sp.)

Houston

New Orleans

ATLANTIC

MIDWAY IS.
(U.S.)

Tropic of Cancer

Gulf of Mexico

BAHAMAS

MAURIT

HAWAIIAN ISLANDS
(U.S.)

MEXICO

Havana

CUBA

CAPE VERDE

Mexico City

Veracruz

DOM. REP.

W. SAHA

SENEGAL

BELIZE

HAITI

PUERTO RICO (U.S.)

Dakar

GUAT.

HOND.

JAMAICA

GUADELOUPE (Fr.)

GAMBIA

EL SAL.

NIC.

Caribbean
Sea

MARTINIQUE (Fr.)

GUINEA-BISSAU

GUINE

PACIFIC

BARBADOS

COSTA
RICA

TRINIDAD AND TOBAGO

SIERRA LEONE

Caracas

VENEZUELA

GUYANA

LIBERIA

PANAMA

Georgetown

SURINAME

Bogotá

FRENCH GUIANA

COLOMBIA

GALAPAGOS ISLANDS
(Ecua.)

Quito

Belém

ECUADOR

Manaus

Fortaleza

KIRIBATI

Equator

SOUTH

BRAZIL

Recife

MARQUESAS IS.
(Fr.)

PERU

AMERICA

OCEAN

Lima

Salvador

OCEA

WESTERN
SAMOA

La Paz

Brasília

AMERICAN
SAMOA

BOLIVIA

TONGA

COOK
ISLANDS
(N.Z.)

TAHITI

FRENCH POLYNESIA

Sucre

PARAGUAY

Rio de Janeiro

Tropic of Capricorn

São Paulo

EASTER ISLAND
(Chile)

Antofagasta

ARGENTINA

Valparaíso

URUGUAY

CHATHAM IS.
(N.Z.)

ARCH. DE JUAN
FERNÁNDEZ
(Chile)

Santiago

Montevideo

Buenos
Aires

FALKLAND IS.
(U.K.)

SOUTH GEORGIA
(U.K.)

Punta Arenas

TIERRA DEL FUEGO

SOUTH SANDWICH IS.
(U.K.)

SOUTH ORKNEY IS.
(U.K.)

Antarctic Circle

SOUTH SHETLAND IS.
(U.K.)

Weddell
Sea

Scale 1:100,000,000; one inch to 1578 miles
Robinson Projection

| 0 | 400 | 800 | 1200 | 1600 | 2000 Miles |

| 0 | 600 | 1200 | 1800 | 2400 | 3000 Kilometers |

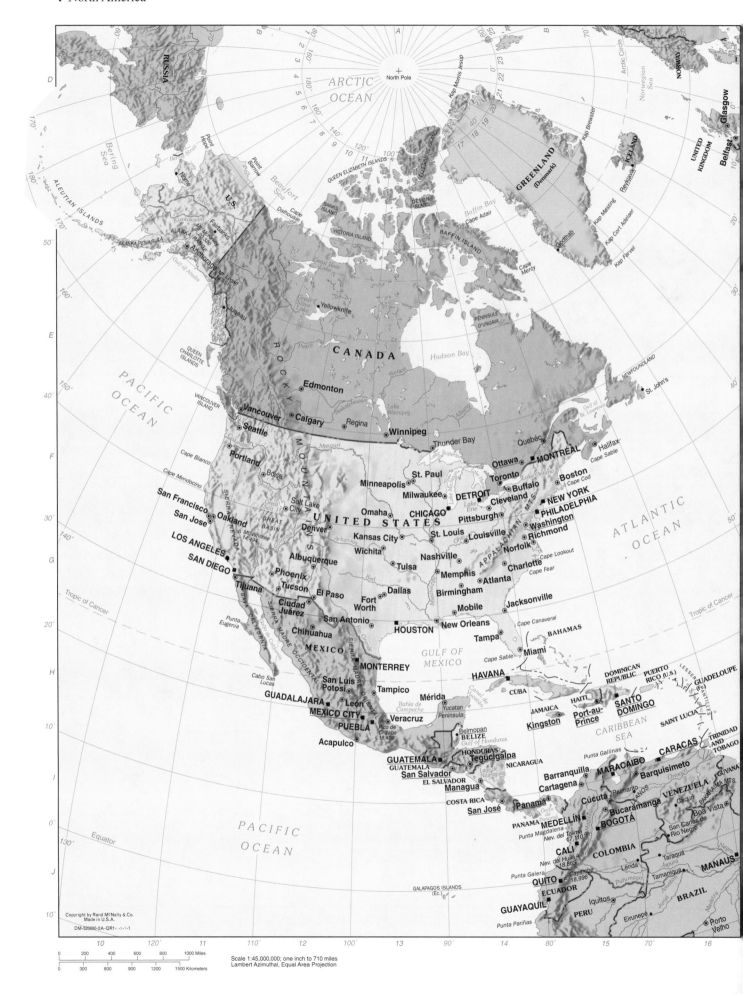

Scale 1:45,000,000; one inch to 710 miles
Lambert Azimuthal, Equal Area Projection

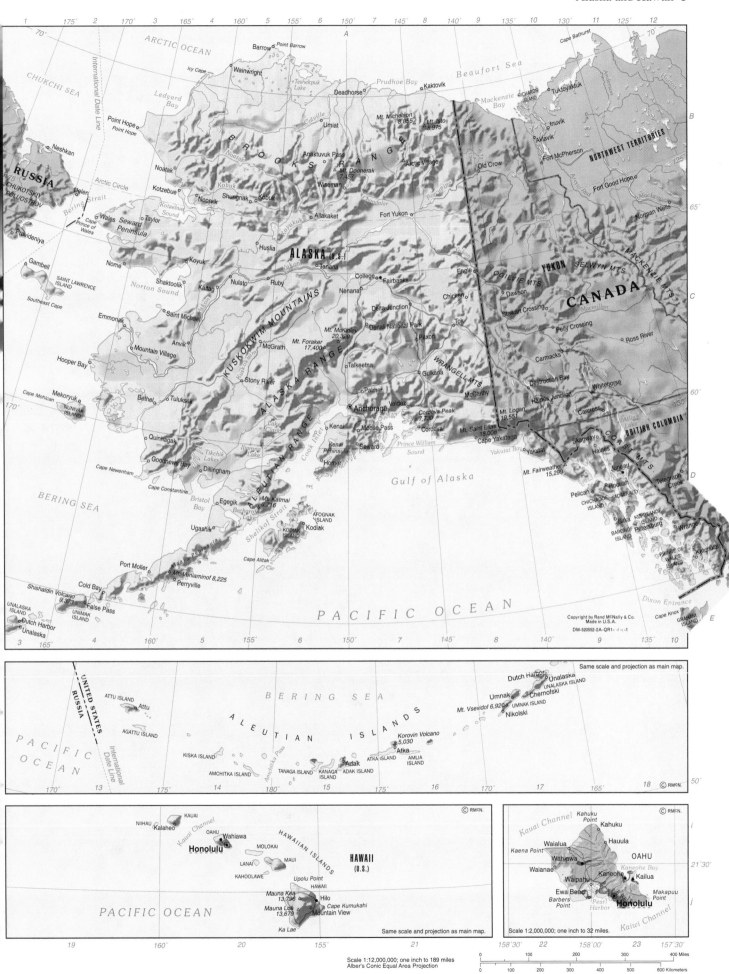

ARCTIC OCEAN
Barrow   Point Barrow

Icy Cape   Wainwright

CHUKCHI SEA   Ledyard   Teshekpuk Lake

Neshkan   Prudhoe Bay   Kaktovik   Beaufort Sea   Cape Bathurst

Deadhorse

Point Hope   BROOKS RANGE   Mt. Michelson 8,855   Mt. Isto 8,975   RICHARDS ISLAND   Tuktoyaktuk

Point Hope   Umiat   Inuvik

Colville   NORTHWEST TERRITORIES

Noatak   Anaktuvuk Pass   Mt. Doonerak 7,457   Arctic Village   Old Crow   Aklavik   Fort McPherson

Kotzebue   Wiseman   Fort Good Hope

Arctic Circle   Noorvik   Shungnak   Kobuk   Allakaket   Fort Yukon   Eagle   Dawson   Norman Wells

Kobuk   Koyukuk   ALASKA (U.S.)   Yukon   OGILVIE MTS   YUKON   SELWYN MTS   MACKENZIE MTS

Huslia   Stewart Crossing   CANADA

Wales   Seward Peninsula   Tanana   College   Fairbanks   Pelly Crossing   Ross River

Cape Prince of Wales   Nome   Koyuk   Nulato   Ruby   Nenana   Chicken   Carmacks

Bering Strait   Shaktoolik   KUSKOKWIM MOUNTAINS   Delta Junction   Tok   Destruction Bay   Whitehorse

Providentiya   SAINT LAWRENCE ISLAND   Kaltag   Mt. McKinley 20,320   Denali National Park   Paxon   WRANGELL MTS   Carcross   BRITISH COLUMBIA

Gambell   Emmonak   Anvik   McGrath   Mt. Foraker 17,400   ALASKA RANGE   Gulkana   McCarthy   Mt. Logan 19,551   Skagway   COAST MTS

Southeast Cape   Norton Sound   Saint Michael   Mountain Village   Stony River   Talkeetna   Palmer   Mt. Saint Elias 18,008   Haines Junction   Haines

Hooper Bay   Cape Yakataga   Atlin

Cape Mohican   Mekoryuk   Bethel   Tuluksak   Anchorage   Valdez   Cordova Peak 7,730   Mt. Fairweather 15,299   Juneau

NUNIVAK ISLAND   Lake Clark   Kenai   Moose Pass   Cordova   Yakutat Bay   Yakutat

Quinhagak   Tikchik Lakes   Iliamna Lake   Kenai Peninsula   Seward   Prince William Sound   Pelican   CHICHAGOF ISLAND

Cape Newenham   Goodnews Bay   Dillingham   Homer   Gulf of Alaska   Hoonah   ADMIRALTY ISLAND

Cape Constantine   Cook Inlet   Sitka   KUPREANOF ISLAND

BERING SEA   Bristol Bay   Egegik   Mt. Katmai 6,716   BARANOF ISLAND   Petersburg   Wrangell

Ugashik   Becharof Lake   AFOGNAK ISLAND   PRINCE OF WALES ISLAND   Ketchikan

KODIAK ISLAND   Kodiak   Telegraph Creek

Port Moller   Mt. Veniaminof 8,225   Cape Alitak

Shishaldin Volcano 9,373   Cold Bay   Perryville   Dixon Entrance   Cape Knox   GRAHAM ISLAND

False Pass   UNIMAK ISLAND

UNALASKA ISLAND   Dutch Harbor   Unalaska   PACIFIC OCEAN

Copyright by Rand McNally & Co.
Made in U.S.A.
DM-520552-2A-QR1- -|-|-1

Same scale and projection as main map.

Dutch Harbor   Unalaska

BERING SEA   Umnak   UNALASKA ISLAND   Chernofski

ATTU ISLAND   Mt. Vsevidof 6,920   UMNAK ISLAND   Nikolski

UNITED STATES   Attu   ALEUTIAN ISLANDS

RUSSIA   AGATTU ISLAND   Korovin Volcano 5,030

PACIFIC OCEAN   International Date Line   KISKA ISLAND   Atka

AMCHITKA ISLAND   Amchitka Pass   Adak   ATKA ISLAND   AMLIA ISLAND

TANAGA ISLAND   KANAGA ISLAND   ADAK ISLAND

KAUAI   Kahuku Point   Kahuku

NIIHAU   Kalaheo   Kauai Channel   Waialua   Hauula

OAHU   Wahiawa   Kaena Point   Wahiawa   Kaneohe Bay

Honolulu   MOLOKAI   HAWAIIAN ISLANDS   Waianae   Waipahu   Kaneohe   Kailua

LANAI   MAUI   HAWAII (U.S.)   Ewa Beach   OAHU   Makapuu Point

KAHOOLAWE   Upolu Point   Barbers Point   Pearl Harbor   Honolulu

HAWAII

Mauna Kea 13,796   Hilo

Mauna Loa 13,679   Mountain View

PACIFIC OCEAN   Ka Lae   Cape Kumukahi   Scale 1:2,000,000; one inch to 32 miles   Kaiwi Channel

Same scale and projection as main map.

Scale 1:12,000,000; one inch to 189 miles
Alber's Conic Equal Area Projection

0 100 200 300 400 Miles
0 100 200 300 400 500 600 Kilometers

Scale 1:16,000,000; one inch to 252 miles
Lambert Conformal Conic Projection

| 0 | 100 | 200 | 300 | 400 | 500 Miles |
| 0 | 200 | 400 | 600 | 800 Kilometers |

Scale 1:12,000,000; one inch to 189 miles
Albers' Conic Equal Area Projection

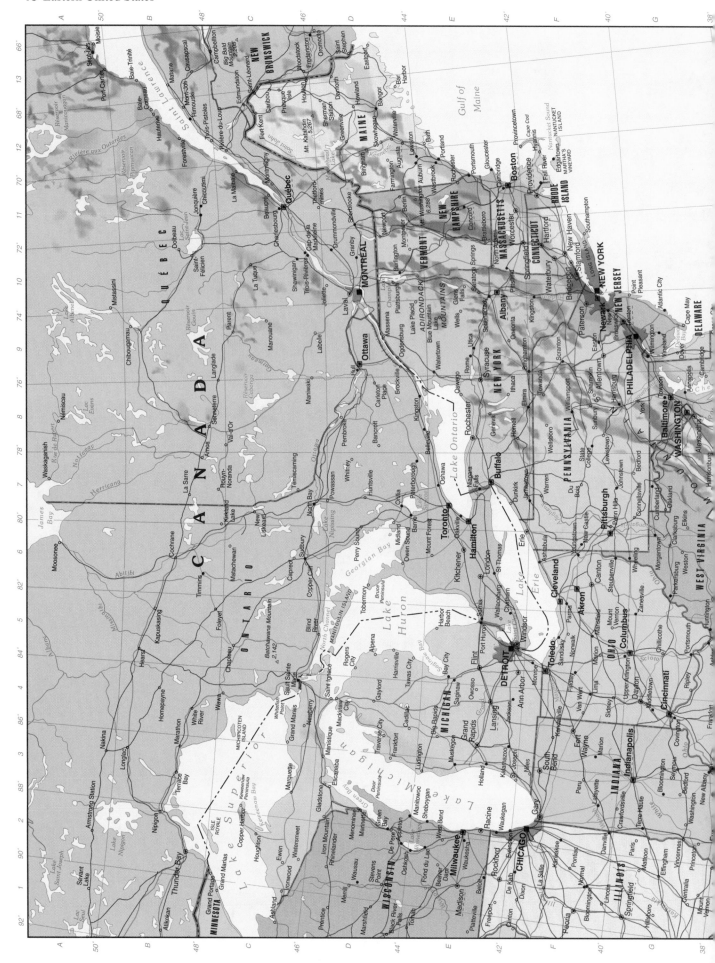

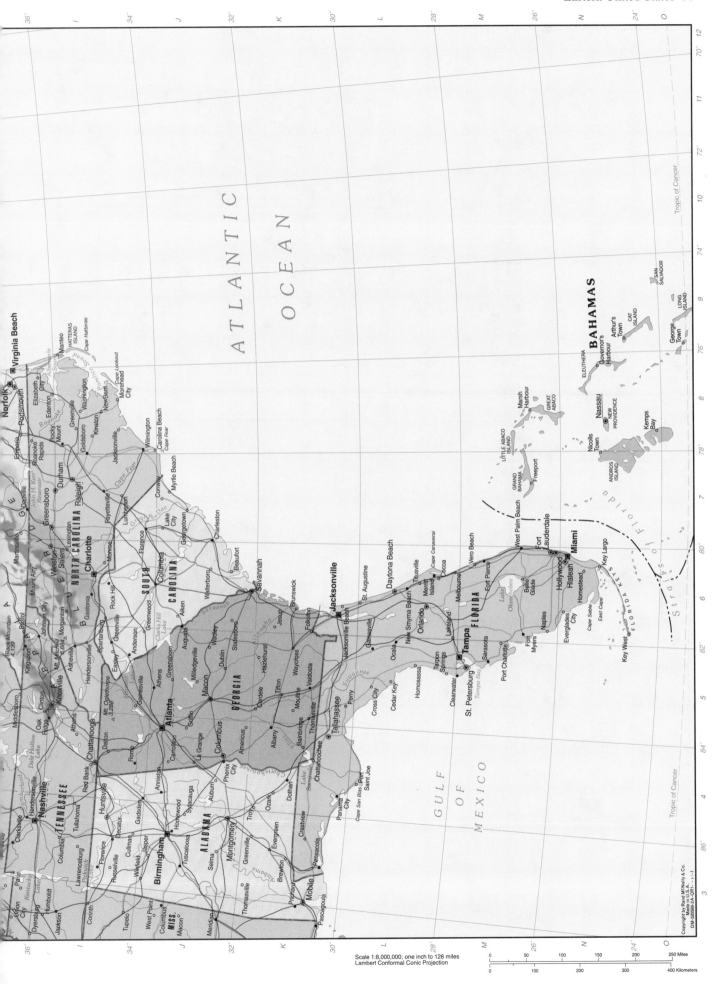

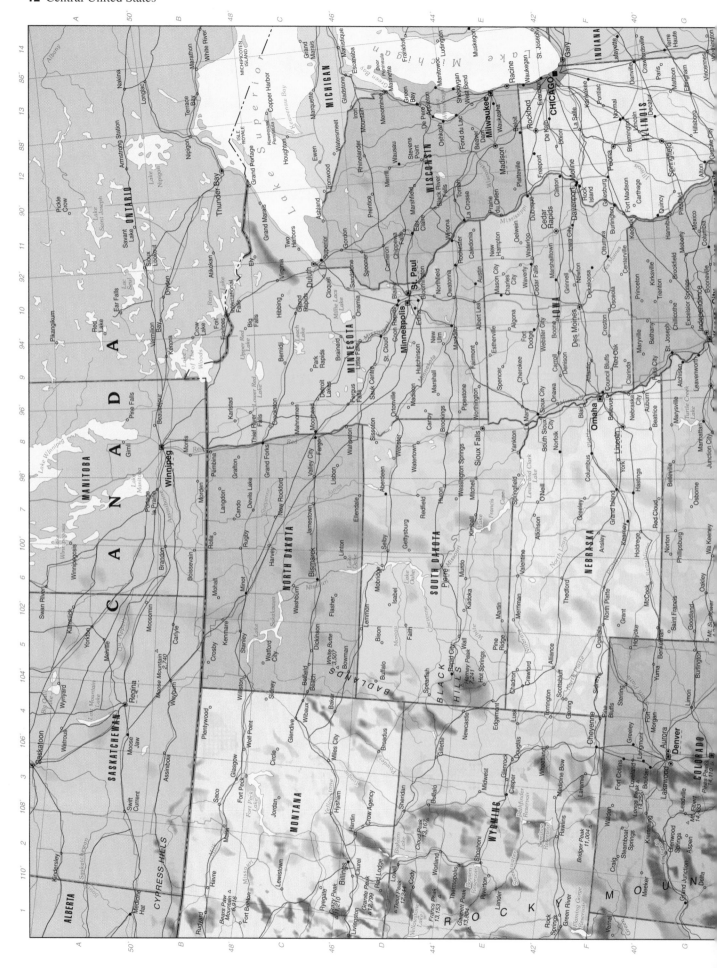

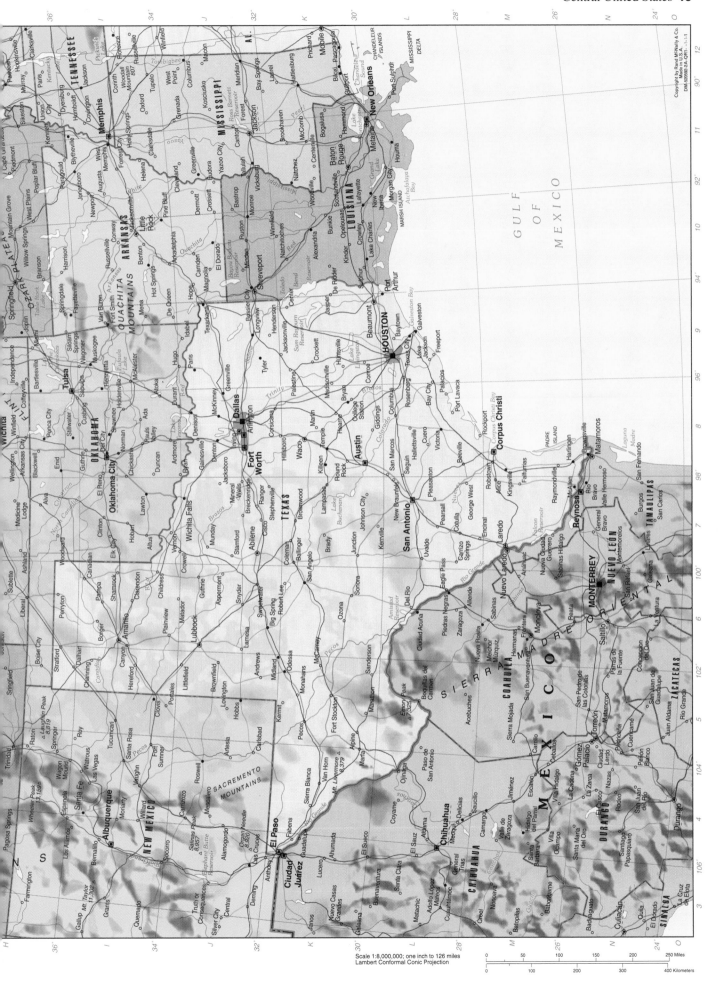

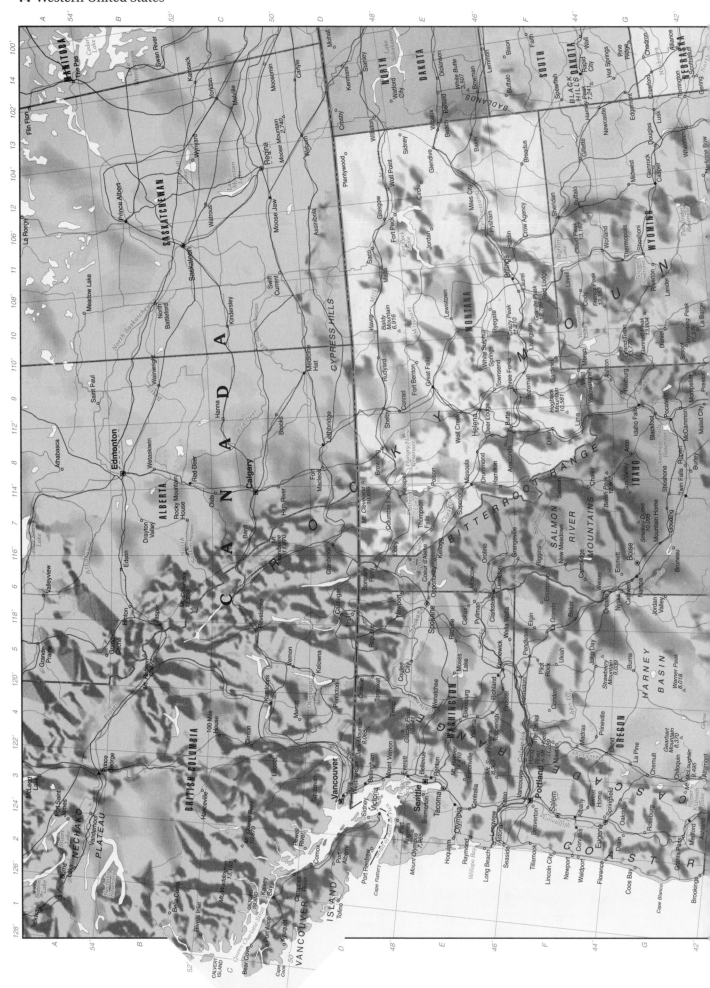

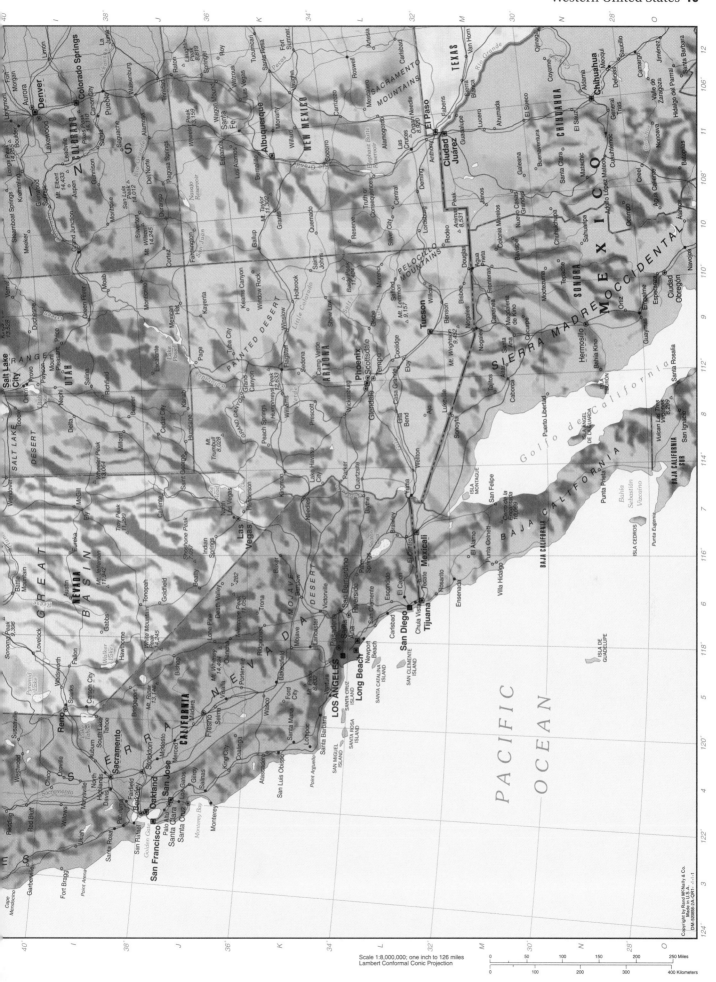

Scale 1:8,000,000; one inch to 126 miles
Lambert Conformal Conic Projection

| 0 | 50 | 100 | 150 | 200 | 250 Miles |

| 0 | 100 | 200 | 300 | 400 Kilometers |

ATLANTIC OCEAN

CARIBBEAN SEA

WEST INDIES

GREATER ANTILLES

LESSER ANTILLES

VENEZUELA

COLOMBIA

PANAMA

GUYANA

BRAZIL

Scale 1:16,000,000; one inch to 252 miles
Lambert Conformal Conic Projection

PACIFIC OCEAN

Scale 1:45,000,000; one inch to 710 miles
Lambert Azimuthal, Equal Area Projection

Copyright by Rand McNally & Co.
Made in U.S.A.
DM-540000-2A-QR1- -1-1-1

| 0 | 200 | 400 | 600 | 800 | 1000 Miles |
| 0 | 300 | 600 | 900 | 1200 | 1500 Kilometers |

BOLIVIA

Tocopilla

Chuquicamata

Tarija

PARAGUAY

Bela Vista

Dourados

Araçatuba

Tupã

Lins

Araraquara

Ribeirão
Prêto

São Carlos

SÃO PAULO

Calama

Cerro
Licancábur
19,409

Ponta Porã

Pedro Juan
Caballero

MATO GROSSO
DO SUL

Presidente
Prudente

Marília

Presidente
Epitácio

Bauru

Piracicaba

São José
dos
Campos

Tropic of Capricorn

Antofagasta

Volcán Llullaillaco
22,110

Salta

San Salvador
de Jujuy

Amambaí

Concepción

Campo
Mourão

Assis

Ourinhos

Maringá

Londrina

Arapongas
Apucarana

Campinas

Sorocaba

SÃO PAULO

Santo
André

Santos

São Vicente

Punta Dos Reyes

Cerro Galán
19,396

Fernando de
la Mora

Asunción

PARANÁ

Telêmaco
Borba

Curitiba

Caxias do Sul

Cianorte

Umuarama

Cascavel

Foz do Iguaçu

Ponta Grossa

Colombo

Punta Ballenita

San Miguel
de Tucumán

Formosa

Pato Branco

União

Curitibanos

Paranaguá

Punta Medio

Punta Cachos

Nevado Ojos del
Salado 22,615

Copiapó

Cerro Bonete
22,546

Concepción

Santiago del
Estero

Presidencia Roque
Sáenz Peña

Resistencia

Corrientes

Villa Ángela

Posadas

Encarnación

Erexim

Chapecó

Rio do Sul

SANTA CATARINA

Joinvile

Itajaí

Brusque

Blumenau

Florianópolis

Vallenar

San Fernando del
Valle de Catamarca

Reconquista

Goya

Uruguaiana

Itaqui

São
Ângelo

Carazinho

Ijuí

Passo
Fundo

Lages

Tubarão

Criciúma

Araranguá

Laguna

Cabo Bascuñán

La Rioja

Santo
Borja

Cruz Alta

Vacaria

Caxias do Sul

Coquimbo

Cerro de las
Tórtolas 20,735

CÓRDOBA

San Francisco

Rafaela

Concordia

Salto

Alegrete

São Gabriel

Santa
Maria

Santana do
Livramento

Santa Cruz
do Sul

Cachoeira
do Sul

Novo Hamburgo

São Leopoldo

Canoas

PORTO ALEGRE

La Serena

Ovalle

San Juan

Alta Gracia

Santa Fe

Paraná

Rivera

Bagé

RIO GRANDE
DO SUL

Punta Lengua de Vaca

Cerro Aconcagua
22,831

Villa Nueva

Mendoza

Villa Alemana

San Martín

Río Tercero

Villa María

Bell-Ville

San Lorenzo

ROSARIO

Concepción del Uruguay

Paysandú

Mercedes

Durazno

Melo

Pelotas

Río Grande

Ponta do Bojuru

San Felipe

Quillota

Villa Nueva

San Luis

Río Cuarto

Villa Constitución

Gualeguaychú

Treinta y
Tres

Viña del Mar

Valparaíso

Santiago

Puente Alto

San Bernardo

Rancagua

Mercedes

Venado Tuerto

Pergamino

Zárate

San Pedro

San José
de Mayo

Florida

Minas

Lagoa
Mangueira

San Antonio

San Fernando

Junín

General San Martín

BUENOS AIRES

Avellaneda

Las Piedras

Maldonado

Cabo Polonio

Punta Topocalma

San Rafael

Lomas de Zamora

La
Plata

MONTEVIDEO

Punta del Este

Curicó

Cerro el Nevado
12,500

Nueve de Julio

Pehuajó

Talca

Linares

Santa
Rosa

Azul

Olavarría

Tandil

Chillán

ARGENTINA

Balcarce

Mar del Plata

Talcahuano

Concepción

Tomé

Coronel

Lota

Los Ángeles

Angol

Tres Arroyos

Bahía Blanca

Punta Alta

Necochea

Punta Morguilla

Temuco

Cipolletti

General Roca

Neuquén

Pedro Luro

Bahía
Blanca

Valdivia

General Conesa

Stroeder

Osorno

Cabo Quedal

San Carlos de
Bariloche

San Antonio
Oeste

Viedma

Punta Rasa

A T L A N T I C

Puerto Montt

Monte Tronador
11,453

Ancud

Castro

Quellón

ISLA GRANDE DE
CHILOE

Puerto Madryn

Trelew

Rawson

Punta Norte

PENÍNSULA
VALDÉS

Punta Delgada

Punta Ninfas

Golfo
San Matías

Golfo
Nuevo

O C E A N

José de
San Martín

Cabo Dos Bahías

Volcán Corcovado
7,546

ARCHIPIÉLAGO
DE LOS
CHONOS

Puerto Aisén

Coihaique

Sarmiento

Lago
Buenos Aires

Comodoro
Rivadavia

Caleta Olivia

PACIFIC OCEAN

PENÍNSULA
DE TAITAO

Cerro San
Clemente 13,314

Perito
Morén

Fitz Roy

Tres Montes

Golfo de
Penas

ISLA BYRON

ISLA CAMPANA

ISLA PATRICIO LYNCH

Lago Posadas

Puerto Deseado

Punta Medanosa

Bahía Laura

Cerro Chaltén
10,959

Monte Fitzroy

Lago San
Martín

Puerto San Julián

Punta Desengaño

ISLA WELLINGTON

ISLA MORNINGTON

Lago Viedma

Puerto Santa Cruz

El Calafate

Lago Santa
Cruz

Bahía Grande

ISLA
MADRE DE
DIOS

El Turbio

Río Gallegos

ISLA DIEGO DE
ALMAGRO

Puerto Natales

Cabo Vírgenes

Punta Catalina

FALKLAND ISLANDS
(U.K.)

Cape Dolphin

Mount Usborne 2,312

Stanley

WEST
FALKLAND

EAST
FALKLAND

Cabo Deseado

ISLA DESOLACIÓN

Punta Arenas

Porvenir

Río Grande

TIERRA DEL FUEGO

Cape Meredith

Punta de Arenas

ISLA RIESCO

Cabo
San Diego

Cabo San Juan

ISLA DE LOS
ESTADOS

SOUTH GEORGIA
(U.K.)

ISLA SANTA
INÉS

Ushuaia

ISLA HOSTE

ISLA
NAVARINO

Falso Cabo de Hornos

Cape Horn
(Cabo de Hornos)

Scale 1:16,000,000; one inch to 252 miles
Lambert Conformal Conic Projection

0 100 200 300 400 500 Miles
0 200 400 600 800 Kilometers

NICARAGUA
COSTA RICA
San José
Puerto Limón
Volcán Irazú 11,260
Puntarenas
Alajuela
San Isidro
Cerro Chirripó 12,530
Volcán Barú 11,401
Golfo de los Mosquitos
Colón
PANAMÁ
Panamá
La Chorrera
David
Puerto Armuelles
Punta Burica
Golfo de Chiriquí
Santiago
Aguadulce
Chitre
Golfo de Panamá
ISLA DE COIBA
Punta Mariato
Punta Mala
ISLA DEL REY
ISLA DE OMETEPE
Lago de Nicaragua
Cabo Santa Elena
ISLA DEL COCO (Costa Rica)
ISLA DE MALPELO (Colombia)
Equator
SAN CRISTÓBAL
GALAPAGOS ISLANDS (ARCHIPIELAGO DE COLÓN) (Ecuador)
PACIFIC OCEAN
Santa Marta
Barranquilla
Cartagena
Ciénaga
Soledad
Sabanalarga
Valledupar
Turbaco
San Jacinto
San Onofre
Sincelejo
Corozal
Plato
Lorica
Cereté
Sahagún
Montería
El Banco
San Marcos
Caucasia
Turbo
Chigorodó
Riosucio
Barrancabermeja
Yarumal
Bello
Puerto Berrío
Itagüí
MEDELLÍN
Envigado
Quibdó
Cabo Corrientes
Punta Marzo
Duitama
Sogamoso
Tunja
Yopal
La Dorada
Honda
Manizales
Pereira
Cartago
Armenia
Nev. del Tolima 17,110
Ibagué
BOGOTÁ
Villavicencio
San Martín
Tuluá
Buga
Espinal
Buenaventura
Punta Magdalena
CALI
Palmira
Neiva
Nev. del Huila 18,865
Popayán
Pitalito
Florencia
Pasto
Ipiales
Tumaco
Cabo Manglares
COLOMBIA
San José del Guaviare
Riohacha
Maicao
Pico Cristóbal Colón 19,029
Cúcuta
San Cristóbal
Pamplona
Bucaramanga
Floridablanca
Pico Bolívar 16,427
Ocaña
La Fría
SERR. DE PERIJÁ
CORD. DE MÉRIDA
Mérida
Machiques
Lago de Maracaibo
MARACAIBO
Altagracia
Cabimas
Punto Fijo
Península de Paraguaná
Coro
Puerto Cumarebo
Golfo de Venezuela
Península de la Guajira
Punta Gallinas
Cabo de La Vela
ARUBA (Neth.)
Oranjestad
NETHERLANDS ANTILLES
CURAÇAO
BONAIRE
Willemstad
Carora
Barquisimeto
Puerto Cabello
Guacara
Valencia
Maracay
Petare
CARACAS
Guarenas
Barcelona
Cumaná
Puerto La Cruz
Porlamar
ISLA DE MARGARITA
Carúpano
Anaco
Valle de la Pascua
El Tigre
San José de Guanipa
Calabozo
Ciudad Guayana
Ciudad Bolívar
Cerro Bolívar 2,631
Cerro Mato 6,112
Trujillo
Valera
Acarigua
Guanare
Barinas
San Fernando
Palmarito
Guasdualito
VENEZUELA
LLANOS
Puerto Ayacucho
Cerro Yavi 6,009
Cacuri
Cerro Marahuaca 8,461
SIERRA PARIMA
San Carlos de Río Negro
SIERRA DE CURUPIRA
Pico da Neblina 9,888
Taraqua
Lérida
Esmeraldas
Punta Galera
Tulcán
Ibarra
Cayambe 18,996
QUITO
Cabo Pasado
Chone
Cotopaxi 19,347
ECUADOR
Manta
Portoviejo
Cabo San Lorenzo
Ambato
Chimborazo 20,702
Riobamba
Jipijapa
Vinces
Babahoyo
Milagro
Vol. Sangay 17,159
Punta Santa Elena
GUAYAQUIL
Golfo de Guayaquil
ISLA PUNÁ
Cañar
Cuenca
Machala
Pasaje
Tumbes
Loja
CORDILLERA OCCIDENTAL
CORDILLERA ORIENTAL
CORDILLERA DEL CONDOR
SERRANÍA DE LA MACARENA
Iquitos
Leticia
Amazon
AMAZONAS
Tamaniquá
Tefé
Talara
Punta Pariñas
Sullana
Piura
Castilla
Sechura
Jaén
Moyobamba
Yurimaguas
Chachapoyas
Lambayeque
Chiclayo
Pacasmayo
Cajamarca
Chocope
Trujillo
ANDES
CORD. ULTRAORIENTAL
Pucallpa
Chimbote
Nev. Huascarán 22,133
Tingo María
Huaraz
Huánuco
Huarmey
Nevado Yerupaja 21,765
Pativilca
Cerro de Pasco
Huacho
PERU
Punta Lachay
Huaral
La Oroya
Tarma
Callao
Lima
Chosica
Vitarte
Huancayo
Mala
Huancavelica
Machupicchu
Cusco
Ayacucho
Abancay
Chincha Alta
Bahía de Paracas
Pisco
Ica
Nevado Auzangate 20,945
Punta Carreta
CORDILLERA DE HUANZO
CORDILLERA ORIENTAL
Nazca
Ayaviri
Punta Parada
Nevado Coropuna 20,686
Juliaca
Nevado Chachani 19,931
Puno
Volcán Misti 19,101
Lago Titicaca
Nev. Illampu 21,066
Arequipa
LA PAZ
Nev. Illimani 20,741
Camaná
Mollendo
Volcán Tutupaca 19,898
Moquegua
Ilo
Tacna
Arica
Nev. Sajama 21,463
ALTIPLANO
Oruro
Cochabamba
Santa Cruz de la Sierra
Sucre
Lago Poopó
Potosí
BOLIVIA
CORD. REAL
CORDILLERA OCCIDENTAL
Pisagua
Iquique
Pozo Almonte
CHILE
Tocopilla
Chuquicamata
Calama
Cerro Licancábur 19,409
ARGENTINA
Eirunepé
Lábrea
Cruzeiro do Sul
ACRE
Rio Branco
Porto Velho
Ariquemes
Guajará-Mirim
Puerto Heath
Puerto Maldonado
Trinidad
SELVAS
90° 85° 80° 75° 70° 65°
10° 5° 0° 5° 10° 15° 20°
0 100 200 300 400 500 Miles
0 200 400 600 800 Kilometers

TOBAGO

TRINIDAD AND TOBAGO
f Spain
Fernando
RINIDAD

Boca Grande

GUYANA
Morawhanna
Marlborough
Charity
Suddie
Parika   Georgetown
Bartica   Enmore
New Amsterdam
Nieuw
Nickerie   Nieuw Amsterdam   Paramaribo
Groningen   Iracoubo
Albina   Sinnamary
Saint-Laurent-   Kourou
du-Maroni   Cayenne
Saint-Élie
Mount Roraima 9,432
Kwakoegron   Guisanbourg
Brokopondo   Quanary
Stuumeer
SURINAME   FRENCH
GUIANA   *Cabo Caciporé*
Juliana Top 4,035   Saûl

GUYANA

Vista
Lethem   *KANUKU MTS.*
KAMOA   *ACARAI MTS.*   TUMUC-HUMAC MOUNTAINS
MTS.   AMAPÁ

ATLANTIC OCEAN

Equator

ILHA DE MARACÁ
Cabo Norte
ILHA BAILIQUE
ILHA DO CURUÁ
ILHA JANAUCU
ILHA CAVIANA DE FORA
ILHA MEXIANA
Macapá   *Cabo Maguari*
ILHA   Soure   *Baía de Marajó*
GRANDE   Bragança
DO GURUPÁ   Capanema   Carutapera
ILHA DE   **Belém**   Castanhal
MANAUS   *MARAJÓ*   Abaetetuba
Manacapuru   Oriximiná   Breves   Cametá   São
Itacoatiara   Faro   Portel   Luís   Parnaíba
Maués   Santarém   Camocim   Itapipoca
Altamira   Pindaré Mirim   Sobral   Fortaleza
Novo   Tucuruí   Bacabal   Coroatá   Caninde   Maracanaú
Aripuanã   *Represa de*   Pedreiras   Codó   Pacajus
S   PARÁ   *Tucuruí*   Caxias   Campo   CEARÁ   Quixadá   Mossoró
Itaituba   *SERRA DOS CARAJÁS*   Marabá   MARANHÃO   Timon   Maior   *Cabo de São Roque*
Conceição   Nazaré   Imperatriz   Teresina   Crateús   Jaguaribe   RIO GRANDE DO NORTE   Natal
Conceiçao   Tocantinópolis   São João dos   Piripiri   Igatu   Caicó   João
Carolina   Patos   Floriano   Picos   Crato   Juazeiro   PARAÍBA   Pessoa
Balsas   Oeiras   Salgueiro   do Norte   Patos   Campina   Timbaúba
SERRA DO PENITENTE   *Represa Boa*   PIAUÍ   Serra Talhada   Grande   Olinda
Conceição   *Esperança*   PERNAMBUCO   Arcoverde   Caruaru   RECIFE
da Araguaia   Curupá   Petrolina   Garanhuns   Palmares
SERRA DOS APIACÁS   Alta Floresta   *SERRA DO ESTRONDO*   Juàzeiro   Paulo Afonso   Palmeira dos   ALAGOAS
CHAPADA DAS MANGABEIRAS   Senhor do   Indios   Maceió
B   R   A   Z   I   L   Palmas   Bonfim   Arapiraca
MATO GROSSO   Porto Nacional   *Represa de*   SERGIPE   Penedo
SERRA FORMOSA   TOCANTINS   Gurupi   *Sobradinho*   Irecê   Jacobina   Aracaju
SERRA DO NORTE   Barreiras   Ibotirama   Feira de   Esplanada
Vilhena   *SERRA DO RONCADOR*   Santana   Santa   Alagoinhas
SERRA DO TOMBADOR   Porangatu   *SERRA DOURADA*   Santana   BAHIA   Itaberaba   Camaçari
PLANALTO   Bom Jesus   Valença   SALVADOR
SERRA DOS PARECIS   DO MATO   da Lapa   Jequié
GROSSO   Guanambi   Ipiaú
Diamantino   Brumado   Itabuna
Cuiabá   Vitória da   Ilhéus
Cáceres   Jaciara   Formosa   Januária   Conquista   Itapetinga
BRASÍLIA   Canavieiras
Barra do Garças   *DISTRITO FEDERAL*   São   Pedra Azul   Belmonte
Jùçara   Luziânia   Francisco   Salinas
Inhumas   Unaí   Almenara
Rondonópolis   Iporá   Anápolis   Montes Claros   Itaobim   Itamaraju
Caiapônia   Goiânia   Paracatu   Teófilo Otoni
Mineiros   GOIÁS   Pires do   João   Bocaiúva   Nanuque   *Ponta da Baleia*
MATO GROSSO   Jataí   Pontalina   Rio   Pinheiro   Pirapora   SERRA DO ESPINHAÇO
Coxim   Itumbiara   Paracatu   MINAS
Corumbá   Rio Verde de   Araguari   Patos de   GERAIS   Governador   São Mateus
DO SUL   Mato Grosso   Harumá   Minas   Curvelo   Valadares
Camapuã   Paranaíba   Campina   Sete Lagoas   Ipatinga   Linhares
Miranda   Verde   Araxá   *Manas*   Colatina
Puerto Bahía   Campo Grande   Frutal   BELO   Ponte Nova   Vitória
Negra   Aquidauana   Uberlândia   HORIZONTE   Vila Velha
SA. DE MARACAJU   São José do   Uberaba   São João   Itaquari
Tres Lagoas   Rio Preto   Franca   del Rei   Cachoeiro de Itapemirim
Bela Vista   Araçatuba   SÃO   Ribeirão Preto   Lavras   Juiz de Fora   RIO DE JANEIRO
Dourados   Tupã   PAULO   Araraquara   Pocos de Caldas   Três Rios   *Cabo de São Tomé*
Presidente   Marília   Lins   São Carlos   Volta   Nova Friburgo
Pedro Juan   Prudente   Assis   Bauru   Campinas   Redonda   Nova Iguaçu
Caballero   Ponta Porã   Piracicaba   Taubaté   Niterói
ARAGUAY   São José dos Campos   RIO DE JANEIRO
Sorocaba   SÃO PAULO   *Tropic of Capricorn*
Santo André   Santos
São Vicente

O BOREAL

Cabo C- Norte

Copyright by Rand McNally & Co.
Made in U.S.A.
DM-549100-2A-QR1- -1-1-1

Scale 1:16,000,000; one inch to 252 miles
Lambert Azimuthal, Equal Area Projection

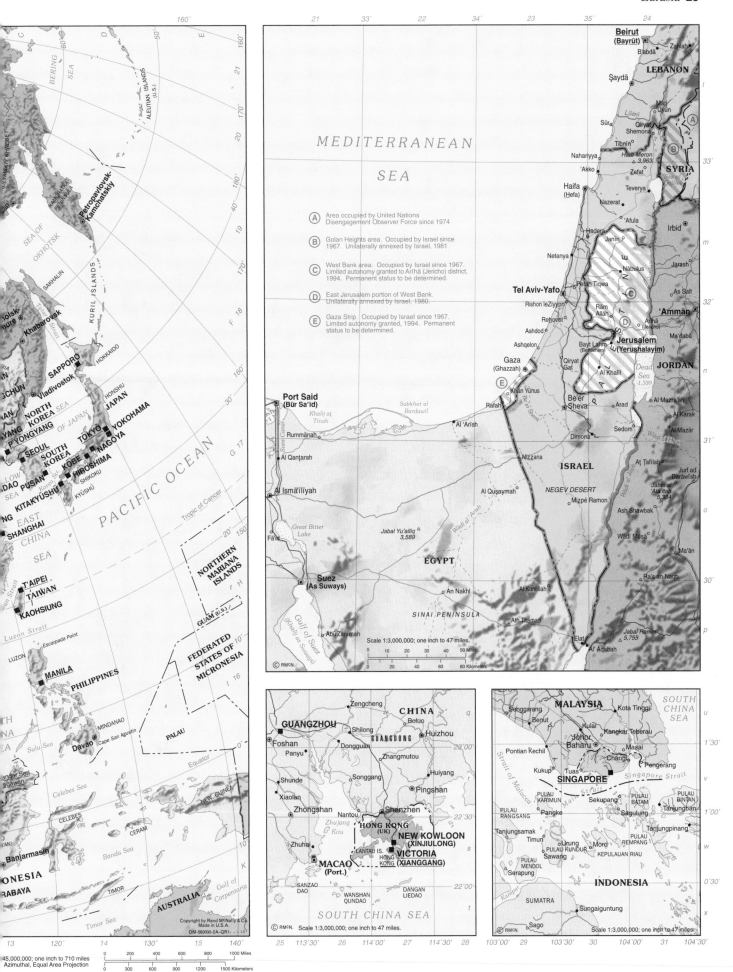

MEDITERRANEAN

SEA

(A) Area occupied by United Nations
Disengagement Observer Force since 1974

(B) Golan Heights area. Occupied by Israel since
1967. Unilaterally annexed by Israel, 1981.

(C) West Bank area. Occupied by Israel since 1967.
Limited autonomy granted to Arīhā (Jericho) district,
1994. Permanent status to be determined.

(D) East Jerusalem portion of West Bank.
Unilaterally annexed by Israel, 1980.

(E) Gaza Strip. Occupied by Israel since 1967.
Limited autonomy granted, 1994. Permanent
status to be determined.

Beirut
(Bayrūt)
B'abdā
Zahlah
LEBANON
Şaydā
Marj
'Uyūn
Şūr
Qiryat
Shemona
Tibnīn
Har Meron
3,963
SYRIA
Nahariyya
'Akko
Zefat
Sea of Galilee
Haifa
(Hefa)
Teverya
Nazerat
'Afula
Irbid
Hadera
Janīn
Jarash
Netanya
Nābulus
Petah Tiqwa
As Salt
Tel Aviv-Yafo
Rishon leZiyyon
Rām
Allāh
'Ammān
Rehovot
Arīhā
(Jericho)
Ma'dabā
Ashdod
Bayt Laḥm
(Bethlehem)
Jerusalem
(Yerushalayim)
Ashqelon
Qiryat
Gat
Al Khalīl
Dead
Sea
-1,339
JORDAN
Gaza
(Ghazzah)
Khan Yūnus
Be'er
Sheva
Arad
Al Mazra'ah
Rafaḥ
Sedom
Al Karak
Port Said
(Būr Sa'īd)
Sabkhat al
Bardawīl
Dimona
Al Mazār
Rummānah
Al 'Arīsh
Nizzana
At Tafīlah
Jurf ad
Darāwīsh
Al Qanṭarah
ISRAEL
Jabal al
'Ata'itah
5,384
Al Ismā'īlīyah
Al Quṣaymah
NEGEV DESERT
Mizpé Ramon
Ash Shawbak
Great Bitter
Lake
Jabal Yu'alliq
3,589
Wadi al 'Araba
Wādī Mūsá
Fā'id
Ma'ān
EGYPT
An Nakhl
Al Kuntillah
Ra's an Naqb
Suez
(As Suways)
SINAI PENINSULA
Ath Thamad
Jabal Ramm
5,755
Abū Zanīmah
Elat
Gulf of Suez
(Khalīj as Suways)
Al 'Aqabah

Scale 1:3,000,000; one inch to 47 miles.
0 10 20 30 40 50 Miles
0 20 40 60 80 Kilometers
© RM©N.

BERING
SEA
ALEUTIAN ISLANDS (U.S.)
50°
KAMCHATKA PENINSULA
Petropavlovsk-
Kamchatskiy
SEA OF
OKHOTSK
SAKHALIN
KURIL ISLANDS
Khabarovsk
HOKKAIDO
SAPPORO
Vladivostok
HONSHU
JAPAN
NORTH
KOREA
SEA
OF JAPAN
YOKOHAMA
PYONGYANG
TOKYO
NAGOYA
SEOUL
KOBE
SOUTH
KOREA
HIROSHIMA
PUSAN
SHIKOKU
KITAKYUSHU
KYŪSHŪ
PACIFIC OCEAN
Tropic of Cancer
EAST
CHINA
SHANGHAI
SEA
T'AIPEI
TAIWAN
KAOHSIUNG
Luzon Strait
NORTHERN
MARIANA
ISLANDS
Escarpada Point
GUAM (U.S.)
LUZON
FEDERATED
STATES OF
MICRONESIA
MANILA
PHILIPPINES
MINDANAO
Cape San Agustin
PALAU
Davao
Sulu Sea
Equator
Celebes Sea
NEW GUINEA
CELEBES
CERAM
Banjarmasin
Banda Sea
Gulf of
Carpentaria
RABAYA
TIMOR
Timor Sea
AUSTRALIA

Zengcheng
CHINA
Botuo
GUANGZHOU
Shilong
Huizhou
Foshan
GUANGDONG
Panyu
Dongguan
Zhangmutou
Huiyang
Songgang
Shunde
Pingshan
Xiaolan
Shenzhen
Zhongshan
Nantou
HONG KONG
(UK)
Zhuhai
Zhujiang
Kou
NEW KOWLOON
(XINJIULONG)
LANTAU IS.
VICTORIA
HONG KONG (XIANGGANG)
MACAO
(Port.)
SANZAO
DAO
WANSHAN
QUNDAO
DANGAN
LIEDAO
SOUTH CHINA SEA
© RM©N. Scale 1:3,000,000; one inch to 47 miles.

Senggarang
MALAYSIA
Kota Tinggi
SOUTH
CHINA
SEA
Benut
Kulai
Kangkar Teberau
Pontian Kechil
Johor
Baharu
Masai
Kukup
Tuas
Changi
Pengerang
SINGAPORE
Singapore Strait
PULAU
KARIMUN
PULAU
BATAM
PULAU
BINTAN
PULAU
RANGSANG
Pangke
Sekupang
Tanjungban
Tanjungsamak
Sagulung
Tanjungpinang
Timun
Urung
Moro
PULAU
REMPANG
PULAU KUNDUR
KEPULAUAN RIAU
Sawang
PULAU
MENDOL
Serapung
INDONESIA
Kampar
SUMATRA
Sungaiguntung
Sago

© RM©N. Scale 1:3,000,000; one inch to 47 miles.

45,000,000; one inch to 710 miles
Azimuthal, Equal Area Projection
0 200 400 600 800 1000 Miles
0 300 600 900 1200 1500 Kilometers

ATLANTIC OCEAN

NORWEGIAN SEA

ICELAND
Reykjavik
Akureyri
Djúpivogur
Stokksnes
Húsar
Hekla 1491
Horn
Rifstangi
Fontur

Arctic Circle

FAEROE IS. (Den.)
Tórshavn

NORWAY
Trondheim
Dombås
Galdhøpiggen 2469
Sognafjorden
Bergen
Stavanger
Oslo
Lindesnes

SWEDEN
Örnsköldsvik
Umeå
Östersund
Härnösand
Sarna
Gävle
Uppsala
Stockholm
Norrköping
Linköping
GOTLAND
Visby
ÖLAND

Kebnekaise 2111
Narvik
LOFOTEN VESTERÅLEN

GULF OF
BALTIC SEA
Klaipėda
Kolka Rags
Lie

SHETLAND ISLANDS
Lerwick
ORKNEY ISLANDS
Wick
Duncansby Head

HEBRIDES
SCOTLAND
Glasgow
Aberdeen
Dundee
GRAMPIAN MTS
Moray Firth
Kinnaird Head
Firth of Forth
Edinburgh
CHEVIOT HILLS
Newcastle upon Tyne

NORTHERN IRELAND
Bloody Foreland
Achill Head
Belfast

IRELAND
Galway
Dublin
Limerick
Cork
Loop Head
Mizen Head
Irish Sea
St. George's Channel

UNITED KINGDOM
Liverpool
Manchester
Kingston upon Hull
BIRMINGHAM
WALES
Leicester
ENGLAND
Cardiff
Hartland Point
Land's End
Lizard Point
Southampton
Plymouth
Portsmouth
LONDON
Strait of Dover
English Channel
CHANNEL IS. (U.K.)

NORTH SEA

DENMARK
Ålborg
Kattegat
Copenhagen (København)
Malmö
BORNHOLM (Den.)
Skagerrak
Grenen
Göteborg
Vänern
Vättern

NETHERLANDS
Amsterdam
The Hague ('s-Gravenhage)
Rotterdam
Kiel
Rostock
Bremer-haven
HAMBURG
Bremen
Hannover
BERLIN
Magdeburg
Essen
BELGIUM
Brussels
Bonn
GERMANY
Leipzig
Dresden
LUX.
Luxembourg
Frankfurt
Mainz

POLAND
Gdańsk
Szczecin
Toruń
Poznań
Łódź
Wisła
WARSAW (WAR)
Wrocław
Katowice
SUDETES
Kra

RU
Kaliningrad

Cherbourg
Le Havre
Rouen
Lille
Reims
Brest
Pointe du Raz
Rennes
Pointe de la Coubre
Nantes
PARIS
Orléans
Tours
Seine
FRANCE
Dijon
Loire
Strasbourg
Mulhouse
Nürnberg
Stuttgart
MUNICH (MÜNCHEN)
CZECH REPUBLIC
PRAGUE (PRAHA)
Plzeň
Ostrava
SLOVAKIA
VIENNA (WIEN)
Bratislava
Győr
Debrec
AUSTRIA
Graz
HUNGARY
BUDAPEST
Szeged

La Coruña
Cabo Ortegal
Cabo de Finisterre
Bay of Biscay
Bordeaux
Limoges
MASSIF CENTRAL
Lyon
Rhône
Zürich
Bern
Genève
Lausanne
SWITZERLAND
Mont Blanc 4807
LIECH.
Bodensee
Säntis 2504

Gijón
Vigo
Oviedo
Santander
Cabo Mondego
Porto
Bilbao
Donostia
Logroño
PYRENEES
Toulouse
Nîmes
Avignon
Nice
MONACO
Marseille
Toulon
Golfe du Lion
Cap de Creus
CORSICA (Fr.)
Ajaccio
Cap Corse

PORTUGAL
Cabo da Roca
Lisbon (Lisboa)
Coimbra
Salamanca
Valladolid
Zaragoza
ANDORRA
Ebro
BARCELONA
Tarragona
Ligurian Sea
La Spezia
Livorno
Turin (Torino)
MILAN (MILANO)
Genoa (Genova)
Bologna
Venice (Venezia)
SAN MARINO
Florence (Firenze)
Ancona
SLOVENIA
Ljubljana
Zagreb
CROATIA
BELGRADE (BEOGRAD)
BOSNIA AND HERZEGOVINA
Sarajevo
Drava
YUGOSL
Split
ADRIATIC SEA

SPAIN
MADRID
Badajoz
Toledo
Tagus
SIERRA MORENA
Córdoba
Sevilla
Granada
SISTEMAS BÉTICOS
Cádiz
Faro
Cabo de São Vicente
Málaga
Almería
GIBRALTAR (U.K.)
Tanger
Ceuta (Sp.)
Strait of Gibraltar
Melilla (Sp.)
Albacete
Murcia
Cartagena
Alacant
Cabo de Palos
Cap de la Nau
BALEARIC ISLANDS
Palma
EIVISSA
MALLORCA
MENORCA
Sassari
SARDINIA (It.)
Cagliari
Capo Spartivento
Capo Comino
TYRRHENIAN SEA
ITALY
ROME (ROMA)
NAPLES (NAPOLI)
Vesuvius 1280
Bari
Taranto
Lecce
Cosenza
Capo Colonna
Catanzaro
Capo Palinuro
Palermo
Messina
Mt. Etna 3340
Catania
SICILY (It.)
Capo Passero
Capo Comino
ALBANIA
Tiranë
IONIAN SEA

ALGIERS (EL DJAZAÏR)
Wahran
Annaba
Qacentina
Tunis
Cap Bon
I. DI PANTELLERIA (It.)
Sousse
Valletta
MALTA

MOROCCO
Rabat
Meknès
Fès
CASABLANCA
Marrakech
Beni-Mellal
Cap Rhir
Tétouan

ALGERIA
El Djelfa
Laghouat
Batna
ATLAS MOUNTAINS

TUNISIA

MEDITERRANEAN SEA

Scale 1:16,000,000; one inch to 252 miles
Lambert Conformal Conic Projection

0   100   200   300   400   500 Miles

0   200   400   600   800 Kilometers

ATLANTIC OCEAN

NORTH SEA

CELTIC SEA

Irish Sea

St. George's Channel

English Channel

Bay of Biscay

LIGURIAN SEA

TYRRHENIAN SEA

MEDITERRANEAN

IRELAND
NORTHERN IRELAND
UNITED KINGDOM
GREAT BRITAIN
ENGLAND
SCOTLAND
WALES
ISLE OF MAN (U.K.)
BRITISH ISLES
GUERNSEY (U.K.)
CHANNEL IS.
JERSEY (U.K.)
ISLES OF SCILLY
DENMARK
NETHERLANDS
BELGIUM
LUX.
GERMANY
FRANCE
SWITZERLAND
LIECHTENSTEIN
MASSIF CENTRAL
PYRENEES
ANDORRA
SPAIN
PORTUGAL
CORDILLERA CANTABRICA
SISTEMA IBERICO
SIERRA MORENA
SISTEMAS BETICOS
BALEARIC ISLANDS (Sp.)
MENORCA
MALLORCA
FORMENTERA
CORSICA (Fr.)
SARDINIA (It.)
ISOLA D'ELBA
VATICAN CITY
MONACO
GIBRALTAR (U.K.)
MOROCCO
ALGERIA
TUNISIA
ATLAS MOUNTAINS

Glasgow
Edinburgh
Belfast
Dublin
Liverpool
Manchester
Sheffield
Nottingham
BIRMINGHAM
Coventry
Cardiff
Bristol
LONDON
Copenhagen (København)
HAMBURG
Bremen
Hannover
Amsterdam
Rotterdam
BELGIUM
Brussels (Bruxelles)
Köln
Bonn
Düsseldorf
Dortmund
Essen
Frankfurt
Mannheim
Stuttgart
Nürnberg
MÜNCHEN (MUNICH)
PARIS
Le Havre
Rennes
Nantes
Tours
Orléans
Dijon
Lyon
Bordeaux
Toulouse
Marseille
Nice
MONACO
Zürich
Bern
SWITZERLAND
MILAN (MILANO)
Turin (Torino)
Genoa (Genova)
Bologna
Firenze
ROMA
La Coruña
Gijón
Bilbao
Oviedo
León
Burgos
Valladolid
Zaragoza
MADRID
SPAIN
BARCELONA
València
Palma
Alacant
Murcia
Córdoba
Sevilla
Málaga
Granada
Cádiz
GIBRALTAR (U.K.)
PORTUGAL
Porto
Lisbon (Lisboa)
Tanger
Rabat
CASABLANCA
MOROCCO
Fès
Meknes
Oujda
ALGIERS (EL DJAZAÏR)
Wahran
Qacentina
Annaba
Tunis
TUNISIA
ALGERIA

Scale 1:10,000,000; one inch to 158 miles
Lambert Conformal Conic Projection

0   50   100   150   200   250   300 Miles
0   100   200   300   400   500 Kilometers

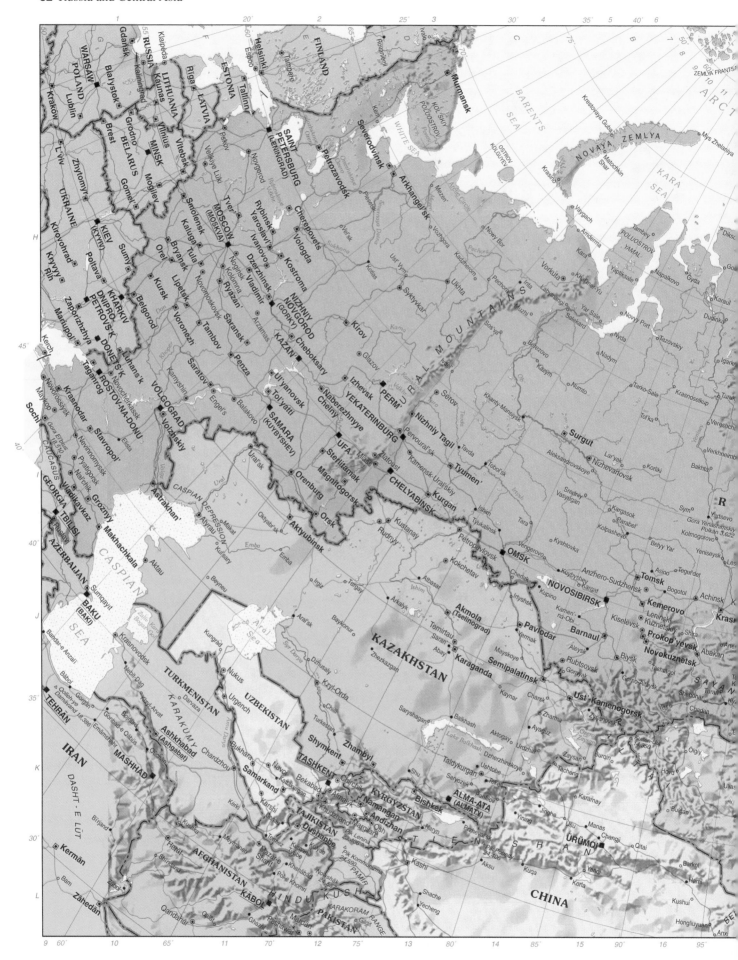

Scale 1:20,000,000; one inch to 315 miles
Lambert Azimuthal, Equal Area Projection

SEA OF OKHOTSK

OSTROV SIMUSHIR

KURIL ISLANDS

OSTROV URUP

OSTROV ITURUP

The southern Kuril Islands are occupied by Russia pending a final peace treaty.

OSTROV KUNASHIR

La Perouse Strait

SAKHALIN

Yuzho-Sakhalinsk

Korsakov

Nevel'sk

Krasnogorsk

Poronaysk

Uglegorsk

Vysokogornyy

RUSSIA

Chita Shilka Sretensk Sosnovo-Ozerskoye

Shkotovo Gulian Mohe Qiqian

Hailar Manzhouli Choybalsan Tamsagbulag Baruun-Urt

WALL OF GENGHIS KHAN Hulun Nur

NEI MONGGOL

Erenhot Abag Qi Abagnar Qi

GREATER KHINGAN RANGE

MANCHURIA

Komsomol'sk-na-Amure

Khabarovsk

Svobodnyy Belogorsk Blagoveshchensk Raychikhinsk Birobidzhan

Svetlaya

Dalnerechensk

Ussuriysk Vladivostok Nakhodka

Olga

Wakkanai HOKKAIDŌ

Rumoi Nayoro Mombetsu

Asahikawa Kushiro

Otaru SAPPORO Obihiro Erimo-misaki

Muroran HAKODATE

Aomori Hachinohe

Hirosaki Morioka Kamaishi

Akita Ishinomaki

Sakata Sendai

Yamagata Fukushima

HONSHŪ Niigata Koriyama Iwaki

Nagaoka Nagano Utsunomiya

Toyama Maebashi TŌKYŌ

Kanazawa Matsumoto KAWASAKI YOKOHAMA

Fukui NAGOYA Mt. Fuji 12,388

KYŌTO Nara Hamamatsu JAPAN

Tottori KOBE OSAKA

Yonago Wakayama

HIROSHIMA Kure Takamatsu Kochi

Shimonoseki Matsuyama SHIKOKU

KITAKYŪSHŪ Oita

FUKUOKA Sasebo Kumamoto

Nagasaki Miyazaki Miyakonojo

KYŪSHŪ Kagoshima

Nishinoomote TANEGA-SHIMA

YAKU-SHIMA

RYUKYU ISLANDS (Japan)

AMAM-O-SHIMA Naze

TOKUNO-SHIMA

OKINAWA-JIMA Nago

Naha

SEA OF JAPAN

NORTH KOREA

Ch'ŏngjin Najin

Kimch'aek Tanch'ŏn

Hyesan Hamhung Hŭngnam

Sinŭiju WŎNSAN

P'YŎNGYANG Namp'o Kaesŏng Sokch'o

SEOUL (SŎUL)

INCH'ŎN Suweon Wŏnju

SOUTH KOREA

TAEJŎN P'ohang

Chŏnju TAEGU Ulsan

KWANGJU Masan PUSAN

Mokp'o Chinju

Korea Strait

Cheju OKI-SHOTŌ

CHEJU-DO (S. Korea)

Yellow Sea

HEILONGJIANG

Yichun Jiamusi Hegang Jixi

QIQIHAR Suihua Harbin Mudanjiang

Baicheng CHANGCHUN JILIN

Tongliao Siping Liaoyuan FUSHUN Yŏnji

JILIN Fuxin SHENYANG Benxi

Chaoyang LIAONING Liaoyang ANSHAN Tŏngdong

Chifeng Jinzhou Yingkou Dandong

Zhangjiakou Chengde Qinhuangdao

BEIJING Tangshan DALIAN Korea Bay

Baoding TIANJIN Lüshun Bo Hai

SHIJIAZHUANG HEBEI Cangzhou Penglai Weihai

Yangquan Dezhou Yantai

Datong Handan Zibo Weifang Shidao

Anyang JINAN Boshan QINGDAO

Xinxiang SHANDONG

Kaifeng Jining Rizhao

ZHENGZHOU HENAN Xuzhou Lianyungang

Luohe JIANGSU

Pingdingshan Fuyang Bengbu Yancheng

Nanyang ANHUI Huainan Yangzhou Nantong

Xinyang Hefei Zhenjiang Wuxi

Huangshi Changzhou SHANGHAI

WUHAN Wuhu Suzhou Jiaxing

Anqing HANGZHOU Ningbo

ZHEJIANG Shaoxing

Nanchang Jingdezhen Wenzhou

CHANGSHA JIANGXI Fuzhou

Zhuzhou Xiangtan Nanchang

Hengyang Ji'an FUJIAN FUZHOU

Chenzhou Sanming Quanzhou T'AIPEI Chilung

GUANGDONG Shaoguan Zhangzhou Hsinchu T'aichung

GUANGZHOU Shantou Xiamen Changhua Hualien TAIWAN

Foshan NEW KOWLOON Chiai Yü Shan 13,114

VICTORIA KAOHSIUNG T'ainan P'ingtung

MACAO (Port.) HONG KONG (U.K.) Oluan Pi

Taiwan Strait

EAST CHINA SEA

PACIFIC OCEAN

Tropic of Cancer

OKINO-TORI-SHIMA (Japan)

IRIOMOTE-JIMA MIYAKO-JIMA Hirara

ISHIGAKI-SHIMA

PHILIPPINE SEA

Luzon Strait

TUNGSHA TAO (Claimed by China, Taiwan)

SOUTH CHINA SEA

BABUYAN ISLANDS

Laoag Aparri PHILIPPINES

Copyright by Rand McNally & Co.
Made in U.S.A.
DM-569700-2A-QR1- -1-1-1

Scale 1:16,000,000; one inch to 252 miles
Lambert Conformal Conic Projection

0 100 200 300 400 500 Miles

0 200 400 600 800 Kilometers

125°   8   130°   9   135°   10   140°   11   145°   12   150°   13

Tropic of Cancer

OKINO-TORI-SHIMA
(Japan)

MAUG ISLANDS

PHILIPPINE
SEA

NORTHERN MARIANA
ISLANDS
(U.S.)

MARIANA
ISLANDS

SARAGON

SAIPAN

PHILIPPINES

PACIFIC OCEAN

GUAM
(U.S.)   Agana

egaspi

SAMAR
Tacloban

LEYTE
olod
Cebu

Tagbilaran

guete

buyan Sea

Butuan

Cagayan de Oro

Bislig

SOROL

YAP

Marawi

MINDANAO
ato   Mount
Apo
9,692   Davao

oronadal

GAFEKUT

FEDERATED STATES OF
MICRONESIA

Cape San Agustin

General Santos

PALAU ISLANDS

Koror

Tinaca
Point

KEPULAUAN
TALAUD

SONSORAL
ISLANDS

PALAU (BELAU)

Tahuna

CAROLINE ISLANDS

MOROTAI
Galela   Wayabula

Manado   Gunung Klabat 6,634
Tondano

HALMAHERA

Equator

Weda

Molucca Sea
(Laut Maluku)

Labuha

Tanjung Libobo

Sorong

Jazirah Doberai

Manokwari

Bosnik

Teba   Tanjung D'Urville
Sarmi

MANUS
ISLAND   Patusi

BISMARCK ARCHIPELAGO

Kavieng

Laiwui

KEPULAUAN OBI

PULAU MISOOL

Teluk
Cenderawasih

Sèrui

Waren

Jayapura

E   S   I   A

KEPULAUAN SULU

Ceram Sea
(Laut Seram)

Kokas

Semenanjung
Bomberai

Piru

CERAM (SERAM)

Bula

PEGUNUNGAN MAOKE

NEW GUINEA

Wewak

Sepik

Bogia

Madang

Namlea
BURU

Ambon

Puncak
Jaya
16,503   Puncak
Trikora
15,584

Puncak
Mandala
15,617

CENTRAL RANGE

Mount Hagen

Mount
Wilhelm
14,793

Aisege

Hoskins

Goroka   Lae

NEW BRITAIN

Tual   Dobo

Birab

Kepi

Mount
Giluwe
14,330

Cape Cretin

Banda Sea
(Laut Banda)

KEPULAUAN
ARU

Tanjung De Jongs

Digul

Lake
Murray

PAPUA NEW
GUINEA

Kerema

Losuia

KEPULAUAN BARAT DAYA

PULAU YAMDENA

Tepa

Saumlaki

PULAU YOS
SUDARSO

Tanjung Vals

Merauke

Fly

Daru

Gulf of
Papua

OWEN STANLEY RANGE

Popondetta

Tufi

Dili   Tutuala

ARAFURA SEA

Mari

Port Moresby

Esa-ala

cussi

TIMOR

Samarai

Soe

Timor Sea

Torres Strait

Bamaga   Cape York

125°   8   130°   9   135°   10   140°   11   145°   12   150°   13

Scale 1:16,000,000; one inch to 252 miles
Sinusoidal Projection

0   100   200   300   400   500 Miles

0   200   400   600   800 Kilometers

A

B

C

D

E

F

G

H

20°

15°

10°

5°

0°

5°

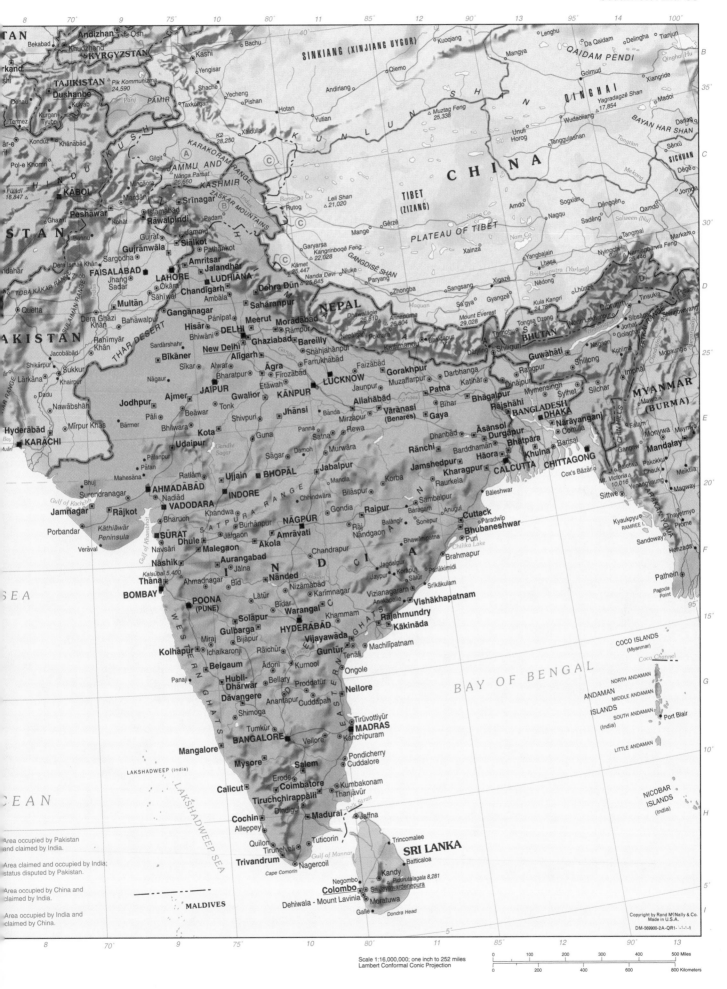

Scale 1:16,000,000; one inch to 252 miles
Lambert Conformal Conic Projection

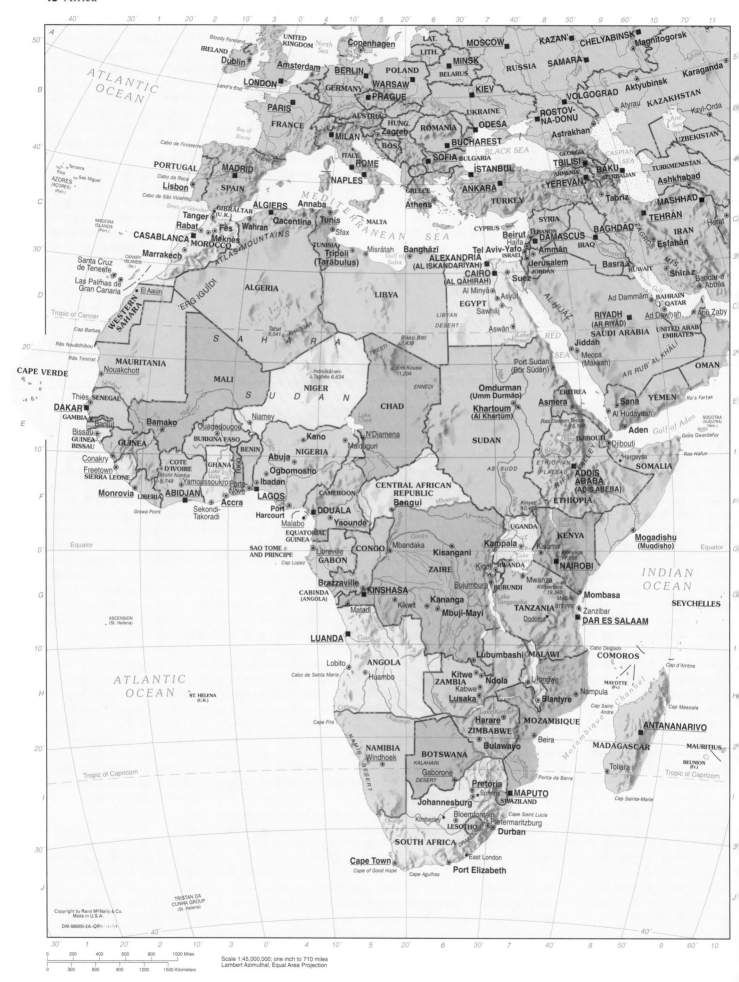

Scale 1:45,000,000; one inch to 710 miles
Lambert Azimuthal, Equal Area Projection

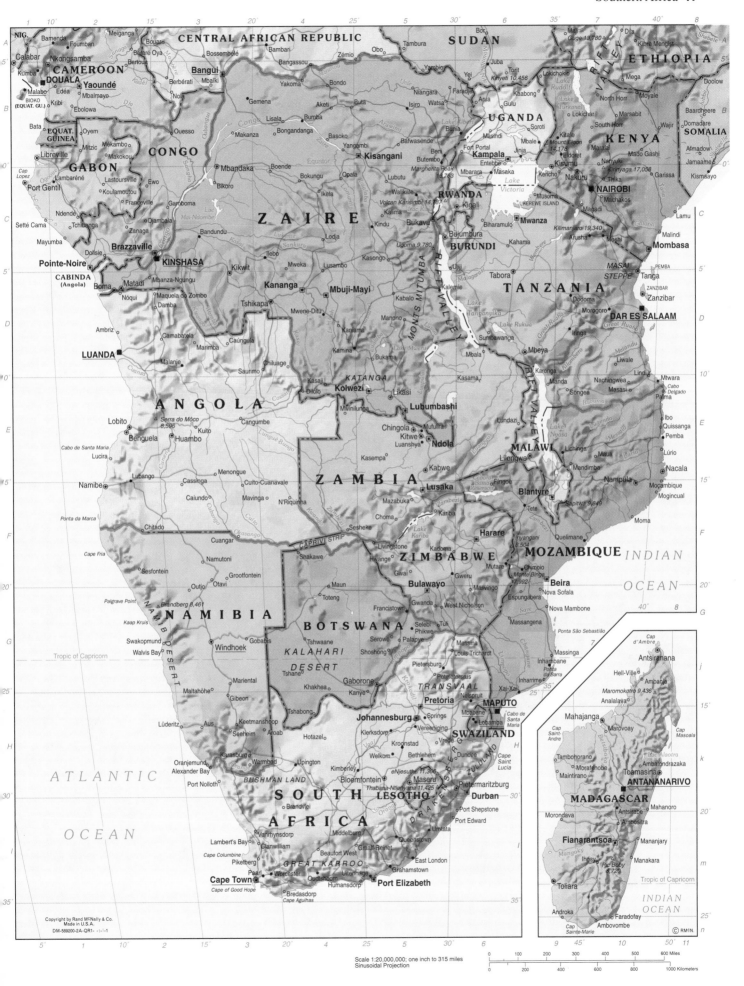

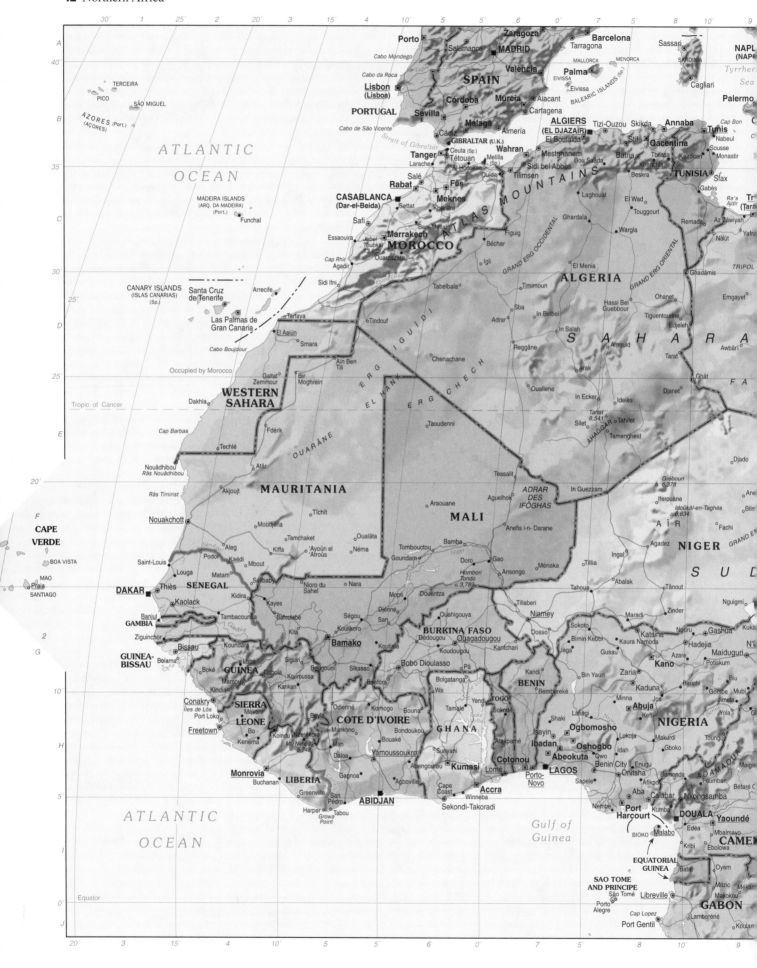

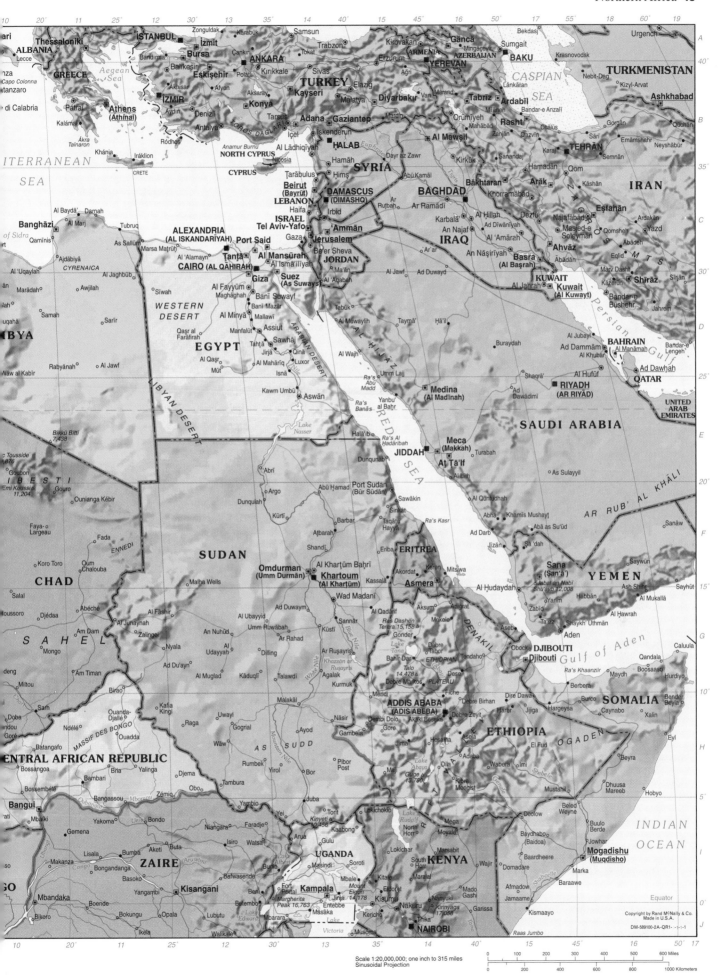

HIMALAYAS
Kathmandu
NEPAL BHU.
INDIA
BNGL.
CHITTAGONG
MYANMAR (BURMA)
YANGON
THAILAND
BANGKOK
CAMBODIA
Phnum Pénh
THANH PHO HO CHI MINH (SAIGON)
Mui Ca Mau
MALAYSIA
Kuala Lumpur
SINGAPORE

CHINA
Chongqing
XI'AN
WUHAN
Yangtze
NANJING
SHANGHAI
GUANGZHOU
Ha Noi
MACAO (Port.)
HONG KONG (U.K.)
Hai Phong
Viangchan
VIETNAM
Da Nang
HAINAN DAO

BEIJING
TIANJIN
SEOUL
QINGDAO
PUSAN
KITAKYŪSHŪ
KYŪSHŪ

SHENYANG
NORTH KOREA
P'YŎNGYANG
SOUTH KOREA
KŌBE
Fuji-san 12,388
YOKOHAMA
TOKYO

RUSSIA
Vladivostok
SEA OF JAPAN
JAPAN
HONSHŪ
SAPPORO
HOKKAIDO
KURIL ISLANDS
SAKHALIN
SEA OF OKHOTSK
Poluostrov Kamchatka
BERING SEA
ALEUTIAN
International Date Line

T'AIPEI
TAIWAN
KAOHSIUNG
Tropic of Cancer

SOUTH CHINA SEA
Escarpada Point
LUZON
PHILIPPINE SEA
MANILA
QUEZON CITY
PHILIPPINES
Cebu
Zamboanga
MINDANAO
Davao
Gunong Kinabalu 13,455
Bandar Seri Begawan
BRUNEI

PACIFIC

MICRONESIA
NORTHERN MARIANA ISLANDS (U.S.)
MARIANA ISLANDS
GUAM (U.S.)
Koror
PALAU ISLANDS
FEDERATED STATES OF MICRONESIA
MARSHALL ISLANDS
KIRIBATI
PALAU (BELAU)
CAROLINE ISLANDS
Equator
NAURU
KI
PHOE

BORNEO (KALIMANTAN)
Gunung Kerinci 12,467
PALEMBANG
Banjarmasin
SUMATRA
INDONESIA
JAKARTA
SURABAYA
JAVA
CELEBES
CERAM
TIMOR

NEW GUINEA
Puncak Jaya 16,503
Mt. Giluwe 14,330
Tanjung Vals
PAPUA NEW GUINEA
Port Moresby
NEW BRITAIN
BOUGAINVILLE
MELANESIA
SOLOMON ISLANDS
Honiara
SANTA CRUZ ISLANDS
TUVALU
T

CHRISTMAS ISLAND (Austl.)
TIMOR SEA
ARAFURA SEA
Cape York
Cape York Peninsula
CORAL SEA

WALLIS AND FUTUNA (Fr.)
W
VANUATU
Port Vila
NEW CALEDONIA (Fr.)
NOUVELLE CALÉDONIE
Nouméa
FIJI
VANUA LEVU
VITI LEVU
Suva

INDIAN OCEAN
Cape Londonderry
Cape Leveque
North West Cape
Carnarvon
Wanneroo
Perth
Cape Naturaliste
Point D'Entrecasteaux

Darwin
Gulf of Carpentaria
Cooktown
Normanton
Cairns
Townsville
GREAT DIVIDING RANGE
Cape Capricorn
Sandy Cape

AUSTRALIA
GREAT SANDY DESERT
Alice Springs
Ayers Rock 2,844
GREAT VICTORIA DESERT
Carnegie
Kalgoorlie-Boulder
Port Augusta
Darling
Adelaide
Cape Arid
Hood Point
Great Australian Bight
Cape Carnot
Cape Jaffa
GREAT DIVIDING RANGE
Brisbane
Newcastle
Sydney
Mt. Kosciusko 7,310
Cape Howe
Canberra
Melbourne
Cape Otway
Cape Grim
TASMANIA
Mt. Ossa 5,305
Hobart
South East Cape

NORFOLK ISLAND (Austl.)
TASMAN SEA

North Cape
Auckland
NORTH ISLAND
East Cape
Mt. Ruapehu 9,177
Cape Farewell
Wellington
NEW ZEALAND
Christchurch
SOUTH ISLAND
Mt. Cook 12,316
CHATHAM I
Cape Providence
STEWART ISLAND

ATLANTIC OCEAN

UNITED STATES

VANCOUVER ISLAND

Seattle
Portland
ROCKY MOUNTAINS
Denver
St. Louis
Memphis
Atlanta
APPALACHIAN MOUNTAINS
Cape Fear
Jacksonville

SIERRA NEVADA
San Francisco
Albuquerque
DALLAS
Mississippi

UNITED STATES

Tampa
Cape Canaveral
Miami BAHAMAS

LOS ANGELES
SAN DIEGO
Tucson
El Paso
San Antonio
HOUSTON
Colorado
Rio Grande
Gulf of Mexico
Cape Sable

OCEAN

Punta Eugenia
Baja California
MONTERREY
HAVANA CUBA

MEXICO
San Luis Potosí
Tampico
Mérida
Yucatan Peninsula
CARIBBEAN SEA
JAMAICA
Kingston

Tropic of Cancer
Cabo San Lucas
Gulf of California

GUADALAJARA
MEXICO CITY PUEBLA
BELIZE

Acapulco
GUATEMALA
GUATEMALA
EL SALVADOR
San Salvador
HONDURAS
Tegucigalpa
NICARAGUA
Managua
COSTA RICA
San José

HAWAIIAN ISLANDS (U.S.)
Honolulu
OAHU
MAUI
HAWAII Hilo

LINE ISLANDS
POLYNESIA

Equator
GALAPAGOS ISLANDS
(ARCHIPIÉLAGO DE COLÓN)
(Ecuador)
Punta Galera
QUITO
ECUADOR
GUAYAQUIL

NORTHERN COOK ISLANDS
RICAN OA
COOK ISLANDS (N.Z.)
SOUTHERN COOK ISLANDS

MARQUESAS ISLANDS
(ÎLES MARQUISES)

FRENCH POLYNESIA
TUAMOTU ARCHIPELAGO
Papeete TAHITI

Punta Pariñas
Chiclayo PERU
ANDES
Nev. Huascarán 22,133
Punta Lachay
Callao
Lima
Punta Carreta
Punta Parada
Arequipa

PITCAIRN (U.K.)

Tropic of Capricorn

EASTER ISLAND
(ISLA DE PASCUA)
(Chile)

PACIFIC OCEAN

CHILE
ARGENTINA

Valparaíso
CÓRDOBA
Santiago

Scale 1:45,000,000; one inch to 710 miles
Lambert Azimuthal, Equal Area Projection

0 200 400 600 800 1000 Miles
0 300 600 900 1200 1500 Kilometers

NEW BRITAIN
Cape Cretin
SOLOMON SEA
Popondetta
OWEN STANLEY RANGE
resby
Sâmarai
Kulumadau
BOUGAINVILLE
CHOISEUL
SANTA ISABEL
SOLOMON ISLANDS
Honiara
MALAITA
GUADALCANAL
SAN CRISTOBAL

TUVALU

CORAL SEA

SANTA CRUZ ISLANDS

VANUATU
ÎLES BANKS
ESPIRITU SANTO
PENTECATE
MALAKULA
EPI
Port Vila
ÉFATÉ
NEW
ERROMANGO
HEBRIDES

WALLIS AND FUTUNA (Fr.)

FIJI
VANUA LEVU
Lautoka
VITI LEVU
Suva
KANDUVU ISLAND

NEW CALEDONIA (Fr.)
NOUVELLE CALÉDONIE
LOYALTY ISLANDS
Nouméa

Tropic of Capricorn

RRIER REEF
Frere
Halifax Bay
Townsville
CLARKE RANGE
Mackay
Mt. Dalrymple 4,431
Blair Athol
Rockhampton
Cape Capricorn
Emerald
Gladstone
Springsure
Theodore
Bundaberg
Maryborough
Sandy Cape
Mitchell
FRASER ISLAND
Gympie
ANDE
Chinchilla
Mt. Kiangarow 3,760
Toowoomba
Redcliffe
mulla
DARLING DOWNS
Ipswich
Brisbane
Warwick
Southport
Bandon
Cape Byron
ke
Lismore
Nyngan
Armidale
Grafton
Tamworth
Coffs Harbour
Dubbo
Taree
W A L E S
Cessnock
Newcastle
Penrith
Parramatta
Sydney
ja
Goulburn
Campbelltown
Wollongong
A.C.T.
Canberra
Jervis Bay
Cooma
tta
Mt. Kosciusko 7,310
Cape Howe
Sale
Wilsons Promontory
TASMAN
FLINDERS ISLAND
Cape Portland
onport
Launceston
SEA
osta
Freycinet Peninsula
TASMANIA
South East Cape

PACIFIC

OCEAN

NORFOLK ISLAND (Austl.)

Cape Maria van Diemen
North Cape
Cape Brett
Whangarei
Needles Point
Mount Roskill
East Coast Bays
Manukau
Auckland
Hamilton
Bay of Plenty
Albatross Point
Tauranga
NORTH ISLAND
Rotorua
East Cape
New Plymouth
Taupo
Cape Egmont
Mt. Ruapehu
Gisborne
Wanganui
Napier
Cape Farewell
Palmerston North
Hastings
The Twins 5,990
Nelson
Porirua
Wellington
Greymouth
SOUTH ISLAND
Waiau
NEW ZEALAND
Jackson Head
Haast
SOUTHERN ALPS
Ashburton
West Cape
Manapouri
Timaru
Christchurch
Invercargill
Oamaru
Foveaux Strait
Dunedin
STEWART ISLAND
CHATHAM ISLANDS (N.Z.)

International Date Line

Scale 1:20,000,000; one inch to 315 miles
Lambert's Azimuthal; Equal Area Projection

0   100   200   300   400   500   600 Miles
0   200   400   600   800   1000 Kilometers

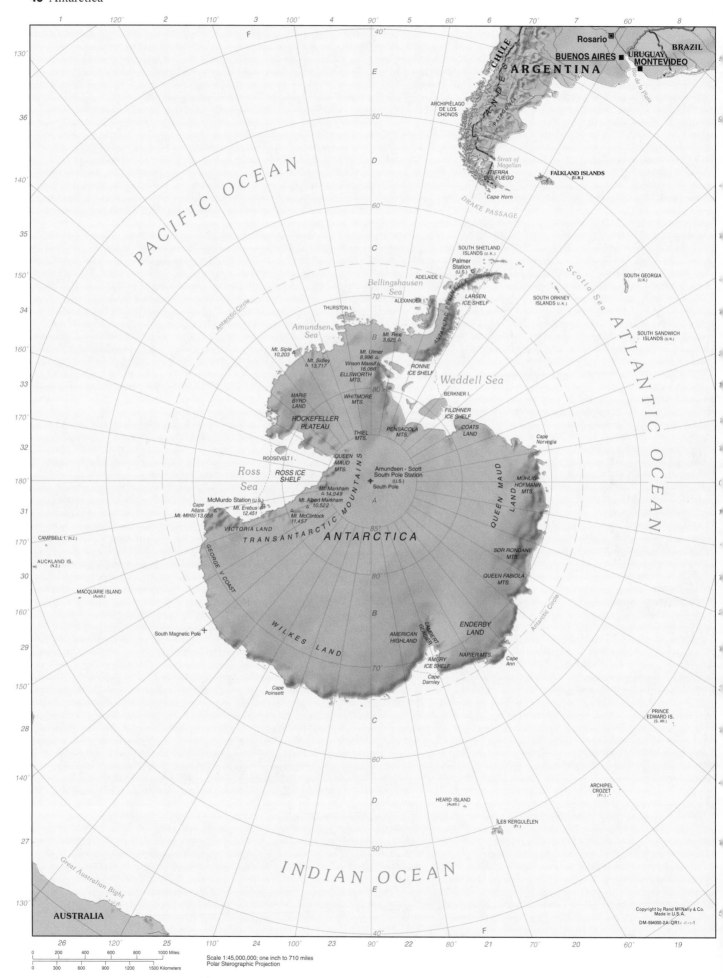

PACIFIC OCEAN

ATLANTIC OCEAN

INDIAN OCEAN

CHILE
ARGENTINA
Rosario
BUENOS AIRES
URUGUAY
MONTEVIDEO
BRAZIL
ARCHIPIÉLAGO DE LOS CHONOS
PATAGONIA
Strait of Magellan
TIERRA DEL FUEGO
Cape Horn
FALKLAND ISLANDS (U.K.)
DRAKE PASSAGE
Scotia Sea
SOUTH GEORGIA (U.K.)
SOUTH SHETLAND ISLANDS (U.K.)
Palmer Station (U.S.)
ADELAIDE I.
ALEXANDER I.
LARSEN ICE SHELF
SOUTH ORKNEY ISLANDS (U.K.)
SOUTH SANDWICH ISLANDS (U.K.)

Bellingshausen Sea
THURSTON I.
Amundsen Sea
Mt. Rex 3,625
ANTARCTIC PENINSULA
RONNE ICE SHELF
Weddell Sea
Mt. Siple 10,203
Mt. Sidley 13,717
Mt. Ulmer 8,996
Vinson Massif 16,066
ELLSWORTH MTS.
BERKNER I.
Cape Norvegia
MARIE BYRD LAND
WHITMORE MTS.
FILCHNER ICE SHELF
COATS LAND
ROCKEFELLER PLATEAU
THIEL MTS.
PENSACOLA MTS.
QUEEN MAUD LAND
MÜHLIG-HOFMANN MTS.
ROOSEVELT I.
QUEEN MAUD MTS.
Amundsen - Scott South Pole Station (U.S.)
South Pole
Ross Sea
ROSS ICE SHELF
Mt. Markham 14,049
Mt. Albert Markham 10,522
TRANSANTARCTIC MOUNTAINS
SØR RONDANE MTS.
McMurdo Station (U.S.)
Mt. Erebus 12,451
Mt. McClintock 11,457
ANTARCTICA
Cape Adare
Mt. Minto 13,658
VICTORIA LAND
QUEEN FABIOLA MTS.
CAMPBELL I. (N.Z.)
AUCKLAND IS. (N.Z.)
GEORGE V COAST
ENDERBY LAND
MACQUARIE ISLAND (Austl.)
WILKES LAND
AMERICAN HIGHLAND
LAMBERT GLACIER
NAPIER MTS.
Cape Ann
South Magnetic Pole
AMERY ICE SHELF
Cape Darnley
PRINCE EDWARD IS. (S. Afr.)
Cape Poinsett
ARCHIPEL CROZET (Fr.)
HEARD ISLAND (Austl.)
ÎLES KERGUÉLEN (Fr.)
Great Australian Bight
AUSTRALIA

Antarctic Circle

Copyright by Rand McNally & Co.
Made in U.S.A.
DM-594000-2A-QR1- -1-1-1

Scale 1:45,000,000; one inch to 710 miles
Polar Sterographic Projection

0 200 400 600 800 1000 Miles
0 300 600 900 1200 1500 Kilometers

Index

Abbreviations of Geographical Names and Terms

Ak., U.S. . . . . Alaska
Al., U.S. . . . . . . Alabama
Ant. . . . . Antarctica
Ar., U.S. . . . . . . Arkansas
Arg. . . . . Argentina
Asia . . . . Asia
Austl. . . . . . . Australia
Az., U.S. . . . . . . .Arizona
b. . . . . *bay, gulf*
Bah. . . . . .Bahrain
B.C., Can.
British Columbia
Bol. . . . . Bolivia
Braz. . . . . Brazil
c. . . . .*cape, point*
Ca., U.S. . . . . . California
Can. . . . . .Canada
Cay. Is. . . Cayman Islands
Co., U.S. . . . . . .Colorado
Col. . . . . Colombia
cont. . . . . *continent*
C.R. . . . . Costa Rica
ctry. . . . . *country*
D.C., U.S.
District of Columbia
De., U.S. . . . . . .Delaware
dep. . . . . *dependency*
Dom. Rep.
Dominican Republic
El Sal. . . . . El Salvador
Eng., U.K. . . . . . . England
Fl., U.S. . . . . Florida
Ga., U.S. . . . . . . .Georgia
Guad. . . . . . . Guadeloupe
hist. reg. . . *historic region*
H.K. . . . . Hong Kong
Hond. . . . . . Honduras
i. . . . . *island*
Ia., U.S. . . . . Iowa
Id., U.S. . . . . Idaho
Il., U.S. . . . . Illinois
In., U.S. . . . . . . .Indiana
Ire. . . . . Ireland
is. . . . . *islands*
Jam. . . . . Jamaica
Ks., U.S. . . . . Kansas
Ky., U.S. . . . . . Kentucky
l. . . . . *lake*
La., U.S. . . . . . Louisiana
Leb. . . . . Lebanon
Ma., U.S. . . Massachusetts
Malay. . . . . . . Malaysia
Md., U.S. . . . . Maryland
Me., U.S. . . . . Maine
Mex. . . . . Mexico
Mi., U.S. . . . . . .Michigan
Mn., U.S. . . . . Minnesota
Mo., U.S. . . . . . . Missouri
Monts. . . . . Montserrat
Mor. . . . . Morocco
Ms., U.S. . . . . Mississippi
Mt., U.S. . . . . . . Montana
mtn. . . . . *mountain*
mts. . . . . *mountains*
N.A. . . . . North America
Nb., U.S. . . . . . .Nebraska
N.C., U.S. North Carolina
N.D., U.S. North Dakota
Newf., Can. Newfoundland
N.H., U.S. New Hampshire
Nic. . . . . Nicaragua
N.M., U.S. . . New Mexico
N.S., Can. . . Nova Scotia
Nv., U.S. . . . . . . .Nevada
N.W.T., Can.
Northwest Territories
N.Y., U.S. . . . . New York
N.Z. . . . . . . New Zealand
Oh., U.S. . . . . .Ohio
Ok., U.S. . . . . . Oklahoma
Ont., Can. . . . . . . Ontario
Or., U.S. . . . . Oregon
Pa., U.S. . . Pennsylvania
Pak. . . . . Pakistan
Pan. . . . . Panama
Para. . . . . Paraguay
pen. . . . . *peninsula*
Phil. . . . . Philippines
plat. . . . . *plateau*
pol. div. . . *political division*
P.R. . . . . . . .Puerto Rico
prov. . . . . *province*
res. . . . . *reservoir*
Sask., Can. Saskatchewan
S.C., U.S. South Carolina
Scot., U.K. . . . . Scotland
S.D., U.S.
South Dakota
Sen. . . . . .Senegal
Sri L. . . . . . Sri Lanka
St. K./N.
St. Kitts and Nevis
stm. . . . . *river, stream*
strt. . . . .*strait*
terr. . . . . *territory*
Tn., U.S. . . . . . Tennessee
Trin.
Trinidad and Tobago
Tx., U.S. . . . . Texas
U.K. . . United Kingdom
Urug. . . . . . . Uruguay
U.S. . . . . . . United States
Ut., U.S. . . . . .Utah
Va., U.S. . . . . . . Virginia
Ven. . . . . Venezuela
vol. . . . . *volcano*
Vt., U.S. . . . . . . Vermont
Wa., U.S. . . . Washington
Wi., U.S. . . . . Wisconsin
W.V., U.S. West Virginia
Wy., U.S. . . . . Wyoming

A

Aba H-8 42
Ābādān C-4 38
Abaetetuba D-9 23
Abakan G-16 32
Abancay F-4 22
Abay H-12 32
Abeokuta H-7 42
Aberdeen, Scot., U.K. . . . D-5 28
Aberdeen, S.C., U.S. D-7 12
Abidjan H-6 42
Abilene J-7 13
Abu Dhaby, see Abū Ẓaby E-5 38
Abuja H-8 42
Abū Ẓaby (Abu Dhabi) .E-5 38
Acámbaro G-9 19
Acapulco I-10 19
Acarigua B-5 22
Accra H-6 42
Achinsk F-16 32
Aconcagua, Cerro, mtn. C-3 21
Acre, state E-4 22
Actopan G-10 19
Ada J-8 13
Adamaoua, mts. H-9 42
Adana H-13 27
Adare, Cape B-31 48
Ad Dammām D-4 38
Ad Dawḩah D-5 38
Addis Ababa (Adis Abeba) H-14 43
Adelaide H-6 46
Aden (ʿAdan) G-4 38
Aden, Gulf of G-4 38
Adirondack Mountains . . . D-9 10
Adrar D-6 42
Adriatic Sea D-7 31
Aegean Sea E-8 31
Afghanistan, ctry. C-7 38
Africa, cont. F-14 3
ʿAfula m-24 25
Agadir C-5 42
Agana C-11 37
Āgra D-10 39
Ağrı Dağı, mtn. H-14 27
Agua Prieta B-5 18
Aguascalientes G-8 18
Aguascalientes, state F-8 18
Ahaggar, mts. E-8 42
Ahmadābād E-9 39
Ahvāz C-4 38
Aiken J-6 11
Ajaccio D-5 30
Ajmer D-9 39
Akita D-16 35
ʿAkko m-24 25
Aklavik C-6 6
Akmola (Tselinograd) . . .G-12 32
Akola E-10 39
Akordat F-14 43
Akron F-6 10
Aktau I-8 33
Aktyubinsk G-12 32
Al Khubar D-5 38
Alabama, stm. K-3 11
Alabama, state J-3 11
Alacant E-3 30
Alagoas, state E-11 23
Alagoinhas F-11 23
Alajuela F-8 17
Al ʿAlamayn C-12 43
Alamogordo L-12 15
Alamosa H-4 13
Åland (Ahvenanmaa), i. C-9 29
Al ʿAqabah p-24 25
Al ʿArīsh n-22 25
Alaska, state B-6 5
Alaska, Gulf of D-7 5
Alaska Peninsula D-5 5
Alaska Range, mts. C-6 5
Albacete E-3 30
Albania, ctry. D-7 31
Albany, Austl. G-2 46
Albany, Ga., U.S. K-4 11
Albany, N.Y., U.S. E-10 10
Albany, Or., U.S. F-3 14
Al Baydaʾ C-11 43
Albert, Lake B-6 41
Alberta, prov. E-10 6
Albert Lea E-10 12
Ålborg D-8 28
Albuquerque K-11 15
Albury H-8 47
Alcalá de Henares D-3 30
Alchev'sk C-11 31
Aldan, stm. F-24 33
Aldanskoye Nagor'ye, plat. F-23 33
Aleksandrovsk-Sakhalinskiy G-26 33
Ålesund C-7 28
Aleutian Islands f-14 5
Alexandria (Al Iskandarīyah), Egypt C-12 43
Alexandria, La., U.S. K-10 13
Alexandria, Va., U.S. . . . G-8 10
Aleysk G-14 32
Al Fāshir G-12 43
Al Fayyūm D-13 43
Algeria, ctry. D-7 42
Algiers (El Djazaïr) B-7 42
Al Hoceïma B-6 42
Al Hufūf D-4 38
Alice Springs E-5 46
Alīgarh D-10 39
Al Ismāʿ īlīyah C-13 43
Al Ismāʿ īlīyah o-21 25
Al Jawf D-11 43
Al Junaynah G-11 43
Al Khalīl n-24 25
Al Kharṭūm Baḩrī F-13 43
Al Khums C-9 42
Al Lādhiqīyah B-2 38
Allahābād D-11 39
Allegheny, stm. F-7 10
Allentown F-9 10
Alma-Ata (Almaty) I-13 32
Almalyk I-11 32
Al Manāmah D-5 38
Al Manṣūrah C-13 43
Al Marj C-11 43
Al-Mawṣil B-3 38
Almería E-3 30
Al Minyā D-13 43
Alor Setar D-3 36
Alpena D-5 10
Alps, mts. C-5 30
Al Qadārif G-14 43
Alta Floresta F-7 23
Altagracia A-4 22
Altai, mts. H-15 32
Altamira D-8 23
Altamont G-4 14
Altiplano, plain G-5 22
Alton G-11 12
Altun Shan, mts. D-6 34
Alturas H-4 14
Altus I-7 13
Amapá, state C-8 23
Amarillo I-6 13
Amazon (Amazonas), stm. D-8 23
Amazonas, state D-6 22
Ambarchik D-30 33
Ambato D-3 22
Ambon F-8 37
American Highland B-22 48
American Samoa, dep. . . . H-12 45
Americus J-4 11
Amiens C-4 30
ʿAmmān C-2 38
Amrāvati E-10 39
Amritsar C-10 39
Amsterdam E-7 28
Amu Darya, stm. I-10 32
Amundsen Sea B-2 48
Amur, stm. G-25 33
Anadyr' E-33 33
Anápolis G-9 23
Anchorage C-7 5
Ancona D-6 31
Andaman Islands C-1 36
Andaman Sea C-2 36
Anderson I-5 11
Andes, mts. . . . .-0 20
Andizhan I-12 33
Andong D-13 35
Andorra, ctry. D-4 30
Andros, i. D-9 17
Angara, stm. F-18 33
Ángel de la Guarda, Isla, i. C-3 18
Angeles B-7 36
Angers C-3 30
Angola, ctry. E-3 41
Anguilla, ctry. E-12 17
Anhui, prov. E-11 35
Ankara H-12 27
Annaba B-8 42
An Najaf C-3 38
Annapolis G-8 10
Ann Arbor E-5 10
Anniston J-4 11
Anshan C-12 35
Antalya H-12 27
Antananarivo k-10 41
Antarctica, cont. A-26 48
Antigua and Barbuda, ctry. E-12 17
Antofagasta A-2 21
Antsiranana j-10 41
Antwerpen E-6 28
A'nyêmaqên Shan, mts. D-8 34
Anyuskiy Khrebet, mts. D-31 33
Anzhero-Sudzhensk F-15 32
Aomori C-16 35
Aôral, Phnum, mtn. C-3 36
Apatzingán H-8 18
Apia H-11 44
Apo, Mount D-8 37
Appalachian Mountains H-6 11
Appennino Mts. D-6 30
Appleton D-12 12
Apure, stm. B-5 22
Aqaba, Gulf of D-1 38
Arabian Desert D-13 43
Arabian Sea F-7 38
Aracaju F-11 23
Araçatuba H-8 23
Arad C-8 31
Arafura Sea B-7 46
Araguaína E-9 23
Arāk C-4 38
Aral Sea H-9 32
Aral'sk H-10 32
Araouane F-6 42
Araraquara H-9 23
Arauca, stm. B-5 22
Arcata H-2 15
Arctic Bay B-16 7
Arctic Ocean A-1 2
Arctic Red, stm. C-7 6
Arctic Village B-7 5
Ardabīl B-4 38
Ardmore I-8 13
Arequipa G-4 22
Argentina, ctry. D-4 21
Argentino, Lago, l. G-2 21
Århus D-8 28
Arica G-4 22
Arīḩā (Jericho) n-24 25
Arizona, state K-9 15
Arkadelphia I-10 13
Arkalyk G-11 32
Arkansas, stm. I-10 13
Arkansas, state I-10 13
Arlington J-8 13
Armadale G-2 46
Armenia C-3 22
Armenia, ctry. G-14 27
Armidale G-9 47
Arnhem, Cape C-6 46
Arnhem Land, region C-5 46
Arrecife D-4 42
Ar Rub' al Khāli, desert .F-5 38
Artemisa D-8 17
Artemovsk G-16 32
Artesia L-12 15
Aruba, ctry. F-10 17
Arviat D-15 7
Arzamas F-6 32
Asahikawa C-16 35
Āsānsol E-12 39
Aseb G-15 43
Ashburton I-13 47
Asheville I-5 11
Ashkhabad (Ashgabat) J-9 32
Ashland G-5 10
Ash Shariqah D-6 38
Ashtabula F-6 10
Asia, cont. D-18 3
Asino F-15 32
Asmera F-14 43
Aspen G-3 12
As Sudd, region H-13 43
As Sulaymānīyah B-4 38
Astoria E-3 14
Astrakhan H-7 32
Asunción B-5 21
Aswān E-13 43
Asyūt D-13 43
Atascadero K-4 15
Aṭbarah F-13 43
Atbasar G-11 32
Atchafalaya Bay L-11 13
Atchison G-9 12
Athabasca F-11 6
Athabasca, Lake E-12 6
Athens (Athínai), Greece .E-8 31
Athens, Ga., U.S. J-5 11
Athens, Tn., U.S. I-4 11
Atlanta J-4 11
Atlantic City G-9 10
Atlantic Ocean E-10 2
Atlas Mountains C-6 42
At Ṭā'if E-3 38
Atyrau H-8 32
Auburn, Al., U.S. J-4 11
Auburn, Me., U.S. E-11 10
Auckland H-13 47
Augsburg C-6 30
Augusta, Austl. G-2 46
Augusta, Ga., U.S. J-6 11
Augusta, Me., U.S. D-12 10
Aurangabad F-10 39
Aurora G-4 12
Austin, Mn., U.S. E-10 12
Austin, Tx., U.S. K-8 13
Australia, ctry. E-5 46
Australian Capital Territory, terr. H-8 47
Austria, ctry. C-6 31
Avellaneda C-5 21
Avignon D-4 30
Ayaguz H-14 32
Ayers Rock, mtn. F-6 46
Ayeyarwady, stm. A-1 36
Azerbaijan, ctry. G-15 27
Azores, is. B-1 42
Azov, Sea of C-11 31
Az-Zarqāʾ C-2 38
Az Zāwiyah C-9 42

B

Bacolod C-7 37
Badajoz D-2 30
Badlands, region D-5 12
Baffin Bay B-20 7
Baffin Island B-17 7
Baghdād C-3 38
Bago B-2 36
Baguio B-7 36
Bahama Islands C-9 17
Bahamas, ctry. C-9 17